COMMENTARY ON KIERKEGAARD'S
CONCLUDING UNSCIENTIFIC POSTSCRIPT
WITH A NEW INTRODUCTION

COMMENTARY ON
KIERKEGAARD'S
CONCLUDING UNSCIENTIFIC POSTSCRIPT
WITH A NEW INTRODUCTION

Niels Thulstrup

TRANSLATED BY
ROBERT J. WIDENMANN

PRINCETON UNIVERSITY PRESS
PRINCETON, NEW JERSEY

Copyright © 1984 by Princeton University Press

Published by
Princeton University Press, Princeton, New Jersey
In the United Kingdom:
Princeton University Press, Guildford, Surrey

All Rights Reserved

Library of Congress Cataloging in Publication Data
will be found on the last printed page of this book

ISBN 0-691-07180-2

(Original work titled *Søren Kierkegaard: Afsluttende
uvidenskabelig Efterskrift udgivet med Indledning og
Kommentar* af Niels Thulstrup, Gyldendal, Copenhagen,
1962, vols. I–II)

The translation of this book has been aided by the
Danish Rask-Ørsted Foundation

This book has been composed in Linotron Bembo

Clothbound editions of Princeton University Press books
are printed on acid-free paper, and binding materials are
chosen for strength and durability. Paperbacks, although satisfactory
for personal collections, are not usually suitable for library rebinding

Printed in the United States of America by
Princeton University Press, Princeton, New Jersey

"You are going on," I said to myself, "to become an old man, without being anything, and without really undertaking to do anything. On the other hand, wherever you look about you, in literature and in life, you see the celebrated names and figures, the precious and much heralded men who are coming into prominence and are much talked about, the many benefactors of the age who know how to benefit mankind by making life easier and easier. . . . And what are you doing?" Here my soliloquy was interrupted, for my cigar was smoked out and a new one had to be lit. So I smoked again, and then suddenly this thought flashed through my mind: "You must do something, but inasmuch as with your limited capacities it will be impossible to make anything easier than it has become, you must, with the same humanitarian enthusiasm as the others, undertake to make something harder." This notion pleased me immensely, and at the same time it flattered me to think that I, like the rest of them, would be loved and esteemed by the whole community.

Kierkegaard, Postscript

CONTENTS

PREFACE   ix

ABBREVIATIONS   xiii

ENGLISH TRANSLATIONS OF KIERKEGAARD   xi

ENGLISH TRANSLATIONS OF HEGEL   xvii

INTRODUCTION   I

1 Speculative Philosophy of Religion in the Ancient World 3

2 The Ancient Church and the Middle Ages   17

3 Speculative Trends in Modern Philosophy   31

4 From Kant to Hegel   40

5 Hegelianism in Germany   62

6 The Situation in Denmark and Kierkegaard's Reaction   70

7 Kierkegaard versus Hegel   91

8 The Theological and Anthropological Premises for
   Kierkegaard's Critique   102

9 The Contemporary Reception of the *Postscript*   117

   GUIDE TO THE COMMENTARY   139

   COMMENTARY   147

   INDEX   395

PREFACE

The *Concluding Unscientific Postscript* is a major work in the history of the philosophy of religion. If we are to circumscribe the position held by Kierkegaard's work it will be necessary to know the origin and development of the chief currents of this history, for these theories form the premises on which it is based and thus constitute its greatest context.

It is in our time a well-known fact that the *Postscript* must be understood in yet another context: in its opposition to nineteenth-century German philosophical Idealism, or speculation, and to the spokesmen and adherents of speculation in the fields of both philosophy and theology. To understand the thrust of the attack the reader must also be familiar with the author's terminology, language, and special treatment of the religious, philosophical, and psychological problems of his time. Even more important, we must consider just what Kierkegaard intended with his work.

A third context emerges when we consider the *Postscript* from the standpoint of its unique position and function in relation to Kierkegaard's other works.

In the Introduction I have concentrated on the broader and more general backgrounds for the work as a whole and on its position in the history of religion. The more specific connections and relationships to other sources, works, and so forth, are presented in the Commentary.

The various philosophical and theological disciplines have grown and developed from a process of differentiation that took centuries.[1] Our modern classification of sciences differs from that of former ages. For example, philosophers of earlier ages did not find it natural to distinguish sharply among metaphysics, epistemology, and philosophy of religion, any more than theologians of that time made the present sharp distinction between metaphysics and dogmatics. Whenever they did make distinctions of this kind they did so merely for

---

[1] See, among other works, Søren Holm, *Religionsfilosofi* (Copenhagen, 1955), especially pp. 11–85; Hans Joachim Störig, *Kleine Weltgeschichte der Wissenschaft*, 2nd ed. (Stuttgart, 1957); A.W.H. Adkins, *From the Many to the One* (London, 1960); and Jørgen Jørgensen, *Filosofiske Forelæsninger som Indledning til videnskabelige Studier*, 3rd ed. (Copenhagen, 1962).

the purpose of again combining philosophy and theology. Thus any attempt to understand this earlier thinking will require a study of the changing views and metaphysical systems from which it issued, along with studies of the particular premises and aims of the thinkers involved.

Today, philosophy of religion covers a wide range of thinking. It is possible to treat traditional and current problems in philosophy of religion with a purely philosophical outlook, for example, along Neo-Thomistic, Neo-Kantian, Neo-Marxist, or analytical lines. If we take this approach we will be able to regard philosophy of religion as a purely philosophical discipline that differs from other philosophical studies in its subject matter rather than in its methods and standards of judgment. It is of course also possible to take the reverse tack and, along with Barth, Bultmann, and others, proceed from a basic theological position, treating philosophy of religion as a purely theological discipline, even though the theologian will in all likelihood encounter philosophical problems en route. In general, however, such modern categories and distinctions prove to be more deceptive than illuminating in connection with an understanding of Kierkegaard and especially his contemporaries.

In Kierkegaard's time it was characteristic that philosophers theologized while theologians philosophized. What thinkers of our time would consider mutually exclusive worlds of thought a German Idealist would have regarded as inseparable: for example, the purely philosophical view according to which only experience and reason may be recognized as legitimate sources of knowledge on the one hand, and on the other the theological view that presupposes revelation as a special source. Sharing a common background and working with the same concepts of science (*Videnskab*), which at the time meant metaphysics, the philosophers and theologians of that era had the same end in view.

It is well known that all of Kierkegaard's pseudonymous works are predominantly devoted to a criticism of one particular tradition in religious-philosophical thought: the idealistic and speculative tradition. From this tradition Kierkegaard borrowed a terminology and conceptual technique that he then turned to his own ends. The basis of that tradition must be sought in a definite point of departure and in specific aims, and within its limits thinkers developed a methodology adapted to attain those aims. Kierkegaard, too, had a definite point of departure and aim, and consequently he developed a way of thinking that was uniquely his own. My purpose in the following introduction is to give an account of these differences in philosophical approach. Emphasis must necessarily be placed on the store of knowledge that Kierkegaard could assume to be available to his readers. Since the author himself is his own best spokesman, a presentation of his ideas and motives can be made all the more briefly. In the conclusion I will deal with some questions concerning the *Postscript* as a whole.

The present work has been composed on much the same principles as those applied in my edition of *Philosophical Fragments* (Princeton, 1962). The information and commentaries presented in the current edition have as far as possible been brought up to date after personal studies based on the latest and most comprehensive Kierkegaard research available to me. Useful supplementary data will be found in my *Kierkegaard's Relation to Hegel* (Princeton, 1980).

It is my pleasant duty to express my gratitude to the many scholars whose investigations have often proved of vital help and support to me. I wish especially to thank Robert J. Widenmann for his painstaking efforts in giving my text English dress and for contributing several valuable items of information. Last but not least, I owe a debt of gratitude both to Director Herbert S. Bailey, Jr., Princeton University Press, and to the expert collaborators at the same Press for their great patience and for their understanding of the difficult nature of this work.

Niels Thulstrup
August 1983

ABBREVIATIONS

ASKB (with item numbers): *Auktionsprotokol over Søren Kierkegaards Bogsamling* ("Auction Catalog of Søren Kierkegaard's Book Collection"), ed. H. P. Rohde (Copenhagen, 1967). The item numbers also correspond to those in my edition: *Søren Kierkegaards Bibliotek* (Copenhagen, 1957).

Breve (with volume and entry number or page number): *Breve og Aktstykker vedrørende Søren Kierkegaard*, ed. Niels Thulstrup, I–II (Copenhagen, 1953–1954).

Enc.: *Encyclopaedia of The Philosophical Sciences*. This work comprises *Logic* (§1–244), with the explanatory notes, or *Zusätze*, supplied by Leopold von Henning; *The Philosophy of Nature* (§245–376) with *Zusätze* by Philipp Michelet; and *The Philosophy of Mind [Spirit]* (§377–577) with *Zusätze* by Ludwig Boumann.

Fragments: *Philosophical Fragments or a Fragment of Philosophy*, my edition; see below.

JP (with volume and entry numbers): *Søren Kierkegaard's Journals and Papers*, ed. and trans. Howard V. Hong and Edna H. Hong, I–VII (Bloomington, 1967–1978). Quotations reprinted by permission from Indiana University Press.

Jub. Ausg. (with volume and page numbers): Georg Wilhelm Friedrich Hegel, *Sämtliche Werke*, Jubiläumsausgabe, ed. Hermann Glockner, I–XX (Stuttgart, 1958–1959).

KW (with volume and page numbers): *Kierkegaard's Writings*, I–XXV (Princeton, 1978—). The English title of the specific work is also given.

ODS (with volume and column numbers): *Ordbog over det danske Sprog*, ed. H. Juul-Jensen et al., I–XXVIII (Copenhagen, 1919–1956; reprint, Copenhagen, 1966–1974).

Pap. (with volume and entry numbers): *Søren Kierkegaards Papirer*, ed. P. A. Heiberg, V. Kuhr, and E. Torsting, I–XI³ (Copenhagen, 1909–1948), and 2nd ed., photo-offset reprint with two supplemental volumes, XII–XIII, ed. Niels Thulstrup (Copenhagen, 1968–1970), and with index, XIV–XVI (1975–1978).

Postscript: Kierkegaard's Concluding Unscientific Postscript; see below.

SV (with volume and page numbers): *Søren Kierkegaards Samlede Værker*, ed. A. B. Drachmann, J. L. Heiberg, and H. O. Lange,

2nd ed., I–XV (Copenhagen, 1920–1936). References in *JP* and *KW* are to the first edition of *Kierkegaards Samlede Værker* (Copenhagen, 1901–1906). H. Nyegaard, however, has published a parallel register in vol. XIV, Part Two, pp. 1–191, of the second edition, giving page and line correlations between these two standard editions. In *Kierkegaard Indices*, compiled by Alastair McKinnon, vol. I: *Kierkegaard in Translation* (Leiden, 1970), there is a composite page and line collation of the second and third Danish editions and the most widely available English, French, and German translations.

W.a.A. (Werke, alte Ausgabe; with volume and page numbers): *Georg Wilhelm Friedrich Hegels Werke*. Vollständige Ausgabe durch einen Verein von Freunden des Verewigten, I–XVIII (Berlin, 1832–1840).

Logic: The Logic of Hegel; see below.

The Science of Logic: Johnston's and Struther's translation; see below.

The Phenomenology of Mind: Baillie's translation; see below.

ENGLISH TRANSLATIONS OF KIERKEGAARD

Armed Neutrality and An Open Letter, trans. and ed. Howard V. Hong and Edna H. Hong. New York, 1969.

Attack upon "Christendom", trans. Walter Lowrie. Princeton, 1968.

Christian Discourses, trans. Walter Lowrie. New York, 1962.

The Concept of Anxiety, ed. and trans. with introduction and notes by Reidar Thomte in collaboration with Albert B. Anderson. Princeton, 1980 (*KW* XIX).

The Concept of Irony, trans. Lee M. Capel. Bloomington, 1968.

Crisis in the Life of an Actress and Other Essays on Drama, trans. Stephen D. Crites. New York, 1967.

The Difficulty of Being a Christian, trans. Ralph M. McInery and Leo Turcotte. Notre Dame, 1969 (based on Jacques Collette's French translation).

Edifying Discourses, trans. David F. Swenson and Lillian Marvin Swenson, I–IV. Minneapolis, 1943–1946.

Either/Or, vol. I trans. David F. Swenson and Lillian Marvin Swenson; vol. II trans. Walter Lowrie, I–II. Princeton, 1971.

Fear and Trembling, trans. Walter Lowrie. Princeton, 1970.

For Self-Examination and Judge for Yourselves!, trans. Walter Lowrie. Princeton, 1968.

The Gospel of our Suffering, trans. A. S. Aldworth and W. S. Ferrie. Grand Rapids, 1964.

Johannes Climacus, or De omnibus dubitandum est, and A Sermon, trans. T. H. Croxall. Stanford, 1967.

The Journals of Søren Kierkegaard, ed. and trans. Alexander Dru. London and New York, 1938.

Kierkegaard's Concluding Unscientific Postscript, trans. David F. Swenson and Walter Lowrie. Princeton, 1941.

Kierkegaard's Writings, ed. Howard V. Hong and Edna H. Hong. Princeton, 1978—.

The Last Years. Journals of 1853–1855, trans. and ed. Ronald Gregor Smith. New York, 1965.

On Authority and Revelation, trans. Walter Lowrie. New York, 1966.

Philosophical Fragments, trans. David F. Swenson. 2nd rev. ed. with introduction and commentary by Niels Thulstrup. Introduction and commentary trans. and 1st ed. rev. Howard V. Hong. Princeton, 1962.

The Point of View of My Work as An Author: A Report to History, trans. Walter Lowrie. New York, 1962.

Purity of Heart Is To Will One Thing, trans. Douglas V. Steere. New York, 1948.

Repetition, trans. Walter Lowrie. New York, 1964.

The Sickness unto Death, ed. and trans. with introduction and notes by Howard V. Hong and Edna H. Hong. Princeton, 1980 (*KW* XIV).

Søren Kierkegaard's Journals and Papers, ed. and trans. Howard V. Hong and Edna H. Hong, I–VII. Bloomington, 1967–1978. Quotations reprinted by permission from Indiana University Press.

Stages on Life's Way, trans. Walter Lowrie. New York, 1967.

Thoughts on Crucial Situations in Human Life. Three Discourses on Imagined Occasions, trans. David F. Swenson. Minneapolis, 1941.

Training in Christianity, trans. Walter Lowrie. Princeton, 1967.

Two Ages . . . A Literary Review, ed. and trans. with introduction and notes by Howard V. Hong and Edna H. Hong. Princeton, 1978 (*KW* XIV).

Works of Love, trans. Howard V. Hong and Edna H. Hong. New York, 1962.

ENGLISH TRANSLATIONS OF HEGEL

Aesthetics: Lectures on Fine Art, trans. T. M. Knox, I–II. Oxford, 1975.

The Difference between Fichte's and Schelling's Systems of Philosophy, trans. H. S. Harris and W. Cerf. Albany, 1977.

Early Theological Writings, trans. T. M. Knox. Philadelphia, 1971.

Faith and Knowledge, trans. H. S. Harris and W. Cerf. Albany, 1977.

Foreword to *Die Religion im inneren Verhältnisse zur Wissenschaft*, by H.W.F. Hinrichs, 1822, trans. A. V. Miller. In *Beyond Epistemology: New Studies in the Philosophy of Hegel*, ed. Frederick G. Weiss. The Hague, 1974.

Lectures on the History of Philosophy, trans. E. S. Haldane and F. H. Simson, I–III. New York, 1968.

Lectures on the Philosophy of Religion. Together with a work on the proofs of the existence of God, trans. E. B. Speirs ·and J. B. Sanderson, I–III. New York, 1968.

The Logic of Hegel (Part I of the *Encyclopaedia*), trans. W. Wallace. New York, 1968.

Natural Law, trans. T. M. Knox. Philadelphia, 1975.

The Phenomenology of Mind, trans. J. B. Baillie. London, 1949.

The Phenomenology of Spirit, trans. A. V. Miller. New York, 1977.

The Philosophy of Fine Art, trans. F.P.B. Osmaston, I–IV. New York, 1975.

The Philosophy of History, trans. J. Sibree. New York, 1956.

The Philosophy of Mind (Part III of the *Encyclopaedia*), trans. W. Wallace and A. V. Miller. New York, 1971.

The Philosophy of Nature, trans. A. V. Miller. New York, 1970.

The Philosophy of Nature, trans. M. J. Petry, I–III. London, 1970.

The Philosophy of Right, trans. T. M. Knox. New York, 1967.

The Philosophy of Subjective Spirit, trans. M. J. Petry. Boston, 1978.

Political Writings, trans. T. M. Knox. Oxford, 1964.

The Science of Logic, trans. W. H. Johnston and L. G. Struthers, I–II. London, 1929.

The Science of Logic, trans. A. V. Miller. New York, 1969.

INTRODUCTION

CHAPTER 1

Speculative Philosophy of Religion in the Ancient World

From antiquity to the time of Hegel and on to the present, religious-philosophical thinking has been dominated, in whole or in part, by cosmology. This cosmology was developed from very different premises in the course of successive ages, so each age operated with its own particular cosmology.

The various mythological views of the universe arose from simple immediate sense perceptions of the environment and were interpreted by a creative imagination. The speculative cosmologies were fashioned in a similar manner, with the difference being that reason took the place of mythical explanations. The unknown was now explained by means of something known[1] instead of by something unknown, and this was subsequently called prime matter or the principle of being (for example, fire, water, or motion). The point of departure for empirical scientific cosmologies remained the same for ages, though later generations added verifiable experience as a means of controlling imagination and reason.

Expressed in modern philosophical terminology, this point of departure was always a complex situation, at least some elements of which were known. For instance, philosophers may have thought of the place where one lives and works, or they referred to the cultivated land supporting small or large human societies that build cities and regulate human affairs. In short, they began with a scheme in which everything was assigned its proper place. Beyond this generally limited horizon the world was in disorder, Chaos instead of Cosmos. As an explanation of this state of affairs it was supposed that good forces reigned over Cosmos and evil ones over a Chaos that constantly threatened to devour Cosmos, just as the oceans threaten to burst dikes or as primeval forests threaten to spread over cleared

---

[1] See especially Wilhelm Nestle, *Griechische Geistesgeschichte von Homer bis Lukian in ihrer Entfaltung vom mythischen zum rationalen Denken dargestellt*, 2nd ed. (Stuttgart, 1944); G. van der Leeuw, *Phänomenologie der Religion*, 2nd ed. (Tübingen, 1956); Friedrich Heiler, *Erscheinungsformen und Wesen der Religion* (Stuttgart, 1961); and Georg Widengren, *Religionsphänomenologie*, 3rd ed. (Berlin, 1969).

areas and cultivated fields. It quite naturally followed that man's duty
did not consist in a mere passive contemplation of the world as it is
but in an active contribution aimed at maintaining and expanding
Cosmos, and thus in remaining on the side of the good powers. So
too, by emphasizing the theoretical rather than the predominantly
practical aspects, philosophers sought within a speculative cosmology
to widen their horizons and attain a mastery of the world through
thought that would reflect man's self-understanding. This view was
analogous to the usual mythological view of the universe as horizon-
tally or vertically stratified, with the earth or human world in the
center, heaven above, and the kingdom of the dead or hell below. It
was accordingly held that beyond this terrestrial existence man has a
form of being before birth and after death. Essentially, speculative
cosmologies are distinguishable from mythological views of the universe merely by their explanations, not by their formal structures.

The Greek philosophers began to develop their cosmologies by
rejecting the mythological explanations in favor of speculative cosmologies, only to end up with the fantastic syntheses proposed by
Posidonius and Proclus. These theories were in turn handed down to
the Middle Ages.[2]

The first questions the Greek philosophers raised and tried to answer by applying reason and experience instead of resorting to myths

[2] An extensive bibliography of works relevant to the philosophers and problems
mentioned in the Introduction is available in my Danish work *Fra Platon til Hegel og
fra Sokrates til Kierkegaard*, 2nd ed., I–III (Copenhagen, 1980), I, 38–113. There exists
no modern collected presentation of the history of religious-philosophical thought.
The following brief outline is aimed only at giving the new reader of the *Postscript* the
most necessary facts; supplemental information must be sought in the works and treatises mentioned in the text. For surveys covering greater periods of time, see for
example the historical sections in Fritz Heinemann, *Die Philosophie im XX. Jahrhundert,
eine enzyklopädische Darstellung ihrer Geschichte, Disziplinen und Aufgaben* (Stuttgart, 1959);
Nicola Abbagnano, *Storia della Filosofia*, 2nd ed., I–III (Turin, 1963); Frederick Cople-
ston, *A History of Philosophy*, I–IX (London, 1946–1975); Émile Bréhier, *Histoire de la
philosophie*, I–III (Paris, 1948); Jacques Chevalier, *Histoire de la pensée*, I–IV (Paris, 1955–
1956); and Richard Kroner, *Speculation and Revelation in the History of Philosophy*, I–III
(Philadelphia, 1956–1961). To these modern and comprehensive presentations of the
history of philosophy must be added Ueberweg's work mentioned in the following
note (a new edition is now in preparation). Monographs and special articles are mentioned in the following notes in connection with the relevant individual points. But
since this presentation is written in accordance with the principle of selection rather
than that of comprehensiveness (which would require several volumes), bibliographical references have been limited to the extent possible. Additional references will be
found in Ueberweg and in the encyclopedias mentioned in the Guide to the Commentary.

was how to explain change, coming into being, and passing away in nature.

Thales of Miletus tried to solve this problem by imagining one prime matter, water, as the bearer of life and thus the cause of change. Making a bold generalization from simple observations, he theorized that water was the prime matter and life-giving principle of all being.[3] This solution did not satisfy Anaximander, who inquired how such a diversity of materials with totally different characteristics could emerge from one basic substance. He came to the conclusion that we must assume that this prime matter is a yet undivided unity of opposite qualities; he thereupon defined his prime substance as the "boundless" (apeiron). His disciple Anaximenes, believing that such a synthesis was realized in the air, accordingly assumed air to be the one and only prime matter.

Unlike his predecessors, Pythagoras fixed upon two principles, the Unlimited and the Limited (peras). He held that the latter was the more important because it qualified and thus determined the identity of every being. It was Pythagoras' theory that these determinations must accord with a law of numbers. Apparently he arrived at this result by observing that musical intervals such as the fourth, fifth, octave, and so forth, depend on definite numerical ratios. According to Pythagoras, the contrasts observable everywhere in nature, from the emergence of things to their passing away, synthesize in a beautiful harmony like that of music and depend on the same numerical ratios. With this observation Pythagoras took a big step, advancing from the assumption of a corporeal basic substance to the abstract

[3] The following works are especially recommended in connection with this and the succeeding passages, for example, Hermann Diels, Die Fragmente der Vorsokratiker, ed. W. Kranz, 7th ed., I–III (Berlin, 1954). The fifth edition of this work has been translated by Kathleen Freeman under the title of Ancilla to the Pre-Socratic Philosophers (Oxford, 1946). Many of the pre-Socratic fragments are translated and supplied with interpretations in Wilhelm Capelle, Die Vorsokratiker, 4th ed. (Stuttgart, 1953) and in G. S. Kirk and J. E. Raven, The Presocratic Philosophers (Cambridge, 1960). Other good works on this subject are Eduard Zeller's older major work, Die Philosophie der Griechen, 2nd ed., I–V (Leipzig, 1879–1892), which is the last edition attended to by the author himself; and Karl Praechter, Die Philosophie des Altertums, 13th ed. (Basel, 1953); this is the same as vol. I of Friedrich Ueberweg's Grundriss der Geschichte der Philosophie, ed. T. Konstantin Oesterreich, 13th ed. (Basel, 1951). See also N. M. Caminero, Historia philosophiae, vol. I: Philosophia antiqua, I–II (Rome, 1960). As to special literature on the pre-Socratic philosophers, see especially Werner Jaeger, The Theology of the Early Greek Philosophers, trans. Edward S. Robinson (London, Oxford, and New York, 1967). The most comprehensive modern standard work is W. E. C. Guthrie, A History of Greek Philosophy, I–V (Cambridge, 1967–1978). See also Adkins, From the Many to the One.

theory of regularity as a principle of being. Since he regarded unity as a principle of numbers, he was now able to posit it as a symbol of rest, immovability, truth, and justice.

Philolaus, a disciple of Protagoras, assumed that there was a globe or counter-earth corresponding to the earth but always in a position opposite to it and thus always invisible He also held that in the center of the universe there is a fire around which ten bodies revolve: the counter-earth, then the earth, the moon, the sun, the five planets known at the time, and finally the sphere of the fixed stars. Since all bodies in rapid motion produce a tone, he conjectured that the same must hold true of revolving spheres, and since a tone's pitch was thought to depend on its distance from the fire in the center of the universe, he accordingly believed that there arose a harmony of the spheres. Like other theories of the pre-Socratic philosophers, this one, too, provided a source of inspiration centuries later for romantic poets and idealistic philosophers.

Heraclitus took a different approach. His thinking consistently focused on the problems connected with coming-into-existence, change, and motion. Noting that fire appeared to be in a constant state of flux, he thus posited fire as the basic principle of being. This perpetual motion was not in his opinion a mere fortuitous phenomenon. On the contrary, he held that although only the external phenomena of change are revealed to us through sense perception, there is in all change an intrinsic regularity and tense harmony (as symbolized by the lyre) that we are able to grasp through reason. Heraclitus therefore regarded perpetual motion as the profoundest secret of being and the mind of the world, and he attached not only cosmological but even ethical importance to this concept. It thus came to be Heraclitus' divinity.[4]

Xenophanes, realizing that the mythological conceptions of the gods bear obvious anthropomorphic traits, developed instead a philosophical and pantheistic monism in which the divinity is one and everything. His disciple Parmenides thereupon came to the conclusion that since only the One exists and it is immutable and immovable, all coming-into-being, change, and motion must be illusory; and inasmuch as our senses merely perceive what is illusory, only reason can yield knowledge of being and hence of truth. Thus being, which Parmenides regarded as something corporeal, can be grasped only by thought. It also follows that a primitive mind incapable of reflection

[4] Concerning the theories of Heraclitus and the Eleatics, see also below, note to p. 336 in the *Postscript*.

would have a world view different from Parmenides'. The plain man is compelled to assume that plurality is possible because things are separated by space. Parmenides' notion excluded such an explanation, for he operated on the premise that empty space did not exist and that instead of many things there existed only one being that is a complete spherical whole. On the basis of this argument motion and change are inconceivable and thus impossible.

Zeno sought to substantiate these Eleatic theories of unity and the impossibility of motion by a series of demonstrations designed to show that opposite hypotheses would lead to absurdity. He reasoned that if there is a plurality of existing objects, each of them obviously must not only have a certain magnitude but also be separated by a certain distance. A part of each object, however, is preceded by another part, which in turn may be divided into parts having a magnitude and preceding each other, so one is finally compelled to admit that each object is infinite in size. If on the other hand what exists has no size, it would not even be, for if we added it to something that also lacked size, the result would clearly be nothing, and no matter how much we add we arrive at the same result: nothing. With these two arguments Zeno sought to prove that plurality was impossible, for things would be both so small as to have no magnitude at all and so large as to be infinite in size.

Zeno attacked theories of motion in a similar way. To move means to traverse a given route between two points, and a route is divisible into an infinite number of sections, so a body must pass through an infinite number of sections to move from one point to the other; but this is impossible in a limited period of time. Zeno illustrated his reasoning by the story of the race between Achilles and a turtle. Achilles, whose greatest asset was his speed, gave the turtle a head start of ten paces—and could not catch up with it. While Achilles was taking the first ten steps the turtle took one, and while Achilles was covering this step his adversary covered one one-hundredth of a step. Thus the distance between them steadily decreased but was never completely eliminated. Zeno also tried to prove that motion of any kind is illusory and that its very concept is rooted in the deceptive perceptions of the senses. He used as an example an arrow in flight. An object, Zeno maintained, is at rest when it occupies a space equal to its own dimensions. Now an arrow in flight occupies such a definite point in space at any given moment, and so it is at rest. We cannot regard motion as a series of states of rest (which would give a cinematographic effect), so to acknowledge motion is to succumb to the absurd thought that the arrow does not occupy a definite space at every given moment. Therefore, there is no such thing as motion.

The problems connected with the obvious contrasts between change and immutability and between unity and plurality remained unsolved, but thinkers persisted in their efforts to do justice to both sides and bring about a conciliation. It was for example clear to Empedocles that being cannot arise from nothing; but since it is plural, it must arise from something with the same characteristic, or at least something composed of elements capable of entering into various combinations and assuming different forms. He consequently assumed the existence of four basic elements: fire, air, water, and earth. Empedocles thereupon maintained that what appears to us as emergence or passing away is in fact merely a mixing or separation of these basic elements, and that the underlying cause of these changes is to be found in two forces or powers: love and hate. Once adopted as basic causal agents, these two forces were deified, thus making a theory of ethics possible. Furthermore, he now developed the epistemological theory that only likes can comprehend each other; or, to use a more modern locution, the subject and object of cognition must conform to each other. This theory was to have a profound effect on later philosophy. Indeed, Plotinus and the German Idealists, especially Goethe and Hegel, transformed Empedocles' theory of conformity into an assertion of identity. Another pre-Socratic philosopher, Anaxagoras, in place of these two powers of love and hate posited Mind (*nous*), a single spiritual force that he saw present in all living things.

In contrast to Parmenides, the Atomists, especially Democritus, accepted the idea of a nothing or a void. Whereas Parmenides held that being was an indivisible unity, the Atomists thought being to consist of an infinite number of very small and indivisible units or atoms that differ in quantity but not in quality. The Atomists were now in a position to explain both the variety of materials and change (or motion) by assigning their cause to various combinations of these atoms in accordance with purely mechanical laws. Democritus too developed an ethics, conformable to his philosophy of nature and metaphysical views.

These speculations in natural philosophy led to divergent and incompatible views (for example, those of Parmenides and Heraclitus), and in practice they resulted in relativism and radical skepticism. It did not seem possible, through either experience or thought, to arrive either at a hypothesis that could be proved beyond doubt or at a universally valid system of ethics. The prospects of achieving an unambiguous cosmology and outlook on life looked dim indeed to those who thought that man was capable of attaining these goals through his own efforts. A beginning had been made by taking a critical attitude to traditional religious interpretations of the external world, but now man himself was turning out to be a problem. Obviously man was unable to master the situation by means of conviction or belief alone; he needed persuasion, and this is where the Sophists came on the scene:

> [They] not only turned against previous and contemporary philosophical efforts to establish what being really is, but doubted man's ability to perceive any universally valid truth whatever. Knowledge could never acquire more than purely subjective validity, and this led to the conclusion that the subjective result of knowledge was valid only for the man who had attained it.[5]

Since the truth was regarded as relative, a harmony between men on matters of faith and ethics could not be based on truth. Men would as a result have to rely on convention or a consensus of opinion or, failing that, on force to persuade others.

Faced with this situation, Socrates (469–399 B.C.) proceeded along a new path. Turning his back on both the speculative thinking in the philosophy of nature and the pragmatically oriented relativism of the Sophists, he aimed his efforts at a reestablishment of ethics.[6] He held that a sound basis for ethics must be sought in true knowledge. He also felt, however, that the greatest obstacle to the acquisition of true knowledge was not acknowledged ignorance but the self-sufficiency and illusion that apparent knowledge causes. He therefore adopted the procedure of making ignorance serve as a point of departure and allowing his apparently knowledgeable victim to disclose his own emptiness. Although our knowledge of Socrates has come to us only indirectly, it would seem safe to assume that he considered it possible to arrive at conceptual definitions by means of induction, for example, the concept of the good. To realize the good one must first have

[5] Johannes Sløk, *Platon* (Copenhagen, 1953), p. 15.

[6] See W. Norvin, *Sokrates* (Copenhagen, 1934); A. Simonsen, *Sokrates* (Copenhagen, 1961); and Povl Johannes Jensen, *Sokrates* (Copenhagen, 1969). Of these three Danish monographs the third is especially remarkable, for it accepts and develops Kierkegaard's positive view of Aristophanes as an important contributor to our knowledge of Socrates as a historical figure. This view has often been criticized and rejected. As to the problems surrounding Socrates, reference is made to V. de Magalhães-Vilhena, *Le problème de Socrate* (Paris, 1952). The subtitle of this work, "Le Socrate historique et le Socrate de Plato," discloses the author's viewpoint. See also Werner Jaeger, *Paideia*, I–III (Berlin, 1954), II, 49–130, and Guthrie, *Greek Philosophy*, III, 323–489.

a knowledge of it, and Socrates maintained that each individual has the potential to accomplish both; the truth is within man, and self-knowledge and knowledge of the truth are identical. This theory became an axiom for all subsequent philosophical idealism from Plato to Hegel. As we know, Kierkegaard proposed an alternative to this theory in the *Fragments*.

There are three distinctive Socratic schools, and with all three of them ethical questions and epistemological problems stand in the foreground. This applies as much to Aristippus as to Antisthenes and Euclid. But it is first and foremost Plato who gives us an appreciation of the scope of what Socrates taught by means of his indirect method and clarification of concepts and what he meant to his disciples personally.

Like Socrates, Plato too inquired into the nature of the good. He defined it as being primarily expediency, as that which can serve as a means to a higher end. The great number of means and ends that it is possible to tabulate, however, will amount to nonsense if we are unable to point out a supreme end that is both inherently good and a supreme good; and it must serve as an idea of goodness in general. It is also possible to comprehend and view truth and beauty in this way.[7]

Under the influence of Heraclitus, Plato became convinced that everything knowable by means of sense perception is subject to change and therefore cannot be a proper object of cognition, for that object must be stable. True rational cognition does not focus on the changeable world known to our senses but on the immutable world of ideas. If we call a certain figure a triangle we do so because we had a concept of what a triangle is beforehand; or, in Plato's terminology, we were familiar with the *idea* of a triangle. Plato solved the old problem of the relationship between knowledge acquired by means of the senses and knowledge gained through reason by assuming that the senses and reason are directed toward different objects, and that objects perceived by the senses are in turn reflections of real existing ideas. The famous metaphor of the cave in *The Republic* (515A ff.) portrays var-

[7] In addition to Werner Jaeger's *Paideia*, II–III, the following may be recommended: A. E. Taylor, *Plato*, 6th ed. (New York, 1957), and Paul Friedländer, *Platon*, 2nd ed., I–III (Berlin, 1954–1960). An important work is Heinrich Barth, *Philosophie der Erscheinung*, I: *Altertum und Mittelalter* (Basel, 1947; 2nd ed. 1966), and II: *Neuzeit* (Basel, 1959). See also David Ross, *Plato's Theory of Ideas* (Oxford, 1951); J. E. Raven, *Plato's Thought in the Making* (Cambridge, 1965); and J. N. Findlay's Gifford lectures, *The Discipline of the Cave* (London and New York, 1966) and *The Transcendence of the Cave* (London and New York, 1967).

ious kinds of cognition ranging from knowledge of what is only apparently real to knowledge of true reality. The same metaphor also illustrates Plato's metaphysics, according to which the world of ideas constitutes true reality and existence. Our material world is merely an image of the ideal world, to which it owes its very existence. Since man is also corporeal, Plato saw him as a prisoner in the material world while his soul or mind is a prisoner of his body. When the soul sees the reflections of the ideal, however, it is able to recollect true reality by drawing on a previous existence in a higher world, and it now aspires to this reality.

In Plato's view true rational cognition concentrates on the ideal world and grasps it as an organized totality or cosmos, using dialectics to achieve this insight. Such an intellect will aspire to ever higher and more comprehensive concepts and will not cease its efforts until it has attained a concept of the one being. The composition of true being corresponds to this conceptual pyramid, and the idea of the good constitutes both the hightest concept and supreme being. Dialectics, however, is also capable of leading us back down the scale to concepts of species and finally to individual specimens, so the path taken by cognition may be said to lead from the particular to the universal and then back to the particular. Besides this structural theory, in the dialogue *Timaeus* Plato also urged space as a principle that is indeterminate and without material characteristics, but which nevertheless is necessary for anything to have physical presence.

To explain the emergence of the empirical world, Plato assumed that there must be a master builder, a creative reasoning power or divine being who used the ideal world as a pattern, thereby creating a material world with limitations. Although this world is thus also imperfect in respect of ethics, it is nevertheless a world in which there is a recollection of perfection and consequently also an appetite and eternal longing for this good. This theory is accompanied by another according to which the soul through a fall has sunk to the material world, which like an evil place imprisons it and prevents it from rising again. There is evidence of an unexplained monism and dualism in Plato's idealistic speculation, as indeed there is in any philosophical idealism. A conception of the world as a hierarchic cosmos in which man occupies a definite position is apparent even here.

Aristotle sought to solve the problem of how to explain change, which in his time had already become a traditional dilemma, by distinguishing between form and matter and between potentiality and actuality (*dynamis* and *energeia* or *entelekeia*). Using a rather complicated argument, he arrived at the conclusion that substance owes its origin to undifferentiated matter that has realized a definite end by receiving a definite form. The means needed to attain this end he called acting or moving causes, and he then went on to postulate four kinds of causes, for any given change: material, efficient (or moving), formal, and final. Thus in the case of a house, the builder and his skill would constitute the moving or efficient cause; the earth and stones the material cause; the concept or plan of the house the formal cause; and the completed work the final cause. Aristotle now applied this method of explanation to all phenomena in the worlds of nature, man, and the divine.[8]

According to Aristotle, every transition from potentiality to actuality must be caused by something actually existing; in other words, a form must combine with real matter. He argued that every substance, God alone excluded, is composed of both form and matter and may assume the role of either cause, depending on its designated function in a specific context or series of changes. Thus a seed is matter when a tree is considered as form, the tree in turn becomes matter in relation to a plank conceived as form, and the plank becomes matter when a house is regarded as form. In the case of a living being, the form and end (or final cause) are identical and in combination constitute the moving or efficient cause, so the soul, which is the essence or form of the body, is also the inherent efficient cause of the living being.

Aristotle included spatial locomotion among the various possible kinds of change. According to his theories in this connection, everything seeks a natural level, with heavy bodies tending toward the center of the earth and lighter bodies away from it; barring obstacles, both proceed in a direct line. The celestial bodies, on the other hand, execute eternal "perfect" movements, which to Aristotle was yet another proof of the eternity of time. This, however, gave rise to another question: How was the potentiality of these circular movements transformed into actuality?

Aristotle solved this problem by arguing that what produces a change

[8] On the subject of Aristotle, whose theories concerning the doctrines of potentiality, actuality, and motion in particular Kierkegaard studied in preparation for his critique of Hegel, reference is made to Werner Jaeger, *Aristotle. Fundamentals of the History of His Development*, trans. Richard Robinson, 2nd ed. (London, Oxford, and New York, 1967); the first German edition of this work appeared in Berlin in 1923. W. D. Ross gives a systematic presentation in *Aristotle*, 5th ed. (London, 1949). The chief work on this subject is now Ingemar Düring, *Aristoteles, Darstellung und Interpretation seines Denkens* (Heidelberg, 1966). See also G.R.G. Mure, *Aristotle*, 2nd ed. (New York, 1964), especially chap. XI, pp. 233–52, "The History and Influence of Aristotelianism."

cannot itself undergo change when functioning as a cause; therefore a prime mover or first cause must itself be unmoved. Now all motion presupposes a prime mover; Aristotle called this first cause God, who is an active being that sustains the eternal perfect movements of the celestial bodies. God is pure form and pure actuality, and because of God's perfection the prime mover is a focal point of attraction; as such, God is both the point of departure and end or final cause of all existence and thus constitutes its supreme reality.

A new cosmology emerged on the basis of Platonism and Aristotelianism and under the influence of the mystery religions and Gnosticism. Let us use a pyramid to illustrate this cosmology. The different levels of the pyramid will represent successively higher degrees of perfection in which everything, man included, is assigned a definite place and specific goals. Inanimate nature will now occupy the bottom level while the next level, which will also be stratified, is reserved for animate matter. Man is relegated to the third level; above him we will find beings occupying an intermediate position between man and the divine; the apex of the pyramid will represent the divine itself, the source and goal of all that is. It was this hierarchically oriented cosmology that so strongly influenced religious and philosophical thinking in antiquity and the Middle Ages.[9]

The Stoic Posidonius (135–51 B.C.) developed this conception into a total view of being that was rigidly deterministic.[10] He held that man's reason participates in divine reason and is capable of comprehending the universe in its entirety. Like Aristotle, Posidonius also maintained that living beings are assigned positions in a sort of ladder arrangement. The bottom step here on earth belongs to men, but once men's souls have been released from their bodies they are able to ascend the ladder and reach the top step, which is occupied by celestial deities. According to Posidonius' theory, heaven consists of a plurality of spheres, each of which is inhabited by a different celestial deity. Thus each sphere has its own spiritual significance, exercises a particular influence, and is capable of conferring a specific trait. For example, Saturn imparts sloth, Jupiter furnishes ambition, and Mars gives bellicosity; the sun contributes intellectual powers, Venus is responsible for erotic desire, Mercury for avarice, and the moon bestows the elementary energy of life. Now all souls owe their origin to the divine heaven, but they leave this heaven and descend

[9] See, among others, Anders Nygren, *Agape and Eros*, 2nd ed., I–II (London, 1937–1939), especially I.

[10] Max Pohlenz, *Die Stoa*, I–II (Göttingen, 1948–1949), I, 208ff., and II, 103ff.

through the different spheres to inhabit bodies, only to aspire once more to their heavenly source. In their descent the souls forget their original purity and are contaminated by increasingly base and more worldly material traits and inclinations. Conversely, they divest themselves of these imperfections in the course of their resurrection and ascent after death, though only the noblest souls are able to complete the journey and return to their original purity and bliss in the eighth heaven. The motivating and life-giving principle in this process is the *Logos*, or divine reason.

> Posidonius' system turns out to be a living pantheism with sufficient room to accommodate the whole of creation, a splendid system comparable to those of Schelling and Hegel. As Hegel used the development of the "Notion" in all its manifestations to make nature emerge from spirit, so Posidonius regards all being as an image of eternal ideas. These ideas are no longer an immutable and supra-sensuous realm, as in Plato, but are God's own thoughts and the content of His consciousness of Himself.[11]

To counter this monistic system the Gnostics developed various dualistic systems. They regarded corporeal and worldly conditions not only as the lowest and most imperfect in the universe but also as an evil state caused by a malevolent power.[12] To the Gnostics, therefore, the task assigned to man consisted of a cultic and ethical process of purification that would emancipate the soul and enable it to return to its exalted origin. They frequently appealed to doctrines of metempsychosis, and one sect, the Carpocratians, whom Kierkegaard mentions in a couple of journal entries,[13] developed a theory to the effect that man ought literally to experience everything evil and sinful, for this sect regarded debasement as a purification process by which man could elevate himself. This theory is a precursor of Hegel's doctrine of the negative.

Plotinus (A.D. 205–270), on the contrary, developed a thoroughly monistic philosophy that was intended as a trenchant polemic against the Gnostics.[14] The following stanza from Heiberg's university song,

[11] Poul Helms, *Fra Tanke til Mystik* (Copenhagen, 1934), p. 107.

[12] See H. Leisegang, *Die Gnosis*, 4th ed. (Stuttgart, 1955). An important work covering this whole period is K. Prümm, *Religionsgeschichtliches Handbuch für den Raum der altchristlichen Umwelt*, 2nd ed. (Rome, 1954).

[13] *Pap.* II A 127 and 599—*JP* I 219 and V 5227, respectively.

[14] See Povl Johannes Jensen, *Plotin* (Copenhagen, 1948), and Émile Bréhier, *La philosophie de Plotin* (Paris, 1968).

which is well known in Denmark, applies to Plotinus as well as to Hegel:

And thought was to itself made clear,
And God to thought became apparent;
So, to a synthesis they tend
Like the brook with its torrential source;
For thought on high did thus ascend
As in itself it took its course.[15]

In Plotinus' philosophy the One occupies a supreme position above any being or existing entity. It is noncomposite and embodies the fullness of all being, but strictly speaking nothing can be said about it because it transcends our world and human language. As the fullness of being it necessarily issues forth from itself in a timeless emanation that first of all produces reason (*nous*). This emanation gives rise to a duality, partly because reason actively acquires knowledge and partly because it is a receptacle for that knowledge. A world soul emanates from reason, dividing and portioning itself out as particular souls in individual animate bodies. The path from the One leads downward from humans to animals, plants, and lifeless nature in a continuous loss of perfection regarding both being and ethics. One may consider as a simile light that appears to be weaker as one withdraws from its source. In Plotinus' cosmos man stands midway between the sheer light of the One and the total darkness represented by matter in its plurality; the task lies in returning to the One along the same path. The means necessary to attain this end consist of self-knowledge, which can teach the soul to turn toward the light, and the exercise of virtue, which will enable man to reach the goal of reuniting with the One and resting in contemplation of it. This means that in Plotinus' view, knowledge of God is fundamentally self-knowledge:

There is no need to go anywhere to partake of real life. One need merely rise up to spirit, which is part of oneself. In other words,

---

[15] From "Cantata ved Universitetets Fest [1839]" in Johan Ludvig Heiberg, *Poetiske Skrifter*, ed. Carl S. Petersen, I–III (Copenhagen, 1931–1932), III. The original text reads:

Og Tanken for sig selv blev klar,
Og Gud for Tanken aabenbar;
De monne sig til Eenhed føie,
Lig Bækken med sit Udsprings Elv,
Thi Tanken opsteg til det Høie,
Dengang den nedsteg i sig selv.

one has only to go within oneself and remain completely alone with one's inmost being.[16]

Along with Spinoza, Plotinus must be regarded as a background and presupposition for German Idealism.[17] Kierkegaard, on the basis of his own premises, was later to deliver a sharp attack against both thinkers.

[16] Jensen, *Plotin*, p. 72.

[17] See, among other works, Carl Roos, *Goethe* (Copenhagen, 1949), and Karl Viëtor, *Goethe* (Bonn, 1949). These two works were published during an anniversary year.

CHAPTER 2

The Ancient Church and the
Middle Ages

The advent of Christianity constituted a further complication of the religious-philosophical issues, so determining the relationship between philosophical knowledge and Christian faith has since been a major problem. Attempts to solve it have been numerous, and of course the means employed to this end have varied in accordance with the philosophy and personal interpretation of Christianity adopted. Even in the time of the Ancient Church there was a clear tendency to regard this relationship as completely lacking in harmony, a view that also prevailed in late Scholasticism and toward the end of the Middle Ages. Nevertheless, the dominant opinion up to the Renaissance and Reformation was that there did not exist any conflict between true philosophy and true faith. In other words, it was felt that there was no conflict between the truth to which man can attain through experience, reason, or mystical insight and the truth revealed through a communication from God. Various arguments were offered in support of this view.[1]

[1] The patristic and medieval religious-philosophical thinking discussed here is presented in its proper context in the histories of philosophy mentioned in chap. 1. Following are some works on these two intimately related periods: A. H. Armstrong, ed., *The Cambridge History of later Greek and Early Medieval Philosophy* (Cambridge, 1967); Émile Bréhier, *La philosophie du Moyen Âge*, 2nd ed. (Paris, 1949); and Étienne Gilson, *La philosophie au Moyen Âge*, 3rd ed. (Paris, 1947). Important material is also available in works on the history of dogmatics, such as Adolf Harnack, *Lehrbuch der Dogmengeschichte*, 4th ed., I–III (Tübingen, 1909–1920); Friedrich Loofs, *Leitfaden zum Studium der Dogmengeschichte*, 4th ed. (Halle, 1906); Reinhold Seeberg, *Lehrbuch der Dogmengeschichte*, 3rd ed. (1920–1922), 4th ed., reprint, I–IV 1–2 (Graz, 1953); J.N.D. Kelly, *Early Christian Doctrines* (London, 1958); and Alfred Adam, *Lehrbuch der Dogmengeschichte*, I–II (Gütersloh, 1965–1968). Other recommended works are Anders Nygren, *Agape and Eros*, 2nd ed., I–II (London, 1937–1939); Gustaf Aulén, *Den kristna gudsbilden*, 2nd ed. (Stockholm, 1941); and Johannes Hessen, *Platonismus und Prophetismus, die antike und die biblische Geisteswelt in strukturvergleichender Betrachtung*, 2nd ed. (Munich, 1955). The articles on "Aristotelismus" and "Augustinismus" in *Theologische Realenzyklopädie*, vols. III and IV (Berlin, 1978–1979), are also valuable. Kierkegaard's relation to these traditions is treated by various authors in *Bibliotheca Kierkegaardiana*, VI: *Kierkegaard and Great Traditions* (Copenhagen, 1981).

Augustine mentions in his *Confessions* that he had obtained some works of the Platonists in Latin translation from a man "bloated with the most outrageous pride." On reading them, he came to this conclusion:

> In them I read—not, of course, word for word, though the sense was the same and it was supported by all kinds of different arguments—that "at the beginning of time the Word already was; and God had the Word abiding with him, and the Word was God. He abode, at the beginning of time, with God. It was through him that all things came into being, and without him came nothing that has come to be. In him there was life, and that life was the light of men. And the light shines in darkness, a darkness which was not able to master it." I read too that the soul of man, although it "bears witness of the light, is not the Light." But the Word [*verbum*; that is, *logos*] who is himself God, "is the true Light, which enlightens every soul born into the world. He, through whom the world was made, was in the world, and the world treated him as a stranger." But I did not find it written in those books [by the Platonists] that "he [the Word, *verbum, logos*; that is, Christ] came to what was his own, and they who were his own gave him no welcome. But all those who did welcome him he empowered to become the children of God, all those who believe in his name."
>
> In the same books I also read of the Word, God, that his "birth came not from human stock, not from nature's will or man's, but from God." But I did not read in them that "the Word was made flesh and came to dwell among us."
>
> Though the words were different and the meaning was expressed in various ways, I also learned from these books that God the Son, being himself, like the Father, of divine nature, "did not see, in the rank of Godhead, a prize to be coveted." But they do not say that he "dispossessed himself, and took the nature of a slave, fashioned in the likeness of men, and presented himself to us in human form; and then he lowered his own dignity, accepted an obedience which brought him to death, death on the cross; and that is why God has raised him from the dead, given him that name which is greater than any other name; so that everything in heaven and on earth and under the earth must bend the knee before the name of Jesus, and every tongue must confess Jesus Christ as the Lord, dwelling in the glory of God the Father."
>
> The books also tell us that your only-begotten Son abides for ever in eternity with you; that before all time began, he was; that

he is above all time and suffers no change; that of his plenty our souls receive their part and hence derive their blessings; and that by partaking of the Wisdom which abides in them they are renewed, and this is the source of their wisdom. But there is no word in those books to say that "in his own appointed time he underwent death for us sinners, and that you did not even spare your own Son, but gave him up for us all.[2]

By "Platonists" Augustine meant first and foremost Plotinus. Clearly, he was able to discern the decisive point of difference between Christianity and an idealistic speculative philosophy such as that of Plotinus. But it is also evident that he did not deny the validity of Plotinus' thinking within certain limits. To Augustine it contained the truth, but not the whole truth. Plotinus had developed a consistently monistic system of philosophy comprising a wholly transcendental concept of God; a doctrine of emanation; a conception of evil as merely a deficiency; and an optimistic theory that man can work out his own salvation. Christianity, on the other hand, insists that God is the Lord of history; man is created; evil is sin or a repudiation of God, and not just an imperfection; and that man cannot save himself. Plotinus not only perceived but also insisted on the incompatibility of these two outlooks. Augustine, on the contrary, although also perfectly aware that these positions were irreconcilable, nevertheless sought to unite them in a synthesis. With the exception of Kierkegaard, philosophers have wandered in Augustine's tracks to this day.

As early as the second century the Apologists[3] endeavored to assert Christianity's equal, or even superior, status in relation to contemporary philosophies. At the same time they felt compelled to struggle for doctrinal purity among their own ranks in order to prepare themselves to contend with various forms of Gnosticism. The most important of the earliest Fathers of the Church were Irenaeus[4] and Tertullian. It was Tertullian who clearly emphasized the impossibility of

---

[2] *Confessions*, VI, 9:13–14; trans. R. S. Pine-Coffin, *Penguin Classics* (London, 1961), pp. 144ff. Augustine quotes rather freely from John 1:1–16, Philipp. 2:6–11, and Rom. 5:6. Whereas Pine-Coffin puts all quotations in italics, ordinary quotation marks have been used here to indicate Augustine's citations from the Bible. Material in square brackets has been inserted by the present author.

[3] The most important texts are collected in E. J. Goodspeed, ed., *Die ältesten Apologeten* (Göttingen, 1914).

[4] Concerning Irenaeus, reference is made to G. Wingren, *Människan och inkarnationen enligt Irenaeus* (Lund, 1947).

becoming a Christian or even preparing oneself for it by means of human wisdom, for the content of Christianity is diametrically opposed to human thinking corrupted by sin. Quite understandably, the expression *credo quia absurdum* has thus often been attributed to Tertullian. A somewhat later thinker, Lactantius, assumed a conciliatory standpoint in his outlook on the relationship between Christianity and Greek philosophy.

An important part in this conflict was played by the Alexandrian school, whose greatest writers were Clement and Origen,[5] pupils of the thinker Ammonius Sakkas, who also taught Plotinus. Obviously stimulated by both Christian thinking and the religious conceptions prevalent among his contemporaries, Origen constructed a theological system that exerted considerable influence. He based his system on a concept of God as a perfect nature followed, in decreasing degrees of perfection, by Christ, the Holy Spirit, and a world of angels populated by incorporeal rational beings. He assumed that the spirits—especially evil spirits—were alienated from God as the result of a fall in the world of angels, and that a visible material world was created for their purification. The angels occupy the uppermost position in this visible world, man occupies the center, and the demons the bottom level. According to Origen, Christ was not only instrumental in bringing about creation, but he also made salvation possible through his teachings about God and God's will and by imparting to the fallen world a higher knowledge that is necessary for salvation. Origen maintained that the process of salvation advances through a sequence of worlds in which the souls are assigned consecutively higher positions according to merit. Ultimately, everything is restored to its original order: Satan himself and his demons are converted, corporeal existence ceases, and God becomes all in all.

Whereas Origen felt that he had to defend Christianity against philosophical attacks, primarily against those of Celsus the Platonist, Eusebius sought to defend it against both paganism (in *Praeparatio evangelica*) and Judaism (*Demonstratio evangelica*). He clearly perceived that there is a difference between the Platonic and Christian dualisms and that the Neoplatonic doctrine of emanation is incompatible with the Christian belief in creation; nevertheless, he held that the Platonic philosophy contained elements of the truth. Another thinker, Gregory of Nyssa, proceeded to stress an intimate connection between philosophical knowledge and Christian belief, strongly emphasizing

[5] On the subject of Origen, reference is made especially to Hal Koch, *Pronoia und Paideusis* (Berlin, 1932).

philosophical clarification of concepts by means of dialectics as a necessary expedient in formulating the truths of faith. Believing it possible to advance from faith to a profounder insight, Gregory proposed to furnish proofs of the truths of faith not only by resorting to authoritative sources but also by means of reason. Like Philo, he described a series of stages in the soul's mystical union with God.[6] The Arian Eunomius tried to go even further than Gregory by interpreting all religious truths as rational truths.[7]

Most of the thinkers whom we have considered thus far were strongly motivated by the Platonic and Stoic traditions and belong both in the history of philosophy and in the history of Christian doctrine. At the same time, however, Aristotelian influence was beginning to make itself felt in the school of Antioch, from which it spread to the Monophysites and Nestorians in Syria in the fifth century. Aristotle's works were translated into Syriac and then in the ninth century from that language into Arabic, so when the Arabs invaded Spain in the twelfth century his works came within the sphere of the Latin language.[8]

Two of the Latin Fathers of the Church in the fourth century deserve special mention: Ambrosius, chiefly because of his work in the fields of ethics, which he patterned on Cicero's *De officiis*; and Marius Victorinus who, besides translating Plotinus and Aristotle into Latin, attempted to combine Aristotelian logic and epistemology with Neoplatonic ontology. The most important and historically most influential thinker, however, was undoubtedly Augustine, whose views of the relationship between Neoplatonism and Christianity were outlined at the beginning of this chapter.

Augustine's attitude toward the complex philosophical tradition did not remain the same throughout his life. Initially, he tended to approve of philosophical knowledge as a means to achieve wisdom and a comprehension of God, and consequently as an aid and preparation for the acquisition of faith. In his later works, particularly in the curious *Retractationes*, written in A.D. 427, he assumed a more critical attitude toward philosophy. In this work he adopted the position that the value of knowledge, which is intrinsically neutral, depends on its application; if put in the service of faith, knowledge must be regarded as something positive. Augustine argued that knowledge

[6] See J. Daniélou, *Platonisme et théologie mystique* (Paris, 1954).
[7] See Johannes Quasten, *Patrology*, I–III (Westminster, Md., 1950–1960), III, 306ff.
[8] See Paul Wilpert's article employed in the above, "Die Philosophie der patristischen Zeit," in Fritz Heinemann, ed., *Die Philosophie im XX. Jahrhundert* (Stuttgart, 1959), p. 144.

alone is worthless, just as it is inadequate merely to have faith as a subjective attitude. In his opinion man's task consists in elevating the content of faith to a cognitive level, but without losing sight of the fact that faith is more comprehensive than, and embodies, knowledge. In this context he defined faith as the acceptance of a thought, thereby interpreting faith as a volitional act and a factor that is necessary even regarding earthly affairs.

Augustine ranked Plato foremost among the philosophers. Clearly, his own concept of God reflects Plato's influence in that he considered God the supreme principle of existence and the source of truth. At the same time he interpreted the Neoplatonic theory of emanation as a theory of creation (*creatio continua*).

Moreover, he anticipated Descartes and modern forms of philosophical idealism by using methodic doubt as a point of departure in his epistemology and by firmly anchoring cognition of the truth in spiritual self-awareness. Augustine believed that there were two areas in which doubt is impossible. First of all, I cannot question the fact that I doubt and thus exist. Nor is doubt admissible in relation to the principle of duality as embodied in a statement like, "the world either exists or does not exist." Since there is no conceivable reason to deny such a statement, there is no reason to call the principle of contradiction into question either. Augustine thought that by embracing these principles he had, in opposition to absolute skepticism, succeeded in establishing the possibility of acquiring knowledge. He also believed, however, that knowledge was not only possible but even indispensable for achieving the aim of life. He reaffirmed the classical conception of eudaemonia as the goal of life, like Ambrosius interpreting happiness as eternal beatitude and participation in God as the supreme truth.[9]

The philosophical thinking of the Middle Ages, as in the patristic period, did not as a rule distinguish sharply between metaphysics and dogmatics. To be sure, distinctions did become increasingly perceptible in the course of time; but even toward the close of the period it was—with few exceptions—generally agreed that the difference between the two disciplines did not imply incommensurability. This assumption was based on adherence to a hierarchical cosmology divided into two main sections, a realm of nature and a realm of grace, with the first realm embracing the created and fallen world and the

[9] See Nygren, *Agape*, II, passim, and especially R. Holte, *Beatitudo och Sapientia* (Stockholm, 1958).

second the redeemed and perfect world. In this scheme earthly existence was regarded as a pilgrimage beginning in the realm of nature
and passing through the realm of grace to reach the goal, the kingdom of glory.

Structurally, this cosmology is of Greek provenance, owing its
origins chiefly to Aristotelianism and Neoplatonism. The explanations of the world of nature advanced by Plato, Aristotle, Ptolemaeus, Plotinus, and their disciples, and the descriptions of the world
of grace given in the Bible and by the Fathers of the Church (among
whom Augustine was considered the greatest),[10] were generally regarded as definitive and authoritative. The primary task facing religious-philosophical thinkers in the Middle Ages was therefore to determine the relationship between these two realms. The thinkers of
this age accordingly felt that philosophy must belong to an inferior
sphere and thus be subordinate to theology, for whereas philosophical cognition is directed toward the realm of nature, theology concerns the superior realm of grace. But if properly understood, philosophy can nonetheless render man valuable, indeed indispensable,
assistance on the way to the heavenly fatherland. In fact, according
to this view it is impossible for man to reach the gates of this kingdom by his own unaided efforts alone; only God's clemency toward
man, the *homo viator*, can lead him all the way to this heavenly goal.

The distinctive and formal character of medieval thinking resulted
from the schools and their curricula, the pedagogical methods then
in use, and the contents of the libraries. The medieval Roman Catholic Church provided a successor to the Roman State school by means
of its monastic and cathedral schools,[11] in which Greek and Roman
culture continued as a living heritage. The universities, which were
founded toward the end of the twelfth and beginning of the thirteenth centuries, were extensions of these schools. Education included the liberal arts (*artes liberales*) and church doctrine. As opposed
to professional or vocational skills, the liberal arts were considered

[10] See Jørgen Pedersen, "Opfattelsen og studiet af middelalderen," *Dansk teologisk
Tidsskrift* (1954), pp. 193–241. An important work is Jean Leclercq, *L'Amour des Lettres
et le Désire de Dieu* (Paris, 1957).

[11] Regarding the systems of education in the Middle Ages, the reader is referred to
William Norvin, *Københavns Universitet i Middelalderen* (Copenhagen, 1929), and
M. Grabmann's important work, *Die Geschichte der scholastischen Methode*, 2nd ed. (Basel,
1961), which is supplemented by the same author's *Die theologische Erkenntnis—und
Einleitungslehre des hl. Thomas v. Aquin* (Freiburg [Switzerland], 1948). An important
work is Olaf Pedersen, *Studium generale. De europæiske universiteters tilblivelse* (Copenhagen, 1979).

unnecessary for the pursuit of a natural life on earth, for they had a higher end: the guidance of man toward an appointed supernatural goal. They consisted partly of three formal arts (*trivium*), that is, grammar, dialectics, and rhetoric; and partly of the four real arts (*quadrivium*), encompassing geometry, arithmetic, astronomy, and music. The Latin terms derive from *tres* and *quattuor viae*, meaning three and four ways—toward man's goal in life. The method of instruction, which was fundamentally quite simple, consisted of studying and explaining recognized authors, and it was this practice that gave rise to the many commentaries of the period.

Disputations, inspired by Peter Abelard and carried on in accordance with very strict rules, made their appearance in the twelfth century and in turn fostered two other literary forms, the so-called *quaestiones disputatae* and the more liberal *quodlibeta*. Owing to considerable difficulties, such as the problems of copying and translating, knowledge of classical literature and philosophy spread slowly. By way of example, Aristotle was primarily known only as a logician until well into the twelfth century while scholars kept to the Neoplatonic tradition as represented by Augustine, Boethius, and Pseudo-Dionysius. When, toward the close of the twelfth and beginning of the thirteenth centuries, scholars became familiar with Aristotle's theories of physics and metaphysics, they found themselves with theories that had been passed on by an Arabian philosophy that was heavily influenced by Neoplatonism.

There is no question but that significant beginnings were made during the first period of Scholasticism, that is, from the sixth to the tenth centuries; nevertheless, this long span must be regarded as essentially a time of preparation. There is only one thinker from this entire period who simply cannot be overlooked in even the sketchiest outline: John Scotus Erigena,[12] who draws on the much earlier Plotinus and prefigures the arrival of Spinoza and the most important thinker of German Idealism, Hegel. In *On the Division of Nature* (*De divisione naturae*) Erigena endeavored to form the first great synthesis of faith and reason to appear in the Middle Ages; what is more, he even proposed to demonstrate their identity.

---

[12] A summary of Erigena's world of thought is given in H. Bett, *Johannes Scotus Erigena* (Cambridge, 1925), and the chief modern work is M. Cappuyns, *Jean Scot Erigène*, 2nd ed. (Paris, 1964), in which the author energetically seeks to interpret him as an exegetic theologian. Of older literature on this speculative thinker, Peder Hjort's (1793–1871) monograph (published in German) is worthy of particular mention: *Johann Scotus Erigena, oder von dem Ursprung einer christlichen Philosophie und ihrem heiligen Beruf* (Copenhagen, 1823).

Erigena intended to use the Neoplatonic theory of emanation, which he adopted in place of the theory of creation, to comprehend the whole of existence, including both nature and God. According to his doctrine, existence passes through four stages in the course of its evolution: an uncreated and creative nature consisting of God as the progenitor of all things; a created and creative nature composed of reason and ideas; created and noncreative nature, which comprehends objects in time and space; and, lastly, uncreated and noncreative nature, or God as the final end to which everything reverts.

Dialectics as logic gradually gained prominence in the field of liberal arts, relegating the other liberal subjects to the background, so the art of disputation was now regarded as alone constituting philosophy, precisely as in the time of the Greek Sophists. This in turn helped to give reason an increasingly independent position in relation to faith.

Berengar of Tours, one of the most important dialecticians of this epoch, advanced the claim that all thought must be noncontradictory. In opposition to him stood Peter Damian (1007–1072), a contemporary and the greatest of antidialecticians, who proclaimed that dialectics was an invention of the Devil, the liberal arts were useless, and all science was folly. Succeeding generations sought to find a compromise between the extremes of Berengar's rationalism and Damian's antirationalism.

The issue of faith versus reason came to a head when Berengar applied his principles to the traditional Eucharistic doctrines. Substance and accident are correlative principles, he argued; if, therefore, the accidents of bread and wine remain unaltered after consecration, their substance cannot undergo any change either. The Church reacted sharply to this repudiation of the Eucharistic doctrines and against dialectics itself, for dialectics had now revealed how dangerous to faith it could be.

Anselm of Canterbury (1033–1109), known as the Father of Scholasticism, subjected the interrelation of reason and faith to new deliberations. He came to the result, first of all, that the Bible embodies the whole truth simply because it explicitly promulgates the truth, and also because it does not deny one single truth. He thereupon concluded that, initially, faith involves an acceptance on the strength of authority; but faith also requires an insight into its content (*fides quaerens intellectum*), which in turn means that the believer will have need of rational ground, experience, and an understanding of what has been accepted by virtue of authority. Furthermore, Anselm considered faith a presupposition for all cognition (*credo ut intelligam*);

cognition is a reward of faith. The means necessary to arrive at an insight into faith (*intellectus fidei*) are in his view first of all rational arguments (*rationes necessariae*), then concentrated studies of natural analogies,[13] and finally ethical purgation.

As is evident from above, the dispute about dialectics did not discourage Anselm. On the contrary, he boldly employed dialectics in the field of theology, both formally and as a means to develop the content of faith itself. He went so far in the latter effort as to arrive at the conviction that it is possible to produce rational arguments in support of the doctrines of the Trinity and Incarnation (*Cur deus homo*). His theory of the interrelation of faith and reason was fundamentally a readaptation of Augustine's thoughts.[14]

Anselm subsequently applied his theory in his famous ontological proof of God's existence.[15] As a Christian, Anselm was fully convinced that God exists and is supreme. But he felt that whoever wishes to elevate this faith to the level of knowledge and know what he believes will have to proceed from the generally accepted conception of God as that beyond which nothing greater is conceivable. It now follows, Anselm argued, that something beyond which nothing greater is conceivable cannot be in the intellect alone, for in that case it would be possible to imagine that it also exists in reality. Now, since what exists in reality is greater than what has conceptual existence, something could be imagined to exist that is superior to the contents of the concept. Thus if it were in the intellect alone, that beyond which nothing greater is conceivable would turn out to be such that something greater than it is in fact conceivable. The concept itself of course precludes this possibility. Therefore, something that is supreme and most perfect, and beyond which nothing greater is conceivable, must exist in both the mind and reality.

This ontological proof of the existence of God was later used in a modified form by Duns Scotus, Descartes, and Leibniz, even though its validity had already been rejected in Anselm's own time by Gaunilon and later by Thomas Aquinas. Kant refuted the argument in the eighteenth century, asserting that existence cannot emerge as the result of a conceptual definition. Hegel followed Anselm.[16]

---

[13] For the historical development of the analogy of being and its use especially in Thomas Aquinas, see in particular Hampus Lyttkens, *The Analogy between God and the World* (Uppsala, 1952).

[14] Concerning Anselm, see especially Karl Barth, *Fides quaerens intellectum*, 2nd ed. (Zollikon, 1958), and J. McIntyre, *St. Anselm and His Critics* (Edinburgh, 1954).

[15] In *Proslogium*. Barth's book mentioned in the preceding note is an interpretation of the proof.

[16] See Dieter Henrich, *Der ontologische Gottesbeweis* (Tübingen, 1960).

Another knotty problem in early Scholasticism concerned the nature and worth of concepts. The controversy between Plato and Aristotle was primarily about metaphysical theories and focused on the question of whether ideas or particular things possess actual being. Medieval thinkers, on the other hand, tackled issues that were predominantly oriented toward epistemology, and so they inquired about whether logic as exemplified in Aristotle's theory of the categories was a formal or real discipline. Some scholars, accepting the Platonic theory of the reality of the Ideas, held that it was a real discipline and were consequently called Realists. Others, adhering to the opposite view, were called Vocalists or Nominalists, thereby indicating that instead of regarding the categories as things, they considered them to be merely words or designations (*nomina*).

Heated debates followed, after which mediation prevailed in the person of Peter Abelard. He subscribed to the views of Aristotle and Boëthius and was influenced by Adelard of Bath, who taught that the universal and particular are merely two aspects of the same reality. Abelard now declared, in agreement with the nominalist thesis, that everything that exists is particular. Mere words are themselves particular things, but they may be uttered about various things and concepts, which in turn may be classified into universal and particular concepts. Although it does hold true that universal concepts exist in the intellect only, they nevertheless conform to existing entities in a definite arrangement, and we cannot call this conformity of things and concepts either a thing by itself or nothing.

Medieval thought underwent further differentiation in the twelfth century, with the cathedral school in Chartres, the monastery in Cîteaux, and the University of Paris developing into centers. Chartres became the center for the secular disciplines; Cîteaux the locus of the medieval mysticism of St. Bernard, which deliberately ignored or was adamantly opposed to the use of dialectical thought; and the University of Paris the home of the Victorines, who were largely influenced by Augustine and sought to fashion a synthesis of secular and religious knowledge, with mystical cognition as the highest stage. At the same time a Jewish and Arab scholasticism developed. Thanks mainly to Avicenna and Averroes, Arab scholasticism came to influence its Christian counterpart in a spirit of Neoplatonism and Pantheism.

When we turn to the thirteenth century we are able to distinguish between five different schools of thought: Averroism; Augustinianism, whose most prominent representative was Bonaventura; the Oxford School led by Roger Bacon; Neoplatonism, which exerted considerable influence on Albert the Great; and Thomism. Through the agency of Albert the Great, moreover, Aristotle came to have a decisive effect on the development of Thomas Aquinas' entire metaphysical philosophy into its definitive form.

Thomas distinguished sharply between faith and knowledge, revelation and reason, and theology and philosophy. Only in this way did he consider it possible to combine these fields into one system without confounding them and making them seem identical.[17]

In Thomas' view knowledge is not innate in man; man is endowed from birth only with a rational faculty enabling him to abstract from particulars and form universal concepts. Cognition takes empirical knowledge as its point of departure and is then able to advance to knowledge of the realm of nature, but it is incapable of proceeding directly to the apprehension of God, for this last form of cognition is native to the realm of grace. Since there is an analogy between the Creator and creation, however, it is possible by means of natural reason to extract proofs of God's existence from creation and to attain to a consciousness of as much of God's essence as can be inferred from this source.[18] But the natural reason is never able to penetrate into the supernatural world of faith. Thomas drew an impassable border between the territories of faith and knowledge, ruling out any possibility of both believing and knowing the same thing; faith and knowledge are two qualitatively different forms of cognition oriented toward qualitatively different objects. For all that, the two faculties are not contradictory, inasmuch as God, being the Creator, is in the final analysis the originator and ultimate goal of both. In Thomas' opinion, the faculty of reason at sinful man's disposal is unable to achieve cognition of God unaided; for this, divine grace is needed.

Thomas did not regard faith as a product of rational cognition but as a supernatural gift bestowed by God. Nonetheless, reason can pave the way for faith by demonstrating that even though the truths of faith transcend reason they are not at odds with it. Likewise, once faith has emerged, reason can play a helpful part in acquiring an

[17] See, among others, M.-D. Chenu, *Introduction à l'étude de Saint Thomas d'Aquin*, 2nd ed. (Montreal, 1954), and the more comprehensive works such as Étienne Gilson, *Le Thomisme*, 5th ed. (Paris, 1947); Gallus M. Manser, *Das Wesen des Thomismus*, 3rd ed. (Freiburg [Switzerland], 1949); P. Reginald Garrigou-Lagrange, *La synthèse thomiste* (Paris, 1950); and Maurice de Wulf, *The System of Thomas Aquinas* (New York, 1959). The relationship between reason and revelation is treated by P. E. Persson in *Sacra doctrina* (Lund, 1957). Another important work is Cornelio Fabro, *Participation et causalité selon S. Thomas d'Aquin* (Paris, 1961).

[18] See Lyttkens, *Analogy*.

analytical knowledge of the truths of faith and toward arriving at a formulation of their contents and mutual relationships.

In *Summa contra gentiles* and *Summa theologica*, Thomas developed his views of the substance and contents of faith and knowledge, and their interrelationship, in keeping with the principles outlined above and on the basis of a teleological view derived from Aristotle. He worked out both the form and content of his *Summa* in harmony with the cosmology discussed in the preceding chapter: everything is created by God and is destined to return to its source. Thomas made this clear right at the beginning of the work.[19] Part One treats of God considered as the cause and end of all things, the One and Triune; then men and angels as rational beings created in the image of God; and finally man's intellect and will. Part Two, which is divided into two sections (*prima secundae* and *secunda secundae*), deals with the movement of the rational creatures back to God. Since man is a created being, Thomas wrote, he is predisposed to make this movement; but because he has fallen into sin he has both lost sight of his supernatural goal and forfeited the capacity for aspiring to it, even though after the fall he still has retained free will and the powers of reasoning and thus is able to strive for relative ends. Only the insight available in faith and conveyed through revelation can enable man to determine what his highest goal is. In the final and actually theological part of the *Summa*, the instrument for attainment of the goal is revealed to be Christ, who reopened the path to God by means of his incarnation, death, and resurrection, and who is present in the Church in the sacraments, the channels through which God's grace flows.

Analyzing in order again to combine, Thomas evolved a harmonious synthesis, a system in which he tried to put everything in its proper place. But his system soon became the object of severe criticism. Duns Scotus and William of Ockham deserve special mention in this regard.

Duns Scotus maintained that most of the assertions that Thomas regarded as demonstrable cannot in fact be proved rationally but derive exclusively from revelation; acceptance of these statements cannot, therefore, be supported by reasoned arguments. In developing an epistemology of his own, Duns Scotus contended that cognition of the particular is prior to cognition of the universal. This was further developed by William of Ockham, who taught that universal

---

[19] I quæ. 2: "tractabimus de Deo, de motu rationalis creaturæ in Deum, de Christo, qui (secundum quod homo) via est nobis tendendi in Deum."

concepts are present in the knowing subject only and not in either God or particular things. To William of Ockham it was thus even less possible to prepare for and substantiate faith by means of rational argumentation than had been the case with Duns Scotus. Gabriel Biel, who has been called the last Scholastic of the Middle Ages, turned Ockham's views to account in theology, and thereby came to influence Luther. Kierkegaard's position is related to the views of these theologians.

Very early in his career, Luther turned against philosophy in general and Aristotle in particular.[20] Melanchthon, however, rehabilitated Aristotelianism, especially in *Oratio de Aristotele* (1544).[21] During the time of orthodoxy Aristotle played an essential role that did not end until the appearance of Leibniz, who was popularized by Wolff, the "schoolmaster" of the rationalistic philosophy that Kant's thinking supplanted under the influence of Hume.[22] Whereas Wolff-ianism only affected theology for a rather short time, Kant's philosophy was epoch-making, and its effects are quite evident even today in issues related to the philosophy of religion. The works on philosophy of religion written by theologians gradually took on the color of apologetics, whereas works on this subject written by philosophers branched off into quite different trends, as will become apparent in the following chapter.

[20] On this subject, see for example Wilhelm Link, *Das Ringen Luthers um die Freiheit der Theologie von der Philosophie*, 2nd ed. (Munich, 1955).

[21] *Melanchthons Werke*, ed. R. Stupperich, I–VI (Gütersloh, 1951–1955), III, 122ff.

[22] The reader is referred especially to Peter Petersen, *Geschichte der aristotelischen Philosophie im protestantischen Deutschland* (Leipzig, 1921); and Max Wundt, *Die deutsche Schulmetaphysik des 17. Jahrhunderts* (Tübingen, 1939) and *Die deutsche Schulphilosophie im Zeitalter der Aufklärung* (Tübingen, 1945; reprint, Hildesheim, 1964).

CHAPTER 3

Speculative Trends
in Modern Philosophy

As it was, even the earliest Italian humanists, such as Petrarch, Salutati, Boccaccio, Lorenzo Valla, and Leone Battista Alberti (to mention just a few), were critical of the Scholasticism in vogue during
their time. Detouring around the Medieval Scholasticism, they turned
instead directly to ancient literature and philosophy as a model.[1] But
the importance of a tradition that had evolved during the course of
more than a millennium could not be destroyed at one fell swoop.
Hence the majority of the works produced by the most outstanding
and influential religious-philosophical thinkers of this period generally provide evidence of a tense relationship between old and new.
Such is the case with Nicholas of Cusa, whose famous *De docta ig-
norantia*, which he completed in 1440, continues the Neoplatonic line
while pointing ahead to Spinoza and German Idealism, though in a
spirit of originality. For example, his theory that everything shares
or participates in the divine is broadly speaking Neoplatonic. So too
Cardinal Bessarion, a famous pupil of Pletho,[2] directed his efforts
toward a revival of Platonism, but in a Plotinian spirit. In 1459, Cosimo Medici reestablished the Academy of Plato in Florence, at which
Marsilio Ficino and Pico della Mirandola became the most prominent
thinkers.[3] Of interest in the present context is the fact that this school

[1] See the still important work by Jacob Burckhardt, *Die Kultur der Renaissance in
Italien* (Vienna, Illustrated Phaidon-Edition, 1960); G. Voigt, *Die Wiederbelebung des
klassischen Altertums*, 3rd ed., I–II (Berlin, 1893); Wilhelm Dilthey, *Weltanschauung und
Analyse des Menschen seit Renaissance und Reformation*, 6th ed. (Stuttgart, 1960); G. C.
Sellery, *The Renaissance: Its Nature and Origins* (Madison, 1950); Paulus Svendsen, *En-
het og mangfold i europæisk kultur* (Oslo, 1980); and my articles in Niels Thulstrup,
Akcept og Protest. Artikler i Udvalg, I–II (Copenhagen, 1981), especially I, 107ff.

[2] An excellent monograph on this unique personality is François Masai, *Pléthon et le
platonisme de Mistra* (Paris, 1956).

[3] See in particular P. O. Kristeller, *The Philosophy of Marsilio Ficino* (New York,
1943). Ficino's chief work, *Commentarium in convivium Platonis de amore*, has been published by R. Marcel with notes, a comprehensive introduction, and a translation into
French under the title, *Commentaire sur le Banquet de Platon* (Paris, 1956). Ernst Cassirer,
ed., *The Renaissance Philosophy of Man* (Chicago, 1948), contains selected texts with
introductions by Cassirer, Kristeller, and J. H. Randall. Concerning Pico, see Johannes
Sløk, *Tradition og nybrud* (Copenhagen, 1957).

was devoted to the preservation of the Alexandrine cosmology and the development of a universal religion containing elements derived from various sources.

Above all, however, the change in the view of man that emerged at this time was of sweeping import. In *Oratio quaedam elegantissima de hominis dignitate* (1486), Pico, the chief spokesman for this nascent view, glorified man's infinite potential and boundless freedom in an unprecedented manner. According to Pico, man is not simply assigned a preordained place and task in the divine scheme of things; on the contrary, man chooses his own place and is then able sovereignly to decide how he will form his own life and mold his environment. In effect, Pico pays homage to man as a god instead of to God who became man. The result of this new attitude was to divert attention from life in the hereafter to life on earth. Just as Marx later turned Hegel's fundamental concepts upside down, so thinkers during the Renaissance inverted Plotinus' ideas, paying warm tribute to an all-embracing, secularized, mystical pantheism. These trends were in turn supported by a revised cosmology. When Giordano Bruno taught that space is infinite, the ancient and Medieval cosmologies, the nicely arranged Cosmos, and the concomitant philosophies and theologies were at once robbed of all meaning. If space is infinite, there is of course no center from which to govern the aggregate; "up" and "down" become merely relative concepts, both literally and figuratively; and any point selected at random can serve as center. So man, who has understood infinity, can also be the center of existence and his own end in life. This novel conception is exemplified by Tommaso Campanella, the last of the Italian Renaissance thinkers, who expanded and used Augustine's epistemological theories of methodical doubt and man's self-awareness to form the basis of his own theory concerning the acquisition of knowledge.

To understand how the issues confronting religious and philosophical thinkers developed until the advent of German Idealism, it is important to be familiar with three trends in the history of philosophy: philosophical rationalism, empiricism, and criticism. The most prominent representatives of these currents of thought were Descartes, Spinoza, Leibniz, Locke, Hume, and Kant. But equally important, especially in connection with German Idealism, is the circumstance that the older tradition dominated by Plotinism remained alive, even if in various adaptations. These speculations, which sometimes could be rather abstruse, likewise contained Gnostic, Cabalistic, and Christian elements.

We encounter speculation in the field of natural philosophy as early as the time of Agrippa of Nettesheim. But in this respect Paracelsus proved to be more significant, for he worked out a system that spread widely and exerted considerable influence, especially on Jacob Boehme, a strange *philosophus teutonicus*.[4]

Boehme set out to solve the puzzles of being by adopting a cosmology that resembled the Alexandrian conception of the world. He proposed that the world proceeded from God's inmost being, nothingness, and evolved through a succession of stages in a downward path to nature, which in turn is governed by seven nature spirits. Boehme solved the problem concerning the origin of good and evil—a recurrent issue in the history of philosophy and religion—by assuming a duality in God permitting the presence of both, an opposition controlling all of being, which for its part strives to overcome the duality. Similar conceptions can be found in Schelling, in Baader, and, in a rationalized version, in Hegel.

In comparison with their Italian contemporaries, the French humanists, Montaigne, Charron, and others,[5] are less significant in the present context. Nor did the new science of nature that arose at this time immediately entail radical changes in approach to the issues current in the fields of religion and philosophy.

The individualism of the Renaissance thinkers, the revised cosmology presented by Copernicus, and the attempts to find a new and unshakable foundation for cognition all left deep marks in religious-philosophical thought.

In his *Discours de la Méthode*,[6] Descartes wrote:

> Of philosophy I will say nothing, except that when I saw that it had been cultivated for many ages by the most distinguished men, and that yet there is not a single matter within its sphere which is not still in dispute, and nothing, therefore, which is above doubt, I did not presume to anticipate that my success would be greater

---

[4] See *Hegel's Lectures on the History of Philosophy*, trans. E. S. Haldane, I–III (London and New York, 1963), III, 188–216. It is evident from these passages that Hegel held Boehme in high esteem. But he nevertheless felt obliged to complain that "because no method or order is to be found in him [Boehme], it is difficult to give an account of his philosophy" (ibid., p. 189). See also *Jub. Ausg.* XIX 296ff., especially H. L. Martensen, *Jacob Boehme, His Life and Teaching*, trans. T. Rhys Evans (London, 1885).

[5] Regarding these philosophers, see especially Henri Busson, *La pensée religieuse française de Charron à Pascal* (Paris, 1933), and *Les Sources et le Développement du rationalisme dans la littérature française de la Renaissance (1533–1601)*, 2nd ed. (Paris, 1957).

[6] In René Descartes, *Oeuvres et Lettres*, ed. A. Bridoux, *Bibliothèque de la Pléiade* (Paris, 1958), pp. 130ff.

in it than that of others; and further, when I considered the numbers of conflicting opinions touching a single matter that may be
upheld by learned men, while there can be but one true, I reckoned
as well-nigh false all that was only probable.

As to the other Sciences, inasmuch as these borrow their principles from Philosophy, I judged that no solid superstructures could
be reared on foundations so infirm.[7]

Descartes thereupon decided to make a fresh beginning and to proceed in accordance with the following four rules:

The *first* was never to accept anything for true which I did not
clearly know to be such; that is to say, carefully to avoid precipi-
tancy and prejudice, and to comprise nothing more in my judgment than what was presented to my mind so clearly and distinctly
as to exclude all ground of doubt.

The *second*, to divide each of the difficulties under examination
into as many parts as possible, and as might be necessary for its
adequate solution.

The *third*, to conduct my thoughts in such order that . . . I
might ascend little by little . . . to the knowledge of the more
complex. . . .

And *last*, in every case to make enumerations so complete, and
reviews so general, that I might be assured that nothing was omitted.[8]

It is of course well known that Descartes consequently concluded that
even if he applied methodic doubt everywhere, doubting both empirical and rational knowledge, it would still be impossible for him
to doubt his own existence.

And . . . I observed that in the words *I think, hence I am*, there is
nothing at all which gives me assurance of their truth beyond this,
that I see very clearly that in order to think it is necessary to exist.[9]

For Descartes, all cognition is rooted in self-consciousness, which in
turn is based on a consciousness of God.

In the next place, from reflecting on the circumstance that I
doubted, and that consequently my being was not wholly perfect
(for I clearly saw that it was a greater perfection to know than to

[7] Translation from *The Harvard Classics*, ed. Charles W. Eliot, vol. 34 (New York,
1911), p. 12.
[8] Ibid., pp. 17ff.
[9] Ibid., p. 29.

doubt), I was led to inquire whence I had learned to think of something more perfect than myself; and I clearly recognized that I must
hold this notion from such Nature which in reality was more perfect.[10]

In other words, God was to Descartes a guarantee, or rather the
condition making true and valid cognition possible. It was on this
foundation that he developed his rationalist system of metaphysics.
The autonomy of the self-consciousness taught by Descartes became
a vital principle in the ensuing development of philosophy and a fundamental axiom in German speculative Idealism.[11]

In his *Lettres à un Provincial*, and more particularly in *Pensées sur la
Vérité de la Religion chrétienne*,[12] Pascal took man's potential for self-
understanding as a starting point. He then described man's ceaseless
striving and extremely limited prospects of acquiring knowledge of
God through empirical or rational means, and of thereby arriving at
a true knowledge of himself. These two works constitute a remarkable and highly contrasting parallel to Kierkegaard's theology and
anthropology. But Pascal was no more successful than Kierkegaard
in steering contemporary religious and philosophical thought toward
new and uncharted paths.

Spinoza's philosophy of identity makes him as much a father of
modern philosophy as Descartes. His philosophy is based on the conviction that thought and actuality conform, thus making it possible
to discern an all-pervasive regularity by rational means. Certainty of
this knowledge depends, according to Spinoza, solely on external
evidence and conclusions; but man also has a capacity for an intuitive
perception that transcends rational cognition and is capable of spon-

[10] Ibid. See also *Descartes' Philosophical Writings*, selected and trans. Norman Kemp
Smith (London, 1952), pp. 115–64.

[11] It may be noted here that Martensen criticized this epistemological principle in
his dissertation from 1837 (see below, chap. 6). An extremely critical view of the
history of philosophy from "the Cartesian Cogito to the Present Day" is expressed
by Cornelio Fabro, *God in Exile. Modern Atheism* (New York, 1968). See my review
of this work, "Gud i Landflygtighed," *Akcept og Protest*, I (Copenhagen, 1981), pp.
153–56.

[12] Jacques Chevalier has provided an excellent edition of Pascal's *Oeuvres complètes*
in *Bibliothèque de la Pléiade* (Paris, 1954). The best existing edition of Pascal's *Pensées*
is, however, that by Louis Lafuma, I–III (Paris, 1951). Of the extensive literature
concerning Pascal, special reference may be made to Arthur Rich, *Pascals Bild vom
Menschen* (Zürich, 1953); and Per Lønning, *Tro og tanke efter Blaise Pascal* (Oslo, 1958),
and *Cet effrayant pari* (Paris, 1980). In Louis Lafuma, ed., *Histoire des "Pensées" de Pascal
1656–1952* (Paris, 1954), the editor has outlined the complex problems connected with
the text and the various editions.

taneously understanding unity and plurality. At this stage, man, apprehending that he is in God, perceives particular things from the vantage point of eternity (*sub specie aeternitatis*). Like his predecessors in modern philosophy, Spinoza was looking for an ultimate causal rather than a teleological explanation; he thought that it would be impossible to end a study of causes unless there existed something that was its own cause. By "its own cause" Spinoza understood "that, the essence of which presupposes existence, or that which by its very nature can only be conceived of as having existence."[13] He was here referring to substance, which he identified with nature, and nature in turn with God. For Spinoza, substance is the only thing that exists per se; what man is able to apprehend, therefore, is either an attribute or a manifestation of substance. Inasmuch as substance in the final analysis constitutes the only reality, and since there is nothing that limits it, it must be infinite and possess an infinite number of characteristics or attributes. Spinoza called this substance God, which turns out to be an impersonal being and identical with nature. Spinoza's Pantheist concept of God clearly influenced German speculative philosophers. For example, Schelling identified spirit with nature in one eternal and divine life, and Hegel maintained that the absolute is the supreme all-pervading actuality. There is, moreover, an obvious and close resemblance among Spinoza's theory of *scientia intuitiva*, Schelling's *intellectuelle Anschauung* (intellectual intuition), and Hegel's dialectical method.

In Spinoza, the unique substance, God, alone owes its existence to itself and is able to comprehend its own essence.[14] This means that no particular being exists independently; a particular thing is simply one of the various modes (*modi*) in which the Substance manifests itself. The divine Substance expresses itself in each particular being as an instinct for self-preservation, which is translatable into a need to assert and confirm one's own nature. Indeed, Spinoza claimed that virtue consists in following this need and acting in harmony with the necessity imposed by one's own nature or essence, so like Hegel he posited an identity between necessity and freedom regarded as freedom from external compulsion. Thus man's aim must be to become autonomous and realize his intrinsic nature. The road leading to this

[13] *Ethica*, P. I, Def. 1: "per causam sui intelligo id, cujus essentia involvit existentiam; sive id, cujus natura non potest concipi nisi existens."

[14] Ibid., P. I, Def. 3: "per substantiam intelligo id, quod in se est, et per se concipitur: hoc est id, cujus conceptus non indiget alterius rei, a quo formari debeat." See H. G. Hubbeling, *Spinoza's Methodology* (Groningen, 1964), and Matthew Spinka, *Christian Thought from Erasmus to Berdyaev* (Englewood Cliffs, N.J., 1962), pp. 34–39.

goal is cognition, which in its highest form will be both knowledge of God and self-knowledge.

By means of a circumscribed and deterministic system Spinoza managed to carry through a rigorous causal explanation of all phenomena. Leibniz (1646–1716), on the other hand, attempted to combine causal and teleological theories, and in so doing he reestablished the link with German Renaissance philosophy.[15] He imagined a universe made up of monads, or centers of force, in which individuality and substantiality permeate each other. Each monad is a reflection of the world, a cosmological mirror and archetype that, insusceptible to external stimuli, is a self-fulfilling principle of activity. The positions of the monads in the hierarchy of existence are determined by the degree of clarity and lucidity (perception and apperception) with which each monad succeeds in mirroring the universe. The lowest monads are in a kind of dream state and appear as insensible matter. The monads of the soul and spirit occupy a higher position and are capable of organizing and subjugating an infinite number of other monads; the monads are thus able to gain mastery over and control a body. Uppermost in the chain of monads is the divine central monad that sustains a harmony between the rest of the monads (*harmonia praestabilita*).

This served as a basis for Leibniz's *Theodicy*, which he published in 1710. He believed it possible to interpret metaphysical and moral evils as inevitable deficiencies that, however, serve to set the good and beautiful into relief. Regarding this world as the best of all possible worlds, he hailed an optimism centered on progress that was passed on to the eighteenth and nineteenth centuries. Hegel in particular was a beneficiary.

Whereas Descartes tried to avoid any conflict between his philosophy and Church doctrine, Spinoza assumed a completely independent attitude. Leibniz, the last great thinker to construe a rationalist system, believed like Pascal that religious truths transcend but do not conflict with reason. This view was developed further by Christian Wolff, among others.

The philosophy of the Enlightenment took divergent courses in England, France, and Germany, but in general it proceeded along well-beaten paths.[16] Of the philosophers of the period who showed

[15] In connection with the following, see my introduction to *Philosophical Fragments* (Princeton, 1962), p. xlvi–lx. See also C. H. Koch, *Den europæiske Filosofs Historie fra Reformationen til Oplysningstiden* (Copenhagen, 1984).

[16] Ernst Cassirer, *Die Philosophie der Aufklärung* (Tübingen, 1932); and P. Hazard, *La crise de la conscience européenne 1680–1715*, 2nd ed. (Paris, 1961), and *La pensée européenne au XVIIIème siècle*, I–III (Paris, 1946).

independence and in various ways influenced subsequent developments, we need here only mention Hamann, Herder, Lessing, and
Jacobi.

Central to Hamann's distinctive style of reasoning is his theory of
God's self-abasement in revealing Himself through nature, human
life, and the Bible. Hamann points to language, a wholly divine and
also wholly human means of communication, as the medium of revelation. Provided that man both has faith and is in a state of innocence, he will be able to hear the word of God and apprehend the
reality created by God in its entirety. But because of original sin man
has lost both his faith and innocence, and as a consequence the mark
of human life is now contradiction; only Christ's redemptive act makes
it possible for human beings to understand themselves and live right-
eous lives. The history of salvation, Hamann insists, is the same for
both mankind considered as a macrocosm and the individual regarded as a microcosm.[17]

Herder was indebted to Hamann for a profound and enduring inspiration, but he converted this impulse into a humanistic religion.
At the same time he developed a philosophy of history that met with
sympathy among the genuine romantics who followed him because
of its all-embracing scope and partiality toward Medieval culture.
The fact that Herder was also influenced by Spinoza is evident from
Gespräche über Gott (1787). Jacobi created a stir especially with *Über
die Lehre des Spinoza, in Briefen an Herrn Moses Mendelssohn* (1785).
He protested against what he considered to be an excessive cultiva-
tion of reason, emphasizing instead faith taken in the usual sense as
the bridge leading from thought to existence itself.

The last philosopher to be mentioned in this chapter is Lessing,
whom Kierkegaard extols in the *Postscript* as an "existing thinker" in
contradistinction to the many philosophers who merely deal in speculation. Lessing took a critical view of orthodox Lutheranism and
the theology of the Enlightenment. As a rule, scholars have hereto-
fore interpreted Lessing's personal standpoint as being predominantly

---

[17] Concerning Hamann, see especially E. Metzke, *J. G. Hamanns Stellung in der Philosophie des 18. Jahrhunderts* (Halle, 1934); W. Leibrecht, *Gott und Mensch bei Johann
Georg Hamann* (Gütersloh, 1958); Ronald G. Smith, *J. G. Hamann. A Study in Christian
Existence* (London, 1960); and Svend-Aage Jørgensen, *Johann Georg Hamann* (Stuttgart,
1976), which contains a good selective bibliography. See also A. Anderson, "Hamann," *Bibliotheca Kierkegaardiana*, X: *Kierkegaard's Teachers* (Copenhagen, 1982). Regarding Herder, see Emanuel Hirsch, *Geschichte der neuern evangelischen Theologie*, I–V
(Gütersloh, 1949–1954), IV. As to Jacobi, see O. F. Bollnow, *Die Lebensphilosophie F.
H. Jacobis* (Stuttgart, 1933).

a rather singular combination of Spinozism, evolutionary optimism, and ethical idealism (*Nathan der Weise*). Recent scholarship, however, led by Thielicke and Otto Mann, seems to have established the fact that in his chief work on the philosophy of religion, *Erziehung des Menschengeschlechts* (1780), Lessing on the contrary gave revelation a position superior to reason and insisted that mankind is still far from having reached the spiritual level of the New Testament.[18]

[18] See my commentary on the *Philosophical Fragments*, pp. xlix ff., with references to relevant literature in note 4, pp. l–li. A capital treatment of Kierkegaard and Lessing is Jacques Colette, *Histoire et absolu* (Paris, 1972). See also Claus v. Bormann, "Lessing," *Bibliotheca Kierkegaardiana*, X: *Kierkegaard's Teachers* (Copenhagen, 1982).

CHAPTER 4

From Kant to Hegel

Kant's works ended one era in philosophy and ushered in a new.[1] It is a well-known fact that Kant took a novel approach to the problems besetting epistemology. He was in no doubt about the feasibility of attaining universally valid, scientific knowledge, for he had noted that pure mathematics and Newtonian physics yield results that are reliable by comparison to the mutually contradictory and uncertain opinions generated by metaphysical philosophy. He therefore posed a new question: What conditions are necessary to make scientific knowledge actually possible?

Kant went about answering that question by applying his famous transcendental method. He reached the conclusion that knowledge of the phenomenal world is rendered possible by space and time, considered as two modes of perception, and by the modes of understanding, of which the two most important are the categories of substance and cause. This does not, however, hold true of the noumenal world, which pure reason cannot make accessible to us. Even though we thus set a limit to the scope of theoretical knowledge, we do not on that account suppress our urge to attain to an ultimate knowledge that encompasses everything and is therefore conclusive and absolute. In our desire to satisfy completely a conscious impulse to synthesize, we comprise everything that exists under one absolute concept, which we call "world," and then conclude our causal explanation by penetrating to the "final cause" of existence, the *causa sui*, or God. At the same time we find that behind the synthesizing activity of consciousness there is a "soul" that, being a self-contained and simple unity, supports this activity. Kant called these three concepts "Ideas of Pure Reason," by which he meant transcendent concepts, that is, concepts

---

[1] Surveys of German philosophy from Kant to Hegel are provided by Nicolai Hartmann, *Die Philosophie des deutschen Idealismus*, 3rd printing, I–II bound in one volume (Berlin, 1960), and Richard Kroner, *Von Kant bis Hegel*, 2nd printing, I–II bound in one volume (Tübingen, 1961). Kant's influence on early Danish philosophy is treated in Anders Thuborg's dissertation, *Den kantiske Periode i dansk Filosofi 1790–1800* (Copenhagen, 1951), and his philosophy is outlined in John Kemp, *The Philosophy of Kant* (London, New York, and Toronto, 1968).

to which nothing in experience corresponds directly.[2] The Ideas of Pure Reason are regulative principles, or principles of validity; they do not exist in the manner of the phenomenal world known to us through the understanding, as metaphysical philosophers both before and after Kant have claimed. In Kant's view, the assumption that ideas of reason have existence in the usual sense leads to antinomies, and these can be resolved only by making use of his distinction between existence in itself and existence as it manifests itself to human cognition.

In *Kritik der reinen Vernunft* (1781) and *Prolegomena zu einer jeden künftigen Metaphysik, die als Wissenschaft wird auftreten können* (1783), Kant sought to surmount the persistent disagreement between rationalism and empiricism by restating the theoretical problems of knowledge and tackling them from a new angle. He likewise raised the question of the conditions necessary for establishing an ethic in *Grundlegung zur Metaphysik der Sitten* (1785) and *Kritik der praktischen Vernunft* (1788). In a subsequent work, *Kritik der Urteilskraft* (1790), he endeavored to bring theoretical and practical reason together in a synthesis. In Kant, theoretical knowledge has the natural world as its proper object, whereas the realm of practical reason is the world of freedom. He now looked to beauty as the sole medium capable of unifying the two corresponding forms of knowledge. Kant finally dealt with religious-philosophical issues in 1793 in *Religion innerhalb der Grenzen der blossen Vernunft*.

As we shall see, the speculative Idealists proposed to go further than Kant. Their efforts were directed toward a synthesis that would embrace not only knowledge of the phenomenal world but also the ideas of reason. Assuming the existence of a divine principle that is the governing power behind all existence and serves as both its starting point and final end, they intended to produce a comprehensive philosophical system of logic in conformity with existence viewed as a complete system.

Now, Kant's theory of knowledge was open to an interpretation according to which its laws were applicable to nature, because nature exists only for the knowing consciousness; it does not have existence in itself. This would imply that nature must necessarily accord with the forms produced by the mind, whereas anything lying beyond the phenomenal world would be beyond the reach of knowledge as well.

[2] In Kant's terminology "transcendental" denotes that which relates to the conditions necessary for knowledge, whereas "transcendent" refers to what lies beyond the reach of knowledge.

But it was also felt that Kant had been inconsistent in suggesting *das Ding an sich* as the cause of phenomena and the source of cognitive material to be interpreted by the consciousness. Kant's own argument rests on the premise that the category of cause is invalid outside the world of phenomena, and thus cannot be used to explain the origin and presence of phenomena in the mind. If we eliminate Kant's "thing-in-itself," however, we will also be able to erase the limit that Kant had imposed on knowledge. It would then be possible, the Idealists argued, to assume that everything is present solely in the mind and that the consciousness, or ego, alone makes knowledge of things possible. This formative ego could thus serve as a basis on which to predicate a creative ego.

In 1794, Fichte ventured just such an undertaking in *Wissenschafts-lehre*.[3] He claimed that the limitation implied by Kant's acceptance of a "thing-in-itself" was in fact a relic from rational dogmatism. In his view, there was no reason whatever for a theory of knowledge to mention anything at all beyond or independent of the mind. To be sure, he admitted, dogmatism cannot be refuted directly; but it cannot be substantiated either. Dogmatism can become a starting point for philosophy only through a deliberate choice. As his own point of departure, however, Fichte on the contrary chose an idealistic approach, inferring everything from the cognitive subject itself, so the free and thinking personality makes a choice that results in a fundamental solipsism. Fichte thus looked on the ego as absolute actuality and not simply as a dormant being in a state of potentiality. The ego's profoundest act, then, consists in consciousness thinking itself; in other words, the ego affirms or posits its own existence.

If we accept the logical axiom that *omnis determinatio est negatio*, it will follow that the ego is only definable in terms of its difference from something else, in this case a non-ego. In Fichte's opinion, this non-ego does not lie outside the mind but is in the cognitive consciousness, to which, however, it appears as a product of the ego. The ego and the newly affirmed non-ego conflict with each other, according to Fichte, and this opposition can be resolved only by adding a third element capable of bringing them together in a higher synthesis. The ego and non-ego will annul each other if predicated absolutely, whereas they can persist as relative concepts.

According to Fichte's three principles, the world confronting the

---

[3] See my introduction to *Philosophical Fragments*, p. liii, note 6, and W. v. Kloeden, "Sören Kierkegaard und J. G. Fichte," *Bibliotheca Kierkegaardiana*, IV: *Kierkegaard and Speculative Idealism* (Copenhagen, 1979), pp. 114–44.

finite and limited ego does not consist of independent entities; rather, the ego produces them and in so doing sets its own limits. The ego unconsciously engenders the world as it does sense qualities, but to the empirical consciousness all this seems to exist and occur necessarily. Now, it must be assumed that the activity that produces a world picture in our consciousness is elevated above all the particular egos. Indeed, Fichte believed that existence can only be apprehended essentially by assuming the existence of an infinite ego that transcends particularity. If we were now to ask Fichte just why such a pure ego should limit its infinite activity, he would resort to practical philosophy and reply that moral acts presuppose something that must be overcome.

Fichte's assertion that a universal ego exploits the unconsciously creative imagination to produce a cosmology was of decisive importance to the Romantic school. The Romantics, however, proceeded to efface the borderline that Fichte had drawn between the universal ego on the one side and the individual ego possessing artistic or poetic genius on the other.[4]

Friedrich Schlegel stated the manifesto of the Romantic school in the periodical *Athenäum*, which he and his brother August Wilhelm published from 1798 to 1800. He claimed that an artist has a clear right to remain aloof from the humdrum of everyday life and from the rules and norms of moral conduct; in fact, he equated this poetic license with moral freedom in his novel *Lucinde*.

Schelling, rather than Fichte, is generally considered to be the most important philosopher of Romanticism, principally on the strength of his philosophy of nature.[5] He objected to the way Fichte had reduced nature to the point where it was merely a stage for the moral activities of the ego. His earliest works indicate that Fichte's three axioms merely served as a springboard in his own pursuit of an ab-

---

[4] See in this regard Kierkegaard's *Concept of Irony* and the various modern scholarly treatments, especially I. Strohschneider-Kohrs, *Die romantische Ironie in Theorie und Gestaltung* (Tübingen, 1960). A brief but precise description of the theoretical basis of the Romantic school is presented in F. J. Billeskov Jansen, *Danmarks Digtekunst*, I–III (Copenhagen, 1944–1958), III, 11ff.

[5] See in this respect especially Rudolph Haym, *Die romantische Schule*, 4th ed., ed. O. Walzel (Berlin, 1920); E. Benz, *Schelling, Werden und Wirken seines Denkens* (Zürich, 1955); and H. Knittermeyer, *Schelling und die romantische Schule* (Munich, 1929). Karl Jaspers, *Schelling* (Munich, 1955), is a sharp and critical polemic, and Walter Schulz, *Die Vollendung des deutschen Idealismus in der Spätphilosophie Schellings* (Cologne, 1955), contains a detailed interpretation and a positive evaluation. See also my "Kierkegaard and Schelling's Philosophy of Revelation," *Bibliotheca Kierkegaardiana*, IV, 144–60.

solute, a harmony between nature and spirit, and a reformulation of the ancient hierarchic cosmos (*Stufenkosmos*).

This tendency first became evident in *Ideen zu einer Philosophie der Natur* (1797) and is developed further in *Von der Weltseele* (1798) and *Erster Entwurf eines Systems der Naturphilosophie* (1799). In these and subsequent works Schelling aimed to achieve an ideal that had been advanced by Nicholas of Cusa and called the "coincidence of [apparent] opposites" (*coincidentia oppositorum*), such as inorganic and organic nature, plants and animals, nature and spirit, necessity and freedom. All of nature evolves according to a basic principle of polarity: a primary unity separates into two opposites that reunite into a whole at a higher level to form an organism. The prime mover behind this entire dynamic process is assumed to be spirit. The history of the development of spirit before it becomes conscious of itself is the history of nature, and the highest of its various subsequent manifestations is art. Schelling presented these views in *Systems des transcendentalen Idealismus* (1800), in which he abolished the opposition between nature and spirit while interpreting art as the profoundest explanation of being. His next step was to conceive of both nature and spirit as modes of expression by which the absolute, or God, is revealed. In other words, Schelling's thoughts had developed into a philosophy of identity. This fact becomes even more explicit in *Bruno, oder über das göttliche und natürliche Princip der Dinge*, in which all opposites eventually merge. Schelling maintained that the absolute can be grasped only by means of an intuitive contemplation in a mystical experience called "the intellectual intuition" (*die intellectuelle Anschauung*), whereby the subject and object of knowledge are regarded as fundamentally identical.

Schelling had thus proceeded along a speculative road leading from inanimate to animate nature and thence to spirit and the identity of spirit and nature. But now he found himself face to face with the problem of how to understand the emergence of the finite material world and its relation to the absolute. In *Bruno* and in a short treatise titled *Philosophie und Religion* (1804) he reverted to the Platonic doctrine of Ideas, regarding the visible world as an aggregate of reflections of a world of ideas that are archetypes; as mere reflections they are thus imperfect. He thereupon combined this with a theory according to which the world has fallen away from the absolute, but he stopped short of accepting either the dualism exemplified in Plato's *Timaeus* or Plotinus' monistic theory of emanation. In providing an explanation of the supposed fall, Schelling, unlike Boehme, wished to avoid placing the cause squarely on the shoulders of the absolute.

Instead, he advanced a fantastic theory to the effect that the absolute bestowed on its reflection freedom in the form of a nothingness whose end product was selfhood (*Jeghed*). This also represented a turning point in universal history, for now the absolute was successfully reconciled with this world through the media of nature, morality, science, and art.

The last great work to be published by the author himself, *Philosophische Untersuchungen über das Wesen der Menschlichen Freiheit und die damit zusammenhängenden Gegenstände* (1809), furnishes ample evidence of Schelling's preoccupation with evil and the strong influence exerted by Boehme in this connection. Like Boehme, he tried to solve this problem by postulating an inner development within the duality present in God; but unlike Boehme, he balked at the prospect of making God the cause of evil. Schelling sought to explain evil as something radical instead of as a mere lack of perfection. Nevertheless, like Hegel and like Goethe in Part One of *Faust*, he considered evil to be a necessary transitional stage on the way to the good, so the freedom that leads man to make the wrong choice is inherently good, too.

Schelling, along with Franz von Baader, succeeded in reviving the mystical and theosophic tradition founded by Jacob Boehme. Moreover, Baader tried to coordinate Boehme's theories and Christianity in the same way that Schelling in his final years worked toward a synthesis in his "positive" philosophy. Baader came to exert as powerful an influence as did Hegel on a certain professor in Copenhagen, Hans L. Martensen, who was one of the prime objects of Kierkegaard's criticism.[6]

The most outstanding theologian among the German Idealists was undoubtedly Schleiermacher. Yet in his own time he was not nearly as influential as the thinkers mentioned above. His *Über die Religion, Reden an die Gebildeten unter ihren Verächtern* appeared in 1799 and again in 1806 in an extensively revised edition. Basic features of the latter edition include, first and foremost, the development of an individualistic, subjective Idealism testifying to a thorough reading of Fichte's *Wissenschaftslehre*. Second, the work is permeated by a mystical pantheism disclosing an influence from Spinoza. But Schleier-

---

[6] See Skat Arildsen, *Biskop Hans Lassen Martensen. Hans Liv, Udvikling og Arbejde* (Copenhagen, 1932), pp. 95ff., 133ff., and passim; H. Brandt, *Gotteserkenntnis und Weltentfremdung* (Göttingen, 1971), and J. H. Schjørring, "Martensen as Søren Kierkegaard's Teacher," *Bibliotheca Kierkegaardiana*, X: *Kierkegaard's Teachers* (Copenhagen, 1982).

macher used both thinkers very freely, just as Lessing and Herder had earlier learned from Spinoza.

Schleiermacher declared that his lectures were written in defense of something quite different from what was commonly accepted as religion at the time. To be sure, historically religion had always been outwardly related to metaphysics and morality. But essentially religion is neither a system of teachings, as the orthodox theologians claimed; nor the set of external rules to which Pietists adhere; nor a complex of rational opinions about God, virtue, and immortality, as the Enlightenment philosophers, and Kant to an extent, held. Finally, religion cannot be identified with morality at all, as Kant had maintained in *Die Religion innerhalb der Grenzen der blossen Vernunft*. Schleiermacher affirmed that religion is on the contrary a spiritual condition in man in which man feels permeated by an immediate sensation of the infinite and eternal, an immediate awareness of the existence of finite being in the infinite, and an instinct for the universe. Schleiermacher viewed the universe as a living organism filled with divine life rather than a mere mechanism lacking a consciousness. During this religious, mystical experience man perceives how the divine principle of life, the universe, unveils itself in nature, history, and the particular individual's inmost being. At the same time, the divine life-force elicits all-inclusive feelings of humility, gratitude, love, pity, and remorse. Compared with this experience, historical revelation with its past testimonies and the conception of a personal God are of no importance whatever to religion. According to Schleiermacher, the various forms of religion that have appeared in the course of history substantiate this fact, each in its own way. Indeed, they prove it by the very circumstance that all of them, Christianity included, are incomplete in one respect or another.

The views that Schleiermacher propounded in *Über die Religion* represented a complete break with every traditional dogmatic interpretation of religion in general and Christianity in particular. Schleiermacher had thus prepared the way for his major work, *Der christliche Glaube*.[7]

Despite disagreements about methods and different results, the theologians of the Ancient Church, the Middle Ages, and the Reformation nonetheless managed to agree that the aim of dogmatics is

---

[7] Dr. Friedrich Schleiermacher, *Der christliche Glaube nach den Grundsäzen der evangelischen Kirche im Zusammenhänge dargestellt* (Berlin, 1821–1822). A second, revised edition came out in 1830. The best critical edition is by M. Redeker, I–II (Berlin, 1960). Schleiermacher's work is available in English, *The Christian Faith*, trans. H. R. Mackintosh and J. S. Stewart (Edinburgh, 1928).

a knowledge of God and a formulation of that knowledge. Thus theology in the proper sense of the word meant to them a teaching about God. Schleiermacher now insisted that, on the contrary, theology is basically psychology, and that it describes and informs us about man and human experience. On the basis of psychological analysis and transcendental deduction, he concluded that religion as such is part of human nature and that the category of the eternal, which is an a priori of religion, is what sustains all human spiritual life. Therefore, he continues, religion is a necessity, and Christianity is the supreme form of religion. Schleiermacher had thus transformed idealistic subjectivism into a system.

He gives us a more detailed explanation of his system in the introduction to *Der christliche Glaube*. Man's consciousness of the world comprises both a feeling of relative freedom that is realized in action and a feeling of relative dependence that surfaces when man is dominated by the world. The feeling of freedom, however, is grounded in a feeling of absolute dependence on the present world, which in turn depends on the power that brought it into being. We can therefore say that religion is the same as the feeling of absolute dependence, and this feeling is again a prerequisite for a consciousness of the world. Man's cultural life, the principal forms of which are art, morality, and science, is based on consciousness of the world, and so Schleiermacher concludes that religion as thus described is a necessary condition for the entire compass of culture. This is of course a purely formal definition of religion. As in *Über die Religion*, Schleiermacher now affirmed that a concrete definition, or the content of religion, is available in the actual empirical religions.

Schleiermacher's next step was to demonstrate that as a historical entity Christianity does not simply furnish the feeling of absolute dependence with elements of contingency and incompleteness; it also gives this feeling a content that is necessary and complete. His procedure consists in undertaking a classification of the religions of history in accordance with their worth. Dismissing as a worthless abstraction the "natural religion" founded during the Enlightenment, he expresses a higher estimation of the monotheistic religions of Judaism, Islam, and Christianity. He then proceeds to an evaluation of these three. The result of his reflections is that Christianity is the greatest teleological religion because it contains a doctrine of redemption.

Schleiermacher identifies the sensation of absolute dependence with consciousness of God. In its most perfect form, this consciousness pervades the consciousness of the world both actively and passively.

But, he continues, worldly consciousness has gained the upper hand in man because the material and corporeal aspects have been allowed to develop to the detriment of spirituality. Man is thus in need of redemption, and an act of redemption can be undertaken only by someone whose consciousness of God dominates his worldly consciousness. Such a man was Jesus of Nazareth, a historical person and the vehicle of divine revelation. Or, in Schleiermacher's words: "As a divine revelation, the appearance of the Redeemer in history is neither something exclusively supernatural nor something which absolutely transcends reason."[8] Redemption in Christ is the condition that makes it possible for man's consciousness of God to conquer his worldly consciousness and thus become the basis of human spiritual life and culture.[9]

Inasmuch as the nucleus of Schleiermacher's theology is a religious experience in the form of a feeling of absolute dependence, religious tenets and dogmatic principles translate into assertions about the condition of faith in man rather than into statements relevant to God. Schleiermacher himself put it this way: "Christian dogmas are interpretations of pious, Christian states of mind put into words."[10]

HEGEL

Hegel is the philosopher who finally undertook to incorporate all preceding religious-philosophical thinking into one grand system designed to be wholly comprehensive and objective. Nonetheless, in spite of its supposed objectivity, the system in fact turns out to be the finest example known of subjectivistic Idealism. Hegel's philosophy of religion can be properly understood only if we are familiar with its position in the system and with the fundamental principles and structure of the entire system itself. Furthermore, this very system of Hegel's is the primary target at which the polemics in the *Postscript* are aimed. It will therefore be appropriate to give here a complete, though brief, account of his philosophical activities and a delineation of his system and philosophy of religion.[11]

---

[8] *Der christliche Glaube*, §13.

[9] See in this respect Anders Nygren, *Dogmatikens vetenskapeliga grundläggning, med särskild hensyn till den Kant-Schleiermacherska problemställning* (Lund, 1922), and Theodor H. Jørgensen, *Das religionsphilosophische Offenbarungsverständnis des späteren Schleiermacher* (Tübingen, 1977), which contains a selective bibliography.

[10] *Der christliche Glaube*, §15.

[11] Employed here is G.W.F. Hegel, *Sämtliche Werke. Jubiläumsausgabe*, ed. Hermann Glockner, 3rd ed., I–XXII (Stuttgart, 1958), hereafter abbreviated as *Jub. Ausg.* This

Georg Wilhelm Friedrich Hegel was born in Stuttgart on August 27, 1770.[12] A bright and hard-working pupil in secondary school (*Gymnasium*), he early took a lively interest in the Roman and Greek classics. In 1788, he entered the University of Tübingen, where he began studies of theology. None of the instructors there seems to have left any mark on him, but decisively important friendships were established with Hölderlin and Schelling, with whom he studied Plato and Kant, and whose enthusiasm for the French Revolution he shared. Hegel graduated from the faculty of theology in 1793 and subsequently accepted an appointment as private tutor with a family in Bern. Here he remained for three years, devoting a good deal of his time to studies of politics and history. Kant's principal work on the philosophy of religion made a rather deep impression on him, so when he left Bern to accept a new position as tutor in Frankfurt am Main he continued his studies, this time concentrating more on theology and metaphysics. Various rough drafts (published for the first time in the present century) indicate that he was already developing original views in, say, the philosophy of religion, and thus was becoming independent in relation to the Enlightenment and Kant's philosophy.

In 1801, he went to Jena, where he was to remain for six years. At that time Jena was a center for both philosophy and literature; Fichte and Reinhold had worked there, and later Hölderlin and Schelling. This same year Hegel produced a work titled *Differenz des Fichteschen und Schellingschen Systems der Philosophie in Beziehung auf Reinholds Beiträge zur leichteren Übersicht des Zustandes der Philosophie des 19. Jahrhunderts.* On his thirty-first birthday, August 27, 1801, Hegel quali-

---

is a photographic reprint of the first completed edition, *Werke alte Ausgabe*, most of the volumes of which Kierkegaard owned (see *ASKB*, hereafter abbreviated as *W.a.A.*). Reference is made here only to some of the milestones in the research on Hegel's philosophy: Karl Rosenkranz, *Kritische Erläuterungen des Hegel'schen Systems* (Königsberg, 1840; reprint, Hildesheim, 1963); Adolf Trendelenburg, *Logische Untersuchungen* (Berlin, 1840; reprint of 3rd ed., Hildesheim, 1964); Rudolph Haym, *Hegel und seine Zeit* (1857; reprint, Hildesheim, 1962); Wilhelm Dilthey, *Die Jugendgeschichte Hegels* (Berlin, 1906; reprinted in Wilhelm Dilthey, *Gesammelte Schriften*, I–XII [Stuttgart, 1957–1960], IV); Hans Leisegang, *Denkformen*, 2nd ed. (Berlin, 1951); Iwan Iljin, *Die Philosophie Hegels als kontemplative Gotteslehre* (Bern, 1946); J. N. Findlay, *Hegel. A Reexamination* (London, 1958); Hans Küng, *Menschwerdung Gottes* (Freiburg, 1970); G.R.G. Mure, *The Philosophy of Hegel* (London, 1965); and Charles Taylor, *Hegel* (Cambridge, 1975). I have outlined Hegel's definitive system in "The System and Method of Hegel," *Bibliotheca Kierkegaardiana*, IV, 52–97. Hermann Glockner's *Hegel-Lexikon*, 2nd ed., I–II (Stuttgart, 1957), is also very useful.

[12] See Franz Wiedmann, *Hegel: An Illustrated Biography*, trans. Joachim Neugroschel (New York, 1968).

fied to give lectures at German universities with a Latin dissertation on the orbits of the planets (*De orbitis planetarum*), a treatise that has since been called a "prototype of speculation." On the basis of purely mathematical and astronomical calculations, he proposed to explain the presence of a "void" in the planetary system between Mars and Jupiter—despite the fact that more than eight months earlier Giuseppe Piazzi had, by empirical means, proved the existence of the asteroid Ceres in this supposed "void."

In the winter semester of 1801–1802 Hegel, now a *Privatdozent* (an unsalaried lecturer), started giving lectures on "Logic and Metaphysics." He added courses on natural law to his program in the summer of 1802, later giving lessons on positive philosophy and the history of philosophy as well. He terminated his earlier studies of politics by writing *Die Verfassung Deutschlands* and then devoted himself exclusively to logic and metaphysics, which he felt even at that time were intimately related. Hegel developed his first system of morality in 1802, and from 1802 to 1803 he and Schelling coedited *Kritisches Journal der Philosophie*, in which he attacked the skepticism exemplified by G. E. Schulze's *Änesidemus . . . oder Verteidigung des Skeptizismus gegen die Anmassungen der Vernunftkritik* (1792). In *Glauben und Wissen* he defended absolute Idealism against the "philosophy of reflection" represented by Kant, Jacobi, and Fichte, whom Hegel maintained were related to each other as thesis, antithesis, and synthesis. In an essay titled "Über die wissenschaftlichen Behandlungsarten des Naturrechts" Hegel developed his thoughts along lines more closely linked to Plato and Aristotle than to Kant and Fichte. He began lecturing on "The System of Speculative Philosophy" in 1803 and 1804, dividing his system into three parts: logic and metaphysics; philosophy of nature; and philosophy of spirit.

It was during this period that the plan matured for the work that constitutes the climax of Hegel's philosophical development—*Phänomenologie des Geistes*,[13] which he finished on October 20, 1806. Printing had already begun in February of that year, and it was finally completed in February 1807. With this work Hegel broke definitively with Schelling and the other Romantics and struck out on his own.

In the spring of 1807 financial difficulties compelled Hegel to accept a position as editor of a provincial newspaper, *Bamberger Zeitung*.

---

[13] In translating this title (*Phänomenologie des Geistes*) as *The Phenomenology of Mind* J. B. Baillie has given the title a much narrower compass than intended by Hegel, for the German word *Geist* is by Hegel endowed with a significance far richer than can be conveyed by the English word "mind." The present translator has generally rendered both *Geist* and the Danish equivalent *Aand* by the more appropriate "spirit."

He kept this position, which did not have very much to do with philosophy, until November 1808, when his close friend Niethammer helped him secure a more suitable appointment as instructor and headmaster at a *Gymnasium* in Nuremberg. Hegel spent eight years there, at the same time preparing, among other writings, a minor introductory philosophical work and, most important, the great *Wissenschaft der Logik*, which came out between 1812 and 1816.

In the summer of 1816 Hegel finally managed to obtain a professorship at Heidelberg, and the following year he published his third major work, *Enzyklopädie der philosophischen Wissenschaften*. This work is a concise and highly concentrated presentation of his definitive philosophical system embracing all of the philosophical disciplines.

On December 26, 1817, the Prussian Minister Altenstein wrote to Hegel, offering him a professorship in Berlin. Hegel accepted in the spring of 1818 and remained in Berlin in this capacity until his death on November 14, 1831.

Hegel published very little while in Berlin. During this period of his life he published *Grundlinien der Philosophie der Rechts* (1820) and a number of rather long reviews and articles in periodicals, besides new editions of the *Enzyklopädie* (in 1827 and 1830). Most of his time was spent preparing his lectures, and after his death these lectures, which as a rule were enlargements of the terse paragraphs in the *Enzyklopädie*, were more or less satisfactorily edited and published by his friends and disciples. Thus the 1830s saw not only new editions of works previously published by Hegel himself but also editions of his lectures on *Philosophie der Geschichte; Aesthetik* in an excellent edition by Heinrich G. Hotho; *Philosophie der Religion*, which was fairly well edited by Philipp Marheineke; and *Geschichte der Philosophie* in a serviceable work done by Karl L. Michelet, who himself wrote a continuation in two volumes, *Geschichte der letzten Systeme der Philosophie in Deutschland von Kant bis Hegel* (Berlin, 1837–1838). Hegel's minor works also appeared at this time.

There is a widespread and epistemologically oriented tradition according to which Hegel's philosophy represents the culminating point of German Idealism and the end of a philosophical development that started with Kant's *Kritik der reinen Vernunft* and terminated in 1831, when Hegel died. In that period Fichte tried to overcome the Kantian dualism between things-in-themselves and their manifestation to human cognition by completely rejecting the concept *das Ding an sich* and ascribing everything to the productive ego. In this way he managed to develop his subjective Idealism. Schelling, intending to work out an objective Idealism, endeavored to demonstrate that there is an absolute identity between the ideal and the real, between spirit and nature. Lastly, Hegel—like Jacob Boehme, who assumed the presence of a duality within the absolute where the negative element may be so to speak regarded as the mainspring of existence—sought to show how the absolute realizes itself as spirit in existence. His purpose in this was to establish an absolute Idealism.

This conception of later philosophical history[14] is traceable to Hegel himself. In the concluding portion of *Lectures on the History of Philosophy*,[15] he summarizes the latest developments in philosophy in such a manner that the dialectical course taken by the idea must begin with Kant, continue on to Fichte and Schelling, and finally end with his own philosophy. "The result is the thought which is at home with itself, and at the same time embraces the universe therein, and transforms it into an intelligent world."[16] This conclusion informs Hegel's own system, which crowns "the strivings of spirit during almost twenty-five centuries."[17]

This immediate background, however, is by itself inadequate as a means to understand the Hegelian system. Hegel did indeed seek, in his *Lectures on the History of Philosophy*, to exhibit the presence of a continuity in the dialectical evolutionary process while recognizing the relative merits of all of the preceding philosophers. In fact he displayed an uncommon virtuosity in accomplishing this, after which he proceeded to the presentation of a system of his own. But students of the history of philosophy and Hegelian scholars in particular have neglected the significance of certain other important points that are essential for an understanding of Hegel. First of all, Hegel's *Phenomenology of Spirit* is not simply his first thoroughly accomplished major work, written after several years of preliminary efforts in various fields. It differs qualitatively from the earlier works by the fact that it presupposes not only study and deliberation but also an experience, a vision of the divine universe given in thought. *The Phenomenology of Spirit* must be understood primarily as a description of this vision,

---

[14] This conception is dominant in Harald Höffding, *A History of Modern Philosophy*, trans. B. E. Meyer, I–II (New York, Toronto, and London, 1955), II, 18–292; in Richard Kroner's well-known work, *Von Kant bis Hegel*, 2nd printing, I–II in one volume (Tübingen, 1961); and in Nicolai Hartmann's otherwise so worthy presentation, *Die Philosophie des deutschen Idealismus*, 2nd printing, I–II in one volume (Berlin, 1961). Justus Hartnack has recently published an original investigation in *Fra Kant til Hegel. En nytolkning* (Copenhagen, 1979).

[15] *Lectures on the History of Philosophy*, III, 545–54; *Jub. Ausg.* XIX 684–92.

[16] Ibid., p. 546.

[17] Ibid.

whereas all of Hegel's later works are a "subsequent rationalization" of it. That project resulted in a definitive system in which all empirical material, including the views of earlier philosophers, was in a modified form incorporated into his system for the sole purpose of contributing to the substantiation of Hegel's fundamental conception.

If this holds true, it spells the end of the old dilemma that has plagued scholars of Hegel: Is *The Phenomenology of Spirit* an introduction to the system or the system itself, but under a certain aspect? Is it merely a theory of knowledge or a philosophy of history? The fact is, one could justifiably read the work in light of all of these aspects because of the way in which it deals with the development of the particular and universal spirit. These two phases of spirit are made identical in a pantheism that Hegel had already acclaimed in *Eleusis*,[18] a poem written in his youth. *The Phenomenology* describes how these phases develop by means of relative antitheses from certainty of the senses (*die sinnliche Gewissheit*) to perception (*die Wahrnehmung*), and then further to force and understanding (*Kraft und Verstand*); next the true nature of self-certainty (*die Wahrheit der Gewissheit seiner selbst*); certainty and truth of reason (*Gewissheit und Wahrheit der Vernunft*); spirit (*der Geist*); religion (*die Religion*); and, ultimately, to absolute knowledge (*das absolute Wissen*).

In its own special way, this progression corresponds to Plotinus' description of the ascent toward the One. The downward path and the divinity's efforts to return to itself are described in the later works, which Hegel has systematically summarized in his tripartite *Encyclopaedia*. Beginning with logic, which concerns the inner trinitarian life of the divinity prior to creation, the *Encyclopaedia* proceeds next to the philosophy of nature, which encompasses the divinity's withdrawal from its original and proper state, and finally to the philosophy of spirit, or the manifestation of spirit as subjective, objective, and absolute spirit. Like each of the preceding stages, absolute spirit is divided into three phases, which in this case are art, revealed religion, and philosophy. The supreme and definitive form of philosophy—Hegel's own—embodies cognition of God in the fully adequate form of a concept. It is a cognition of God that is identical to self-knowledge, and thus it corresponds completely to Plotinus' view. To Hegel's mind, this entire cosmic and individual process takes place with absolute necessity and through a dialectical development that is

---

[18] This poem is readily accessible in *Dokumente zu Hegels Entwicklung*, ed. Johannes Hoffmeister (Stuttgart, 1936), pp. 380–83.

grasped by means of the dialectical method, which in turn performs the same function as Schelling's intellectual intuition.

Two traditions within religious and philosophical thought fuse together[19] in Hegel's system. In my presentation above I have described the first of them by bringing forward philosophers like Posidonius, Plotinus, John Scotus Erigena, Nicholas of Cusa, Jacob Boehme, and Schelling.[20] The reader will remember that the second and principal current is represented by the rationalist thinkers from Aristotle to Spinoza. Now, in combining these two traditions, Hegel attached primary importance to the experience, hierarchic structure, and life of the divine. He attached only secondary importance to his description, adaptation, and subsequent rationalization—though this is what leaps to the eye when one reads Hegel for the first time.

The goal for Hegel's labors in philosophy was an adequate cognition of God. He intended to reach this goal by means of a conception of the absolute as a self-active spirit that, during its ascent, develops according to steadily advancing self-determinations from a unity filled with contrasts to plurality, and finally to a new and higher synthesis. As a consequence, the human thought that is supposed to follow this dialectical process must be *flüssig* (fluid). In other words, the concepts (the instruments of thought) must be dynamic rather than static precisely because they are rich in contrasts. Supported to some degree by Fichte's dialectical method, Hegel now took a new approach to the problem concerning change and its relation to thought, a quandary that had occupied the pre-Socratic philosophers, Plato, and Aristotle so much. He felt that the negative element that every concept is supposed to contain causes the concept to pass over into its opposite, but the two opposites are then reunited in a higher unity or synthesis. If, for instance, we think the concept of being in its purity by abstracting from it everything that has existence, it will turn out to be nothing. The concepts of being and nothing are then mediated to form a synthesis called becoming (*Werden*). The new and higher concept in its turn functions as a thesis from which an antithesis emerges, whereupon the two latter are "sublated" in a new synthesis. This process continues until the spirit has produced the world as a totality.

[19] Hegel generally used the words "reconcile" and "reconciliation" (*versöhnen, Versöhnung*), whereas Danish Hegelians and Kierkegaard preferred the terms "mediate" and "mediation" (*mediere, Mediationen*).

[20] See, in addition to the work by Benz mentioned above in note 5, Wilhelm Dilthey, *Weltanschauung und Analyse des Menschen seit Renaissance und Reformation*, 6th printing (Stuttgart, 1960).

In his own way Hegel set out to create a synthesis of the fundamental theories of Heraclitus and Parmenides, but he did so at the
price of abandoning the principles of contradiction and identity. Simple perception views its object or what is immediately concrete as a
totality, whereas reflective philosophy or philosophy based on the
understanding (which in Hegel's estimate includes Kant's philosophy) is incapable of holding on to a totality. Speculative thought,
however, advancing beyond these positions, grasps the unity of the
contrasts and formulates that unity in a concrete concept. Inasmuch
as the highest being consists of thought formulated conceptually, the
concrete concept serves as both the instrument and the aim of thought.

The origin of Hegel's distinctive methodology must be sought in
his early preoccupation with the Bible, especially the Gospel according to St. John and the mystical tradition and interpretations of that
tradition.[21] The Johannine Logos teaching and the identification of
God, spirit, truth, life, and the way furnished Hegel with the inspiration he needed to arrive at his fundamental conception—the divine
idea. This idea, which is spirit and was at the beginning, is the God
who became flesh; it is life and light, and it will guide the world back
to God. He also derived the idea of reconciliation or mediation of
opposites from the Gospel of St. John.[22] Hegel's logic must thus be
interpreted as a genuine Logos doctrine, for his intention was to
combine the Greek speculative Logos with the Biblical world of ideas.[23]
Furthermore, he regards the Biblical world as

> the System of Pure Reason, as the Realm of Pure Thought. *This
> realm is the Truth as it is without veil.* One may therefore express it
> thus: that this content *shows forth God as he is in his eternal essence
> before the creation of Nature and of a Finite Spirit.*[24]

Hegel believed that after creation the dialectical development in
history and time had reached a point that he called the "speculative
Good Friday,"[25] and that it is in fact God's nature to die and return
to life. He thought that it now devolved on him to allow for God's

---

[21] In this connection see Wilhelm Dilthey's epochal work, *Die Jugendgeschichte Hegels*, 2nd printing (Stuttgart, 1959). His groundwork on this point has been continued
by Hans Leisegang in *Denkformen*, 2nd ed. (Berlin, 1951), especially in chap. IV, "Der
Kreis von Kreisen." See also Iwan Iljin, *Die Philosophie Hegels als kontemplative Gotteslehre* (Bern, 1946), especially pp. 48ff.

[22] See for example John 12:24.

[23] See on this subject C. H. Dodd, *The Interpretation of the Fourth Gospel* (Cambridge,
1953), pp. 263ff.

[24] *The Science of Logic*, I, 60, modified; *Jub. Ausg.* IV 45–6.

[25] In *Glauben und Wissen*, I, 433, mentioned above.

resurrection from the dead and to provide an instrument that would make it possible to acquire knowledge of the living God. This, then, was the purpose of his philosophy. To Hegel, the world regarded as a divine emanation is a living organism. Thus if reasoning is to apprehend this totality with respect to its source, the thought must conform to its object, which like life itself unfolds in an eternally repeated cycle. Life, he observed, is initially concentrated in a seed that bursts forth and develops into a plant with stalk, leaves, and flowers; as the flowers produce fruit with seeds that fall to the ground, the entire process begins again. Now, since spirit in Hegel's philosophy is identical with life, it follows that thought, the loftiest activity of spirit, must develop exactly like a living organism, which means that in its own proper sphere it must make its way through thesis, antithesis, and synthesis. Pure thought, the Logos, returns to itself once it has engendered the world and made it intelligible in Hegel's distinctive philosophical system, a system that embodies all knowledge. Hegel has expressed this as follows in the concluding paragraph of his *Science of Logic*:

> By reason of the nature of the method which has been demonstrated the science is seen to be a circle which returns upon itself, for mediation bends back its end into its beginning or simple ground. Further, this circle is a circle of circles; for each member, being inspired by the method, is intro-Reflection which, returning to the beginning, is at the same time the beginning of a new member. The various sciences, of which each has a before and an after, are fragments of this chain; or rather, each *has* only a before, and in its conclusion shows its after.
>
> Thus the Logic too in the Absolute Idea has returned to this simple unity which is its beginning.[26]

This mode of thought has rightly been called a typical "integral thought" (*Ganzheitsdenken*). Characteristically, it always springs from the living fullness of a totality, and it is able to grasp particulars only by means of an abstraction that tends to isolate. Moreover, the antitheses in an object that result from such an act of abstraction appear to be contradictory, whereas they prove to be merely relative opposites when regarded from a total viewpoint. This may be compared with Spinoza's third step in the process of cognition and with the dominant recurring theme in Leibniz's *Theodicy*.

In Hegel's view, the speculative conceptualization of a totality by

---

[26] *The Science of Logic*, II, 484ff.; ibid., V, 351.

proceeding from a totality and employing "living" concepts that contain opposites should not merely be understood figuratively or be likened to Kant's epistemological theories. On the contrary, it is nothing less than the divine spirit's progress toward self-knowledge, and it has found its first adequate and definitive expression in Hegel's system. Inasmuch as God and reason are everything to Hegel—as they were to Spinoza—one is equally justified in attaching the labels of both Pantheism and Panlogism to the Hegelian system. Hegel is distinguishable from "atemporal" Pantheists like Plotinus and Spinoza by his attempt to incorporate time and thus history into his philosophy and by the dialectical method, which is inseparable from his system.

As mentioned above, the system is divided into three parts: logic, the philosophy of nature, and the philosophy of spirit. These correspond respectively to the science of the idea in-and-for-itself (*an und für sich*); the science of the idea withdrawing from and external to itself (*in ihrem Andersseyn*); and of the idea returning to itself (*in ihrem Beysichseyn*).

Hegel's is not simply a formal logic but rather a concrete logic or, as expressed above, the teaching of God's inner trinitarian life prior to creation. This theory embodies a logic of being, essence, and concepts; the first two constitute objective logic, whereas the logic of concepts is Hegel's subjective logic. In Hegel objective logic takes the place usually occupied by metaphysics,[27] for the predominant perspective is ontological. Hegel paid no heed whatsoever to Kant's critique of reason.

In nature the divine idea is regarded as having withdrawn from the realm proper to it, so nature is the idea in the form of otherness. It now arranges itself, as Hegel put it in the *Encyclopaedia*,

> as a *system of stages*, one arising necessarily from the other and being the proximate truth of the stage from which it results: but it is not generated *naturally* out of the other but only in the inner Idea which constitutes the ground of Nature.[28]

In the first part of his philosophy of nature Hegel deals with mechanics, whereupon he turns to physics and then to organic physics. Taken as a whole, then, the philosophy of nature discusses first, unconscious nature in which the idea is in a world completely alien to

[27] Ibid., I, 74; ibid., IV, 64.
[28] *Hegel's Philosophy of Nature*, trans. A. V. Miller, Foreword by J. N. Findlay (Oxford, 1970), p. 20.

it; second, conscious nature in which the idea begins to achieve a
consciousness of itself; and third, self-conscious nature, that is, man.

The dialectical development in logic, the first main part of the
system, is dominated by a metaphysically construed determinism that
is every bit as rigorous as was the case with Spinoza. This also holds
true of both the second part, the philosophy of nature, and the third,
the philosophy of spirit. The philosophy of spirit begins where the
philosophy of nature concludes—with man, who comprehends himself through the manifestations of the divine spirit. "The goal of nature," Hegel insists,

> is to destroy itself and to break through its husk of immediate,
> sensuous existence, to consume itself like the phoenix in order to
> come forth from this externality rejuvenated as spirit. Nature has
> become an other to itself in order to recognize itself again as Idea
> and to reconcile itself with itself.[29]

The upward path thus already begins in the philosophy of nature.

In the realm of spirit, as in logic and nature, there are three phases:
subjectivity, objectivity, and absolute spirit. The theory of subjective
spirit, which Karl Rosenkranz treats more extensively,[30] encompasses
first of all the concept of soul, which in turn is divided into three
elements: the natural or physical soul, the feeling soul, and the actual
soul (die natürliche, die fühlende, und die wirkliche Seele, respectively).
The actual soul shows the emergence of spirit as an organic principle
that transforms itself from a cosmic principle into one of individuality; as a result the soul becomes conscious of itself as an ego and
thus as subjective spirit. Initially this consciousness is immediate and
sensory (see The Phenomenology of Spirit); it develops, however, into
the understanding (der Verstand), which breaks down the immediately
given totality into particular objects but is unable to reunite them and
grasp them as a totality. The subjective spirit thereupon turns its
attention from the objective world to its own cognitive abilities, as
in Kant. In Hegel this implies that consciousness becomes self-consciousness, initially in an individual or single limited and therefore
inadequate form, and subsequently as universal consciousness, thereby
attaining to the stage of reason or spirit. Reason (die Vernunft) too
makes its first appearance in the form of individual reason producing
speculative cognition (der theoretische Geist) and then as practical spirit.

[29] Ibid., p. 444.
[30] Karl Rosenkranz, Psychologie oder die Wissenschaft vom subjectiven Geist (Königsberg, 1837, ASKB 744). This work made a strong impression on Kierkegaard.

At its highest stage practical spirit sets its sights on heavenly bliss (*die Glückseligkeit*). Being incapable of reaching this goal,[31] however, it is necessarily sublated in a synthesis consisting of theoretical and practical spirit, that is, free spirit (*der freie Geist*), which in turn seeks to make its own freedom actual as a new world. At this more elevated level the idea passes from the particular to the universal and in this form realizes itself in objective spirit. To Hegel objective spirit constitutes the world of freedom; he treats this even more fully in *The Philosophy of Right*, which is a systematic continuation of his *Lectures on the Philosophy of History*.

As mentioned above, the doctrine of objective spirit, which also covers Hegel's treatment of ethics in *The Philosophy of Right*, comprises the objective world of freedom, but it is a world ruled by dialectical necessity. In his exposition Hegel begins with the concept of right, the subject of which is a juristic person who, by means of a concept of things (that is, through possession and property), lives in a sphere of external freedom that is negated by the concept of injustice. Injustice gives rise to crime, but this is in turn negated by punishment, thereby restoring justice. Inasmuch as punishment is an expression of the universal will, it represents morality, a disposition to will what is right and hence a good will. Morality turns into arbitrariness and thus a form of evil[32] whenever it is determined purely subjectively. On the other hand, it becomes moral or ethical conduct (*die Sittlichkeit*) when justice and the good are made actual in the fundamental structures of society, that is, in the family, civil society, and the highest expression for a spirit that has succeeded in objectivizing itself—the state.

Strangely enough, Hegel gave the limited national state priority over the universal state, making it the goal of the future. In *The Philosophy of History*, however, which continues the theoretical discussion presented in *The Philosophy of Right*, the main point of view is that during the course of time the world spirit manifests itself in various national spirits, each of them possessing a distinctive trait. In keeping with the theory of organism (which was later adopted by Spengler and others) every national spirit springs from an embryonic stage and matures, thereby surpassing the levels attained by preced-

[31] *Hegel's Philosophy of Mind [Spirit]*, trans. William Wallace with the *Zusätze* trans. A. V. Miller (Oxford, 1971), §480, p. 238.

[32] See *Hegel's Philosophy of Right*, trans. with notes by T. M. Knox, 2nd ed. (Oxford, 1957), §140, pp. 93–103; *Jub. Ausg.* VII 220ff. This is the famous section in which Hegel deals with the moral evils resulting from subjective morality: hypocrisy, falsity, probabilism, good intentions, subjective opinion, and irony.

ing societies, until ultimately it too perishes in the vain contest waged by old age against anything that is young, novel, or in the process of emergence. Unlike absolute spirit, the objective spirit cannot become universal and thus reach the final and most exalted stage in the system's *Stufenkosmos*. In fact, the dialectical process actually founders, for it can only be imagined to unfold within the boundaries prescribed by "the objective spirit."

Hegel's theory of absolute spirit encompasses art, religion, and philosophy. In art, the absolute spirit emerges as contemplative. In harmony with this view, Hegel defined esthetics as the manifestation of the absolute to sensate contemplation in the form of beauty and in the form of the idea in a particular configuration; as such, it also appears as an ideal.[33]

Religion is the next and higher phase in the self-development of absolute spirit, for it makes its appearance in forms of pictorial thought (*die Vorstellung*), images, and symbols. As in the preceding stages, this occurs with necessity:

> It lies essentially in the notion of religion,—the religion i.e. whose content is absolute mind—that it be *revealed*, and, what is more, revealed *by God*. Knowledge (the principle by which the substance is mind) is a self-determining principle, as infinite self-realizing form—it therefore is manifestation out and out. The spirit is only spirit in so far as it is for the spirit, and in the absolute religion it is the absolute spirit which manifests no longer abstract elements of its being but itself.[34]

Supranaturalism, such as Hegel knew and understood it, was characterized by him as inadequate because it interprets dogmas as intuitive, literal expressions of the absolute. He also contended that theological rationalism emasculates the concept of God and that Schleiermacher had remained within the confines of individual subjectivity. Hegel then proceeded to sublate these two standpoints, which he called thesis and antithesis respectively, by apprehending the essence and function of religion in a speculative concept. He arranged the different religions in a series of stages in which absolute spirit gradually unveils itself until it arrives at the stage of absolute religion—which Hegel equated with Christianity—whereupon it informs itself as spirit. This spirit is inherently the Father, whereas

---

[33] Hegel explains this view in greatest detail in *Vorlesungen über die Aesthetik*, ed. H. G. Hotho, I–III (Berlin, 1835); *Jub. Ausg.* XII–XIV. See *Hegel's Philosophy of Fine Art*, trans. F.P.B. Osmaston, I–IV (London, 1916).

[34] *Hegel's Philosophy of Mind [Spirit]*, §564, pp. 297ff.

nature is the Son, and the Holy Ghost coincides with spirit's return to itself. The midpoint of Christianity is the historical Incarnation that brought about the union, atonement, and mediation of the spirits of God and man.

The iliad and odyssey of spirit come to an end in Hegel's philosophy and speculative cognition. Unlike art, philosophy does not merely make the absolute spirit intuitable, nor does it simply render it apparent as religion does; on the contrary, philosophy comprehends the absolute. The contents of philosophy and religion are the same, but the form of religion turns out to be inadequate compared with philosophy's adequate form. In the latter, the absolute spirit dwells on itself during the course of its dialectical development from logic, through nature, and back to itself; in other words, it reflects on the system with the help of the dialectical method, the very life nerve of that same system. At its highest level, which is the stage occupied by speculative knowledge, philosophy is the same as cognition of God. Knowledge of God is in turn identical to the self-cognition of the human spirit and to its necessary self-development in a microcosmic as well as a macrocosmic sense. Both types of development are described in *The Phenomenology of Spirit*.

CHAPTER 5

Hegelianism in Germany

Hegel exercised tremendous influence on both philosophy and theology during the span of an entire generation. From Berlin his influence spread like ripples on a pond, until it simply melted away or was broken—as by Kierkegaard.

Unless one is familiar with this Hegelianism it is scarcely possible to penetrate to the basic motive behind the *Postscript* and its composition, or to the reason why Kierkegaard made such extensive use of the entire conceptual apparatus and terminology of speculation. It must not be forgotten that this Hegelianism and its later modification constitute the real backdrop for the polemic that Kierkegaard aimed at what he variously called "Speculation" and "the System."

It is no more possible in Hegelianism to make a sharp distinction between philosophy and theology than it was in the case of earlier speculative movements; indeed, they have common premises and similar aims. Nevertheless, it might be practical to discuss Hegelianism in the field of philosophy first and then turn to theology.

A Hegelian school[1] already began to take shape in Hegel's own lifetime. One of Hegel's first disciples was Georg A. Gabler, who had attended Hegel's lectures in Jena and who, in compliance with

[1] The most detailed exposition of philosophical Hegelianism is provided by J. E. Erdmann in *Grundriss der Geschichte der Philosophie*, 3rd. ed. (Berlin, 1878), whereas the Hegelian philosophy of religion is presented by O. Pfleiderer in *Religionsphilosophie auf geschichtlicher Grundlage* (Berlin, 1878), pp. 63ff. More recent works deal with the entire movement. See for example W. Moog, *Hegel und die hegelsche Schule* (Munich, 1930), pp. 406–87, and Karl Löwith's important work, *Von Hegel zu Nietzsche* (Stuttgart, 1941), which is also available in several later editions. The standard modern work, however, is still T. K. Oesterreich, *Die deutsche Philosophie des XIX. Jahrhunderts und der Gegenwart,* in Friedrich Ueberweg, *Grundriss der Geschichte der Philosophie,* 13th ed. (Basel, 1951), IV; a new edition of this work is in preparation. Still worth reading is also the Danish presentation by Harald Høffding, *Philosophien i Tydskland efter Hegel* (Copenhagen, 1872). A complete presentation of Hegelian theology has yet to appear, but a brief outline is available in Horst Stephan, *Geschichte der deutschen evangelischen Theologie seit dem deutschen Idealismus,* rev. and ed. Martin Schmidt (Berlin, 1960), pp. 74ff. In H. L. Martensen's memoirs, *Af mit Levnet,* I–III (Copenhagen, 1882–1883), I, 85–231, there is an admirable description of the German universities from 1834 to 1836, and Skat Arildsen, *Biskop Hans Lassen Martensen. Hans Liv, Udvikling og Arbejde* (Copenhagen, 1932), is important for an understanding of the era of speculation.

Hegel's wishes, succeeded him to the professorship in Berlin. Another was Friedrich Wilhelm Carové, who attached himself to Hegel in Heidelberg. Hermann F. W. Hinrichs was a more important follower, and Hegel even wrote the prologue[2] to his *Die Religion im inneren Verhältnisse zur Wissenschaft* (1822), availing himself of the opportunity to direct a sharp attack against Schleiermacher. During this time Hegel also established a relationship with Karl Daub, a systematic theologian. In Berlin Philipp K. Marheineke, after encountering Hegel's philosophy, revised his own dogmatic work to make it accord with the dialectic method. Among the many other disciples whom Hegel gained in Berlin, the following are worthy of mention: Leopold von Henning, Eduard Gans, Karl L. Michelet, Heinrich G. Hotho, and Heinrich T. Rötscher. In 1827 the Hegelians began their own periodical, *Jahrbücher für wissenschaftliche Kritik*, to which Hegel himself contributed several rather extensive reviews[3] in his later years.

Insofar as the faithful adherents, sticking closely to Hegel's view, interpreted his philosophical system as the embodiment of being in its entirety and in an adequate and definitive form, there could of course be no question of advancing even further than the system but only of defending it against attacks and putative misunderstandings. Before long, however, various attempts were being made to employ Hegelian views in areas that the master himself had not treated too fully. By way of example, in history of philosophy Zeller's experiments in his presentation of Greek philosophy and Kuno Fischer's in connection with modern philosophy soon broke through the limits that Hegel had imposed on the concepts. As might be expected, problems finally arose concerning the correct interpretation of specific points in the system. Hegel's disciples very quickly split up into a right wing, a center, and a left wing, depending on whether they interpreted Hegel in conformity to the traditional view of Christianity, whether they simply left this question in abeyance, or whether from their explanations of his ideas they drew conclusions that conflicted with Church doctrine. There were many shades of difference, and each explanation had more or less self-thinking representatives.

Many of the problems concerning logic, metaphysics, religion, and philosophy that are tackled in the *Postscript* are the very same issues that were so heatedly debated in both Germany and Denmark in the 1830s and 1840s. This will become evident in the following pages

---

[2] Reprinted in *Jub. Ausg.* XX 1–29.
[3] Ibid., pp. 57–445.

and in the commentary on relevant sections and passages in the *Post-script*.

The first assaults on Hegel's logic occurred in his own lifetime. Hegel intended to refute five of them in *Jahrbücher für wissenschaftliche Kritik*, but he managed to compose only long-winded and sarcastic reviews of the first two[4] in 1829, though unfortunately not of the most important of them, *Ueber den gegenwärtigen Standpunkt der philosophischen Wissenschaft, in besonderer Beziehung auf das System Hegels* (1829), by C. H. Weisse. Weisse criticized Hegel's logic because it does not include time and space (which are indeed treated in the system, but not until the second part) and because it does include actual being. He thus felt that the system contains both too little and too much. He kept up his criticism of Hegel in later writings, gradually developing as his own standpoint an ethical theism that conflicted with Hegel's philosophy. Weisse characterized Hegel's philosophy as monistic pantheism, and with his views he approached the outlook held by other philosophers, including Immanuel Hermann Fichte. Beginning in 1837, this group published *Zeitschrift für Philosophie und spekulative Theologie*, and under Fichte's leadership the periodical not only served as their forum but quickly became a rallying point for Hegel's opponents. It is worth observing that this was the only German philosophical journal to which Kierkegaard subscribed without interruption from its start in 1837 until his death in 1855.[5]

A lawyer, Karl F. Göschel, whom Hegel had praised in 1829 for his *Aphorismen über Nichtwissen und absolutes Wissen im Verhältniss zum christlichen Glaubensbekenntnis*, acted as Hegel's apologist in 1834 with *Der Monismus des Gedankens*. Weisse then maintained in *Die philosophische Geheimlehre über die Unsterblichkeit des menschlichen Individuums* (1834) that Hegel failed to include the idea of individual immortality in his system. Göschel replied to this with *Von den Beweisen für die Unsterblichkeit der menschlichen Seele im Licht der spekulativen Philosophie* (1835) in which he set forth three proofs of personal immortality corresponding to the traditional proofs of the existence of God.[6] Weisse's position was adopted by J.F.F. Billroth in his lectures on the philosophy of religion, which Johann Eduard Erdmann published posthumously in 1837.[7]

---

[4] Ibid., pp. 314–93.

[5] See *ASKB* 877–911.

[6] Concerning the debate about immortality, see below, note to p. 152 in the *Postscript*.

[7] J.F.F. Billroth, *Vorlesungen über Religionsphilosophie*, ed. Dr. Johan Eduard Erdmann (Leipzig, 1837; *ASKB* 428).

Fichte the Younger expressly sought to develop a conciliatory standpoint in his first works, *Sätze zur Vorschule der Theologie* (1826) and the first edition of *Beiträge zur Charakteristik der neuern Philosophie* (1829). With his three-volume work *Ueber Gegensatz, Wendepunkt und Ziel heutiger Philosophie* (1832–1836), however, and especially with a thoroughly revised edition of *Beiträge*, to which he added the subtitle *kritische Geschichte* ("critical history"), Fichte made it clear that he stood opposed to Hegel. Kierkegaard owned this edition and several other works by Fichte.[8] He was also acquainted with C. Philipp Fischer's anti-Hegelian works and with thinkers like Julius Schaller.[9] Moreover, his library contained additional anti-Hegelian writings, as those by A. Günther and J. H. Pabst,[10] plus a selection of works by other contemporary German thinkers.

Hegel's logic and metaphysics were attacked and subsequently defended by various writers. For example, Adolf Trendelenburg, whose works were highly appreciated by Kierkegaard, attacked Hegel, whereas Karl Werder, whose lectures Kierkegaard attended in Berlin,[11] undertook to defend Hegel in *Logik. Als Commentar und Ergänzung zu Hegels Wissenschaft der Logik* (1841). As mentioned above, the question of the individual's immortality soon arose, and both religious-philosophical and dogmatic views were advanced in an effort to solve this problem. We have already discussed Göschel and Weisse. Of the many other participants in this debate, we may mention Ludwig Feuerbach, who in 1831 published an anonymous work, *Gedanken über Tod und Unsterblichkeit*,[12] in which he proposed to demonstrate that the consequence of Hegel's basic theory could only be that the finite perishes because it is annulled in the infinite. Friedrich Richter took an analogous position in *Die Lehre von den letzten Dingen* (1833–1844). Whereas Göschel thus represented "right-wing" Hegelianism and Weisse anti-Hegelianism, Feuerbach, Richter, and others developed a "left-wing" Hegelianism, and thinkers like Erdmann and Rosenkranz formed a center position. Immanuel Hermann Fichte upheld the immortality of the individual in *Die Idee der Persönlichkeit und der individuellen Fortdauer* (1834).[13] Although employing an argument

[8] *ASKB* 500–11.

[9] See Dr. Julius Schaller, *Die Philosophie unsere Zeit, zur Apologie und Erläuterung des Hegelschen Systems* (Leipzig, 1837; *ASKB* 758).

[10] See *ASKB* 520–24.

[11] See *Pap.* III C 28ff.

[12] *Gedanken über Tod und Unsterblichkeit, aus den Papieren eines Denkers, nebst Anhang theologisch-satyrischer Xenien*, published by one of his friends (Nuremberg, 1830).

[13] See *ASKB* 505.

similar to Göschel's, Fichte nevertheless agreed with the other anti-Hegelians and insisted that Hegel's system did not contain a theory of individual immortality, either implicitly or explicitly.

The left-wing Hegelians continued to draw increasingly far-reaching consequences from Hegel's ratiocinations and finally succeeded in annulling the identity between faith and knowledge—in other words, between theology and philosophy—that had been so important to Hegel. It is well known that in his two-volume work *Das Leben Jesu kritisch bearbeitet* (Tübingen, 1835–1836) David Friedrich Strauss declared that the evangelical narratives were the product of myths that had furnished the eternal idea with historical form. In his efforts to demythologize, Strauss sought to deny that Jesus' historical reality was decisively important to religion. Inspired by Hegel, he based his reasoning on the view that the individual is insignificant and only the idea matters; in Strauss's view the idea cannot come to realization in any one individual but only in mankind at large. This conception is in complete agreement with the view set forth by Hegel in his key work, *The Phenomenology of Spirit*, and Strauss like Hegel contended that his particular method merely elevated the truth of Christianity from the inadequacy of representative thought to the adequacy of a concept; this also corresponded to Hegel's conception of dialectical development. In his next work, *Die christliche Glaubenslehre in ihrer geschichtlichen Entwicklung und im Kampfe mit der modernen Wissenschaft*, I–II (Leipzig, 1841–1842),[14] Strauss proposed to demonstrate that the development of dogma amounts to the history of its dissolution; that "dogma is the product of the idiotic consciousness"; and that Christianity as a theism and dualism is incompatible with Hegel's modern philosophy, which is a pantheism and monism originating from Spinoza. Strauss thus began by using Hegelian premises, but he went much further than Hegel would have liked, drawing conclusions that Hegel would never have drawn and thereby disrupting the Hegelian reconciliation of faith and knowledge.

In Feuerbach, whose work on immortality is mentioned above, Hegel's concept of an absolute divine spirit changes into its opposite. Hegel held that speculative knowledge is the equivalent of cognition of God, which in turn is identical to the human spirit's self-knowl-

---

[14] Frederik Schaldemose's Danish translation of *Das Leben Jesu kritisch bearbeitet* was not published until 1842–1843. A Danish translation of *Die christliche Glaubenslehre . . . Wissenschaft*, however, appeared almost immediately: David Friedrich Strauss, *Fremstilling af den christelige Troeslære i dens historiske Udvikling og i dens Kamp mod den moderne Videnskab*, trans. Hans Brøchner, I–II (Copenhagen, 1842–1843). Kierkegaard owned a copy of this work (*ASKB* 803–04). See my commentary on the *Fragments*, p. 204.

edge. Feuerbach, on the other hand, claimed in *Das Wesen des Chris-tenthums* (Leipzig, 1841)[15] that cognition of God is nothing but man's self-knowledge combined with an erroneous assumption according to which self-knowledge is related to something external to it. Con-sciousness of God is quite simply self-consciousness:

> The being of man as distinct from that of an animal is not only the basis but also the object of religion. However religion is conscious-ness of the finite; thus religion is and can be nothing but man's consciousness of his own being, not indeed of his finite and limited being but of his infinite being.[16]

Feuerbach then added:

> Man is nothing without an object . . . but the object to which a subject establishes an essential and necessary relationship is none other than the objective being of this very same object.[17]

Whereas the left-wing Hegelians thus used Hegel's philosophy as a basis to arrive at the above conclusions in their own philosophies of religion, some representatives of the center and especially those belonging to the Hegelian right wing sought to interpret his philos-ophy in conformity to the traditional conception of Christianity. In fact, they even tried to employ Hegel's dialectical method in theo-logical disciplines, especially in systematic subjects, and to go even further than Hegel. This was the case with Hans L. Martensen in particular.

Carl Daub adhered to Kant's philosophy at the beginning of his career, then switched to Schelling, and eventually ended up as a con-vinced Hegelian. In his memoirs Martensen has given a vivid descrip-tion of his meeting with Daub that sets the latter's imposing person-ality into clear relief.

> I looked up Daub as soon as possible [after arriving in Heidel-berg]. Here then stood before me the man who had given new life to speculative theology, a venerable old man with a skull cap on his head, enkindling respect. He has not been compared to an old eagle without reason. My personal impression of him formed a complete contrast to the one I had of Schleiermacher. Schleier-

[15] Kierkegaard owned the second edition (Leipzig, 1843; *ASKB* 488). See also Eu-gene Kamenka, *The Philosophy of Ludwig Feuerbach* (London, 1970), especially pp. 35–68.

[16] *Das Wesen des Christenthums*, 3rd ed. (Leipzig, 1849), p. 25.

[17] Ibid., p. 28.

macher was small and delicately built, Daub was tall and powerful. There was something gigantic about him, and one realized that here there were bones with marrow. Schleiermacher's speech was distinguished by an impressive refinement and often conveyed a tinge of irony. Daub's was frank and coarse and he went directly to the heart of the matter, often displaying a striking sense of humor in his vigorous bass voice. The conversation soon turned to dogmatics, and thus also upon Schleiermacher. He spoke very disparagingly about Schleiermacher's dogmatics. He said that as concerns a dogmatic work he first of all asked what it could teach him about the triune God. When he had perceived that Schleiermacher only touched on this article [of faith] in an appendix and in fact provided nothing new, he exclaimed: "If you can't tell me anything *de deo triuno* [about the divine trinity], I've got no use for you." He thereupon tossed the book into his "critic's office," by which he meant a place on the floor of his room where he deposited books that he did not care to read. As I had expected, I received the impression from our conversation that Daub could not be content with the purely subjective but demanded objective truth, and that he would not settle for man's religious feelings but insisted on God's revelation and an insight into that revelation.[18]

Martensen also relates how he painstakingly worked his way through Daub's principal work from his final period, *Die dogmatische Theologie jetziger Zeit oder die Selbstsucht in der Wissenschaft des Glaubens und seiner Artikel*, which came out in 1833 and was dedicated to the memory of Hegel. This book, Martensen tells us, was patterned on Hegel's *Phenomenology of Spirit*; its intention was, with the doctrine of the trinity serving as a focal point, to substantiate the fact that traditional Church doctrine is both rational and intelligible. One of Daub's last works was a long essay induced by Strauss's *Das Leben Jesu*, in which Daub strongly emphasized that the very fabric of Christianity is inseparably woven together with historical revelation. This essay made an impression on young Kierkegaard, who incidentally seems only to have owned Daub's posthumously published lectures.[19]

Philipp Konrad Marheineke, however, acquired greater influence

[18] H. L. Martensen, *Af mit Levnet*, I, 114ff.

[19] Carl Daub, *Philosophische und theologische Vorlesungen*, ed. Marheineke and Dittenberger, I–VII (Berlin, 1838–1844; *ASKB* 472–472g). The most important of these lectures concern philosophical anthropology (vol. I) and an introduction to dogmatics (vol. II). See also Emanuel Hirsch, *Kierkegaard-Studien*, I–II (Gütersloh, 1930–1933), II, 539ff.

at this time through his presentation of the basic teachings of Christian dogmatics regarded as a science.[20] Like Hegel he distinguished between faith in the lower sphere of pictorial thought and knowledge in the superior sphere of the concept. To Marheineke the purpose of dogmatics is to apprehend the content of faith:

> Purely historical faith is . . . an unswerving belief in authority, indeed not only with regard to the content which renders this faith true, but also with respect to the form in which it limits its own free thought and makes itself untrue. Christian truth has been given and presented to us in the teachings of the Scriptures and the Church, and this conception of truth is both sufficient for a rational faith and the truth itself. These scriptural and ecclesiastical truths of faith are by themselves profounder than what is available through the medium of a conception, for they are speculative and spring from absolute knowledge. The task facing science is therefore to discover by means of speculation the sources of the truth of this conception and then the source of the conception of the truth, in order thereby to arrive at a true conception.[21]

Marheineke defined the essence of religion as the idea of God made manifest in the mind in the various forms of historical religions. Christianity, to which the doctrine of the trinity is central, is the purest and most perfect of these religions. He consequently arranged his dogmatics according to a trinitarian principle, first treating God the Father as God's intrinsic being (*das In-sich-Seyn Gottes*), then the Son as God's external being (*das Aus-sich-Seyn Gottes*), and finally the Holy Spirit as God's being-for-Himself (*das Für-sich-Seyn Gottes*).

[20] Dr. Philipp Marheineke, *Die Grundlehren der christlichen Dogmatik als Wissenschaft*, 2nd ed. (Berlin, 1827; *ASKB* 644).
[21] Ibid., §105.

CHAPTER 6

The Situation in Denmark
and Kierkegaard's Reaction

The philosophical atmosphere in Denmark differed somewhat from that in Germany where, as we have seen, Hegel continued, directly and indirectly, to dominate the philosophical debate for several years after his death. In both countries, however, it applies to adherents as well as opponents that their understanding of Hegel and their resultant positive and negative evaluations generally lacked a crucial perspective; they failed to take into account the intrinsic life of the divine idea, its withdrawal from itself, and its return to itself with dialectical necessity via the realms of nature and history. As a consequence, they did not bring out with sufficient clarity the conformity between Hegel's theory and the earlier tradition whose premises and forms are briefly discussed in the foregoing. Probably on the basis of his own statements,[1] Hegel was customarily regarded as a thinker whose most important background had to be sought in Kant. Scholars were unable, however, to appreciate sufficiently the fact that Hegel reached behind Kant, Descartes, and the chiefly epistemologically oriented issues of recent philosophy and seized the ontological thinking of antiquity and the Middle Ages that endeavored to embrace the whole world.

Generally speaking, these are the circumstances that prevailed in Denmark when Kierkegaard wrote the first volumes of his pseudonymous works in general and the *Postscript* in particular. A rather broad survey of the state of philosophy and theology in Denmark in the 1830s and beginning of the 1840s will help to make this situation more intelligible.

At the time of Kierkegaard, Danish theologians were in most cases not influenced by Hegel but by other currents and trends. The Hegelian system and, more broadly speaking, speculative philosophy and theology played an appreciable and positive role only for a small group of clergymen and theologians, and mainly in Copenhagen. We

---

[1] See chap. 5.

may observe the clergy and bishops, and mention Jacob Peter Mynster as a leading figure; we may consider the only faculty of theology in the country at that time, the one at the University of Copenhagen; or we may take a unique personality like N.F.S. Grundtvig and the circle of young, often clever, but invariably argumentative theologians who surrounded him; furthermore, in this connection we could even take into consideration the influential faculty of philosophy or include the Danish poets and estheticians from the 1830s and 1840s. On the basis of all of these observations we would be forced to the conclusion that it is only possible to find *one* representative spokesman for Hegelianism in its purest form—apart from a few epigones, of course.[2]

Let us consider the clergy and bishops first. Here the theological standpoint was overwhelmingly conciliatory, and sharply pronounced views were the exception. To be sure, there were still a few decided rationalists around in the 1830s, for example, Archdeacon H. G. Clausen of the Cathedral of Copenhagen, and some equally rabid Supranaturalists, or orthodox theologians, as they were commonly called at the time. But characters like Hengstenberg in Germany turned up only rarely (A. G. Rudelbach is the only one who comes to mind), and they had extremely limited possibilities of as-

---

[2] Anathon Aall gives a concise outline of the history of Danish philosophy in Friedrich Ueberweg, *Grundriss der Geschichte der Philosophie*, 13th ed. (Basel, 1951), V, 259ff., and there is a brief but clear description in F. J. Billeskov Jansen, *L'Âge d'Or* (Copenhagen, 1953). The bulk of the material written on this subject is, however, available only in Danish, of which a selection follows. The history of the Danish Church is accessible in Hal Koch, *Den danske Kirkes Historie* (Copenhagen, 1954); I have reviewed this work in *Dansk teologisk Tidsskrift* (Copenhagen, 1956), pp. 233ff. The history of the faculty of theology in Copenhagen is given by Leif Grane in *Københavns Universitet 1479–1979*, ed. Svend Ellehøj and Leif Grane, I–XIV (Copenhagen, 1980—), V: *The Faculty of Theology*, pp. 325–78. A short treatment of the philosophers will be found in Harald Høffding, *Danske Filosofer* (Copenhagen, 1909). Surveys of the history of Danish literature during this same period are given by Valdemar Vedel in *Guldalderen*, 2nd ed. (Copenhagen, 1948); Vilhelm Andersen in *Illustreret dansk Litteraturhistorie*, I–IV (Copenhagen, 1925–1929), III; and by F. J. Billeskov Jansen in *Danmarks Digtekunst*, III (Copenhagen, 1958). There exists an important series of recent monographs of the prominent personalities of that time: Niels Munk Plum, *Jakob Peter Mynster som Kristen og Teolog* (Copenhagen, 1938); Skat Arildsen, *Biskop Hans Lassen Martensen. Hans Liv, Udvikling og Arbejde* (Copenhagen, 1932); J. Larsen, *Henrik Nicolai Clausen* (Copenhagen, 1945); K. Baagø, *Jacob Christian Lindberg* (Copenhagen, 1958); Vilhelm Andersen, *Poul Martin Møller* (Copenhagen, 1944); Dr. J. Himmelstrup, *Sibbern. En Monografi* (Copenhagen, 1934); and Morten Borup, *Johan Ludvig Heiberg*, I–III (Copenhagen, 1947–1949).

I have given a more detailed account of Hegelianism in Denmark in *Kierkegaard's Relation to Hegel* (Princeton, 1980).

serting themselves in church life and theological debates. Danish theologians were of course familiar with writers like Schelling, Baader,
Fichte the Younger, and even Schleiermacher, but none of these
thinkers seems to have made much of an impression. In Denmark,
romantic idealism usually turned into a down-to-earth romantic na-
tionalism in which peace and mutual understanding reigned over the
intellectual lives of the clergy and laity. Mynster is typical in this
regard, and he was far more important to the educated circles in the
capitol than Martensen, not least by reason of the fully justified respect he commanded as an upright, reserved, distinguished, and conservative person.

Mynster (1775–1854) intended to stand for a Supranaturalist interpretation of Christianity, but he refrained from disputing the mild
form of rationalism that was still fairly widespread up to the middle
of the century. On the other hand, he vigorously attacked the
Grundtvigians and revivalist movements. To Mynster, Christianity
depended first and foremost on the individual soul's inward encounter with God. Inwardness and romantic contemplation were to him
natural forms of life. His best known and most widely read book is
fittingly titled "Reflections on the Doctrines of the Christian Faith";[3]
this work has seen several printings. He begins the first chapter with
the question, "Where is my weary soul to find repose?"[4] On the next
page he asks, "Where is my restless heart to find peace?" Mynster
then goes on to explain that in the human soul there is a yearning
for what is sublime and noble and a craving for action and self-development. Man, however, always stands face to face with inevitable
death:

> There is a monstrous power that is the enemy of life, and that is
> stronger than life. How often it has made encroachments, even on
> the intimate circle of those whom I called mine! It tore even my
> dearest friend, whose very being had become one with mine, from
> vainly protesting arms, away from a bleeding heart. Restraining
> the tears in my eyes, I beheld with an unswerving gaze until I saw
> as far as the eye can reach and caught sight of my friend's and my
> own final, ineluctable destiny, saw decay followed by the annihi-

[3] Dr. J. P. Mynster, *Betragtninger over de christelige Troeslærdomme*, 2nd printing, I–II
(Copenhagen, 1837; *ASKB* 254–55). The first printing came out in 1833. See Cornelio
Fabro, "L'attività oratoria, dottrinale e pastorale ei . . . J. P. Mynster," *Ricerche di
storia sociale e religiosa* (Rome, 1973), pp. 41–108, and my article on Mynster in *Bibliotheca Kierkegaardiana*, X: *Kierkegaard's Teachers* (Copenhagen, 1982), pp. 15–70.

[4] Mynster, *Betragtninger*, I, 1.

lation that leaves no trace. Further my sensuous eye did not reach. Is there nothing in me that sees further? Is there no light in this black night? Is there no voice from heaven when the earth is mute?

All these reflections led me to religion. Yet I cannot say that this was what led me to it from the very beginning. Everything considered, I cannot say that I sought religion from the very beginning at all; rather, it sought me out.[5]

Mynster maintains that religion corresponds both to man's yearning for an ideal and to his conscience and reason, so it is capable of creating harmony:

If what I call my own reason were enough for me, I would not need any instruction. But if I am going to receive instruction, if it is to benefit me and really merge with my being, then how am I to grasp it, if not with reason? Instruction does not address itself to unreasonable people, and if it addresses itself to me it does so because I am sensible of its power and can understand what it teaches, for there is something in me that can grow light when a light shines therein.[6]

In accordance with this view, Mynster regarded faith as both a divine gift and a human obligation, since man fulfills his destiny by believing. Mynster ascribed far less importance to historical proofs of the truth of Christianity than to the psychological aspect; he felt that only Christianity can really satisfy man's needs. To Mynster there was a continuity rather than a breach between human idealism and Christianity, and both address themselves equally to the individual's feelings, reason, and will. In *Betragtninger*, which furthermore is composed in the form of edifying discourses on various points of traditional dogma, Mynster did not attach much importance to church community, or the sacraments. Nevertheless, as concerns the external forms of pious life, he always regarded the state church as the best framework for the religious life of the individual, for it secures the individual's personality against new and changing trends. With his manner of thinking, he was scarcely able to view the various efforts at outward reforms with much sympathy, for example, changes in the liturgy or the hymnal. In this respect, Kierkegaard completely agreed with him. In fact, Mynster's outlook on both ecclesiastical and political affairs was strictly conservative. He participated in the theological and philosophical debates of his time, making sound and

[5] Ibid., p. 5.
[6] Ibid., p. 8.

clearly formulated contributions, but he did not take part in a controversy against the practical application of rationalism in the Church, even though his own conception of Christianity was based on Supranaturalism. On the other hand, he was, as mentioned above, strictly on his guard against the revivalists and Grundtvig, for he believed that they displayed a self-satisfaction and intolerance that would lead them to abolish the individual's freedom in church matters if they ever acquired the power they sought. In this Mynster was hardly mistaken. He had no respect for either Hegel or speculative theology and attacked them directly at the first opportunity.

If we turn our attention to the subject of theology, we will discover that the prevailing attitude in the theological faculty at the University of Copenhagen may be characterized as conciliatory. Theologians clung to traditional dogmatics and moderate Supranaturalism, but at the same time they insisted that historical criticism of traditional views was in principle justified. They attached considerable importance to the study of the Bible, but they also emphasized that the importance of the Bible had everything to gain and nothing to lose from a sober historical criticism.[7] Some, like Mynster, turned against the revivalists' and Grundtvig's theological notions, regarding them as a kind of fanatical Neo-orthodoxy. Altogether, they avoided extremist views, with the result that neither Ferdinand Christian Baur, David Strauss, nor Ludwig Feuerbach ever came to exert much influence on the theological and ecclesiastical world in Denmark.

Henrik Nicolai Clausen (1793–1877) was indisputably the most prominent member of the theological faculty from the 1820s until well into his waning years. His special fields were systematic theology, which at the time was practically synonymous with dogmatics, and the New Testament. For a while he was to some extent influenced by Schleiermacher, but in the course of time his standpoint on dogmatics gradually drew close to a mitigated form of orthodoxy. Clausen was unsympathetic toward Hegel and speculative theology.

Something new finally appeared on the scene during the winter semester of 1837–1838 when Hans Lassen Martensen (1808–1884), just returned from his prolonged travels abroad, received an appointment at the university as lecturer in systematic theology. He had been very close to Grundtvig's narrow circle for a while in the beginning of the 1830s, a fact that he preferred not to be reminded of later;

---

[7] See for example C. E. Scharling, *Hvad er Hensigten, Betydningen og Resultaterne af Theologernes videnskabelige Undersøgelser om det Nye Testamentes Skrifter?* (Copenhagen, 1833), which Kierkegaard owned (*ASKB* 761).

indeed, in his memoirs he mentions it only in passing.[8] Frederik Christian Sibbern's lectures on the philosophy of Christianity, which were slightly influenced by Schleiermacher, were of great consequence to him. During his trip abroad, Martensen met many intellectuals, including Steffens, Marheineke, Daub, and Strauss. The poet Nikolaus Lenau was of some importance to him, and Schelling and especially Baader had a tremendous influence on him. Martensen's dissertation, *De autonomia conscientiæ sui humanæ in theologiam dogmaticam nostri temporis introducta* (Copenhagen, 1837), was specifically intended to signify a break with Hegel, but it hardly ended Martensen's enduring admiration for him. While upholding Anselm's principle of *credo ut intelligam* the youthful author sought to refute the principle of autonomy, which he thought was predominant in modern philosophy from Descartes to Hegel, with the sole exception of Leibniz. Man's conscience, which Martensen equated with self-consciousness, is in essence a consciousness shared with God, a coknowledge in which man is first and foremost known to God. (The agreement with Baader's way of thinking is evident here.) Martensen argued that man is incapable of apprehending the truth by his unaided efforts alone. Knowledge of the truth is possible only if we proceed from a theocentric point of view, and man is unable to rise to this position because he is a created being and burdened with sin. It thus follows that all cognition is based on revelation and faith. Baader and Martensen concurred that whenever these prerequisites are present it will be possible to attain to true speculative knowledge and develop a Christian speculative system.[9]

In the winter of 1837–1838 Martensen began lecturing on modern philosophy from Kant to Hegel, and then after Poul Møller's death he gave lectures on moral philosophy, which he quickly published under the title of *Grundrids til Moralphilosophiens System* (Copenhagen, 1841). Of all Martensen's works, this one bears the clearest witness to his affirmative attachment to Hegel. He likewise held lectures that were first announced as "Prolegomena to Speculative Dogmatics" but later changed to "Christian Dogmatics." Out of these and subsequent lectures grew his famous and chief work on dogmatics, which did not see the light of day until July 1849.[10] Although this writing,

[8] H. L. Martensen, *Af mit Levnet*, I (Copenhagen, 1882), pp. 26ff.

[9] Kierkegaard's attitude toward Martensen's theology, especially in the *Postscript*, is treated by Arild Christensen in "Efterskriftens Opgør med Martensen," *Kierkegaardiana*, IV (Copenhagen, 1962), pp. 45–62. See also J. H. Schiørring, *Kierkegaardiana*, X: *Kierkegaard's Teachers* (Copenhagen, 1982), pp. 177–208.

[10] Dr. H. Martensen, *Den christelige Dogmatik* (Copenhagen, 1849; *ASKB* 653). See

too, shows considerable influence from Hegel, especially in its method, it is incorrect to describe it as a purely Hegelian work. Baader still meant a great deal to Martensen, and we should not overlook the indicative and pregnant fact that in his youth he wrote a book about Meister Eckhart and in his later years one about Jacob Boehme. Both books show his appreciation for speculative mysticism and theosophy.

During the proportionately short span of time from the end of the 1830s to 1854, when he succeeded Mynster as Bishop of Zealand, Martensen left his mark on the students of theology, who gathered before his lecture platform in great numbers. His speculative thinking, however, was of profound and lasting significance to relatively few, and they exercised only a limited influence on their contemporaries.

Without any doubt, the theory of speculative thought attracted a great deal of attention in both the theological and philosophical faculties, especially at the beginning of the 1840s. This is obvious both from the many works that appeared during these years and from contemporary and later descriptions of conditions at the time. We will quote only two of these accounts here. The first is by Clausen, who in 1877, a generation after the period under discussion, wrote the following in his memoirs:[11]

> The reign of terror that had controlled every aspect of life with a power that is conceivable only in that land of ideologies came to an end with Hegel's death in November 1831. There stood "The System," the exclusive key to the kingdom of redemptive truth and at the same time the only path leading to honor and power on the bureaucratic ladder. But the disciples, about whom the master is said to have declared that the whole lot of them either did not understand him or misunderstood him, for a long time continued to gnaw at the literary remains, until the school was split by sharp clashes and bitter internal strife.[12] The spiritual and intellectual upheaval caused by Hegelianism, which shook the intellectuals south of the Eider [River] and enthused them to the point of fanaticism,

---

also Dr. H. Martensen, *Christian Dogmatics. A Compendium of the Doctrines of Christianity*, trans. William Urwick, M.A. (Edinburgh, London, and Dublin, 1874). In his introduction the translator observes (p. v) that Martensen, being dissatisfied with a German translation of his work, rewrote it himself in German. The English version is a translation of the German edition prepared by Martensen.

[11] H. N. Clausen, *Optegnelser om mit Levneds og min Tids Historie* (Copenhagen, 1877), pp. 210–13.

[12] See chap. 5.

hardly affected life in the North. This alone is a pretty fair indication that there is a fundamental difference in mentality between
Germans and Danes, or rather, Scandinavians. Hegel's philosophy
was not subjected to public examination until 1838, when Sibbern
wrote *Hegels Philosophie i Forhold til vor Tid*, that is, long after the
epoch-making phenomenon had culminated in the Fatherland. J. L.
Heiberg's endeavors to introduce Hegelian categories into esthetic
criticism, and even into his own poetic works, did not really catch
on either—all his ingenious efforts notwithstanding. As to theology, it was all the more fortunate that this delayed transplantation
across our borders took place through the medium of a personality
who not only possessed an uncommon intellectual refinement and
keenness, but in addition was firmly anchored to a Christian standpoint. It was in the autumn of 1837 that [Martensen's lectures on]
"Speculative Dogmatics" . . . were introduced into our university.
The novelty of the subject lent support to his brilliant lectures.
Indeed, no matter how great the modifications made to the Hegelian costume that emerged here, the result could after all only be
that the contents of Christian revelation came to look like something hitherto unknown and unheard of, and this new form of the
Gospel evoked the greatest interest among the students. . . . But
the speculative movement was transmitted to us and brought into
relation to theology in such a manner that it undoubtedly incited
a great number of students to think more liberally and independently, and to acquire a deeper understanding of religion. Yet a
dangerous illusion lay very close at hand. Many believed that by
means of a specious initiation into the secrets of speculation they
could be elevated to the peak of cognition, thus rendering the la-
borious acquisition of constructive knowledge superfluous. It is an
obvious and readily explainable fact that in those years interest in
the exegetic studies gradually diminished, while the vast majority
of the students found cheap compensation in the philosophical no-
menclature that played such a great part in the Hegelian movements. "The favorite philosophy of the times" soon became, to
use one of Søren Kierkegaard's phrases, "the childish philosophy
of the times." People found youthful pleasure in this beating of
drums, and they became an object of their own admiration when
they heard themselves cavorting with these hollow nuts. Or, to
use Goethe's words of wisdom: "Wherever ideas are wanting, words
will take their place in due time." Our mother tongue in particular
groaned beneath a linguistically corrupt submersion in speculative
German. This overwhelming and extremely oppressive barbarity

confronted me during the written exercises that I held for a great number (one hundred or more) of students in those years.

Clausen wrote as an outsider. We have a similar report, however, from one of those who allowed themselves to be swept along by this current of enthusiasm. Johannes Fibiger (1821–1897), who studied theology from 1837 to 1845, wrote in his memoirs as follows:[13]

> One had to have lived at that time to be able to form an idea of its [speculative theology's] peculiar ways, in fact, simply to be able to believe in the possibility thereof [that is, of its soaring flight]. Laboring under the absolute rule of German philosophy, all our thinkers were zealously engaged in building a fantastic tower of Babel, and all we heard around us was that every braggart had made it his immediate mission in life to build an even higher tower. The universe with all its big and little recesses had been reconnoitered and clarified in concepts, all the riddles were solved; Hegel and his host of disciples in Berlin had consummated the work. But this also disclosed the artifice and exhibited the price of battle. It was thought that the system could be imitated and extended; to become a great noble in the intellectual world one needed only to construct a system of one's own and advance beyond Hegel.[14] We soon ceased to breathe any other air. The only thing we heard at the university, and it rang like a voice from out of the future, was Martensen's oratory, which contained more than enough airy stones to build an edifice of that kind.

One of the first definite Hegelians in Denmark of the type described above was Adolph Peter Adler (1812–1869), who was later to occupy a good deal of Kierkegaard's attention.[15] Adler gave a faithful account of Hegel's philosophy in his first two books, *Den isolerede Subjectivitet i dens vigtigste Skikkelser* (Copenhagen, 1840) and *Populaire Foredrag over Hegels objective Logik* (Copenhagen, 1842). What he called "isolated subjectivity" corresponds to Kierkegaard's romantic ironist or esthetician, and it has, he says (*Subjectivitet*, §10),

> no place in a rational and real world. . . . When it thus halts and remains at the stage of its own particularity, seeking only to realize

---

[13] Johannes Fibiger, *Mit Liv og Levned*, ed. and abridged by [the author's stepson] Karl Gjellerup (Copenhagen, 1898), p. 73.

[14] Compare with this Kierkegaard's incessant ridicule of those who, like Martensen, wanted "to go further."

[15] "Bogen om Adler" (*Pap.* VII²). In English, *On Authority and Revelation*, trans. Walter Lowrie (Princeton, 1955).

this, it is wild nature, infinite instinct and desire, an unlimited condition, self-accentuated inwardness, an unconstrained ego, and an isolated, abstract subjectivity in all its forms. As the negation of all objectivity, it sets the singleness of its will above all universality and its isolated subjectivity as the highest. It allows all subjectivity to yield to the conditions imposed by the ego, and in its empty, infinite, unconstrained, and hollow freedom it proceeds to enter into empty infinity.

Adler follows up these conceptual definitions by presenting the typical forms and features of isolated subjectivity, in the main using statements he had found in Hegel.[16] His second "Hegelian" book gives evidence of even less originality than did his dissertation.

Rasmus Nielsen (1809–1884) intended his dissertation for the licentiate degree in theology[17] to be an improvement on Hegel's system in a manner akin to that of Martensen. In 1841 Nielsen started publication of *Den speculative Logik i dens Grundtræk*, but in 1844 he stopped at the fourth installment—right in the middle of a sentence. In *Den propædeutiske Logik* (Copenhagen, 1845) he began to criticize Hegel for being a formalist, and during the years immediately following he drew closer to Kierkegaard. As we know, he attacked Martensen in 1849 when the latter published his work on dogmatics. Neither this affair nor Nielsen's later works, however, will be discussed here.

One of Denmark's few left-wing Hegelians was A. F. Beck (1816–1861), "Mynster's unhappy lover," as Kierkegaard calls him in the *Journals and Papers*.[18] In *Begrebet Mythus eller den religiøse Aands Form* (Copenhagen, 1842) Beck subscribed to Strauss's and Bruno Bauer's view that the Gospels were intentionally falsified by the authors, that all of the Pauline Epistles are spurious, and that Christianity is on the whole demoralizing.

The Hegelian centrists were represented in Denmark by Peter Michael Stilling (1812–1869) during these years. After writing carefully prepared reviews of Nielsen's and Martensen's first books, he won his master's degree with a dissertation titled *Den moderne Atheisme eller den saakaldte Neohegelianismes Conseqvenser af den hegelske Philosophie* (Copenhagen, 1844). He enters into a discussion of Feuerbach's theories mentioned above, and on page 89 he concludes that among

[16] See *Pap.* X² A 401; *JP* IV 4555.
[17] *De speculative historiae sacrae tractandae methodo commentatio* (Copenhagen, 1840). In Danish, *Om den speculative Methodes Anvendelse paa den hellige Historie*, trans. B. C. Bøggild (Copenhagen, 1842).
[18] *Pap.* VII¹ B 87, p. 285.

other things they amount to "a complete philosophical bankruptcy and an absurdity scarcely worth the trouble of dwelling on."

If we turn our attention from these men and concentrate on more important thinkers like Sibbern, Poul Møller, and Heiberg, we will immediately perceive that the first two clearly reflect a manner of thought that differs widely from Hegel's, and in fact they came to reject Hegelian philosophy. Heiberg alone remained faithful to his former teacher.

Frederik Christian Sibbern (1785–1872) became professor at the University of Copenhagen in 1813, the year Kierkegaard was born, and did not relinquish his position until 1870, fifteen years after Kierkegaard's death. During his long tenure at the university, he assiduously kept abreast of everything that went on in the fields of philosophy, theology, and literature. At the same time he himself produced a long list of works, eventually managing to present expositions of nearly all the different branches of philosophy. He has since been esteemed above all as a psychologist.

As a young man, Sibbern was imbued with the spirit of Romanticism in philosophy, religion, and poetry, but he always, even in extreme old age, contrived to remain open and receptive while tirelessly pursuing his own development. Rather than continue along the path of romantic speculation, he sought, especially in the early 1840s, to base a cosmology on experimental psychology and the science of nature, and so he energetically went about the task of mastering these subjects. He gradually evolved a liberal or unorthodox religious view of life as an alternative to a predominantly orthodox Christian view. The older he became and the more independence he gained as a philosopher, the more his influence nevertheless declined; in his final years he was regarded by many as a curiosity who had long since outlived his day. We have pointed out the fact that his lectures on Christian philosophy (which remain unpublished) had a stimulating influence on Martensen; but Martensen is only one example. It would certainly not be an exaggeration to say that for some time Sibbern meant as much to the students of theology as the professors in their own faculty did. He was by nature open and kind, and most of his contemporaries felt that he also was charmingly naive.

In the following we shall briefly touch only two aspects of Sibbern's thought: first, his philosophy of Christianity; and second, his attitude toward Hegel's philosophy.

Sibbern endeavored to combine religion and speculation in his lectures on Christian philosophy, which Kierkegaard attended in the winter semester of 1833–1834.[19] He assumed in these lectures that it is feasible to develop a true Christian philosophy that can substantiate the truth of Christianity independently of any authority. Even more, he insists that any true speculation must inevitably lead to what is proclaimed by Christian doctrine.

In Sibbern's opinion, the prerequisite for a Christian philosophy is from an objective viewpoint the truth and rationality of Christianity, whereas the subjective premise is that the Christian philosophy must be thoroughly permeated by the spirit and doctrine of Christianity. The point of departure for a philosophy of Christianity must be faith regarded as primary and as the focal point of Christian existence. By comparison, thought is a secondary though not inessential basic element. We have true faith only when it is a living, thoroughly determinative principle of spiritual life, and it will bring salvation only if the truth of Christianity is established as the truth for man by means of evidence produced within man himself. Compared with this inward evidence, which has its parallel in Mynster, all other external proofs recede into the background, as they are merely based on authority. On the other hand, Sibbern holds that it is possible to develop this inward evidence into rational knowledge and to employ philosophy in our efforts to arrive at an understanding of the triune God's redemptive revelation in Christ. In other words, Christianity and philosophy should be combined. When Sibbern asserts that Christ is the universal principle in both life and philosophy he is not inferring that the purpose of a philosophy of Christianity is to afford an alternative to revelation, for he rejects the idea that philosophical cognition can replace either revelation or the Scriptures in which this historical fact is recorded. Nor can philosophical knowledge abolish faith, since faith serves as the basis and final goal of cognition.

It has been mentioned that Sibbern continued to broaden and deepen his store of knowledge throughout his long life. This also holds true with respect to the natural sciences. He studied mathematics, physics, crystallography, zoology, and physiology, and he always underscored how important experience is for thought. This background alone was enough to make Hegel's system appear unsatisfactory to him, and indeed a predominantly critical attitude toward Hegel broke the surface in 1838 when he published "Bemærkninger og Undersøgelser fornemmelig betræffende Hegels Philosophie, betragtet i Forhold til vor Tid" in *Maanedsskrift for Litteratur*.

Heiberg had sought with little success to propagate Hegel's phi-

[19] See Skat Arildsen's reconstruction of Sibbern's lectures, *Martensen*, pp. 42ff.

losophy in Denmark in *Perseus*, Heiberg's own philosophical journal. He reproached Poul Møller for having broken with Hegel in a long essay on the problem of immortality, a work that will be discussed in more detail below. Sibbern defended Møller in his article mentioned above, praising him as one of those thinkers whom Hegelianism merely serves as a temporary stage. Heiberg, faithfully sticking by Hegelianism, was now duly informed by Sibbern that he is merely a dilettante in the field of philosophy.

In his long essay Sibbern upbraids Hegel for speaking contemptuously of experience. He claims that too much is taken for granted in Hegel:

> He seems to take it for granted that there are such things as a consciousness, a conscience, cognitive and volitional actions, a philosophy, and so forth. Doubt certainly did not preside when his philosophy was taking shape.[20]

Sibbern then goes on to accuse Hegel's philosophy of nature of being the system's "*partie honteuse*, though by no means its *partie modeste*." It is "just as baroque as it is *affreux* . . . and [it] presents not a few significant discrepancies in connection with what physics and physiology have to offer."[21]

Sibbern's objections to Hegel's dialectical method are equally noteworthy. "Although it cannot be denied that it might be interesting and illuminating to be guided through the whole domain of philosophy in such a manner, even if one-sided,"[22] the method itself nonetheless commits a logical error at its very source. Sibbern asserts that rejection of the universal validity of the principle of contradiction, which is the logical cornerstone of the method, must "as a consequence lead to the denial of this very rejection, and thus to the reestablishment of its validity."[23] Further, it may be all well and good to insist that *reines Seyn* (pure being) is *Nichts* (nothing), but

> this [definition] is after all really only a simple reflective remark that informs us about the first concept posited. But it cannot in addition be the first advance made, nor can *Nichts* now turn out to

[20] F. C. Sibbern, "Bemærkninger og Undersøgelser fornemmelig betræffende Hegels Philosophie, betragtet i Forhold til vor Tid" in *Maanedsskrift for Litteratur* (Copenhagen, 1838), p. 10.
[21] Ibid., p. 28.
[22] Ibid., p. 79.
[23] Ibid., p. 81.

be an Other and different from *Seyn*, by which this pure *Seyn* comes to be determinate [being].[24]

Sibbern also objects to the idea that a third concept, becoming (*das Werden*), can emerge from such a dialectic. He then adds:

Moreover, these altogether vacillating initial definitions in Hegel are not very important. In order in Hegel to find soil where there is a foothold and room to move around, one could just as well proceed from the concept of *Seyn* directly to the concepts of *Andersseyn* and *Daseyn*, omitting the intermediate [concept of nothing], which is both meaningless and baseless. It is important to Hegel only insofar as its presence has prevented the concept of becoming from being exposed to discussion and deliberation, which after all would have befitted this inherently rich concept.[25]

Sibbern thereupon criticizes Hegel's philosophy of religion, in particular because of the positions assigned to Christianity and the doctrine of the Trinity:

Under the heading of *"der absolute Geist"* Hegel concludes his entire system with this triad: art, revealed religion, philosophy. If it already seems remarkable that revealed religion is here assigned a position between art and philosophy, it is absolutely astonishing to find that the whole Trinity has been classified as the middle term of this trilogy. Just imagine! The whole Trinity, hence that which is of the greatest and most comprehensive significance in the world, the entire basis of totality, is listed as the *middle* term in a *Hegelian* trilogy![26]

It may also be mentioned that Sibbern very well understood those tendencies in Hegel on which the left-wing Hegelians could enlarge.

In contrast to Sibbern, Poul Martin Møller (1794–1838) was in the 1830s still under considerable influence from speculative philosophy. In his final years, however, he turned away from it. It is regrettable that Møller left behind little more than fragments of his work as a philosopher, for with them as a basis it is not in every respect possible to arrive at an idea of what form his overall philosophical outlook would have taken had he lived longer. Furthermore, he was as much a poet as a thinker, and in his personal life he was very much a bohemian—and a pedant.

[24] Ibid., p. 36.
[25] Ibid., p. 38.
[26] Ibid., p. 138.

Møller considered the importance of speculation to lie in the fact that it consistently maintained and explored one definite point of view, thereby eliminating possible sources of confusion. But he did not believe that speculation could be used to solve problems:

> By means of speculative philosophy we do not so much obtain answers to the questions posed by common sense, but come to realize that since the questions are themselves based on concepts that contain no truth they are no longer applicable.[27]

Moreover, Møller felt that speculative philosophy lacked an appreciation of the significance of the individual. Differences in individuals can be disclosed only by empirical means; but why, Møller asks, does speculation then regard this kind of cognition as an imperfect form of knowledge?

Of special importance in the present context is Møller's long essay from his final years, "Tanker over Muligheden af Beviser for Menneskets Udødelighed, med Hensyn til den nyeste derhen hørende Litteratur," which appeared in *Maanedsskrift for Litteratur*, no. 17 (Copenhagen, 1837), pages 1–72 and 422–53.[28] This article contains a wealth of factual information about the debates on immortality that were carried on by Hegelians in Germany, and it thus proved very useful to Kierkegaard.

In his essay Møller emphasizes that man cannot attain perfect knowledge. If we avail ourselves of the empirical sciences to summarize all the existing subjects and their modes of existence in a complete system of concepts, we will never be finished. Even if we agree that such a conceptual system is feasible within a given limited area of experience, the summary could be made only with the aid of universal concepts, whereby full perception would be lost. We could on the other hand depart from the path of experience and cling to the most abstract views, and in this way we might be able to arrive at a clear consciousness of the general and fundamental conditions of existence; but we will still fail to exhaust the entire infinitude of definitions (qualities). Further, man does not have at his disposal a third and higher form of cognition that can embrace both the particular and the universal and give each its due. In spite of this, Møller holds that it is possible to develop a philosophy of life that not only asserts

[27] Poul Møller, "Strötanker [Aphorisms] 1826–1837" in *Efterladte Skrifter*, 3rd ed., III (Copenhagen, 1856), p. 117.

[28] Reprinted in *Efterladte Skrifter af Poul Møller*, [ed. with biography by F. C. Olsen], 2nd ed., I–VI (Copenhagen, 1848–1850), V, 38–140. See Gregor Malantschuk, "Søren Kierkegaard og Poul M. Møller," *Frihed og Eksistens* (Copenhagen, 1980), pp. 101–14.

the individual's reality and significance but also substantiates the fact that the individual is immortal. In giving a more detailed presentation of these views Møller approaches the Christian outlook. Although he does speak of Hegel with respect as a man who sought to accomplish something great, he feels compelled to reject him, but he does so with the humorous touch that Kierkegaard admired so much in the unforgettable teacher of his youth.

Mynster, Clausen, Sibbern, and finally Møller became opponents of "the system," and Martensen wanted "to go further" than Hegel, as Kierkegaard expresses it. But Hegel's philosophy had one confirmed adherent in Denmark: Johan Ludvig Heiberg (1791-1860).

To Heiberg belongs the honor of being the one who introduced Hegel's philosophy into Denmark. He had studied under the master himself in Berlin, and he has related[29] the experience he underwent on his homeward journey, when the fundamental ideas of the system suddenly appeared to him in full clarity and in their proper context. In the years following his return to Denmark, Heiberg wrote a considerable number of books and articles that made him the Danish spokesman of the system. It is worth mentioning that before Hegel's lectures on esthetics were published Heiberg had already developed an esthetics of his own along the lines of Hegelian views.

Heiberg was convinced that it was possible to bring unity and coherence into intellectual life, that is, into art, religion, and philosophy, only by applying the basic ideas of Hegel's system. He has explained this clearly in his work *Om Philosophiens Betydning for den nærværende Tid* (Copenhagen, 1833). In this writing Heiberg maintains that the times suffer from an excess of ideas; for example, in addition to art, poetry, and religion, the natural sciences and politics were becoming increasingly popular and important. He thought that the problem, to which only Hegel's philosophy is capable of providing a solution, consisted in relating all these ideas and interests to each other and reducing them to a coherent system. This in turn means that philosophy does not contribute anything new; it rather consists in a deliberation on or knowledge of something already given. Because of this, philosophy is a part of man's common sense, and it yields cognition of the truth contained in the variety of human experiences and in man's efforts with respect to nature, the state, art, and religion. A philosophy does not evolve, Heiberg maintains, until we reflect on a completed period of development, and then philosophy makes this development continuously present to us and conse-

[29] See below, pp. 247-48.

quently eternal by translating the developed content of the period in question into conceptual terms.

By thus opening our eyes to what we in fact already possess, philosophy remedies spiritual maladies. Indeed, Heiberg perceived just such an ailment among his contemporaries; the age, he noted, suffered from a conflict between ideality and reality and between the infinite and the finite, with the result that finite and opposing pursuits had thrust the infinite and the eternal beyond reach. What we now must learn from philosophy is to be able to perceive that it is precisely the infinite and the eternal that underlie individual and finite endeavors, so what we seek is granted to us even while we are searching. In Heiberg's opinion this is how Hegel's philosophy reconciles the ideal with reality.

Heiberg believed that basically the conflicts arising from contrasting endeavors and activities could be found in the Hegelian system of logic, in which everything is supposed to be represented by a corresponding concept.[30] He does not seem to show the same interest in Hegel's philosophy of nature, but he did make a separate study of the third part of the system, the philosophy of spirit, including, as mentioned, the fine arts and at least part of the philosophy of religion. He compared the three parts of the system with hell, purgatory, and paradise as delineated in Dante's *Divine Comedy*.

In the present discussion we will only deal peripherally with one of Heiberg's views, and that merely to indicate how he thought. As a true Hegelian, Heiberg was naturally convinced that philosophy and religion have a shared content but are different in form. He wrote a so-called "apocalyptical comedy," *En Sjæl efter Døden* (1841), a social satire in which he asserts that a person can be saved in two ways: either by becoming immersed in the historical figure of Christ, or by understanding God speculatively. The second method alone is perfect, and one must repeatedly return to it for support if religion is to have any force, for only that which can be put into a conceptual form has validity. Philosophy cannot be used as a means to prove the existence of God, Heiberg maintains, which indeed cannot be proved at all unless it is presupposed a priori. On the other hand it is possible by means of philosophy to convert an image of God into a concept and to think of God as the absolute that has no antithesis, because the absolute is the one synthesis that renders all contrasts and all other important syntheses of contrasts possible. Heiberg finds that the

[30] Heiberg describes this logic in *Philosophiens Philosophie eller den speculative Logik*, I–II (Copenhagen, 1831–1832).

Christian doctrine of the Trinity contains points of agreement with Hegel's philosophy. He says:

> The trilogy that constantly permeates the Hegelian system is the reflection of the Trinity itself in the realms of thought, nature, and spirit, and this is the absolute condition for all philosophy.[31]

If we are to think of God as an infinite being, we must not simply interpret the infinite to mean an unlimited temporal and spatial dimension in a permanent state of transition from something finite to something infinite, that is, as a sum of finite points or what Hegel called "the bad infinity." True infinity embodies a plenitude whose elements stand in an inner and necessary interrelation; for example, self-consciousness contains an inner relation between subject and object. Heiberg regarded this as a revolving circle in which nothing is permanent or immutable, first or last, or cause or effect. The true infinity cannot, however, remain in an external and thus finite relation to a finitude that has temporal and spatial extension, for the finite would consequently set a limit to infinity, whereby the latter would of course cease to be infinite. To avoid this, the infinite must reveal itself within the realm of the finite and make the finite serve as a necessary form through which the finite itself is thoroughly defined. This, Heiberg claimed, is exactly what Christianity teaches: God enters into the finite world by means of the Incarnation. The second person in the Trinity denotes both diversity and the finite, insofar as finitude is able to accommodate God. The third person, the Holy Ghost, signifies the perfect harmony between the infinite and the finite.

Heiberg thought that with these arguments he was past the dispute between the rationalists and the Supranaturalists. In his opinion the rationalists placed the infinite outside the compass of the finite, whereas the Supranaturalists conversely kept the finite beyond the sphere of the infinite. According to speculative logic both views involve a self-contradiction. From this it is evident that Heiberg must be classified as a right-wing Hegelian.

As mentioned above, the various theological and philosophical standpoints then represented in Denmark were set into sharp relief on a particular occasion. That occasion was the dispute concerning logical principles that occurred at the close of the 1830s and the be-

[31] In the article "Recension over Hr. Dr. Rothe's Treenigheds og Forsoningslære" in *Perseus, Journal for den speculative Idee.* Ed. J. L. Heiberg, no. 1 (Copenhagen, June 1837), p. 11.

ginning of the 1840s. The outward cause of the dispute was an apparently insignificant remark by one of Martensen's good friends and fellow partisans, Johan Alfred Bornemann, who also acted as official examiner at the oral defense of Martensen's dissertation. In a rather long review of that same dissertation Bornemann wrote as follows: "Both rationalism and Supranaturalism are antiquated standpoints in theology [since the appearance of Martensen's thesis] and now belong to a bygone age."[32] This statement provoked Mynster to write "Rationalisme, Supranaturalisme" in protest.[33] Mynster's purpose in writing this article was to demonstrate that both rationalism and Supranaturalism still existed as historical phenomena and that the two represented contradictory and not simply contrary views. In other words, Mynster supports the principle of contradiction while delivering overt attacks on both Hegel and Heiberg, though his emphasis in this work is on the validity of the principle of exclusion. Sibbern and Kierkegaard were on Mynster's side in this controversy. Kierkegaard, however, did not define his position clearly until a later date, first in *Either/Or*[34] and then in an undated entry from about May 1844 in *Journals and Papers*. This important entry is here quoted *in extenso*:

N.B.

It is not difficult to comprehend that in a certain sense the principle of identity is higher than the principle of contradiction and the basis for it. But the principle of identity is only the limit for human thought; it is like the blue mountains, like the line the etchers call the base—the drawing is the main thing. As long as I live in time, the principle of identity is only an abstraction. Therefore nothing is easier than to delude oneself and others into thinking the identity of all by abandoning diversity. Nevertheless one might ask such a person how he conducts himself with regard to living, since in identity I am beyond time. Suicide is therefore the only ethical consequence of the identity-principle adhered to in time. The confusion arises only from living in categories different from those used in writing books—O, wretched book-writing!

As long as I live, I live in contradiction, for life is contradiction. On the one side I have eternal truth, on the other side manifold existence [*Tilværelse*], which human beings as such cannot penetrate, for then we would have to be omniscient.

---

[32] *Tidsskrift for Litteratur og Kritik*, I (Copenhagen, 1839), pp. 3ff.
[33] Ibid., pp. 259ff.
[34] *Either/Or*, I, 37; *SV* I 25.

The uniting link is therefore faith.[35]

[*Addition to above*:]

Identity can never become *terminus a quo* but is *terminus ad quem*; one always comes to it only through abstraction.[36]

Both Heiberg and Martensen went on the offensive against Mynster.[37] Heiberg narrowed down the principles of exclusion and contradiction to the point where they were valid only in the sphere of reflection, which is *eo ipso* the equivalent of saying that they are overcome and abolished in the superior sphere of speculation. In his contribution to the debate Heiberg limited himself to the logical principles involved, whereas Martensen was interested in the purely historical aspect concerning the professed irreconcilable conflict between rationalism and Supranaturalism. To be sure, Martensen did concede that in this instance it will be possible to retain the contrasts between the two; but in agreement with the Hegelian interpretation of concepts as antithetical entities and in total disagreement with Mynster, he held that a higher mediated point of view could be developed on the basis of these two historical phenomena. More concretely, this point of view gives expression to the assumption of a fundamental harmony between rational or speculative philosophy on the one hand and faith based on revelation on the other. Neither Heiberg nor Martensen could agree that the principles of contradiction, exclusion, or even identity are fully applicable in the fields of either epistemology or history. Both men were only willing to admit that the validity of these three principles was limited to the sphere of formal thought and to the subordinate and imperfect sphere of human life.

Hegel, Heiberg, Martensen, and Kierkegaard all seemed to concur on at least one point: the principle of contradiction is applicable only within certain areas. This also denotes, however, the limit of their agreement. Hegel, Heiberg, and Martensen maintained that it is possible for man to transcend these spheres in life and thought (which in their philosophies become identical) and to rise to the higher sphere of speculation. Like Mynster and Sibbern, Kierkegaard claimed that it is altogether impossible for man to reach a stage where the logical principles of contradiction, exclusion, and identity are annulled. He firmly insisted that the logical principles apply unconditionally—both

[35] *Pap.* V A 68; *JP* I 705.

[36] *Pap.* V A 69; *JP* I 706.

[37] Heiberg with "En logisk Bemærkning i Anledning af H. H. Hr. Biskop Dr. Mynsters Afhandling" and Martensen with "Rationalisme, Supranaturalisme og principium exclusi medii."

formally and in factual existence—whenever we are dealing with the only type of thought and being possible for man in an existence in the present created world. The dispute about the logical principles[38] thus leads us to the question of anthropology in speculative idealism and in Kierkegaard.

[38] Works concerning this rather local debate are available only in Danish. The controversy was treated for the first time by Viktor Kuhr, *Modsigelsens Grundsætning* (Copenhagen, 1915). It was then examined in a broader perspective by Jens Himmelstrup in *Søren Kierkegaards Opfattelse af Sokrates* (Copenhagen, 1924), pp. 218ff. In addition, the reader is referred to P. P. Jørgensen, *H. P. Kofoed-Hansen (Jean Pierre). Med særligt Henblik til Søren Kierkegaard* (Copenhagen and Christiania [Oslo], 1920), pp. 161ff.; Skat Arildsen, *Martensen*, pp. 142ff.; and H. Høirup, *Grundtvigs Syn paa Tro og Erkendelse* (Copenhagen, 1949), passim.

CHAPTER 7

Kierkegaard Versus Hegel

The fundamental disagreement between Kierkegaard on the one side and Hegel along with his Danish proselytes on the other is conveyed even more clearly in the *Postscript*. This can be demonstrated by means of a closer examination of a few pivotal concepts in logic and metaphysics. As indicated at the end of the preceding chapter, the next questions to arise concern, first of all, the premises on which their disagreements are based and, second, the effect that their differences of opinion have on the method Kierkegaard employs in the *Postscript* to present the religious and philosophical issues.[1]

Kierkegaard writes as follows in the *Postscript*:[2] "(A), a logical system is possible; (B), an existential system is impossible." He then furnishes this comment:

> In the construction of a logical system, it is necessary first and foremost to take care not to include in it anything which is subject to an existential dialectic, anything which is, only because it exists or has existed, and not simply because it is. From this it follows quite simply that Hegel's unparalleled discovery, the subject of so unparalleled an admiration, namely, the introduction of movement into logic, is a sheer confusion of logical science. . . . And it is surely strange to make movement fundamental in a sphere where movement is unthinkable.

This brings us to the crux of the matter, for this quotation contains rather more implicitly than explicitly what Kierkegaard means by logic, a logical system, and existence (*Tilværelse*). A comparison of Kierkegaard's concepts with similar concepts in Hegel will make it

---

[1] There still remains the historical problem of how well Kierkegaard was acquainted with the religious and philosophical traditions sketched in the preceding chapters and, in particular, with the shape given them by Hegel. This question lies beyond the scope of the present introduction to Kierkegaard's work. I have examined the problem more closely, however, in *Kierkegaard's Relation to Hegel* (Princeton, 1980) and "Kierkegaard's Kenntnis der philosophischen und theologischen Tradition," *Theologische Zeitschrift* (Basel, 1979), pp. 351ff.

[2] *Kierkegaard's Concluding Unscientific Postscript*, trans. David F. Swenson and Walter Lowrie (Princeton, 1941), pp. 99ff.; *SV* VII 97.

obvious that the two thinkers disagree completely. It will therefore be necessary to return to some points in Hegel's logic that were merely touched on above.

In Hegel's view, as in Aristotle's, logic is not merely a formal discipline but also a concrete logic and epistemology.[3] As we have already pointed out, it is manifestly clear from his two principal works, *The Science of Logic* and *Encyclopaedia of the Philosophical Sciences*, that to him logic *sensu eminenti* is a doctrine of the divine reason or logos and concerns this divinity's inner triune life before creation. This life, which Hegel regards as a dynamic process, is presented in his *Science of Logic*. The withdrawal of the divine idea from its own proper sphere is then described in *The Philosophy of Nature*. In his *Philosophy of Spirit*[4] Hegel sets forth the divine idea's efforts to return to its own realm after its endeavors to absorb the fullness of the empirically concrete world.

We have already observed that Hegel's logic is itself divided into three parts: "The Doctrine of Being," "The Doctrine of Essence," and "The Doctrine of the Concept." He defines it as follows: "LOGIC IS THE SCIENCE OF THE PURE IDEA; pure, that is, because the Idea is in the abstract medium of Thought."[5] What this definition involves becomes evident from a statement in *The Science of Logic*:

> Logic is . . . to be understood as the System of Pure Reason, as the Realm of Pure Thought. *This realm is the Truth as it is, without husk in and for itself.* One may therefore express it thus: that this content *shows forth God as he is in his eternal essence before the creation of Nature and of a Finite Spirit.*[6]

In Hegel's opinion God's nature or essence develops in the following manner. When conceived in its pure state, being is identical to nothing. These two concepts are then mediated in a third concept, becoming, thereby giving rise to the concept of determinate being (*Daseyn*). This implies that being faces a limit, for the dialectical development of thought and being (which are identical) has also ad-

[3] See also above, chap. 6.

[4] *The Logic of Hegel*, trans. William Wallace, 2nd ed. (Oxford, 1892), §18, p. 28 (hereafter abbreviated as *Logic*); *Jub. Ausg.* VIII 64; *The Philosophy of Mind [Spirit]*, §385, p. 20.

[5] *Logic*, §19, p. 30. Compare Jens Himmelstrup's definition in *SV* XV 711ff.

[6] *Hegel's Science of Logic*, trans. W. H. Johnston and L. G. Struthers, I–II (London and New York, 1929), I, 60 (hereafter designated as *The Science of Logic*); *Jub. Ausg.* IV 45–6.

vanced to the concept of "somewhat" (*Etwas*), and this concept, because it simply is, limits itself in relation to the concept of otherness (*Anderes*). The limit applied here gives us the concept of finitude, and Hegel interprets this in turn as a contrast to an endless progression that he calls the wrong or bad infinity (*die schlechte Unendlichkeit*).

We are now presented with a series of qualitative definitions of self-subsistent units called "ones." By means of these determinations the development proceeds to the concept of magnitude (*Grösse*) and then further to the concept of measure (*Mass*), which is a synthesis of quality and quantity. Each limited quantity, or quantum, however, can become so large as to exceed its qualitative character,[7] and when this occurs one measure may be employed to measure another, thereby allowing the process to continue to the doctrine of essence. This constitutes the second part of the logic, and it is in this section that Hegel deals with essentialist or reflective qualifications and definitions, including the principles of contradiction and excluded middle (*principium exclusi medii*). It is also the section that has constantly been the target of criticism ever since the days of Trendelenburg and Kierkegaard.

Being is that which is immediate in our consciousness, whereas essence refers to the mediacy involved in thought. As we reflect on this relationship, our thought progresses from immediate being to annulled being, which is the essence of being. Briefly, the result of this conceptual movement is that thought at this stage necessarily proceeds from one pair of concepts to the next, whereas it was only able to move from one concept to another when it was at the level of immediate being. As opposed to being, which is conceived by thought as something composite, the concept of essence is apprehended as a unity, but at the same time thought also grasps it as something containing a difference. Opposition presupposes something that has been posited beforehand, and we can call what has been presupposed the "positive," whereas that which has been posited may be called the "negative." Thus the concept of essence embodies negativity. In Hegel's logic the two contradictory terms, the positive and negative, predispose each other as ground and consequence. This also applies to the concepts of matter and form, which are reflective qualifications in terms of essence; and it holds true once again of force and its manifestation, a pair of concepts that develop into outer and inner. When outer and inner unite, actuality emerges

---

[7] Note in this connection Kierkegaard's discussion of the anecdote about Chrysippus' and Carneades' argument about how to stop a sorites in the *Fragments*, p. 53.

as the adequate manifestation of essence; we have thus left the sphere of reflection (the understanding) and arrived at the stage of reason. Hegel claims that at this stage thought regarded as the inner and being as the outer become identical, so we are now able to move on to the sphere of the concept. This is then treated in the third part of his logic.

One of the characteristic traits of Hegel's view of the concept is that in his opinion it contains contradictions and more than one meaning. This is of course diametrically opposed to Kierkegaard's view and to the rules of classical formal logic, which require that concepts be unique in their reference and free of contradictions. Hegel never considers these contradictions, however, to be contradictory in fact but simply contrary terms. The contradiction contained in each concept constitutes the negative element that propels the developmental processes of both being and essence. This is how, as Kierkegaard puts it, movement finds its way into logic, thereby entering an area in which he believed it definitely does not belong; for he viewed logic as a static discipline rather than as a dynamic process. We have already observed that in Hegel's linguistically symbolic cosmos his speculative concept with its intrinsic contradictions is identical to the living creative divinity. Hegel thereupon identifies the divinity with science and this in turn with the speculative philosophy that his own system embodies.

Hegel begins the third part of his logic with the doctrine of the subjective concept (*der Begriff*), which not only contains antitheses but also serves as a basis for them. These are in turn qualified by means of the judgment (*das Urtheil*) and the end or final cause. Hegel's dialectic then proceeds to the doctrine of the objective concept, which leads to a teleological cosmology and ultimately to the doctrine of the idea. The fully evolved absolute idea marks the end of Hegel's presentation of logic, but the absolute idea embraces the entire preceding development from beginning to end, and since its content may be said to consist of the whole system of logic itself, arrival at this stage also implies a return to the beginning. Thus the circle is closed.

This gives us an extremely sketchy outline of Hegel's logic, the discipline that he identifies with his theology. As indicated above, within this logical framework he also discusses traditional formal logic and its axioms. He limits the validity of these axioms, however, to a definite subordinate sphere while rejecting their applicability altogether in the field of strictly speculative logic.

It seems suitable at this point to inquire into just what Hegel means by a system of logic. In answering this question I am reminded of Kant's famous definition:

> In accordance with reason's legislative prescriptions, our diverse modes of knowledge must not be permitted to be a mere rhapsody, but must form a system. Only so can they further the essential ends of reason. By a system I understand the unity of the manifold modes of knowledge under one idea. This idea is the concept provided by reason—of the form of a whole—in so far as the concept determines *a priori* not only the scope of its manifold content, but also the positions which the parts occupy relatively to one another. The scientific concept of reason contains, therefore, the end and the form of that whole which is congruent with this requirement. The unity of the end to which all the parts relate and in the idea of which they all stand in relation to one another, makes it possible for us to determine from our knowledge of the other parts whether any part be missing, and to prevent any arbitrary addition, or in respect of its completeness any indeterminateness that does not conform to the limits which are thus determined *a priori*. The whole is thus an organised unity (*articulatio*), and not an aggregate (*coacervatio*). It may grow from within (*per intus susceptionem*), but not by external addition (*per appositionem*). It is thus like an animal body, the growth of which is not by the addition of a new member, but by the rendering of each member, without change of proportion, stronger and more effective for its purposes.[8]

Hegel's explanation of the meaning of a system makes Kant's ideal more concrete in some respects:[9]

> The thought, which is genuine and self-supporting must be intrinsically concrete; it must be an Idea; and when it is viewed in the whole of its universality, it is the Idea, or the Absolute. The science of this Idea must form a system. For the truth is concrete; that is, whilst it gives a bond and principle of unity, it also possesses an internal source of development. Truth, then, is only possible as a universe or totality of thought; and the freedom of the whole, as well as the necessity of the several sub-divisions, which

---

[8] *Immanuel Kant's Critique of Pure Reason*, trans. Norman Kemp Smith (London and New York, 1964), pp. 653ff. (A832ff.; B861ff.).

[9] *Logic*, §14–15, pp. 24–25. In this and the notes immediately following the same paragraph numbers also apply to German editions of the *Encyclopaedia of the Philosophical Sciences*. See also *The Phenomenology of Mind [Spirit]*, pp. 81, 86; *Jub. Ausg.* II 14.

it implies, are only possible when these are discriminated and defined.

In the next paragraph he adds:

> Each of the parts of philosophy is a philosophical whole, a circle rounded and complete in itself. In each of these parts, however, the philosophical Idea is found in a particular specificality or medium. The single circle, because it is a real totality, bursts through the limits imposed by its special medium, and gives rise to a wider circle. The whole of philosophy in this way resembles a circle of circles. The Idea appears in each single circle, but, at the same time, the whole Idea is constituted by the system of these peculiar phases, and each is a necessary member of the organisation.

It is true that these quotations do not afford explicit evidence that Hegel was thinking exclusively of a logical system. Nevertheless, as indicated above, logic in the strict sense of the word clearly means to Hegel speculative logic. Moreover, in his opinion the absolute idea both can and absolutely must develop with metaphysical necessity according to the rules of speculative logic. It is therefore evident that the system that Hegel discusses can only and must on all accounts be a speculatively logical system.

If in conclusion we examine Hegel's interpretation of being and existence, we can indeed obtain a definition, but it will be necessary to preface this definition with an observation. According to Hegel, determinate being (*Daseyn*) belongs under the part of the philosophical system that pertains to *The Science of Logic*. This means that anything stated in respect of determinate being also applies to the divinity prior to the creation of the world; what is more, to be consistent it can apply *only* to the divinity. If we forget this or merely adhere to colloquial usage, as Hegel himself sometimes does, we may easily get the mistaken idea that Hegel's intention in his logic is simply to discuss a phenomenon belonging to the actual created world. This mistake is, by the way, extremely common.

We have previously noted that the doctrine of determinate being is found in the first section of Hegel's logic. Here it becomes part of the first conceptual triad (called "quality") in which it constitutes the negation of being and as such impels the speculative-dialectical development toward "being-for-self" (*Fürsichseyn*). Determinate being is then defined as follows:

> In Becoming the Being which is one with Nothing, and the Nothing which is one with Being, are only vanishing factors; they

are and they are not. Thus by its inherent contradiction Becoming collapses into the unity in which the two elements are absorbed. This result is accordingly *Being Determinate* (Being there and so).[10]

Hegel elaborates on this in the following paragraphs. First of all, "Determinate Being is Being with a character or mode" (*Bestimmtheit*) which "as reflected into itself in this its character or mode . . . is a somewhat, an existent."[11] Furthermore, "Somewhat is by its quality—firstly *finite*, secondly *alterable*; so that finitude and variability appertain to its being."[12] In the course of the development, "Something becomes an other: this other is itself somewhat: therefore it likewise becomes an other, and so on *ad infinitum*."[13] This infinite progression (*"ad infinitum"*) is the "bad" or negative infinity and is simply a negation of finitude. Hegel then proceeds to rectify the situation: "What we now in point of fact have before us, is that somewhat comes to be an other, and that the other generally comes to be an other."[14] The results are, among other things, a correction of the course taken by the bad infinity and a further determination of being:

> Thus essentially relative to another, somewhat is virtually an other against it: and since what is passed into is quite the same as what passes over, since both have one and the same attribute, viz. to be an other, it follows that something in its passage into other only joins with itself. To be thus self-related in the passage, and in the other, is the genuine Infinity. Or, under a negative aspect: what is altered is the other, it becomes the other of the other. Thus Being, but as negation of the negation, is restored again: it is now *Being-for-self.*[15]

We have now indicated, both explicitly and implicitly, that by logic Hegel understands a speculative logic containing contradictions, a logic embracing theology, which in turn is the same as Hegel's philosophy. We have also shown what Hegel means by a logical system and how he interprets determinate being or existence. Furthermore, we have on the authority of Hegel's own words made it clear that determinate being is hardly more than an extremely limited phase in the dialectical development of reason, the idea, and the divinity. By

[10] *Logic*, §89, p. 169.
[11] Ibid., §90, p. 170.
[12] Ibid., §92, p. 172.
[13] Ibid., §93, p. 174.
[14] Ibid., §95, p. 176.
[15] Ibid.

the same token, it is likewise obvious that in Hegel's opinion a system must be totally comprehensive and thus include much more than *Daseyn*, and that to accord with his notion of logic it must in any case be a logical system.

If we now confront those views with a few assertions made by Kierkegaard, various differences and parallels in respect of terminology, form, and content will immediately leap to the eye. In addition, this will enable us to shed a revealing light on his attitude to the Hegelian logic and thus of his view of the entire system, for the crucial parts of the system are precisely logic and the dialectical method.

Kierkegaard allows that it is possible to establish a logical or philosophical system of the kind described by Kant in the definition quoted above. Unlike Hegel, however, Kierkegaard interprets a system of logic to mean a system devoid of contradictions and consisting of linguistically formulated statements rather than a system based on contradictions. At present we are discussing only Kierkegaard's interpretation of logic strictly speaking and not his broader application of the word. Given this restriction, we can say that logic is in Kierkegaard's opinion synonymous with formal classical logic, according to which no philosophical system may be at variance with logical axioms. It follows that whereas Hegel in accordance with the principle of identity regards concepts as both the instruments and the goals of thought, Kierkegaard maintains that concepts must be unique in their reference and thus cannot contain the negative elements necessary to keep a process going. This has the effect of debarring movement from logic, a point that Kierkegaard indeed underscores. He is therefore certainly willing to concede that a logical system is possible, but above all he does not mean by this a speculative logic in the Hegelian sense of the term, and so he denies the legitimacy of Hegel's system. As a matter of fact, Kierkegaard adopts the view of logic that Sibbern and Mynster at the time advocated in Denmark during their controversy with Heiberg and Martensen. Kierkegaard nevertheless does agree with Heiberg that the classical logical axioms are applicable only within one definite sphere, that of existence.

We have seen that Kierkegaard's understanding of existence, especially in the sense of human existence, differs widely from Hegel's view of *Daseyn* and *Existenz*, respectively. It is therefore a foregone conclusion that there will also be a fundamental difference between their philosophies of religion with respect to their points of departure, methods, and results. Kierkegaard gives expression to this lack of accord in the following passage:

A system of existence is impossible. Does this mean that no such system exists? By no means; nor is this implied in our assertion. Existence [*Tilværelsen*] itself is a system—for God; but it cannot be a system for any existing [*existerende*] spirit. System and finality correspond to each other, but existence is precisely the opposite of finality. It may be seen, from a purely abstract point of view, that system and existence are incapable of being thought together; because in order to think existence at all, systematic thought must think it as abrogated, and hence as not existing [*tilværende*].[16]

In the very next paragraph Kierkegaard refers his readers to the one part of his works that is devoted to a cogent philosophical argumentation in support of the assertions quoted above: to the "Interlude" in the *Fragments*.[17] The main purpose of the "Interlude" was quite simply to bring home the fact that God acts freely and reveals Himself when and where He wishes. Making liberal use of elements drawn from Aristotle, ancient skepticism, and Leibniz, Kierkegaard aims a frontal attack against Hegel's speculative determinism by developing fundamental philosophical considerations of the nature of historical phenomena and the only possible conception that man can have of these phenomena. His formal point of departure is Plato's idealist philosophy, and in his argument he at least partly employs an Aristotelian terminology.

Kierkegaard begins by asking what happens when something comes into existence, that is, when something makes its entry into worldly existence; or, in theological terms, when it becomes part of the cre-

---

[16] *Postscript*, p. 107, translation modified; *SV* VII 106. By "existing spirit" in this quotation Kierkegaard of course means a human being who is content to live in existence and who does not try to transcend it speculatively.

[17] *Fragments*, pp. 89–110; *SV* IV 264–80. In this connection there are two themes that can only be noted in passing: the dialectic of freedom and, as mentioned above, anthropology. They can only be understood correctly when regarded as part of Kierkegaard's theology, which in turn is fundamentally decisive for his conception of the nature and scope of logic.

With reference to what follows, see the introduction (pp. xlv ff.) and commentary (pp. 239ff.) in my edition of the *Fragments*; Paul Holmer, "Kierkegaard and Logic," *Kierkegaardiana*, II (Copenhagen, 1957), pp. 25–43; Gregor Malantschuk, "Frihedens Dialektik hos Søren Kierkegaard," *Frihed og Eksistens* (Copenhagen, 1980), pp. 19–32; Régin Prenter, "L'homme, synthèse du temps et de l'éternité d'après Søren Kierkegaard," *Studia theologica*, II (Copenhagen, 1949), pp. 5–20; and Johannes Sløk, *Die Anthropologie Kierkegaards* (Copenhagen, 1954). This last work is discussed by me in *Theology Today* (Princeton, October 1955), pp. 297ff. Sløk's book, *Kierkegaard, humanismens tænker* (Copenhagen, 1978), correctly emphasizes the incompatibility of Kierkegaard's thoughts with speculative theories.

ated world. In other words, what change is involved here? Anything that comes into existence must be presumed to have had a prior existence in the form of a plan and thus in the form of potentiality. When it came into existence it received the form of actuality. The question of what change took place can of course apply only under the assumption that the plan itself remains the same, otherwise the change will not attach to coming into existence but rather to a change in essence, which would merely confuse matters. Kierkegaard's reply to the question is that the change involved in coming into existence is a transition from potentiality to actuality, hence a change in being, and that everything that undergoes this transition does so through an act of freedom. He operates under the assumption that, as he expresses it: "Every cause terminates in a freely effecting cause."[18] This postulate, a self-evident presupposition incapable of and requiring no verification, forms the basis of Kierkegaard's entire demonstration.[19] God is the freely effecting cause. Inasmuch as every cause is referable to this freely effecting cause, only the distraction occasioned by observing intermediate causes could induce someone to reply that the change attaching to coming into existence takes place with necessity. In these passages Kierkegaard regards necessity as a purely logical term rather than as a historical or metaphysical category, and potentiality and actuality as two forms of factual existence.

Once something has come into existence, it has not only done so through an act of freedom; it has also become historical and thus part of empirical actuality, but in this case we are dealing with a past actuality. Whatever is necessary is on the contrary atemporal; it has neither past nor future but is ever in the present and as such belongs under the category of eternity. The fact that something cannot subsequently be changed once it has become a historical actuality gives rise to the question of whether immutability possesses the character of necessity. Kierkegaard gives a negative reply to this question, and it follows from his answer that it is no more legitimate to apprehend the course of past events as having occurred with necessity than it is possible to prophesy future events. All past, present, and future events pass from the form of potentiality to the existential form of actuality, and this always takes place through an act of freedom. If this postulate obtains, Hegel is mistaken in his attempt to amalgamate logical, metaphysical, and historical categories in his system, with the result

---

[18] *Fragments*, p. 93; *SV* IV 267.
[19] See Kierkegaard's remarks concerning the Hegelian beginning without presuppositions: *Postscript*, pp. 102ff.; *SV* VII 100ff.

that he is compelled to classify historical events under the category of necessity.

In the conclusion of the "Interlude" Kierkegaard poses the problem of how the past should be interpreted. He proceeds here by first distinguishing between the phenomena of nature, which belong to the category of space, and historical phenomena, which pertain to the category of time. He then asserts that inasmuch as these phenomena did not eventuate with necessity, our conception of them must not allow us to make it seem as though they belong within the category of necessity and thus within the timeless category of logic; for in fact such events lie within the category of freedom. Freedom is the sphere of the whole of reality, whereas human existence has additional distinguishing marks.

It is manifest from the above that Kierkegaard rejected the idea that it might be possible for any human being to develop a system of existence. On the one hand existence consists of everything that has become actual and thus itself partakes of existence; on the other, a logical and hence atemporal system may not include "anything which is subject to an existential dialectic, anything which is, only because it exists or has existed, and not simply because it is."[20] Man himself lives in existence, from which he is unable to withdraw to gain an overall view and begin building systems of this same existence. Thus in Kierkegaard's view the scope of logic is limited to what lies beyond the temporal. By contrast, Hegel felt that logic in the guise of his speculative logic not only reigns supreme in the realm of timelessness (God's inner trinitarian life) but is also designed to rule the phenomena of space and time, as is the case in his philosophies of nature and spirit. It is, however, necessary to add in this connection that in Hegel the idea informs both space and time fundamentally, and that these two categories must therefore be viewed in this light.

Hegel does not discuss a system of existence but a speculatively logical system. Kierkegaard denies that it is possible to achieve a system of existence but concedes that a logical system is feasible. Kierkegaard's view of logic, however, differs essentially from Hegel's.

[20] Ibid., p. 99; *SV* VII 97.

CHAPTER 8

The Theological and Anthropological
Premises for Kierkegaard's Critique

It is already obvious from the few examples presented above that Kierkegaard makes very extensive use of traditional religious and philosophical terminology in the *Postscript*, as he also does in his other pseudonymous works. This circumstance could scarcely have caused the work's first (few) readers any difficulties in a technical sense. For a present-day reader, however, it undoubtedly presents an obstacle not only with respect to language but also with respect to the subject matter and content.

Kierkegaard did not use this ready-made terminology without reflecting on what he was doing, or because it was after all the one he happened to know best and he did not feel like going to the trouble to invent a new one. On the contrary, he used it to a specific end, making it serve as a medium for indirect communication. In *The Point of View for My Work as An Author*, which constitutes a direct rather than indirect communication, Kierkegaard lets us in on the secret of the art of helping others: "if real success is to attend the effort to bring a man to a definite position, one must first of all take pains to find *him* where he is and begin there."[1] This was precisely Socrates' method.

Kierkegaard exploited this traditional conceptual instrument of philosophy as a means to impart something that was untraditional at that time. In other words, his intention in the pseudonymous works, which culminate with the *Postscript*, was not "to go further" than Hegel or back to an older form of speculative thought. Like Pascal and Hamann, he wished instead to return to the Bible and its exegesis of man's relationship to God.

It is a matter of common knowledge that the aim of the theological research of the last generation, which in some instances is directly inspired by Kierkegaard and in particular by his *Fragments*, has been

---

[1] *The Point of View for My Work as An Author: A Report to History*, trans. Walter Lowrie, ed. Benjamin Nelson (New York, 1962), p. 27; *SV* XIII 568. Although written in 1848, this work did not come out until 1859, when it was published by Kierkegaard's brother Peter Christian Kierkegaard.

to elucidate the differences between the Biblical world of ideas and the way of thinking that prevailed in antiquity, especially in idealistic philosophy.[2] The very fact that there were such distinctions, however, was by no means a matter of course to Kierkegaard's contemporaries, and when they did acknowledge them they did not feel that such differences as there were implied incompatibility. As a rule, mediation came to mean a compromise between vague concepts.

More often than not, the derivation and development of religious and philosophical thought were implicitly or explicitly indebted to a specific cosmology for their orientation. Thinkers began with a certain total situation and on the basis of this they proceeded to develop their views of man, their philosophical anthropologies, and their definitions of man's place in existence, man's mission in life, and the capacities and possibilities available for the accomplishment of this mission. Kierkegaard on the contrary assumed that it is impossible to achieve a complete understanding of what it means to be a human being—that is, a particular existing human being—either by means of self-knowledge, as maintained by all philosophical idealism,[3] or through studies of the environment, nature, or history. He held that knowledge of man must be based on the Biblical presentation of divine revelation. Kierkegaard's conception of God, the world, and man is therefore basically different from Hegel's, but his view is to a great extent couched in the language of speculation.

It has been pointed out that since Aristotle's philosophy does not allow for the idea of creation, the thinkers of the High Middle Ages initially encountered considerable difficulties in their efforts to make his metaphysics fit into scholastic philosophy. Indeed, if we try to locate the decisive difference between Greek and Biblical thinking,

---

[2] Outstanding examples are Karl Barth, *Der Römerbrief* (Zürich, 1919), and especially the epoch-making second edition (Zürich, 1922); Emil Brunner, *Der Mittler* (Tübingen, 1927); and Anders Nygren, *Agape and Eros*, vol. I in the original Swedish edition of 1930. Johannes Hessen, *Platonismus und Prophetismus* (Munich, 1939), may also be mentioned in this connection.

Since the 1920s these differences have been taken as a matter of course by most prominent representatives of Scandinavian theology. See for example Regin Prenter's dogmatic work, *Creation and Redemption*, trans. Thomas J. Jensen (Philadelphia, 1967); N. H. Søe, *Kristelig Etik*, 4th ed. (Copenhagen, 1957) and *Religionsfilosofi*, 2nd ed. (Copenhagen, 1963). See also Horst Stephan, *Geschichte der deutschen evangelischen Theologie seit dem deutschen Idealismus*, 2nd ed., ed. Martin Schmidt (Berlin, 1960); John Macquarrie, *Twentieth-Century Religious Thought*, 2nd ed. (London, 1982); and Leif Grane in *Københavns Universitet 1479–1979*, V (Copenhagen, 1980.) See also V. Lindström, "The First Article of the Creed," *Kierkegaardiana*, XII (Copenhagen, 1982, pp. 38–50.

[3] This point is treated in detail in the *Fragments*.

we will find it in the very fact that in the Bible both the world and man are regarded as products of creation, a point that has been strongly emphasized in modern times. Of course this means, first, that the world does not exist and abide by virtue of its own powers; it came into existence from nothing on the strength of God's life-giving word alone, and if it is God's will, it can once again vanish into nothing. Second, it implies that according to the views of the Old and New Testaments the world is an object for ethical consideration instead of an object of cognition, as the Greeks held.[4] In the Biblical conception man is created in the same manner as his environment and is assigned the specific task of making himself master of the rest of the world, but he can accomplish this task only if he has a correct relation to God. Both the world and man are, in this view, inseverably bound to God; a relation to God is inevitable even if man rebels against God and tries to become his own master as well. A correct relation to God consists in faith and obedience, whereas infidelity and disobedience constitute the fundamental characteristics of sin and are an indication that man has rejected God's truth in order to lead a life of his own in error.

Let us suppose that man is in error and God's truth enters into the historical world in a unique mode as a definite person, and that this person then shows us how we both can and must live our human lives in accordance with God's will. It follows that man will not be referred to another round of introspection or to observations of his environment; he will be referred to that person. What is more, his relation to God and to himself, his self-understanding, and his relation to the rest of the world—all this will be qualified by his relation to that person.

Kierkegaard expresses these rather uncomplicated ideas and their consequences in many different ways in both the pseudonymous works, of which the *Postscript* is both the midpoint and the turning point, and in the works published under his own name. There are several points of departure[5] to choose among if we wish to illustrate the parts

---

[4] See for example the articles αἰών and κόσμος in Kittel, *Theologisches Wörterbuch zum Neuen Testament*, I–X² (Stuttgart, 1933–1979), I, 197ff., and III, 867ff.

[5] Of the extensive literature on this subject the following may be recommended as examples: Valter Lindström, *Stadiernas teologi* (Lund, 1943), and Johannes Sløk, *Die Anthropologie Kierkegaards* (Copenhagen, 1954).

I have intentionally made the presentation in this chapter as brief as possible and refrained from entering into a direct discussion with the many scholars who have already worked with these same difficult problems. More detailed investigations are presented in the notes to the introduction to my edition of and commentary on the *Fragments*, especially p. xcvi. In addition, special reference may be made to Per Løn-

played by the theory of creation and the inevitability of a relation to God in Kierkegaard's world of thought. We might start as follows.

The ethically minded Judge in the second half of *Either/Or* emphasizes to his young friend, who is a romanticist and esthete, that man is in an inescapable situation in which he both can and must make a choice, and that even a refusal to do so involves a choice. The Judge then adds that "in making a choice it is not so much a question of choosing the right as the energy, the earnestness, the pathos with which one chooses."[6] In this way man fulfills his destiny and is "brought into immediate relation to the eternal Power whose omnipresence interpenetrates the whole of existence."[7] This power is of course God, who created and now sustains the universe. Whoever refuses to make a choice lives basically in despair, which Kierkegaard calls "the sickness unto death." Despair and anxiety are negative signs of the inevitability of the God-relationship; faith is, on the contrary, the positive sign. God is present in the created world in nature, history, and man; but since God is not immediately recognizable, it is impossible to obtain knowledge of God by empirical or rational means. Furthermore, Kierkegaard says, as the prerequisite for all human life, God has a subjective rather than an objective reference to life.[8] It follows that if a thinker, proceeding along the lines of speculative philosophy, attempts to acquire a knowledge of God but forgets to take into account the fact that he himself is a single existing individual, he will in reality merely attain to a self-knowledge that is distorted because he has neglected existence and the ethical task imposed by existence. In Kierkegaard's view, this is the reason why the system actually fails to include ethics.

As mentioned above, Kierkegaard makes wide use of traditional philosophical terminology in his descriptions of existence. He speaks, for example, of specimen, individual, and kind; possibility, actuality,

---

ning, "*Samtidighedens Situation*" (Oslo, 1954); Anna Paulsen, *Søren Kierkegaard, Deuter unserer Existenz* (Hamburg, 1955); Gregor Malantschuk, *Kierkegaard's Thought* (Princeton, 1971); R. H. Johnson, *The Concept of Existence in the Concluding Unscientific Postscript* (The Hague, 1972); Mark C. Taylor, *Kierkegaard's Pseudonymous Authorship* (Princeton, 1975); John W. Elrod, *Being and Existence in Kierkegaard's Pseudonymous Works* (Princeton, 1975); Gregor Malantschuk, *Fra Individ til den Enkelte* (Copenhagen, 1978); and Vincent A. McCarthy, *The Phenomenology of Moods in Kierkegaard* (The Hague, 1978). Articles treating various aspects of this subject will be found in *Kierkegaardiana*, I–XI (Copenhagen, 1955–1980), and *Bibliotheca Kierkegaardiana*, ed. Niels Thulstrup and Marie Mikulová Thulstrup, I–XVII (Copenhagen, 1978—).

[6] *Either/Or*, II, 171; *SV* II 181.

[7] Ibid.; *SV* II 182.

[8] *Postscript*, p. 178; *SV* VII 185.

and necessity; time, eternity, and the moment; and body, soul, and spirit. As Sløk in particular has pointed out,[9] however, these concepts have another content and function in Kierkegaard than they do in idealistic speculative philosophy. As a case in point, when Kierkegaard mentions the absolute self or the self in its eternal validity, he is not referring to the ego in its divine aspect but to a concrete and particular created self. This concept also embraces the idea that God has given each self the task of realizing its purpose in existence, and that if it fails to accomplish this task in its given state, the requirement will act as a judgment that will annihilate the self and plunge it into despair. In this case the self will be realized, all right, but negatively,[10] thereby opening the door to a rebirth and hence a new life.

The exposition of this new life and what living as a Christian entails is presented in the works that follow the *Postscript*. The intention of the works up to and including the *Postscript* is on the other hand to define man's course from the stage of immediacy to Christianity, or to "Religiousness B," as it is called in the *Postscript*.

The ethical elaborations presented by the Judge in *Either/Or* and by Climacus in the *Postscript* are based on a theory of creation that is intimately connected with the conception that the single individual's principal task consists in realizing his purpose in life. Kierkegaard sometimes expresses this by saying that the infinite or God's creative will must be actualized in the finite world. The esthete, who in Kierkegaard is the equivalent of a romanticist, seeks to evade this task by refusing to choose himself in his eternal validity; so evasion of the fundamental choice in existence comes to be synonymous with choosing to live a life in unfreedom instead of in freedom. In Kierkegaard's theory, man is a synthesis of soul and body sustained by a created spirit, and each individual has the task of actualizing this synthesis. A person leading an ethical life at least makes an effort to realize this synthesis, whereas the individual whom Kierkegaard classifies as an esthete—and this is a rather comprehensive category—makes no attempt at all in this direction. The only person who has fully succeeded in accomplishing this task is Jesus Christ, in whom the eternal and temporal are united in the paradoxical moment.

Kierkegaard's discussion (via his pseudonymous authors) of man as a synthesis is closely linked to his concepts of the self and spirit. These in turn denote that man is a created being consigned to existence, where he is confronted with the task of realizing a definite

---

[9] In *Die Anthropologie Kierkegaards*.
[10] *Postscript*, p. 230; *SV* VII 244.

purpose in life. Before an individual can know that he has such a task, however, he must have arrived at consciousness of the fact that he is a single human being possessing a unique self before God. Kierkegaard holds that it is also man's duty to acquire both this self-awareness and a consciousness of God, and that failure in either respect will entail guilt and result in the psychological symptoms of spiritlessness, anxiety, and the lower forms of despair. At a deeper level, sin emerges whenever an individual refuses to acknowledge his purpose in life, but an individual who is still in one of the lower stages of life will be unable to perceive that his shortcoming is a sin and not simply a matter of guilt or some minor transgression. Consciousness of sin is attainable only in the highest stage of life, which Kierkegaard calls "Religiousness B."

If on the basis of Kierkegaard's theory of creation we regard man as a synthesis, then man's very existence becomes synonymous with realizing the task imposed by the synthesis. In other words, man must employ his own existence to bring the two terms of the synthesis, which may also be called the eternal and the temporal, into a properly balanced relation. Thus an existing human being is always striving, as Kierkegaard puts it in the *Postscript* and with reference to Lessing. In Kierkegaard's view, a person who is constantly preoccupied with speculative thought is by contrast unable to achieve the passion necessary for this striving and hence is in a state of stagnation; and only a person who has comically misunderstood what it means to be human could be content to remain in this situation. The person who both exists and thinks—"the existing thinker"—looks on his existence as a task that lies before him, whereas the individual who merely speculates tends to regard existence in general as something past and finished, and thus as intelligible. Kierkegaard expresses this relation in various ways. For instance, he asserts that the eternal corresponds to the future as the goal toward which we strive by means of repetition, and not to the past, which is accessible to us through the medium of recollection. Since the eternal is the future, it moreover represents uncertainty as far as objective thought is concerned. Kierkegaard maintains that it can be grasped and realized only through the venture involved in the act of faith, in other words, by means of a leap. When a person makes this venture he also renounces his absolute dependence on the relative ends in the created world. In fact, he reverses his relationships. His previously relative relation to his absolute end now becomes fittingly absolute, whereas his absolute relation to relative ends is reduced to a correspondingly relative level. Kierkegaard also expresses this by saying that a casual God-relation-

ship is turned into a serious or earnest relationship. Inasmuch as Kierkegaard interprets faith as a venture that involves a choice and thus
a leap, he refutes the theory that doubt is an epistemological concept
that can be overcome by simply making a logical inference. Kierkegaard holds that doubt is an ethical category that emerges as the result
of a resolve, and it can therefore be conquered only by the same
means.

As mentioned above, man is faced with the task of existing, and
in his existence he must establish a correct relation to the two terms
of the synthesis that constitutes his being. Kierkegaard makes the
observation that a plain man is able to accomplish this without any
apparent difficulty. The person whom Kierkegaard calls the simple
wise man differs from the plain man only because he is cognizant of
the nature of his task. In other words, if a person is also an existing
thinker, then unlike the plain man he will be faced with the additional
obligation of understanding both himself in existence and the task
imposed by existence. Or, in Kierkegaard's terminology, the simple
wise man must succeed in reduplicating the task in his existence.
Between the task assigned to each individual and the accomplishment
of that task lie the difficulties that men avoid, evade, or try to solve
in various ways. The specific attitude taken to the task indicates the
particular stage in which the person in question is living.

Let us disregard for a moment Kierkegaard's first two books, *From
the Papers of One Still Living* and *The Concept of Irony*, neither of
which Kierkegaard himself counts as part of his opus. It will then be
possible to draw a schematic outline and see how Kierkegaard starts
by positing an alternative in *Either/Or* between the esthetic (or romantic) and ethical attitudes of life. In this book Kierkegaard has not
yet made a distinction between the ethical and the religious stages;
he has only set the esthetic apart from the ethical stage. He has intentionally limited the Judge's horizon, only permitting him to assert
that man is capable of attaining to a self-understanding by dint of his
own efforts and through despair and repentance. The Judge is thus
made to represent immediate ethical optimism. Two new elements
are added in *Fear and Trembling* and *Repetition*: the double movement
of infinity, comprising resignation and faith, and repetition in the
religious sense of a rebirth through faith.[11] In *The Concept of Anxiety*
the first or humanistic-religious ethics represented by the Judge is

---

[11] See in this connection my introduction to *Frygt og Bæven*, 2nd ed. (Copenhagen,
1983) and Gregor Malantschuk in his edition of *Gjentagelsen* (Copenhagen, 1961). These
are annotated Danish editions of *Fear and Trembling* and *Repetition*, respectively.

differentiated from the Christian ethics, which "presupposes dogmatics and with it hereditary sin."[12] The first ethics runs aground on sin and founders, whereas the second presupposes it. Sin radically impedes man's efforts, and it can only be overcome by faith, which is the direct opposite of sin and a condition or prerequisite bestowed by the absolute paradox in the person of Jesus Christ.[13]

Kierkegaard was now in a position to draw up and define a series of stages ranging from the immediate consciousness to Christianity, and this he does in the greatest detail in the *Postscript*.[14] It was consequently also possible for Kierkegaard to focus his attention on man's way to Christianity regarded as a given presupposition and then to describe this movement under the viewpoint of "becoming subjective."[15]

The *Postscript* is thus based on three premises. First, there is the idealistic speculative philosophy of religion that supplied the terminology used in the book. Second, it rests on the Biblical doctrines of man as a created being with an ethical requirement to realize his purpose in life; of man as a sinner; and of God's redemptive revelation in Jesus Christ as an object of faith and the condition necessary for the realization of human existence in accordance with God's will. The third premise is Kierkegaard's coherent analysis of the stages from immediacy to Christianity, an analysis that constitutes an attack aimed directly at speculation.

The principal theme in the *Postscript* is extremely simple and may be briefly formulated as follows: How can a single existing human being who is infinitely interested in his eternal salvation establish a true relation to the message brought by Christianity? Kierkegaard considers this message in the light of the *Fragments*, in which he had already taken pains to delineate its decisive traits and distinguish it from all the idealistic theories about truth and the possibility of achieving knowledge of it.

We should first of all remember that the author of the *Postscript* is the pseudonymous Johannes Climacus, a humorist who knows what

---

[12] *The Concept of Anxiety*, ed. and trans. Reidar Thomte and Albert B. Anderson, vol. VII of *Kierkegaard's Writings* (Princeton, 1980), p. 20; translation modified to include a phrase omitted. *SV* IV 325.

[13] *Fragments*, p. 73; *SV* IV 259.

[14] *Postscript*, pp. 259ff.; *SV* VII 279ff.

[15] Unlike most of the religious and philosophical thought outlined in the preceding chapters, Kierkegaard's thinking is not oriented toward any definite cosmology. Nor does he proceed in accordance with the a priori method of reasoning founded by Kant. In this respect, I am unable to agree with Elrod and Malantschuk, who maintain that Kierkegaard's methods are influenced by and resemble Kant's methodology.

Christianity is but does not dare to call himself a Christian. In Part One he asserts that in attempting to reply to the above question, in the first place it will make no difference at all whether historical research manages to confirm or invalidate the Biblical reports. In the second place, it does not matter if scholars seek to prove the truth of Christianity by traditional means, as both Catholics and the Grundtvigians have tried to do. In the third place, whether or not the truth of Christianity is acknowledged in speculative philosophy of religion is also immaterial. The issue and central theme of the work do not indeed concern either the objective problem of whether Christianity is true or untrue, or the methods previously applied to prove or disprove the truth of Christianity. The *Postscript* tackles the subjective problems of how the ego, the single existing human being, can establish a relation to Christianity and how Christianity can become the truth for the individual.

In Part Two Climacus presents the subjective rather than the objective path to Christianity. The relation to the truth of Christianity consists in an incessant striving in this earthly existence. Men may assume different attitudes toward their task, but as we have set forth in greater detail above, the very fact that no man is able to escape from existence makes it humanly impossible to develop a system encompassing the whole of reality. Like human existence, reality as a whole is unfinished, and the thinker who proposes to devise such a system is himself part of that incomplete existence. Kierkegaard concedes that the attainment of objectivity is an ideal with respect to empirical sciences such as philology and history, but he insists that the ideal of objectivity is on the contrary a serious obstacle to the acquisition of knowledge of the truth in connection with the stages of existence. The way to the goal here consists in becoming subjective. This is the only path to a realization of the fact that the truth of Christianity does not consist of a system of philosophical doctrines; rather, it means participation in existence. It is therefore a communication of existence, as Kierkegaard phrases it. Kierkegaard does not believe that it is possible for man to attain to this truth by means of introspection, which at most can lead to recognition of the fact that sin has separated man from the truth.

In Kierkegaard's view, if a person is to make the leap into the sphere of faith he will require pathos (passion). The pathos involved in the act of faith is simply the single existing individual's concern about his eternal happiness, a concern that was evident even before the inception of Christianity. Kierkegaard asserts that the difficulties involved in the pathetic aspect of faith are compounded by the addition of dialectical elements. First, we have the historical and paradoxical revelation in Christ, which are already presented in the *Fragments*. Then there is the dialectical element attaching to the contents of faith. Finally, we must also consider the believer's position in regard to faith, which may be expressed by using traditional dogmatic terminology and saying that *fides quae* determines *fides qua*.[16]

In Kierkegaard's scheme, neither the romanticist nor the speculative thinker relates to this paradoxical truth. What is more, they do not know the meaning of sin and faith and fail completely to establish an ethical relation to their own existence. The ethicist in the humanistic-religious sphere maintains that it is on the contrary possible to arrive at a recognition of guilt by means of self-knowledge. Not until we reach the next stage, however, which Kierkegaard calls "Religiousness A" in the *Postscript*, does it become possible to realize that man's guilt in failing to fulfill his determination is total because it is guilt before God. At this stage man's existence is informed by a consciousness of the fact that his total guilt, impotence, and responsibility, and his consequent suffering, are all caused by the distance that he himself has placed between his actual existence and his purpose in existence. This means in turn that he has acquired an insight into the distance separating God from man. Therefore, the ethical attitude at this stage does not yield a perceptible external change; whatever change takes place does so only in inwardness.

Let us assume that one specific condition has been established as necessary before a person can attain to eternal happiness, a condition that man as a created being does not himself possess even though he may be conscious of his total guilt. The condition is faith in Jesus Christ as the absolute paradox. This prerequisite will place a gulf between all the preceding stages from immediacy to Religiousness A on the one hand and Christianity on the other. It is Christianity itself that posits this condition, but the condition is also given to man in Christianity—along with the task of holding it fast in his existence and against the dictates of reason. The only alternative will now be to take offense at this truth, thereby disclosing the fact that what the individual had previously understood as total guilt is in reality total sin. In Kierkegaard's Christian psychology this is also the road to the

[16] An outstanding analysis of the *Postscript* is to be found in Pierre Mesnard, *Le vrai visage de Kierkegaard* (Paris, 1948). See also Cornelio Fabro's introduction to his Italian translation, *Postilla non scientifica*, I–II (Bologna, 1962; 2nd ed., Florence, 1972), and George E. and George B. Arbaugh, *Kierkegaard's Authorship* (London, 1968).

depths of despair. The way out is, first of all, faith both in Christ as the truth and in His gift of total forgiveness. Second, it consists in recognition of the fact that Christ, who in total suffering obeyed God's commandment to live as a human being, also demands that he be imitated and that men achieve contemporaneity with Him.[17]

In speculative philosophy of religion, and especially in Hegel's version, the single existing individual vanishes in the necessary development of world history. Kierkegaard, on the other hand, regards the individual as free and responsible for the sphere of existence in which he lives.

The situation in Denmark was taken as a point of departure in the preceding pages. We then saw how the controversy about the principles of logic inaugurated a reckoning with fundamental aspects of Hegelian speculation and how this was continued in the *Postscript*. I have also shown that the basic cause of the disagreement about logical principles is to be found in the different views of anthropology held by Hegel and his opponents. In Kierkegaard's case, theology serves as the basis of his anthropology. The *Postscript* thus proceeds from a total situation that has two main components: the single existing human being and Christianity. The aim of the work is now to render an account of how to establish a correct relation between these two elements, whereas the means applied to reach this objective are determined by the stage occupied by the pseudonymous author, for this in turn defines the viewpoint from which the work was written.

In connection with both the *Postscript* and the other pseudonymous works, scholars, finding support in Kierkegaard himself, attached great importance to clarification of the pseudonymous authors' precise relation to their progenitor.[18] They then deemed it relevant to distinguish between "genuine" pseudonymous authors who do not represent Kierkegaard's own views and "mock" pseudonymous authors who do express Kierkegaard's opinions. The question of genuine or mock pseudonymity, however, is irrelevant with respect to comprehension of any particular work taken as a whole, inasmuch as it is really only important to ascertain the stage occupied by the respective pseudonymous author and then to interpret the significance of this. I

---

[17] In this connection compare the quotation in chapter 2 above from Augustine, who like Kierkegaard perceived the differences between philosophical idealism and Christianity but who nevertheless strove for a synthesis. See Jørgen Pedersen, "Augustine and Augustinianism," *Bibliotheca Kierkegaardiana*, VI: *Kierkegaard and Great Traditions* (Copenhagen, 1981), pp. 54–98.

[18] See my introduction to the *Fragments*, pp. lxxxv ff.

have therefore in the present work not respected Kierkegaard's express desire in this connection.[19]

Johannes Climacus is named as the author of the *Postscript*, an assignment that he also received in the case of the *Fragments*. Climacus repeatedly professes to be a humorist,[20] and so he both qualifies the humoristic point of view in an absolute sense in relation to Christianity, or Religiousness B, and defines its relative position within the sequence of the stages.

In the *Postscript*[21] Kierkegaard distinguishes between three stages or spheres of existence: the esthetic, the ethical, and the religious. He then inserts irony as a sphere between the esthetic and the ethical,

---

[19] In this regard, Lars Bejerholm, *"Meddelelsens Dialektik"*. *Studier i Søren Kierkegaards teorier om språk, kommunikation och pseudonymitet* (Lund, 1962), is especially recommended. Emanuel Hirsch (*SK-Studien*, II, 747ff.) has, with a decided inclination toward hair-splitting, displayed erudition and penetration in explaining the pseudonym Johannes Climacus. In both the Introduction and Commentary I have disregarded Kierkegaard's express request (*Postscript*, p. 552; *SV* VII, no pagination) to mention only the pseudonymous authors by name and not mention Kierkegaard himself. The reason for this is that the distinction between the author and the creator of the author is not important to understand the work itself. Even if the *Postscript* had been written anonymously, without place and date of publication, it would still be possible to comprehend the work in agreement with Kierkegaard's intentions. If on the contrary we do adhere to this distinction, we will have to regard the author of the *Fragments* as a mock pseudonym and the author of the *Postscript* as a genuine pseudonym.

Kierkegaard himself has made numerous entries in the *Journals and Papers* on the problem of pseudonymity. Only the following from 1849 (*Pap.* X[1] A 531; *JP* VI 6440) will be cited here:

In margin: The significance of the pseudonyms.
The Significance of the Pseudonyms
All communication of truth has become abstract: the public has become the authority; the newspapers call themselves the editorial staff; the professor calls himself speculation; the pastor is meditation, no man, none, dares to say *I*.

But since without qualification the first prerequisite for the communication of truth is personality, since "truth" cannot possibly be served by ventriloquism, personality has come to the fore again.

But in these circumstances, since the world was so corrupted by never hearing an *I*, it was impossible to begin at once with one's own *I*. So it became my task to create author-personalities and let them enter in [*sic*] the actuality of life in order to get men a bit accustomed to hearing discourse in the first person.

Thus my task is no doubt only that of a forerunner until he comes who in the strictest sense says: *I*.

But to make a turn away from this inhuman abstraction to personality—that is my task.

[20] *Postscript*, pp. 402 and 545; *SV* VII 439 and 608.
[21] Ibid., p. 448; *SV* VII 492.

and humor as a sphere separating the ethical from the religious. The religious stage is subdivided into two more stages: the universally religious stage and the Christianly religious stage. Kierkegaard himself presents and qualifies all of these stages in both the *Postscript* and the pseudonymous works that preceded it, and they have been repeatedly discussed in the literature about Kierkegaard. I shall therefore restrict myself to a brief characterization of the humorist's viewpoint.

In *The Concept of Irony*[22] Kierkegaard makes a distinction between two specific stages. On the one hand we have irony as a purely humanistic outlook on life with two basic forms: Socratic and romantic irony. On the other we have humor as an outlook on life that presupposes the existence of Christianity. He retains this distinction in the *Postscript*, but with the difference that the humorist is acquainted with some of the essential features of the religious stage and the specifically Christian attitude toward life, although he himself does not exist in this stage.[23] The humorist represents the highest stage within "immanence" and thus within the compass of the created world. Although he consequently personifies the last stage prior to the religious, in which the suffering and guilt indigenous to existence are accepted in responsibility to God, he nevertheless shies away instead of making the leap into religiousness. He is perfectly aware of the significance of suffering, but instead of accepting it as an integral part of existence he revokes it in the form of a jest.

The fact that the view in the *Postscript* is based on Climacus' humoristic perspective tends to qualify and limit the thoughts that are included in the work. Furthermore, it is a factor that determines how these thoughts are expressed and what artistic effects are used to bring them home to the reader.[24] This of course gives rise to many questions, some of which are treated in the *Postscript* itself.[25]

Socrates did not proceed from the lower stage that he occupied, and he did not imitate philosophers of nature and the Sophists by delivering lectures in a direct form. Instead, he made use of interrogation and experimentation to produce an indirect form of communication that he employed to impart the highest truth available to him. So too, in the pseudonymous works the indirect method, which in this case is motivated by and developed on the basis of a stage

---

[22] *The Concept of Irony*, pp. 341–42; *SV* XIII 428.

[23] *Postscript*, pp. 243ff.; *SV* VII 259ff.

[24] See in this respect especially F. J. Billeskov Jansen, *Studier i Søren Kierkegaards litterære Kunst* (Copenhagen, 1951; reprint, 1979), pp. 51ff.

[25] Especially pp. 67ff. and 312ff.; *SV* VII 60ff. and 338ff.

higher than that to which Socrates had access, is designed to be a form of communication suitable to the knowledge of the truth attainable at each of the stages represented by the various pseudonymous authors. Now, the humorist represents a vantage point from which he can survey the preceding lower standpoints, and he also has an insight into the higher stages that follow his own. As a consequence, his existential experience enables him to present not only his own outlook but also the lower standpoints, including the comic misunderstandings of speculative philosophy. At the same time, he is by means of his experiments able to give us some idea of the contents of the higher spheres.[26] The humorist thus indicates the way to Christianity, serving as a guide on the road to the highest existential sphere attainable by a single individual. Like Lessing, however, he himself does not venture to make the leap across the chasm.

The key to Kierkegaard's works is *The Point of View for My Work as An Author*, which was mentioned at the beginning of this chapter. In this book, which as we also have mentioned is in the form of direct communication, Kierkegaard assigns the *Postscript* a special position as a turning point within his opus.

> This work concerns itself with and sets "the Problem", which is the problem of the whole authorship: how to become a Christian. So it takes cognizance of the pseudonymous works, and also of the eighteen edifying discourses which are interlaced into these works, showing that all of this serves to illuminate the Problem—without, however, affirming that this was the aim of the foregoing production. Such an affirmation would have been impossible, since it is [written by] a pseudonym who interprets the other pseudonyms. . . . The *Concluding Postscript* is not an aesthetic work, but neither is it in the strictest sense religious. Hence it is by a pseudonym, though I add my name as editor [as he did in the *Fragments*]—a thing I did not do in the case of any purely aesthetic work. This is a hint for him who is concerned about such things and has a flair for them.[27]

The earlier works described the road leading from the esthetic position back to Christianity. The *Fragments* and the *Postscript* now de-

---

[26] On this subject see Gregor Malantschuk, *Indførelse i Søren Kierkegaards Forfatterskab*, 2nd ed. (Copenhagen, 1979); Cornelio Fabro, "La 'communicazione della verità' nel pensiero di Kierkegaard," *Studi Kierkegaardiani* (Brescia, 1957), pp. 125–65; and Lars Bejerholm, "Communication," *Bibliotheca Kierkegaardiana*, III: *Concepts and Alternatives in Kierkegaard* (Copenhagen, 1980), pp. 52–60.

[27] *The Point of View*, p. 13; translation modified; *SV* XIII 557ff.

scribes a second way back, a retreat from the system and a speculation that sought to advance from faith to intellectual comprehension. The way of faith does indeed represent an advance, but to suffering.

This would seem adequate to fit the *Postscript* into its proper context as concerns both antecedent philosophy and traditions and the thought that was contemporary with the work. The only thing left in the present connection is to relate how the work was received by Kierkegaard's contemporaries and how Kierkegaard reacted to this reception. At the same time we will briefly outline the various later editions, translations, and so forth.

CHAPTER 9

The Contemporary Reception
of the Postscript

The *Postscript* met with a reception that might be called typical of the Royal City of Copenhagen. No one worthy of note in the world of literature, in the Church, or at the University of Copenhagen broke with a time-honored rule that imposes silence about an outsider's achievements. Not until several years later was the *Postscript* finally made the subject of debate, and then only because of Rasmus Nielsen's attack on Martensen's dogmatics. But as soon as this controversy subsided Kierkegaard's book was relegated to oblivion along with his other works.

Dr. H. L. Martensen at that time held the chair of professor extraordinary in theology at the university. Without mentioning his opponents by name, he proceeded in the Preface to the first edition of *Den christelige Dogmatik* to indulge in a polemic against those "who lack an instinct for coherent thought and are instead able to find satisfaction by thinking in the form of asides, aphorisms, whims, and brief flashes of wit."[1] In the summer of 1850 Martensen gave more elaborate expression to his sentiments in the following unforgettable words:

> Now, as to Johannes Climacus and the other pseudonyms, they are of absolutely no interest to me in the present context. I must confess that my opinion of these works differed from the opinion held by the reviewer [Professor Rasmus Nielsen]. It did not seem to me that the intention of these works was to provide us with a new system or to establish any school of philosophy whatever. I was least of all able to adopt the point of view that the author's intention was to justify a reform of dogmatics. I rather suspected from my slender knowledge of them that the purpose was in a Socratic fashion to set a profounder skepticism in motion in the reader. This would serve to arouse the reader to seek a problem that is higher and greater than any of the philosophical or theolog-

---

[1] Dr. H. Martensen, *Den christelige Dogmatik* (Copenhagen, 1849; *ASKB* 653), p. iii. The preface is dated July 1849.

ical issues presented by the various schools. By this I mean the personal problem of life that no system is able to impart or solve for us, a problem that each individual alone must pose and solve for himself on the basis of his God-given uniqueness. I therefore assumed that these works took a direction altogether different from the one adopted by Nielsen, for Professor Nielsen obviously tends toward Scholasticism and would like to guide us to a new treatment of theology based on a new epistemology. I do not, however, attach any importance at all to this, which is my own interpretation of the pseudonymous works, my knowledge of this voluminous literature being, as said, extremely poor and fragmentary. This is among other reasons due to the fact that the course of my studies and my personal intellectual outlook make me less receptive to an experimental presentation of the highest truths. I thus seek instruction in these truths chiefly from authors who employ direct communication. . . . I have absolutely no use for the doctrines [in the works by Climacus] that the reviewer has sought to impart to me with such great insistence. Rather I am compelled in this case to apply an old proverb: "The truths contained in them are nothing new, and what is new is not true."[2]

The *Postscript* had hardly been out a week when *Corsaren* was quite naturally on the spot with an article titled "Den store Philosoph."[3] The article, whose author preferred to remain anonymous, begins with a discussion of Kierkegaard's acknowledgement of responsibility for the pseudonyms and then continues in the following vein:

but I wonder just how the public must feel about such a cloudburst of authors. We find an analogy to this in the mountains when the snow melts in the spring. Every single snowbank dissolves, converging into one huge, foaming, rapid mountain stream. This mountain stream is the one and only Søren Kierkegaard, and there stands a stupefied public gazing on his mighty dialectical leaps.

Let this tremendous cataract thunder in turbulent pathos; let it plunge with superhuman force from the dizzying heights of spec-

---

[2] H. Martensen, *Dogmatiske Oplysninger* (Copenhagen, 1850; *ASKB* 654), pp. 12ff. The controversy that arose in connection with Martensen's dogmatics is presented by Skat Arildsen, *Biskop Hans Lassen Martensen* (Copenhagen, 1932), pp. 245ff.

[3] That is, "The Great Philosopher." It appeared in the issue for March 6, 1846. *Corsaren* is now available in an excellent photographic print: *Corsaren 1840–1846. M. A. Goldschmidts årgange*, ed. Uffe Andreasen, Det danske Sprog- og Litteraturselskab and C. A. Reitzel Publishing House, I–VII (Copenhagen, 1977–1982). Volume VII consists of an index to the entire work.

ulation down into the profoundest depths of thought; let its roll-
ing waves of dialectic transform the blackest masses of granite into
the whitest dust and fling it into the eyes of man and beast—that's
all right with us! We intend to keep our feet on the ground and
watch. . . .

Our Magister also profits from the occasion . . . to offer his
opinion on praise and reproach. He does not care to be praised
because it would be an inconvenience to him. It would be the same
as if someone were to take his hat off to him in the street. He
would be obliged to return the gesture, and this would be too
much of a bother. Such being the case, you might suppose that he
would allow himself to be praised, as then he need not disturb his
hat—but, no, this does not suit him either. . . . Bishop Mynster
has the monopoly on praising him; anyone who interferes with
this privilege may expect to be brought to court and heavily fined.
And so the rest of us are of course supposed to keep our mouths
shut.

It certainly seems strange that a man who purchases a book and
lays out three rix-bankdollars and sixty-four shillings[4] is not allowed to dispose of his book as he sees fit. Suppose Mag. Kierkegaard were to invite a man home for a cup of coffee and then
say to his guest: "You're going to taste the most delicious coffee
you've ever had in your life. But I expect your transports of delight
to make you absolutely speechless. You must not praise it. Bishop
Mynster is the only one allowed to praise my coffee. And don't
find fault with it either, or I'll kick you down the stairs." In this
case Mag. Kierkegaard would be quite within his rights; if the man
refuses to accept the conditions he gets no coffee. Likewise, not
until our Magister has a book printed for private circulation and
makes a present of it to a friend does he have the right to accompany it with this question: "Do you acknowledge this book to be
something so perfect, so fine and delicate, that a mere whiff of
human judgment would defile it?" If the friend swears to God that
this is so, he should be given a copy bound in morocco leather and
decorated with gilded edges. *Sub poena praeclusi et perpetui silentii*
[under the penalty of exile and perpetual silence]. A man gets a
very strange feeling, however, when he has quite honestly paid his
three rix-bankdollars and is then told: "Read it as you read your
Bible! If you don't understand it, read it again, and if you still don't

---

[4] The currency used in Denmark in Kierkegaard's time. See below, note to the
preface in the *Postscript* (pp. vii ff.).

understand it, you might as well blow your brains out right away."
There are moments when a man's thoughts are confused and he
thinks that Nicholas Copernicus was a fool to have insisted that
the earth orbits around the sun. Quite the contrary. It is heaven,
the sun, the planets, earth, Europe, and Copenhagen that revolve
around Søren Kierkegaard, who stands silently in the middle and
does not even take his hat off in token of the honor shown him.

The anonymous journalist then proceeds to discuss Kierkegaard's
person instead of the *Postscript*. Rather than quote this portion of the
article, we may permit ourselves a slight digression and by way of
example quote a few lines from J. L. Heiberg's poem *En Sjæl efter
Døden*. The contents of the final part of the article closely parallel the
thoughts and desires expressed by the Soul in the following lines:

> For I'm not too much engaged
> By the work a poet has staged;
> But often I feel my heart burn
> With a longing for his person to learn,
> To know how he eats and tipples,
> How he hiccups, how he sniffles;
> In short—to know him right privately.[5]

The Soul asks Mephistopheles if the residents of the hell of spiritlessness also subscribe to Claudius Rosenhoff's periodical, *Den Frisindede*:

> For it was my favorite of them all.
> In triflings it is capital;
> It keeps away from what is grand,
> Which not all at once can understand.[6]

---

[5] Johann Ludvig Heiberg, *Poetiske Skrifter*, X, 231.

> Thi jeg bekymrer mig ikke stort
> Om Værket, som en Poet har gjort,
> Men tidt jeg føler mit Hjerte brænde
> Af Begjærlighed efter ham selv at kjende,
> At vide, hvordan han spiser og drikker,
> Hvordan han nyser, hvordan han hikker,
> Kort sagt, at kjende ham ret privat.

[6] Ibid., p. 225.

> Thi fremfor Alle var den mig kjær.
> Den gaaer saa fortrinligt i det Smaa,
> Og holder saa godt sig fra det Store,
> Fra Det, som ei Alle strax kan forstaae.

It could scarcely be expected that Climacus' express desire not to be reviewed might deter this incredible hack in *Corsaren*, and on March 10, 1846, he adorned the front page of his sheet with a review in verse that maintains the following tone throughout:

It's no book for the great, even less for the little person;
Far too thick just to amuse, much too thin for comprehension.
Though not a poem, there is no want of inventiveness;
Jests with tears it recounts, mixed with smiles of earnestness.
Just when one thinks, now you'll weep, one must heartily guffaw;
Should a footnote glide sprightly into joy, soon will the text this
    fallen snow then thaw.
It has thoughts without contents, action without device,
And he who wants can cull good hints, but base advice.
This idea with ideas to squander is replete;
Events of the day it uses just where meet.
Learned it is; upon its gist the typesetter no light could likely throw,
Though in the Danish tongue it has richness close to overflow.
What it desires understood I cannot clearly see,
But in wonder I must cry: How great is man's ability![7]

Using "Prosper naturalis de Molinasky" as a pseudonym, Peder Ludvig Møller (1814–1865), who at the time was well known in Denmark, wrote a review that ran in two issues of *Kjøbenhavnsposten* (March 27 and 28, 1846).[8] It contains attacks on Kierkegaard's person, which were prompted by an article titled "En omreisende Æsthetikers Virksomhed, og hvorledes han dog kom til at betale

---

[7] Det er ingen Bog for Store, endnu mindre for de Smaa;
Alt for tyk til kun at more, alt for tynd til at forstaae.
Det er intet Digt, ei heller mangler den dog Phantasie.
Spøg med Taarer den fortæller, blander Alvors Smiil deri.
Naar man troer, nu skal Du græde, maa man just af Hjerte lee;
Glider Noten let i Glæde, Texten tøer den faldne Snee.
Den har Indhold ei, men Tanke; den har Handling uden Traad,
Og Enhver, som vil, kan sanke gode Vink, men slette Raad.
Den Idee har til Ideer noksom til at rutte med,
Bruger, Hvad der daglig skeer, netop paa det rette Sted.
Lærd den er; den skriver Noget, som vist Sætter ei forstod
Og har dog paa Dannersproget Rigdom fast til Overflod.
Hvad den have vil forstaaet, derpaa jeg mig ei forstaaer
Men med Undren jeg udbryder: Hvad dog Mennesket formaaer!

[8] Møller later published his article in *Kritiske Skizzer* (Copenhagen, 1847), Part Two, pp. 253ff.

Gjæstebudet"[9] that appeared in *Fædrelandet* on December 27, 1845. Written under the pseudonym of Frater Taciturnus, this essay by Kierkegaard was a biting reply to "Et Besøg i Sorø," an article that Møller later included in his annual of esthetics[10] and in which he attacked Kierkegaard's earlier pseudonymous works. Toward the close of Kierkegaard's article, Frater Taciturnus gives voice to the following desire:

> Now if only I might soon get into *Corsaren*. It is really hard on a poor author to be pointed out as the only one (assuming that we pseudonyms are one person) in Danish literature who has been abused there. Unless my memory fails me, my superior, Hilarius Bookbinder, was praised in *Corsaren*; Victor Eremita even had to suffer the ignominy of being immortalized—in *Corsaren*! And yet, I have indeed already been there; for [just as] *ubi spiritus, ibi ecclesia,* [so] *ubi* P. L. Møller *ibi Corsaren.*[11]

This amounted to a public exposure of the fact that Møller was a contributor to Goldschmidt's publication. Møller himself later confirmed that he was merely the author of "several satirical critiques and poems"[12] in *Corsaren*.

Møller begins his essay by characterizing Kierkegaard as a dialectician *par excellence*. He thereupon describes himself as "an altogether simple and ordinary man of nature" who from time to time derives amusement by perusing works of literature, and who has lately entertained himself by giving consideration to the *Postscript*. After a few introductory gibes, Møller continues as follows:

> So the essential contents of the work consist in a presentation of "the problem invested in historical costume" [taken from the *Fragments*], which in turn splits up into two problems. The first or objective problem respecting the truth of Christianity does not really

---

[9] "The Activities of a Travelling Esthete. How He Happened to Pay for the Banquet After All." Reprinted in *SV* XIII 459–67.

[10] P. L. Møller, *Gæa* (Copenhagen, 1846), pp. 144–87. The word *Gæa* means "earth" and was obviously chosen to contrast with the title of Heiberg's annual, *Urania*, which means "the heavenly" or "celestial." Reprints of both works are now in preparation by The Danish Language and Literature Society and are to be published in 1984.

[11] *SV* XII 467. "for [just as] the spirit is present wherever the Church is, [so] wherever P. L. Møller is we have *Corsaren*." This article appeared in *Fædrelandet* on December 27, 1845.

[12] In *Almindeligt dansk Forfatterlexikon for Kongeriget Danmark med Bilande,* ed. Thomas Hansen Erslew, I–III (Copenhagen, 1843–1853), II, 406. This article was revised by Møller himself.

concern the author personally and is therefore treated by him with the utmost brevity. The second problem, however, the subjective question of how J. Climacus . . . can become a shareholder in eternal happiness, is in the main an issue that interests only him. This problem is accordingly subjected to a very detailed investigation, whereas if worse comes to worse others can always leave it out. He has so to speak from the cradle advanced beyond what is called believing with the simplicity of the heart. This whim is one of those extravagances that usually accompany genius, and it allows him to enjoy beatitude only in accordance with a dialectical chain of reasoning proving that our Christian heritage—which at the same time is both historical and nonhistorical—is an absurdity and a paradox. Not until he has reached this point is he able with the aid of a "leap" to arrive at faith in Christianity and the beatitude it promises. For the sake of those who fail to understand completely the terms "dialectical" and "dialectics," their meaning may be depicted most clearly as a zig-zag movement toward a goal that ordinary undialectical people would reach by following a straight line. . . . The dialectical aspirant to an eternal happiness must be concerned solely about himself, must emancipate himself from so-called civic or human duties, all private emotional relationships, and so forth, for these are nothing but "esthetics". . . . In the interest of his personal welfare after death the individual is even obliged to "hate father and mother," indeed, to do whatever the devil may be necessary.

Møller then draws his readers' attention to what he claims is

a not imperceptible sign of the times . . . a sort of system closely following the same principles has recently been published in Germany, but tending in the opposite direction (M. Stirner, *Der Einzige und sein Eigenthum*).[13]

The critic now makes particular note of the fact that the *Postscript* is permeated by antagonism toward the public, both the orthodox members of the clergy and those given to esthetics, and especially toward speculative philosophers. He explains to the innocent readers of his sheet that a subjective existential thinker like the author of the *Postscript* is "the sort of person who communicates everything that crosses his mind in the way it crosses his mind. This is in fact the way he exists himself." Møller then interprets this as the explanation for

[13] This was Kaspar Schmidt's left-wing Hegelian work published in Leipzig in 1845.

his strange form as well as the previously puzzling aspect of his horrible productiveness. It is not only easiest for our author to jot down everything he thinks, but inasmuch as "subjectivity is the truth" he even feels it his duty to do so. If other authors did likewise and for example published all their scrapbooks, perhaps we would soon be in a position to admire an equally astounding productiveness on the part of many more.

This then is the characterization that Møller is able to give of Kierkegaard's form of communication. He thereupon devotes a few remarks to the style and manner of exposition employed in the *Postscript*, observing that first we hear

> Platonic pathos, then gossipy coffee fiends, next the simplicity and rhythm of the Bible, at another moment the small talk of a Copenhagen tea-room. . . . Everything is there, mixed up in the most divine potpourri.

The reviewer of course does not fail to include a few personal affronts to Kierkegaard. He mentions Kierkegaard's request that only the name of the respective pseudonymous author be used when quoting from his works, and on the basis of this Møller manages to draw the following conclusion:

> it would almost seem that the author is only willing to assume the name of Frater Taciturnus and so on when he is not afraid of getting hit on the head. But as long as there is no danger afoot he is on the contrary quite willing to be called S. Kierkegaard.

As we know, in the humoristic Preface to the *Postscript* Kierkegaard reflects at some length on the difficulties to which an author may be exposed if his work has aroused admiration. The Conclusion of the *Postscript* contains, in a final explanation that is not humoristic, an expression of gratitude to Bishop Mynster ("The signature Kts"). In his review Møller extracts statements from these two parts of the book, and by comparing them manages to detect evidence of an implicit grudge against Mynster. He regards "the author's much discussed modesty and humility," together with his joy in having only one reader, as plagiarisms of a thought uttered by Socrates in Plato's *Gorgias*. As to Kierkegaard's modesty, this is bluntly declared to be nothing but poorly concealed vanity. The reviewer concludes his article with the assertion that the humoristic revocation in the *Postscript* makes all of his own critical observations superfluous.

The following day Peter Wilhelm Christensen published an article titled "Troen og Dialektikken" in Rasmus Theodor Fenger's and C. J. Brandt's Grundtvigian periodical.[14] Christensen's express intention was

> merely to demonstrate the fact that plain Christian faith in our holy, universal Church is quite justified, in contradistinction to any dialectical hocus-pocus or mimic-pathetic abracadabra that may be practiced outside the Church. It is not my intention to engage in any discussion with Mr. Kierkegaard, for I owe him the same attention I desire and expect from him—none at all. I simply want to give vent to my anger at him. Without any "obligate encroachments" whatsoever on his freedom, I propose to show his readers and those of *Dansk Kirketidende* that I do not hesitate to snap my fingers at all his philosophical tricks, because I have the faith of the Church in my heart and its confession on my lips. Besides, I am completely unfamiliar with his philosophy and do not understand it.

To avoid any possible misunderstandings, Christensen is careful to request that his readers be sure to notice this declaration of his ignorance of Kierkegaard's philosophy. He then follows it up with still another to the effect that he has only read part of the *Postscript* and has not read the *Fragments* at all. Having thus by way of anticipation disposed of any potentially distracting elements, he proceeds to deliver an attack on Climacus' criticism of Grundtvig and Lindberg, finding that like "any dialectic practiced outside the Church" it is "completely irrelevant to the matter at hand." Christensen's intention with this article of March 29, 1846, was in reality to dismiss Kierkegaard's book as a piece of trivial literature, but about six months later, on September 20, he attempted to refute the *Postscript* with another essay in the same journal. This article will be discussed briefly later on.

On March 30 and 31 the daily newspaper *Nyt Aftenblad* carried some replies to Møller's review in *Kjøbenhavnsposten* mentioned above; although undoubtedly well meant, they were not exactly successful. By way of introduction the *Postscript* is called one of the most serious and profound works ever produced in Danish literature, a work "containing a wealth of truths that our age especially should take to heart." The author solemnly reproaches the editor of *Kjøbenhavns-*

---

[14] In *Dansk Kirketidende*, March 29, 1846. Christensen (1819–1863) was for a time Kierkegaard's secretary and copyist. See *Pap.* III xvii, and the editors' notes to *Pap.* IV A 141 (*JP* V 5688).

posten for "allowing the first immature boy who comes along to use his newspaper to concoct the most wretched piece of trash about a work of such great merit, and on top of that in the most indecent tone." The writer then promises to make a thorough study of the *Postscript* and in the course of "a half score or score of articles to give the public a notion of the wealth of serious and holy truths contained in the book." For reasons unknown, however, this plan never came to fruition. The following day brought merely a brief recapitulation and another diatribe against *Kjøbenhavnsposten* and its reviewer, P. L. Møller.

In addition to these public responses to the work, there were a couple of personal reactions that are of less importance but nevertheless deserve mention. Kierkegaard sent dedication copies of the *Postscript* to several notables, including Anders Sandøe Ørsted (whose copy still exists), Sibbern, Heiberg, his brother Peter Christian Kierkegaard, and presumably several others. In a letter dated March 19, 1846,[15] to his brother, who had thanked him for the present in a letter that is no longer extant, Kierkegaard revealed a disinclination to engage in discussion "even with a clever dialectician." In all likelihood, Peter Kierkegaard, who received his copy on March 1, was, like Christensen, in complete disaccord with his brother on the subject of Grundtvig and Lindberg. Nevertheless, Kierkegaard in the very first lines of his letter rules out any possibility of a discussion, inasmuch as he fears "that it will take too long for us to arrive at a mutual point of departure."

Kierkegaard sent Mrs. Gyllembourg a copy of his little *A Literary Review* (which came out on March 30, 1846) by way of Heiberg, who also received a copy. Heiberg thanked Kierkegaard for both books in a letter dated April 2, 1846,[16] in which he abstained, however, from taking a position on the *Postscript*. Morten Borup, the editor of Heiberg's letters, is certainly correct in asserting that this was a diplomatic move.

This was then the reaction that followed immediately on publication of the *Postscript*. We have still to consider only Christensen's article "Om Troens Dialektik," which as mentioned above appeared in *Dansk Kirketidende* on September 20, 1846, and was intended as a valid refutation of the *Postscript*. The reader will remember that in his previous article Christensen had been content merely to dismiss the

---

[15] *Breve og Aktstykker vedrørende Søren Kierkegaard*, ed. Niels Thulstrup, I–II (Copenhagen, 1953–1954), I, no. 133; II, 69ff.; hereafter abbreviated as *Breve*.

[16] *Breve*, I, no. 135.

book from the scene. In the later article Christensen quite rightly asserts that Climacus' real self-imposed task in the *Postscript* consists in raising the question, "How am I to become a Christian?" He is able to agree that Climacus' criticism of scripturalists and speculative theologians in Part One is pertinent, but he insists that it does not apply to "the clergy,"

> for they [Grundtvig and Lindberg] of course simply affirm that the answer already lies at hand, but only for whoever inquires. Furthermore, they hold that the contents of Christianity as expressed in the Church's confession of faith are alone the truth leading to salvation, but only those who believe and have been baptized are in a position to avail themselves of this truth. Here we see how Grundtvig and Lindberg have borne witness in the name of Our Lord. How else could we interpret them? But by inquiring as he does, the author of course is no more able to reach an agreement with these men than with the Lord Himself.

Assuming a somewhat solemn attitude, Christensen then declares that he proposes "to commend this humorist [Climacus] to Satan . . . purely and simply so that I might be able to love Mag. Kierkegaard, whom I cannot help loving."

So ends Christensen's criticism of Part One of the *Postscript*. He then passes over to an examination of Part Two and the thesis that truth resides in inwardness, which is the equivalent of earnestness, and that everything depends on the assimilation of this truth in existence. Proceeding from his failure to understand the principle of subjectivity, he maintains that this view too is altogether un-Christian. Christensen's lack of comprehension on this point may perhaps be explainable by the circumstance that he did not read either the *Fragments* or the *Postscript* thoroughly before taking up his pen. He therefore accuses Climacus of having "gone astray by failing to refer thought back to its very source; that is, to the fact that only Christianity is the truth leading to salvation." He asserts that Climacus has committed the additional error of using his own assumptions as a source from which to draw typically pietistic conclusions. Christensen had evidently misunderstood Kierkegaard's objections to misuse of the baptismal covenant and the confession of faith. At least he fails to take note of them in his article and so simply upholds the view that both baptism and the confession of faith yield objective certainty. As a result, he is compelled to reject every interpretation that is not in agreement with Grundtvig's. The article also concludes on a note of disapproval, as Christensen raises a few objections to Climacus' method of indirect communication.

Kierkegaard prepared several drafts in response to the various articles and reviews but refrained from publishing anything. For example, he drafted a letter to *Aftenbladet*[17] in which he animadverts on Møller's

> lies and falseness in reporting the contents of a book being reviewed, the most unscrupulous extraction of particular words, the impudence of interrupting a quoted passage in the middle to extract just the opposite from it, and so forth—such conduct should never be tolerated by any decent newspaper.

In this same draft Kierkegaard also reproaches the editor of *Kjøbenhavnsposten* for his inability to perceive "that there is something wrong here, and that only a savage spite would vent itself in such mendacities." He maintains that if the editor really thinks it worthwhile to print an article of that kind, he at the very least should see to it that the author's name is affixed to the article. This brings Kierkegaard again to the subject of Møller:

> take Mr. P. L. Møller's name. Just let it appear beneath an article and see how quickly the reader will put the newspaper aside and allow his attention to wander to any other object whatever.

Following these introductory remarks concerning the current problem of Møller's review, Kierkegaard enters into more important issues.

> I truly mean it when I say that I do not desire any reviews. It appears to me that the idea of what it means to be an author is gradually being confused, and in the end people will be less concerned to read a book than to grade it and give it a mark. Before long writing a book will be confounded with taking an examination, so that ultimately importance will be attached to the examination rather than to the book, and instead of intending [to promote] assimilation on the part of the reader one will be curious about the outcome of the examination. But good Lord, I really do not write for that reason. . . . I derive my joy and satisfaction from writing the book, and once it is written I desire peace and quiet to enable the single individual to find out whether he may be benefited in any way by reading it. . . . What I have to say is not something new by any means, and the only thing required on the

---

[17] *Pap.* VII[1] B 86, pp. 279, 283.

part of a reader is therefore inwardness in reading it; and this is something that [every] review [after all avoids (?)].[18]

Kierkegaard added the following in connection with his relation to the reader:

As things are now I am in a rather favorable position. The right time for my reader is not when it has become fashionable to read my books. No, when it is in vogue to leave them unread and a man must feel ashamed to admit that he has read them—then is the moment for *my* reader.[19]

In reply to Christensen, Kierkegaard prepared a draft for an article that was to be titled "An Unhappy Lover in *Dansk Kirketidende*."[20]

Besides smoke, drafts, and vermin, I know of nothing more calamitous than to become the object of another's fixed idea, or to have somebody get the idea to occupy himself purely personally with his presumed relationship to one. . . .

His first article . . . was written to show me that he was not afraid to write against me. And he was so eager to display this courage that he himself admits to not having read the book he discusses.

Mr. Chr. has in issue no. 52[21] once again turned author for my sake concerning the same book (*Concluding Postscript*), and again for purely personal reasons: because he finds it impossible not to love me . . . these unhappy lovers are the most alarming people . . . [and] since he provides no information as to how much of it he has read now, it [is] his own fault if one is compelled to assume that he still has not read it. But as he once wrote about it to show me his courage, so now he writes to show me his love.

Since the book has thus become a trivial matter, I can leave it out of account altogether. It can, however, certainly be defended; but not before it has found a reader with sufficient skill to be able to read it and who then tries to attack it, but mind you, not in a couple of unbridled columns in a periodical intended to be read like any newspaper.

[18] The square brackets in the last sentence were inserted by the editors of *Papirerne* as a suggested reading of an illegible portion of the manuscript. The square brackets above are the translator's.

[19] *Pap.* VII¹ B 86, p. 283.

[20] *Pap.* VII¹ B 87, pp. 285ff.

[21] The article of September 20.

In November of the same year Kierkegaard prepared several outlines for an article to have been titled "Self-Defense Against Unwarranted Recognition."[22] The target of this proposed article was "that
raging Roland, that quarrelsome Magnus Eirikson, who caresses me
in the most gruesome manner with the most obligate and appreciative utterances."[23] Magnús Eiríksson, as the name is properly spelled,
had on November 19 and 20, 1846, inserted a notice in *Adresseavisen*
about his latest book, which bore the following title: *Dr. H. Martensens trykte moralske Paragrapher, eller det saakaldte "Grundrids til Moralphilosophiens System," i dets forvirrede, idealistisk-metaphysiske og phan-
tastisk-speculative, Religion og Christendom undergravende, fatalistiske,
pantheistiske og selvforguderske Væsen, belyst og bedømt af Magnús Eiríksson.*[24] The purpose of this work was quite simply to bring about
Martensen's dismissal, an ambition that elicited the following observation from Kierkegaard:[25]

> And he has with the might and main of the devil managed to hook
> my *Concluding Postscript to the Philosophical Fragments* up with these
> efforts of his in *Adresseavisen. Pro dii immortales!* [Alas, immortal
> Gods!]. A poor, defenseless, experimenting humorist who for the
> sake of thought alone thinks a few problems through at a distance
> of 100,000 miles, or rather at the distance separating an idea from
> a moment; and who simply arranges everything maieutically in the
> disinterested sphere of ideality—such a humorist acquires a scream-
> ing party-liner and with the aid of admiring utterances of recog-
> nition is connected with the most despicable sort of attack possible
> against an individual. By imputing to me motives of which there
> is not a trace in the book, which indeed does not mention or name
> Prof. Martensen with one single word,[26] and by appealing to a few
> students with whom M.E. is supposed to have spoken: he manages
> in a bestial manner to get that out of it.
>
> To be given recognition and admiration in that way is what I
> call literary assault and battery. . . . Nor do I know whether or

[22] *Pap.* VII¹ B 88–92.

[23] *Pap.* VII¹ B 88, p. 287. See also *Breve*, I, nos. 163–64; II, 79ff.

[24] The title in English: "The Moral Articles Published by Dr. H. Martensen, or His
so-called 'Outline For a System of Moral Philosophy.' Its Muddled, Idealistically
Metaphysical and Fantastically Speculative Characteristics, Which Strike at the Very
Roots of Religion and Christianity; And Its Fatalistic, Pantheistic and Self-Worship-
ping Nature. Elucidated and Evaluated by Magnús Eiríksson."

[25] *Pap.* VII¹ B 88, p. 289.

[26] This is true, but both Martensen and Heiberg are frequently mentioned in the
drafts.

not M.E. has read the book; but if he has, then I know that he has absolutely misunderstood it in a mendacious and presumptuous fashion.

In another draft of the same article Kierkegaard has the following to say about his debate with speculation:

Insofar as an occasional polemic against Hegel does appear in my work, the whole thing is deliberately maintained in such a way that the book could just as well have been written in Germany as in Copenhagen. It is not my fault that M.E. knows no more about Hegel than the fact that Prof. M. has studied him.[27]

Eiríksson published another work in 1849, this time with the title *Speculativ Rettroenhed, fremstillet efter Dr. H. Martensens "christelige Dogmatik," og Geistlig Retfærdighed, belyst ved en Biskops Deeltagelse i en Generalfiskal-Sag.*[28] He asserts in a footnote on page 108 that Kierkegaard had in the *Postscript* mocked and insulted Martensen's theology. Once again Kierkegaard went to work on a draft for an article. He reaffirms his aversion to entering into a personal debate, adding that in the *Postscript*

the scene is deliberately sustained in such a way that rather than being in Denmark it is in Germany, where, after all, the speculation that "goes beyond" originates. . . . Everything is kept as poetic as possible, because as the editor I am no friend of finite squabbles.[29]

Kierkegaard has more than once expressed his opinion on the *Postscript*, both in the *Journals and Papers* and in subsequent published works. For our present purposes we may limit ourselves to mention of the most important journal entries only, taking them in chronological order.

It is evident from an entry made some time prior to February 7, 1846,[30] that Kierkegaard entertained momentary doubts as to whether or not, in view of his conflict with *Corsaren* and the resultant town gossip, he ought to have left the disclosure of his responsibility for the pseudonymous authors out of the *Postscript*. He came to the con-

[27] *Pap.* VII¹ B 91, p. 303.
[28] The title in English: "Speculative Orthodoxy Presented According to Dr. H. Martensen's *Christian Dogmatics*, and Ecclesiastic Justice. Illustrated by Reference to a Bishop's Participation in An Action Brought by the Public Prosecutor."
[29] *Pap.* X⁶ B 128; *JP* VI 6596.
[30] *Pap.* VII¹ A 3; *JP* V 5872.

clusion, however, that respect for the truth demands that he disregard such external circumstances.

The next entry to be considered is extremely important:

> It is now my intention to qualify as a pastor. For several months I have been praying to God to keep on helping me, for it has been clear to me for some time now that I ought not be a writer any longer, something I can be only totally or not at all. This is the reason I have not started anything new along with proof-correcting [in connection with the *Postscript*] except for the little review of *The Two Ages* [by Mrs. Gyllembourg], which, I repeat, is final.
>
> February 7, 1846[31]

It is a well-known fact that this plan was quickly renounced, not least because of his conflict with *Corsaren*, the beginnings of which are related above. Kierkegaard continued to write. But whereas his principal aim in the first part of the authorship had been to provide an account of how the particular individual may *become* a Christian, in his later works Kierkegaard concentrated on the problem of how a man is to *live* as a Christian. He frequently discusses these two positions directly in many later journal entries. The following from 1848 may be taken by way of example.[32]

> To be a Christian involves a double danger.
>
> First, all the intense internal suffering involved in becoming a Christian, this losing human reason and being crucified on the paradox.—This is the issue *Concluding Postscript* presents as ideally as possible.
>
> Then the danger of the Christian's having to live in the world of secularity and here express that he is a Christian. Here belongs all the later productivity.

He clarifies this in the last paragraph of the entry:

> This means that the grief of sin must be very deep within a person, and therefore Christianity must be presented as the difficult thing it is so that it may become entirely clear that Christianity only is related to the consciousness of sin. To want to be involved in becoming a Christian for any other reason is literally foolishness—and so it must be.

In 1849, after having written *The Point of View For My Activities as An Author*, which however he left unpublished, Kierkegaard ex-

---

[31] *Pap.* VII¹ A 4; *JP* V 5873.
[32] *Pap.* IX A 414; *JP* I 493.

plained in another entry that up to then he had not made any public statements about himself directly, not even in "A First and Last Declaration" in the *Postscript*. He had merely assumed responsibility for the pseudonyms: "The information given in *Concluding Postscript* about the structure of the pseudonyms is by a third party."[33] Kierkegaard is here of course referring to the author of the work, the humorist Johannes Climacus, of whom he in turn stands as author. Later in the same year Kierkegaard offered the following observation on the subject of the work and its reception in Copenhagen:

> What an accomplishment the *Concluding Postscript* is; there is more than enough for three professors. But of course the author was someone who did not have a career position and did not seem to want to have one; there was nothing worthy of becoming a paragraph in the system—well, then, it is nothing at all.
>
> The book came out in Denmark. It was not mentioned anywhere at all. Perhaps fifty copies were sold. . . . And in the meantime I am caricatured by a scandal sheet that in the same little country has 3,000 subscribers, and another paper (also with wide circulation, *Flyveposten*) continues the discussion about my trousers.[34]

He elaborates on this theme in another entry[35] made later that year. In an entry made shortly thereafter in relation to Rasmus Nielsen's aforementioned criticism of Martensen's dogmatics, Kierkegaard complains that people have failed to understand why the *Postscript* is humoristic. Instead, he says, like Nielsen they "think they can improve on the matter by taking occasional theses and switching to a direct lecture."[36]

In still another important entry, also from 1849,[37] Kierkegaard makes a comparison between Feuerbach and Johannes Climacus. Kierkegaard proposes in this entry that Feuerbach did not actually attack Christianity per se; rather, he attacked the individual members of the Church by demonstrating that they do not actually live their lives in harmony with the teachings of their religion. He thus concludes that Feuerbach in fact unwittingly prepared a defense of Christianity. Climacus, too, Kierkegaard affirms, undertook to defend Christianity, in the course of which he went to such extremes in his dialectic that "to many it may seem like an attack." Climacus does mount an at-

---

[33] *Pap.* X¹ A 161; *JP* VI 6366. See also the *Postscript*, pp. 225ff. (*SV* 237ff.).

[34] *Pap.* X¹ A 584; *JP* VI 6458.

[35] *Pap.* X² A 124.

[36] *Pap.* X² A 130. See also *Breve*, I, nos. 208–10, on Nielsen.

[37] *Pap.* X² A 163; *JP* VI 6523.

tack, but against "an established Christendom" that "has taken illegal possession of Christianity by a colossal forgery." In this same entry Kierkegaard also has the following to say about the *Postscript* and his relation to it:

> This book has an extraordinary future.
> And I, the author, am in a way held up to ridicule as always. I manage to do things the entire significance of which I do not understand until later.

The idea of retiring after publication of the *Postscript* surfaces again in the *Journals and Papers* in 1850.[38] The *Postscript* is of course also mentioned in the draft for *My Activities as An Author*,[39] and is referred to in various drafts for articles related to Martensen's dogmatics. In the latter case Kierkegaard once more took pains to define the importance of his book.

> it makes a turn into faith, and if it is necessary to make an advance on that it will not be toward a Christian speculation, as Martensen would have, but toward martyrdom for the sake of Christianity.[40]

By 1851 Kierkegaard's attitude toward Bishop Mynster had changed radically. One of the chief reasons for this was Mynster's comparison of Kierkegaard with Goldschmidt in *Yderligere Bidrag til Forhandlingerne om de kirkelige Forhold i Danmark*, which came out in Copenhagen on March 13, 1851. In consideration of his dispute with *Corsaren*, such a comparison could serve only to embitter Kierkegaard. He thus found reason to regret having expressed gratitude to Mynster in "A First and Last Declaration," as now he understood "what a slow-witted [*in margin*: credulous] fool I was."[41] In March 1854, Kierkegaard again mentions the *Postscript* in connection with Mynster, who died on January 30 of the same year. The entry in question bears the title: *"My Relationship to Bishop Mynster in the Shortest Possible Resume."*[42] Kierkegaard writes:

> When I had completed the esthetic part of my writing, when on the largest possible scale I had made room for Bishop M. (in a postscript to *Concluding Postscript*), made room for him as the one

---

[38] *Pap.* X³ A 318 (*JP* VI 6660) and X⁶ B 249.
[39] *Pap.* X⁵ B 168. This work came out on August 7, 1851.
[40] *Pap.* X⁶ B 114.
[41] *Pap.* X⁶ B 182, p. 293.
[42] *Pap.* XI³ B 15; *JP* VI 6854.

and only in Denmark, I went to him. I said: I am in complete disagreement with you, as much as is possible. . . .
 Bishop Mynster answered: You are the complement to me.

The last journal entry to mention the *Postscript* is dated June 29, 1855, and consists of a scrap of paper on which Kierkegaard noted that he had personally presented Mynster with a copy of the book.[43] He reminisces over the fact that "it was the first time I went to see him after my appearance as an author."

An extremely comprehensive and detailed investigation would be required to give an account of the influence the *Postscript* has had up to the present, both on theologians and on philosophers. To be as brief as possible, we may say that the liberal theology that assumed a leading position at German and Scandinavian universities following the demise of axiomatic speculative theology was imbued with an idealistic principle of subjectivity. But this principle differed completely from that expounded in the *Postscript*. Kierkegaard was accordingly either circumnavigated or reinterpreted. Theologians with, for example, Grundtvigian or Lundensian tendencies, or those of a so-called dialectical school, occupied themselves chiefly with objective problems while leaving the question of assimilation and appropriation in abeyance. Very few scholars felt that they were able to make use of the *Postscript*—and then only to devise a new system.
 Of the many philosophical trends that have emerged during the past generation, only the existential philosophers have really employed Kierkegaard's works in general and the *Postscript* in particular. They proceed, however, in an altogether different mode of treating the problem. Whereas Kierkegaard raised the question of how a single individual can become a Christian, the existential philosophers are more concerned with the question of how man in general is to become a human being. Our philosophers, far from having abandoned their optimism, have thus "gone further."[44]

---

[43] *Pap*. XI² A 419.

[44] I have outlined Kierkegaard's influence and the inspiration he imparted to modern philosophy in "Kierkegaard's Socratic Role for Twentieth Century Philosophy and Theology," *Kierkegaardiana*, XI (Copenhagen, 1980), pp. 197–211, and in "Presenza e funzione dei concetti kierkegaardiani nella teologia contemporanea scandinava e germanica," *Liber Academiæ Kierkegaardiensis*, I (Copenhagen, 1980), pp. 29–40. Anton Hügli, J. Heywood Thomas, Alastair McKinnon, and I have all contributed toward elucidating this topic, and it is treated in *Bibliotheca Kierkegaardiana*, VIII: *The Legacy and Interpretation of Kierkegaard* (Copenhagen, 1981).

οὐδεὶς ἕτερος ἑτέρῳ ταὐτὸ ἐννοεῖ
Plato, *Gorgias*

GUIDE TO THE COMMENTARY

The Commentary has been prepared along the same lines as my edition of *Philosophical Fragments*, with Introduction and Commentary (Princeton, 1962), and my commentaries in German on Kierkegaard's philosophical and theological writings, though in a more concise form. Some changes, however, have been made because of the special form and contents of the *Postscript*. For example, instead of including an outline of the entire work in the Introduction, I have considered it more practical to preface the commentary on each major section with a résumé of the contents of the particular section.

Here, as in my edition of the *Fragments*, I have observed a European practice according to which "commentary" has the meaning of *commentarius perpetuus*, that is, explanatory and illustrative information given page by page and line by line. This usage, which emerged in the seventeenth century with the publication of Greek and Latin classical works, is still current among exegetes who work with the Old and New Testaments. "Commentary" is thus not used here in the more restricted sense of a series of liberal interpretations—which in the case of the *Postscript* would require several volumes.

Kierkegaard's work is of great importance today, and not merely to the reader familiar with modern religious and philosophical thought. There is accordingly very good reason to accentuate how the work in its entirety and its details, and with its thousands of interwoven threads, is linked to its own past and contemporary ages and to their metaphysical, epistemological, and religious problems, ways of thought, and language. It is my experience that apart from a very restricted circle of specialists, readers of Kierkegaard generally know and view these relationships almost exclusively through Kierkegaard's spectacles. Or, Kierkegaard is studied by means of compendiums that in many cases are unfortunately written by modern scholars whose own philosophical or theological positions are far removed from Kierkegaard's and his contemporaries' views and ways of thinking. As a result, the reader acquires an inadequate understanding. I have therefore in the Commentary endeavored to bridge the gap separating the present-day reader from Kierkegaard and his contemporaries. I have sought to accomplish this partly by allowing the sources themselves to be heard extensively and partly by explaining to a certain degree the terminology and modes of thought employed by both Kierkegaard and those thinkers with whom he conducted his debate.

Account has to a great extent been given for Kierkegaard's demonstrable acquaintance with the various philosophers, theologians, poets, and writers, and for the philosophical and theological movements, schools, and issues discussed by him and on which he takes a position in the *Postscript*. As far as possible, and where they are not obvious, the sources quoted are those that were immediately available to Kierkegaard, but which in several instances are not identical with the primary sources. One of the principal sources of research into his literary background is *Katalog over Søren Kierkegaards Bibliotek* (Copenhagen, 1957), which I have edited with an introduction.

Although the main lines of the *Postscript*'s broader, religious-philosophical setting are presented in the Introduction, in the Commentary special importance has been attached to a detailed explanation of Kierkegaard's relation to German speculative Idealism and to his predecessors and contemporaries. On the other hand, an explanation of the liaisons with current religious and philosophical topics, as well as an evaluation of the theories presented by Kierkegaard, lie outside the scope of this work. Information on these subjects must be sought elsewhere. Reference is made in this respect especially to the periodicals *Kierkegaardiana*, edited by me (Copenhagen, 1955–1980), and *Kierkegaard-Study*, edited by Masaru Otani (Osaka, 1964—); to the series *Bibliotheca Kierkegaardiana*, edited by Marie Mikulová Thulstrup and Niels Thulstrup, I–XVII (Copenhagen, 1978—); and to *Liber Academiae Kierkegaardiensis*, edited by Alessandro Cortese and Niels Thulstrup (Copenhagen and Milan, 1980—).

Among the sources of which most frequent use is made the following may be mentioned here:

The Bible is quoted, unless otherwise indicated, from *The New American Catholic Edition* (New York, 1961). The edition most generally used by Kierkegaard is the authorized Danish translation of 1819, commonly called "King Frederik VI's Bible."

Plato is quoted from *The Dialogues of Plato*, translated by B. Jowett, I–IV (New York, 1871 and later reprints), and the pagination used is that of the Stephanus edition. Further information is provided wherever it is required for a more exact apprehension of a quotation or allusion.

Aristotle is as a rule quoted from the translations in *The Loeb Classical Library*, although in some instances, especially where the works of logic are concerned, W. D. Ross's complete translation, *The Works of Aristotle*, I–XII (Oxford, 1928–1952), has been taken into account.

As with Plato, the pagination of Bekker's edition has also been retained here for practical reasons.

Hegel is quoted from those English translations that have been available in Denmark, but where such have not been obtainable the German text has been rendered into English by the present translator. Reference is under all circumstances made to *Georg Wilhelm Friedrich Hegel. Sämtliche Werke*, Jubiläumsausgabe, edited by Hermann Glockner, I–XX, photomechanical reprint (Stuttgart, 1958–1959). Since Glockner has undertaken various regroupings (especially of Hegel's minor works) to arrive at a chronological arrangement, references in the Commentary are made not only to volume and page numbers in this edition but also as a rule to the older collected edition that Kierkegaard used (see note on pp. 177ff. in my edition of the *Fragments*).

As implied in the opening lines of the preceding paragraph, a special problem arose in conjunction with the preparation of the English text. This edition, which also represents a thorough revision of the original Danish version, was entirely prepared and translated in Denmark. Now, when determining their principles for acquisitions of books in languages other than Danish, the two major scholarly libraries in Copenhagen, The Royal Library and Department I (the humanities) of The University Library, for centuries assumed as a matter of course that their readers had a firm grasp of not only modern European tongues but also the languages of classical antiquity and the Middle Ages. It is only in recent times that these libraries—as a concession to the spreading decay in liberal arts education—have begun to make exceptions, for example, by obtaining English translations of German philosophers. Lacking authoritative translations from other languages, the translator of my work has therefore in many instances, and especially in the case of quotations, been compelled to assume responsibility for these translations as well.

I have not attempted to provide an exhaustive bibliography but have focused on special studies of Kierkegaard in connection with the relevant topics. Reference is in general not made to the well-known standard works that were constantly consulted during the preparation of the Commentary. These are listed below.

WORKS ON PHILOSOPHY

The Encyclopedia of Philosophy. Ed. Paul Edwards, I–VIII. New York, 1967.

Eisler, Rudolf. *Wörterbuch der philosophischen Begriffe*. 4th ed., I–III. Berlin, 1927–1929.

Historisches Wörterbuch der Philosophie. Ed. Joachim Ritter and Karl-fried Gründer, I–V [A–Mn]. Darmstadt, 1971–1981.

Philosophisches Wörterbuch. Ed. G. Schischkoff. Stuttgart, 1957.

Ueberweg, Friedrich (ed.). *Grundriss der Geschichte der Philosophie*. 13th ed., I–V. Basel, 1953.

Philosophen-Lexikon. Ed. W. Ziegenfuss and G. Jung, I–II. Berlin, 1949–1950.

Enciclopedia filosofica. I–IV. Rome, 1957.

WORKS ON THEOLOGY

Realencyklopädie für protestantische Theologie und Kirche. 3rd ed., I–XXIV. Leipzig, 1896–1913.

Kirke-Leksikon for Norden. I–IV. Copenhagen, 1900–1929.

Nordisk teologisk Leksikon. I–III. Copenhagen, 1952–1957.

Die Religion in Geschichte und Gegenwart. 3rd ed., I–VI. Tübingen, 1957–1962.

Lexikon für Theologie und Kirche. 3rd ed., I–X. Freiburg, 1957–1962.

Theologische Realenzyklopädie. I–X [A–Fak]. Berlin, 1977–1983.

Theologisches Wörterbuch zum Neuen Testament. I–X². Stuttgart, 1932–1979.

The Oxford Dictionary of the Christian Church. London, 1957.

OTHER IMPORTANT WORKS

Nouvelle Biographie Générale, depuis les temps les plus reculés jusqu'à 1850–60. Ed. Dr. Hoefer, I–XLVI. Reprint, Copenhagen, 1963–1969.

Dansk biografisk Leksikon. 2nd ed., I–XXVII. Copenhagen, 1933–1944; 3rd ed., I–XII [A–Sca]. Copenhagen, 1979–1983.

The Oxford Classical Dictionary. Oxford, 1950.

Ordbog over det danske Sprog ("Dictionary of the Danish Language"). Ed. H. Juul-Jensen et al., I–XXVIII. Copenhagen, 1919–1956; reprint, Copenhagen, 1966–1974. This work is indispensable for research on Kierkegaard.

OTHER SPECIAL LEXICA

Ast, F. *Lexicon Platonicum*. I–III. Leipzig, 1835–1838; reprint, Bonn, 1956.

Bonitz, H. *Index Aristotelicus*. Berlin, 1870; reprint, Berlin, 1961.

Eisler, R. *Kantlexikon*. Berlin, 1930; reprint, Berlin, 1961.

Glockner, Hermann. *Hegel-Lexikon*. 2nd ed., I–II. Stuttgart, 1957.

Himmelstrup, Jens. *Terminologisk Register til Søren Kierkegaards Værker.* 2nd ed. Copenhagen, 1964.

Søren Kierkegaard. International Bibliografi. Ed. Jens Himmelstrup. Copenhagen, 1962.

Jørgensen, Aage. *Søren Kierkegaard-litteratur 1961–1970.* Aarhus, 1971; and *Søren Kierkegaard-litteratur 1971–1980* (in *Kierkegaardiana*, XII. Copenhagen, 1982, pp. 129–235).

Lapointe, François H. *Søren Kierkegaard and His Critics. An International Bibliography of Criticism.* London, 1980.

In addition to the works mentioned above, the following have also proved to be very useful: A. B. Drachmann's notes to the *Postscript* in *Søren Kierkegaards Samlede Værker,* 2nd ed., VII (Copenhagen, 1925); the commentary on the selections included in F. J. Billeskov Jansen's anthology, *Søren Kierkegaard. Værker i Udvalg,* I–IV (Copenhagen, 1950), IV, 163–79; and the notes in H.-M. Junghans's German translation, *Abschliessende unwissenschaftliche Nachschrift zu den Philosophischen Brocken,* vols. 16¹–16² of *Sören Kierkegaard. Gesammelte Werke* (Düsseldorf, 1957). For reasons of language it has unfortunately been impossible for me to take into consideration either Masaru Otani's annotated Japanese translation of the *Postscript* or Cornelio Fabro's Italian version, *Briciole di filosofia e Postilla non scientifica,* I–II (Brescia, 1962); revised edition in Kierkegaard's *Opere* (Florence, 1972).

The drafts and manuscripts are printed in the Commentary primarily to indicate important deviations from the final work, including omissions and the mention of persons by name. They also serve to show us how Kierkegaard prepared and developed his work, especially from a stylistic point of view.

References in the Commentary are to the Swenson-Lowrie edition of the *Postscript* mentioned in the list of English translations of Kierkegaard in the pages preceding the Introduction and are indicated by page and line number (100:10) followed by the *cue-word* in italics. There are, however, some discrepancies where the Swenson-Lowrie (S/L) translation either deviates unduly from the original meaning or omits the cue-word or passage under commentary. In these cases the translation has been amended, with the S/L translation given in brackets. Notes added by the present translator are indicated by the initials "R.J.W."

MANUSCRIPTS, EDITIONS, AND TRANSLATIONS

Both the various drafts and the fair copy of the *Postscript* have been preserved and are now part of the manuscript collection in the Royal

Library of Copenhagen, along with Kierkegaard's other manuscripts and his personal copy of the work, which contains remarks written in the margin. The collection also includes the first set of proofs for the entire work with corrections made by Israel Levin (1810–1883), Kierkegaard's secretary at the time,[1] besides several sheets of the second proof. Volumes VI B 13–99 and VII[1] B 74–92 of my edition of *Søren Kierkegaards Papirer*[2] include everything from these different sources that is important for understanding the work's conceptual content and mode of formation, and these sources are in turn quoted below in the Commentary on the basis of an evaluation made in each case.

There are three—and only three—editions of the *Postscript* in which the Danish text has philological value in its own right. The first is of course the original edition of 1846. The second, edited by A. B. Drachmann (1860–1935), a classical philologist, appeared in 1902 as vol. VII of *Søren Kierkegaards Samlede Værker* and contains a critical supplement[3] showing variant readings in the different drafts and proofs. The third, prepared by the same editor, is the improved edition that came out in 1925 as vol. VII of the second edition of the *Samlede Værker*. In this work, which is printed in the Gothic script of Kierkegaard's time, Drachmann even went to the point of preserving Kierkegaard's peculiarities and inconsistencies in orthography and punctuation, and he also added an excellent critical supplement.[4] Drachmann himself has given a detailed account of the principles that he applied when editing Kierkegaard's works.[5] His second edition of the *Postscript*, which represents a model of scholarly scrupulousness, has been used as the basis for my Commentary.

None of the other Danish editions possesses any intrinsic philological value, and thus only a few of them will be briefly mentioned here. In 1874 Kierkegaard's brother Peter Christian Kierkegaard saw to a second printing that followed the original edition but introduced some errors. Several photomechanical reprints were made of Drachmann's two critical editions, and my Danish edition of 1962 follows his text. Peter P. Rohde also adhered to Drachmann's text in his edition of 1963, but this edition and subsequent reprints[6] contain nu-

---

[1] See, among other references to Levin, *Breve*, I, nos. 127–30.

[2] These two particular volumes came out in Copenhagen in 1968.

[3] *SV* VII 553–61 (first edition).

[4] *SV* VII 1–13, secondary pagination (second edition).

[5] A. B. Drachmann, "Tekstkritik, anvendt paa Søren Kierkegaards Skrifter," *Udvalgte Afhandlinger* (Copenhagen, 1911), pp. 154–74.

[6] *Søren Kierkegaards Samlede Værker*, ed. Peter P. Rohde, I–XX (Copenhagen, 1962–1964), vols. IX and X.

merous errors and interchanged lines. All of these editions were published in Copenhagen where about ninety-eight percent of all Danish books were published in Kierkegaard's time, just as they are today.

There are many translations of the *Postscript* into the major modern languages. In the following we will mention only translations that are accompanied by introductions and notes of some worth. The others can be dealt with summarily, for readers with an interest in such matters will easily be able to find all the bibliographical information they may desire in any good scholarly library throughout the world.

The following annotated German translations are available: *Sören Kierkegaard. Gesammelte Werke*, vols. 16¹–16²: *Abschliessende unwissenschaftliche Nachschrift zu den philosophischen Brocken*, translated by H. M. Junghans (Düsseldorf, 1957–1958), and *Sören Kierkegaard. Philosophisch-theologische Schriften: Philosophische Brosamen und Unwissenschaftliche Nachschrift*, translated by B. and S. Diderichsen in collaboration with Niels Thulstrup . . . edited by Hermann Diem and Walter Rest (Cologne, 1959). The latter edition contains my brief notes and was reprinted as a pocketbook in Munich in 1976. In Italian we have *Briciole di filosofia e Postilla non scientifica*, edited by Cornelio Fabro, 2 vols. (Bologna, 1962), which contains a full introduction and brief notes. Fabro later revised and reprinted this work in his edition of Kierkegaard's *Opere* (Florence, 1972). The *Postscript* appears in French in Paul Petit's translation, *Post-Scriptum aux Miettes philosophiques* (Paris, 1949), and *Søren Kierkegaard: Œuvres complètes*, vols. X–XI: *Postscriptum définitif et non scientifique aux Miettes philosophiques*, translated by P.-H. Tisseau and E.-M. Jacquet-Tisseau (Paris, 1977). Most of the notes in the second of these two editions are taken from Drachmann, and a few derive from F. J. Billeskov Jansen's volume of notes in *Søren Kierkegaard. Værker i Udvalg*, vol. IV (Copenhagen, 1950). The *Postscript* was translated into Japanese by Masaru Otani in two volumes (Tokyo, 1959–1961), which appeared as vols. 10 and 11 of *Christian Classical Series*. Another translation, likewise in two volumes, was later made by Sugiyama, Yoshima, and Ogawa Keiji (Tokyo, 1969–1970).

When David F. Swenson died on February 11, 1940, he left behind the greater part of his manuscript of an English translation of the *Postscript*. This was "Completed after his death and provided with Introduction and Notes by Walter Lowrie." It was published in Princeton, N.J., in 1941 and has since been photographically reprinted many times.

COMMENTARY

Résumé (pp. Title Page–20)

Climacus opens his book by taking a peremptory look at the reception given the *Fragments*, his first work. Noting that it was completely ignored and thus escaped being drawn into speculation's hullabaloo, the author feels encouraged to continue his work. The only thing he fears is a sensation, especially if it brings cries of appreciation in its wake, for although criticism can be ignored, approval and admiration impose a reaction and a reply, or perhaps an expression of gratitude. Climacus did not make any promise of a sequel to his *Fragments*, since a sequel would in fact be inconceivable. It is possible, however, to invest the problem presented in that work in a historical costume, as that would only require learning and scholarship. Of course, if handled improperly, the application of learning and scholarship to the problem might also have a distracting effect.

Now if the problem concerns an individual existing person's transition from the status of nonbeliever or non-Christian to that of believer or Christian, and if this transition can occur only via a leap and consequently entails a discontinuity, then neither proficiency in world history, nor rhetoric, nor speculative systematic philosophy can be of any help. The last of these is even so strangely constituted that it maintains that Hegel's system (or the one bearing Hegel's impress) is not yet complete, which is the equivalent of saying that it is not a system at all. Climacus insists that the scholarly introduction to Christianity and to the problem of arriving at a decision distracts the individual because of its very learnedness; the rhetorical lecture distracts by intimidating the dialectician, who in this case is the author himself; and the systematic tendency distracts by promising everything and keeping nothing.

The problem that concerns the author, and which is the same for each and every person, does not come to light at all in any of these ways, and least of all whenever one takes the systematic approach. The system, which philosophers insist is without presuppositions, simply presupposes faith as something preexistent and given. The problem as set forth in the *Fragments* was whether a man can base an eternal happiness on historical knowledge. The question therefore concerns the individual's relationship to Christianity and not simply the truth or falsity of Christianity. From the standpoint of Christi-

anity the only wholly unpardonable offense is to regard this relationship as having been determined beforehand.

To clarify the problem the author proposes to present first what
he calls the objective problem, whereby the historical will receive its
just due, and then the subjective problem. Book One is thus sequen-
tial to the *Fragments*, whereas Book Two "is a new attempt of the
same general tenor as the *Fragments*, a new approach to the problem
of that piece" (p. 20).

*   *   *

According to a bill from the printer, the manuscript for the *Postscript*
was delivered to Bianco Luno's printing office on December 30, 1845.
See *Søren Kierkegaards efterladte Papirer*, ed. H. P. Barfod and
H. Gottsched, I–VIII (Copenhagen, 1869–1881), II, 269 note; this
volume covers the period 1844–1846. Kierkegaard writes in *Pap.* VII[1]
A 2 (*JP* V 5871):

> The entire manuscript, lock, stock, and barrel, was delivered to
> the printer *medio* December, or thereabouts, 1845. —"A First and
> Last Declaration" was dashed off on a piece of paper in the original
> manuscript but was laid aside to be worked out in detail and was
> delivered as late as possible lest it lie around and get lost in a print
> shop.

The work with its present title came out on February 28, 1846, on
consignment with C. A. Reitzel and was printed by Bianco Luno in
an impression of 500 copies. Kierkegaard's expenses for paper and
printing were 461 *Rdl.* 1 *Mk.* 3 *Sk.*,[1] to which must be added 100

---

[1] *Rdl.* is the abbreviation for *Rigsdaler* (rixdollar), a monetary unit that was introduced into Denmark by decrees of 1541 and 1544 during a reorganization of the monetary system. On May 4, 1625, it became the basic monetary unit and was officially
divided into six marks of sixteen shillings (*Skilling*) each. In accordance with a decree
of 1873 it was replaced by the present decimal system of crowns (*kroner*) and *øre* in
January 1875. Both the Danish unit and the American dollar owe their names to the
Joachimsthaler, a silver coin first struck in the early sixteenth century in the town of
Sankt Joachimsthal (Jáchymov) in Bohemia, Czechoslovakia. *Joachimsthaler* was soon
shortened to *Thaler* and in this form found its way into several western European
languages. In Danish the word *daler* is still used to denote two crowns, even though
this particular coin went out of circulation in 1978.

Because of various elusive factors it is impossible to translate the *Rigsdaler* or *Rigsbankdaler* (*Rbdl.*) into precise terms of present-day purchasing power. A very rough
estimate, however, based solely on comparisons of prices of land and precious stones,
would put one *Rigsdaler* of Kierkegaard's time at 100 Dkr. today. At present rates of
exchange this would be the equivalent of about US $11.40. See Astrid Friis and Kristof
Glamann, *A History of Prices and Wages in Denmark 1660-1800*, 1— (London, 1958—),

Rdl. in proof fees. Kierkegaard discusses this subject in an entry in his journal (*Pap.* X¹ A 584 from 1849; *JP* VI 6458), but the information provided by him is very approximate. A statement of accounts that he sent to the publisher in July 1847 indicates that 119 copies had been sold, leaving a stock of 381 copies. See Frithiof Brandt and Else Rammel, *Søren Kierkegaard og Pengene* (Copenhagen, 1935) and *Breve*, no. 152. In August of the same year Reitzel bought this remaining stock from Kierkegaard, together with the unsold copies of the other books that this same publisher held on consignment. Kierkegaard received thirty-three percent of the market value paid in installments, the last of which was paid to him in May 1849.

1   The title page did not receive its final form until the printed manuscript was completed. In the first draft it appeared as follows (*Pap.* VI B 89):

Logical Problems

by

Johannes Climacus

edited

by

S. Kierkegaard.

The second proposal for a title was (*Pap.* VI B 90):

Concluding (Simple) Postscript

An Elaborate Though Superfluous Postscriptum

To

The Philosophical Fragments

by

Johannes Climacus

Edited

by

S. Kierkegaard.

Copenhagen 1845

At Reitzel's.

I, 1–7, and Richard G. Doty, *Money of the World* (London, 1978), p. 138. (Note by R.J.W.)

Furthermore, an outline of Kierkegaard's plans for the first few sections of the book have come down to us in *Pap.* VI B 13–18 (*JP* V 5787–92).

1:1   *Concluding.* Kierkegaard's intention with this work was to crown the pseudonymous authorship. This is evident not only from his private papers, for example, *Pap.* X⁶ B 249, but also from "A First and Last Declaration" at the end of his book.

1:1   *Unscientific.* In the second draft to the title page (quoted above) "unscientific" is replaced by "simple." The change was probably made to indicate the polemical and antagonistic position of Kierkegaard's work to a speculative thinking that was not merely purported to be scientific but also the only thinking that was entirely scientific. In several passages Hegel employed the words philosophical, speculative, and scientific synonymously. Only a single quotation is required to give an impression of Hegel's and his disciples' linguistic usage and concept of science. In the programmatical preface to *The Phenomenology of Spirit*, pp. 70ff., Hegel says (*W.a.A.* II 6; *Jub. Ausg.* II 14):

> The systematic development of truth in scientific form can alone be the true shape in which truth exists. To help to bring philosophy nearer to the form of science—that goal where it can lay aside the name of *love* of knowledge and be actual *knowledge*—that is what I have set before me.

On the next page he adds:

> When we state the true form of truth to be its scientific character—or, what is the same thing, when it is maintained that truth finds the medium of its existence in notions or conceptions alone—I know that this seems to contradict an idea with all its consequences which makes great pretensions and has gained widespread acceptance and conviction at the present time.

Hegel thereupon acknowledges that with this statement he has set himself in opposition to the theoreticians of the Romantic school, Schelling included. As concerns Hegel's idea of science, special reference is made to B. Heimann, *System und Methode in Hegels Philosophie* (Leipzig, 1927); I. Iljin, *Die Philosophie Hegels als kontemplative Gotteslehre* (Bern, 1946); and W. Becker, *Selbstbewusstsein und Spekulation* (Stuttgart, 1972).

Kierkegaard's concept of science, which is neither Romantic nor Hegelian (nor a positivism bearing an imprint of the natural sciences), is developed most fully in the introduction to *The Concept of Anxiety*. As in the *Postscript* and *On Authority and Revelation* (pp. 3–196; *Pap.*

VII² B, pp. 5–311), it is a polemic aimed at the Hegelian view. In complete agreement with the *Postscript*, a remark added to a draft of "The Dialectic of Communication" (*Pap.* VIII² B 82:8; *JP* I 650:8) reads:

> Modern philosophical science has become imaginary or fantastic (pure knowledge)† and confusingly learned (the apparatus).
>
> † *In margin*: Especially since abandoning Kant's honorable way of giving, if I dare say so, the well-known 100 dollars to become theocentric.
> Mad combinations of this: in the same book to treat pure thought *sub specie æterni* and afterwards to regret that one has not gotten around to consider an assistant professor's little discussion in a newspaper.*
> *In margin: The historicizing method.

We lack an analysis of Kierkegaard's conception of science, but important contributions to the clarification of this problem have been made by Gregor Malantschuk in "Frihedens Dialektik hos Søren Kierkegaard," *Dansk teologisk Tidsskrift* (Copenhagen, 1949), pp. 193ff.; "Das Verhältnis zwischen Wahrheit und Wirklichkeit in Søren Kierkegaards existentiellem Denken," *Symposium Kierkegaardianum* (Copenhagen, 1955), pp. 166–76; "Søren Kierkegaards Teori om Springet og hans Virkelighedsbegreb," *Kierkegaardiana*, I (Copenhagen, 1955), pp. 7–15; *Frihed og Eksistens* (Copenhagen, 1980); and *Kierkegaard's Thought* (Princeton, 1971).

1:4   *A Mimic-Pathetic-Dialectical Composition. An Existential Contribution.* Vilhelm Andersen has aptly and concisely explained the title page as follows in *Illustreret dansk Litteraturhistorie*, II (Copenhagen, 1924), pp. 686–87:

> The task in the new book is to transform the logical problem of the *Fragments* . . . into a question of life. This is accomplished by concentrating all the preceding works, whose authors at different times speak from behind a mask (mimic), as a poet (pathetic), and as a thinker (dialectical), thereby forming a contribution that is existential. In other words, the contribution is by a living person and about a living person, because it makes clear the fact that Christianity is not a form of thought but a form of life, that it does not mean speculating but existing, and that it is not a science but a passion.

The word "mimic" may have been taken from an example given by Hamann in *Sokratische Denkwürdigkeiten* (Amsterdam, 1759).

1:7   *Johannes Climacus.* Concerning this pseudonym see Emanuel Hirsch, *Kierkegaard-Studien*, I–II (Gütersloh, 1930–1933), II, 747ff., and my edition of the *Fragments*, pp. 148ff.

2   *The motto.* The draft (*Pap.* VI B 91) has the following concerning the motto:

(Better well hung than ill wed!)
As a motto I will use the last line by Hippias in the dialogue *Hippias* [The Greater] and the first part of Socrates' reply thereto.

The Greek reads in translation: "But really, Socrates, what do you think all this amounts to? It is really scrapings and parings of systematic thought, as I said a while ago, divided into bits" (304A). In his edition of Plato with the Greek texts, *Platonis Opera*, ed. Astius [Ast], I–XI (Leipzig, 1919–1932; *ASKB* 1144–54), Kierkegaard read as the quotation indicates, although he as usual left out the accent marks in the original edition of the *Postscript*. It may be observed that Burnet has συνάπαντα and κνήσματά.

3:8   *The motto: "Better well hung than ill wed."* An explanation of the meaning of this will be found in my edition of the *Fragments*, p. 152. This line stems originally from Shakespeare's *Twelfth Night*, Act I, Scene 5: "Many a good hanging prevents a bad marriage." Junghans remarks in his note to this passage that "hung" may be interpreted as "left alone"; but this interpretation hardly covers the case fully. Undoubtedly such an interpretation does seem likely in view of the ensuing "than by an unfortunate marriage to be brought into systematic relationship with the whole world." But even though the pseudonym Johannes Climacus provides this explanation in the Preface to the *Postscript*, the earlier work is not written by a genuine pseudonym. The *Fragments* was both written and originally intended for publication under Kierkegaard's own name, and contemporaneity with Christ, a thought that is given increasing prominence in the subsequent authorship, is a central theme whose consequence for Kierkegaard and for his mock pseudonyms in the *Fragments* is simply that he would prefer to be left alone with the truth, Christ, than to share company with an untruth, the crowd. As a matter of principle, Kierkegaard cannot here in the *Postscript* allow the genuine pseudonym Johannes Climacus to come forth with the whole explanation, for Climacus avows that he is not a Christian. See Per Lønning, *Samtidighedens Situation* (Oslo, 1954) and note the expression "being crucified on the paradox" in *Pap.* IX A 414 (*JP* I 493).

3:15   *the incessant forebodings of . . . Speculation.* This may conceivably be an allusion to a Hegelian of that time, Rasmus Nielsen (1809–1884), a professor of philosophy who from 1841 to 1844 published *Den speculative Logik i dens Grundtræk*. Of this unfinished work, however, only twenty-six paragraphs appeared, the last of which ends in the middle of a sentence.

3:24   *the promised hero incognito*. Very likely this is a reference to J. L. Heiberg's famous vaudeville, *Kong Solomon og Jørgen Hattemager* (1825).

3:28   *the book . . . neither reviewed nor mentioned anywhere*. This is not quite true. The *Fragments* was reviewed in *Neues Repertorium für die theologische Literatur und kirchliche Statistik* in April 1845, but Kierkegaard discovered it rather late (see the *Postscript*, pp. 245–46, and my note thereto in the present volume). It was reviewed in Denmark by J. F. Hagen in C. T. Engelstoft's *Theologisk Tidsskrift*, but not until May 1846; and as mentioned above the *Postscript* was published on February 28 of the same year. The German review is reprinted in M. Theunissen and W. Greve, *Materialen zur Philosophie Sören Kierkegaards* (Frankfurt am Main, 1979), pp. 212ff., and by me in *Kierkegaardiana*, VIII (Copenhagen, 1971), pp. 212–16.

3:34   *magic . . . false alarms*. An allusion to the title of Holberg's comedy *Hexerie eller blind Allarm*.

4:6   *Baggesen's words*. In *Thomas Moore eller Venskabs Seir over Kjærlighed*, which Kierkegaard read in the first edition of *J. Baggesens danske Værker*, ed. his sons and C. J. Boye, I–XII (Copenhagen, 1827–1832; *ASKB* 1509–20), I, 329:

> Og slige skrækindjagende Personer,
> Som, for Exempel, de, hvis Vaaben er en Sax,
> Som skaber Mennesker, men dræber dem igjen
> Med Regninger paa Skabelsen.
> [And such terrifying persons,
> Those whose scissors are their weapons,
> Who create men, but slay them again
> With their bills for the creations.]

4:15   *Aristotle*. A quotation from *Rhetoric* 1416b. Kierkegaard used a German translation, *Aristotelis Rhetorik*, trans. Carl Ludvig Roth (Stuttgart, 1833; *ASKB* 1092), which he bought on January 30, 1843. See *Pap*. IV A 207 (*JP* IV 4254) and *Pap*. V C 2–5 (*JP* II 2346–47). The quotation has the following form in Roth's translation (pp. 289ff.):

> Jetzt stellt man die lächerliche Regel auf, die Erzählung müsse schnell seyn. Und doch trifft hier Das zu, was Einer dem Brodtkneter, der ihn fragte, ob er einen rauhen oder zarten Teig machen solle,

antwortete: wie denn? ist's denn nicht möglich, einen guten zu machen?

4:34   *Pereat.* "Down with him!" This was said in contrast to *vivat,* "may he live." *Pereat* was in earlier times commonly used by Danish students.

5:38   *silence.* The complete isolation of prisoners in cells without occupation, a principle practiced under the so-called "Philadelphia System," had too severe an effect, and to remedy this situation the Auburn System was introduced into American prisons in 1823. At night the prisoners were to be isolated in separate cells, whereas during the day they were to work together in workshops, but in complete silence. Where Kierkegaard acquired his knowledge of such matters has not come to light, but his earlier literary plans to sketch a "masterthief" (*Pap.* I A 11ff.; *JP* V 5061ff.) show his interest in subjects of this kind. Possibly his acquaintance with Police Inspector Jørgen Jørgensen was a contributing factor, and his library included such books as the very popular *Udvalg af danske og udenlandske Criminelsager og af mærkelige Forhandlinger om saadanne,* ed. F. M. Lange, I–VI (Copenhagen, 1835–1841; *ASKB* 926–31). See Sejer Kühle, *Søren Kierkegaard: Barndom og Ungdom* (Copenhagen, 1950), pp. 136–38.

6:4   *proprio marte, proprio stipendio, propriis auspiciis.* "By one's own hand, on one's own behalf, at one's own expense." A like expression is used by Cicero in *Philippics,* II, 37, 95. See *Pap.* V B 24:84, where Kierkegaard uses the same expression in a draft to the preface to the *Fragments* (p. 154 in my edition).

6:13   *"the peasant boy in pawn."* An allusion to Holberg's comedy of the same title, *Den pantsatte Bondedreng,* in which a stupid peasant boy is exploited by a debt-ridden vagabond who in the end leaves him in the lurch.

13:4   *(p. 162).* In the original edition; p. 137 in my edition (*SV* IV 301).

13:10   *in optima forma.* In the best form.

14:20   *investing the problem in historical costume.* Whereas the *Fragments* basically speaks only "algebraically," mentioning by name neither Christianity nor the individual, this work speaks concretely about Christianity and about the individual as personified in, "I, Johannes Climacus, thirty years old, a common, ordinary human being."

14:37   *Essentially there is no sequel.* That is, as a matter of principle and as viewed from a systematic vantage point. It will become apparent from what follows that some of the main problems presented in the *Fragments* are treated again in the *Postscript* from a different viewpoint.

15:7ff.   *exceptional learning, the orator, the systematic philosopher.* With these phrases Kierkegaard in all probability intends his former professors at the university, Martensen and Bishop Mynster, and in particular H. N. Clausen. Note the following remark and what follows on p. 15: "whose guidance he could wish that he might have been able to follow in his student years."

15.21   *to construct a quantitative approach to faith.* In other words, it is impossible to arrive at a conviction of faith either empirically through studies of history or rationally through rational argumentation, since it cannot be attained by an inference or a conclusion but only by a resolve or a choice, that is, by a leap. See Gregor Malantschuk, *Way to Truth* and *Fra Individ til den Enkelte* (Copenhagen, 1978).

15.29   *the leap of faith.* Although transitions in Hegel take place through a quantitative dialectic, with necessity and continuity, all transitions occur according to Kierkegaard by means of a qualitative leap—either dialectically or pathetically—with freedom and involve a discontinuity. Here the question thus concerns a pathetic leap from the status of nonbeliever to that of believer.

16:1   *discrimen.* Decisive test [S/L: line of demarcation].

16:34   *the system is not yet finished.* By "the system" must here as elsewhere in the work be understood the theory of Hegel and his devotees. The statements relevant to the system's lack of completion must be interpreted in the light of criticisms leveled at it in the *Postscript* itself, especially pp. 99ff., to which the reader is referred.

17:36   *give unto Caesar his due.* Matt. 22:21.

18:9   *The system presupposes faith as something given.* Kierkegaard very likely has in mind passages in Hegel where faith is identified with immediate knowledge, for example, in the *Encyclopaedia of the Philosophical Sciences*, §63 (*W.a.A.* VI 128; *Jub. Ausg.* VIII 166; *Logic*, p. 123): "But, seeing that derivative knowledge is restricted to the compass of finite facts, Reason is knowledge underivative, or Faith." Hegel, however, does not identify this "Faith" with Christian faith: "The two things are radically distinct. Firstly, the Christian faith comprises in it an authority of the Church: but the faith of Jacobi's philosophy has no other authority than that of a personal revelation" (ibid., p. 125).

Kierkegaard asserts here and in *Fear and Trembling* and *Stages on Life's Way* that Hegel reduces faith to something that a man possesses through the necessity of nature and that stands on a par with indeterminate feelings and random moods. As a rule, Hegel defines immediacy as synonymous with what is given by nature, as that with which a person must begin and to which he must assume an attitude of conscious opposition if he is not to stagnate in his spiritual development and revert to evil. The charge that Kierkegaard here makes against Hegel is essentially that Hegel does not let faith acquire the status of the very category that is to be achieved and lived in. Kierkegaard claims that in Hegel religion and faith are rather subordinated to philosophy in such a way as to endow speculative knowledge with a position that is superior to faith, so speculation becomes the category to which the concept of faith must be elevated. Religion is, with respect to form, subordinate to speculative philosophy, for it is the property of the multitude who have not succeeded in elevating themselves to speculative contemplation.

It is Hegel's view that the value of speculative thought lies in demonstrating the necessity of the content of religion, thereby providing a rational certainty that is unattainable at the immediate stage of faith. Thus Hegel consistently refuses to justify the true content of faith through either tradition or ecclesiastical authority; he does so only by way of thought, that is, by philosophical speculation. Kierkegaard's critical question concerning this tenet is not only whether or not religion in general and Christianity in particular are altered in form by this process, but also whether or not this transfer into the sphere of speculative knowledge causes a radical change in the content of faith. Kierkegaard's own reply to the question is to the effect that Hegel spiritualizes (*spiritualiserer*) the content of faith and deceives his readers by presenting the matter as if he simply absorbs the traditional Christian content of faith into his philosophy. There is no doubt that Hegel himself regards his philosophy as the supreme development of Christianity, as well as the best possible defense of its validity. Yet he in fact explains away specific historical revelation—the very cornerstone of Christianity—and this entails an erroneous definition of both sin and faith.

See especially Torsten Bohlin, *Søren Kierkegaards dogmatiska åskådning i dess historiska sammenhang* (Stockholm, 1925), pp. 379ff.

18:10   *in a system that is supposed to be without presuppositions!* Kierkegaard was here and on p. 101, where the problem is treated more circumstantially, thinking in particular of Hegel's explanations in the beginning of *The Science of Logic*, in "With What Must the Science Begin?" (vol. I, 79ff.; *W.a.A.* III 59ff.; *Jub. Ausg.* IV 69ff.). Kierkegaard's reasoning is that the beginning of logic, and with it that of philosophy, finds itself in a dilemma that even the ancient skeptics were acquainted with and had declared to be unsolvable. Either this beginning is mediated or it lies in immediacy. If it is mediated, the beginning is lacking, for the mediation, the grounds, and the argumentation can be prolonged indefinitely; if on the other hand the beginning lies in immediacy, there is no proof that it really is a beginning. This dilemma will persist as long as philosophy begins with a statement or an assertion, that is, a postulate; conversely, there will no longer be a dilemma if philosophy, as taught by Fichte (in *Grundlage der gesammten Wissenschaftslehre*, 2nd ed., Tübingen, 1802), begins with a requirement, a decision, an act.

In Hegel the beginning is both knowledge and will. The knowledge constituting the beginning is both mediated and immediate, he insists, since everything immediate is the result of an act of mediation: what exists does so after having come into existence. One must regard the beginning of Hegel's *Logic* as mediated by the entire *Phenomenology of Spirit*, the end result of which was pure knowledge. This pure knowledge *is* now, according to Hegel, but it has come into existence through spirit's own dialectical process of development. It *is*, yet it has the property of immediacy; it is completely indeterminate and undeveloped, and its potential content will finally be defined and developed in *The Science of Logic*. The beginning is thus the concept (or "Notion," in Hegelian English) Being, a conception of "to be," but it also holds true that philosophy cannot advance any further without a decision: "Nothing is there except the decision (which might appear arbitrary) to consider Thought as such" (*The Science of Logic*, vol. I, 82).

18:18   *The problem posed and formulated.* The problem appears on the title page of the *Fragments* and the quotation on p. 137. See my commentary on the *Fragments*, pp. 149ff.

18:34   *once dealt with by theologians.* In the prospectus for the theological curriculum sent out in the fall of 1831 (printed in *Tidsskrift for Kirke og Theologie*, I, 1832, pp. 305ff.) by the faculty of theology at the University of Copenhagen it was announced that lectures on natural theology and apologetics would be offered every other year. Kierkegaard did not own the earlier Danish work by Peter Erasmus Müller, *Kristelig Apologetik eller Videnskabelig Udvikling af Grundene for Kristendommens Guddommelighed* (Copenhagen, 1810) but instead Dr. K. H. Sack, *Christliche Apologetik* (Hamburg, 1829; *ASKB* 755). This work, however, does not seem to have made much of an impression on Kierkegaard, who merely (*Pap.* II C 60; *JP* V 5350) makes mention of the same author's *Christliche Polemik* (Hamburg, 1838; *ASKB* 756), and then only once. On the other hand, the right-wing Hegelian Karl Rosenkranz's *Enzyklopädie der theologischen Wissenschaften* (Halle, 1831; *ASKB* 35) has left traces here and there.

The history of apologetics is presented in O. Zöckler, *Geschichte der Apologie des Christentums* (Gütersloh, 1907), and another recommended work on this subject is the essay in *Theologische Realenzyklopädie*, III (Berlin, 1978), pp. 371–429.

19:13   *this theocentric age . . . nineteenth century . . . universal history.* Kierkegaard is here thinking especially of Hegel's speculative philosophy. Hegel sought to arrange every single phenomenon in its proper setting within the quantitative, dialectical, world-historical evolution and by this means to arrive at a contemplation of the whole of existence from the vantage point of the divine or of eternity. In Kierkegaard's view, this is impossible for an individual existing in finitude. This point of view is clearly emphasized in several passages in the *Postscript*. The word "theocentric" itself does not seem to appear in Hegel's works.

19:14   *speculatively significant. . . .* The words "speculative" and "speculation" derive from the Latin *speculatio*, which corresponds to the Greek *theoria* (θεωρία), basically meaning perception, contemplation, intuitive cognition of objects beyond experience. It is found with this meaning in, for example, Aristotle (*Metaphysics* 1025b 18, 1050a 10 and passim), in the Neoplatonists, and in the Neoplatonic-Augustinian tradition of the Middle Ages. A similar meaning is conferred by Schelling on the expression "intellectual intuition" (*intellectuelle Anschauung*). In his *Philosophische Briefe über Dogmatismus und Kriticismus* (1795; here quoted from Schelling's *Werke*, ed. Manfred Schröter, I [Munich, 1927], p. 242) Schelling explains as follows:

> There dwells within us a concealed and wonderful capacity to draw our naked ego out of the vicissitudes of time in our inmost being, away from all that supervenes from outside, and then under the form of immutability to perceive the Eternal in us.

> This "intuition" is the point at which knowledge of the absolute and the absolute itself merge (*Darstellung m. Syst.*, §2), in other words, where thought and its object become identical. In Hegel the expression "speculative cognition" has the same import. Among the many concordant explanations of "speculation" and "speculative cognition" scattered by Hegel throughout his works the following may be quoted from the *Enzyklopädie der philosophischen Wissenschaften* (*W.a.A.* IV 159; *Jub. Ausg.* VIII 197; *Logic*, pp. 153ff.):

> the speculative is in its signification, neither preliminarily nor even definitely, something merely subjective: . . . on the contrary, it expressly rises above such oppositions as that between subjective and objective, which the understanding cannot get over, and ab-

sorbing them in itself, evinces its own concrete and all-embracing nature. . . . Speculative truth, it may also be noted, means very much the same as what, in special connexion with religious experiences and doctrines, used to be called Mysticism.

The reason underlying the appearance here of "speculatively significant" must rest, as Junghans notes in his commentary on this passage, in the fact that it is intended to mean "significant within the compass of speculation." Hegel's own concept of the historical unfolding of philosophy was that his own absolute idealism succeeded Fichte's subjective and Schelling's objective idealism, thereby concluding a history of philosophy that had begun with the Seven Sages and now culminates with Hegel's own system. This is the system containing the very speculation—that is, the speculative cognition of the truth—that was asserted to be the same as the absolute itself (see the Introduction, chapter 4).

In a journal entry from 1849 written a few days after publication of Martensen's dogmatics, Kierkegaard, fully consonant with the main theme of the *Postscript*, observes (*Pap.* X^1 A 554; *JP* II 1132):

> As I have said so often, speculation can comprehend everything—except how I arrived at faith or how faith has come into the world. But philosophy continuously takes faith to mean a sum of doctrinal propositions. . . . However it is certainly ridiculous to note the cocksureness with which a dogmatician sits and arranges a system—and God knows whether faith is found in the world.

19:28   *conditio sine qua non.* An indispensable condition—without which one does not come into relationship to Christianity.

19:29   *hates father and mother.* Luke 14:26. See *Fear and Trembling*, pp. 82ff. (*SV* III 135ff.) where Kierkegaard claims "that the words [in the Bible] are to be taken in as terrible a sense as possible." Bretschneider's Greek Lexicon to the New Testament defines this word as "to love less," "to put in a subordinate position," and so forth. See Niels Thulstrup's "Kierkegaard og K. G. Bretschneider," *Festskrift til Søren Holm* (Copenhagen, 1971), pp. 31–42. As to the concept μισέω, see Kittel, *Theologisches Wörterbuch zum Neuen Testament* IV (Stuttgart, 1942), pp. 687–99, especially 694ff., in which the connection with usage in the Wisdom literature of the Old Testament is underscored.

19:33   *outlines of universal history.* With this Kierkegaard may have had an eye not only on Hegel's *Philosophy of History*—probably one of the first of Hegel's works with which he became acquainted—but also on Grundtvig's *Kort Begreb af Verdens Krønike i Sammenhæng* (Copenhagen, 1812) or his *Udsigt over Verdens Krøniken, fornemmelig i det Lutherske Tidsrum* (Copenhagen, 1817; *ASKB* 1970). With reference to Grundtvig's works, see William Michelsen, *Tilblivelsen af Grundtvigs Historiesyn* (Copenhagen, 1954) and *Den sælsomme forvandling i N.F.S. Grundtvigs liv* (Copenhagen, 1956).

20:8   *the five foolish virgins.* Matt. 25:1–13.

Résumé (pp. 23–35)

When viewed objectively Christianity is a given entity, the truth of which is investigated without personal interest or commitment. In this context truth can mean two things: first, historical truth, and second, philosophical truth. But an objective inquiry does not consider the subjective truth, that is, the assimilated truth. It follows that the problem formulated by the author, which implies a decision, is not raised at all.

Johannes Climacus thereupon demonstrates this point more explicitly, first by considering the Bible and a case in which a scholar seeks to assure himself of the greatest possible reliability. No matter how much diligence and learnedness the scholar displays he nevertheless will remain stuck in an approximation and will never obtain a result that yields absolute certainty. Nor can inspiration, the dogmatic guarantee that has been advanced, be of any assistance to historical certainty, for inspiration relates to faith only, not to knowledge.

This implies that the philologist is quite within his rights in pursuing his research according to his own methods. On the other hand, what the author calls "the learned, critical theology" suffers from an equivocalness because this theology always makes it appear as though a result relevant to faith might emerge from the efforts made on its behalf. This is an illusion that has been passed on from generation to generation. No one has in fact clarified just what the dispute is all about. If it is merely a philological-historical debate, it has nothing to do with faith; nor will it concern faith if other elements such as dogmatics are drawn into the debate. Now if we assume that a so-called conservative theologian has succeeded in substantiating everything about the Bible that he could possibly wish to prove, and if we accordingly were to raise the question whether or not the believer has thereby gained anything with respect to his faith, the reply would have to be in the negative, because knowledge concerning the Scriptures is not identical with Christian faith.

If, conversely, we assume that another, adversarial quarter has succeeded in disproving all this, and if we now inquire as to whether Christianity on that account is eliminated, the reply once again will be negative. Not until faith ceases to be faith do proofs become imperative, that is, when the categories of faith and knowledge have been merged or confounded. The result of the thinker's deliberations is, then, that the more he strives for objectivity the further the problem concerning his eternal happiness recedes in the distance, for it is a problem that is not related to objectivity but to subjectivity, since the decision involved lies in subjectivity only.

*   *   *

23:1   *res in facto posita.* Something given; a given fact.

23:14   *a subjective truth.* For example, a truth that is appropriated by the individual in inwardness and through a choice. Subjective truth is equivalent to edifying truth, a truth that, coming from outside, builds up or fortifies the life of the individual. The principal treatment of this concept is to be found on pp. 169ff., to which the reader is referred.

25:7   *anything historical . . . approximation.* The pregnant and concise statements here must be understood in context with "The Interlude" in the *Fragments*, especially pp. 93ff. Whatever is essentially historical has come into existence in time and points back to a freely working cause, God. (Note, to cite but one example, Thomas Aquinas' theory of the freely working cause.) A conception of the past, or in other words knowledge of the historical, is for that reason contingent on a belief understood as a sense for coming-into-existence. As such, knowledge of the past embodies an irreducible element of uncertainty that excludes the possibility of a deterministic philosophy of history.

It may be observed that several modern scholars of history, although proceeding from different philosophical backgrounds, share the view advanced in this passage: that it is only possible to attain to an approximation in the apprehension of events and their sequence. Of the literature relating to this problem the following may be recommended: Henri-Irénée Marrou, *De la connaissance historique* (Paris, 1954); Rudolf Bultmann, *Geschichte und Eschatologie* (Tübingen, 1958); H. U. von Balthasar, *Theologie der Geschichte* (Basel, 1965); R. G. Collingwood, *The Idea of History* (London, Oxford, and New York, 1961); John Herman Randall, Jr., *Nature and Historical Experience: Essays in Naturalism and in the Theory of History* (New York and London, 1958); Richard McKeon, *Freedom and History* (New York, 1952); *The Philosophy of History in Our Time: An Anthology*, selected and ed. Hans Meyerhoff (Garden City, N.Y., 1959); René Sédillot, *L'histoire n'a pas de sense* (Paris, 1965); and *Die Religion in Geschichte und Gegenwart*, I–VI (Tübingen, 1952–1965), II, 1473–96, which gives a summary and a comprehensive bibliography.

See in this respect Howard V. Hong's observations in the *Frag-*

ments, pp. 101 and 108ff., concerning the Danish word *Tro*, which may be translated as both "faith" and "belief."

25:19   *epigram.* Here to be taken more properly in the sense of a derisive verse.

26:9   *topics that come up for consideration.* This refers to the issues treated in the history of literature in scholarly introductions to studies of the Old and New Testament (isagogics). Thus H. Mosbech writes in *Nytestamentlig Isagogik* (Copenhagen, 1946–1949), p. 791:

> The Greek word χανών (canon) actually means "pipe," but in a figurative sense it also means "measuring stick," "ruler," "guide" or "register," "list." In the East, the word was from Athanasius' time used to denote a catalogue (κατάλογος) of those writings regarded by the Church as divinely inspired. But as the word gradually gained acceptance in the western Church it also came to signify that these writings were to be applied as a rule and guide for Christian doctrine and life; this is currently the common meaning of the word "canon." In conjunction with this, however, scholars persisted in the thought that the canonical scriptures are normative, for they contain God's revelation, giving it such a mode of expression as to assign the scriptures a special position within the Christian Church, a status that is essentially different from all other writings. Thus in the concept "canon" there is the notion of a sharp demarcation: these definite writings, and no others. This factor was of decisive importance when, about A.D. 90, the extent of the canon of the Old Testament was definitely established. The desire to sort out the divinely inspired writings while repudiating all others likewise played a significant role when the canon of the New Testament was at last defined about A.D. 400.

Kierkegaard's textbook on this subject, which as a discipline in its own right does not antedate The Age of Enlightenment, was the solid and matter-of-fact work by W.M.L. de Wette, *Lehrbuch der historisch kritischen Einleitung in die Bibel Alten und Neuen Testaments*, 4th ed., 4 parts in one vol. (Berlin, 1833; *ASKB* 80). Kierkegaard read a concise outline of these problems regarded in their formal structure in the right-wing Hegelian Karl Rosenkranz's *Enzyklopädie der theologischen Wissenschaften* (Halle, 1831; *ASKB* 35), §60ff. Here these questions are treated in exactly the same sequence as in the *Postscript*: authenticity, integrity, and the trustworthiness of the authors (*Axiopistie*), in that order. The history of research on this subject is comprehensively presented by W. G. Kümmel in *Das Neue Testament,*

Geschichte der Erforschung seiner Probleme (Freiburg, 1958); see especially pp. 145–243 for the first half of the nineteenth century.

26:12   *Inspiration.* Kierkegaard obviously has in mind here the orthodox theory of verbal inspiration rather than Schleiermacher's theory of personal inspiration. On this entire question see H. Cremer's essay in *Realenzyklopädie für protestantische Theologie und Kirche*, 3rd ed. IX (Leipzig, 1901), pp. 183–203, and G. Schrenk's article "γραφή" in *Theologisches Wörterbuch zum Neuen Testament*, I (Stuttgart, 1933), pp. 750–69, and in *Die Religion in Geschichte und Gegenwart* III (Tübingen, 1959), pp. 773ff.

26   *authority.* The idea of authority (*Autoritet*) acquired through study
(note †):5   and from knowledge is intimately connected with the concept of authority (*Myndighed*) in the sense of an invested power, and both were very important to Kierkegaard personally as well as theoretically throughout his authorship. They are developed especially in the essay "On The Difference Between A Genius and An Apostle" (1847), which was published in the anonymous *Two Minor Ethico-Religious Treatises* (in *The Present Age*, trans. Alexander Dru and Walter Lowrie [New York, 1940], pp. 73ff.; *SV* XI 109ff.). See also *The Point of View for My Work as An Author*, p. 142 note (*SV* XIII 558 note). As to relevant literature, reference is made to P. A. Heiberg, *Søren Kierkegaards religiøse Udvikling* (Copenhagen, 1925), pp. 238–85; Eduard Geismar, *Søren Kierkegaard*, I–VI (Copenhagen, 1926–1928), IV, 45ff., 81ff.; Emanuel Hirsch, *Kierkegaard-Studien*, I–II (Gütersloh, 1930–1933), II, 852ff.; and C. Fabro's introduction to his translation of *The Book on Adler, Dell'autorità e della rivelazione* (Padua, 1976).

26:13   *tunnel under the Thames.* The English engineer Brunel started digging the first tunnel under the Thames in 1825, but owing to several mishaps—seeping water, among others—it was not completed until 1842.

27:12   *the scholarly critical theology.* Kierkegaard has in mind here the Protestant conservative exegesis represented by names such as Hermann Olshausen in Germany and C. E. Scharling in Denmark. Like Theodor Zahn at a later date, both of them turned against the radical views of the Tübingen school. See W. G. Kümmel's history of research mentioned above and Jørgen Pedersen, "Kierkegaard's View of Scripture," *Bibliotheca Kierkegaardiana*, II (Copenhagen, 1978), pp. 27–59.

27:17   *When a philologist.* This is very likely an allusion to Johan Nicolai Madvig's voluminous annotated edition of Cicero's *De finibus bonorum et malorum* (Copenhagen, 1839). See Povl Johannes Jensen, *J. N. Madvig, et Mindeskrift* (Copenhagen, 1955).

27:32   *keeps us in suspense.* In other words, he prevents us from arriving at a decision.

28:11   *Luther's rejection of the Epistle of James.* The allusion here is to Luther's famous assessment of the Scriptures of the New Testament in the preface to his translation of the Bible of 1539. See *Deutsche Schriften,* Erlanger ed. I–LXVII (Erlangen, 1826–1886), LXIII, 115, where Luther asserts that "the Epistle of Saint James [is] a rather insipid epistle." See also Thestrup Pedersen, *Luther som Skriftfortolker,* I (Copenhagen, 1959).

29:1   *the learned rescue corps.* Kierkegaard may have had in mind F. C. Baur and the so-called Tübingen school who, by adopting some of the Hegelian views of historical evolution, sought to implement a methodical investigation of the sources of primitive Christianity and in the course of their work to repudiate most of the Scriptures of the New Testament. A series of conservative scholars ("the learned rescue corps") by contrast defended the traditional interpretations. See the work by W. G. Kümmel mentioned above. There is a résumé in Horst Stephan, *Geschichte der deutschen evangelischen Theologie seit dem deutschen Idealismus,* 2nd ed., ed. Martin Schmidt (Berlin, 1960), pp. 154ff., and a modern refutation of the Tübingen school is J. Munck, *Paulus und die Heilsgeschichte* (Aarhus, 1954).

29:3   *Wessel said.* . . . This is from Johan Herman Wessel's *Kierlighed uden Strømper,* Act IV, Scene 2: "Jeg pleier ellers gaa derfra hvor Slagsmaal er" ("I usually leave where there is a brawl").

29:18   *claudatur.* That is, *claudatur parenthesis* or, "terminate the subordinate clause." In this case it is used in the sense of "conclusion."

29:21   *e[x] concessis.* On the basis of mutual concessions.

29:27   *I assume . . . have succeeded in proving about the Bible.* See in this connection the quotation from Strauss in my edition of the *Fragments,* pp. 150ff.

29:31   *as if every letter were inspired.* 2 Tim. 3:16: "All scripture is inspired by God."

30:4   *runs into danger everywhere.* From Hans Adolph Brorson's hymn (1734) that begins with "Jeg gaar i Fare, hvor jeg gaar" ("I walk in danger wherever I walk").

30:25   *ubique et nusquam.* Everywhere and nowhere.

30:28   *lurks at the door of faith.* Compare Gen. 4:7.

30:32   *a profitable schoolmaster.* See Gal. 3:24: "Therefore the Law has been our tutor unto Christ, that we might be justified by faith."

31:1   *that faith is abolished in eternity.* 1 Cor. 13:12–13: "We see now through a mirror in an obscure manner, but then face to face. Now I know in part, but then I shall know even as I have been known." See also 2 Cor. 5:7.

31:37   *a confusion of the categories.* That is, of the categories of faith and knowledge.

31:38   *The vanity of faith.* This expression is from Ex. 20:7.

32:14   *Poor unlearned Peer Ericksen.* A colloquialism originating from Holberg's *Den Stundesløse,* Act III, Scene 5.

32:23   *zealousness* [S/L: fanaticism]. The Zealots were an extremist nationalist party among the Pharisees during the time of Jesus. The words "zealotry" and "zealousness" (Danish *Zelotismen*) with the meaning "fanatical devotion," especially in relation to trivialities, have thus been borrowed by most of our Western languages, Danish included. Kierkegaard is here applying the word to the devotees of the theory of verbal interpretation in its orthodox form.

33:8   *subject . . . subjectivity.* As Junghans correctly observes in his commentary on this passage, with Kierkegaard these two words have two fundamental meanings in relation to Christianity. First of all, they mean the personal passion whereby the message of Christianity is grasped; in this case "Subjectivity is the truth." Second, they indicate that subjectivity implies a human being, an individual, a subject, and in this sense "Subjectivity is untruth" because the subject is a sinner and does not possess the essential truth.

33:20   *while the grass grows under his feet the inquirer dies.* From the Danish proverb, "Medens Græsset groer, døer Horsemor" ("While the grass grows the stud starves"). The meaning here is that the development proceeds so slowly that the result arrives too late to be of any benefit.

33:37   *the significance of mediation.* Whereas Hegel's Danish disciples generally employed this word, Hegel himself used the terms *Vermittlung* or *Versöhnung* (reconciliation or, as used in English translations of Hegel, mediation and sublation. The Danish word derives from the French *la médiation.*—R.J.W.) to indicate a reconciliation of two relative opposites. Hegel everywhere accentuates the fact that the opposites that present themselves are only contraries, not contradictions, and are relative, not absolute. In Hegel's view they can and therefore must be made to combine in a higher synthesis with inherent necessity. If for example the concept being is thought in its purest possible state so that everything determinately existent is abstracted from it, the concept or notion must be empty; in other words, it has passed over into its opposite, nothing. These two concepts, being and nothing, are now mediated to form a third, the concept becoming. A modern monograph is H. Niel, *De la médiation dans la philosophie de Hegel* (Paris, 1945).

Kierkegaard had very early assumed an extremely critical attitude to Hegel's theory of mediation. In a well-known entry from 1839 he writes (*Pap.* II A 454; *JP* II 1578):

> All relative contrasts can be mediated [*medieres*]; we do not really need Hegel for this, inasmuch as the ancients point out that they can be distinguished. Personality will for all eternity protest against the idea that absolute contrasts can be mediated . . . for all eternity it will repeat its *immortal* dilemma: to be or not to be—that is the question (Hamlet).

In a later entry he notes (*Pap.* II A 108; *JP* III 3072) that "Philosophy's idea is mediation—Christianity's the paradox." This thought is reiterated in several other entries: *Pap.* III A 211 (*JP* II 2277); IV B 117, pp. 228ff., 294; C 55, 81, 97 (*JP* II 1242, 1603; V 5601); V B 47:14; VI B 54:33 (*JP* III 3307:33); VII[1] A 158 (*JP* V 5944). In these entries he makes equally decisive thrusts against the theory of mediation in the various fields in which Hegel and his disciples had applied it. This concept does not properly belong either to logic or to ethics but rather to dogmatics in which atonement, in lieu of taking place with necessity, occurs through a free volitional act on the part of God.

34
(note *):1   *The skepticism . . . inherent in the Hegelian philosophy.* By philosophical skepticism is generally meant a way of thinking that makes doubt its most important principle, in particular doubt concerning the certitude of the cognition of truth. Ancient skepticism arose as a reaction against a metaphysical dogmatism, making its appearance first with Pyrrho (which is why initially skepticism generally was called Pyrrhonism) and next with Arcesilaus and Carneades in the Academy (see note below). Aenesidemus and more particularly Sextus Empiricus are well known among the later skeptics. See A. Goedeckemeyer, *Die Geschichte des Griechischen Skeptizismus* (Leipzig, 1905); R. Richter, *Der Skeptizismus in der Philosophie* (Leipzig, 1904–1908); E.-A. Preyre, *À l'extrême du skepticisme* (Paris, 1947); and G. Schnurr, *Skeptizismus* (Göttingen, 1964).

In modern philosophy, Descartes has established doubt as the one and only basic methodical principle of thought (*de omnibus dubitandum*). But ordinarily Montaigne, Charron, Sanchez, and others are designated as the skeptics or Pyrrhonists of modern philosophy; especially well known is Montaigne's "Apologie de Raymond Sebond" in *Essais*, II, 12ff. Kierkegaard's knowledge of ancient skepticism stems in part from readings of Sextus Empiricus, whose writings he owned in an edition from 1621 (*ASKB* 146), and partly from Diogenes Laërtius, as well as from the histories of philosophy by Tennemann, Hegel, and others (see notes on pp. 193 and 209–211 in my edition of the *Fragments*).

In mentioning here the skepticism inherent in Hegelian philosophy, Kierkegaard is alluding to what in modern usage is called relativism, as the subsequent pertinent characterization and assessment indicate. The earliest and most prominent representatives of this outlook were the Sophists Gorgias and Protagoras, to whom Kierkegaard makes specific reference a little further on.

34
(note *):2

according to Hegel, truth is. There does not seem to exist here an allusion to any definite passage in Hegel, but Kierkegaard obviously has in mind a fundamental thought in such works as *The Phenomenology of Spirit* and *The History of Philosophy*.

34
(note *):6

the role of Imprimatur. Imprimatur means "may be printed." The phrase appearing in this passage is from Holberg's *Erasmus Montanus* (Act II, Scene 3) in which Per, a half-studied rural parish clerk, mistakes the word *imprimatur* for a title and tries to impress some farmers by asking Erasmus who the Imprimatur is this year. As late as the eighteenth century the dean of the philosophical faculty had to grant his countersignature on academic treatises before they could go to print. Both *imprimatur* and the dean's name were then affixed to a flyleaf in the printed book.

34
(note *):7

skeptical. In this case the word is used in the sense of a relativism denoting the theory of skepticism as a practical standpoint.

34
(note *):9

as illusory as happiness was in paganism. Herodotus relates (I, 32 and 86) that when the Lydian King Croesus stood at the height of his power the sage Solon said to him during the course of a conversation (quoted from the edition owned by Kierkegaard, *Die Geschichte des Herodotus*, trans. Friedrich Lange [Berlin, 1811; *ASKB* 1117], p. 19): "You are, I see, immensely wealthy and lord over many peoples. But I cannot answer your question [about his (good) fortune] until I have learned whether or not you have ended your life happily. . . . " Croesus was later taken prisoner by the Persian King Cyrus who intended to have him executed by fire. When, from the stake, Croesus cried "Solon!" three times, Cyrus, learning what lay behind this, spared the life of his enemy.

34 (note
*):11

The greatest secret of the system . . . same as the Sophism of Protagoras. The Greek Sophist Protagoras' tenet, the so-called *homo-mensura* ("man is the measure"), is an expression for a total subjectivism and relativism in epistemology. According to this theory, a universally valid truth is unattainable. Protagoras' statement is quoted in my commentary on the *Fragments*, pp. 210ff.; see also *Ancilla to The Pre-*

Socratic Philosophers, trans. Kathleen Freeman (Oxford, 1948), p. 125, and B. Schultzer's outline in *Relativitet* (Copenhagen, 1957), pp. 48ff.

It may be observed that the description that Kierkegaard here gives and, with a certain reservation ("pretty much the same"), applies to Hegel's system would not be acceptable to Hegel himself, for Hegel had in fact repudiated Protagoras (see my commentary on the *Fragments*).

34 (note *):15   *Plutarch's Moralia*. A quotation from *Moralia*, 220D. Besides the Greek edition of Plutarch's moral works, Kierkegaard owned *Plutarchs moralische Abhandlungen*, translated from Greek by J.F.S. Kaltwasser, I–V (Frankfurt am Main, 1783; *ASKB* 1192–96), in which the relevant passage reads (II, 348ff.):

> Eudamias, a son of Archidamus and brother of Agis, saw the already aged Xenocrates discoursing in the Academy with his students and inquired as to who the old man was. When told that he was a wise man in search of virtue, he replied, "And when will he use it, if he is only now looking for it?"

34 (note *):17   *The Academy* was the name given to a school for philosophy that Plato founded in Athens. It existed from 385 B.C. until A.D. 529, when Emperor Justinian abolished it. To the so-called older Academy belonged, among others, Xenocrates (ca. 396–314 B.C.), a Platonist under the influence of Pythagoreanism, with whom Kierkegaard also became acquainted in Dr. W. G. Tennemann, *Geschichte der Philosophie*, I–XI (Leipzig, 1798–1819; *ASKB* 815–26), III, 10ff.

34 (note *):24   *ataraxy*. The word means "imperturbability," "calmness," "equanimity" (from the Greek ἀτάρακτος and ἀταραξία). Ataraxy had been stressed as a principal virtue as early as Democritus. See Hermann Diels, *Fragmente der Vorsokratiker*, 7th ed., ed. W. Kranz, I–II (Berlin, 1954), II, 129, no. 16; English translation in *Ancilla to the Pre-Socratic Philosophers*, p. 92.

It was chiefly with the skeptics, however, that ataraxy became associated with *epoche* in the sense of "reserve" or "abstention"; that is, abstention from making judgments about things. Diogenes Laërtius describes it as follows (IX, 107ff.; trans. R. D. Hicks, *Loeb Classical Library*, II, 517ff.): "The end they [the skeptics] hold to be suspension of judgement, which brings with it tranquility like its shadow. . . . " The Stoics' doctrine of apathy is related to this. Kierkegaard owned a Danish translation of Laërtius, *Diogen Laërtses filosofiske Historie*, trans. B. Riisbrigh, ed. posthumously B. Thorlacius, I–II (Copenhagen, 1811–1812; *ASKB* 1110–11), in which the above quotation appears in vol. I, 448.

34 (note
*):30

Socrates proposed. This is an allusion to Plato's *Apology*, 41B: "Above all, I shall be able to continue my search into true and false knowledge; as in this world, so also in that [that is, in Hades]; I shall find out who is wise, and who pretends to be wise, and is not."

34 (note
*):35

biography of Poul Møller. "Poul Møller's Levned, med Breve fra hans Haand," by F. C. Olsen in *Poul Møllers efterladte Skrifter,* ed. F. C. Olsen, I–III (Copenhagen, 1839–1843; *ASKB* 1574–76), I, 3–115. The biographer relates that Møller

> began more and more to withdraw from Hegel, while following with a lively interest the opposition against this philosopher and his devotees, indeed even getting himself into an irritable mood, though in fact only concerning the devotees. . . . A friend once asked him to try and see if he could not in one short sentence state the basic all-important point in the Hegelian philosophy. Poul Møller kept silent awhile, stroking his chin as he lay on his sofa, and then said: "Well, Hegel is really crazy. He suffers from a monomania and thinks that the concept is able to spread out like this." Here he made some expansive movements with his hands, and said no more.

On the subject of Kierkegaard and Poul Møller see Frithiof Brandt, *Den unge Søren Kierkegaard* (Copenhagen, 1929), pp. 336ff.; Gregor Malantschuk, *Frihed og Eksistens* (Copenhagen, 1980), pp. 101–14; and H. P. Rohde in *Bibliotheca Kierkegaardiana,* X (Copenhagen, 1982).

The author begins this section by pointing out that Danish scholars, having abandoned the certainty afforded by the Bible as their objective and unshakable anchor, now resort to the Church. Climacus is here referring, as he expressly affirms, to Grundtvig's "matchless discovery" (p. 36) of "the living word in the Church, the Apostles' Creed, and the word in connection with the sacraments" (p. 37).

If the problem is treated objectively the same dilemma will emerge as we previously had in the case of the Bible, and it will be further complicated by the fact that the problem really concerns the subject's own relationship. The author insists that had Grundtvig only been acquainted with Greek skeptical philosophy he would have realized that the certainty afforded by sense perception and historical research amounts to no more than an approximation.

It is indeed an irrefutable fact that whereas the New Testament is historical when viewed objectively, the Church is a contemporary institution. But whenever we postulate an identity between the present-day Church and the primitive Church, a difficulty will arise in connection with a Church theory, for an assertion of this kind will require corroboration. It will not help to appeal to the Apostles' Creed because the historical problems concerning its sincerity, trustworthiness, and so forth—indeed the very same dilemmas as those we encountered in relation to the Bible—will immediately surface. Our progress toward a solution of these problems will be blocked by the circumstance that it is basically impossible to advance beyond the point of approximation or probability. Nor will it help to concentrate our attention on the sacrament of baptism and seek to base an eternal happiness on this. The crux of the problem is, concludes Climacus, that in relation to any historical phenomenon whatever, it is fundamentally impossible to obtain more than an approximation—and an eternal happiness cannot be based on anything that is basically uncertain.

If we assume that the course of history in itself affords a proof of the truth of Christianity we will first have to appreciate the fact that it is impossible to deal with this line of argument in its essentials. A hypothesis may certainly gain in probability through having endured for several centuries, "but it does not on that account become an eternal truth, adequately decisive for an eternal happiness" (p. 45). If we nevertheless insist that it does, this simply indicates that we have commingled and confused the categories of quantity and quality while remaining in the dark as to just what constitutes the possibility of a transition, that is, a leap.

✳   ✳   ✳

35:16   *letter-fanaticism . . . Don Quixote.* In a draft to the *Fragments* Kierkegaard writes (*Pap.* V B 1:5):

> The apologetical questions of the Bible and the Church amount to one and the same thing. People do not deny that the Church exists; but its claim to have existed and, what is more, to be apostolic is after all surely a historical question.

He then adds (*Pap.* V B 1:6; *JP* III 3047):

> For a long time now rigid letter-of-the-law orthodoxy has reverted to being a counterpart to Don Quixote, whose various ridiculous hair-splitting sophistries will provide excellent analogies.

Kierkegaard owned both Heinrich Heine's German and Dorothea Biehl's Danish translations of Cervantes' work (*ASKB* 1935–40). The import of the parenthetical phrase, "for the comic interpretation is always the concluding one," must be sought in Kierkegaard's interpretation that the comic consists in contradiction (see *Pap.* V A 85; IX 279, 280; *JP* II 1741, 1754–55, respectively). Thus in this case the solemn seriousness takes itself so seriously as to become its own travesty, thereby rendering itself impossible. The statement may be understood in connection with the episode related in the foregoing about Poul Møller's attitude to Hegelianism in his final years. The humoristic treatment of speculation once again reveals a parallel: this treatment is the "concluding" one. See Masaru Otani, "The Comical," *Bibliotheca Kierkegaardiana*, III (Copenhagen, 1980), pp. 229–36.

36:12   *"matchless discovery."* N.F.S. Grundtvig uses this expression in connection with the "independent universal validity of the Apostles' Creed" in "Troesbekjendelsens selvstændige Almeen-Gyldighed," *Maanedsskrift for Christendom og Historie*, I (Copenhagen, 1831), p. 609. The article was a review of Mynster's *Om Begrebet af den christelige Dogmatik* (Copenhagen, 1831). Grundtvig claims that "a discovery . . . that opens the most brilliant perspectives . . . for a free unfolding of Force the world will have to call matchless." By the beginning of the 1840s the expression had already become a byword among

Grundtvigians. H. Høirup maintains in articles in *Kristeligt Dagblad* for March 2, 1953, and *Nationaltidende* for March 8 of the same year that Grundtvig himself did not use this term anywhere but that it originated from Kierkegaard.

36:18   *Delbrück.* Ferdinand Delbrück (professor of philosophy in Bonn) in *Philip Melanchthon, der Glaubenslehrer: Eine Streitschrift* (Bonn, 1826). Part of this work was translated by Grundtvig and annotated in *Theologisk Maanedsskrift*, 10 (Copenhagen, 1827), pp. 122ff. (pp. 179ff. in the original German edition). *Theologisk Maanedsskrift* was edited by A. G. Rudelbach (1792–1862), who at the time was an adherent of Grundtvig but later joined the established Lutheran Church. The following quotation is from Grundtvig's translation.

On The Apostles' Creed

As a Christian Rule of Faith

(By Delbrück)

———

May be printed

Copenhagen Police Court, the 20th September 1827

P. Eberlin[1]

———

Finding support in the testimony of the oldest Fathers of the Church, Lessing held that the quintessence of the doctrine of Christian faith is embodied in the teachings promulgated as fundamental by the Church during the first three centuries, and that these were handed down in the form of a rule of faith (that is, the Apostolic). This rule was not deduced from the books of the New Testament, and it is moreover older than the Church. Not only did it completely gratify the first Christians in the days of the Apostles, but for three whole centuries it was accounted by their descendants as being perfectly satisfactory.

It is therefore not the Scriptures but the rule of faith that is to be respected as the rock on which the Church is built, all the more so because the writings of the New Testament were unknown to the first Christians. Later, the laity either did not read them at all or read them very seldom. What is more, the Ancient Church itself judged the value and authenticity of the Apostolic writings in accordance with the rule of faith. It did not prove but in passing only corroborated and illuminated the truths of faith by means of these

---

[1] Grundtvig was subjected to censorship from 1826 to 1837.

writings. Indeed even in this respect the Church attributed to them no basic importance (*urkundliches Ansehn* [authentic aspect]), but in view of their advantage let them persist by placing these Apostolic writings at the head of the writings of the old Fathers. In this position they constitute the oldest supplement to the rule of faith, though not its source. What these Scriptures contain in excess of the rule of faith was not considered necessary for eternal happiness. In all this the Ancient Church deserves to be imitated, for it is easier to substantiate the divine source (*unmittelbare göttliche Einge-bung* [immediate divine inspiration]) of the rule of faith than that of the Scriptures taken as a whole.

What moved Lessing to advance these proposals and champion them so zealously was none other than the hostile attack against the Scriptures in the *Wolfenbüttel* fragments, which are by an unknown author; for this sally against the Bible convinced Lessing of the necessity of making the fundamental theses of our faith independent of the Scriptures and their documentation. Hence these theses came to rest on a foundation where objections against the Scriptures did not strike them at all! And this necessity, which he felt so deeply—how much more compelling it has become in our day, now that our theologians have begun (and stalwartly continue) to cast doubt on the authenticity of one book of the Scriptures after another; to say nothing of the fact that as usual they pursue a course in the interpretation of the Scriptures whereby they can find all kinds of things (*alles machen aus allem* [anything is possible from any of them]) in any book whatever.

To anyone who feels very strongly about the well-being of our Church it must necessarily be a source of joy to learn that, as Lessing had desired, the statements by the Church Fathers unanimously bear witness to the fact that during the first three centuries the Church really did seek the source of its unchangeable fundamental doctrine, a doctrine that is perfectly valid without additional proofs (*keines Beweisses fähigen und bedürftigen* [capable of and requiring no proofs]). The Church made its search in a rule of faith communicated by Christ directly to the Apostles, and from this rule of faith the Apostles were to extract all of their verbal and written instructions. It followed that in relation to the fundamental doctrine, the Scriptures were merely employed as a means of further elucidation, and proofs were drawn from them only as concerns the derived, changeable (*nicht unveränderliche* [not unchangeable]) doctrines. Even so, the development of the fundamental doctrines and the definition of the derived doctrines were by no means unconditionally subject to the authority of the written word (*des Schriftsworts*). This authority was only permitted to serve as a guiding principle during such Christian investigations as were governed by the Holy Spirit. The authority and the outcome (*Ergebnisse*) of the research would have to conform; if not, the scholar would be presuming to guess at a secret meaning that was at variance with the written word.

Now if a close investigation of Lessing's proposition as here interpreted and more precisely defined were to bring out the greatest degree of probability possible in matters of this kind (which I hardly doubt), an extremely important consequence would follow: it would show that two churches drifted equally far from the Ancient Church, though in opposite directions. One church made not only conclusions (*die abgeleiteten Lehren* [the derived or deduced doctrines)] but also basic doctrines dependent on a tottering interpretation of the Scriptures, so everything became changeable. The other declared not only the fundamental doctrines but even a whole sequence of conclusions to be unchangeable. The only difference between the two churches is that it would be easier for one of them to instate the simple basic doctrines in the prestige they deserve. The other church would on the contrary find it harder to deprive the so completely deformed and complicated (*vielfach verschlungene und verzweigte* [frequently interlaced and ramified]) didactic propositions of a prestige that has endured throughout the centuries, and thus to return to the original freedom of faith!

36:19   *Lessing . . . Socratic doubt.* Kierkegaard may have had in mind Lessing's statement toward the end of *Axiomata VII*, where he writes (*G. E. Lessings sämmtliche Schriften*, I–XXXII [Berlin, 1825–1828; *ASKB* 1747–62], VI, 80ff.):

The Apostolic Creed has obviously arisen from an oral, handed-down doctrine rather than been drawn directly from the Scriptures. If the latter were the case, certain parts would be more complete, others more determinate. This not being so, it can be explained even less from the conjecture that the Creed is supposed to be merely a formula intended for catechumens than from the fact that it has arisen from an oral and traditional faith that was regarded as complete and taken for granted. For when this faith was composed, the books of the New Testament had not yet been so carefully sifted; nor had anyone perceived why they ought to be.

36:32   *Mag. Lindberg.* See the Index.

36:37   *hiatus.* Actually, "yawning." The draft (*Pap.* VI B 21:28) has "hiatically roaring." Kierkegaard, who frequently criticizes Grundtvig's mannerisms especially in his *Journals and Papers*, here intends something in the way of "bellowing" or "howling."

36:37   *more accessible to common sense.* The following may be quoted from Kierkegaard's draft (*Pap.* VI B 29):

> Grundtvig is a poet to the core, an original and sonorous hymn writer,[1] useful outside the party if the public will defray the cost of having him shaved. He has a forceful nature, even if so forceful that he seems to need strife and opposition. He is a profound man whose assertions at times are confirmed[2] in the strangest way, a bearer of witness who, intensely moved in the passion of immediacy, has worked day and night with an uncommon perseverance. He is a man with many, many abilities, even though these are not always exactly under control. As such, Grundtvig will ever assert his importance. That does not, however, concern this investigation (here I am only concerned with him as a thinker), which only deals with a single Grundtvigian idea. As a thinker, Grundtvig is a genius. But he is so immediate a genius that the genial inspiration, or the suffering a genius undergoes in connection with an idea, has with respect to his spiritual constitution something in common with what an attack of apoplexy is to the corporeal. An idea grips him, he is surprised, stirred, he will give all of mankind eternal bliss in his matchless discovery. He lacks, however, the dialectical versatility required in order in a reflective relationship to look into what he has discovered and see whether it is something great or something vacuous. Therefore, although his ideas are many, very different, and of extremely varying qualities, they all possess a common impress, a birthmark whereby they are recognizable at once—the mark of absoluteness, an undialectical or apoplectical absoluteness. Everything that Grundtvig says is absolute. The very moment he has any opinion at all it is absolute, matchless, the way to eternal bliss. Sometimes the idea, having interrupted the train of thought, does not actually come into being. Rather it becomes a motive for a lyrical effusion in which the poetical is unmistakable, whether it is a description of the total ignorance of the times, his bright promise of a matchless future, or a naive amazement at himself over once again having made a matchless discovery. He does not become a thinker when influenced [*berørt*] by an idea, but poetic in relation to the apoplectic obscurity enveloping the influ

ence [Berørelsen]. Should he revoke an [in margin: earlier] idea, he once again fails to become dialectical in relation to it; instead, he revokes the idea absolutely—because now he has been imbued with the opposite idea absolutely. The idea is [in margin: in the most variant forms of lyrical affirmation] at once ascribed such a matchless absoluteness that each and every conceptual qualification [Tanke-Bestemmelse] despairs of becoming involved with it. Just as the Mohammedans are unwilling to deal with Allah directly but simply cry, "Allah is great!"—so Grundtvig's absolute idea too can only be worshipped. Such shabbiness, a parish clerk's shriek of adoration, a bawling recognition, which as an interjectory achievement linguistically achieves everything and humanly speaking a little more than one might wish on the part of rational beings, does of course turn up once in a while. This meaningless shriek, a combination of all sorts of interjections, is however always significant as long as care is taken to shriek in the right way. For one becomes familiar with a discovery not only by observing the discovery but also by taking note[3] of whom the discovery has quite matchlessly satisfied, on whom it caused a matchless light to dawn and illuminate world history and the future of the human race. Grundtvig, who is so rigidly orthodox, is not altogether innocent of a certain superstition concerning the tremendous category of the absolute, a category that is however very treacherous. There is about it something like opening one's mouth wide to speak aloud. Of course if a man wishes to talk he cannot keep his mouth closed, but he may also open it so wide that nothing at all gets said; his mouth just stays wide open. It is possible for such an absoluteness to befall Grundtvig, which in other respects is unusual. For it is not so unusual for a genius to have a devotee who parodies him, but Grundtvig is so absolute that he is his own caricature, with his absoluteness as much a parody as his style. All that is needed is a painstaking reproduction of his style—either polemically as some time ago by Poul Møller, or in admiration as by Siegfried Ley [that is, Christian Sigfred Ley]—and we have a parody, so by doing the same thing friends and enemies produce the same effect. Indeed, even if these innocent and insignificant remarks were to stir Grundtvig, causing him to invest himself with the strength of the Ases, I am sure that he would slay me so absolutely that I would escape altogether unharmed. Understood spiritually, in order to slay what in a spiritual sense is only a very relative size, one must pay close attention to the relative. If one does not, the living man will easily satisfy himself that it is not *he* who has been slain but rather one of the monstrous absolutes against which Pastor Grundtvig defends himself, the mother tongue, the native soil, and the North—an absolute just as Grundtvig is absolutely absolute.

As a psychological curiosity this Grundtvigian absoluteness might require a more detailed elucidation. Here its treatment can be afforded only very little space, since chiefly only a particular idea is being taken into consideration, an idea for which Grundtvig once again has earned the dubious merit of absoluteness. Absoluteness is characteristic of Grundtvig even in petty things, and it is [his use of] absolutes in relation to petty things that is really most interesting to observe from a psychological point of view. It is a well-known fact that an author once in a while employs italics with a few words, either to assist the reader to follow better the course of the development or to give a particular word its proper due. But if italics are to be used successfully one must have an understanding of the relative, for the idea of italicizing is precisely relative. Instead of this relative understanding Grundtvig has a matchless understanding: he italicizes absolutely, so finally those words that are not in italics are the outstanding ones. Of course, this is really an exaggeration—by Grundtvig, not by me, and the truth as well as esthetic considerations demand that one take care not to exaggerate when speaking of Grundtvig. Grundtvig is not very economical with the relative; as soon as he uses it he does so absolutely. Italics seem to be especially on the increase in his recent works.

Now and then an author alludes to a scope of ideas that is certainly rather unfamiliar, but that is nevertheless so well known that it is pleasantly refreshing to the reader to be reminded of a previous thought instead of being presented with a novel thought in a new garb. A good author does this sparingly and prudently; Grundtvig does it absolutely. His style, especially in his more recent writings, does not embody a rousing allusion to Nordic mythology now and then. No, it has become a gobbledygook containing pixies, trolls, Dalby-Mølle [Dalby Mills], a junk-shop inventory of a hackneyed poetic phraseology, and God knows what else. One must read him with a dictionary at hand or be prepared to be unable to understand him when he interlards his style with chattels, such as skippers interlace their speech with naval terms.

A prose author with a knowledge of art employs hyphenated words at rare intervals, but with great care and usually comically, because this linguistic form does not belong to prose. But Grundtvig does everything absolutely; he and his imitators use hyphenated words with matchless affectation. Even Aristotle (in his *Rhetoric*) counsels against the employment of hyphenated words in prose, since they make an impression on the multitude only and in addition constitute a poetic reminiscence. Plutarch (in *Moralia*) recounts that King Philip was insulted because someone addressed him in hyphenated words, for he held the opinion that only a crowd should be addressed this way. In his lectures held here in 1803 Heinrich Steffens intoned a brief and epigrammatical pronouncement on the Romans; Nero was the last Roman, not Brutus. Even though the statement might be unjust, which is explainable by a partiality for the Greeks, it is nevertheless brief, ingeniously expressed, and rousing. But take Grundtvig's mile-long, italicized, and annually recurrent lectures on the Roman yoke. Is there in all that he says on this subject any additional qualification by thought? And after having cudgeled Hamann in the guise of the Romans, he generally appends to his lectures a hearty and touching peroration on life and the living, life and spirit, the school of life, the High School in Soer, in the North, on [the hill called] Skamlingsbanken—but first and last on the High School. *Posito*, I assume that all these rousing lectures have aroused us all and that we now stand ready to realize Grundtvig's idea. Might it not perchance turn out that he is simply at a loss for a more concrete idea, having principally concentrated on giving alarm? His absolute hatred of the Roman yoke and the Romans corresponds to his absolute predilection for the Greeks, who have by Grundtvig in his capacity of prophet been engaged in order, in an alliance with the Icelanders, to figure in a future world-historical season. The present writer must always admit his inferiority when his knowledge is compared with a linguistically proficient philologist's erudite acquaintance with the Greek mind [*Græciteten*]. Nevertheless this writer, through readings of the Greeks and by having many times recalled the mentality [*Sjælstilstand*] of that people, is in the situation of having found a reassurance he perhaps would never have found elsewhere. He has found a guidance beneficial to his perhaps errant and perhaps also misguided thinking, and he is in a position of not having occupied himself with any man so much as with the greatest intellectual hero of Greece—Socrates. I wonder if Socrates would have understood one, single word about the matchless future for which Grundtvig vouches. On the other hand, has Grundtvig said anything about Greece that contains definitions arrived at by thought? And at the same time he holds everything German in contempt, including the service rendered by German philologists and philosophers to Greek schol-

arship. Does his style, presentation, or behavior give evidence that
he has learned anything from that plastic representative of beauty,
art, intellectuality, and a fortunate equanimity?

So his genius as a thinker finally culminates in *"the living word"*.[4]
Anyone reasonably well acquainted with Pastor Grundtvig's writings [*in margin*: though assiduous reading] will easily be able to
imitate his mysterious [*mystiske*, also "mystical"] lecture on the
living word without exactly needing extraordinary talents, since
like witches' formulas and the like, it is cooked up by haphazardly
tossing several strong hyphenated words together. But how much
thought there is in this matchless discovery is anybody's guess. *Is
it an esthetic discovery* concerning the relationship between the written and the spoken word? Even Aristotle engaged in such investigations, and a connoisseur would be able to indulge in toothsome
and illuminating observations of this relationship. Moreover, the
observations would be valuable psychologically because maturity
of spiritual development stands in proportion to this relationship;
the living word decreases in proportion to the increase in intellectuality, a circumstance of which Aristotle was already aware. But
in Grundtvig one seeks development and thought in vain. For him
the living word has acquired the nugatory worth of absoluteness.
The written word, the dead letter, and the black lines on white
paper are dead and powerless, entirely worthless, and incapable of
producing a spark of life in a man's soul. It is like a death in which
one is living now (except for the noise made in the Danish Society
and aboard steamers)—because people write books. Compared with
such a state of affairs there was a matchless life here in the North
in antiquity when no books were written—perhaps because nobody could write. In an esthetic sense the discovery that there is a
difference between the spoken and the written word would be of
the same species as the discovery that the sun rises: matchless!—
matchless, that is, that anyone could take it into his head to call it
a discovery. The gain can therefore derive only from the performance and shrewd observation, lest the gain come to consist in reducing the discovery to nothing at all with the aid of absoluteness.
This easily happens to Grundtvig because he has a superstition concerning the tremendous category of absoluteness. He does not seem
to realize that this category is a treacherous term, that it can likewise mean nothing at all. . . . Southern nations also speak in categories of absoluteness, precisely because they lack abstraction. They
employ superlatives, measuring everything by the measuring stick

of the moment, whereby the matchless becomes a meaningless category. It may seem more vivid to speak in this way, but it is only
a less perfect image of what life really is. Anyone acquainted with
the fuss [*Væsen*] the Grundtvigians make over life and the living,
as well as with the odious practice [*Uvæsen*] they pursue with these
expressions, will easily perceive that the whole secret lies in attaining a southern childishness that, unacquainted with abstraction,
without the concentration necessary to learn from experience, and
without being disturbed by dialectical continuity, is Quakerishly
blissful in an apoplectic absoluteness.[5] Is the theory of the living
word a *discovery in the ethico-psychological field?* Does the discovery
refer to the word's power to release silent inwardness, that is, passion, next [to release] inclosedness [*Indesluttethed*], and then the demonic? Who would not gratefully read (for only Grundtvig has an
aversion to reading) what has been written on this subject by capable observers? But here again the gain would derive from the
performance. Nor would it be possible to think an absolute distinction between the written and the spoken [word], just as it would
hardly be advisable for any thinker to pretend to have thought an
absolute difference between subdivisions under the same fundamental concept.

Is it a *metaphysical discovery?* Does it concern the relationship between essence [*Væsen*] and form, that is, that the word is the essential form of thought and that this relationship embodies an absolute commensurability? Is the discovery perchance a pendant to
the Hegelian one that the outer is the inner and the inner the outer?
Alas! It [would be] extremely profitable to be able with acumen to
unravel this part of the border dispute between the logical and the
ontological. If this is the discovery, the absolute distinction again
becomes inexplicable, and any gain in connection with the discovery will attach exclusively to the performance.

Is it a *dogmatic discovery?* When talking about the living word the
speaker's tone rises in the following crescendo: the living word,
life and spirit, the mother tongue, woman's heart, Denmark's lovely
meadows [*Danmark, deiligst Vang og Vænge*, the first line of an old
and popular patriotic song], the Word of the Church, Martin Luther, the matchless discovery, the Word as it was in the beginning.[6] This last is, as everybody knows, an allusion to The Gospel
According to John 1[:1–3]. Now an allusion to that work is not
exactly a matchless discovery reserved for a world-historical genius; a Neoplatonic gnosticizing by fits and snatches is unfortunately not matchless either. Just as there were times when pagans

worshipped numbers, and just as a lottery player still concentrates
his entire conjecture on a number, so too the phrase "the word as
it was in the beginning" was and is used to produce an effect of
profundity simply by mentioning it with a hollow voice. Wherever
the dialectical and real development through thought are wanting,
a convenient short cut is taken toward the most desperate opposite
position: the profundity of the profound thought is rendered obvious by scowling,[7] by yodeling, by raising one's eyebrows, by
gazing straight ahead, by assuming a deep F in the bass scale. The
profundity ought to consist in a more concrete understanding.
Modern Speculation has also dealt with the λόγος. Trend[e]lenburg,
who owes his excellent culture and education to the Greeks, accordingly cites the following passage from a modern work as an
example of an erroneous inference (Erlaüterungen [zu den Elementen
der aristotelischen Logik (Berlin, 1842)], p. 69): "Gott ist das Wort; die
Categorie ist ein Wort; also ist die Categorie Gott." ["God is the Word;
the category is a word; therefore the category is God."] Now
Grundtvig is rarely guilty of an erroneous inference; he is much
too absolute, much too lively to respect the Roman yoke of the
syllogism. As I have said, here there would be no discovery at all,
for to discover that "the Word" is used in the New Testament
with a special pregnancy and κατ' ἐξοχήν [in an eminent sense]
would be inadvisable in the nineteenth century—in particular now
that Christianity has endured for eighteen hundred years. Is it a
historico-dogmatic discovery? So much acumen has been displayed
concerning this concept that it will take a distinguished thinker to
make discoveries. Not even Mag. Lindberg seems to have succeeded; indeed, one dares not even expect such from Grundtvig.
So without venturing with certainty to say what the living word
is according to Grundtvig's matchless discovery (and who would
venture to have an opinion about it with certainty?) I allow myself
the following hypothesis: the mystery-word is a motive enabling
Grundtvig to give free reign to his imagination.

[Pap. VI B 22,98ff.] Although what I have set forth here has led
me somewhat astray from my project, I nevertheless consider it
pertinent to throw a little light on Grundtvig. The indignation of
several devotees over my method of approach will not surprise me.
On the other hand, I would feel bad if someone to whose judgment I attribute importance were merely to marvel at the fact that
I have taken the trouble to look for thought in Grundtvig's ideas;
if he simply were to marvel at this while acquiring a lower opinion
of me than he otherwise might have had, because it seemed as

though I had expected to find something. But there is another reason that has determined me. With a worried and profound air, one moment weeping, the next heralding, then prophetic, now blissful over the fulfillment of the prophecy—in this way Grundtvig thrusts himself forward everywhere as a religious individuality with a desire to be important. Yet just as a mocker of religion may sometimes be dangerous, so too, for converse reasons, may such a figure as Grundtvig, because he is especially cut out to arouse offense. A more private concern about the religious will readily feel painfully affected by the Grundtvigian maladroit indomitability. A mixture of a distinguished poetic individuality and a vaudevillian character is a dangerous sight when people really become aware of him.

[*Pap.* VI B 29,111.] What is propounded here in one way digresses from my project yet in another is pertinent to it as a preparation for the negligible returns that Grundtvig's matchless ecclesiastical theory yields for thought. The indignation of several devotees over my method of approach will not surprise me; nor do I fear that Grundtvig, invested with the strength of the Ases, will slay me. He generally slays his opponent so absolutely [*Pap.* VI B 30,112ff.] that the slain lives on completely unharmed and untouched, for in order to hit the mark—especially to hit the mark dangerously—the lethal blow must always contain a bit of relativity. On the other hand, I would feel bad if someone to whose judgment I attribute importance were to misunderstand me, as if, seeing as there simply is nothing to be found in the Grundtvigian ideas, there were no reason even to say so. With a worried and profound air, one moment weeping, the next heralding, then prophetic, now blissful over the fulfillment of the prophecy, Grundtvig thrusts himself forward everywhere as a pretentious religious individuality who is more than willing to let himself be called Rabbi and Guide (Matt. 23:10). Yet just as a mocker of religion sometimes may be dangerous, so too, for converse reasons, may such a figure as Grundtvig, because he is especially cut out to arouse offense. A more private concern about the religious, each and every more inward understanding that in fear and trembling employs ethical categories against itself in self-concern [*Selvbekymring*], would readily feel painfully affected by that world-historical, Ale-Norse [*ølnordiske*] lack of constraint, which nonchalantly is busy only with great visions and matchless discoveries. It must feel painfully affected by that Grundtvigian maladroit indomitability: a peculiar mixture of a distinguished poetic individuality and a vaudevillian character.

[*Pap.* VI B 29,111ff.] So much for Grundtvig in general. Even though it may be doubtful whether this is the suitable place (which is why the space allotted is restricted as much as possible), nevertheless the present moment seems to be propitious now that Grundtvig has come into fashion. Of course our age, which is so strongly moved and in ferment, can always find use for an extraordinary person, a seer, a prophet, a man of strength, a supervisor, a martyr, and so forth. And when fortunately it so happens that one man is able with equal bravura to take charge of this entire repertoire of extraordinariness—and Grundtvig, whose existence has never suffered from monotony, can do this in a manner perfectly satisfactory to our age—well, no wonder he is appreciated. First with an apostolic, saintly aura about his transfigured countenance, then unrecognizable in Old–Norse [*oldnordisk*] shagginess, always a noisy personality, godly, worldly, Ancient Nordic, Christian, High Priest, Ogier the Dane; one moment jubilant, the next weeping, ever prophetic, even when things turn out so ironically that he is contemporary with a fulfillment not eyed until in some remote future—Grundtvig is not an imperceptible phenomenon. But it is open to question just how much Christian Orthodoxy has benefited from being defended with might and main by such a fantastic figure, who in the capacity of defender of Orthodoxy may readily arouse offense. A more private concern about the religious, each and every more inward understanding that in fear and trembling is disciplined by self-concern, will readily feel painfully affected by this lack of constraint, which nonchalantly is busy only with great visions and matchless discoveries. And whoever holds that one must learn by living and that to exist is an art will not exactly rejoice over the Grundtvigian result: that one can reach the age of sixty-five and still remain just as undialectical in oneself, just as extroverted, and just as noisy as in youth. This means that he is able to be a genius and become an old man without learning the least thing existential from life, even though one is polite enough to assume that the genius has taught everybody else, a situation essentially reserved only for God, who teaches others without Himself learning—and now [along comes] Grundtvig.

[1] although eccentric.

[2] *Note.* Sometimes [the confirmation is] also strange, as if what is perpetually repeated about the written word being dead and matchless [*mageløst*] were con-

firmed by a pronouncement at Court and by constitutional law—that Grundtvig's written words are "dead and powerless [*magtesløse*]."

[3] *Note.* As a rule the conclusion would be correct. But empirically one may happen to draw an incorrect conclusion if in reality a special case has arisen and one is unaware of it. Such a special case would exist if a person who is quiet and introspective in a noble sense, someone eminently gifted and in possession of an uncommon erudition and education, were decisively to join a party. This would be a special case that would have to be regarded as a psychological phenomenon whose explanation *in concreto* may be sought in different ways, or perhaps ought to be given up altogether. Only the following conclusions are indefensible and must not be made: from the eminence of the individual to that of the party, or from the genius of the party *en masse* to the insignificance of the individual. Whoever is and can be important to himself can only incidentally belong to a party in a religious sense. This is especially so with a party such as the Grundtvigian, which on an average is made up of some volunteer geniuses who, by means of a "sticky" relationship to the universal genius, take a short cut around the more humble positions in the world of spirit to pompous employment as virtual genius with a virtually "almost matchless eye for world history" in a virtually "manifest and universally genial licensed tongue." For Grundtvig is pure genius; or, if anyone prefers, unadulterated genius—we'll not quibble about words. With a relationship to him his followers remain virtually the same.

[4] *In margin*: And so finally the theory of *the living word*, which stands in the most intimate connection with the theory of the Church, since it is with the living word that the Church forms a contrast to the dead words of the Scriptures.

[5] *In margin*: Or is the living word perhaps *the mother tongue*? Does the discovery signify that everyone after all really speaks only one language and never learns another language as well as that one? Does it also mean that the originality available to the native in his mother tongue is capable of releasing his entire spiritual development? No one could care to learn more about this than I, who often enough have had to own up to the fact that I at least have been unable to learn other languages. But here again further particulars will be needed to decide whether the discovery amounts to anything or whether it is completely matchless. Until further particulars arrive, only so much is certain: Grundtvig *qua* author has not exactly enriched the mother tongue but has rather impoverished it, for he has employed many a good expression with such exaggeration and affectation that one is disgusted by them and is nearly tempted to stop using them. If such a conduct is to be called a preference for the mother tongue, it must be taken in a very particularistic (and separatistic) sense. A genuine son's lovable preference for his mother tongue is recognizable rather by his regaining the language's lost sons, by regenerating those words that have become extinct and trite through constant use and misuse, and by his restoring to them their lost originality.

[6] *Note.* This long string of words does not so much indicate the process of thought, which I do not make so bold as to do; but it is to be regarded as a prescription according to which the mysterious [*mystiske*] lecture may be prepared.

[7] *Note.* The mimical has absolutely no meaning in relation to thought. Yet such an importance is ascribed to it once in a while. I recall a man [A. P. Adler] who presumably had his entire content of thought packed into one logical proposition that he propounded as a formula. When I made a slight objection he repeated the formula; when I again made a slight objection he repeated the formula, now saying that I had not understood it and that everything essentially depended on the voice

in which the proposition is uttered. He thereupon bade me listen. Striking a sort of pose, he began to recite it three times in a row in a false voice* (half chanting). Naturally, I now conceded to him that I had understood it; what will one not do to escape from a madman?

* which to the ear produced a monotony akin to what appears to the eye when one reads ancient manuscripts, in which the writing continues on and on without any interpunctuation whatsoever.

37:12   *abusive epithets to the Bible.* The thought here may possibly concern isolated, disconnected expressions by Grundtvig, for example, in *Skal den Lutherske Reformation virkelig fortsættes?*

> By itself the Bible cannot manifest itself, for it is neither a god nor a human being nor a spirit, but only a book. Hence it is a dead object without a consciousness of its own and that spiritually as well as bodily must allow itself to be treated at the discretion of men; so to forget this and speak about the Bible as if it were able to think, talk, and perform miracles is simply a remnant of Medieval superstition. Even if this is not so obviously ridiculous as what is recounted by old priests and monks . . . it is after all really neither more Christian nor wiser. [Quoted and translated from *Grundtvigs Værker i Udvalg*, ed. Hal Koch, I–X (Copenhagen, 1940–1949), III, 286.]

37:22   *the living word*—in contrast to the "dead" written word. On this subject reference is made especially to the article by Grundtvig quoted above and to the aforementioned work by H. Høirup, more particularly to pp. 249ff.

37:28   *the aged Grundtvig.* Grundtvig was born in 1783, Kierkegaard in 1813.

38:3   *so matchless a future for Greece.* Kierkegaard is referring to Grundtvig's *Haandbog i Verdens-Historien*, I (Copenhagen, 1833), p. 321, where among other things he asserts that, "Christianly enlightened, spirit will continue its glorious course, which has been perverted and interrupted."

38(note *):3   *the inference from essence to existence is a leap.* By essence must be understood here ideal, timeless being, and by existence (*Tilværelse*) factual being in time, in history (equivalent to the two concepts *essentia* and *existentia*). The transition between the two occurs by means of a free act and with a leap. For an interpretation of this passage reference is also made especially to "The Interlude" in the *Fragments* and to Søren Holm, *Søren Kierkegaards Historiefilosofi* (Copenhagen, 1952), pp. 21–30, and Gregor Malantschuk, "Søren Kierkegaards Teori om Springet og hans Virkelighedsbegreb" in *Frihed og Eksistens* (Copenhagen, 1980), pp. 38ff.

39:29   *the pixie also moves.* The nearest English equivalent to the Danish *Nisse* [S/L: Kobold], which is sometimes conceived as a guardian spirit and at others as a mischievous one. The expression is taken from a Danish proverb that goes: "Det nytter kun lidt, at Bonden flytter, naar Nissen huser i hans Gaard, hans Kjælder, thi Nissen flytter med, som man fortæller." ("It helps but little that the farmer moves when a pixie quarters in his farmhouse or in his cellar, for the pixie also moves, as the story goes.")

40:2   *the primitive character of the Creed.* From the beginning of the 1840s things took place exactly as described in this passage. Grundtvig himself, Peter C. Kierkegaard, and J. C. Lindberg sought to provide historical proof of the correctness of the theory of the Creed as "the little word from Our Lord's own mouth" spoken by Christ to the Apostles during the forty days between the Resurrection and the Ascension. Grundtvig's chief contribution to this debate was an article, "Kirkelige Oplysninger, især for Lutherske Christne," printed in Peter C. Kierkegaard's periodical *Tidsskrift for christelig Theologie* (1840–1842) and reprinted in, among others, *Grundtvigs Værker i Udvalg,* ed. Hal Koch, I–X (Copenhagen, 1940–1949), III, 359–447. With Grundtvig the argument always proceeds from the Wolffian *demonstratio apagogica* in the following manner: It would be self-contradictory if there was a Christian Church with a creed that was not of divine origin; there exists a Christian Church as a present indisputable fact; *ergo,* the Creed must be of the origin mentioned above! See H. Høirup, *Grundtvigs Syn paa Tro og Erkendelse* (Copenhagen, 1949), pp. 36ff. and 358ff. Concerning Peter C.Kierkegaard the reader is referred to O. Holmgaard, *Peter Christian Kierkegaard, Grundtvigs Lærling* (Copenhagen, 1953), especially pp. 47–69 and to my article "The Brother Peter Christian" in *Bibliotheca Kierkegaardiana,* XII (Copenhagen, 1983), pp. 26–30.

Lindberg (1797–1857) attached himself while yet a student to Grundtvig, who at that time upheld a strict Lutheran view of the Bible. As a student Lindberg dedicated himself chiefly to Semitic philology, a subject in which he became an expert. In 1825, when Grundtvig in his polemical writing *Kirkens Gienmæle* attacked H. N. Clausen because of his work *Catholicismens og Protestantismens Kirkeforfatning, Lære og Ritus,* Lindberg immediately took the side of Grundtvig, persecuting Clausen with fanatic zeal. Clausen's standpoint was interpreted as rationalism in treatises and articles in *Theologisk Maanedsskrift, Maanedsskrift for Christendom og Historie,* and es-

pecially in *Den nordiske Kirketidende*, which Lindberg edited from 1833
to 1840. He quickly sought contact with the Moravian Brethren
(*Brødremenigheden*) in Stormgade in Copenhagen—a circle that Kierkegaard's father and the Boesen family are also known to have fre-
quented—and was a close acquaintance of Kierkegaard's older brother,
Peter. Lindberg also held Christian meetings in his own home. Owing to his sharp tongue and pen, Lindberg naturally fell into disfavor
with the clerical and secular authorities. With respect to Lindberg
reference is made especially to K. Baagø, *Magister Jacob Christian
Lindberg* (Copenhagen, 1958), the aim of which is "to establish Lindberg's central position in the history of earlier Grundtvigianism from
ca. 1825 to 1840 and his decisive influence on the ecclesiastical life of
that period" (p. 18). As a motto the book uses Kierkegaard's appreciative statements about Lindberg in the *Postscript*.

40:27   *recourse to ancient books.* J. C. Lindberg in "Om den christne Troes-
Bekjendelses Form i den sidste Udgave af den danske Alterbog,"
Nordisk Kirketidende (Copenhagen, 1834), cols. 829ff., where he refers
to, among others, Bois-Clair, *Le cathécisme évangélique en trois langues,
françoise, danoise et allemande* (Copenhagen, 1697).

40:29   *a new renunciation.* That is, besides the renunciation that is pronounced before the Creed: I renounce the Devil with all his works
and pomps.

41:6   *the subsequent-historical.* In other words, the intervening time in the
history of the Church from the Ascension to the present.

41:19   *the variation in the reading of the confession, which Lindberg has himself
discussed exegetically.* The reference here is to *Nordisk Kirketidende* (Copenhagen, 1834), cols. 828ff. (1836), cols. 305ff., as well as to the article
"Frimodig Gjendrivelse af Hr. Biskop J. P. Mynsters Forsvar for den
privilegerede Vaisenhuus-Cathecismus" (Copenhagen, 1836). The
dispute about "the little 'e' " is presented by Baagø in the work mentioned above, pp. 232–38. In the New Book of Common Prayer
(Copenhagen, 1830) *den hellige Aand* appears in place of the previous
den Helligaand (both mean the Holy Spirit), whereupon Lindberg
maintained that the new form implied a repudiation of the Holy Spirit
as a person (Baagø, *Magister Lindberg*, p. 233).

41(note   *presume to judge infallibly the secrets of the heart.* It was characteristic
†):2   that the official ecclesiastical and secular authorities attacked Lindberg's person just as violently as they did his views, and they even
accused him of harboring unscientific motives. It may be mentioned
in this connection that a generation later H. N. Clausen, discussing
the dispute that arose as a result of Grundtvig's attack on him, had

this to say about Lindberg in his memoirs, *Optegnelser om mit Levneds og min Tids Historie* (Copenhagen, 1877), p. 117:

> Now, after so much has intervened and moss has even grown above his grave, that man [Lindberg] is to me simply a psychological curiosity. He knew how to keep the dispute going for *five whole years* with the unfailing talent of an attorney. Every time it seemed to be on the verge of dying out he was ready with a new pamphlet; he had an inexhaustible supply of variations on the same theme and he knew how to speculate in the tastes of the reading masses with piquant titles and the most insulting accusations.

Later Clausen speaks of Lindberg's manner of disputing as "perfidious." Baagø (*Magister Lindberg*, pp. 15–17) mentions several contemporary and later evaluations of Lindberg.

41(note †):3   *with which sort of judgment Lindberg has always been pursued.* See H. N. Clausen, *Den theologiske Partiaand* (Copenhagen, 1830), in which Lindberg is repeatedly accused of distortions, and so forth. For example, he states on page 83:

> first by exchanging its expressions with others, then by omitting, now by adding one or several words without distinguishing them by means of quotation marks, and all this with such judicious selection as to make the entire observation look hard and cutting or paradoxical and offensive.

41(note †)   The printed manuscript reads (*Pap.* B 98:14):

> so the difference between the two men is this: Lindberg is a brilliant and clever man with an uncommon erudition and exceptional dialectical power of endurance who has tendered a service with intelligent moderation; Grundtvig, on the other hand, is (as a thinker) a bewildered genius who is absent from himself in loftiness, profundity, and the world-historical. In circumstances of life the difference has always been that Lindberg has been scorned, mocked, and insulted at every opportunity, probably because his power has indeed made itself felt; whereas Grundtvig has enjoyed a meaningless recognition under the azure category of: Genius, Seer, Bard, Prophet.

42:28   *attach his eternal happiness to it.* That is, to the confession of faith.

42:36   *baptism.* Julius Købner (1806–1884) and an engraver, Peder Christian Mønster, were the first leaders of the Baptists in Denmark. A small circle of adherents gathered around Mønster, and on October 27, 1839, the group was baptized by immersion in Lersøen, a lake just outside Copenhagen, by the leader of the Baptist Church in Hamburg, J. G. Oncken (1800–1884). In consequence of this, a lawsuit was inaugurated on the part of the public, for a royal decree of January 13, 1741 (the so-called Conventicle Mandate, described by Johannes Pedersen in *Den danske Kirkes Historie*, I–VIII, ed. Hal Koch and Bjørn Kornerup [Copenhagen, 1950–1966], V, 200ff.) requiring that religious assemblies be convoked under the leadership of the clergy and a royal ordinance of March 15, 1745 were directed against the Separatists and Anabaptists. According to these prescripts, the practice of the Baptists was illegal, and since they refused to cease their practices Mønster was arrested on December 2, 1840.

Negotiations were then started through the inducement of Elisabeth Fry, the famous English Quaker who visited Denmark in 1841 to obtain information on conditions in the Danish prison system. On April 14, 1842, E. C. Tryde, Archdeacon of The Church of Our Lady (Vor Frue Kirke), received authority to discuss with Mønster, who was still being held under arrest, the possibility of producing a Baptist confession of faith. Mønster firmly insisted that the Baptists had withdrawn from the state church, and that the latter's baptism was a sinful act with which the Baptists could have nothing to do. The decisive point for them was not the form of baptism (sprinkling or immersion) but the confession made prior to baptism. Pursuant to the discussions, Tryde himself made the proposal that the Baptists be permitted to let their children remain unbaptized until the age of nineteen, which according to a royal ordinance of May 25, 1759, was the utmost age limit for confirmation. Bishop Mynster, on the other hand, steadfastly maintained that the Danish Christian community is identical with the Danish Evangelical Lutheran Church and that every child born had therefore to be reckoned as a member of that religious society, the only community recognized by the state. Consequently, such children should be baptized, if necessary by compulsion. A royal resolution of December 23, 1842, in agreement with Mynster's point of view ordained that the children of Baptist parents were to be baptized, whereupon the Baptist children of Copenhagen were by force or cunning removed from their homes and brought to Trinity Church, there to be baptized against the will of their parents.

In his writing *Om Religions-Forfølgelse* (Copenhagen, 1842) Grundtvig expressed himself trenchantly against the use of civil compulsion in religious matters, and Peter C. Kierkegaard, then vicar in Pedersborg-Kindertofte near Sorø, refused to comply with the resolution on compulsory baptism. When the matter once again became current in 1845, the Chancellery followed Mynster's view and in a letter dated February 11 gave Peter Kierkegaard fourteen days in which to choose between compulsory baptism of Baptist children or dismissal from his position (see Kierkegaard's letters to his brother Peter in *Breve*, nos. 116, 117, 118). Faced with this option, Peter Kierkegaard nevertheless decided not to baptize the Baptist children by force— but nothing happened to him. King Christian VIII and the Chancellery did not dare to implement coercive measures.

Kierkegaard took the side of Mynster in this affair, whereas against Mynster stood (besides those mentioned above) H. N. Clausen, D. G. Monrad, H. L. Martensen, A. S. Ørsted, and Mynster's son-in-law, J. H. Paulli. After various discussions, in which the clerical conferences of both Roskilde and Copenhagen were implicated, the Chancellery received authorization to submit a proposal for the abolition of the provision for compulsory baptism. Before the proposal for a new royal decree was worked out, however, D. G. Monrad as March-Minister (1848) and his successor, J. N. Madvig, had carried through religious freedom by law. With the constitution of June 5, 1849, compulsion on the part of the established Church was eliminated, so the Baptists were also recognized as a religious community. See Michael Neiiendam, *Frikirker og Sekter*, 3rd ed. (Copenhagen, 1948), pp. 76–85, and Hal Koch, *Den danske Kirkes Historie*, VI (Copenhagen, 1954), pp. 304ff.

43:15   *simply in order to make sure.* The printed manuscript has (*Pap.* VI B 98:15):

> *Note.* Prof. Martensen, who is otherwise equipped with the fortunate prerequisites for becoming a dogmatic thinker, has not exactly legitimated himself as such in his little booklet on baptism. The professor establishes baptism as decisive for eternal happiness; but for safety's sake* he however adds: that anyone not baptized can also be eternally happy. It is scientific to stand ready to serve in every way with fine sand and gravel. All that is needed is for many readers of this booklet to become reassured in the matter of their eternal happiness,** and as to this I (most respectfully) have no doubt. This is what is called satisfying the demands of the times and being understood by the times. Without infinitely interested passion the whole question and all the talk about an eternal happiness are coquetry; but God help the person with an infinite and passionate interest who is put away in a lonely cell with such dogmatic guidance.

> * *In margin*: he seems (naively) to assume, and that without making sure by using dialectical safety measures.

** *In margin*: Strangely enough, in our age it is not difficult at all to reassure people with respect to their eternal happiness; rather it is difficult to make them uneasy about it.

43:37   *the children of Abraham*. See Rom. 9:7.

44:24   *to have Grundtvig as an ally*. Compare the unpublished continuation in the draft quoted above.

45:10   *Pastor Grundtvig enjoys . . . tribute of admiration and accidentalia*. The Danish Ecclesiastical Ordinance of 1539 decreed that clerics were to enjoy the same privileges as before. The farmers were to yield a tenth of their corn and cattle, and every vicar was to retain his vicarage with all its privileges and adjoining lands, along with his right to receive offerings on the three most important feasts. Shortly thereafter it was prescribed that everyone was in addition to give an offering on the occasions of the first churching of a woman, a marriage, and a burial, in accordance with fixed rates. Kierkegaard's remarks, which are to be taken figuratively, refer to these fixed and accidental offerings, hence offerings on "accidental," irregular occasions. In Kierkegaard's time these offerings still constituted an appreciable portion of a clergyman's income.

45:16   *Seer, bard, skald, prophet, and so forth*. Compare the following from Kierkegaard's draft (*Pap*. VI B 33):

As a poet, as a hymn writer, as a speaker, as a forceful nature who, intensely moved in the passion of immediacy, has worked day and night with exceptional perseverance, as a man with many, many talents, even if these are not exactly under control, Grundtvig will always be of consequence; but as a thinker his significance is very dubious. Suppose there existed a contractual relationship between readers and authors. If a youth obediently and perhaps even with unusual admiration has recourse to the study of an author and is justified in complaining when he feels disappointed, then such a person would probably have that right against Grundtvig. The absolute world-historical alarm is sounded, it can be heard across more than one kingdom, the rush is on—one reads, and even if it were a matter of life and death one would be in no position to extract any definitions by thought from it all. Now, in time one can grow accustomed to this contemporary noise, just as with living next door to a coppersmith. In time one can learn how to avoid being taken in, even though willingly conceding that Grundtvig is at one's service in every way wherever there may seem to be need of a supervisor, a seer, a bard, or a prophet. His existence does not suffer from monotony but is rich in exceptional variety. First he makes his entry into the contemporary age weeping, weeping over the darkness and ignorance of the age; then he opens up bright and smiling prospects of a golden year to come; one moment he is as old as if born at the time of the Reformation; the next he traipses youthfully with a light flourish of his hat, and although his hair is turning gray his eyes sparkle with (he says) the fire of youth; and so he stands on Mount Tabor and prophesies but understands that it will not be the lot of the prophet to set foot in the Promised Land; he will not himself partake of the matchless future he eyes at a distance of one or two centuries—until suddenly on the occasion of a popular amusement he discovers that the prophecy has been fulfilled and that now it is time to knock off work. Is it any wonder that he has become so popular lately? A generation so deeply moved as the present indeed always has use for an ambassador *extraordinarius*, whether seer, skald, martyr,§ prophet, or hero of the present. And when fortunately it just so happens that one man is able to play all these roles with equal bravura, that he merely needs to shave his beard off † in order no longer to be a prophet but a standard bearer*—no wonder this man is an indispensable performer!

As a thinker his genius consists, among other things, in abrogating the concept when intending to posit it. Although it is therefore often enough seen in this world that a genius has a follower by his side who parodies him, Grundtvig as a thinker offers the rarer phenomenon of being a genius who at the same time is his own caricature—so absolute is he.

§ a strong man.
† or put an imitation nose on.
* for young Denmark.

The printed manuscript (*Pap.* VI B 98:17) continues with:

His existence is itself a parody to such an extreme that it need merely be narrated quite simply, and one has written a satire. In like manner his style is so parodic that merely a painstaking rendering of it constitutes a parody, for instance, the polemical version done once by Poul Møller or the enthusiastic version by Siegfried Ley [Christian Sigfrid Ley]. The fact that friend and enemy by doing the same thing produce the same effect simply provides excellent proof that Grundtvig's style is intrinsically a parody.

46(note   *Jean Paul.* (Jean Paul Richter, 1763–1825). It has not been possible
*):1   to verify this statement. Kierkegaard writes in the manuscript (*Pap.*
            VI B 25; *JP* III 3607):

> Jean Paul is the one who has said that even if we eliminated all
> the proofs for the truth of Christianity, there would still remain
> the fact that Christianity has endured for 18 centuries.

46:36   *weighed and found wanting.* Dan. 5:27.

47:17   *Icelander.* Efforts to throw light on the source of this have been to
            no avail.

47:34   *they know not what they do.* Luke 23:34.

Besides the works mentioned above reference for the entire section
is made to Carl Weltzer, *Grundtvig og Søren Kierkegaard* (Copenhagen,
1952); Søren Holm, *Grundtvig und Kierkegaard* (Copenhagen and Tübingen, 1956) and Jørgen K. Bukdahl's review of this work in *Kierkegaardiana*, III (Copenhagen, 1959), pp. 116–21; and Jørgen Bukdahl
(Sr.), "Grundtvig og Kierkegaard," *Kierkegaardiana*, IX (Copenhagen, 1974), pp. 196–219. See also my article on Grundtvig in *Bibliotheca Kierkegaardiana*, XIII (Copenhagen, 1983).

Climacus begins this portion with reflections on the relationship between speculative philosophy and Christianity. From a speculative point of view, he writes, Christianity is regarded as a historically given entity. The speculative philosopher endeavors to solve the problem of the eternally valid truth of Christianity—or its philosophical quality of truth—by interpenetrating this truth with thought. The result of these efforts is an insistence on an identity between atemporal thought and Christianity as a historical presence.

The speculative philosopher maintains that his thinking begins without presuppositions. In this instance, however, he presupposes Christianity as something taken for granted. He also assumes that we are all Christians, even though it is really a matter of indifference to him whether anyone accepts Christianity or not.

Following this outline of the speculative position, Climacus notes that it may conceivably be altogether impossible to consider Christianity in accordance with the speculative philosopher's intentions. The reason may perhaps be that by rights Christianity must be interpreted to mean subjectivity or an actualization of inwardness (*Inderliggørelsen*), so it is impossible to learn anything at all about Christianity with the disinterest required by objective thought, for "only the like is understood by the like" (p. 51).

Climacus concludes that the problem raised in the investigation cannot arise at all for the speculative observer, any more than it could in paganism. He also ascertains that an identity between the divine and the human, which the speculative philosopher insists on, is an illusion. Man is a synthesis of the temporal and the eternal, so as long as he lives in time he cannot be purely eternal, as our speculative philosopher would have it.

*   *   *

49:7   *bittweise*. As a petition, beggingly. The German word is actually a translation of what according to Roman law is said to be possessed *precario* (from *precari* to pray) and refers to what has been acquired by means of prayer and favor and which therefore can only be possessed through the goodness of others. In *The Science of Logic* (I, 86; *W.a.A.* III 69; *Jub. Ausg.* IV 79) Hegel employs the word *bittweise* to denote scientific disciplines that, unlike his speculative philosophy, do not begin without presuppositions, but which

> presuppose their object, and take leave to assume [*bittweise*] that everyone has the same idea of it, and is likely to discover in it roughly the same determinations that they themselves indicate and extract from the object in various ways by analysis, comparison, and other forms of reasoning.

Hegel began his logic with the doctrine of being, which in its abstract purity turns out to be identical with nothing. See above, Introduction, chap. 4, and Kuno Fischer's presentation in *Geschichte der neuern Philosophie*, 2nd printing, I–X (Heidelberg, 1904–1912), VIII[1], 448ff.

50:29   *Socrates says.* In Plato's *Apology*, where Socrates defends himself against Meletos' accusation of atheism (27B):

> Did ever any man believe in horsemanship, and not in horses? or in flute-playing, and not in flute-players? No, my friend; I will answer to you and to the court, as you refuse to answer for yourself. There is no man who ever did. But now please to answer the next question: Can a man believe in spiritual and divine agencies, and not in spirits or demigods?
> He cannot.

50:36   *advanced beyond Christianity.* A jab at the right-wing Hegelians, for example, Martensen—who wished to advance beyond Hegel. See my edition of the *Fragments*, p. 156, and Hermann Brandt, *Gotteserkenntnis und Weltentfremdung* (Göttingen, 1970).

50:39   *à la Münchhausen.* See for example *Wunderbare Reisen . . . des Freiherrn von Münchhausen* (Copenhagen, 1813).

51:20   *quidquid cognoscitur. . . .* "Whatever is known, is known in the mode of the knower." The expression is undoubtedly a quotation, but it has been impossible to verify. Thomas Aquinas uses a similar expression in *Summa Theologica*, III, quest, 10:2.

52:10   *where God is negatively present in subjectivity.* As Junghans points out in his note 127, this may mean either that God as the final presupposition for all cognition cannot Himself be known, or that through a consciousness of guilt and sin God has given man to understand his distance from God. Of these two possible interpretations, the latter—conformable to the intention of the *Postscript*—is preferable to the first, which would be to interpret Kierkegaard from Schleiermacher's point of view.

52:16   *philosophy has arrived at an understanding of the necessity of the histori-*

cal. In Hegel's system it is an axiom that the historical course of events proceeds with metaphysical necessity, which is supposed to reflect the unfolding of the idea in time according to the law of dialectics. So too nature is the unfolding of the idea in space. Hegel emphasizes this axiom especially in *The Phenomenology of Spirit* and *The Philosophy of History*. See the Introduction, chap. 4, and my article in *Bibliotheca Kierkegaardiana*, IV (Copenhagen, 1979), pp. 84–87.

52:36   *Hegelian principle, that the external is the internal*, and so forth. In *The Science of Logic*, where the following appears in the section on "Appearance" (II, 158ff.; *W.a.A.* IV 183; *Jub. Ausg.* IV 661; *Enc.*, §133; *Logic*, pp. 242–44):

> Inner, as simple intro-reflected identity, is the immediate, and consequently is as much Being and externality as Essence; and Outer, as manifold and determinate Being, is only Outer, that is, it is posited as unessential and as having passed back into its Ground—in other words, as Inner. This transition of each into the other is their immediate identity as foundation; but also it is their mediated identity; for each is through its Other what it is in itself, the totality of the Relation. Or conversely the determinateness of each side is mediated with the other determinateness through the fact that in itself it is the totality; thus the totality mediates itself with itself through form or determinateness, and the determinateness mediates itself through its simple self-identity.

52:39   *to abolish . . . the distinction between the visible and the invisible Church*. The Greek word *ekklesia* actually means all those called out, and in classical Greek denotes in particular the Athenian popular assembly in which all free citizens had a seat and a vote. Similarly, *ekklesia* as used in the New Testament does not mean merely a group of Christians, but all Christians. In addition, the Greek translation of the Old Testament, *Septuaginta* (generally abbreviated as LXX; see my edition of the *Fragments*, p. 254) employs *ekklesia* as the usual translation of the Hebraic *qaha'l*, which in turn signifies the whole of Israel when convoked for worship or war. The Greek word thereupon acquired a sacred association and was adopted by the Christian Church. In the New Testament the word thus primarily denotes the totality of Christians; and, second, it may be applied to a local congregation. In the narrative in *The Acts of the Apostles* (2:41ff.) about the first congregation in Jerusalem the word occurs with both meanings and always as a mark of respect intended to characterize Christians as the true people of God, the new Israel, the chosen, the holy. The most salient aspect of this Church is that it exists only in and by virtue of Christ. In some passages in the New Testament this is expressed by calling the Church the body of Christ, just as Christ is called the Head of the Church (see in this respect É. Mersch, *La théologie du corps mystique*, 2nd ed., I–II [Paris, 1946]). The founding of the Church is traceable to Matt. 18:16 and Acts, chap. 2, and it is scarcely possible to posit a Church theory without stressing the fact that its basis is Jesus of Nazareth as Lord and Christ. Modern research on the New Testament (especially the Swedish with A. Fridrichsen and his pupils and O. Linton, and the Swiss with O. Cullmann, as the leading names) emphasizes the Church theory as fundamental in the New Testament while stressing the fact that the New Testament makes no distinction between a visible and an invisible church.

Augustine was the first to make this distinction. With him the Church is in one respect the visible institution of salvation. But in another respect it is the *congregatio sanctorum*, the community of the holy encompassing the pious who belong to the Church in the proper sense of the word and who, living within the visible Church, cannot be visibly distinguished from it. In the strictest sense, the Church to Augustine's mind consists of those predestined for salvation; but since these need not necessarily belong to the visible Church, the Church in the proper sense of the term is invisible.

More than a millennium later Calvin differentiated between a visible and an invisible Church in a similar fashion: the invisible embraces those whom God has decided to select for salvation, whereas the external and visible organized Church comprises both the chosen and the rejected. So too the Lutheran Orthodoxy makes a distinction between the visible Church comprising the baptized who adhere to the pure doctrine, and within this visible Church—which by virtue of the pure doctrine is the true Church—the invisible Church consisting of the true believers. See for example D. Hollazius, *Examen theologicum acroamaticum vniversam theologiam theticopolemicam complectens*, ed. R. Tellerus (Leipzig, 1750), Part IV, chap. I, quest. IX, pp. 1281ff.: "*an ecclesia recte diuiditur in visibilem et inuisebilem?*" The Pietists tried to make this invisible Church visible by gathering the true believers into small Christian communities called *ecclesiolae in ecclesia*. In the Age of Enlightenment the visible Church was understood as a purely human organization, so the invisible Church came to be an abstract principle.

Kierkegaard's reference in the *Postscript* is probably to the latter distinctions, with which he was acquainted mainly from Karl Hase's textbook of dogmatics, *Hutterus redivivus oder Dogmatik der evange-*

lisch-lutherischen Kirche, 4th ed. (Leipzig, 1839; *ASKB* 581), §124: "Ecclesia visibilis et invisibilis." It may be mentioned that Martensen maintains in his *Den christelige Dogmatik* (Copenhagen, 1849; *ASKB* 653), §191, that "the true Church is at the same time invisible and visible." Hegel also differentiates between a visible and invisible Church, though only as two aspects of the same thing (see *W.a.A.* XVIII 205; *Jub. Ausg.* III 226).

Concerning Kierkegaard's view of the Church the reader is referred to Valter Lindström, *Efterföljelsens teologi hos Sören Kierkegaard* (Lund, 1956), pp. 187–227, and P. Wagndal, *Gemenskapsproblemet hos Sören Kierkegaard* (Lund, 1954).

53:31   *sure spirit of faith.* This expression is from Ps. 51:12 (see also Ezek. 11:19).

53:38   *recessive self-feeling of the subject.* The "self" according to Kierkegaard may mean both the natural and the God-given self, and room is made for the self given by God to the same degree that natural self-esteem (*Selvfølelse*) diminishes (recedes).

54:14   *the money-changers in the forecourts of the temple.* Matt. 21:12.

54:19   *Aristotle. Nicomachean Ethics.* 1177a–1178b.

54:34   *Since man is a synthesis. . . .* Synthesis actually means to put together or combine. Kant in particular employed the concept of synthesis and Fichte established a triad, thesis/antithesis/synthesis, as his method in pursuing speculative thought. Hegel, on the other hand, called the third term "the higher unity": that is, mediation.

Kierkegaard's concepts of anthropology and synthesis differ from those of speculative idealism, as is evident especially from *The Concept of Anxiety* and *The Sickness Unto Death.* In *The Concept of Anxiety* (*SV* IV 348; *KW* VIII 41), he writes: "Man is a synthesis of the psychical and the physical; however, a synthesis is unthinkable if the two are not united in a third. This third is spirit."

See Gregor Malantschuk, *Indførelse i Søren Kierkegaards Forfatterskab* (Copenhagen, 1953), pp. 16ff.; Johannes Sløk, *Die Anthropologie Kierkegaards* (Copenhagen, 1954); Arild Christensen, "Om Søren Kierkegaards Inddelingsprincip," *Kierkegaardiana,* III (Copenhagen, 1959), pp. 21–28; Paul Sponheim, *Kierkegaard on Christ and Christian Coherence* (London and New York, 1968); and Mark C. Taylor, *Journeys to Selfhood* (Los Angeles, 1981).

As an exemplification of the issues under investigation, Climacus now chooses Lessing. Lessing in fact isolated himself in subjectivity, and it is impossible to find or formulate his result concerning Christianity. Religious subjectivity entails just such an isolation, for the "course of development of the religious subject has the remarkable trait that it comes into being for the individual and closes behind him" (p. 62). Both Lessing's style and his conduct when confronted by Jacobi and Lavater, who tried to pin him to a definite view, were compatible with this proposition.

This being the case, the author may now urge Lessing as an example, though of course without certainty that he is justified in doing so. A subjective existing thinker must be alert to the dialectic of communication; in other words, whereas objective thought takes no interest in the thinking subject, the subjective thinker must on the contrary be personally involved in his thinking. A corresponding antithesis becomes manifest in that objective thinking is interested in results, whereas the subject is interested in the method and a coming-into-existence (*Tilblivelsen*) and is thereby prohibited from concerning himself with results. The subjective thinker's method corresponds to the lack of a conclusion in the earlier Platonic dialogues. He must first think the universal, and this constitutes his first reflection. But as he concentrates his efforts on existing in what he thinks, a second or double reflection emerges and isolates him. A third antithesis between the two forms of thinking turns up in the question regarding the form of communication. Whereas objective thought requires an immediate or direct form, subjective thought must use the reflective or immediate, for inwardness precludes the application of a direct form of communication. Now inasmuch as the existing subject exists he is in a process of coming-into-existence, and so his form of communication must correspond to that of existence. It is quite a different matter for those who claim to possess a positive insight. Their brand of positivism, however, cannot lead to the truth, for the certainty of sense perception is deceptive, historical certainty is a delusion, and speculative certainty and its supposed results are an illusion (p. 75).

The subjective existing thinker properly speaking is neither purely negative nor purely positive, but both; for he has the eternal in him even though he exists in them. This may also be given expression by saying that he has as much of the comic as he has of pathos; or, if a definition of existence is desired, Climacus would comply with our request by asserting that it is "the child that is born of the infinite and the finite, the eternal and the temporal, and [which] is therefore a constant striving" (p. 85).

Following these introductory remarks concerning essential issues, the author turns to a discussion of considerations that "are more definitely referable to Lessing" (p. 86). Lessing first of all asserted that accidental, historical truths can never become proofs for eternal truths of reason; and second, that the transition whereby one bases an eternal happiness on historical testimony takes place by means of a leap.

Climacus now undertakes an examination of these two propositions. Placing them in relation to *Philosophical Fragments*, he arrives at the conclusion that the paradox of Christianity must consist in the fact that as concerns both revelation and the single individual it always posits a relationship between time and the historical on the one hand and the eternal on the other (p. 88). It is in this context that Lessing's observations are of consequence in the religious and philosophical debate, for it was he who repudiated the idea of a direct transition from what is historically trustworthy to an eternal decision. Climacus also maintains that all the talk in modern or Hegelian philosophy of a direct transition has even been modified to imply that the eternal is quite simply the historical. As mentioned above, Lessing speaks on the contrary of the transition as a leap; but Climacus is not quite sure whether Lessing intended this expression to be anything other and more than merely a linguistic turn of speech (p. 96).

*   *   *

59:29   *Peter the Deacon.* In Holberg's *Erasmus Montanus* (Act I, Scene 2) Per Degn (Peter the Deacon), a smatterer, tells the parents of the student Erasmus that to become a parson one must first be a deacon or parish clerk (*Degn*).

60:8   *bluster of the world-historic.* Aimed at Grundtvig.

60:8   *violence of the systematic.* Aimed at Hegel.

60:19   *Lessing . . . a scholar . . . a librarian.* Lessing spent his last ten years as a librarian at the ducal library in Wolfenbüttel, where he occupied himself with his literary, historic, and religious-philosophical writings. Kierkegaard may have acquired his knowledge of Lessing's biography from, among others, Johann Friedrich Schink, "Lessings Leben," in vol. I of the edition of Lessing's works that he owned (see *ASKB* 1747–62 and note following).

60:31   *line of demarcation . . . between poesy and the formative arts.* An allusion especially to Lessing's "Laokoon," which Kierkegaard read in G. E. *Lessings sämmtliche Schriften,* I–XXXII (Berlin, 1825–1828; *ASKB* 1747–62). Lessing distinguishes between the formative arts in the dimension of space and poetry in the dimension of time. See O. Mann, *Lessing* (Hamburg, 1949), pp. 81–160.

60:37   *unpretentious dress of the fable.* Lessing's own fables and translations of others (for example, Aesop's Fables) are found in vol. XVIII of the edition of his works mentioned in the note above.

62:6   *town-criers and docents.* That is, Grundtvigians and Hegelians.

63:23   *systematic railway of world history.* In Hegel's posthumously published *Lectures on the History of Philosophy* (III, 404ff.; *Jub. Ausg.* XIX 529ff.) Lessing is mentioned only in passing in a few passages.

64:16   *in verba magistri.* In the words of the teacher. See Horace, Ep. I, 1, 14.

64:28   *the traveller.* See p. 545 in the *Postscript* where the anecdote is repeated.

64:36   *And now his style!* Lessing's style was a prototype for that used in the *Postscript.*

65:11   *the heretics.* An allusion to *Repetition* (*KW* VI 225; *SV* III 287) in which Constantin relates Clement of Alexandria's well-known practice of writing in a way that was incomprehensible to heretics.

65:30   *Jacobi's enthusiastic eloquence.* This refers to the well-known conversation that F. H. Jacobi (1743–1819) had on June 6, 1780, and that he has related in "Briefe über die Lehre des Spinoza," *Sämmtliche Werke,* I–VII (Leipzig, 1812–1815; *ASKB* 1722–28), IV^1, 37ff. This copy is preserved in the Kierkegaard Archives in the Royal Library of Copenhagen. See also H. Thielicke, *Offenbarung, Vernunft und Existenz, Studien zur Religionsphilosophie Lessings* (Gütersloh, 1957), pp. 105ff.; and Jacques Colette, *Histoire et absolu* (Paris, 1972), pp. 159ff.

65:31   *Lavater's . . . concern for his soul.* Johann Casper Lavater owes his reputation as a theological author to three works: *Aussichten in die Ewigkeit, Pontius Pilatus,* and *Nathanael,* which were published between 1769 and 1786. Kierkegaard owned his *Physiognomische Fragmente zur Beförderung der Menchenkenntnisz und Menchenliebe* (Leipzig and Winterthur, 1775–1778; *ASKB* 613–16). The statement that Lavater is supposed to have made about Lessing has been sought in vain.

65:33   *his last words.* See page 91ff. in the *Postscript.*

65(note *Hegel.* It has been impossible to bring the source of this to light.
*):1

Karl Rosenkranz, who describes Hegel's final hours in *Hegels Leben* (Berlin, 1844), pp. 422–28, communicates nothing on this subject.

66:7   *Cato Uticensis*. The reference here is to the elder Cato's statements according to Plutarch's *Apopthegmata reg. et imp. Cato*, XVIII: "Concerning people who took ridiculous things seriously, he said that they would be ridiculous in serious situations." Kierkegaard owned several editions and translations of Plutarch (*ASKB* 1172–1200), including *Plutarchs moralische Abhandlungen*, trans. J.F.S. Kaltwasser, I–V (Frankfurt am Main, 1783; *ASKB* 1192–96).

66:19   πολύμητις 'Οδύσσευς. That is, the ingenious Ulysses. The expression appears in several passages in Homer; for example, *Iliad*, I, 311.

66:21   *Darin haben Sie recht*. . . . "In that you are right; if only I had known."

68:11   *a double reflection*. A result of thought is formulated by deliberation or reflection, whereas the second or double reflection concerns the relation of the result to the individual. See also Jens Himmelstrup, "Terminologisk Register," *SV* XV 553ff.

68:35   *process of becoming*. This phrase is used throughout to render the Danish *i Vorden*, where *Vorden* means "becoming" in the sense of genesis. In *The Concept of Irony* (*SV* XIII 128 note) Kierkegaard equates it with the Greek γένεσις. (Note by R.J.W.)

69:26   *worship . . . in truth*. Compare John 4:23.

71.27   *the vineyard*. The expression is taken from the parable in Matt., chap. 20.

72:19   *Adresseavis* [S/L: newspapers]. *Adresseavis* ("The Advertiser") was orginally a medium for advertisements and was called *Kjøbenhavns Adresse-Comptoirs Efterretninger*. It was started in 1706 by F.v.d. Osten's licenced advertising office and in 1726 was taken over by printer J. Wielandt, who the year before had begun publication of *Addres og Notifications Relation*. The paper did not acquire much importance, however, until 1759 when Hans Holck assumed control of it. He began to print general news as well but subsequently eliminated the news material, and until 1888 the paper remained a mere advertiser. It ceased publication entirely in 1908.

74:8   *Socrates . . . his demon*. Socrates discusses his demon in many passages in Plato's dialogues. See for example *Apology* 27, 31; *Phaedon* 99.

In Greek popular religion demons were inferior divine beings in a sense that often closely approximates "fate" or "guardian spirit." See M. P. Nilsson, *Geschichte der griechischen Religion*, 2nd ed., I–II (Munich, 1940–1950), I, 216–22; *Theologisches Wörterbuch zum Neuen Tes-*

tament, II, 1ff.; William Norvin, *Sokrates* (Copenhagen, 1934), pp. 94–110; and Paul Friedländer, *Platon*, 2nd ed., I–II (Berlin, 1957), I, 34–63.

With Socrates the demonic voice is heard "only as a warning when the soul is about to enter on a wrong course. This means conversely that the soul feels that it is on the right path in its *logos* as long as the voice does not make itself heard" (Norvin, *Sokrates*, p. 104). Norvin regards this as an expression for Socrates' profound religiousness, and even more, for his unconditional, religious honesty: If only I will listen to God's voice he will help me to find the right path to the good and he will give me assurance that I am taking this path, but he will not lift the veil from the absolute (ibid., p. 106). To Norvin this is an expression of something characteristic of Socrates, a "subjectivity [that] is the profoundest truth" (p. 108). Socrates himself says in Plato's *Apology* 31D:

> Some one may wonder why I go about in private, giving advice and busying myself with the concerns of others, but do not venture to come forth in public and advise the state. I will tell you the reason of this. You have often heard me speak of an oracle or sign which comes to me, and is the divinity which Meletus ridicules in the indictment. This sign is a voice which comes to me and always forbids me to do something which I am going to do, but never commands me to do anything, and this is what stands in the way of my being a politician.

74:9   *as I suppose.* Kierkegaard uses the Latin *posito.*

74:13 *a maieutic artistry.* Actually, to assist in giving birth, like a midwife. Here the meaning is to assist in self-redemption.

74:30 *Now everyone . . . the dialectic of becoming, through Hegel.* Kierkegaard had in mind Hegel's *Science of Logic* (I, 95–120; *W.a.A.* III 78–111; *Jub. Ausg.* IV 88–121), the section on "Becoming," where the thesis is as follows (p. 95):

> Pure Being and pure Nothing are, then, the same; the truth is, not either Being or Nothing, but that Being—not passes—but has passed over into Nothing, and Nothing into Being. But equally the truth is not their lack of distinction, but that they are not the same, that they are absolutely distinct, and yet unseparated and inseparable, each disappearing immediately in its opposite. Their truth is therefore this movement, this immediate disappearance of the one into the other, in a word, Becoming; a movement wherein both are

distinct, but in virtue of a distinction which has equally immediately dissolved itself.

In "Observation I" to this Hegel adds (ibid., p. 97):

> What was said above about immediacy and mediation (which latter contains a relation and therefore negation), must also be said of Being and Nothing: that neither in heaven nor on earth is there anything not containing both Being and Nothing. Since we are speaking of a Something, of an actual fact, these determinations admittedly are no longer found in that complete untruth in which they manifest themselves as Being and Nothing: they have already been further determined and are taken, for example, as positive and negative, the former being posited and reflected Being, the latter posited and reflected Nothing: now of positive and negative, the former has Being and the latter Nothing for abstract basis.

75:1   *that they are not like those negative ones.* The expression itself is an allusion to Luke 18:11 about the Pharisees and the publican. As to the subject matter, reference is in all likelihood to Schelling, who called the latest phase of his philosophy positive in contrast to his previous negative philosophy in the lectures he gave in Berlin from 1841, and which Kierkegaard attended for a while.

75:6   *the Greek skeptics.* See above, note to p. 34 note.

75:6   *the entire treatment of this subject in the writings of modern idealism.* Possibly the reference is to Hegel's *Phenomenology of Spirit,* pp. 149ff. (*Jub. Ausg.* II 81ff.).

75:27   *sub specie aeterni.* From the vantage point of eternity. The expression is from Spinoza's *Ethics,* in which he postulates three stages of cognition: vague or accidental experience (*experientia vaga*); rational cognition (*ratio*); and finally immediate intuition (*scientia intuitiva*), in which the particular phenomena are perceived as links in a totality from the vantage point of eternity (*sub specie aeternitatis*; see for example *Ethics,* V, Prop. XXIX, XXX, and XXXI). The element of time is no longer applicable in the third stage of cognition.

Kierkegaard's usage diverges somewhat from Spinoza's, as Walter Lowrie points out in his note in *Kierkegaard's Concluding Unscientific Postscript,* trans. David F. Swenson and Walter Lowrie (Princeton, 1941), p. 560:

> The Danish editors [of *SV*] remark that this phrase is "derived from Spinoza." Doubtless it is, but Spinoza's word in the *Ethica* (where it occurs 14 times) is *aeternitatis.* By this phrase he describes the *tertium cognitionis genus,* which is intuition of God, leading to

the true knowledge and to *amorem Dei intellectualem*. The manuscript delivered to me made an attempt to correct S.K. and to conform this phrase to Spinoza's usage; but since S.K. was a good Latinist and the form he uses is an agreeable one (whether it is supported by precedent I do not know), and since friends in the faculties of Classics and Philosophy at Princeton unite in counselling me not to alter it, I do not presume to do so.

As a rule—and likewise here—Kierkegaard uses this term to denote the standpoint of speculative idealism as opposed to that of the existing thinker.

76:38   *Diogenes tells us.* Diogenes Laërtius, II, 5, 21, tells us that Socrates "discussed moral questions in the workshops and the market-place, being convinced that the study of nature is no concern of ours." (Translation by R. D. Hicks, *Loeb Classical Library*, I, 151.) See *Diogen Laërtses filosofiske Historie*, trans. B. Riisbrigh, ed. [posthumously] B. Thorlacius, I–II (Copenhagen, 1811–1812; *ASKB* 1110–11), I, 66.

76:39   *Socrates . . . stood still.* In Plato's *Symposium* 220C the following story is told about Socrates:

> One morning he was thinking about something which he could not resolve, and he would not give up, but continued thinking from early dawn until noon—there he stood fixed in thought; and at noon attention was drawn to him, and the rumor ran through the wondering crowd that Socrates had been standing and thinking about something ever since the break of day. At last, in the evening after supper, some . . . (I should explain that this was not in the winter but in the summer) brought out their mats and slept in the open air that they might watch him and see whether he would stand all night. There he stood all night as well as the following morning; and with the return of light he offered up a prayer to the sun, and went his way.

77:2   *star-gazing.* This is most likely a jab at Heiberg, who from the beginning of the 1840s acted as an amateur astronomer and from 1844 to 1846 published *Urania*, a three-volume yearbook dedicated to the subject of astronomy. See M. Borup, *Johan Ludvig Heiberg*, I–III (Copenhagen, 1947–1949), III, 55–64.

77:6   *article in the periodical from Funen.* An article titled "Orest og Ødip eller Collisionen" ("Orestes and Oedipus, Or the Collision") in *Det fyenske Tidsskrift for Litteratur og Kritik*, a quarterly published by the Literary Society of the Diocese of Funen and edited by L. Helweg

(1818–1883), brother of the author of the article. It was written by a Grundtvigian, Friedrich Helweg (1816–1901) and appeared in vol. III (Odense, 1845), pp. 55–60. Here Socrates is described as "the historical Oedipus," but the author does not discuss Socrates' irony.

77:24 *Socrates says somewhere.* Kierkegaard is obviously referring from memory, and none too accurately, to Socrates' statement in *Gorgias* 511D, which reads:

> For he [the pilot] is a philosopher, you must know, and is aware that there is no certainty as to which of his fellow-passengers he has benefited, and which of them he has injured in not allowing them to be drowned. He knows that they are just the same when he disembarked them as when they embarked, and not a whit better either in their bodies or in their souls.

77:31 *Plato and Alcibiades.* For instance in *Symposium* 215A and *Alcibiades* 106A: "Your silence, Socrates, was always a marvel to me . . . and now that you have begun to speak again, I am still more amazed."
77:33 ἄτοπος means, as indicated in the text, strange, remarkable, odd.
78:1   *Privatdocent.* The draft continues with (*Pap.* VI B 35:19; *JP* V 5795; "[intended]" inserted by present translator):

> The subjective existing thinker who has the categories of infinitude in his soul has them always, and therefore his form is continually negative. Suppose such a person devoted his whole life to writing one single book, suppose he published it, suppose he assumed there was a reader—he would then express his relationship to a reader negatively and without qualification; whereas a positive assistant professor who scribbles a book in fourteen days blissfully and positively addresses himself to the whole human race. That negative thinker, on the other hand, could never achieve any kind of direct relationship to his reader. He therefore would probably say: I can just as well recommend the reading of this book as advise against it, because, bluntly speaking, there is no direct gain from reading and no direct loss from not having read it.*
> The subjectively existing thinker is therefore just as negative as he is positive. Among the negative ones there are a few. . . .

> * *Note.* For the sake of caution I must beg everyone not to be bothered about what he reads here. It is written for idle people; yes, the serious reader will easily perceive that it is a joke [intended] to tease Lessing.

A privatdocent was in Germany an unsalaried university teacher or lecturer whose income depended on fees paid to him by the students.

A docent was on the other hand employed and remunerated by a university. Kierkegaard was well aware of this distinction, as is evident in part of a long entry concerning Magnús Eiríksson and titled "Self-Defense Against Unwarranted Recognition" (*Pap*. VII¹ B 88, pp. 293ff.):

> True, Holberg was of the opinion that in his time much too much debating was being done by many too many, so all this debating became an empty and vain show. But if in his time a teacher in the art of disputation had been employed by a university, would not Holberg, I wonder, have found it ridiculous for this man to train the youth entrusted to him in debating, in his capacity of teacher and with pedagogic seriousness? It is my opinion that the misfortune of our age, as well as its comical side, consists in the fact that much too much lecturing [*doceres*] is being done by many too many. But from this (and consequently also from presenting it) it however certainly does not follow that there should be anything comical in the fact that a regularly appointed teacher at a university lectures when he has students to guide; and if there is nothing comical in this there certainly can be nothing comical either in his doing it well and with talent. Insofar as there is an occasional polemic against Hegel in my writings, and insofar as they always take aim at all this lecturing, the whole thing is done diligently and, I can also safely say, with artistic correctness in such a way that the book could just as well have been written in Germany as in Copenhagen. What is more, *the privatdocent*, the typical figure I have always used—if not with the same success then at any rate similarly as Holberg used the Magister—is actually not found in Denmark at all. The privatdocent is a genuinely German character; and yet I am convinced that had Holberg lived in our time he would have immortalized the privatdocent. There is an infinite difference between a docent and a privatdocent, especially such as I have characterized the latter. The privatdocent is lecturing frothiness, a lightly armed encyclopedist, he has a sort of quick scientific mind, and he is neither teacher nor capable of independent thought. In a way he is the same as Holberg's Magister, except that he lectures instead of debating. As Holberg's Magister might be absolutely superstitious about the effects of one single syllogism, so a privatdocent is superstitious with respect to the system. A privatdocent would find himself in the most embarrassing situation of all if he became a real docent, in exactly the same sense as the political tinker [in Holberg's play *Kandestøberen*, "The Tinker Turned Politician"] was in an extremely embarrassing position when

he really became mayor. The privatdocent is halfheartedness, he has the pretentious form of the lecturing address [docerende Foredrags], and essentially he has nothing to say; or he has a brief rigmarole in relation to which he in turn is joint owner with all the other privatdocents. I think I have found expression for this halfheartedness in the very word "privat-docent"—one who essentially does not belong on a lectern but lectures away. The privatdocent is a completely fantastic figure who does not accomplish anything; all he does is fan the air, especially with the help of promises and announcements. As an author the privatdocent essentially belongs to the literature of subscription plans and dust covers. If a real docent begins to try his hand at any such thing he to that extent—but only to that extent—must be regarded as a privatdocent.

78:29   the wound of the negative. According to Hegel's view, "the conceptual determination is strictly speaking an arbitrary method of differentiation; it is like an incision in living material, which does indeed segregate what is cut away but also inflicts a wound" (Himmelstrup's Terminologisk Register, SV XV 649–50). The concept as positive is thus separated from the negative.

79:23   "moves the waters of the language." John 5:11.

80:1   Lucian. In Charon, chap. 6. The edition owned by Kierkegaard, Lucians Schriften aus dem Griechischen übersetzt [translator anon.], I–IV (Zürich, 1769; ASKB 1135–38), II, 291, has the following version:

One of his friends asked him to be his guest the next evening, if I am not mistaken. "Very, well," he said, "I'll come." But just as he was saying this a tile fell from the roof, I know not how, and killed him. I could not help laughing at his being prevented in such a way from keeping his promise.

80:15   differential knowledge. That is, knowledge that separates one person from another, for example, knowledge of a language that one of the two does not speak.

83:3   bifrontal. With a visage on both sides of the head, like the god Janus (bifrons).

83(note *):2   Let us try. Compare 2 Cor. 8:8 and 13:5.

83(note *):10   oracle. In Plutarch's De Pythiae oraculis, chap. 19.

83(note *):17   Magister Kierkegaard. In the dissertation The Concept of Irony, pp. 200ff. (SV XIII 276ff.).

83(note *):19   citing the dialogue Alcibiades II. That is, 138B and C.

83:15   *the scriptural injunction.* Matt. 6:17.

84:1   *its inexpressible sighs.* Compare Rom. 8:26.

84:14   *Hauptpastor [Goeze] . . . ergötzlich.* J. M. Goeze (1717–1786) was Lessing's well-known orthodox opponent in the dispute concerning Reimarus' *Wolfenbüttler Fragmente.* Kierkegaard owes his acquaintance with him to Lessing's polemical writings, *Eine Parabel, Nöthige Antwort auf eine sehr unnöthige Frage, Axiomata,* and *Anti-Goeze* (nos. I–II), which he read in *Lessings sämmtliche Schriften,* I–XXXII (Berlin, 1825–1828), VI.

Ergötzlich means diverting, delightful.

85:14   *Symposium.* 203B:

> On the birthday of Aphrodite there was a feast of the gods, at which the god Poros or Plenty, who is the son of Metis or Discretion, was one of the guests. When the feast was over, Penia or Poverty, as the manner was, came about the doors to beg. Now Plenty, who was the worse for nectar (there was no wine in those days), came into the garden of Zeus and fell into a heavy sleep; and Poverty considering her own straitened circumstances, plotted to have him for a husband, and accordingly she lay down at his side and conceived Eros

85:14   *Plutarch . . . Isis and Osiris.* See above, note to p. 100.

85:17   *Hesiod.* This is not found in the auction catalogue of Kierkegaard's books.

85:24   *This was Socrates' meaning.* The draft continues with (*Pap.* VI B 35:24; *JP* V 5796):

> This is what Socrates develops in the *Symposium.* In his dissertation, Magister Kierkegaard was alert enough to discern the Socratic but is considered not to have understood it, probably because, with the help of Hegelian philosophy, he had become superclever and objective and positive, or had not had the courage to acknowledge the negation. Finitely understood, of course, the continued and the perpetually continued striving toward a goal without attaining it means rejection, but, infinitely understood, striving is life itself and is essentially the life of that which is composed of the infinite and the finite. An imaginary positive accomplishment is a chimera. It may well be that logic has it, although before this can be regarded as true, it needs to be more precisely explained than has been done up to now, but the subject is an existing [*existerende*] subject, consequently is in contradiction, consequently is

in the process of becoming, consequently is, if he is, in the process of striving.

85:38   *that objective thought has validity.* That is, it is justifiable within its own domain.

86:7   *Lessing has said.* Kierkegaard's references to and quotations from Lessing are all taken from *Lessings sämmtliche Schriften* (*ASKB* 1747–62). The present quotations are from *Ueber den Beweis des Geistes und der Kraft.*

86:10   *leap.* See above, note to p. 15. Under this heading the main issue being considered is the pathetic leap, the qualitative transition from objective acceptance to subjective conviction. With regard to the leap, reference is made especially to J. Himmelstrup's *Terminologisk Register* (*SV* XV 697ff.) and to Gregor Malantschuk's essay "Søren Kierkegaards Teori om Springet og hans Virkelighedsbegreb," *Frihed og Eksistens* (Copenhagen, 1980), pp. 38ff.

86:25   *the reading of the schoolboy.* When lessons were to be read aloud by the whole class in unison, it was considered a joke to jabber instead, "I'm pretending that I'm reading, but I'm not reading anyway."

86:35   *quasi-dogma.* In his Journal from 1845, Kierkegaard, occupied with the same problem, wrote (*Pap,* VI A 62; *JP* III 3633):

> In a way the eternity of hell-punishment is easy to prove, and in any case it can be shown again how difficult it is to get a historical point of departure for an eternal happiness in time, and also how thoughtlessly men behave. The first (the problem of *Fragments*) is supposed to be so easy to understand that everyone grasps it. The second (the eternality of hell-punishment—that is, an eternal unhappiness) no one will accept [this explains the expression "*quasi-dogma,*" an apparent dogma or one not widely accepted] and the Church teaches it in vain [see for example *Confessio Augustana,* art. 17], for it may be assumed quite safely that no one believes it. Well, well, well, what thinkers! It is absolutely the same problem. If anyone is able to think the one (eternal happiness decided in time), then he has *eo ipso* thought the second. If time is able to be an adequate medium for deciding an eternal happiness, then it is also an adequate medium for deciding an eternal unhappiness. Here is the core of the problem, although the proofs which the orthodox have propounded [Kierkegaard may have read about this in Karl Hase, *Hutterus redivivus,* §132; *damnatio et beatitudo aeterna* (*ASKB* 581)] are devoid of all elementary concepts.
>
> The core is simply that the eternal eludes decision in time because it presupposes itself.

The reason why Kierkegaard mentions this problem precisely here is probably connected with the fact that in vol. V of Lessing's works (the volume with which he was working at the time) he may have read Lessing's essay from 1770, "Leibniz von den ewigen Strafen" (pp. 3–48).

87:13   *Miraculous human thoughtfulness.* The draft has the following additional note (*Pap.* VI B 35:25; *JP* II 1638):

> Rare thinking! If a historical point of departure can decide an eternal happiness, then it can also *eo ipso* determine eternal perdition. We easily understand the one, and we cannot understand the other—that is, we do not think either of the parts but talk our way glibly into the first and are a little shocked by the second. If anyone can think the one (the deciding in time of eternal happiness through a relationship to a historical phenomenon), then he has *eo ipso* thought the other. If time and the relationship in time to a historical phenomenon can be an adequate medium for determining eternal happiness, then it is *eo ipso* adequate for deciding an eternal perdition. To that extent, then, all the extremely curious proofs with which a pious orthodoxy has fenced in this dogma are a misunderstanding, just as the proofs are also quite curious and completely devoid of the specific concept and its consequences.

88:2   *balk — gjør Opbud.* An expression from the seventeenth century meaning "to declare oneself bankrupt."

88:5   *all thinking is rooted in the principle of immanence.* In his use of the two concepts immanence and transcendence, Kierkegaard takes his point of departure—as he predominantly does in his technical terminology—in idealistic, speculative usage, according to which the term "logical immanence" expresses logical, systematic consistency. Any philosophy that argues that it is possible by means of (experience and) reason alone to apprehend the totality of existence, including man and his place therein, may be called a philosophy of immanence. Such a philosophy will not contain anything transcendental or extrinsic, and even less anything paradoxical.

Of importance in this connection is the elucidation given in "On the Difference Between a Genius and An Apostle" (*SV* XI, especially, pp. 112ff.; *The Present Age*, pp. 137ff.). See also Emanuel Hirsch, *Kierkegaard-Studien*, II (Gütersloh, 1933), pp. 803ff.; Valter Lindström, *Stadiernas teologi* (Lund, 1943), pp. 268ff.; and Gregor Malantschuk, "Wahrheit und Wirklichkeit in Søren Kierkegaards existentiellem Denken," *Frihed og Eksistens* (Copenhagen, 1980), pp. 47ff.

88:18   *But now.* Kierkegaard quotes in German.

88:31   *the Fragments.* Pages 68ff. in my edition.

88:33   *Lessing says that from the historical accounts.* Page 76 in the edition mentioned above, where Lessing adds: "If I had lived at the time of Christ, the prophecy fulfilled in His person would at any rate have made me very attentive to Him."

89:3   *quotation from Origen.* From the apologetic writing Κατά Κέλσου.

89:14   *ex concessis.* Proceeding from concessions made (to an opponent). Kierkegaard as usual writes "*e concessis.*"

89:22   *which Christianity has abolished.* Kierkegaard had in mind Biblical passages such as Gal. 3:28; Rom. 10:12; 1 Cor. 12:13; Col. 3:11.

89:24   *singled out for special emphasis.* Kierkegaard writes "has spaced" (*spatieret*). Since the Gothic print of Kierkegaard's time did not have italic letters, words were emphasized by spacing the letters. (Note by R.J.W.)

89:24   *zufällige Geschichtswahrheiten.* . . . "Accidental historical truths can never become proofs of necessary truths of reason." From the edition mentioned above, vol. V, 80.

90:6   *the whole misunderstanding . . . in recent philosophy.* Kierkegaard is referring to Hegel in particular, who maintained that the development of the divine idea in time (as well as in space) proceeds with logical necessity. On this subject see especially "The Interlude" in my edition of the *Fragments,* pp. 89ff. and 124ff.

90:15   *Understood in this manner, the transition.* Following this, the draft continues with (*Pap.* VI B 35:30):

> I shall now take the words where he speaks of the leap. Contemporaneity or noncontemporaneity does not make any essential difference; a historical (and the fact that the god exists [*er til*], that is, exists by having come into existence [*være bleven til*], is a historical fact for the contemporary, too) point of departure for an eternal decision is and remains a leap.

90:17   μετάβασις εἰς ἄλλο γένος. Transition from one conceptual sphere to another. In *Analytica posteriora* (75b) Aristotle explains that proofs valid in one discipline cannot simply be transferred to another, adding by way of example that geometric truths cannot be proved arithmetically. Kierkegaard has taken the expression from Lessing, who quotes it.

90:23   *"Das, das ist der garstige breite. . . ."* "That is the ugly broad trench that I cannot cross, however often and earnestly I have attempted to make the leap."

90:25   *that the word Sprung is merely a stylistic phrase.* Compare *Pap.* V B 1:3; *JP* III 2342): "Lessing uses the word *leap*; whether it is an expression or a thought is a matter of indifference—I understand it as a thought."

90:32   *Lady Macbeth's passion.* Kierkegaard was thinking about these lines in Shakespeare's *Macbeth* (Act V, Scene 1), following the murder of King Duncan: "Here's the smell of the blood still: all the perfumes of Arabia will not sweeten this little hand." He may have used *"Macbeth" efter Shakespeare og Schiller*, trans. and ed. Peter Foersom (Copenhagen, 1816), which was the text employed for performances at The Royal Theater in Copenhagen from 1817 on. Kierkegaard has obviously confused these lines with the following from *The Life and Death of King Richard II* (Act III, Scene 2):

> Not all the water in the rough rude sea
> Can wash the balm from an anointed king.

The confusion is probably due to the Danish renditions, which literally retranslated into English read:

> Here [it] smells always—always ever of blood!
> All the myrrh in the East cannot remove
> The stench of cadaver from this little hand.

And from *King Richard II*:

> Not all the waters in the wild sea
> Can remove the balm from an anointed head.

91:31   *Jacobi.* Kierkegaard owned F. H. Jacobi's *Sämmtliche Werke*, I–VI (Leipzig, 1812–1825; *ASKB* 1722–28). Jacobi's conversation with Lessing took place in July 1780, six months before Lessing's death. Originally he had communicated the content of the conversation in a letter to Mendelssohn, to whom the letter was sent via their mutual friend, Elise Reimarus. The exchange of letters with Mendelssohn was published by Jacobi in 1785 in *Ueber die Lehre des Spinoza, in Briefen an Herrn Moses Mendelssohn*. In this work Elise Reimarus is called Emilie. Kierkegaard read the letter in Jacobi's *Collected Works*, vol. IV[1], from which he cites what follows in the text.

92:6   *catechumen.* This word derives from the Greek *katechein*, to instruct, and was a designation for people who went to baptismal instruction (*Katechese*), especially in the Ancient Church. They were assigned special places in the church and were not permitted to be present at the consecration in the mass.

92:37   *every human being is taught . . . by God.* From 1 Thess. 4:9.

93:11   *only the strength of woman, which is weakness.* Compare Shakespeare's *Hamlet*, Act I, Scene 2.

93:22   *"Gut, sehr gut. . . ."*

Good, very good! I can use all that, too; but I can't do the same thing with it. In general your somersault [*salto mortale*] doesn't seem bad to me, and I can understand how a man with a good head can go head over heels like that to get underway. Take me with you, if possible.

Jacobi's reply reads: "If you'll just step up on the elastic spot it will go of itself."

94:3   *Lessing's last words.* "To that there also belongs a leap, which I no longer may expect of my old legs and heavy head."

94:7   *speaking of meat and drink.* This is an allusion to Callicles' reply to Socrates in *Gorgias* 490C: "You talk about meats and drinks and physicians and other nonsense; I am not speaking of them."

94:8   *Although . . . the leap is itself.* To this the draft adds (*Pap.* B 35:33):

Had Jacobi been a Polos he might have answered as the latter answered Socrates on a similar occasion: How tiresome you are, Lessing, always talking about your old legs and your heavy head. As to his irony with the assistance of dialectics, the following may be observed. Despite the fact. . . .

94(note   *to be taught earnestness by the parish priest.* Kierkegaard may here be
*):4 hinting at the then widely known affair involving the author Thomas C. Bruun (1750–1834). In 1783 he published some indelicate rhymes titled *Mine Frie-Timer eller Fortællinger efter Boccaccio og Fontaine*, whereupon the Copenhagen Bishop N. E. Balle (1744–1816) recommended that the authorities forbid the author to release the yet unsold copies of the book. Prime Minister O. H. Guldberg (1731–1808) in the meantime prepared a Cabinet order instructing the Chief of Police to confiscate the book and fine the author 100 *Rdl.* The order also contained the following:

seeing that it may be inferred that he is an evil, corrupted, and offensive person, quite unversed in religion and Christianity, you [the Chief of Police] are to see that he be convened before Our Bishop Balle, where in the presence of two clergymen he is to be instructed in religion and Christianity; and should he, as may be presumed, be found ignorant and unconversant with same, then in the event that none of the priests will undertake to give him the proper instruction a school master shall be appointed to whom he shall continue to go until he has acquired the requisite knowledge. Should he on the other hand be found unwilling or obstinate We desire to be informed thereof in order that he, being an offensive and evil person, may be confined in prison or in the house of correction.

Bruun met with the bishop on December 19, 1783, and before Archdeacon Dr. J. C. Schönheyder and Rector of the Church of The Holy Spirit Peder Vogelius he acknowledged his fault in having published poems of a "depraved and nefarious nature." He was then examined in proficiency in Christianity and his "knowledge was found to be such that he could not be considered as being unenlightened." See Bjørn Kornerup, *Den danske Kirkes Historie*, V (Copenhagen, 1950), pp. 376ff.

95:2   *in playing with prepositions.* [S/L: propositions] Kierkegaard presumably read Hegel's extensive review of vol. III of Jacobi's *Werke* (in *W.a.A.* XVII, which was published in 1835; *Jub. Ausg.* VI 313–47; see also *Lectures on the History of Philosophy*, III, 410–23). Having criticized some of Jacobi's definitions of concepts, Hegel then writes (*Jub. Ausg.* VI 343):

> Such determinations, especially the more obscure, that are contained in the naked prepositions—for example, besides me, above me, and so forth—cannot serve, I dare say, to remove the misunderstanding; the result has rather shown that they sooner induce and augment such [misunderstandings]. For the product of the understanding that first of all is thereby expressed, and that in a less perfect manner in the preposition, is moreover repugnant to the governing idea of spirit.

95:8   *Jacobi thus relates.* A verbatim quotation from *Werke*, IV, 1, p. 74: "with a half smile": "he himself may perhaps be the Supreme Being and presently in a state of utmost contraction."

95:14   *Gleim.* J. W. Gleim (1719–1813) was a popular lyricist and fabulist who founded the Anacreontic style in Germany. See Wilhelm Kosch, *Deutsches Literaturlexikon*, 2nd ed., I (Bern, 1949), p. 664.

95:16   *Lessing said to Jacobi. . . .* "With a half smile": "You know, Jacobi, perhaps I'll do that." The draft instead of concluding here adds (*Pap.* VI B 35:34):

> The jest would not be less if perhaps L. even intended with this to refer to a passage in Aristophanes [*Clouds*, v. 366ff.] in which Strepsiades is given lessons by recent philosophy in how rain is produced, whereas he had believed that it was Jupiter who made it rain (and in his own way).

95:20   *to transcend itself . . . thought.* Compare the *Fragments*, pp. 76ff., with the commentary, pp. 230ff.

95:24   *entered into the heart of man.* Compare 1 Cor. 2:9.

95:27   *Mendelssohn says*: "To doubt whether there is anything that not only transcends all concepts but lies completely beyond the concepts—this I call a leap beyond oneself."

95(note *):3   *whether he was a human being.* Compare *Phaedrus* 229E–230A.

95(note †):5   *Edelmann, Bettelmann. . . .* The German equivalent of

Rich man, poor man, beggar man, thief,

Doctor, lawyer, merchant, chief.

96:1   *Mendelssohn of course bets to be excused.* The draft has (*Pap.* VI B 38; *JP* I 632):

> Double-reflection is already present in the communication itself, in the fact that the subjectivity (who wants to express the life of the eternal*) existing [*existerende*] in isolation wants to communicate himself, something he cannot possibly do directly, since it is a contradiction.
>
> One may very well want to communicate himself, like the person in love, but always indirectly.
>
> Every finite certainty is simply a deception; to demand this of God is only to make a fool of him. It is like the unfaithfulness in an erotic relationship which consists not in one's loving another girl but in having lost the idea.**

> * Where all sociality and all communication are inconceivable, because motion is inconceivable. Trend[e]lenburg's contribution to the category; the passage in the conclusion about Isis and Osiris, which are noted in my copies.
>
> ** If such a girl were to long for the wedding day because it would give finite certainty, if she wanted me to understand that now she was certain, I would deplore her unfaithfulness, for then she would have lost the idea of love.

96:11   *before I came to read the volume of Lessing.* Kierkegaard may have taken the word "leap" from Lessing through the medium of D. F. Strauss's *Die christliche Glaubenslehre* (see my commentary to the *Fragments*, pp. 149ff.), but he had earlier worked with the concept. See the account in Gregor Malantschuk's "Søren Kierkegaards Teori om Springet og hans Virkelighedsbegreb," *Frihed og Eksistens* (Copenhagen, 1980), pp. 38ff.

96:13   *Κατ' ἐξοχήν.* In an eminent sense. See *Fear and Trembling*, p. 53 note (*SV* III 105 note).

96:16   *the intellectual intuition of Schelling.* See especially Schelling's *System des transzendentalen Idealismus* in *Werke*, ed. M. Schröter, I–VI (Munich, 1927–1928), II, 369, and the conclusion of the fourth lecture in his *Vorlesungen über die Methode des akademischen Studiums* (ibid., III, 277).

96:19   *the inverse procedure of the method.* In other words, the result is posited at the outset, so the dialectical development in fact ends in its presupposition. Hegel himself says that such is the case in his thinking (*W.a.A.* III 64; *Jub. Ausg.* IV 74; *The Science of Logic*, I, 82ff.):

> If it is considered that progress is a return to the foundation, to that origin and truth on which depends and indeed by which is produced that with which the beginning was made, then it must be admitted that this consideration is of essential importance.

This peculiarity had already been pointed out by Sibbern in his extensive critical essay on Heiberg and Hegel's philosophy in *Maanedsskrift for Litteratur* (Copenhagen, 1838), p. 301, and in several other places. See my *Kierkegaard's Relation to Hegel* (Princeton, 1980), pp. 150ff.

Résumé (pp. 97–113)

Lessing had also accentuated a continued striving in preference to possession of the truth. Climacus now turns this statement, too, against the system by repeating that system and finality are synonymous, so an unfinished system is no system at all. To be sure, Climacus continues, it is possible to construe a system, but in doing so nothing may be admitted into it that belongs in this earthly existence, for existence is always in a process of becoming and involved in a coming-into-existence; in short, it is constantly undergoing change and striving toward a goal. Earthly existence is dynamic, whereas logic is static. It therefore follows that Hegel's attempt to introduce motion into logic is in principle impossible and in practice a source of confusion, since existence and logic are categorically different and incommensurate.

Having developed his main point, Climacus then directs his criticism against details in the system. The system is said to begin with the immediate; it is supposed to be without presuppositions, so its beginning is an absolute beginning. To this assertion Climacus makes the objection that this beginning is reached only through a reflection, which in turn raises the question of how this reflection is halted in order to make a beginning, for reflection as such is infinite and does not stop by itself. Reflection is not stopped by drawing a logical conclusion but only by making a resolve, which involves ethics. This would seem to imply that a beginning without presuppositions must be abandoned—and also that speculative philosophy has sidestepped the entire problem. It has also failed to clarify another major problem: How is the empirical "I" or ego that is to make the resolve related to a pure self-identity ("I = I")?

It is impossible for any human being to grasp existence as a system; such a system exists only for God. Man is himself a link in existence and thus obviously cannot regard it as finished or concluded, or as a closed system. In other words, he himself exists whether he wants to or not; he has, to employ a modern locution, been consigned to existence, and since existence consists of movement and striving, ethics will acquire decisive significance for him. This in turn means that the existing subject's striving is simply an expression for his ethical view of life, which transcends the logical.

This concept of existence is emasculated especially in the so-called pantheistic systems of philosophy. The moment we emphasize existence itself, however, we are also compelled to assert that there is no such thing as a humanly understandable system of existence. Although the speculative philosopher seeks to demonstrate the unity of the subject and object of cognition, existence interposes a cleft between them, separating being and thought. Thus instead of calling the objective tendency (speculation) an impious pantheistic self-deification, our author would prefer to view it as an essay in the comic, since an objective thinker who follows such a line of philosophy has in fact become so distracted that he ignores human existence—from which any and all attempts on his part to escape will nevertheless be in vain.

*   *   *

97:8   *Lessing's words are:*

If God held the whole truth in His right hand and in His left the unique, ever-active impulse toward truth, although with the pendant that I might go astray for all eternity, and said to me, "Choose!" I would fall with humility on His left hand and say, "Father, give! Pure truth is indeed for Thee alone!"

The quotation is from *Eine Duplik* (1778). Kierkegaard quotes a bit inaccurately in the original: *helte* for *hielte* and *spreche* instead of *spräche*. In 1849 Kierkegaard disavowed Lessing toward the end of a long entry (*Pap.* X¹ A 478; *JP* IV 4375):

But he [Lessing] was wrong insofar as this is a little too erotic and smacks a little too much, also in relation to truth, of wanting to regard the price as being more valuable than the truth. But this is really a kind of selfishness and can easily become dangerous, yes, a presumptuous error.

97:25   *Selections that Lessing had had published.* That is, from Hermann Samuel Reimarus' rationalist, never-completely published *Apologie oder Schutzschrift für die vernünftigen Verehrer Gottes.* Lessing published portions of this work during the years 1774–1778—the so-called "Wolfenbüttler Fragments"—thereby bringing about the controversy in which the previously mentioned Goeze was his chief orthodox opponent. As to Reimarus, see for example Albert Schweitzer, *Geschichte der Leben-Jesu-Forschung,* 6th ed. (Tübingen, 1951), pp. 13ff.

99:6   *Agent Behrend.* J. J. Behrend, businessman, broker, and somewhat of a character (d. 1821). Kierkegaard made note of this anecdote in his diary as early as September 1839 (*Pap.* II A 571; *JP* I 140). Presumably he had read it in L. N. Bjørn, *Dumriana eller Indfald, Anecdoter og Characteertræk af Claus Dumrians Levned* (Copenhagen, 1821), p. 19.

Nanking was the name of a sort of yellowish cotton material that was originally produced in China or the East Indies.

99:22   *(A.) a logical system is possible.* As noted by Gregor Malantschuk in "Søren Kierkegaard og Poul Møller," *Frihed og Eksistens* (Copenhagen, 1980), pp. 101ff., the criticism of Hegel here is an intensified continuation of the animadversions advanced by Poul Møller in his last philosophical essay, "Tanker over Muligheden af Beviser for Menneskets Udødelighed . . . ," *Efterladte Skrifter af Poul M. Møller,* 2nd ed., I–VI, ed. F. C. Olsen (Copenhagen, 1848–1850), V, 62ff.:

> Philosophy has a purely a priori element, the simply ontological. Here the dialectical unfolding of the concept carried through by Hegel with enormous energy is of the greatest importance. It is really possible to develop the universal determinations of thought in such a dialectical context that one category leads to the next; with this method of proceeding it is feasible to bring about an a priori system of determinations for the whole of existence [*Tilværelse*]. . . . In the so-called speculative logic, the idea of which Hegel had grasped, we have a revival of the metaphysics or ontology that had been superseded by the critical philosophy; but with this science the purely a priori part of philosophy indeed comes to an end. This [science] expresses a sum of universal and necessary determinations for everything existing, but it does not however [N.B.] demonstrate the necessity of the actually existing world with its infinite determinateness. The actually exsiting world can only be known experientially, and no philosophy is able a priori to prove the necessity of the inexhaustible wealth of determinations with which it appears. Ontology, however, like mathematics, embodies a sum of hypothetical propositions, yielding an a priori development of all the predicates that may be propounded of everything that is supposed to be able to exist; but that something actually does exist must be apprehended in another way.

99:30   *the introduction of movement into logic.* See above, Introduction, chap. 4, and regarding this entire section, Paul L. Holmer, "Kierkegaard and Logic," *Kierkegaardiana,* II (Copenhagen, 1957), pp. 25–43. Of older literature see especially Adolf Trendelenburg, *Logische Untersuchungen,* I–II (Berlin, 1840; *ASKB* 843), the chapters titled "Die dialektische Methode" (I, 23–109) and "Die Bewegung" (I, 110–23).

99(note
*):1

systematists concede. It has not been possible to ascertain to whom allusion is being made here.

99(note
*):6

the Method is supposed to be everything. Of Hegel's programmatic statements relevant to the "method" the following may be quoted from the preface to *The Phenomenology of Spirit* (p. 106; *Jub. Ausg.* II 45):

> It might well seem necessary to state at the outset the chief points in connexion with the *method* of this process, the way in which science operates. Its nature, however, is to be found in what has already been said, while the proper systematic exposition of it is the special business of Logic, or rather is Logic itself. For the method is nothing else than the structure of the whole in its pure and essential form.

On this subject, reference may be made especially to B. Heimann, *System und Methode in Hegels Philosophie* (Leipzig, 1927).

100:11

Trendlenburg. Adolf Trendelenburg (whose name Kierkegaard consistently misspells), *Logische Untersuchungen,* I–II (Berlin, 1840; *ASKB* 843). Kierkegaard bought this work on January 15, 1844, but he had already obtained a series of Trendelenburg's other works in February and May 1843, including *Die logische Frage in Hegel's System* (Leipzig, 1843; *ASKB* 846); see *Pap.* IV B 40 note. In March 1844 Kierkegaard began to study Trendelenburg in earnest, as may be noted from *Pap.* V A 74, 98, and passim (*JP* III 2341, 3300). Concerning the relationship between Kierkegaard and Trendelenburg, see Hermann Diem, *Kierkegaard's Dialectic of Existence,* trans. Harold Knight (Edinburgh and London, 1959), pp. 32ff.; James Collins, *The Mind of Kierkegaard* (Chicago, 1953), pp. 109ff.; and H. Küng, *Menschwerdung Gottes* (Freiburg, 1970), pp. 324ff.

Kierkegaard studied Aristotelian logic under the guidance of Trendelenburg's *Elementa logices Aristotelicae,* 2nd ed. (Berlin, 1842; *ASKB* 844), and *Erläuterungen zu den Elementen der aristotelischen Logik* (Berlin, 1842; *ASKB* 845). It is possible to accompany Kierkegaard step by step with the aid of *Pap.* V C 11:1–34, which consists of excerpts of quotations from Aristotle that Kierkegaard underlined in his copy of *Elementa logices Aristotelicae.* By this means, Kierkegaard became acquainted with *Prior Analytics, Posterior Analytics, Topica, On Interpretation, The Categories,* and parts of *Metaphysics,* thereby acquiring support and a scheme for many of his own thoughts. (Note by R.J.W.)

100:17

Plutarch's work on Isis and Osiris. Kierkegaard possessed several editions of Plutarch (*ASKB* 1172–1200), and he read Plutarch while preparing the *Postscript.* Plutarch, interpreting the Egyptian myths of Isis and Osiris, maintains that matter is the same as Isis, the feminine principle of existence, who aspires to reach the divine spirit, Osiris, just as plurality struggles to arrive at oneness. He also proposes that since the Greek words for motion (striving, yearning) are cognates, it may be inferred (chap. 60) that thought and motion are identical. Zeller has characterized Plutarch as a "pythagoreanizing Platonist" in *Die Philosophie der Griechen*, 3rd ed. I–V (Leipzig, 1881–1892), V, 159–202. For the mythical story of Isis and Osiris, see C. E. Sander-Hansen in *Illustreret Religionshistorie*, ed. Johannes Pedersen (Copenhagen, 1948), pp. 91ff.

101:12   *the categories . . . an abridgement of existence.* In other words, a formula for existence.

101:19   *the beginning is, and again is not.* See Hegel's *Science of Logic* (I, 86; *W.a.A.* III 68; *Jub. Ausg.* IV 78):

> And further, that which is-beginning, already is, and equally, as yet, is not. The opposites Being and Not-being are therefore in immediate union in it: in other words, it is the undifferentiated unity of the two.

See Trendelenburg, *Logische Untersuchungen*, I, 23ff.

101:22   *The system . . . begins with the immediate.* Both here and in the succeeding passage Kierkegaard had his eye on Hegel's *Science of Logic*, in particular the section titled "With What must the Science Begin?" (I, 82; *W.a.A.* III 59ff.; *Jub. Ausg.* IV 69ff.), where Hegel gives the following explanation:

> The beginning must be an absolute, or, what is here equivalent, an abstract beginning: it must presuppose nothing, must be mediated by nothing, must have no foundation: itself is to be the foundation of the whole science. It must therefore just be something immediate, or rather the immediate itself. As it cannot have any determination relatively to Other, so also it cannot hold in itself any determination or content; for this would be differentiation and mutual relation of distincts, and thus mediated.—The beginning therefore is Pure Being.

102:12   *pure being, is a pure chimera.* In other words, it is the same as nothing because when the concept of being is thought in its purity by abstracting from all concrete existence it passes over into its opposite—nothing.

102:27   *the bad infinite.* The bad or quantitative infinite is in Hegel's *Logic* (pp. 174–76; *W.a.A.* III 263ff.; *Jub. Ausg.* IV 273ff.) an endless development in which each new term contains no more than the pre-

ceding. This negative infinity can be symbolized by a line without
beginning or end, whereas the qualitative or correct and positive infinity can be symbolized by a circle. In the latter case new content is
absorbed in each successive term.

J. L. Heiberg espouses Hegel's distinction in *Perseus. Journal for den
speculative Idee* (Copenhagen, 1837; *ASKB* 569), pp. 3–89, especially
21ff., in which Heiberg published a review of W. H. Rothe's theological dissertation, *De Trinitate et Reconciliatione* (Copenhagen, 1836).
Kierkegaard owned this work in a Danish translation, *Læren om
Treenighed og Forsoning* (Copenhagen, 1836; *ASKB* 746). Rothe was
strongly influenced by Schelling.

103:8   *I ask him for a resolve.* For illumination of this problem see Kuno
Fischer's interpretation of Hegel's theory of the beginning of philosophy in *Geschichte der neuern Philosophie*, 2nd ed., I–X (Heidelberg,
1904–1912), VIII, 447:

> The beginning of logic and philosophy generally finds itself in a
> dilemma that even the ancient Skeptics had recognized and de-
> clared insoluble. Either this beginning is mediated or it is imme-
> diate: in the first instance the beginning is wanting, since media-
> tion, the grounds, and the proof continue without end; in the second
> the grounds are lacking. In the first case we have a proof without
> a beginning, in the second a beginning without a proof, and in
> neither is the science able to begin. This dilemma will persist as
> long as philosophy begins with an assertion or a statement; it is
> eliminated as soon as the beginning of philosophy is no longer
> made by a statement or an assertion but, as Fichte taught, by a
> requirement, a resolve, an act. . . . With Hegel the beginning of
> philosophy (logic) bears the character of knowledge as well as the
> will or a resolve. With him it is knowledge that makes the begin-
> ning, mediately as well as immediately, everything immediate being
> the result of a mediation: it is, after having become. The beginning
> of logic must be regarded as mediated through the entire *Phenom-
> enology [of Spirit]*, the ultimate result of which was pure knowl-
> edge. Pure knowledge has now come into being: it is, and it has
> the character of immediacy, but it is still completely undetermined
> and undeveloped. What it is must first be determined and devel-
> oped, and it is precisely in this that indeed the task and theme of
> logic reside.

See also Fischer's interpretation of Fichte, ibid., VII, 315–19.

103:27   μετάβασις. . . . Transition to another sphere. See the Index.

103(note
  *:3   εὐθύς. . . . Because an indeterminable and difficult infinity of
         worlds at once met those that exceeded the number one.

103:31   *Hegelian logicians.* The views of the Hegelian logicians are presented
         most fully in Johann Eduard Erdmann, *Grundriss der Geschichte der
         Philosophie,* 3rd ed., I–II (Berlin, 1878), II, 605–44, to which the reader
         is referred. Possibly there is an allusion here and in other passages in
         this section to A. P. Adler, *Populaire Foredrag over Hegels objective
         Logik* (Copenhagen, 1842), in which Adler writes in §10:

> Being is immediate. . . . The expedient that gives it to us is ab-
> straction, and what abstraction leaves behind, what even the most
> extreme abstraction is unable to annihilate, is the most immediate
> of all; it is a being to which thought has not been able to put an
> end. Being is thereby the utmost immediately self-imposing ne-
> cessity.

104:11   *[what the system says, that it begins] with nothing.* Compare Hegel's
         Science of Logic (I, 85; *W.a.A.* III 68; *Jub. Ausg.* IV 78):

> The Beginning is not pure Nothing, but a Nothing from which
> Something is to proceed; so that Being is already contained in the
> Beginning. The Beginning thus contains both, Being and Nothing;
> it is the unity of Being and Nothing, or is Not-being which is
> Being, and Being which also is Not-being.

105:4   *leap.* See above, notes to pp. 90–97.
105:6   *a kinship with Trop.* In J. L. Heiberg's vaudeville, *Recensenten og
         Dyret,* Scene 3, Trop, "an old law student in his sixtieth year," says:
         "At any moment whatever I can procure a certificate to the effect
         that I came close to passing my Latin law examination. This is at any
         rate something." The vaudeville was performed annually in Copen-
         hagen from 1826 to 1853.

105:30   *Rötscher.* H. Theodor Rötscher in *Aristophanes und sein Zeitalter*
         (Berlin, 1827), p. 31:

> Since the drama forms the apex of poetry, it is also the final
> phenomenon in its own evolution, for it contains both of the other
> kinds [of poetry] as its presupposition and combines their elements
> in itself. The roots of this poetry thus lie in Athens, the city that
> comprises the other tribal spirits [*Stammgeister*] of Greece. Now the
> drama is divided into tragedy and comedy, but in such a fashion
> that Attic comedy by its very nature presupposes the forces of
> tragedy as something overcome and forms the conclusion of dra-
> matic poetry.

105:34   *explaining Hamlet.* H. T. Rötscher, *Cyclus dramatischer Charaktere,*
I–II (Berlin, 1844–1846; *ASKB* 1802–03), II, 99–132.

106:19   *the philosophical controversies of a recent past.* Most likely Kierkegaard
was thinking primarily of Hegel's controversy with Schelling over
the beginning of philosophy. There is an echo of this debate in Hegel's *Science of Logic* (I, 79; *W.a.A.* III 60; *Jub. Ausg.* IV 70):

> The modern embarrassment about a beginning arises from yet
> another need with which those are unacquainted, who, as dog-
> matists, seek a demonstration of the principle, or who, as sceptics,
> seek a subjective criterion with which to meet dogmatic philoso-
> phy;—a need which, finally, is entirely denied by those who begin
> with explosive abruptness from their inner revelation, faith, intel-
> lectual intuition, and so forth, and desire to dispense with Method
> and Logic.

Then again, Kierkegaard might have had in mind Frederik C. Sibbern's critique of Hegel in his long article, "Bemærkninger og Undersøgelser, fornemmelig betræffende Hegels Philosophie, betragtet
i Forhold til vor Tid," which appeared in *Maanedsskrift for Litteratur*
(Copenhagen, 1838) and later as a special reprint, which Kierkegaard
owned (*ASKB* 778); see especially pp. 315ff. and 326ff. and above,
Introduction, chap. 6, and my *Kierkegaard's Relation to Hegel* (Princeton, 1980), pp. 150–54.

106:20   *the significance of Hegel's Phenomenology for the system.* See the Introduction (chap. 4) to the present volume. The problem concerning the
relation of *The Phenomenology of Spirit* to the rest of Hegel's works
was a subject of debate in Kierkegaard's time. See for example Adolf
Trendelenburg, *Die logische Frage in Hegels System* (Leipzig, 1843; *ASKB*
846), pp. 23ff.

106:29   *a big book has been written about it.* This may be an allusion to C. L.
Michelet, *Geschichte der letzten Systeme der Philosophie in Deutschland
von Kant bis Hegel,* I–II (Berlin, 1837–1838; *ASKB* 678–79), II, especially pp. 616ff., or to I. H. Fichte, *Beiträge zur Charakteristik der
neuern Philosophie,* 2nd ed. (Sulzbach, 1841; *ASKB* 508), pp. 798ff.
Kierkegaard owned both works.

107:4   *the I = I?* Kierkegaard had in mind Fichte's epistemology, according to which the beginning of all consciousness consists in the ego
positing itself, and this was formulated as "I am I." In formal logic
this is expressed by A = A, where the subject and predicate are identical; this applies to all content of the consciousness and serves to
assert the principle of identity and the category of reality. The ego
thereupon posits a non-ego, without which the former is unthinkable,

and as a consequence the principle of contradiction and the category of negation are now asserted. We acknowledge in this synthesis a unity of the ego and the non-ego in a primal subjectivity, the absolute ego.

107:18 *such a youth . . . enthusiasm enough.* This may be compared with H. N. Clausen's depiction of the period 1835–1839 in *Optegnelser om mit Levneds og min Tids Historie* (Copenhagen, 1877), pp. 212–13, which I have quoted in the Introduction, chap. 6. As to Kierkegaard's own earlier position with respect to Hegel's philosophy, see his long essay *Johannes Climacus, or, De omnibus dubitandum est,* trans. T. H. Croxall (Stanford, 1958), pp. 112–55 (*Pap.* IV B 1).

107:30 *existing spirit.* A human being.

107:30 *System and finality.* See on this point my article in *Theologische Zeitschrift* (Basel, 1957), pp. 219ff.

107:39 *Fragments.* See my edition, pp. 95ff. (*SV* IV 268ff.).

108:17 *the world has stood now for six thousand years.* Ever since the time of the Ancient Church people reckoned that the world was created about 4000 B.C. A celebrated theologian, J. A. Bengel, even maintained in 1741 that he was able to prove that creation was inaugurated on October 10, 3943 B.C. On this subject see O. Linton, "Skapelsens år, månad och dag," *Lychnos* (Lund, 1937).

108:27 *quodlibet.* In the Middle Ages a scholar who entered into a discussion of any subject was occasionally called a *quodlibetarius.* The word is related to the scholastic forms of literature. Out of the commentaries on the recognized authors grew the summaries, and from disputations between the teachers and pupils arose the *quaestio* literature, which in turn had two subdivisions: the *quaestiones disputatae* and the *quodlibetalia.* At the universities the so-called *disputatio ordinaria* were held regularly twice a month, and from this derived the *quaestiones disputatae.* The *quodlibetalia* were the result of the disputative exercises that took place twice a year and that turned first on one subject then on another (*quaestiones de quodlibet*).

Kierkegaard has the word from one of his theological textbooks. On August 8, 1839, he noted in his diary, "If only I were soon finished with my exams so that I could be a *quodlibetarius* again." (*Pap.* II A 534; *JP* V 5406, modified.)

108:29 *another author.* Frater Taciturnus in *Stages on Life's Way,* the entry dated midnight, May 2 (*SV* VI 244).

109:5 *identity of subject and object.* The theory of the identity of the subject and object of cognition is common to the greatest thinkers of speculative idealism (see the Introduction). It is already evident in Fichte in 1794; see *J. G. Fichtes sämmtliche Werke,* ed. I. H. Fichte, I–XI

(Berlin and Bonn, 1834–1836; *ASKB* 489–99), I, 98 note. Here he states that "The ego is the necessary identity of subject and object (subject-object), and it is simply this, without further mediation." It appears in Schelling, for example, in *System des transcendentalen Idealismus* (*Werke*, ed. M. Schröter, II [Munich, 1927], pp. 388ff.). To Hegel the theory is the presupposition and end of his system.

109:35   *these words of Lessing.* Quoted on p. 97 in the *Postscript*.

110:23   *Platonic interpretation of love.* In *Symposium* 200.

110:32   *One could then . . . always wanting to be a learner.* Junghans is of the opinion (note 291) that the allusion here is to the following statement that is ascribed to Solon: "I am growing old and always learning many things." It is not to be found, however, either in Diogenes Laërtius or in W. Capelle's *Vorsokratiker*.

110:39   *But Greek philosophy always had a relation to Ethics.* The reference here is to Socrates. See the Introduction, chap. 1.

111:7   *So-called pantheistic systems.* For example, that of Spinoza or even as early as Plotinus in which evil is but an intermediate stage on the way toward the good, or is regarded as something inferior and imperfect. See the Introduction.

111:18   *in tumultuous aphorisms.* Intended here are perhaps Franz v. Baader's attacks on Hegel in, among other works, *Revision der Philosopheme der Hegelschen Schule bezüglich auf das Christenthum* (Stuttgart, 1839; *ASKB* 416).

111:24   *systematists.* The printed manuscript continues with (*Pap.* VI B 98:30):

> If an age hit on the idea of wearing trunk hose and it was regarded as a matchless discovery to such a degree that anyone who did not wear them was despised—but it would be carrying things too far to command that not a word be uttered unless it concerned some further improvement or other, another new button or some such thing in the trunk hose.

113:3   *telluric conditions:* earthly conditions.

113:16   *cellar-dweller.* In Danish *Kjeldermand*, which in Kierkegaard's time was still a designation for someone who ran a restaurant or detail business in a cellar (*Kjelder*). But as in this passage this term was also used concerning an unenlightened, ignorant person.

113:23   *his talents and his learning, and so forth.* The printed manuscript has in addition (*Pap.* VI B 98:31; the ellipsis is Kierkegaard's):

> If a privately practicing thinker, a speculative crotcheteer, lived like an unfortunate lodger in a little garret in a huge building. . . .
> —but why does he want to keep on living there? Yet where is he

COMMENTARY TO PAGES 97–113

then to go, all alone in this wide world? Oh, if he dared knock at Lessing's door; but L. is a difficult man. He is so popular compared with the systematists that anyone in a hurry is able to understand him directly. But the man who meditates on him will not be able to understand him, although this is not to be so understood directly, since on the contrary it is to that man an enthusiastic expression of the fact that he perhaps does understand Lessing after all. With the systematists it is the reverse: the first understanding is hard, the second on the other hand—well, it is sad for those who had placed their hopes on it. But in that case Lessing has indeed put the unfortunate lodger into a pretty fix; he has made him even more displeased with his lodgings and bolder in being displeased— and then on top of that he leaves him in the lurch. Maybe this is how things stand, perhaps in his loneliness he is longing for the little garret and the distracting noise and bustle in the big building—perhaps, who knows? I do not know, for of course I am not the lodger.

Résumé (pp. 115–167)

The author begins this section by juxtaposing objective and subjective methods of approach. Whereas objectively we consider only a matter at issue, subjectively our regard is fixed on the subject and subjectivity, which in this case turns out to be the all-important question. Therefore the supposed guidance offered by science or speculation as a means of solving the problem is misguidance. The speculative view is that the way to a solution of the problem consists in becoming objective, whereas Christianity teaches that it lies in becoming subjective, in truly actualizing the potential that man possesses as a created being. Feeling that both poets and the clergy have failed to understand this, the author seeks to clarify his position by posing the question of what judgment ethics would have to pronounce if the greatest task imposed on each individual was not to become a real subject (p. 119).

Climacus thereupon concentrates on the scholar's preoccupation with world-historical knowledge, which he claims may readily become a distracting and demoralizing esthetic diversion for the subject, since the great and significant in history are not straightway identifiable with the good. Only the will, not historical results, can be judged ethically, and "for the study of the ethical, every man is assigned to himself" (p. 127); this task is indeed quite sufficient in itself. The ethical, the author continues, is just like the absolute: it is "infinitely valid in itself, and does not need to be tricked out with accessories to help it make a better showing" (p. 127).

Just as preoccupation with world history may produce confusion, another kind of confusion may arise when the function of ethics is misunderstood. (Here our author has brought his sights to bear on Hegel's *Philosophy of Right*; see chap. 4.) Such is the case when one holds that the ethical is actualized and made concrete in a particular social order, the individual being left the task of acknowledging and occupying his place in the given society.

The author then proceeds to elaborate on how according to his opinion the world-historical consideration viewed as a cognitive act is merely an approach or approximation that may prevent the scholar from making a beginning (p. 134). Now the question arises, What does the world-historical actually imply? World history may be considered as the history of the human race, but since the ethical is not intended for the race but for the individual it will be impossible to discern the ethical in world history.

The task as the author has postulated it, which is to become subjective, will suffice for a whole life. This, the author continues, will be extremely difficult for an intelligent man to understand, precisely because it is so simple. The plain man will know this simple fact essentially and directly. The only difference between the two is that if the wise man does know it, he is also conscious of his knowledge; but the knowledge shared by the two men is identical in this field.

The ethical, however, is not merely knowledge; it is a doing or an act with a relation to knowledge. This the author demonstrates with some examples: what it means to die, to be immortal, to thank God for the good He has bestowed on me, what marriage entails, and so forth.

The author now pokes fun at Heiberg's (Dr. Hjortespring's) miraculous conversion to Hegelian philosophy and then relates how he himself hit on the idea of trying his hand as an author whose aim it is to make difficulties everywhere (p. 147).

*   *   *

116:21 *a greater Christian joy in heaven.* From Luke 15:7.

118:8 *Storm Street (Stormgade).* Like Storm Bridge (*Stormbro*) this street is so named to commemorate the Swedish assault (*Storm*) on Copenhagen on February 11, 1659. The attack took place at this very point.

119:1 *to assign China a place different.* Most likely Kierkegaard had in mind here Hegel's *Lectures on the Philosophy of History*, where China is discussed in Part One, "The Oriental World" (*W.a.A.* IX 141–69; *Jub. Ausg.* XI 163–91; *The Philosophy of History*, pp. 116–67). Neither Hegel's description nor his placement of China in world history, however, deviates significantly from earlier philosophers of history. Besides, Kierkegaard is merely being ironic with respect to those philosophers who occupy themselves with insignificant historico-philosophical problems while ignoring the essential or ethical and religious issues.

119:8 *the way and the truth.* An allusion to John 14:16.

119:15 *the Fragments called attention.* In the "Interlude" between chapters IV and V; in my edition, pp. 89–110.

119:17 *the world-historical progress of the idea.* The following observation appears in the margin of the provisional draft but is crossed out with vertical pencil lines (*Pap.* VI B 40:3; *JP* II 1607):

If I attempted to point out how the Hegelian ordering of the world-historical process perpetrates caprices and leaps, how it almost involuntarily becomes comical when applied to more concrete details, I would perhaps get the attention of a few readers. Essentially the interest would be in arranging world history, and perhaps I am the one who should do it. If I were merely to state this, I would probably cause quite a stir. But to regard all this interest as curiosity is, of course, ethical narrow-mindedness; yes, even to regard interest in astronomy as curiosity and silly dilettantism, which in order to advance further disappoints by moving into another discipline, would also be regarded as ethical narrow[-]mindedness. Yet I am happy at this point to remember Socrates "who gave up astronomy and the study of heavenly things as something which did not concern man."

119:26   *A Sophist has said.* Verification of this statement has been sought in vain.

121:26   *syllogist* [S/L: logician]. Syllogism (Greek συλλογισμός) actually means a reckoning all together, collecting from premises, an inference from premises. Aristotle introduced the syllogism into logic in *Prior Analytics.* See I. M. Bochénski's history of problems, *Formale Logik* (Freiburg, 1956), pp. 74ff., and Sir David Ross, *Aristotle,* 5th ed. (London, 1964), pp. 32–38.

121:27   μετάβασις εἰς ἄλλο γένος. See above, note to p. 90.

122:10   *For every human being is an unprofitable servant.* See Matt. 25:30 and Luke 17:10.

122:26   *pro virili [parte].* [S/L: As in him lies]; as far as a man is able.

123:10   *the divine madness.* An allusion to Plato, who in *Phaedrus* (244B and 256B) speaks of μανία, that madness; or rather, the divine inspiration that leads men beyond the purely rational. See Paul Friedländer, *Platon,* 2nd ed., I–III (Berlin, 1954–1960), III, especially pp. 209ff.

123:25   *the outward is the inward, the inward the outward.* See the Index and quotation from Hegel.

124:6   *In fables . . . there is mention made of a lamp.* Kierkegaard was very likely thinking specifically of Aladdin and the magic lamp in Adam Oehlenschläger's *Poetiske Skrifter* (Copenhagen, 1805).

124:29   *numbered the hairs of your head. . . .* These phrases stem from Matt. 10:30 and Rom. 9:27.

125:26   *gratitude . . . bestowed upon a barber's apprentice.* As Junghans suggests, this may be an allusion to E. Theodor A. Hoffmann, *Klein Zaches, genannt Zinnober,* 2nd ed. (Berlin, 1824; ASKB A II 268).

126:4   *another author.* Kierkegaard's pseudonym, Frater Taciturnus, in *Stages*, Part Three, p. 402 (*SV* VI 467).

126:4   *a depth of seventy thousand fathoms.* The numerical quantity itself, which Kierkegaard employs as a finite expression of the infinite, is probably a loan from Hegel's *Philosophy of History* (p. 163; *W.a.A.* IX 200; *Jub. Ausg.* XI 222), in which Hegel maintains that the mythical Indian kings "had reigned 70,000 years, or more."

126:10   *die Weltgeschichte ist das Weltgericht.* "World history is the Last Judgment." This is from Schiller's poem *Resignation* (1784), in which the meaning according to Carl Roos's interpretation is that every choice of one of life's two great possibilities involves the loss of the other. This judgment is passed by experience or by world history.

126:22   *access to the realm of the historical.* The import of this passage is that one becomes famous and is enrolled among the other world-historical celebrities on the basis of achievements, visible results, or something else that is measurable, and these are all quantitative factors. Such quantitative results—for example, a king's conquests—never lead to a new quality, however, for they say nothing about the ethical status of the celebrity.

126:29   *King Solomon and Jørgen the hatmaker. Kong Solomon og Jørgen Hattemager*, a vaudeville by Heiberg in which Salomon Goldkalb, an impoverished Jew from Hamburg, is in Korsør and is confused with Baron Goldkalb, his rich namesake from Frankfurt.

127:25   *a dance of cranes.* Perhaps a reference to Hostrup's student comedy, *En Spurv i Tranedands* (1816).

127:31   *The ethical . . . is infinitely valid in itself.* See the note on Kant's ethics in my edition of *Frygt og Bæven* (Copenhagen, 1961; 2nd rev. ed., 1983).

127:36   *words of the poet.* Schiller in his poem *Die Götter Griechenlands, Schillers sämmtliche Werke*, I–XII (Stuttgart and Tübingen, 1853–1857), I, 87–91. The entire line reads in the original "Dienst sie knechtisch dem Gesetz der Schwere" and means "Serves the law of gravity submissively."

128:28   ($\nu\eta\sigma\tau\epsilon\acute{\nu}\epsilon\iota\nu$ $\varkappa\breve{\alpha}\varkappa\acute{o}\tau\eta\tau o\varsigma$). "To fast from evil." Plutarch cites this rule by Empedocles in *De cohibenda ira*, chap. XVI. The meaning is that one must break one's habit of transgression by refraining from such acts for a definite period of time, in the same way that one goes on a diet.

129:4   *another confusion.* The polemic here is directed against Hegel's doctrine of the objective spirit, hence against *The Philosophy of History* and *The Philosophy of Right.*

129:10   *every age has its own moral substance.* This is Hegel's view, especially in *The Philosophy of History.*

129:15   *what will not the Germans do for money.* "Hvad giør dog Tydsken ei for Penge?" It is from Johan Hermann Wessel's comic narrative, "Stella," which appeared in his versified weekly, *Votre Serviteur,* V (1785), p. 7.

129:32   *a prophet . . . a world-historical swashbuckler.* See the Index: Grundt-vig, his "matchless discovery," and so forth. The end of this passage is, however, addressed equally to Hegel.

130:5   *deriving his instruction from a reformatory.* This may be related to a recollection from Kierkegaard's trip to Jutland after his degree examination. In *Pap.* III A 57 (*JP* V 5457) he writes that Rev. A. F. Boesen's wife told him how

> she and her husband visited the prison [in Viborg]. In a separate cell they found five or six adult gypsies (about 25 to 30 years old) who were being taught the alphabet in order to be prepared for confirmation.

Their teacher was a former private tutor imprisoned for thievery.

130:21   *in the popular ethic.* Kierkegaard hardly had a particular publication in mind. A number of books on this subject appeared during his time. See the Section *Moral,* Dept. I, in the University Library, Copenhagen.

130:33   *the amiable king's pious wish.* King Henry IV of France. Among the stories that were part of the school curriculum is the one of how Duke Carl Emanuel of Savoy once asked the King how great a profit he makes on France. The King replied:

> As great as I want; for since I have my subjects' love I can demand of them as much as I desire. But I hope, that is, if God will grant that I live yet a while longer, to arrange matters so that there will not be a farmer in the kingdom who will not have a chicken in his pot at least every Sunday.

See K. F. Becker, *Verdenshistorie,* rev. J. G. Woltmann, trans. J. Riise, I–XII (Copenhagen, 1822–1829; *ASKB* 1972–83), VIII, 119.

131(note *):2   *understand his necessity.* According to Hegel's deterministic philosophy of history, which is based on metaphysics, Socrates necessarily had to appear as representing a definite phase in the unfolding of the idea in time. Indeed, Hegel says as much in just this way in his posthumously published *Lectures on the History of Philosophy* (I, 384–448; *W.a.A.* XIV 42–122; *Jub. Ausg.* 42–122).

131(note
*):4
by an oracle. Plutarch writes about this oracle in *De genio Socratis,* chap. 20.

132(note
cont.):1
condemned by a majority of just three votes. Plato's *Apology* 36A. The preferred reading now is τριάκοντα (thirty). τρὶς (three) appears in only one manuscript, the *Codex Venetus,* but this was the reading adopted by Bekker, whose textual edition Kierkegaard owned.

132(note
cont.):6
Antoninus philosophus. Marcus Aurelius Antoninus. Kierkegaard possessed both a textual edition and a German translation (*ASKB* 1218–19) of his well-known self-observations.

132(note
cont.):15
Xenophon. Kierkegaard's memory has failed him. It is in Plato's *Gorgias* (473E) that Socrates says to Polus:

> O Polus, I am not a public man, and only last year, when my tribe were serving as Prytanes, and the lot fell upon me and I was made senator, and had to take the votes, there was a laugh at me, because I was unable to take them.

Compare this with Kierkegaard's observations in "The Individual" in *The Point of View for My Work as An Author,* p. 136 (*SV* XIII 653).

132:5
"a glass of water." This is a reference to *Le verre d'eau* ("The Glass of Water"), one of Eugène Scribe's numerous plays that J. L. Heiberg translated for performance at the Royal Theater. It is based on the familiar story that the Duke of Marlborough was overthrown because his wife accidentally spilled a glass of water on Queen Anne's dress. See Ronald Grimsley, *Søren Kierkegaard and French Literature* (Cardiff, 1966), p. 121.

133:28
a daring venture where much is lost. In Danish, "Dristigt vovet, halvt vundet," which is also the title of a play by J. L. Heiberg (1817). The phrase is a proverb meaning "fortune favors the bold" and is formed after the fashion of the Virgilian *audaces fortuna juvat* (*Aeneid*, X, 284). Compare Terentius in *Phormio*, I, 4: *fortes fortuna adjuvat.*

134:22
valore intrinsico. According to its intrinsic worth.

134(note
*):3
Schelling's intellectual intuition. Hegel touches on this in both the preface to *The Phenomenology of Spirit* (pp. 77ff.) and *The Science of Logic* (I, 89ff.), from which the following may be cited (translation by R.J.W.):

> No element of intellectual intuition that is eternally or absolutely present at the *beginning* of the science can be anything but a primary, immediate, and simple determination; this also holds true even though the object of this intuition is called the eternal, the divine, or the absolute. Even if we give it a name richer in content than that expressed by mere being, the only matter for considera-

tion will be how such an absolute enters into *thinking* knowledge and the expression of this knowledge. True, intellectual intuition is the forcible rejection of mediation and of demonstrative external reflection. But if it asserts more than simple immediacy, it asserts something concrete, something containing differences in determination. As we have already observed, the expression of representation of such a thing is, however, a mediating movement that begins with *one* of the determinations and proceeds to another, even when it returns to the former; furthermore, such a movement must not be either arbitrary or assertoric. Thus anything that *begins* with such a representation is not concrete but merely a simple immediacy from which the movement starts. Moreover, if something concrete is taken as a beginning, the proof needed to connect the determinations contained in the concrete will be lacking.

134(note †):10   *only one Chinaman*. In the section on China in Hegel's *Philosophy of History* both Confucius and Lao-Tse are mentioned.

135:1   *Monomotapa*. A negro kingdom in southeast Africa in the modern countries of Zimbabwe and Mozambique that arose in the fifteenth century and was still of some importance in the eighteenth century. Kierkegaard may have been thinking of the Danish historian, Christian Molbech (1783–1857), who had a considerably greater empirical and a materially less philosophical ballast than Hegel did and who from 1840 to 1841 published his lectures on the philosophy of history. See Morten Borup, *Christian Molbech* (Copenhagen, 1954), pp. 351ff. Hegel does not mention this kingdom. See Robert W. July, *A History of the African People*, 2nd ed. (New York, 1974), pp. 151–56.

135:6   *Christmas Eve*. Holberg's comedy *Julestuen* (Scene 12):

> *Schoolmaster*: . . . for just as the bird Phoenix, which is found in Arabia, lives thousands of years in solitude and burns herself up as soon as she hatches her young to avoid living in the society and company of her own kind, we people ought on the contrary to enjoy social intercourse and merriment to make it plain that we are not related to such dumb creatures.

135:16   *ethical narrow-mindedness*. The draft has in addition (*Pap.* VI B 40:5; *JP* II 2286):

> Yes, even wanting to regard interest in astronomy as curiosity, silly dilettantism, or even intellectual swindling, which in order to advance and advance does not penetrate into anything but merely makes variations of the sciences and intellectual disciplines—this, also, would be regarded as ethical narrow-mindedness. Socrates, it seems, was also narrow-minded in this way: "He gave up the study

of astronomy because he perceived that the heavenly things do not concern us." But at that time Professor Heiberg had not proved that astronomy was what the times required. Now he has proved it, and so it certainly is. Earlier Claudius Rosenhoff expressed something similar, and at Tivoli an observatory has been erected where we can entertain ourselves astronomically for two shillings while poor folk occupy themselves with astronomy free at the Round Tower. And thus it has also been proved that world history is what the age demands.

Yet joking is one thing and earnestness another. Praise be to science and learning. Praise be to daring to begin and despondently abandoning because human limitations frighten a person back.* An objection which merely dreads [frygter] the insurmountable work or merely dreads that it is insurmountable without having anything higher to put in its place is not worthy of attention. Therefore the objection is not formulated in that way. The objection comes from the ethical. It says. . . .

* *In margin:* Learned science does not want to see the ethical in the historical, still less to extract from all this what the ethical is; scholarly research is solely in the interest of knowledge.

135:35   *driving the cattle away.* This sentence is reminiscent of Jesus' cleansing of the temple in John 2:14.

136:29   *Falstaff. King Henry IV, First Part,* Act II, Scene IV. Kierkegaard has the gist of it if not the exact wording.

Prince Henry: Go, hide thee behind the arras:—the rest walk up above. Now, my masters, for a true face and good conscience.
Falstaff: Both which I have had; but their date is out, and therefore I'll hide me.

137:16   *quod desideratur.* What is desired, that is, needed.

137:17   *quod erat demonstrandum.* What was supposed to be proved.

137:19   *But it is all the more remarkable.* The draft supplements this with (*Pap.* VI B 40:6):

N.B. (This is to be expanded.) Though with the exception of a noble philology,* which simply delves into a particular aspect scientifically—and does not make itself guilty of speculatively trying to confound the task of every single individual with the world-historical task of the entire race.

* even though it may be demanded of a philologist that he be clear about and conscious of himself ethically before proceeding to

his science, and that he develop himself ethically during all his scientific pursuits.

137:24   *the dog who looked at himself in a mirrored reflection.* In *Phaedrus Fables,* no. 5, the dog saw a reflection of his piece of meat in the water, snapped at the reflection—and lost the piece of meat.

137:38   *Kofod's history.* That is, Hans Ancher Kofod's vivid exposition, *Historiens vigtigste Begivenheder,* which was first published in 1808. Kierkegaard read this work while preparing for his university entrance exam; see *Breve,* II, 4.

138:7   *whether everything is speculatively fused indistinguishably together.* The draft has in addition (*Pap.* VI B 40:7):

> *Note.* In this way Prof. Rasmus Nielsen in the capacity of systematic Peer Degn and *Imprimatur* would undoubtedly find room for Archdeacon Tryde. Indeed Tryde too is reported really to know his stuff systematically inside out; he is also supposed to have rendered the service of bringing the System into people's homes; and finally he probably differs from real Hegelians in that he assumes that world history has managed to prolong its Deer Park season somewhat and will be finished only with Prof. R. Nielsen. On the other hand Candidate Barfoed might perchance find room for Pastor Helveg, who as Chaplain *pro persona* ought to be included too.

The printed manuscript has this version (*Pap.* VI B 98:34):

> *Note.* In this way Prof. R. Nielsen in the capacity of systematic Peer Degn and *Imprimatur* would undoubtedly find room for Archdeacon Tryde. Indeed Tryde too is reported really to know his stuff systematically inside out, and in addition is supposed to have rendered the service of bringing the System into people's homes; and finally he has the strange characteristic of differing from the German systematists by assuming that world history has managed to prolong its Deer Park season, so that it will be over only with R. Nielsen. I am not saying this to claim credit for having pointed out that the Archdeacon should be included in the world-historical process, but it seems to me that *qua* systematist Tryde has long since qualified to be mentioned with praise.

138:29   *complicity with God.* The expression (*Samviden*) itself was used especially by Martensen in connection with Franz von Baader's use of the word *conscientia.* With Martensen it denotes the "participatio creaturae in cognitione divinae essentiae." See Martensen's dissertation for the Licentiate degree, *De autonomia conscientiae sui humanae, in theologiam dogmaticam nostri temporis introducta* (Copenhagen, 1837; *ASKB*

648), p. 65. In Baader's view, God's knowledge is primary and exemplary, whereas man's, being secondary and like an image, is derived from and coparticipant in the divine and can therefore be designated as *con-scientia*, that is, coknowledge or complicity (*Samviden* or *Medviden*). See Skat Arildsen, *Biskop Hans Lassen Martensen: Hans Liv, Udvikling og Arbejde* (Copenhagen, 1932), I, 122ff. and 133ff. [*Samviden*, which is now archaic, was also once used in the sense of "conscience" (*Samvittighed*).—R.J.W.]

138:37 τέλος. *Telos* means end, goal. Kierkegaard has surely taken the word from Aristotle.

140:3 *God is the God of the living.* Matt. 22:32.

141:15 *existing spirit.* That is, a human being.

141:18 *drama dramatorum.* The drama of all dramas.

142:20 *he dies and leaves the scene.* This entire passage recalls to mind Ps. 78:39: "He remembered that they were flesh, a passing breath that returns not."

142:27 *as numberless as the sand of the sea.* Compare Gen. 22:17.

144:16 *Socrates.* See my edition of the *Fragments*, p. 201 (note to p. 38).

144:18 *astronomy, which the age now demands.* A gibe at J. L. Heiberg, who, as already mentioned, from 1844 to 1846 published *Urania* (see *ASKB* U 57–8), his annual of astronomy, which Kierkegaard makes fun of in *Forord*, no. IV (*SV* V 31–4); *Prefaces (Forord)* is a little humorous book (as yet untranslated). Kierkegaard compares himself with Socrates, who turned from the philosophy of nature to ethics. See the omitted portion of the draft (*Pap.* VI B 40, 5; *JP* II 2286).

144(note *): 2 *On the Ethical Virtues.* A quotation from *De virtute morali*, chap. I.

145:21 *Luther.* For example, in "Auslegung des vierzehnten, funfzehnten und sechszehnten Capitels St. Johannis" (1538), in *Luthers sämmtliche Schriften*, ed. J. G. Walch, I–XXIV (Halle, 1740–1753), VIII, 609:

> But when I want to speak and pray to my God for myself there are already a hundred thousand hindrances ere I arrive at that point. Then the Devil is able to cast all sorts of reasons in the way, hindering and obstructing me from all sides, so that I give way and never think of it.

Compare the Weimar edition, vol. XLVI, 78ff.

145:26 *one of the greatest actors is said to have remarked.* The statement has been attributed to the English actor David Garrick (1717–1779).

145:32 *quantum satis.* A sufficient quantity.

145:34 *Lot's wife.* See Luke 17:28–32.

145:37 *the parable of the trees.* See Judges 9:7–15. Kierkegaard's memory, however, is at fault; the trees asked every possible tree *except* the Cedar to be their king.

146:24   *systematician . . . astronomer.* Another poke at Heiberg. See the Index.

146:25   *water-inspector.* A person who in larger cities supervised, cleaned, and repaired the water conduits. It might be mentioned that the drinking water available in Copenhagen in Kierkegaard's time was so polluted that even the city authorities advised against drinking water without taking steps to purify it. Eels and other assorted marine animals could even be pumped directly into the kitchen through the faucet. See Villads Christensen, *København 1840–1857* (Copenhagen, 1912), pp. 159–70.

147:11   *theologues.* With this Kierkegaard always means the grade school teachers whom academic men of the time generally held in contempt as smatterers, which they in fact were.

147:23   *riding on the railway.* In German in the original (*"Auf der Eisenbahn"*). See letters numbered 81 and 186 in *Breve*, where the same theme occurs.

147:29   *reputation of being slow.* The printed manuscript continues with (*Pap.* VI B 98:35):

> Imagine that tailor about whom Hoffmann tells the story that he had taken balloon-gas; suppose he had taken a smaller quantity so that he had not immediately sought a route through the open window and out into the open by taking a relatively oblique course; suppose he had taken a smaller quantity so that he might still have been able to restrain himself; would it be a sign of wisdom for him to assume that to restrain himself was no art but that it was an art to fly out the window, which he of course could easily achieve by taking another little dose?

147:39   *a dose of sulphuric acid.* The draft has in addition (*Pap.* VI B 40:10):

> [I know that if I take] 4 shillings' worth of sulphuric acid I will die, and that Napoleon and Alexander always had poison with them, that a man died in Berlin from getting a little hot sealing-wax under his fingernail while another went through all the ailments without dying, that one can die of anything, and that what killed the smith can save the baker.

148:2   *that Juliet in Shakespeare poisoned herself.* In *Romeo and Juliet,* Juliet as part of a strategy drinks a sleeping potion that makes her appear to be dead. Romeo, believing that she really is dead, commits suicide by taking poison, whereupon Juliet, awakening and seeing his lifeless body, kills herself with his dagger.

148:3   *the Stoics regarded suicide as a courageous deed.* The prevalent Stoic view was that if a person were not otherwise able to proclaim his independence he ought to take his own life. Seneca says (*Ep.* 12:10): "Let us thank God that nothing can keep us in this life."

148:18   *a velvet inset.* When worn on clerical gowns this inset indicates a doctorate of theology.

149:4   *commensurable with the uncertainty of death.* Junghans interprets this to mean that uncertainty of the time of death must also be included when thinking of the concept.

149:13   *Soldin.* A second-hand bookseller with a bookstore in Pilestræde and known as a character. The following is one of several anecdotes told about his absent-mindedness: A customer came into the store and while Soldin was on a ladder fetching a book the customer spoke a few words to Soldin's wife in an imitation of Soldin's voice. Soldin thereupon turned to his wife and asked, "Is it I who am speaking?"

Kierkegaard had already made note of this anecdote in 1837 (*Pap.* I A 33 and 340; *JP* I 118 and II 1541, respectively). See Carl Roos, *Søren Kierkegaard og Goethe* (Copenhagen, 1955), p. 104, and his reference to Camillus Nyrop's *Den danske Boghandels Historie*, II (Copenhagen, 1870).

149:39   *Diedrich Menschenschreck.* In Holberg's comedy of the same title (Scene 20) the principal character, a braggart of an officer, discloses that he is also a thoroughly henpecked husband.

150:12   *anticipando.* Preconceived.

152(note *):1   *The reduplicated presence of the thought.* Reduplication (actually a redoubling) indicates the objective relation produced by reflection (Himmelstrup) in the sense that one exists in what one understands (see *SV* XII 144; *Training in Christianity*, p. 124).

153:11   *some have found immortality in Hegel.* The Hegelian school was divided over the problem of whether or not individual immortality was taught in the system or whether it perhaps was a consequence of the system (see above, Introduction, chap. 5). Hegel made several comments on this problem, but he generally did so in a historical rather than a systematic context. Thus in his posthumously published *Lectures on the Philosophy of Religion,* I, 200 (*W.a.A.* XII 269; *Jub. Ausg.* XVI 269) he offers the following interpretation of the myth that man will become immortal if he eats of the Tree of Life:

> Man is immortal in consequence of knowledge, for it is only as a thinking being that he is not a mortal animal soul, and is a free,

pure soul. Reasoned knowledge [*Das Erkennen*], thought, is the root of his life, of his immortality as a totality in himself.

In 1829 H. E. Schubart published his *Ueber Philosophie überhaupt und Hegel's Enzyklopädie der philosophischen Wissenschaften insbesondere* in which he reproached Hegel for having rejected the immortality of the individual. Hegel made the following reply to Schubart in a review printed in *Jahrbücher für wissenschaftliche Kritik* (*Jub. Ausg.* XX 314ff.; quotation pp. 378ff.):

> The author allows his confusion to take the most sublime bounds . . . on the occasion of his tirade against faith and the immortality of the soul. . . . To the author it is not galimatias to call the universe one whole consisting only of components in which each component nevertheless is itself supposed to be a whole. The greatest truth of each component is [in turn] supposed to consist in a lack of reference to the other components, so each part (since the whole abides in the interrelationship of the components) is without reference to the whole of which it is a component. Such logic is supposed to teach faith in the immortality of the soul.

Friedrich Richter proposed in his *Die Lehre von den letzten Dingen* (Breslau, 1833) to demonstrate that the consequence of Hegel's philosophy was the denial of the soul's immortality. C. F. Göschel in 1835 assumed the opposite standpoint in his essay "Von den Beweisen für die Unsterblichkeit der menschlichen Seele im Lichte der spekulativen Philosophie" in which he advanced three proofs of the immortality of the soul, corresponding to the cosmological, teleological, and ontological proofs of the existence of God. Several others besides the foregoing participated in the debate, among whom were L. Feuerbach, C. H. Weisse, and I. H. Fichte ("the Younger"). Kierkegaard was not particularly well acquainted with all of this from original sources; but he found a thorough orientation in Poul Møller's long historico-critical essay, "Tanker over Muligheden af Beviser for Menneskets Udødelighed, med Hensyn til den nyeste derhen hørende Litteratur," which appeared for the first time in *Maanedsskrift for Litteratur* (Copenhagen, 1837), where Kierkegaard immediately read it (*Pap.* II A 17 dated February 4, 1837; *JP* V 5201). In this essay Poul Møller broke definitively with Hegel.

A striking example of how the debate occupied people's minds is found in Johanne Luise Heiberg, *Et Liv gjenoplevet i Erindringen*, 4th ed., I–IV (Copenhagen, 1944), I, 243, where she writes:

Martensen often visited us in the evening and the conversation between the two gentlemen turned heated and lively on Hegelian philosophy, which we two women [Johanne Luise Heiberg and Mrs. Gyllembourg] of course had difficulty in following. Something or other, however, occurred to our minds, making us uneasy. When Martensen took his leave, we stormed in to Heiberg with questions. His mother in particular flew into such a passion over what she had grasped of this doctrine, that she kept returning from her bedroom to advance her objections. One evening is unforgettable to me. Both of the gentlemen had discussed Hegel's view that the individual's immortality consisted in being merged with the entire great universe. This made Heiberg's mother completely beside herself. Again and again she came in, in a worsening state of disarray, attacking the doctrine. To this attack Heiberg made no reply other than, "Go to bed, it's late."

"Fuse together!" she screamed, "do you think I want to be fused together with all those many nasty drops?"

"Go to bed!"

Besides the work by Poul Møller mentioned above, reference may also be made to Harald Høffding, *Philosophien i Tydskland efter Hegel* (Copenhagen, 1872), pp. 17ff., and Johann Eduard Erdmann, *Grundriss der Geschichte der Philosophie*, 3rd ed., I–II (Berlin, 1878), II, 677ff.

153:14 *sub specie aeterni*. From the viewpoint of eternity or, for example, elevated above the categories of time and space and above human existence. See the Index: Spinoza.

153:20 *A Soul after Death*. Heiberg's poem *En Sjæl efter Døden* with the subtitle *en apocalyptisk Comedie* was published in *Nye Digte 1841*. He was plainly influenced by August von Platen's fragment *Die neuen Propheten* (Leipzig, 1822), Aristophanes' *The Frogs*, and the pact scene and the scene between the student and Mephistopheles in Goethe's *Faust*.

153:20 *commentary of Archdeacon Tryde*. That is, the always well-meaning but somewhat naïve Archdeacon E. C. Tryde (1781–1860), who was vividly interested in philosophy and belonged to Heiberg's intimate circle of acquaints. In his review of *En Sjæl efter Døden*, in *Tidsskrift for Litteratur og Kritik* (1841), pp. 174–95, Tryde indulged in deliberations about whether the soul of the Philistine whom Heiberg had condemned to the Hell of Boredom (along with all of Sibbern's books!) could be saved in a Christian sense. Martensen too raised this question in his review in the newspaper *Fædrelandet* in January 1841.

153:33 *I am not a learned man*. Holders of a doctorate were privileged with the title "Highly Learned" (højlærd). Kierkegaard had a Magister's Degree of Philosophy, which is roughly equivalent to a Ph.D.

153:34   *Professor Poul Møller.* See above.

153:38   *Tom, Dick and Harry strung upon a thread.* Compare Poul Møller's observation in the article mentioned above:

> The most unscientific manner in which people lately have sought to promote the doctrine of immortality is by publishing collections of excerpts taken from writings of other ages on this subject. I am thinking in this connection especially of the booklets published by Dr. Hubert-Becker containing extracts of works from the sixteenth and seventeenth centuries on the state of the soul after death.

154:3   *well-trained.* Danish *dresseret*, a word usually used only in connection with animals, for example, a trained or performing dog. (Note by R.J.W.)

155:25   *Gessler's hat.* See Schiller's *William Tell*, Act I, Scene 3. Kierkegaard was undoubtedly thinking of Rossini's opera of the same title, which was performed at the Royal Theater from 1842 on. Kierkegaard owned *Schillers sämmtliche Werke*, I–XII (Stuttgart and Tübingen, 1838; *ASKB* 1804–15), but neither in the *Journals and Papers* nor in the published works are there many traces of readings of Schiller.

155:31   *Mars in the armor which rendered him invisible.* This is most likely a confusion with Hades' helmet, which renders the wearer invisible and which Athenia put on to assist her hero Diomedes in his fight against Ares (Latin, Mars), the god of war. See the *Iliad*, V, 845ff.

158:6   *another author.* Kierkegaard's pseudonym Vigilius Haufniensis in *The Concept of Anxiety* (*KW* VIII 138ff.; *SV* IV 448ff.).

159:5   *Privy Councillor Andersen.* Privy Councillor (*Kammerraad*) was originally the title of a member of the Exchequer (*Skatkammerkollegiet*) with a higher rank than that of Privy Assessor (*Kammerassessor*). But even in Kierkegaard's time the title Privy Councillor was merely nominal, placing its bearer in subsection two of the sixth order of preference.

159:17   *in Lent at evensong.* What Kierkegaard means here is simply something that occurs regularly or habitually. Neither in the present nor in the older lenten collects is "the Second Sunday in Lent at evensong" given special emphasis.

160:2   *authority of the first instance.* The clergy.

160:17   *the pneumatic and the psychosomatic.* That is, the spiritual and the soul (or mind) and body. Concerning these anthropological terms in Kierkegaard, see Johannes Sløk, *Die Anthropologie Kierkegaards* (Copenhagen, 1954), pp. 77–89, and Arild Christensen, "Om Søren Kierkegaards Inddelingsprincip," *Kierkegaardiana*, III (Copenhagen, 1959), pp. 21–7.

161:15   *rejoicing in the jollity.* Rom: 12:15.

161:17   *impressia vestigia.* Footsteps. See Cicero, *De oratore*, 12.

161:17   *humble before God.* A quotation from Assessor Vilhelm's essay in *Stages*, p. 111 (*SV* VI 117).

163:13   *separation.* Compare Eph. 2:14.

163:24   *solitary communion with itself.* This should be followed by: "His presence is an eternal contemporaneity." The original edition and the first edition of the Collected Works in Danish (*SV* VII 152) have *Samvittighed* (conscience) instead of *Samtidighed* (contemporaneity). Kierkegaard later corrected it in his own copy of the work. See *Pap.* VII¹ B 85:9. The entire phrase was then omitted in S/L. (Note by R.J.W.)

163:31   *snivel and wail before the tribunal.* Before judgment is passed Socrates says in Plato's *Apology* 34C:

> Well, Athenians, this and the like of this is nearly all the defense which I have to offer. Yet a word more. Perhaps there may be someone who is offended at me, when he calls to mind how he himself on a similar, or even a less serious occasion, had recourse to prayers and supplication with many tears, and how he produced his children in court, which was a moving spectacle, together with a posse of his relations and friends; whereas I, who am probably in danger of my life, will do none of these things.

163:35   *the fortunate lot of Dr. Hartspring.* That is, J. L. Heiberg. Just why Kierkegaard dubbed Heiberg "Dr. Hartspring" (*Dr. Hjortespring*) has not come to light. In his *Autobiografiske Fragmenter* (November–December 1839) Heiberg tells the following story:

> Now I had settled down in Hamburg during my journey home [from Berlin where he had met Hegel] in the summer of 1824 . . . and was at the time continually ruminating over what [in Hegel's system] was still obscure to me. One day I was sitting in my room in the [Hotel] König von England with Hegel on my table and Hegel in my thoughts, at the same time listening to the almost incessant music of the beautiful psalms emanating from the chime of bells of St. Peter's Church. Suddenly, in a way such as I have never experienced before or since, I happened to be seized by a momentary inner vision, just like a flash of light, that all at once illuminated the entire region for me, awakening in me the previously concealed central thought. From that moment the major

contours of the system were clear to me, and I was thoroughly convinced that I had grasped its inmost core, however many details might remain that I still had not assimilated and perhaps never would assimilate. I can truly say that that wonderful moment was something close to the most important epoch in my life, for it gave me a peace and security and a self-awareness that I had never known before.

163:35   *Dr. Hartspring.* In the printed manuscript this is changed from "Dr. Marcussen," which had in turn been changed from "Prof. Heiberg" (*Pap.* VI B 98:36).

163:37   *(of which the waiters were unaware).* The printed manuscript has the following in the margin (*Pap.* 98:37):

> *In margin*: whereas the barber, who had arrived that very moment to shave the professor's beard off, found him in a solemn mood with three subscription plans in his hand that the Spirit is assumed to have inspired in him.

163:38   *the Hegelian philosophy which assumes that there are no miracles.* Neither Heiberg nor Hegel says directly that there are no miracles. Hegel has the following to say about them in *Lectures on the Philosophy of Religion* (II, 338; *W.a.A.* XII 200; *Jub. Ausg.* XVI 200):

> Miracles are changes connected with the world of sense, changes in the material world which are actually perceived, and this perception is itself connected with the senses because it has to do with changes in the world of sense. It has already been remarked in reference to this positive element of miracles, that it undoubtedly can produce a kind of verification for the man who is guided by his senses; but this is merely the beginning of verification, an unspiritual kind of verification by which what is spiritual cannot be verified.

164:3   *The conversion of Paul.* Acts 9:1ff.

164:9   *same Easter morning . . . in Goethe's Faust.* In Part One, especially V, lines 765ff., where Faust says (translation by Walter Kaufmann, *Anchor Books*):

> Although I hear the message, I lack all faith or trust;
> And faith's favorite child is miracle.
> For those far spheres I should not dare to strive,
> From which these tidings come to me;
> And yet these chords, which I have known since infancy:
> Call me now, too, back into life.

164:16   *poetic requital.* The meaning is retribution or settlement. This may in turn be interpreted to mean that in practice Heiberg makes a fool of himself by romanticizing his miraculous conversion to a philosophy that repudiates miracles and denies the very romanticism to which he succumbs.

164:18   *the romantic.* In the printed manuscript this is changed from (*Pap.* VI B 98:39):

> just as later in addition to becoming an astronomer he became a Christmas buck [*Julebuk*], which is a perfect indication of how his speculative and astronomic spiritual existence significantly makes its mark on the external world.

A *Julebuk* was a person who at Christmas time dressed in a buck's or goat's costume, kissed children, and distributed gifts. Both the word and the custom have long since gone out of use. The word *Buk* also means "blunder." See *ODS*, IX, col. 900.

164:32   *the café in the Frederiksberg Garden.* Josty's, which still exists. See Villads Christensen, *Søren Kierkegaard og Frederiksberg* (Copenhagen, 1959), pp. 24ff.

164:38   *a queen's remembrance.* The widow of Frederik VI, Sophie Frederikke (1767–1852), who after the king's death in 1839 usually resided at Frederiksberg Castle.

165:3   *that poetical hero.* The printed manuscript has (*Pap.* VI B 98:41): "*Changed from:* of that celebrated systematic prize hero, Professor Heiberg."

165:6   *literature on the subscription plan.* The target here is undoubtedly J. L. Heiberg's *Perseus, Journal for den speculative Idée,* the only two issues of which appeared in June 1837 and August 1838. The periodical had 133 subscribers, including Kierkegaard, and the two issues contained six articles all told: four by Heiberg, one by Martensen, and one by Carl Weis. Compare Kierkegaard's *Forord,* no. VIII (*SV* V 55ff.).

166:16   *as Aladdin.* In *Adam Oehlenschlägers poetiske Skrifter,* I–II (Copenhagen, 1805; *ASKB* 1597–98).

166:21   *pereat.* Down with him! *Crucify:* see Luke 23:21.

166:33   *material support.* There is an untranslatable play on words here. The Danish word *Underholdning* means both "amusement" and "income" (*ODS*, XXV, cols. 1212ff.).

166:35   *laid out money on it.* See above, note to title page, and Hirsch's remarks in his translation of Kierkegaard's *Briefe* (1955), p. 146. In the cost of production of the books on consignment must be included secretarial assistance in copying the manuscripts, costs of proofs, in-

cidental expenses, the purchase of books, and the cost of living. Kierkegaard's fortune was in the main spent, directly or indirectly, on
the production of his works.

167:6   *a lottery of tasteful gifts.* Compare Kierkegaard's *Forord*, no. I (*SV* V
21ff.):

> When a man wants to publish a book he will next make sure
> that he is rendering a service. To that end he will ask a publisher
> or someone with a philosophical mind, his barber or a passerby,
> just what it is the age demands. Failing this he will himself hit on
> something, and he will not forget to announce that this is what the
> age demands. For not everyone is endowed with the mental for-
> titude to understand the demand of the age, even less since it might
> seem to a doubter that the requirement of the age is manifold and
> that just like Maren Amme [in Holberg's *Barselstuen*, Act 3, Scene
> 5] the age, though one, has several voices.
>
> You see, I have done all this and I am therefore happy to present
> an esteemed public with my New Year's gift, which in every re-
> spect is especially elegant and dainty. I have neglected nothing and
> thus dare flatter myself that it will come at a time seasonable to
> the reading world and especially to every family that celebrates
> Christmas Eve and New Year's Eve, since it is in every way serv-
> iceable as a tasteful present and can even be put on a Christmas
> tree with the help of a silk bow attached to the gilt binding.

Résumé (pp. 169–224)

The author begins this section with observations concerning different ways of approaching the truth. We may define it empirically as the agreement of thought with being, or idealistically as the agreement of being with thought. Regardless of which definition we prefer, we must first ascertain what we mean by "being." If we are speaking of empirical being the truth will remain an approximation because concrete empirical being is constantly undergoing change. If we take the idealistic approach we end up with a tautology, for in this case we are dealing with a purely conceptual being in which the terms thought and being mean the same thing. In the first case something else besides thought must intervene; in the second we get nowhere at all.

A third possibility will appear if an existing individual—an existing spirit, as the author phrases it—raises the question of the truth. In this event truth will be defined not as something objective but as a process of assimilation, as inwardness or subjectivity, and if thus defined the task of the subject will consist in becoming engrossed in that truth existentially.

The path taken by objective reflection leads away from the subject and toward abstract thought, for example, to mathematics or historical knowledge. This kind of reflection is supposed to possess or be able to attain a certainty that lies beyond the grasp of subjective thought, because a purely subjective definition of the truth supposedly makes it impossible to distinguish between truth and error, since both may be rooted in inwardness. Thus madness and truth would become indistinguishable. In this connection the author exposes two forms of madness. The first, of which Don Quixote serves as a prototype, is a form of madness produced when the passion of inwardness is attached to a particular finite image; the second form arises when inwardness is absent precisely where and when it ought to be present (p. 175). The speculative definition of truth as the identity of being and thought is false, since it is impossible to escape from existence.

Having rendered this account of the possible definitions of truth, the author introduces a distinction between what he designates as nonessential and essential cognition. In Climacus' view, such knowledge as concerns existence may be called essential, and this will in turn mean that only ethical and ethico-religious knowledge are essential (p. 177).

The author thereupon recapitulates his view (p. 178), exemplifying it with the problem concerning the cognition of God. If the question is raised objectively it will concern the problem of whether or not this is the true God, whereas if raised subjectively it will concern how the individual is to be related to something undefined so that the relationship will be a true God-relationship (p. 178).

There is no truth in mediation, for the truth lies in inwardness. Such is also the case with regard to the problem of immortality (p. 180).

In principle it holds true that if a man makes an objective inquiry he attaches importance to *what* he says, whereas if he inquires subjectively the emphasis will be placed on *how* he says it (p. 181). The passion of infinitude is the truth itself, and this will in turn mean that subjectivity is the truth. The author then expresses this in the form of a definition: *"An objective uncertainty held fast in an appropriation-process of the most passionate inwardness is the truth*, the highest truth attainable for an *existing* individual" (p. 182). This is also a paraphrase of what faith is (p. 182); and if subjectivity, or inwardness, is the truth an objectively defined truth will become a paradox when it relates to an existing individual.

In this connection the author discusses the Socratic position (pp. 183–84). Unlike in the *Fragments*, however, he in the present work distinguishes between Socrates and Plato, characterizing Socrates as a philosopher who wanted to exist and Plato as one who was interested in speculation.

Climacus now poses the question whether it might not be possible to find a more inward expression for the definition of truth as subjectivity. Indeed it is possible, he affirms, but in that case the definition would have to begin in this manner: "subjectivity is untruth" (p. 185). The assumption behind this definition is that subjectivity—a term the author frequently uses in the personalized sense of "subject," that is, the particular existing human being—has become or becomes untruth in time and thus is living and existing in error. Now if we call this untruth or error sin we must also assume that the individual is born in sin and as a sinner, and consequently that he is in a condition called Original Sin.

The paradox comes into being when the eternal essential truth relates itself to an existing individual, which means that here the paradox is defined by the relationship rather than by any content. The eternal truth becomes a paradox whenever it enters into time, and it is to the truth in this guise that the individual must establish a relationship. Should the paradox then become paradoxical in itself it will repel the individual by virtue of the absurd. Faith as the passion of inwardness corresponds to this.

The author now identifies the paradox and the absurd. The absurd is, he declares, the fact that the eternal truth has come into existence in time; consequently the way of objectivity is impracticable (pp. 188ff.), for an objective approach will never advance further than to an approximation. Moreover, the author explains, Christianity has proclaimed itself to be the eternal essential truth that has come into existence in time, and it has served notice that it is a paradox that requires the inwardness of faith in relation to what to the Jews was an offense and to the Greeks was foolishness—and to reason is absurd.

Now if we assume that a revelation in a strict sense must be a mystery, it will follow that the maximum understanding possible is the realization that it cannot be understood (p. 192). Speculation, however, manages to emasculate the concepts of revelation, the paradox, and man's absolute difference from God. This absolute difference inheres in the circumstance that a man is a particular existing being, whereas God is the infinite who is eternal (p.195).

The speculative philosopher seeks to explain the paradox, but instead he merely corrects it by declaring that it is not a paradox; in other words he simply abrogates the paradox. He does not maintain that Christianity is not the truth; he insists rather that it is his speculative understanding of Christianity that substantiates its truth. As an example of the treatment Christianity receives at the hands of speculation, the author now considers (pp. 201ff.) the paradox of the forgiveness of sin, in relation to which certainty is available only in eternity. In attempting to explain this paradox speculative philosophy once again fails to respect the difference between the plain man's and the plain wise man's knowledge of what is simple, for the speculative philosopher arrives at the conclusion that the paradox is valid for the plain man but eliminated in the case of the philosopher. This is the result of claiming that Christianity is true only to a certain degree—the most stupid thing ever said about Christianity.

Such being the situation, the author found it necessary to regard it as his task to elucidate what existence and inwardness are, and this in the face of the enormous knowledge and speculative results available in his time. But if inwardness is the truth it will be impossible to communicate any result, and the author's form of communication will have to be indirect. The author is therefore in a situation that is quite different from that of the Apostles, who had the task of proclaiming a hitherto unknown truth.

A direct God-relationship is paganism, the author writes, because a direct relationship between two spiritual beings is inconceivable where the essential truth is concerned (p. 221).

Climacus' principal thought was that, owing to an excess of knowledge, people in his time had forgotten the significance of inwardness and what it means to exist. From this it ought to be possible to derive an explanation of the misunderstanding between speculation and Christianity (p. 223). His own method of proceeding in this situation must above all not be didactic. With Socrates and Hamann as formal prototypes the author thus resolved to commence, and his first job would be *"to exhibit the existential relationship between the aesthetic and the ethical within an existing individual"* (p. 224). In short, he set out to present it in a mimic form (see the subtitle of the book).

*   *   *

169:15   *desideratum.* Something desired and hence lacking.

169:30   *the pure I-am-I.* This was the point of departure for Fichte's philosophy of identity. See the Introduction, chap. 4 and the Index.

169:32   *in the manner indicated.* That is, on p. 98.

170:16   *copula.* This word actually means "band." In a sentence—especially a proposition containing a logical judgment—the copula links the concepts inherent in the subject and predicate. Colloquially, this is generally expressed by means of a verb such as "is" or "has."

In Hegel's ontologically oriented logic, however, the copula "to be" does not simply relate subject and predicate, as in Aristotelian logic, but is primarily an expression of being: " 'This action is good': the copula denotes that the predicate belongs to the Being of the subject, and is not connected with it merely externally" (*The Science of Logic*, II, 261; *Jub. Ausg.* V 69). It is this view among other logical concepts that Kierkegaard has in mind here and in the following passage. See Robert Widenmann, "Copula," *Concepts and Alternatives in Kierkegaard*, vol. III of *Bibliotheca Kierkegaardiana* (Copenhagen, 1980), pp. 14–17.

170:16   *reduplication.* The concept of reduplication has been analyzed by Gregor Malantschuk in an essay in *Frihed og Eksistens* (Copenhagen, 1980), pp. 73–83, titled "Fordoblelse." The following is quoted with a view toward an understanding of Kierkegaard's present use of this term:

Reduplication according to Kierkegaard expresses a fusion of two different qualities into a synthesis. Insofar, reduplication is intimately related to Kierkegaard's concept of a synthesis, with but the important difference that by means of the word reduplication one is constantly reminded of the doubleness of a relationship, that is, in which two different qualities are linked to each other. Reduplication as such will thus always be determined by the two qualities forming the reduplication. Kierkegaard then distinguishes sharply between the kind of reduplication in which both terms lie "within the identity of immanence" and the reduplication of which one term is transcendental. To Kierkegaard the latter reduplication is reduplication properly speaking, and it is this reduplication that pertains to the sphere of Christianity. . . . First we have a "simple reduplication" within immanence: a teacher proposes a doctrine while at the same time reduplicating this doctrine in his life. This reduplication [*Reduplikation*] constitutes a redoubling [*Fordoblelse*], for it embodies two different elements that now merge to form a synthesis: the teacher's original attitude and the requirement exacted of him by the doctrine. Another form of reduplication within immanence arises insofar as every content of thought, if it is not "to be a figment of the imagination," must also evince the possibility of being. In this way we acquire a reduplication in which the two different elements, being and essence, form a synthesis. But since in such instances these two aspects are grasped in the language of abstraction, this difference will only be a "tautology." Therefore Climacus is also able to say [in the present passage in the *Postscript*] that this abstract reduplication annuls itself the moment it is posited.

171:20   *custom clerk.* Kierkegaard is here thinking of the town clerk responsible for issuing certificates for goods passing through the gates in the ramparts, which at that time still encircled Copenhagen. This anecdote is also mentioned in *Pap.* X^5 A 10 (*JP* III 3170).

171:37   *mediation.* Concerning this concept and Kierkegaard's criticism of it see the Index.

172:24   *subject-object.* According to Fichte's *Wissenschaftslehre* (*SW* I, 98 note) "subject-object" expresses a pure self-identity or "I=I". See the Introduction, chap. 4.

173:20   *Hamlet.* Act III, Scene 1.

174:35   *the question of Pontius Pilate.* "What is truth?" John 18:38.

175:2   *Privatdocent . . . de omnibus dubitandum est.* Kierkegaard is here clearly referring to Martensen. In the winter semester of 1837–1838 Kierkegaard attended Martensen's introductory lectures on speculative dogmatics in which Descartes' principles were expressly made the object of special attention (see *Pap.* II C 18, dated November 29, 1837). Shortly thereafter Kierkegaard wrote a little unpublished play titled *Striden mellem den gamle og den nye Sæbekielder* ("The Conflict Between the Old and the New Soapcellars"; *Pap.* II B 1–21) in which he used Martensen's lectures as a backdrop. Kierkegaard's unfinished work, *Johannes Climacus eller de omnibus dubitandum est* (*Pap.* IV B 1–17; *Johannes Climacus, or, de omnibus dubitandum est,* trans. T. H. Croxall [Stanford, 1958], pp. 112ff.) must be interpreted in the same light. I have analyzed Kierkegaard's little play in *Kierkegaard's Relation to Hegel* (Princeton, 1980), pp. 180–200; reference is also made to Arild Christensen, "Efterskriftens Opgør med Martensen," *Kierkegaardiana,* IV (Copenhagen, 1962), pp. 45–62.

175:29   *walking stick . . . Døbler . . . chamber organ.* The following appears in the draft of this passage (*Pap.* VI B 40:21):

> It makes one think of that ingenious poem by J. Kerner about a stick that belonged to a privatdocent and that through constant association with its owner finally became a privatdocent just like him.

Kierkegaard is referring to Justinus Kerner, *Die Dichtungen* (Stuttgart, 1834; *ASKB* 1734).

By "Døbler" Kierkegaard undoubtedly means Ludwig Döbler (born in Vienna October 3, 1801), an Austrian engraver who studied physics and chemistry, which he then put to use in exhibitions of magic. His magic was novel in that it was based on recent inventions as the oxyhydrogen microscope, Stampfer's stroboscopic plates that made projected pictures move, Drummond's special light for enlarging dissolving views, and other such contraptions. He accompanied his tricks with didactic lectures, and during a tour of twenty years throughout Europe he enjoyed tremendous popularity, performing before royalty, Goethe, Metternick, and other notables. Later in life he reverted to his profession as engraver and produced works of art that were highly appreciated. He died in Gstettenhof in Lower Austria on April 17, 1864.

Döbler's travels brought him to Copenhagen in August 1841. On the 13th he performed before the King and Queen and then on August 16, 19, 24, and 27 he played to packed houses in the Royal Theater. After having pretty nearly turned Copenhagen on end (to judge from contemporary newspaper articles), he departed August

31 aboard the *S/S Frederik den Sjette* for Travemünde—with Elisabeth Fry and her entourage as fellow passengers.

There is no direct evidence that Kierkegaard ever saw Döbler perform, and it is unknown whether a "walking stick" of the kind mentioned by Kierkegaard ever formed part of Döbler's show. This particular contraption may be a figment of Kierkegaards's imagination, or it may have come from another source—as indicated by the draft quoted above—and been ascribed to Döbler as a matter of style.

See *Österreiches biographisches Lexikon*, ed. Leo Santifaller and Eva Obermayer-Marnach, I–VII (Grasz-Cologne and Vienna, 1957–1978), I, 190; *Allgemeine deutsche Biographie*, I–LVI (Leipzig and Munich, 1875–1912), V, 272; *Kjøbenhavnsposten* for August 7, 13, and 14, 1841; and *Berlingske politiske og Avertissements-Tidende* for August 16, 17, and 28, 1841. (Note by R.J.W.)

175:31   *drinking a toast of brotherhood with the public hangman.* In Holberg's *Mester Geert Westphaler eller den meget talende Barbeer* (Scene 8) the main character boasts that on the only trip he ever made to Kiel he drank a toast of brotherhood with a man who turned out to be "the hangman of Slesvig."

176:5   *an expectation of the creature.* Rom. 8:19.

   a fantastic rendezvous in the clouds. Probably an allusion to Ixion, who according to Greek mythology intended to embrace Juno but embraced a cloud instead.

177:20   *Peter Deacon.* In Holberg's *Erasmus Montanus*, Act III, Scene 3. See the Index.

177:22   *this great philosophicum.* In Kierkegaard's time the student entrance examination was given by the university and was called *examen artium*, or "first examination" (see *Breve*, no. VII, and note). After a semester the students were to take the "second examination," often called "the major philosophicum," the first part of which included tests in Latin, Greek, Hebrew, History, and Mathematics. After still another semester the students found themselves faced with the second part, which included Practical Philosophy, Physics, and Higher Mathematics.

177:29   *quantum satis.* As much as necessary.

177:38   *the truth becomes a paradox.* By "truth" we must here understand the message of Christianity that comes from without and that brings the possibility of salvation with it. Since it comes from without, it does not originate in the heart of any man; moreover, it is the opposite of what reason would expect and therefore of what paganism had imagined. Reason, of which speculative philosophy is representative, seeks to arrive at a *theologia gloriae*, whereas God reveals Himself in a state of abasement. Since we know God only through His revelation, all genuine theology must consequently be *theologia crucis*. Reason will thus be offended at the fact that the truth as something not comprised in the categories of time and space has nevertheless become historical and that the individual encounters it in a specific historical situation, hearing it as a message "from the past." This message persists as a thought that is foreign to the ego, incommensurable with human reason, and always "repellent," that is, paradoxical.

On "paradox" see especially N. H. Søe, "Søren Kierkegaards Lære om Paradoxet," *Nordisk teologi, idéer och män. Till Ragnar Bring* (Lund, 1955), pp. 102–22; Henning Schröer, *Die Denkform der Paradoxalität als theologisches Problem* (Göttingen, 1960), pp. 55–92; J. Heywood Thomas, "Paradox," *Concepts and Alternatives in Kierkegaard*, vol. III of *Bibliotheca Kierkegaardiana* (Copenhagen, 1980), pp. 192–219.

179
(note *):1

God . . . a postulate. See Valter Lindström, *Stadiernas teologi* (Lund, 1943). In the draft (*Pap.* VI B 40:23) Kierkegaard mentions H. Hemsterhuis, and in a note the Danish editors of the *Journals and Papers* refer to his *Vermischte philosophische Schriften*, I–III (Leipzig, 1782; *ASKB* 573–75), II, 127ff., 185ff., 216ff., and 236ff.

180:13

Socrates. Kierkegaard apparently had in mind the description of life after death in *Phaedo* where Socrates, having spoken of punishment for evil and reward for good, continues with (114D):

> I do not mean to affirm that the description which I have given of the soul and her mansions is exactly true—a man of sense ought hardly to say that. But I do say that, inasmuch as the soul is shown to be immortal, he may venture to think, not improperly or unworthily, that something of the kind is true. The venture is a glorious one, and he ought to comfort himself with words like these, which is the reason why I lengthen out the tale.

Kierkegaard is unjustified in putting an "if" into Socrates' mouth.

180:17

one of our modern thinkers with the three proofs? This is an allusion to C. F. Göschel's writing mentioned above (see the Index), especially chap. II, "Von der Triplicität der Beweise für die Unsterblichkeit im Lichte der Spekulation."

180:32

many a wedded matron. The draft adds (*Pap.* VI B 40:24):

> Many a wedded matron has on the other hand had her husband guaranteed by the formalities of wedding vows, and so forth, has had innumerable proofs of love [*Elskoven*], has more than once

yielded to the tenderest expressions of love, and yet was not in love [*forelsket*].

181:23   *to annul the difference between good and evil, together with the principle of contradiction.* See the Index: contradiction.

181   *Stages on Life's Way, Note on p. 426.* This corresponds to p. 366 in (note *):1   the original edition and to *SV* VI 495. This footnote, which is from *Stages* and to which Kierkegaard merely makes reference, does not belong in the *Postscript* at all.

182:23   *I contemplate the order of nature in the hope of finding God.* Compare Pascal's statement in *Pensées* (fr. 229, ed. L. Brunschvicg):

> La nature ne m'offre rien qui ne soit matière de doute et d'inquiétude. Si je n'y voyais rien qui marquât une Divinité, je me déterminerais à la négative; si je voyais partout les marques d'un Créatur, je reposerais en paix dans la foi. Mais, voyant trop pour nier et trop pour m'assurer, je suis dans un état à plaindre. [Nature offers me nothing that might not be a matter of doubt and disquiet. If I saw nothing there that indicated a Divinity I would settle on the negative; if I saw everywhere the indications of a Creator I would peacefully repose in faith. But seeing too much to deny and too much to assure me, I am in a state to be pitied.]

See Per Lønning, *Cet effrayant pari* (Paris, 1980).

183:1   *In the principle.* This passage has the following form in the draft (*Pap.* VI B 40:26):

> When subjectivity, inwardness, is the truth and this subjectivity exists [*er existerende*] (this must never be forgotten), and when from this point of view the question of truth is raised objectively, the truth must be the *paradox.* The eternal truth is a paradox to the existing individual and his only true relationship to it is in passion. True, a mathematical principle is no paradox, but a mathematical principle is not an essential truth, either, and it does not so relate to an existing individual as to make his existing essential.
>
> Viewed eternally there is no paradox and when the eternal truth relates itself to an Eternal being [*den Evige*] there is no paradox. Quite right. But with all respect I must say that I am not an Eternal being either, nor was the deceased Hegel while he lived; even though he was a great man and I am an insignificant person we however have one thing in common—each of us is a particular existing human being. Let us never forget that simple principle that we certainly all know from our textbooks. Any eternal truth, which in announcing itself to existing individuals does not do so as a para-

dox, is *eo ipso* not an eternal truth. What comforts me with respect to the system is that it will probably go out of fashion again and the systematists will most likely remake their robes and once more be in fashion; for there is an eternal youthfulness in their noble efforts.

The eternal truth must not be understood in an abstract sense but as the essential truth that has an essential relationship to existence, or more properly, to the existing individual. Precisely for this reason it must be simultaneously eternal and temporal and as such be the eternal truth in *time* for an existing individual. (For it is not so difficult to understand that the eternal truth is the eternal truth in the *species aeterni* of abstraction, and speculation has made things rather easy for itself by obtaining something far easier to answer under the high-flown name of speculation, which is supposed to be something quite different from faith.) This existing individual is not a fantastic I = I but an everyday altogether plain human being such, for example, as myself, Johannes Climacus, born in Copenhagen, of average stature, black hair and brown eyes, presently 30 years old. Just as the eternal essential truth is a paradox in relation to an existing individual, so an existing individual's relationship to it is again a paradox, in the same way as faith too was determined in the foregoing.

With this all the bombastic chatter to the effect that eternally there is no paradox and that true speculation does not remain standing with the paradox is repudiated; for all suchlike is readily wafted away merely by putting the accent of the question in the right place; that is, whether or not a man is speculation, or whether the speculator has ceased to be a human being, an individual human being, an existing human being, and whether or not the existing individual must have the goodness to content himself with existing. The speculator's meritorious deed of annulling the paradox speculatively is not so meritorious after all, but is only a self-accusation betraying the fact either that the eternal truth is no longer the eternal essential truth that essentially concerns the existing individual, or that he himself has been fantastically transformed into a chimeric I = I.

Now Christianity has precisely declared itself to be the essential eternal truth and, furthermore, proclaimed itself as a paradox, having with this also intended to be of essential significance to the existing individual through his assimilating it in existing [*exister-ende*] and by existing in it. The truth abides in inwardness only, and therefore only therein is Christianity essentially in truth. Faith is consequently Christian truth, and viewed essentially it consists of how one believes. The paradox is the crucifix of reason (the uncertainty of objectivity) and faith is the passion of inwardness despite the paradox. This is really how things must stand, as sure as a human is a human and as long as a human is an existing human. If the honorable speculating professor wants to understand it differently, perhaps he will do me the favor of discontinuing his speculative explanation of Christianity for a moment and explain to us who he then is, to which species of beings he belongs. After all, it can scarcely be assumed that the essential eternal truth came into the world because it felt a need of being explained by a speculator; it would be better to assume that the eternal essential truth came into the world because men were in need of it. And why were they in need of it? Surely not to explain it so that they might have something to do, but in order to exist in it. But if this is why it came into the world and if it has itself implied this by proclaiming itself to be a paradox, not to give clever heads a nut to crack but because it cannot be anything else to existing beings [*existerende Væsener*] as long as they exist, while at the same time it is the very guidance in their existence—if this is so, the gain of modern speculation becomes a phantom that goes the same way as the I = I, pure being, and the like.

In margin:

Paganism culminates in the principle that subjectivity is the truth. Socrates' ignorance embodies more truth than any pagan knowledge. Within this principle lies in turn Christian truth.

From a pagan standpoint it is paradoxical that an eternal truth is supposed to relate itself to an existing individual—the Christian standpoint is that the eternal truth as a paradox relates itself to an existing individual. Christian knowledge is not knowledge about the paradox but knowledge about it in passion, and the knowledge of the wise man consists in the fact that it can only be known in passion. Thus, the fact that subjectivity is the truth is by all means expressed objectively when the truth proclaims itself to be a paradox.

Socrates therefore does not by any means have Christian faith, which naturally is not to be found in paganism, but his is an analogy to it. His paradox is merely an expression of the passion of inwardness with which he relates himself to the eternal truth, which only becomes a paradox when it concerns an existing individual and is assimilated by an existing individual. In this sense the paradox of faith was to believe that a god exists [*er . . . til*], which is still by no means Christian faith. The Christian paradox is the passion of inwardness in relation to an eternal truth that declares itself to be a paradox, where the passion of inwardness in its turn finds its most paradoxical expression in the fact that the individual is himself a sinner—and thus is not prevented from knowing the eternal truth merely by the circumstance that he exists. The objective paradox is on the contrary formed by the fact that the eternal truth, which itself proclaims itself to be a paradox, embodies within itself a historical element [and] has come into existence [*er bleven existerende*]. Just as the Socratic paradox appeared because the eternal truth was related to an existing individual, so the Christian paradox appears because the eternal truth has entered into existence [*er bleven existerende*] and now in turn relates itself to an existing individual in paradoxical passion.

183:9   *"But to have made an advance. . . . "* A quotation from *Fragments*, my edition p. 139 (*SV* IV 302).

183:38   *the category of the absurd.* Here in the sense of "the absolute paradox."

184:19   *integer.* Untainted (by sin).

184 (note *):1   *a difficulty in the plan of the Fragments.* Regarding this plan see the introduction to my edition, pp. lxvii ff.

184(note *):10   *distinguish between Socrates and Plato.* Concerning this altered evaluation of Socrates concomitant with a modified view, reference is made especially to Jens Himmelstrup, *Søren Kierkegaards Opfattelse af Sokrates* (Copenhagen, 1924), pp. 117ff.

185 (note* cont.):12   *sensu eminentiori.* In a more eminent sense.

185(note cont.):18   πίστις. Faith. Concerning the use of this word in classic Greek, reference is made to Bultmann's article in Kittel's *Theologisches Wörterbuch zum Neuen Testament*, VI (Stuttgart, 1960), pp. 175ff.

185(note cont.):20   *a work of Aristotle. Rhetoric* 1355a ff., where the word denotes something that brings about conviction. Kierkegaard bought Carl L. Roth's German translation (Stuttgart, 1833; *ASKB* 1092) of this work on January 30, 1843, and read it chiefly in 1845. See *Pap.* V A 1; IV A 207 (*JP* II 1111; V 5572; IV 4254). See also Cornelio Fabro, "Aristotle and Aristotelianism," *Kierkegaard and Great Traditions*, vol. VI of *Bibliotheca Kierkegaardiana* (Copenhagen, 1981), pp. 27–53.

185:8   *Subjectivity, inwardness . . . truth . . . untruth.* In the second clause of this sentence "subjectivity" indicates an existing individual who, Christianly regarded, always has the truth outside of himself and is for example never able to grasp it by means of recollection. In the first clause subjectivity means the personal passion and earnestness with which one believes. The concept of truth as employed here is treated in most of the presentations of Kierkegaard's world of thought. Here only a few references will be made: Emanuel Hirsch, *Kierke-gaard-Studien*, II (Gütersloh, 1933), pp. 768ff.; the brief outline in Gregor Malantschuk, *Indførelse i Søren Kierkegaards Forfatterskab* (Copenhagen, 1953), pp. 39ff.; Valter Lindström in *Festskrift till Ragnar Bring*, pp. 85–102; and J. Heywood Thomas, *Subjectivity and Paradox* (Oxford, 1957).

Kierkegaard has several times spoken out against the prevalent misunderstanding of the principle of subjectivity in the sense that traditionally makes it the equivalent of individual arbitrariness. The following journal entry of 1849 is an example (*Pap.* X² A 299; *JP* IV 4450):

> In all the usual talk that Johannes Climacus is mere subjectivity etc., it has been completely overlooked that in addition to all his other concretions he points out in one of the last sections that the remarkable thing is that there is a How with the characteristic that when the How is scrupulously rendered the What is also given, that this is the How of "faith." Right here, at its very maximum, inwardness is shown to be objectivity. And this, then, is a turning of the subjectivity-principle, which, as far as I know, has never before been carried through or accomplished in this way.

186:5   *deeper in subjectivity.* To this the draft adds (*Pap.* VI B 45; *JP* III 3085):

> The forgiveness of sin is indeed a paradox insofar as the eternal truth is related to an existing person; it is a paradox insofar as the eternal truth is related to the person botched up in time and by time and who nevertheless is an existing person (because under the qualification of sin existence is registered and accentuated a second time), but forgiveness of sin is really a paradox only when it is linked to the appearance of the god [*Guden*], to the fact that the god has existed [*existeret*]. For the paradox always arises by the joining of existing and the eternal truth, but the more often this occurs the more paradox.*
>
> *Note. Reminiscent of *Fragments*, in which I said that I do not believe that God has existed [*er til*, eternally is], but know it; whereas I *believe* that God has existed [*har været til*] (the historical). At that time I simply put the two formulations together in order to make contrast clear and did not emphasize that even from the Greek point of view the eternal truth, by being for an existing person,

becomes an object of faith and a paradox. But it by no means follows that this faith is the Christian faith as I have now presented it.

188:32   *idolatry*. The printed manuscript also has the following (*Pap*. VI B 98:43):

> [He was] so unrecognizable that not even the precursor knew him immediately but only from his words, and the disciples did not know him immediately because there was nothing to see but [knew him] only from the words of the precursor (John 1:31, 33ff.).

188:35   *sensu strictissimo*. In the strictest sense.
188:35   *in the Fragments*. In the "Interlude," pp. 97–110 (*SV* IV 264–80).
189:3   *In relation to the absurd*. The draft adds (*Pap*. VI B 42; *JP* II 2287):

> In relation to the absurd, objective approximation is nonsense; for objective knowledge, in grasping the absurd, has literally gone bankrupt down to its last shilling.
>
> In this case the way of approximation would be to interrogate witnesses who have seen the God [*Guden*] and have either believed the absurd themselves or have not believed it, and in the one case I gain nothing, and in the other I lose nothing—to interrogate witnesses who have seen the God perform a miracle, which for one thing cannot be seen, and if they have believed it, well, it is one further consequence of the absurd.—But I do not need to develop this further here; I have done that in the *Fragments*. Here we have the same problem Socrates had—to prevent oneself from foundering in objective approximation. It is simply a matter of setting aside introductory observations, and the old reliables, and proofs based on effects, and pawnbrokers, and all such in order not to be prevented from clarifying the absurd—so that a person can believe if he will.
>
> If a speculator would like to give a guest performance here and say: From an eternal and divine point of view there is no paradox here—this is quite right; but whether or not the speculator is the eternal who sees the eternal—this is something else again. If he then continues his talking, which does have the eternal in the sense that like the song it lasts for an eternity, he must be referred to Socrates, for he has not even comprehended Socrates and even less found time to comprehend, according to his own position, something which goes beyond Socrates.

Another part of the draft also has a bearing on this passage (*Pap.* VI B 43; *JP* III 3084):

> Christianity does not want to be understood—but the rude speculator does not want to understand this. He cries incessantly: "From the standpoint of the eternal, there is no paradox."
>
> Christianity entered into the world not to be understood but to be existed in. This cannot be expressed more strongly than by the fact that Christianity itself proclaims itself to be a paradox. If the horror in the beginning of Christianity was that one could so easily take offense, the horror now—the longer the world exists—is that Christianity, aided by culture, abundant knowledge, and objectifying, can so easily become sheer nonsense. The longer the world continues the more difficult it becomes to become a Christian.

189:4   *like the comedy, Misunderstanding upon Misunderstanding. Misforstaaelse paa Misforstaaelse,* a comedy from 1828 by Thomas Overskou (1798–1873) who imitated Kotzebue. It is printed in *Overskous udvalgte Komedier,* I–II (Copenhagen, 1850–1851), II, 135–80.

190:18   *Fragments.* Pages 114ff.; *first part of this book*—the present section recapitulates the part mentioned.

190:24   *the public pawnbrokers and guarantors.* The public pawnbroker (*Assistenshuset*) in Copenhagen was an institution founded in 1688 to make loans against security, and it was directly responsible to the Minister of Finance. It was abolished March 29, 1974. *Guarantors* is here used in the sense of "reliable witnesses."

191:14   *an offense to the Jews.* 1 Cor. 1:23.

191:24   *subjectivity is in the first instance.* In connection with this point see the important observation in the *Fragments,* p. 78 (*SV* IV 255): "although as soon as the condition is given, the Socratic principle will again apply."

191:31   *sensu laxiori.* In a broader sense.

191:33   *intellectual talent in relation to the misunderstanding.* By this Kierkegaard means the talent for speculation that misunderstands.

192:24   *the policemen said to Geert Westphaler.* In the five-act edition of 1753, Act IV, Scene 2, "two constables" say to Geert Westphaler, a very talkative barber: "We are very sorry to have to come to you on such an errand [namely, to serve a writ]."

193:31   *a fool in the eyes of the world.* 1. Cor. 1:23 and 4:10.

193:36   *sacrifice all his wealth.* Compare Matt. 13:45ff.

194:11   *over-earthly and under-earthly beings.* These phrases are of course humoristic and used in a figurative sense. As Junghans interprets them, the "over-earthly" are the speculative idealists, the "under-earthly" the empirical philosophers, and, if we extend the image, the "earthly" is the existing thinker.

194:18   *a professor makes public.* Possibly this reference is simply to the custom prevalent among professors at the time (especially in Germany) of letting the first edition of a work serve in reality as a trial edition. It is also quite conceivable, however, that specific reference is being made to Martensen and his *Grundrids til Moralphilosophiens System* (Copenhagen, 1841; *ASKB* 650). See my commentary on the *Fragments*, pp. 156ff.

194:37   *if it assumes to be Christianity.* The draft continues with (*Pap.* VI B 40:27):

> [. . . which] by its principal teaching and at every point proclaims itself to be a paradox. Christianity's doctrine that God was a human being, a particular human being, that He lived in time for a certain number of years, ate, and drank—this is surely the most frightful paradox that can be offered to an existing human being, who precisely as existing [*existerende*] is himself in a process of becoming and hence is unable to understand eternally because he is not himself eternal, but is only existing.

195:28   *The modern mythical allegorizing tendency.* This is the view upheld by David F. Strauss in *Das Leben Jesu*, I–II (Berlin, 1853–1836); see above, Introduction. Kierkegaard owned *Begrebet Mythus eller den religiøse Aands Form* (Copenhagen, 1844; *ASKB* 424), a work written by A. F. Beck, who was one of Strauss's Danish adherents. See also my edition of the *Fragments*, p. 204.

197:22   *abrogated.* Kierkegaard uses three words in this passage to produce an untranslatable play on words. The verb *at hæve* means "to annul," "to abrogate"; *Ophævelsen* ("abrogation") also means "a fuss about nothing"; and *Hævelse* generally means a swelling such as caused by a bruise, but it can also mean the inflation that a self-centered person feels. (Note by R.J.W.)

197:31   *God is a highest conception.* Compare Spinoza's definition of substance (*sive Deus; Ethica*, I, def. III): "per substantiam intelligo id quod in se est et per se concipitur; hoc est id, cuius conceptus non indiget conceptu alterius rei, a quo formari debeat." ("By substance I understand that which exists in itself and is conceived by itself; that is, something the concept of which does not require the concept of something else from which it must be formed.")

197:33   *the highest principles.* See especially vol. II, 330ff., in Trendelenburg's work mentioned by Kierkegaard in the following journal entry (*Pap.* V A 74; *JP* III 2341):

Basic principles can be demonstrated only indirectly (negatively). This idea is frequently found and developed in Trendlenburg's *Logische Untersuchungen*. It is significant to me for the leap, and to show that the ultimate can be reached only as a limit.

198:8   *the fullness of time.* This expression originates from Gal. 4:4, but here it is used ironically.

198:15   *an unutterable joy.* This expression is borrowed from 1 Pet. 1:8.

198:21   *a truly surprising surprise.* The source of this is a line in Heiberg's vaudeville, *Recensenten og Dyret,* Scene 15: "the surprising surprise of those surprised" (De overraskedes overraskende Overraskelse).

198:23   *an existing human being is a synthesis of the infinite and the finite.* Gregor Malantschuk gives an excellent explanation of Kierkegaard's view of man as a composite being or synthesis in *Kierkegaard's Way to the Truth,* trans. Mary Michelsen (Minneapolis, 1963), pp. 20ff.:

> Kierkegaard designates these two universal qualities, the components of every human being, by such terms as time and eternity, the finite and the infinite, body (and soul) and spirit, necessity and freedom, etc. These coupled terms all say the same thing—that man's being consists of two antithetical qualities. . . .
>
> Kierkegaard derived his understanding of man as a composite of two completely different qualities from Christianity. . . .
>
> We discover first of all something quite obvious to Kierkegaard—that one of the elements of the synthesis must be of greater value than the other. The Eternal must be higher than the temporal, the spirit higher than body and soul, and so on. Secondly, it follows that when the two components stand in the right relationship to each other, the higher component must be the dominant one. Thirdly, because of the qualitative difference between the two components, man is faced at the outset with the task in existence of relating the two factors in the right manner.
>
> Kierkegaard tries to include all the possibilities and contradictions of human life under this formulation: man is a synthesis. Out of this grows his theory of the stages, which is only a historical cloak for the synthesis and a corroboration of its truth. By reflecting on the different possibilities over against which the components of the synthesis place man, we get in abridged perspective a glimpse of the whole structure of the stages.

See also the following works: Regin Prenter, "L'homme, synthèse du temps et de l'éternité d'après Søren Kierkegaard," *Studia theologica* (Lund, 1949), pp. 5–20; Johannes Sløk, *Die Anthropologie Kierkegaards*

(Copenhagen, 1954), pp. 19–89; Louis Dupré, "The Constitution of the Self in Kierkegaard's Philosophy," *International Philosophical Quarterly*, III, 4 (1963), pp. 506–26; Vernard Eller, *Kierkegaard and Radical Discipleship* (Princeton, 1968), pp. 140ff.; Paul Dietrichson, "Kierkegaard's Concept of the Self," *Inquiry*, VIII, 1 (1965), pp. 1–32; Ralph Henry Johnson, *The Concept of Existence in the Concluding Postscript* (The Hague, 1972).

199:15   *aufheben has various and even contradictory meanings.* Compare Hegel in *The Science of Logic* (1, 119ff.; *W.a.A.* III 110; *Jub. Ausg.* IV 120):

> To transcend (*aufheben*) has this double meaning, that it signifies to keep or to preserve and also to make to cease, to finish. To preserve includes this negative element, that something is removed from its immediacy and therefore from a Determinate Being exposed to external influences, in order that it may be preserved.— Thus, what is transcended is also preserved; it has only lost its immediacy and is not on that account annihilated. . . . It is a joy for speculative thought to find words which in themselves have a speculative meaning; the German language has several such.

The Danish equivalent is the verb *at ophæve*, to annul, abrogate, repeal, revoke, nullify, and so forth. According to *ODS*, XV, cols. 841ff., it also once meant to lift, elevate, preserve, swell, and so on, but this usage was archaic even during Kierkegaard's time. G.R.G. Mure writes in *The Philosophy of Hegel* (London, 1965), p. 35, that

> in synthesis the antithesis . . . is cancelled *qua* contradiction but also thereby preserved. It is *aufgehoben*, says Hegel, availing himself of the fact that the verb *aufheben* has both these meanings. "Sublated" will serve as a translation.
>
> In "sublation" the reader will at once recognize double negation. [Note by R.J.W.]

199:31   *tollere . . . conservare.* To abrogate or annihilate and to preserve or conserve, respectively. Compare Cicero: *tollendum esse Octavium.*

200:1   *mean reduction, the status of a relative moment, as is also usually said.* This is Hegel's meaning in *The Science of Logic* (I, 120; *W.a.A.* III 111; *Jub. Ausg.* IV 121): "The more precise meaning and expression which Being and Nothing receive, now that they are moments, must result from the consideration of Determinate Being as the unity in which they are preserved." In other words, since the original position is abrogated it is reduced to a relative "moment" or phase in the development and only possesses conditional validity.

200:20   *Christianity which is and was and remains the truth.* John 14:6 and Apoc. 1:8.

200:27   *κατὰ δύναμιν* [S/L: When the potential . . .]. Potentially, according to possibility. Viewed as a teaching, the truth of Christianity was merely potential until speculative thought brought it to light and explained it.

201:18   *sensu strictiori.* In a stricter sense.

201 note *):1   *the Romans . . . at Zama.* P. Cornelius Scipio Africanus Major conquered the Carthaginians at Zama in 202 B.C., thereby ending the Second Punic War. But the Roman recorders of history and war say nothing about the fact that the Romans on this occasion are supposed to have fought with wind and dust in their eyes. Probably Kierkegaard's memory failed him concerning the location of the battle, which took place at Canne, not at Zama—and at Canne the Romans suffered their worst defeat. This is narrated both in Polyaen's *Stratagemata* (IV, 38:4) and in Livius (XXII, 46) who tells us that "The sun was at an angle appropriate to both parties, whether they were intentionally deployed in this manner or whether they stood in this position by accident. The Romans faced the south, the Carthaginians the north." As the day waned, the Romans had increasingly to fight with the sun in their eyes, and of this Livius writes: "The Romans had the wind—which the natives of the region called *volturnus* [named after Mount Vultur, that is, an east-southeast wind]—in their faces, and it blew much dust in their faces, depriving them of their sight." Junghans, who quotes this passage, is correct in pointing this out as Kierkegaard's primary source. Kierkegaard offered the first five books of Livius for his entrance examinations, and he owned a couple of editions (*ASKB* 1251–56).

202:9   *before a distinguished public.* The addressee is Martensen, who in 1845 had received an appointment as Court Preacher.

204:2   *intermediate staff of clever brains.* In Danish: *et Mellemstab af gode Hoveder.* The word *Mellemstab* is an archaic military term that designated the portion of the staff embracing physicians, veterinarians, attendants, and so forth; hence the nonmilitary or civilian part of the staff.

205:33   *then he is stupid.* The following is added in the margin of the printed manuscript (*Pap.* VI B 98:44):

> and a Christian would probably call him unhappy; for a deceived man is of course always unhappy, and of those deceived the one who deceives himself is the unhappiest, and of such deceived persons the unhappiest is in turn he who in contrast to the piously deceived would have to be called the presumptuously deceived.

206:5   *whoever is neither cold nor hot.* St. John the Apostle, commanded to write to the Church at Laodicea, says: "I know all your ways; you are neither hot nor cold. How I wish you were either hot or cold! But because you are lukewarm, neither hot nor cold, I will spit you out of my mouth." (Rev. 3:15ff.)

206:7   *Pilate.* Pilate's question in John 18:38.

206:12   *his wife who was made anxious.* Matt. 27:19.

206:17   *washing the hands.* Matt. 27:24.

206:39   *sets his hand to the plow.* This phrase is taken from Luke 9:62.

207:8   *dullness in the grain market* [S/L: stock-market]. *Flauhed* (modern *flovhed*) can also mean shame; embarrassment, awkwardness, sheepishness; dullness, slackness; insipidity, and so forth, which leaves Kierkegaard abundant possibilities for a play on words. See *ODS*, IV, cols, 1233ff., and Hermann Vinterberg and C. A. Bodelsen, *Dansk-Engelsk Ordbog*, I–II (Copenhagen, 1966), I, 319.

207:12   *not bought it dear enough.* "For you have been bought at a great price" (1 Cor. 6:20 and 7:23). The Greek word τιμῆς is here in the absolute and signifies "payment"; hence, "You have been bought and paid for." The expression is known from the sacral emancipation of slaves. Compare A. Deissmann, *Licht vom Osten* (Tübingen, 1923), pp. 270ff.

207:38   *"I am not like these three."* Compare Luke 18:11.

208:9   *the Greek poet.* Sophocles. This episode is related by Cicero in *De senectute*, VII, 22 (trans. W.W.A. Falconer, *Loeb Classical Library*, 1959):

> Sophocles composed tragedies to extreme old age; and when, because of his absorption in literary work, he was thought to be neglecting his business affairs, his sons haled him into court to secure a verdict removing him from the control of his property, under a law similar to ours, whereby it is customary to restrain heads of families from wasting their estates.

This passage is cited by Lessing in his biography of Sophocles in *G. E. Lessings sämmtliche Schriften*, I–XXXII (Berlin, 1825–1828; *ASKB* 1747–62), X, 133. Since Kierkegaard was engrossed in the writings of Lessing while working on the *Postscript*, it is very likely that he read about this episode there.

208:35   *speaks only of livelihood and wife.* Luke 14:16ff.

210:1   *that Christianity is the truth.* After this the printed manuscript has the following continuation in the margin (*Pap.* VI B 98:45; *JP* II 1610):

> A person can be a great logician and become immortal through his services and yet prostitute himself by assuming that the logical

is the existential and that the principle of contradiction is abrogated in existence because it is indisputably abrogated in logic; whereas existence is the very separation which prevents the purely logical flow. Hegel may very well be world-historical as a thinker, but one thing he has certainly lacked: he was not brought up in the Christian religion, or he was mediocrely brought up. For just as the person brought up to believe in God learns that even if every misfortune falls to his lot in life and he never sees a happy day, he must simply hold out, so also the person brought up in Christianity learns to regard this as eternal truth and to regard every difficulty simply as a spiritual trial [*Anfægtelse*]. But Hegel's concept of Christianity is so far from bearing the imprint of this primitivity of childhood inwardness that his treatment of faith—for example, of what it is to believe—is nothing but pure foolishness [corrected from *stupidity*]. I am not afraid to say this. If I had the cheek to say of the most simple man alive that he is too stupid to become a Christian, this would be a matter between God and myself, and woe unto me! But to say this of Hegel remains a matter only between Hegel and myself, and at most a few Hegelians, for the stupidity is of another kind, and to say this is no blasphemy against the God who created man in his image, consequently every man, and against the God who took human form in order to save all, the most simple of men as well.

210:6   *my mission of judgment.* This expression is borrowed from the teachings of Orthodox dogmatics about Christ's triple mission (*munus Christi triplex*), that is, as prophet, high priest, and king (judge). See for example Karl Hase, *Hutterus Redivivus . . .* , 4th ed. (Leipzig, 1839; ASKB 581), §§99–102. The following is added in the draft (*Pap.* VI B 40:33; *JP* V 5797):

> that, like the Wandering Jew in a beautiful legend, I should lead the pilgrims to the promised land and not enter myself, that I should guide men to the truth of Christianity and that as my punishment for going astray in my younger days I myself would not enter in but would venture only to be an omen of an incomparable future.

210:19   *The story is quite a simple one.* The draft continues with (*Pap.* VI B 40:34):

> Although *already several years ago* I had my sights on Christianity, and although when I then *began 3 years ago* with the fancy of wanting to be (N.B.) an author I at once aimed at it, I nevertheless have no such thing to plead. On the contrary, the beginning is quite simple. Now it was probably about 8 years ago, it was a

Sunday—well, now perhaps the reader will not believe me because it was again a Sunday, but it is nonetheless quite certain that it was Sunday. It was late afternoon, evening was already beginning, the beginning of its leave-taking was thereby intimated, though it has often tempted me to the misunderstanding that one ought to remain in its company.†

In margin: N.B.: perhaps the whole thing could be used best by itself under the title An Unsuccessful Author's Attempt to be a Reader—and in this the pseudonymous books could be examined.
†In margin: to be thoroughly worked out.

211:25   *inwardness is merely a phase.* Which is what inwardness according to its nature precisely must not be, since it is a total qualification.

212:7   *an opportunity to breathe in peace.* The draft adds (*Pap.* VI B 49; *JP* I 56, modified):

Evening's leave-taking (from the day and from the one who has experienced the day) is puzzling [*changed from*: has a remarkable ambiguity]; its reminder is like the careful mother's instruction to the child to go home, and its invitation is like an inexplicable hint, as if now for the first time the true life was beginning. Man is blended in the same way—finitude is like the child for whom it is expedient to come home early; infinitude is like the adult who wants to stay out at night—and the evening's leave-taking is puzzling. Sometimes one would like to interpret it as an invitation persuasively insinuated by the night wind as it monotonously repeats itself and searches the forest and fields as if looking for something, persuasively insinuated by the far echo of stillness in itself (as if it had a presentiment of something), persuasively insinuated by the sublime tranquility of heaven (as if it were found) and by the audible silence of the dew, as if this were the explanation of this, and the refreshment of infinitude, the fruitful visit of the quiet night concealed in the lifting fog.
In margin: As if one first found rest by remaining out for a nocturnal rendezvous, not with a woman but, with the infinite.

212:29   *the river Niger in Africa.* The source of the Niger, where Sierra Leone, Liberia, and French Guinea border each other, was not located until 1879. The river empties into the Gulf of Guinea in a huge swampy delta, as was demonstrated by the two explorers Clapperton (in 1825 and 1827) and Lander (in 1830).

212:32   *the rest of the family . . . removed by death.* When reading this passage we must remember Kierkegaard's own family history. In 1822 Maren

Kirstine Kierkegaard died, in 1832 Nicoline Christine, and in 1834 Petrea Severine. His brother Peter Christian's first wife, Elise Marie (née Boisen), died in 1837, two older brothers, Søren Michael and Niels Andreas, died in 1819 and 1833, respectively. His father Michael Pedersen's first wife, Kirstine Nielsdatter (née Royen), had died in 1796, and his second wife, Ane Sørensdatter Lund, died in 1834. See Olaf Kierkegaard and P. F. Parup, *Fæstebonden i Sædding Kristen Jespersen Kierkegaards Efterslægt* (Copenhagen, 1941).

212:35   *the names of the many dead.* The draft then has (*Pap.* VI B 40:35):

> For it actually happened, and from it one can see how easy it is to be an observer and how much cause people have to be angry with such a person for stealing from them, for every man is usually a poetic figure whom the observer steals.
>
> In all likelihood they had been talking together before I came, but I heard the following. In a voice affected by emotion the old man said to the little one whom he held by the hand: Poor child, now I am the only one you have left; you don't have a father any more and I can't be one to you; even though I love you more than anything my days are after all numbered, and I myself long to depart from this world and find rest. But there is a God in heaven after whom all fatherliness on earth is named, He is more your father than both Father and Grandfather; keep close to Him, He won't desert you; and yet there is one name in which there is salvation, the name of Jesus Christ; don't ever forget it, and don't forget my admonition.

213:7   *bring my gray hairs in sorrow to the grave.* From Gen. 42:38.
214:6   *because he himself is an old man.* The draft adds (*Pap.* VI B 40:36):

> [. . .] because his years were numbered. There have probably been times—and it is an appalling thought—when death came upon a person who had something infinitely important to say, depriving him of speech, so he was unable to utter it; but here it was as if death came and fastened itself upon the old man and he had one single person whom he loved, one single person to whom he wished to say what he believed concerned that person's temporal and eternal good, but the person to whom he had to talk was a child, and a child and an old man are indeed not equals who grow up together—they simply part company.
>
> It is a delicate matter to make a child give a promise or to put a child under oath that way. Therefore something else happened. As I stood deeply moved by the whole episode, it seemed to me at

one moment as if I myself were the young man whom the father buried with tears, and the next as if I were the child who was making that sacred promise. Yet I was of course neither, nor could it affect me that way essentially.

The father now left with the little one and I stayed behind; then the impression began to concern me more clearly. I thought, Here is a task for you. Now you are after all tired of life's diversions, tired of girls, so you only love them in passing and don't even care to chase them. Even if Christianity were not such a gigantic phenomenon and whether it ever becomes everything to you or you are offended by it, the sorrow and concern of such an honorable man and such a promise and the exaction of such a promise, which would move a stone, must move you; there must be a property of faith and a hostile power that seeks to wrest this from the believer and give him something else instead. Let it then be your task to regard Christianity as an entrusted good so that what Christianity is and what it is not might really become clear. So now you have something to do, and after all one must have something with which to pass the time, and at least this is not something evil.

The old man had left, so even if I wanted to initiate him into my thoughts it was now too late. O, well, it is not necessary either; I am not fond of handshakes but of the quiet dedication of a resolve. After all, the inwardness of spirit always lives in the body as a stranger and foreigner—so why all the gestures? I think as Brutus in Shak[e]speare: no promises, for a promise concerns only myself. So the old man never learned that he also bound me by an oath, and if we ever happen to see each other he will immediately, such is my hope, learn of my promise and that I have kept it to the best of my abilities.

In margin: Only once in my life has an oath been required of me, and then I laughed and said: This is silly—for I was suspicious of the person who had demanded the oath of me. But while laughing I said to myself: You'll promise it anyway. And it is quite possible to do this, it being a *reservatio mentalis* in a good sense, perhaps even out of care for the one who demands the oath, lest it become ridiculous afterwards.

214:33   *The womanish is always dangerous.* There is the following in the margin of the printed manuscript (*Pap.* VI B 98:46; *JP* I 926):

There is such deep and beautiful truth in what Socrates says to Crito (in *Phaedo*), when in the solemn moment of taking leave he asks with spontaneous intimacy if there is anything the dying one in the moment of departure wishes him to do. Socrates answers: Nothing—only that you attend to your own selves, even if you promise me nothing now; but if you are indifferent to your own selves and do not follow in life the track of what has been set forth now and at other times, then you achieve nothing at all even though you promised ever so much and ever so solemnly. (See para. 115 in *Phaedo*.)

214:37   *Shakespeare makes Brutus say.* In *Julius Caesar*, Act II, Scene 1. Kierkegaard quoted from Peter Foersom's Danish translation of 1807 (*ASKB* 1889–96). As a rule he read Shakespeare in Schlegel's and Tieck's German translations (*ASKB* 1883–88), though sometimes he used Ortlepp's (*ASKB* 1874–81). Compare Johannes Sløk, *Shakespeare og Kierkegaard* (Copenhagen, 1972).

215:18   *reservatio mentalis.* Here in the sense of "mental reservation."

216:16   *my landlady.* This situation is formed as a parallel to Heiberg's experience in connection with Hegel's philosophy. See pp. 247–48.

217:26   *an enthusiastic genius.* Compare *SV* XI 109–27 (*The Present Age*, pp. 71ff.), "On the Difference Between a Genius and an Apostle."

217:28   *the nota bene of reduplication.* That is, that one must live in truth.

217:30   *valore intrinsico.* Intrinsic worth.

220:25   *"without God in the world."* Eph. 2:12.

220(note   *a Greek author.* Kierkegaard had in mind the following passage from
*):3   Plato's *Phaedo*, 111B:

and in a word, the air is used by them as the water and the sea are by us, and the other is to them what the air is to us. Moreover, the temperament of their seasons is such that they have no disease, and live much longer than we do, and have sight and hearing and smell, and all the other senses, in far greater perfection, in the same degree that air is purer than water or the ether than air. Also they have temples and sacred places in which the gods really dwell, and they hear their voices and receive their answers, and are conscious of them and hold converse with them, and they see the sun, moon, and stars as they really are, and their other blessedness is of a piece with this.

221:34   *happy about his favorable outward appearance.* In Xenophon's *Symposium*, chap. V, Socrates and Critobulus discuss which of them is the most handsome. Critobulus insists that the most efficacious is the most beautiful. Socrates then ironically concludes that in that case his eyes must be the most beautiful, for they are distinctly protuberant, thereby enabling Socrates to see not only straight ahead but also to the sides like a crab. So too with his nose, for the purpose of a nose is to smell, and Socrates' nostrils turn outward instead of merely downward like other people's.

222:12   *he bore the sins of the world.* John 1:29.

222:20   *a number of growths on the forehead.* Regarding Socrates' appearance, see Kierkegaard's notes to *The Concept of Anxiety* (*Pap.* III B 30; *JP* IV 4246).

222:26   *dancing master in the Friendly Society. Det venskabelige Selskab of 3. Januar 1783* (The Friendly Society of January 3, 1783) was a club that held weekly concerts during the winter season and arranged annual balls that were conducted by "Ball Inspectors." See the Society's laws of 1819, IV, §12, and C. Bruun, *Kjøbenhavn,* I–III (Copenhagen, 1887–1901), III, 646.

222:27   *in toto.* On the whole.

222:29   *private call.* (*privat Kald.*) Under absolutism in Denmark in the seventeenth century the King alone had the right of nomination (*Kaldsret,* that is, advowson), but the church patrons, among whom were major landed proprietors, usually had the right to make proposals (*jus proponendi*). The constitution of 1849 abolished this system.

222:36   *had essentially to do with himself.* The draft then has (*Pap.* VI B 40:38):

> "for when a child must be weaned, the mother blackens her breast" and of course an ethical individual must no longer be a child. And likewise, to recall the *Fragments,* if the god wishes to reveal himself in human form and has the least thing conspicuous about him— then he deceives and the relationship fails to become one of inwardness, which is truth. But if he looks just like this particular human being, altogether like any other man, he will deceive only those who think that catching sight of the god has something in common with going to Tivoli.

The quotation with which Kierkegaard begins this portion of the draft is from *Fear and Trembling,* p. 28 (*SV* III 64).

223:19   *But above all it must not be done in a dogmatizing manner.* The draft has (*Pap.* VI B 40:39):

> But that could not be brought out by lecturing [*docerende*], for that very moment I would have qualified myself in essential conformity with speculation's deviation; what it is to exist had to be elucidated, not in its concept or in knowledge about it but in inwardness in existence [*Existents*].

223:36   *Holstein carriage.* This was an open and awkward horse-drawn carriage with a body made of wicker-work and usually with four seats suspended from leather straps.

224:7   *poor Hamann . . . reduced to a paragraph by Michelet.* The reference is to Karl Ludvig Michelet (1801–1893) who belonged to the Hegelian center—though with leanings to the left—and who edited Hegel's *Lectures on the History of Philosophy* in three volumes (*W.a.A.* XIII–XV; *Jub. Ausg.* XVII–XIX). In 1837 and 1838 he published his own *Geschichte der letzten Systeme der Philosophie in Deutschland* in two thick volumes. Among other things, the work was intended as a continuation in Hegel's spirit of the master's philosophy of history. Hegel's work concludes with a discussion of Schelling, and Michelet continues with a discussion of Solger and ends with Hegel. In vol. I, 300–86, under the title "Glaubensphilosophie" ("The Philosophy of Faith"), he deals with Hamann (pp. 300–18), Herder (pp. 318–39), and in conclusion Jacobi. It is a known fact that in 1828 Hegel had published in his *Jahrbücher für wissenschaftliche Kritik* a very comprehensive but condescending criticism of F. Roth's edition of Hamann's writings (printed in *W.a.A.* XVII 38–110; *Jub. Ausg.* XX 203–75). Michelet, however, is the first to have allowed Hamann an independent position in the history of philosophy and to have discussed his thinking with comprehension and recognition. See my essay "To af Forudsætningerne for Hamanns Opgør med sin Samtid," *Dansk teologisk Tidsskrift* (Copenhagen, 1960), pp. 78ff.

224:26   *satisfactio vicaria.* Substitute satisfaction. The expression is employed in orthodox theology concerning Christ's death of atonement.

Résumé (pp. 225–266)

Climacus now reviews the pseudonymous works. He is pleased to note that they seem to have realized the goal he had set for himself. He undertakes to interpret them but expresses some reservation, since it is impossible for him to know for certain whether or not his reading will agree with the authors' views (p. 225). At any rate, he finds that the pseudonymous authors have been alert to the relation between communication and the truth qualified as inwardness. According to Climacus, *Either/Or* explicitly permits the existential relationship between the esthetic and the ethical to come into being in an existing individuality (as he expresses it), and in this Climacus espies an indirect polemic against speculation; for speculation is indifferent to existence. He interprets the fact that there are no results or final decisions in these works as an indirect expression of the truth qualified as inwardness; and this may also imply a polemic against the truth defined as knowledge.

The first part of *Either/Or* presents an existential possibility that cannot develop into an actual concrete existence; it is a melancholy that requires further ethical processing (p. 226). The second part sets forth an ethical personality that exists by virtue of the ethical. To Climacus it is striking that *Either/Or* ends precisely with an edifying truth. He would have preferred to see it emphasized more strongly, "in order that the individual stages on the way toward a Christian religious existence might be clearly set out" (p. 229). Christian truth considered as inwardness is also edifying, but from this it does not follow that any edifying truth is Christian; edification is a broader and more comprehensive concept.

The work mentioned above was succeeded by *Two Upbuilding Discourses* and then *Three Upbuilding Discourses*. These were definitely not Christian sermons, since they did not use the doubly reflected religious categories inherent in the paradox but solely the ethical categories of immanence. The author then criticizes (pp. 229–30) the fact that some people summarily called the edifying discourses sermons, and he also has a few critical remarks to make about "a possibility" in *Either/Or*.

The definition of truth as inwardness implies that whoever wishes to edify a reader must write so that he first frightens his reader away, alienating him and awakening consternation. We can readily discern points of resemblance here with other theories, for example, Melanchthon's doctrine of *usus secundus legis*. Climacus feels that *Fear and Trembling*, another pseudonymous work, succeeds in producing such a repellent effect; in this book secrecy is presented "as something so fearful that aesthetic secrecy becomes child's play by comparison" (p. 234). The concept of repetition is a correlative of this, and the pseudonymous author of *Repetition* also realized that it is fundamentally an expression of immanence. Climacus is of the opinion that the pseudonymous authors constantly had their sights trained on the problem involved in existing, and so they kept up an indirect polemic against speculation (pp. 236).

The next work to be interpreted is *The Concept of Anxiety* (p. 240), and in this connection Climacus shows a special interest in the treatment of sin. He contends that sin must not be conceived in abstract terms, since this would make it impossible to arrive at a decisive understanding of this important qualification, for we would immediately encounter the problem involved in the fact that sin is essentially related to our very existence. Climacus of course quickly notices that *The Concept of Anxiety* is distinguishable from the other pseudonymous works in that its form is direct and it is even given to lecturing a bit (p. 241).

So finally along came the author's own work, *Philosophical Fragments*. Meantime, Magister Kierkegaard's edifying or "upbuilding" discourses had been steadily following step with the pseudonymous works, all of which the reading world assumed were written by the same man. The last four edifying discourses had a tinge of humor, thereby indicating that they gave expression to the stage of life immediately preceding the Christian position.

Climacus claims that speculation seems to perform the trick of understanding the whole of Christianity. But instead of arriving at a Christian understanding it proffers a speculative interpretation that is nothing but a misunderstanding. He readily admits that to combat this tendency on the part of speculation he purposely designed *Philosophical Fragments* according to a plan that would make it a parody of speculation in both form and content.

The author allows himself a little digression to consider the difference between an edifying discourse and a sermon. He asserts that basically this difference must issue from the circumstance that only an ordained clergyman has the right to give a sermon.

Returning to his main topic, Climacus now proposes that the pseudonymous works taken as a whole represent a movement toward

Christiantity. In this respect it is important to remember that although Christianity is inwardness it is "not every and any type of inwardness" (p. 251). The form of presentation in these works, however, makes it impossible to give an abstract of them, Climacus says, because an abstract would simply eliminate their most important aspects and transform them into a lecture in the worst sense of the word (p. 252). As to the *Fragments*, Climacus' own work, he discloses that it made a decisive approach to Christianity but without mentioning either Christianity or Christ by name.

The next work to appear was *Stages on Life's Way* (p. 252). Our author concentrates his attention on the third part of this book, "Guilty?/Not Guilty?"—which is a story of suffering. This work differs from *Either/Or* in that it is divided into three parts or stages: the esthetic, the ethical, and the religious. These are in turn defined as pleasure and perdition; action and victory; and suffering.

✳   ✳   ✳

225: title   *APPENDIX.* When reading this section we must constantly bear in mind that its interpretation of the earlier works is written from the standpoint of Johannes Climacus in the guise of humorist and differs from the view later held by Kierkegaard himself. Kierkegaard expresses his view in, for example, *The Point of View for My Work as An Author*, which he wrote in 1848 and which was published posthumously by his brother in 1859.

225:1   *Either/Or.* Published on February 20, 1843.

226:7   *no result and no final decision.* It would seem safe to assume that this shows a formal influence from the earlier Platonic dialogues, for example, *Eutyphro, Ion, Hippias Minor, Hippias Major, Laches, Charmides, Lysis,* and *Protagoras,* which are generally regarded as ending without a result. To take *Protagoras* as an example, this is done by giving the dialogue the aim of defining the concept of virtue, but Socrates and the Sophist who has given the dialogue his name fail to reach an agreement, so Socrates concludes by exclaiming (361C):

> Now I, Protagoras, perceiving this terrible confusion of ideas, have a great desire that they should be cleared up. And I should like to carry on the discussion until we ascertain what virtue is, and whether capable of being taught or not.

In a significant journal entry from 1846 (*Pap.* VII¹ A 74; *JP* IV 4266) Kierkegaard declares:

The fact that many of Plato's dialogues end without a result has a far deeper basis than I had thought earlier [for example, in *The Concept of Irony*]. They are a reproduction of Socrates' skill which makes the reader or hearer himself active, and therefore they do not end in a result but in a sting. This is an excellent parody of the modern rote-method which says everything the sooner the better and all at one time, which awakens no self-action but only leads the reader to rattle it off like a parrot.

See Jens Himmelstrup, *Søren Kierkegaards Opfattelse af Sokrates* (Copenhagen, 1924), pp. 52ff. and 100ff.

226:13   *The first of the Diapsalmata.* Below is a collation of the references on this page, all of which are from *Either/Or.*

Original edition	SV		English edition	
Part One, p. 3	I	3	I	19
Part Two, p. 217	II	227	II	214
bottom				
Part Two, p. 368	II	381	II	356

226:24   *autopathic.* Or idiopathic; something innate, peculiar to the individual. Here it is used as an antonym to sympathetic, compassionate.

227:13   *has despaired.* Kierkegaard's references to *Either/Or*, II, on this and the following line are omitted in S/L.

Original edition	SV		English edition	
Part Two, pp. 163–227,	II	171–236	II	150–214
pp. 239ff.	II	249ff.	II	235ff.
Part Two, p. 336	II	347ff.	II	336

227:39   *ethical pathos.* The draft continues with (*Pap.* VI B 40:41): "ethical pathos with which to embrace (*omslutte*) the ethical truth with infinite passion."

228:1   *quiet, incorruptible.* This expression is from 1 Pet. 3:4.

228:15   *de omnibus dubitandum.* One must doubt everything. See the Introduction, chap. 3.

229:10   *Caesar burned the entire Alexandrian library.* During Caesar's campaign in Alexandria in 47 B.C. the Alexandrian library, which had been founded by the elder Ptolemaists and is reported to have contained about half a million scrolls, was burned by accident. It was divided into two departments, a major department in the castle and a minor one in the Temple of Serapis. Following the destruction of the major section, Antony as a replacement presented Cleopatra with the library founded by Eumenes II in Pergamon.

Kierkegaard has mixed this up with the very dubious tradition according to which Caliph Omar is supposed to have ordered the destruction of the library in Alexandria, with this motive: "Either these works contain what is embodied in the Koran, in which case they are superfluous, or they contain other things, in which case they are ungodly." Quoted and translated from K. F. Becker, *Verdenshistorien*, rev. J. G. Woltmann, trans., J. Riise, I–XII (Copenhagen, 1822–1829; *ASKB* 1972–83), IV, 93.

229:22   *Two Upbuilding Discourses.* Published May 16, 1843.

229:23   *three more.* Published October 16, 1843.

229:38   *some . . . called the edifying discourses sermons.* Under his usual label "Kts" Bishop Jakob P. Mynster wrote an article titled "Kirkelig Polemik," which made its first appearance in J. L. Heiberg's *Intelligensblade.* He wrote among other things (IV, 122): "Whoever has read that beautiful discourse—or let us rather call it a sermon. . . . "

230:11   *uno tenore.* Without interruption.

230(note   *impetus.* Flight.
*):6

231:23   *neither in heaven [nor] on earth.* Compare Phil. 2:10.

232:1   *This had become clear to me,* and so forth. The draft continues with (*Pap.* VI B 40:43):

> It is at this point that the religious rests. This had now become clear to me, and I was merely waiting for the spirit to come upon me so that I might bring it out in the inwardness of an existing individuality with the greatest possible passion, though concealed in a deceptive form, which always serves as a dynamometer [*Kraft-Maaler*] of inwardness. What happens? Well, I§ really cut a ridiculous figure, because I am like an unsuccessful author whom fate pursues: then out came. . . .
>
> §*In margin:* Mag. K. and I cut ridiculous figures in different ways.

232:10   *China . . . Persia.* The allusion here is to Hegel's *Philosophy of History,* which begins with an exposition of China, India, and Persia, and their positions in the world-historical dialectical development (pp. 116ff.; *Jub. Ausg.* XI 158ff.).

232:29   *Mary.* Luke 2:19.

234:4   *Fear and Trembling.* Published on October 16, 1843.

234:12   *terminus a quo.* Here, point of departure.

234:13   *terminus ad quem.* Here, goal.

234:15   *the lyricism of the book.* The draft then has (*Pap.* VI B 40:44):

> and now [he] breaks out in lyricism; or Joh. de Silentio is a deceptive author who himself has experienced or believes he has experienced this collision, who himself exists in the telescopic distance

from the universal that this terror entails, and now seeks relief for a moment in this mystification under the form of double reflection, so his meaning and other such things remain outside, but the impression of such an existing individual's suffering is placed as close to existence as possible. For apart from the contradiction inherent in such an existing individual wanting to communicate himself, all direct communication of the truth as inwardness is, as has been developed, a misunderstanding, a confusion, and consequently any production in these spheres ought to embody in its form the reduplicated repetition of the content.

In margin: Kts' *"die erhab[e]ne Lüge."*

234:15   *the way Johannes has described himself.* The printed manuscript also has (*Pap.* VI 98:49):

Whether or not this is a deception remains to be seen, whether or not he himself has experienced or believes he has experienced this collision, whether or not he himself, existing in this frightful telescopic distance from the universal, now for a moment seeks relief in this mystification under the form of double reflection.

234:16   *"eine erhabene Lüge."* An exalted lie.

234:17   *the signature Kts.* As mentioned above, this was Mynster's pseudonym (Jakob Peter Mynster). In his article "Kirkelig Polemik" (see above) Mynster has the following to say about *Fear and Trembling*:

I have also read that remarkable work *Fear and Trembling* and I certainly was not at a loss for a profound religious foundation or a mind powerful enough to bring the greatest problems of life under observation. It reminded me vividly of this famous passage in Jacobi: "Ja, ich bin der Atheist und Gottlose, der, dem Willen der Nichts will zuwider, lügen will, wie Desdemona sterbend log, lügen und betrügen will, wie der für Orest sich darstellende Pylades u.s.w." ["Yes, I am an atheist and a godless man who, contrary to wanting to will nothing, wishes to lie just as Desdemona lied while dying, who wishes to lie and cheat as Pylades did when presenting himself to Orestes, and so forth."] The book is, however, by no means an imitation or echo of Jacobi's statement.

The above is quoted from Mynster's *Blandede Skrivter,* I–VI (Copenhagen: 1852–1857; *ASKB* 358–63), I, 466f. The quotation from Jacobi was a statement which he had made to Fichte and appears in *Friedrich H. Jacobis sämmtliche Werke,* I–VII (Leipzig: 1812–1825; *ASKB* 1722–28), III, 27.

234:37   *vapeurs.* Hysterical feelings.

235:1   *Reitzel.* Carl A. Reitzel (1789–1853), who started his business in 1819, was the most prominent bookseller and publisher during the Danish "Golden Age." Kierkegaard was a steady customer in the bookstore from his student days, and several of his own books were published by Reitzel, some of them on commission. See Frithiof Brandt and Else Rammel, *Søren Kierkegaard og Pengene* (Copenhagen, 1935), pp. 12–26. Reitzel's bookstore and publishing house still exist.

235:1   *Repetition.* Published on October 16, 1843.

235:6   *Constantine Constantius.* Kierkegaard's memory has failed him. It is Vigilius Haufniensis who calls *Repetition* "a witty book" in *The Concept of Anxiety* (*KW* VIII 17; *SV* IV 322 note).

236:20   *Later a new pseudonym.* The draft then has (*Pap.* VI B 40:45; *JP* I 633):

> Later I again found illumination of the meaning of the experiment as the form of communication.
>
> If existence [*Existents*] is the essential and truth is inwardness, if it is precisely the dubiousness of speculation to have overlooked this, if the misfortune it brings upon men is precisely that life becomes meaningless to them unless perhaps they take two or three years to read the system, and even if one has entertained himself with it for a long time, it nevertheless still makes individual existence [*Existents*] meaningless to the existing individual [*existerende Individualitet*] himself—then it is always good that this be said, but then it is also good that it be said in the right way. But this right way is precisely the art which makes being such an author very difficult; therefore it pleases me that the pseudonymous authors have overcome the difficulties which I had almost despaired over. If this is communicated in a direct form, then the point is missed; then the reader is led into misunderstanding—he gets something more to know, that to exist [*at existere*] also has its meaning, but he receives it as knowledge so that he keeps right on sitting in the *status quo.* . . . Thus the system, too, is well disposed; it says: Heavens, there is room enough; we can readily take it up into the system.* Alas, yes, in the system there is plenty of room.
>
> * This happened to Hamann, for example, in Michelet. Jacobi has also become a paragraph in the system.

236:22   *Stages on Life's Way.* Pages 460ff. (Original edition, p. 340; *SV* VI 460ff.)

236:33   *a love story.* The draft continues with the following notations (*Pap.* VI B 41:1–10):

1. A little about why the pseudonymous authors especially use marriage to throw light on the ethical.

2. A little about why they use an engagement with respect to the erotic; for an engagement is dialectically altogether different from a broken relationship where the highest has been consummated.—The thoughtlessness and immorality of calling it a "promise" when a man makes a girl pregnant and then abandons her; such conduct does not allow the exercise of dialectics, and sound common sense tells us that here there are at least 4 crimes: making the girl pregnant before one has married, making the child thus an illegitimate child, then to abandon the girl, and so to commit adultery in the event one takes up with somebody else.

3. A trial [Prøvelse] is only a transitory phase [Moment].

4. The Concept of Anxiety—a little on the lecturing side.

5. Sin as a qualification of existence [Existents].
The inwardness of sin as anxiety in the existing individual [Individualitet] is the greatest possible distance from the truth when the truth is subjectivity.

6. Nicolaus Notabene, a merry author, perhaps to divert attention from the fact that The Concept of Anxiety lectured a bit.

7. Mag. Kierkegaard's last 4 edifying discourses had a certain humorous tinge, maybe as a sign that here he had achieved what he wanted—the humorous is easily produced by using immanence and letting time reflect itself incorrectly in immanence, so eternity lies behind. The religious lies in the fact that eternity is behind and is thus essential; the humorous consists in the fact that time becomes as a feigned movement.

> Viewed from my standpoint, this is just the transition to the paradox.

8. Then I thought, now or never—and so out came the Fragments, which Mag. Kierkegaard had had the goodness to edit.

Without ever having forgotten that incident by the grave, I at that very time was reminded quite vividly of the venerable old man. Speculation has dealt with Christianity ambiguously, having said that it understood the truth of Christianity; but I have shown above that if this is understood a little more accurately it is the same as saying that Christianity does not become the truth until speculation has comprehended it. To make this really clear, I thought, you must venture to the limit, you must make that willful presumptuousness become really plain by pretending that Christianity is a conceptual experiment that originated in your head. Any direct attack on speculation will lead to nothing—for the system has indeed plenty of room and so an attack will be accommodated along with everything else. No, you must advance beyond speculation. But in using this presumptuously ironic form against speculation you must be careful so that instead of obtaining something exceedingly modern, a new religion perhaps, you will achieve what that sorrowing old man esteemed as the highest, extract the strictest orthodox features from it, and extract them in such a way as to make it clear that it is inaccessible to speculation. On the other hand, by means of the form of an experiment you must manage to make an existing individual inquire about it, and bring the issue as close to existence as possible so that it will not become a little more knowledge that a knowledgeable person can acquire and add to his abundant knowledge, but a primitive impression of his existence. And this, to repeat once more, can never be done indirectly, since in that case the recipient receives it through his knowledge, and things are left the way they were.

9. An apology to the pseudonymous authors for having in a way reviewed them; they are justified in not wanting to be reviewed, it being impossible to review them because the form here is so important, and they had better be content with a few readers, rather than with many who with the help of a report get something to run with. Zeno, seeing that Theophrastus had so many disciples, said: "His chorus is larger, mine more harmonious." (Plutarch concerning how one may presume to praise oneself in a permissible way, a work that I at this *very time* have been reading with great interest.)

10. A story of *suffering*; suffering is precisely the religious category.

> In *The Stages* the esthete is no longer a brilliant man walking around in B's living room—a hopeful person, and so forth, because he is still only a possibility. No, he is existing [*existerer*].

"it is exactly the
same as *Either/Or.*"

Constantin Const. and the young man put together in the quidam of the experiment (humor advanced).

> as a point of departure for the beginning of religiousness.
> —just as the tragic hero who used to demonstrate faith.

Three stages and yet an either/or.

237:16　　*according to the Scriptures*. Matt. 19:9: "And I say unto you, Whosoever shall put away his wife, except it be for fornication, and shall marry another, committeth adultery: and whosoever marrieth her which is put away doth commit adultery."

237:18 *the words of the Scriptures.* Here again Kierkegaard must have had in mind Matt. 19:9, which he read in the Danish translation of 1819.

237:23 *second protocol of the criminal courts.* As pointed out in a note to this passage in the first edition of the collected works in Danish, the thought here most likely concerns the so-called "Second Criminal Chamber," which was instituted in accordance with public notice of January 5, 1842, and belonged to the Lower Court of Copenhagen (*Hof- og Stadsretten*). Like the previous Inquisitional Commission, which it replaced, it had the right to arrest persons under suspicion.

237(note *):4 *in modern poetry.* Efforts to ascertain just which examples Kierkegaard had in mind here have been to no avail. There are several passages in the works of Thomasine Gyllembourg (1773–1856) in which such topics are treated in a way that was considerably audacious according to the general notions of the age. See in this respect E. Hude, *Thomasine Gyllembourg og Hverdagshistorierne* (Copenhagen, 1951), and F. J. Billeskov Jansen, *Danmarks Digtekunst*, I–III (Copenhagen, 1944–1958), III.

238:33 *in which God tempts a man.* Gen. 22:1.

239:5 *But it is as if it were nothing.* Following this the manuscript has (*Pap.* VI B 98:51).

and if the clergy do not even distinguish themselves by having faith (*fides*), nevertheless several clergymen do so all the more by uttering everything they say *bona fide* [in good faith], namely, without thereby thinking the slightest thing, although some of them nonetheless are speculative, too.

239:10 *free from the law of God.* Kierkegaard's usage here is somewhat careless and gratuitous. He was thinking of Rom. 6:20: "When you were slaves of sin, you were free from the control of righteousness." See also Rom. 7:4 (*The New English Bible*):

So you, my friends, have died to the law by becoming identified with the body of Christ, and accordingly you have found another husband in him who rose from the dead, so that we may bear fruit for God.

239:24 *the ethicist in Either/Or.* Vol. II, 242ff. (*SV* II 257ff.).

240:3 *In Fear and Trembling.* On p. 72 (*SV* III 125).

240:6 *The Concept of Anxiety.* Published June 17, 1844.

240:15 *quodlibet.* Anything whatever.

241:3 *the prophecy concerning Esau and Jacob.* Gen. 25:23.

241:16   *found a little favor.* This may refer to some appreciative remark made to Kierkegaard or to mention in an article or a book. *The Concept of Anxiety* was not reviewed. See Erslew's *Forfatter-Lexicon*, Supplement, vol. II (1864), p. 36, and Martin Heidegger, *Being and Time*, trans. John Macquarrie and Edward Robinson (Oxford, 1967), p. 494, *"Division Two, Section 45,"* note vi.

241:19   *a merry little book by Nicolaus Notabene. Forord*, which also came out on June 17, 1844.

241:19   *The pseudonymous books are generally ascribed to a single origin.* Very shortly after Kierkegaard had started his authorship more or less outspoken conjectures were made regarding the author behind the pseudonyms, but in general the pseudonymity was respected officially. In Thomas H. Erslew's *Almindeligt Forfatter-Lexicon*, which was published in installments (1843ff.), mention is made (vol. II, 25) that Kierkegaard "is presumed to be the author of *Either/Or . . . Repetition . . .* [and] *Fear and Trembling.*"

241:23   *And so finally came my Fragments. Fragments* appeared on June 13, 1844.

241:26   *Magister Kierkegaard's upbuilding discourses had steadily followed suit.* Collections of edifying or "upbuilding" discourses appeared on May 16 and October 16, 1843, March 5, June 8, and August 31, 1844.

241:29   *the four last.* These were published on August 31, 1844 (*SV* V 79–193).

242:4   *some said . . . one could very well call them sermons.* Kierkegaard may have had in mind here Mynster who in the aforementioned article, "Kirkelig Polemik" (*Blandede Skrivter*, I, 471), wrote the following about Kierkegaard's edifying discourses: "what the son [Kierkegaard] learned from his father he wrote in a sermon that will appeal to and refresh every sensitive heart."

242(note *):24   *the genius of Socrates . . . dissuading.* See the Index.

243:2   *terminus a quo.* Literally, the border from which or, in other words, the final station before the goal.

243(note *):1   *Intelligencer.* The reference is to *Intelligensblade* (Copenhagen, 1844), pp. 112ff., and to Mynster's article mentioned above in which he argues against a demand for more philosophically oriented sermons for the educated.

243(note *)   The printed manuscript has the following addition (*Pap.* VI B 98:52):

It is indeed a fact that the discourse about Job differs from the others,* and it is always a joy to see a judge like the firm of *Kts*, which hits the mark. The Magister himself has told me why it is different. In *Repetition* "Job" was employed in such a way (thus drawn into passion) that it might easily have produced a confusing effect on some reader or other who is accustomed to find a more peaceful edification in contemplation of that pious man.** Therefore the Magister resolved to do his bit to preserve Job as a religious prototype also for the reader who has not been tested in the extremes of passion, or who does not want this to be presented experimentally. This is also why the edifying discourse was published a few weeks after *Repetition*.

* *In margin*: not that this makes it exactly a sermon.
** *In margin*: although one would have to approve of the use [of Job] in that work both psychologically and poetically.

244:4   *"unto edification."* Kierkegaard made several comments in the journals for the immediately following years on the distinction between "the poetic category" of edification and the Christian category "unto edification." See especially *Pap.* VIII¹ A 15 and X¹ A 510 and 529 (*JP* V 5975; VI 6431, 6438, respectively).

244:13   *character indelebilis.* An ineradicable mark. According to Roman Catholic doctrine (*Concilium Tridentinum*, sess. VII. can. 9) the three sacraments of baptism, confirmation, and ordination transmit an indelible character and therefore cannot be repeated:

> Si quis dixerit, in tribus sacramentis, baptismo scilicet, confirmatione et ordine, non imprimi characterem in anima, hoc est signum quoddam spirituale et indelebile, unde ea iterari non possunt: A[nathema] S[it].Whoever maintains that the three sacraments of baptism, confirmation, and ordination do not imprint a distinctive mark on the soul, that is, a spiritual and ineradicable sign that makes a repetition [of these sacraments] impossible, shall be excommunicated.

The above is quoted from Denzinger, *Enchiridion symbolorum*, no. 852. The doctrine is formulated in conformity with Thomas Aquinas' *Summa theologica*, III, q. 63, art. 6. Kierkegaard incorrectly writes *caracter*, a Danish word that cannot be used interchangeably with "mark" or "character."

244:21   *Whether . . . in this little piece.* The draft has (*Pap* VI B 51):

> Now whether or not I have thus succeeded in the piece (*Philosophical Fragments*). . . .† If I have succeeded, so much the better; if not, well, the misfortune is not very great, for such a piece can be written quickly—and the misfortune will be even less if it becomes clear to me that I should not write at all, for that is the easiest of all.

† The review in the German *Repertorium* (the concluding remark is silly, for it would have been correct if the *Fragments* had been sheer earnestness; but of course there is indeed irony in the book—from this, however, it does not follow that the book is irony).

The draft also has the following addition (*Pap.* VI B 52):

In relation to communication it is also important to be able to deprive in the event the recipient is in the position of knowing too much. One clothes it [the communication] in such a completely foreign manner that he will not recognize it, and that very moment he is deprived of what he knows, for now he does not know it.

245(note *):2 *Allgemeines Repertorium. Neues Repertorium für die theologische Literatur und kirchliche Statistik*, II, 1 (Berlin, 1845), pp. 44–48. This review of the *Fragments* has been reprinted in *Kierkegaardiana*, VIII (Copenhagen, 1971), pp. 212–16, and in *Materialien zur Philosophie Søren Kierkegaards*, ed. M. Theunissen and W. Grieve (Frankfurt am Main, 1979), pp. 127ff.

247:15 *Socrates . . . in the Gorgias.* Kierkegaard is thinking in particular of 465E where Socrates terminates a rather prolix elucidation with the following:

I may have been inconsistent in making a long speech, when I would not allow you to discourse at length. But I think that I may be excused, as you did not understand me, and could make no use of my shorter answer, and I had to enter into an explanation. And if I show an equal inability to make use of yours, I hope that you will speak at equal length; but if I am able to understand you, let me have the benefit of your brevity, for this is only fair; and now this answer of mine is much at your service.

248:8 *Potemkin enchanted Catherine.* Kierkegaard may have read about this in K. F. Becker, *Verdenshistorien*, XI, 207ff.

In 1787 Catherine [II; 1729–1796] undertook . . . a voyage to these regions [among others to the Crimea] to cheer herself up, and during the voyage the magnificence of the entire Orient was set before her. In Kiev, where she stayed several months on account of ice on the Dnieper [River], she boarded a ship in a little fleet of fifty vessels and approached the new countries and creations around which Potemkin [1739–1791] was able to cast an illusion of rapid growth. Masses of people were collected from an area of about 190 miles to give an appearance of a dense population in various places. Once they had served this brief creation the people were left to perish from hunger. Herds of cattle were driven from one place to the other in order to impress on the Empress, who had seen the same herds several times, that the painted villages that she could see in the distance were prosperous.

248:25   *its veil was rent in twain*, and so forth. Matt. 27:51.

250:8   *vis comica*. The power of the comic.

250:16   *the assertion of a zealous Hegelian*. As is evident from *Pap*. V B 60, p. 137, Martensen is the target:

> Some teach that eternity is comic, or more correctly, that in eternity a man will preserve his comic consciousness of the finite. This wisdom is due especially to the last 3 or 4 paragraphs of Hegel's *Esthetics*. With us it has been interpreted by Prof. Martensen in one of the newspapers. Although ever since his first performance in *Maanedsskrift for Litteratur* after his return home the good professor has invariably felt it incumbent upon him to *assure* us that he has advanced beyond Hegel, he nevertheless has not made any advance here. In general, Prof. M. differs from the philosophers who make promises only in that he gives assurances.

The interpretation referred to by Kierkegaard was in Martensen's famous review of Heiberg's *En Sjæl efter Døden* in *Fædrelandet*, no. 398, January 10, 1841.

250:19   *a bookkeeper out of Holberg*. Erich Madsen in *Den Stundesløse*.

250:39   *a policeman's shield*. Here in the figurative sense of legitimation or authority.

251:1   *agent*. In past times "agent" was not only the designation for a commissioner, a middleman, or a traveling businessman but was for example also used as a title when addressing prominent merchants.

252:5   *the pseudonymous authors have again and again asked to be excused from being reviewed*. See *Fear and Trembling*, p. 24 (*SV* III 70), *Repetition*, p. 150 (*SV* III 288), and *Stages*, p. 184 (*SV* VI 203).

252:14   *Zeno*. That is, the Stoic of Citium (ca. 336–264 B.C.).

252:14   *Theophrastus*. Theophrastus of Eresus (ca. 372–288 B.C.). When Aristotle died in 322 B.C., Theophrastus, in accordance with Aristotle's wishes, assumed leadership of the peripatetic school. Kierkegaard's knowledge of these philosophers stems from (besides Plutarch's work mentioned below) especially Tennemann's and Hegel's presentations of the history of philosophy.

252:16   *Plutarch*. In *De se ipso citra invidiam laudando*, 17. Kierkegaard usually read Plutarch in a German translation, *Plutarchs moralische Abhand-lungen*, trans. J.F.S. Kaltwasser, I–V (Frankfurt am Main, 1783; *ASKB* 1192–96).

252:36   *(as it prognosticates about itself)*. Original edition, pp. 309, 376; *Stages*, pp. 363, 437ff. (*SV* VI 419, 507ff.).

253:28   *Socrates*. Callicles says in Plato's *Gorgias* 490E: "How you go on, always talking in the same way, Socrates!" Socrates: "Yes, Callicles, and not only talking in the same way, but on the same subjects."

253(note †):1   *"How easy it is."* Original edition, p. 16; *Stages*, p. 43 (*SV* VI 39). *"This may suffice."* Original edition, p. 86; *Stages*, p. 122 (*SV* VI 130).

253(note †):7   *This motto, which is also quoted in Pap.* VI A 78 (*JP* V 5283), origi-nates from Carl Maria von Weber's opera *Preciosa*.

254:14   *Either/Or* was first printed in 525 copies, published in February 1843, and was almost sold out in December 1844. As early as 1845 the publisher, Reitzel, suggested a second printing but Kierkegaard was reluctant. See *Pap.* VIII¹ A 84 (*JP* V 5997 375):

> Yesterday Molbech wrote to me (in a note dated April 29, 1847) that the sell-out of *Either/Or* is "a phenomenon in the literary his-tory of our day which may need to be studied." And why? The Councillor of State did not know that it has been sold out for a long time, he did not know that a year ago Johannes Climacus in *Concluding Unscientific Postscript* expressed his opinion in the matter, that two years ago Reitzel talked about a new edition, that I am the obstacle; he has no idea of how I work against myself in the service of the dialectic of inversion and, if possible, in a somewhat cleansing service of truth.

In August 1847 Kierkegaard entered into negotiations regarding a new printing of *Either/Or*, and it came out in May 1849. Christian Molbech (1783–1857) was a Danish historian and philologist.

254:18   *New Year's present.* See *Forord*, nos. III and IV (*SV* V 30ff.). The allusion is to Heiberg.

254:20   *Tivoli entertainments.* Tivoli is a pleasure garden in Copenhagen that was opened in 1843. The draft has in addition (*Pap.* VI B 53:10):

> Let Oehlenschläger try to rewrite his poem about Valborg. As soon as the reading world sees the name Valborg it will say: Bor-ing. And then to endow her with the enthusiasm of love [*Elskov*], an altogether new vegetation of pathos, without such distracting diversions as a new name or different circumstances—the poet will very soon learn that this business of the same is extremely difficult.

254(note
*):6

Oehlenschläger . . . Valborg . . . Signe. Kierkegaard is here thinking of Oehlenschläger's *Axel og Valborg* (1810), a romantic tragedy about the fidelity of love, and *Hagbarth og Signe* (1815), another tragedy.

254(note
†):2

Lichtenberg. In his essay "Ueber Physiognymik wider die Physiognomen," *Vermischte Schriften,* ed. G. C. Lichtenberg and F. Kries, I–IX (Göttingen, 1800–1806; *ASKB* 1764–72), III, 479, Lichtenberg makes the following statement quoted in German by Kierkegaard: "Such works are looking-glasses. If a monkey peeps at itself, it cannot turn out to look like an Apostle."

255:31

in Trebizond and R—. "R—" refers to *Røven,* a vulgarity meaning "backside" or "arse." It is taken from Holberg's comedy *Mester Geert Westphaler eller den meget talende Barbeer* (Scene 7 in the one-act version) in which the Danish *Røven* is a mispronunciation of the French city of Rouen. The line reads: "Why, Anders Christensen has been in Bordeus [Bordeaux] and Røven [Rouen] in France three or four times, what's more, the devil knows where in Trapezund or Cattesund [the Cattegat]. . . ." Compare Kierkegaard's comments on the natural sciences in the first paragraph of *Pap.* VII¹ A 200 (*JP* III 2820, modified), in which he uses language that would not be acceptable in most Danish homes even today:

> It does no good at all to get involved with the natural sciences. We stand there defenseless and utterly without control. The researcher immediately begins to distract us with his particular projects; one moment we must go to Australia, the next to the Moon, then down into a hole under the ground, now the devil knows where into the backside—looking for an intestinal worm [*nu Fanden i Vold i Røven—efter en Indvoldsorm*]. First we must use a telescope, then a microscope. Who the devil can stand it! [*hvo Satan kan holde det ud!*].

255(note
*):2

pp. 268 . . . 367ff. Stages, pp. 319, 428 (*SV* VI 365, 497). These references were omitted from the note in the Swenson/Lowrie edition of the *Postscript.*

256:9

Goethe's Leiden. See Carl Roos, *Kierkegaard og Goethe* (Copenhagen, 1955), especially pp. 28ff.

256:19

pp. 353ff. . . . paragraph no. 5. Stages, pp. 411ff., 415ff. (*SV* VI 477ff., 483ff.). Omitted from the Swenson/Lowrie edition.

257:19

himself (§3). This should read: "(cf. p. 340; §3, p. 343)." *Stages,* pp. 396, 399 (*SV* VI 460, 464).

257:23

The "Story of Suffering" was called an experiment. This is illuminated in *Pap.* VII¹ B 83 (*JP* V 5865):

For p. 217.[1] A note which was not printed because it was prepared later, although it was rough-drafted, and for certain reasons I did not want to change or add the least thing to the manuscript as it was delivered lock, stock, and barrel to Luno the last days of December, 1845.

Note. This experiment (" 'Guilty?'/'Not Guilty?' ") is the first attempt in all the pseudonymous writings at an existential dialectic in double-reflection. It is not the communication which is in the form of double-reflection (for all pseudonyms are that), but the existing person himself exists in this. Thus he does not give up immediacy, but keeps it and yet gives it up, keeps erotic love's desire and yet gives it up. Viewed categorically, the experiment relates to "The Seducer's Diary" in such a way that it begins right there where the seducer ends, with the task he himself suggests: "to poetize himself out of a girl." (See *Either/Or*, I, 470.)[2] The seducer is egotism; in *Repetition* feeling and irony are kept separate, each in its representative: the young man and Constantin. These two elements are put together in the one person, Quidam of the experiment, and he is sympathy. To seduce a girl expresses masculine superiority; to poetize oneself out of a girl is also a superiority but must become a *suffering* superiority if one considers the relationship between masculinity and femininity and not a particular silly girl. Masculinity's victory is supposed to reside in succeeding; but the reality [*Realitet*] of femininity is supposed to reside in its becoming a story of suffering for the man. Just as it is morally impossible for Quidam of the experiment to seduce a girl, so it is metaphysically-esthetically impossible for a seducer to poetize himself out of a girl when it is a matter of the relationship between masculinity and femininity, each in its strength, and not of a particular girl. The seducer's egotism culminates in the lines to himself: "She is mine, I do not confide this to the stars . . . not even to Cordelia, but say it very softly to myself." (See *Either/Or*, I 446.)[3] *Quidam* culminates passionately in the outburst: "The whole thing looks like a tale of seduction." What is a triumph to one is an ethical horror to the other.

5866 [*Pap.* VII[1] B 84]

Addition to 5665 [sic] (VII[1] B 83): The experiment, however, is precisely what is lacking in *Either/Or* (see a note in my own copy);[4] but before it could

---

[1] In the original edition, *SV* VII 274.

[2] English edition, I 440; *SV* I 479.

[3] English edition, I 419; *SV* I 455.

[4] See *Pap.* IV A 215; *JP* V 5628.

be done absolutely right, an enormous detour had to be made.

The experiment is the only thing for which there existed [*existeret*] considerable preliminary work before it was written. Even while I was writing *Either/Or* I had it in mind and frequently dashed off a lyrical suggestion. When I was ready to work it out, I took the precaution of not looking at what I had jotted down in order not to be disturbed. Not a word escaped, although it came again in a superior rendering. I have not gone through what I had jotted down, and nothing was missing, but if I had read it first, I could not have written it. The experiment is the most exuberant of all I have written, but it is difficult to understand because natural egotism is against adhering so strongly to sympathy.

257:25   *Repetition.* References to pp. 313 and 339 are omitted from S/L. *Stages*, pp. 366, 395 (*SV* VI 424, 459).

258:1   *jest and earnest.* A long sentence followed by references to pp. 327 and 328 in *Stages* are omitted from S/L. *Stages*, pp. 381ff. (*SV* VI 444).

258:3   *Constantine . . . partes.* The expression *at tage partes* means "to take sides" and "to take part in"; here the former is intended.

258:30   *the comical and the tragic.* The printed manuscript adds the following (*Pap.* VI B 98:53):

> and [Quidam] has thus in a supreme form achieved what the esthete in *Either/Or* esthetically asked of the gods: "that he might always have the laugh on his side" (see vol. I, the last Diapsalm, p. 30).[5]

258:36   *terminus a quo.* Actually, departing-point. Here it is used in the sense of the final stop before reaching a goal.

258:37   *In modern philosophy humor. . . .* What Kierkegaard is aiming at here has been sought in vain. Perhaps he was thinking of J. E. Erdmann's assertions concerning religious irony in *Vorlesungen über Glauben und Wissen* (Berlin, 1837; *ASKB* 479), pp. 80ff.

258(note   *periissem nisi periissem.* "I would have perished [in a higher eternal
*):2 sense] had I not perished [in a worldly human sense]." Kierkegaard undoubtedly came by this expression in one of Hamann's letters in which Hamann applies the saying to himself. See *Hamann's Schriften*, ed. F. Roth, I–VIII (Berlin, 1821–1843; *ASKB* 536–44), III, 224: "*periissem nisi periissem*—I also hope to be able to say this again some day." Kierkegaard had already jotted this down in 1843 (*Pap.* IV A

---

[5] English edition, I 42; *SV* I 31.

123; *JP* V 5673), and he used it as a motto for his own life in 1848 (*Pap.* IX A 48; *JP* VI 6154).

259:14   *no advance beyond faith.* The Danish *Gaaen ud over* means both "transcending" and "to make a victim of," or, in the present context, "faith is not made the victim." (Note by R.J.W.)

259:35   *The fact that faith. . . .* The draft then continues with (*Pap.* VI B 53:13; *JP* II 1668):

> That Christianity is like this, that it is preceded by humor, shows how much living out of life [*Udlevelse*] it presupposes in order rightly to be accepted. Christianity was certainly not proclaimed to children but to the world of superannuated philosophy, science, and art. For this reason the paradox is something else than, say, the marvelous, just as the hope Christianity proclaims is opposed to understanding. But the dialectic of hope goes this way: first the fresh incentive of youth, then the supportive calculation of understanding, and then—then everything comes to a standstill—and now for the first time Christian hope is there as a possibility. The fact that ecclesiastical chatterboxes have confused this as well as all Christian speech is none of my business.

259:38   *an experience of life.* Danish *Udlevelse*, an archaic word meaning "decrepitude," "worn out with age," the state of having lived out one's time. *ODS* (XXV, col 511), however, referring to this very passage in the *Postscript*, interprets it to mean a state of maturity (experience of life) or self-development (*Livsudfoldelse*). Compare the quotation immediately above.

260:5   *a Bible passage.* Mark 10:15 and Luke 18:17.

260:18   *small children weeping in Elysium. Aeneid*, VI, 426ff. (here taken from J. Loft's Danish translation):

> Voices were continuously heard, an eternal
>   wimpering of small children;
> Weeping, their souls lay here on the foremost
>   threshold.

Compare with this the esthete in *Either/Or*, II, 39 (*SV* I 28): "It was only in the happy days when the world was young, that men could imagine infants weeping in Elysium, because they had died so early." The esthete in his misery wishes himself dead.

260:29   *an offense to the Jews.* 1 Cor. 1:23.

261:12   *gathers wrath over the heads of the men.* Rom. 2:5.

261:16   *a radical cure.* This is an older medical expression that was used when referring to a treatment that aimed at a basic cure, in contradistinction to a palliative that merely weakens the malady or gives relief in case of pain but does not remove the cause.

261:20   *Solomon Goldkalb's opinion.* In J. L. Heiberg's vaudeville, *Kong Salomon og Jørgen Hattemager* (1825), Scene 26, Salomon Goldkalb, who has a poor knowledge of German, says: "*Ich* means *vieles* for *und* against *und* also yes *und* no." (Heiberg's *Poetiske Skrifter*, V, 252.)

262:17   *ancipiti proelio.* With a double front.

262:37   "*with whom it was impossible. . . .*" *Either/Or*, II, 8 (*SV* II 10): "One cannot really become angry with you. Evil has in you, as it had in the medieval conception, a certain seasoning of good nature and childishness."

263:1   "*a possibility of everything.*" Compare *Either/Or*, II, 17 (*SV* II 20), reading: "an epitome of every possibility," and Plato's *Republic* 561:

> A man so various that he seems to be
> Not one, but all mankind's epitome.

263(note   *The Hegelian philosophy culminates.* Hegel writes in *The Science of*
†):1   *Logic* (II, 155; *Jub. Ausg.* IV 656), Section C, "The Relation of Outer and Inner," that "Outer is not only *equal* to Inner in content, but both are but one Fact." Applied to Hegel's ethics this means that the state realizes the will of the individual. In the discussion of the commandment concerning charity in *The Phenomenology of Spirit* (pp. 443ff.; *Jub. Ausg.* II 325) Hegel gives the following explanation:

> Another celebrated commandment runs: "Love thy neighbour as thyself." It is directed to an individual standing in relation to another individual, and asserts this law as a relation of a particular individual to a particular individual, i.e. a relation of sentiment or feeling (*Empfindung*). Active love . . . aims at removing evil from someone and bringing him good . . . i.e. we have to love him intelligently. Unintelligent love will do him harm perhaps more than hatred. Intelligent, veritable (*wesentlich*) well-doing is, however, in its richest and most important form the intelligent universal action of the state—an action compared with which the action of a particular individual as such is something altogether so trifling that it is hardly worth talking about.

See in this connection the instructive interpretation in Eduard Geismar's *Søren Kierkegaard . . .* , III, 8–21.

264:    *pp. 87, 88, 89. . . .* All of these references to *Stages on Life's Way*
19–20   plus some relevant portions of the text are omitted from S/L after "melancholy of thought." On line 20 "thought" should be followed by: "(the ethicist explains him on pages 87, 88, and 89)." On the

same line "understanding" should be followed by: "(cf. the ethicist, page 90. Constantine's view of jealousy is encountered on the bottom of page 99 and top of page 100)." On line 21 "irony" should be followed by: "(cf. The ethicist on pages 107 and 108. Victor's attack on marriage appears on page 85)."

Original edition	SV	English edition
pp. 87, 88, 89	pp. 131ff.	pp. 123ff.
p. 90	p. 135	pp. 126ff.
pp. 99 and 100	p. 147	pp. 136ff.
pp. 107, 108	p. 157	p. 145
p. 85	p. 128	pp. 120ff.

265:15   *fancy gold stuff on the cover.* Once more an allusion to Heiberg's annual of astronomy, *Urania*, which was printed on extremely heavy paper. Each page was bordered by a thick black margin, and the book was bound in white with gold ornaments. Kierkegaard's pseudonym has the following comments to make in *Forord*, no. IV (*SV* V 31):

> As we know, in the month of December the business writers begin their literary New Year's larks. Several especially elegant and dainty books, intended for children and Christmas trees but particularly suitable as tasteful presents, dart past each other. After they have created a furor for fourteen days a polite critic assigns them a place in some collection of samples as inspiring copy for all the esthetic calligraphers. For esthetic calligraphy is the watchword and an extremely serious matter; it is something a person educates himself in by abandoning ideas and thoughts.
>
> O! Ye great Chinese gods! I would never have thought it possible. Is not Prof. Heiberg in the running this year? Yes, sure enough, it is Prof. Heiberg. Well, when a man is so well equipped it is all very well for him to make an appearance before admiring crowds. Not even Salomon Goldkalb in all his finery was dressed like this; why, this is pure gold. If no one else buys this book the Chamber of Art will.

265:21   *the sophistic proposition that everything is true.* Kierkegaard was in all likelihood thinking of Aristotle's *Metaphysics* 1007b, 19ff., where Aristotle writes as follows concerning the Sophist Protagoras' relativistic epistemology (translation by Hugh Tredennick, M.A., *Loeb Classical Library*):

> Again, if all contradictory predications of the same subject at the same time are true, clearly all things will be one. For if it is equally

possible either to affirm or deny anything of anything, the same thing will be a trireme and a wall and a man; which is what necessarily follows for those who hold the theory of Protagoras. For if anyone thinks that a man is not a trireme, he is clearly not a trireme; and so he also is a trireme if the contradictory statement is true. And the result is the dictum of Anaxagoras, "all things mixed together"; so that nothing truly exists.

266:3   *"This author represents inwardness."* Following this the draft has (*Pap.* VI B 53:16; *JP* II 2115):

Inwardness. If anyone were to give an account of Hegel and say that he represents thinking, we would have the right to answer: Well, that says nothing at all; I must have a better idea of which thoughts he represents. So also with inwardness. To say he represents it is to make a fool of oneself and the one under review, for *loquere ut videam*[6] applies here, and I have to have an idea of *how* he represents it.

266:16   *the Docents are not silent.* The draft then continues with (*Pap.* VI B 53:17):

and an old proposition often comes to mind: *si tacuissent, philosophi mansissent.*[7] And although I normally believe that sufferings and other such things may help as regards inwardness and style, yet I think that most docents are so flounder-like that one could easily skin them—without torturing one passionate word out of them.

[6] "You speak so that I may see." Hongs's note no. 631, II 604.
[7] "If they had kept quiet, they could have been taken for philosophers." See Boethius, *De consolatione philosophiae*, II, 17.

Résumé (pp. 267–312)

The first three parts of this chapter deal with fundamental problems concerning existence, such as potentiality and actuality and the existing individual's relation to them. The author opens with an attack on the speculative approach to factual existence. Thought, to be truly speculative, must abstract from existence and view it from the vantage point of eternity (*sub specie aeterni*). In so doing, abstract thought must ignore what is concrete, that is, the coming-into-existence and process of becoming that existence involves. This holds true as well of logical thinking, which employs the language of abstraction and thus also views existence from the vantage point of eternity, thereby abrogating existence. Concretion, however, is a problem that the existential thinker cannot disregard, for it constitutes his predicament in life.

So too in an abstract sense it may not be difficult to raise and answer the question of what is implied in saying that a definite something is an actuality; but the answer will remain abstract. The difficulty lies in combining something factual with the ideality of thought. In other words, thought is not concerned with particulars but with universals, and yet the individual must somehow bring a particular something into the orbit of his thought. This is a contradiction that vanishes for the abstract thinker but that is very real to an existential thinker.

It is impossible to manage this difficulty in the realm of abstract thought, which becomes evident when we consider the problem of immortality. The abstract thinker is able to talk about immortality in general terms, but he is unconcerned about whether or not a particular existing individual is immortal. Thus abstract thought is for all practical purposes an essay in the comic in connection with Christianity and the problems inherent in existing. By way of example, the author points to those Hegelian philosophers who insist that they have annulled the principle of contradiction. So far so good, providing the philosophers remain in the realm of pure thought and pure being; but this claim is invalid when applied to existence. It is therefore necessary to exercise caution when dealing with Hegelians and to ascertain with whom or with what one is conversing, whether with an existing human being or the pure "I = I."

The Greek philosophers, Climacus maintains, never forgot that thinking must have a bearing on the thinker's life. Hegelians have on the other hand forgotten this relationship, with the result that their so-called positive thinking constitutes a terrible form of skepticism. An indirect attack on this philosophy will be the most effective. For instance, if a man passionately and enthusiastically tries to use pure thought as a guide in life he himself will unsuspectingly be a satire on Hegelian philosophy and thus indirectly its worst enemy.

Existence entails coming-into-being, a process of becoming, and motion. For the existing individual this in turn implies an ethic to control these movements and changes. Thus in abstracting from existence Hegelians are also compelled to disregard ethics.

As indicated above, existence consists in movement, but we must have something that can give continuity and cohesion to movement. To say that everything is in movement is to deny movement. To solve this problem Aristotle postulated an unmoved mover that is the end and measure of all motion; he called this prime mover God. Climacus, at this point considering only the individual's existential situation, asserts that an absolute continuity is impossible for an existing individual because both his thinking and his willing must at some time or other be broken off. Man can "anticipate" a continuity, however, by employing the concrete eternity inherent in "idealizing passion."

Now abstract thought is without interest or commitment, whereas the existing thinker is passionately interested in existence, for he is concerned with ends and goals. The existing individual does of course think, but in existence thinking must be put together with the very fact that he exists. Thus pure thought, which is detached from the individual's existence, may be regarded as a phantom with no relation whatever to the individual's composite existence, which to him is actuality. As a result, abstract thought is completely unconcerned with the difficulties pertaining to existence, and the philosopher's so-called pure thought ends up as a mere distraction, for pure thought is incapable of clarifying what it means to exist as a human being. Speculative philosophers, our author continues, have failed to realize that knowledge about actuality is nothing more than a possibility; it is not actuality. The only actuality to which an existing individual may have more than a cognitive relation is his own, that is, the fact that *he* exists. This actuality constitutes an absolute interest in which he is totally committed.

The author then considers the reliability of sense perception, which he regards as illusory, a fact that both Greek skepticism and modern idealism have adequately demonstrated. So too knowledge of a historical actuality is also deceptive, for to understand a historical actuality the thinker must first transform it into a possibility. The actual subject (*Subjektivitet*) is not the subject who is merely thinking, for when he is thinking he is in the realm of possibility. An actual subject may be defined as a person who exists ethically and subjectively, and this existence constitutes an actuality from which he cannot escape.

The next section (pp. 282ff.) consists of apparently disconnected paragraphs, each of which deals with a particular subject matter.

The author asserts that when viewed from a poetic or intellectual standpoint, possibility is superior to actuality. From an ethical standpoint, however, actuality must take precedence over possibility. Ethically, only one contemplation has meaning, and that is self-contemplation. In relation to every actuality external to the existing individual it holds true that the individual is able to grasp it only through thought; in other words, an outside actuality can be apprehended intellectually only in the category of possibility. Now if the thinking individual encounters an actuality that he cannot translate into terms of possibility he will have to suspend his thinking, and thus he will have a paradoxical rather than a conceptual relation to that actuality.

Climacus states (p. 287) that "The How of Truth is precisely the truth." According to the author, therefore, everything depends on inquiring in a medium suitable to both the inquiry and the reply. In the case of actuality inquiry can only be made ethically, and then only concerning the single individual. Conversely, it is a misunderstanding to raise such a question intellectually or esthetically.

In the fields of esthetics and the intellectual it is true that an actuality is understood and thought only when its *esse* has been resolved into its *posse*. Ethically, on the other hand, a potentiality is understood only when each and every *posse* has been really transformed into an *esse*.

Actuality is not externality but inwardness, which in turn means an infinite interest in one's own existence (p. 288).

The proper object of faith is not a teaching but someone else's actuality, that is, the teacher himself, and in face of this actuality faith must decide pro or con.

Now to exist means first of all to be a single individual. Abstract thought must therefore ignore factual existence, for it is possible only to think universals, not particulars. So the actuality of the god's existence as a particular individual must be an object of faith. Faith is not "an asylum for the feeble-minded" but constitutes a very special sphere in its own right. It is therefore possible to recognize at once any misunderstanding of Christianity by the fact that it always entails an intention to transform Christianity into a philosophical doctrine and thus bring it into the sphere of intellectuality.

Climacus readily grants that the philosophical proposition concerning the identity of thought and being should not be interpreted as referring to imperfect forms of existence. But this leaves us with the unanswered question of whether it is applicable to higher orders of existence, for example, the Ideas. Climacus acquiesces here too, but he adds that in this case the proposition is valid only because being and thought mean one and the same thing, for now we are dealing with a conceptual being whose only existence is in thought (pp. 293ff.).

In the pages that follow, Climacus, applying Aristotelian categories, gives a more elaborate criticism of Hegelian thought, especially in connection with Kant.

Let us assume that speculation is justified in its derision of the earlier tripartition of man into soul, body, and spirit. Let us also concede to speculation the merit of having defined man as spirit within which the elements of soul, consciousness, and spirit are interpreted as developmental stages in the same subject. Nevertheless, Climacus adds, there is on that account no reason to grant that all this can be transferred from world-historical evolution directly to the single individual (p. 308). According to modern speculation the individual's development is supposed to be purely and simply dependent on the universal human spirit. If this view were right, however, it would imply that only defective specimens of human beings are born in each generation.

Ethics presents every human being with the task of becoming that for which he is intended and created, that is, of realizing and actualizing his potential. In this connection thought is not superior to feeling and imagination. On the contrary, the three are coordinate and of equal importance, and the task consists precisely in uniting these elements of life in contemporaneity. Truth is not superior to the Good and the Beautiful; rather the truth and the Good essentially belong to each and every individual. Furthermore, the existing individual is not simply supposed to think the truth, the Good, and the Beautiful; it is his duty to exist in them (p. 311).

* * *

267:4 *sub specie aeterni.* From the vantage point of eternity. The expression is from Spinoza's *sub specie aeternitatis.* See the Index.

267:6 *a synthesis of the temporal and the eternal.* Kierkegaard's concept of synthesis is analyzed most clearly by Gregor Malantschuk in *Kierke-gaard's Way to the Truth* (Minneapolis, 1963), to which the reader is referred. See above, note to p. 207, and the Introduction.

267(note *):3   *Trendlenburg*. Adolf Trendelenburg in *Logische Untersuchungen* (Berlin, 1840; *ASKB* 843), chap. II ("Die dialektische Methode"), pp. 57ff.

267(note *):5   *"die Existenz. . . . "* "Existence is the immediate unity of reflec-tion-into-itself and reflection-into-another. It follows from this [?] that existence is the indefinite multitude of existents." Taken from Hegel's *Encyclopaedia of the Philosophical Sciences*, §123 (*W.a.A.* VI 250ff.; *Jub. Ausg.* VIII 288ff.; *Logic*, p. 230). The question mark in parentheses is of course Kierkegaard's.

268:11   *the doctor in Holberg*. In *Barselstuen* (Act III, Scene 5):

> *Doctor*: . . . I once had a patient . . . who had a fever and abstained from both food and drink for six days.
> *Woman in confinement*: Then I suppose he died.
> *Doctor*: Of course! What else? But on the other hand the fever left him completely, and all we wanted was to get rid of it.

268:23   *such a thinker's life*. Perhaps the reference here is to Karl Rosen-kranz, *Hegel's Leben* (Berlin, 1844), or to *Erinnerungen an Karl Daub* (Berlin, 1837; *ASKB* 743). Kierkegaard was familiar with the second work, and he respected Daub as a thinker. See *Pap.* II A 96, 97 (*JP* III 3605 and I 279), and Franz Wiedmann, *Hegel: An Illustrated Biog-raphy*, trans. Joachim Neugroschel (New York, 1968).

268:31   *pathos or pathological*. "Pathos" means passionate. In the present context "pathological" should be given the same meaning and not that of a deviation connected with morbidity or disease. Pathos de-rives from the Greek πάσχειν, to suffer or be affected by something, and from πάθος, a suffering, passion, emotion.

268(note *):1   *When you read in his writings*. Kierkegaard may have had in mind various passages in Hegel's works where the thought mentioned in the text is given expression. See for example *Enc.*, 88 (*Jub. Ausg.* VIII 214ff.; *Logic*, p. 168), where Hegel postulates an abstract identity of being and thought, noting expressly that "in the case of being, we are speaking of nothing concrete: for being is the utterly abstract." In other words, being is the equivalent of thought thinking itself.

269:16   *If it is the case that an abstract thinker. . . .* The draft continues with (*Pap.* VI B 54:3; *JP* I 925):

> If it is taken for granted in this way that Hegel* lacked a sense of the comic, then this is *eo ipso* proof that all his thought is but the feat of a talent which has simply followed its talent. The ethical

act of reflection is in the last analysis decisive. However great, however glorious everything else is, it does not help. Everything higher than the universal must first have tested itself in the ethical act of reflection, which is the measure of the universal. Briskly to follow a talent, to choose a brilliant distinction, even if one amazes the world ten times over, means to remain behind. Ethical reflection is the authorization; if it is secured, then the distinction can be celebrated. If a merchant sells yard-goods by the thousands of yards and a poor widow measures out only a single yard once in a while— the decisive thing is the authorized yard which legally makes the sale a lawful sale. Similarly, ethical reflection and going through the universal involved in it first makes each human existence a truly authentic existence. The distinction of talents is in itself a sad affair.

* *Obliquely in margin*: abstract thinkers.

270:17   *Hegel himself.* Kierkegaard is here alluding to Hegel's essay, "Glauben und Wissen oder die Reflexionsphilosophie der Subjektivität" (*W.a.A.* I 3–157; *Jub. Ausg.* I 279–433), to the "Period of The Thinking Understanding" in modern philosophy in *Lectures on the History of Philosophy* (III, 217–356; *W.a.A.* XV 328–534; *Jub. Ausg.* XIX 328–534), and especially to "Contradiction" in *The Science of Logic* (II, 58ff.; *W.a.A.* IV 57ff.; *Jub. Ausg.* IV 535ff.).

270:22   *Jens Skovfoged in Kallundborgs-Krøniken.* That is, "Kallundborg Krønike eller Censurens Oprindelse," in *Jens Baggesens danske Værker*, ed. the author's sons and C. J. Boye, I–XII (Copenhagen, 1827–1832; *ASKB* 1509–20), I, 235. In this rhymed narrative by Baggesen (1764– 1826) Jens Skovfoged, whose last name means assistant forester or gamekeeper, rides past a gallows on which a thief had been hanged.

Then along came Jens Skovfoged, clip-clop, clip-clop,
Riding his horse at a trot,
Past that horrible spot
Where, 'tis known, devils keep watch
Over that trophy of justice.

Although hanged the thief was not yet dead. On hearing his cry for help Jens takes pity on him, cuts him down, and brings him home with him. The thief then rewards his savior by stealing a pair of boots—whereupon Jens quite cold-bloodedly hangs him again. Kierkegaard made note of these lines in 1837 (*Pap.* II A 35; *JP* V 5208).

270:23   *the Hegelians have several times been on the warpath, especially after Bishop Mynster.* The manuscript (*Pap.* VI B 54:4) mentions "Martensen and Heiberg" point-blank. Kierkegaard has in mind here the debate about logical principles that took place in Denmark at the end of the 1830s and beginning of the 1840s. On July 12, 1837, Martensen defended his dissertation for the licentiate, *De autonomia conscientiæ sui humanæ in theologiam dogmaticam nostri temporis introducta*. This dissertation indeed very clearly stamps its author as a disciple of Hegel, but it also bespeaks an even heavier dependence on F. von Baader. It was reviewed by Martensen's respondent, his good friend and a sharer of his views, J. A. Bornemann (1813–1890), who in 1854 succeeded him as professor of systematic theology. In his review (in *Tidsskrift for Litteratur og Kritik* I, 1–40) Bornemann stated that: "In theology, both rationalism and Supranaturalism are antiquated standpoints belonging to a bygone age." These words induced Mynster to react with a sharp and clear essay in the same periodical, titled "Rationalisme, Supranaturalisme" (reprinted in Mynster's *Blandede Skrivter*, II, 95ff.). Mynster defended both the distinction between rationalism and Supranaturalism and the principles of classical logic against Hegel's and his adherents' insistence on the abrogation of the principles of contradiction and exclusion. Heiberg now made himself heard, opposing Mynster in "Om Contradictions- og Exclusions-Principet. En logisk Bemærkning" (reprinted in Heiberg's *Prosaiske Skrifter*, II, 167ff.). In his article Heiberg maintains among other things that "the unmediated opposites . . . are found neither in immediacy nor in the concept but only in the intermediary field of reflection, hence only in the logical region representing the finite and empirical" (pp. 171ff.). Finally Martensen entered the fray with his article, "Rationalisme, Supranaturalisme og principium exclusi medii." Like Heiberg, he expresses his veneration for Mynster while objectively disagreeing with him regarding logic and theology. After this the conflict turned into an exchange of opinions between Martensen and Mynster, with Mynster once again (in 1842) elaborating on and giving a more explicit formulation of his standpoint in "Om de logiske Principer" (reprinted in *Blandede Skrivter*, II, 116ff.). On Mynster's side stood F. C. Sibbern and, as is evident from the text in the *Postscript*, Kierkegaard. See also the Introduction, chap. 6.

270:39   *Like the giant*. Antaeus. Kierkegaard refreshed his school instruction in mythology by means of W. Vollmer, *Vollständiges Wörterbuch der Mythologie aller Nationen* (Stuttgart, 1836; *ASKB* 1942–43), which contains comprehensive articles about both Antaeus and Hercules (pp. 245ff., 832ff.).

271:11   *something that is true in theology which is not true in philosophy*. An allusion to the late Scholastic doctrine of the double truth. The prop-

osition concerning the double truth is clearly formulated by the Ock-
hamist Robert Holkot (a Dominican from Cambridge; d. 1349), who
distinguished between a *logica naturalis* and a *logica fidei*. According to
this view the natural or Aristotelian logic does not apply in all areas.
It does not hold true in the sphere of faith, and especially not with
regard to the doctrine of the Trinity where the principle of contradiction loses its validity. See his *Super quattuor libros Sententiarum* (Lyon,
1497), I, q. 5H:

> Rationalis logica fidei alia debet esse a logica naturali. . . . Oportet
> ponere unam logicam fidei . . . modo philosophi non viderunt,
> aliquam rem esse unam et tres . . . paucae regulae vel nullae, quas
> ponit in libro Priorum et alibi, tenent in omni materia, Causa est,
> quia Aristoteles non vidit, quod una res esset una et tres. [A ra-
> tional logic of faith ought to be distinguished from natural logic
> . . . (and) a logic specific to faith will have to be established. . . .
> The philosophers have simply failed to realize that it is possible for
> a definite thing to be both one and three; . . . few rules—perhaps
> none at all—are applicable under all the conditions with which he
> (Petrus Lombardus) operates in Part One and other passages. The
> reason is that Aristotle does not allow for the fact that one thing
> is (both) one and three.]

The history of this conception is presented by among others Karl
Heim in "Geschichte des Satzes von der doppelten Wahrheit," *Glaube
und Leben* (Tübingen, 1926), pp. 73ff.

272:20   *"everything is and nothing comes into being."* Kierkegaard's knowl-
edge of the Eleatics' philosophy originates for the most part from
Diogenes Laërtius (IX, 2–5) as presented by W. G. Tennemann in
Geschichte der Philosophie, I–XI (Leipzig, 1798–1819; *ASKB* 815–26),
I, 150–209, and Hegel in *Lectures on the History of Philosophy* (I, 239–
78; *W.a.A.* XIII 280–327; *Jub. Ausg.* XVII 296–343). See the Index.

272(note   *a parallel has been drawn between Hegel's doctrine and that of Heraclitus.*
*):2   Just who undertook this comparison has not come to light.

273:37   *abrogating the principle of contradiction.* See note above. Hegel and his
adherents, among others Martensen and Heiberg, held that it was
unnecessary to uphold the classical principle of contradiction, since it
could be so formulated as to coincide with the principle of identity.
The Hegelians then transferred the term "principle of contradiction"
to the principle of exclusion and repudiated the validity of the latter.

274:14   *a Pythagorean dying away from the world.* See Plato's *Phaedo* 61D ff.
The Pythagoreans taught that man is the property of God and that

suicide is inadmissible, for God as the providential guardian will himself determine when a man is to leave this life.

274:28   *a phantom.* The draft has the following (*Pap.* VI B 54:7):

> [. . .] such as what one becomes with the help of speculative philosophy. Even if everything it said were true, it nevertheless turns the existing individual into a phantom and a dummy—which no existing individual can permit unless speculative philosophy explains itself more clearly. As soon as it begins to do this it will have to engage in a completely different kind of dialectic, the Greek, and then I dare say we will come to terms. It is in the very first beginning that one must restrain oneself, at the point where the thinking individual ceases to be an existing individual in order to think *sub specie æterni*, and at this point one merely needs the courage to be altogether humanly simple and dimwitted, and things will be all right.

275:14   *one still living* [S/L: living individual]. This is perhaps a reference to Kierkegaard's first book, *Af en endnu Levendes Papirer* ("From The Papers of One Still Living," *SV* XIII 45–100; not translated into English), from 1838. This entire paragraph is retrospective.

275:23   *conceited and foolish enough.* See Matt. 25:2.

275:35   *a steel pen-point.* They came into use in Denmark in the 1830s.

276:5   *Socrates said.* See the commentary on the *Fragments*, p. 207.

277:4   *everything is motion.* The draft continues with (*Pap.* VI B 54:8):

> [for to say] that everything is in motion is just an attempt to think movement under the form of rest. Now whereas abstract thought straightaway annuls all movement, passion is to the existing individual exactly the residual maximum he needs to restrain himself, and the passion itself is in turn the impulse of the movement.

For Kierkegaard's concept of motion and its interconnection with several other important concepts, as well as his use of Aristotle in this respect, the reader is referred to Klaus Schäfer, *Hermeneutische Ontologie in den Climacus-Schriften Sören Kierkegaards* (Munich, 1968).

277:6   τέλος and μέτρον. [Greek words omitted by S/L.] Measure and final end, respectively.

277:9   *Aristotle.* In *Metaphysics* 1071b ff. See my commentary on the *Fragments*, pp. 196ff.

277(note *):1   *the discipline of Heraclitus.* Kierkegaard has this story from W. G. Tennemann, *Geschichte der Philosophie*, I, 220, where reference is made to Plato's *Cratylus* 402A. Tennemann writes:

Heraclitus explained a thing's change by means of a mental image: one cannot go through the same stream twice. One of his followers, finding even this too much of a concession, added as a corrective: "One cannot even do it once."

277(note
‡):1
Art and poetry . . . disinterested. See Kant, *Kritik der Urteilskraft,* Part I, Section 1, Book 1, §5 (*Werke,* ed. Cassirer, V, p. 279): "Taste is the faculty of judging an object or an image by means of pleasure or displeasure, without any interest at all. The object of such a pleasure is called beautiful."

277(note
‡):1
anticipation of the eternal. The expression itself had previously been employed by Poul Møller, who in his essay on immortality wrote (*Efterladte Skrifter,* 3rd ed., V [Copenhagen, 1856], p. 90): "True art is an anticipation of the blissful life." Kierkegaard used the expression in *The Concept of Anxiety* (*KW* VIII 153; *SV* IV 463), the very work dedicated to the deceased poet-philosopher. See Gregor Malantschuk, *Frihed og Eksistens* (Copenhagen, 1980), pp. 101–40. The theory of art as an anticipation received its classical expression in Schiller's poem *Das Ideal und das Leben.*

278:9
Telos. Final goal; νοῦς θεωρήτικος, contemplative or theoretical thought, differs in aim from νοῦς πράκτικος, which designates thought directed toward action. Aristotle writes in *On The Soul* 433a (trans. W. S. Hett, *Loeb Classical Library*): "But the mind in question is that which makes its calculations with an end in view, that is, the practical mind: it differs from the speculative mind in the end that it pursues."

278:25
reflection-in-itself. Another reference to *Encyclopaedia of the Philosophical Sciences,* §123. See the Index and Hegel's *Science of Logic,* II, 25–70 (*W.a.A.* IV 7–73; *Jub. Ausg.* IV 485–551).

278:37
But pure thought. The draft continues with (*Pap.* VI B 54:9): "while pure thought hovers in mystical suspension and wants to answer everything within itself, thereby making it impossible to answer what is actually being asked."

278:38
as the saying is. Kierkegaard has in mind the section in Hegel's *Science of Logic* titled "With What Must the Science Begin?" (I, 79–90; *W.a.A.* III 59–74; *Jub. Ausg.* IV 69–84), where Hegel writes (p. 82 in the English edition):

The beginning must be an absolute, or, what here is equivalent, an abstract beginning: it must presuppose nothing, must be mediated by nothing, must have no foundation: itself is to be the foundation of the whole science. It must therefore just be something immediate, or rather the immediate itself. As it cannot have any determination relatively to Other, so also it cannot hold in

itself any determination or content; for this would be differentiation and mutual relation of distincts, and thus mediation.—The
beginning therefore is Pure Being.

279:10   *inter-esse*. An intermediate being. See *Pap.* IV B 1, p. 148; *Johannes
Climacus or, de omnibus dubitandum est*, trans. T. H. Croxall (Stanford,
1958), pp. 151ff.

279:11   *the hypothetical unity of thought and being*. See Hegel's *Encyclopaedia*,
§88 (*W.a.A.* VI 171–77; *Jub. Ausg.* VIII 209–15; *Logic*, pp. 163–69).

279:12   *Abstract thought considers both possibility and reality*. This conception
is found in Hegel's *Science of Logic*, Part II, Section 3, Par. A, "Contingency, or Formal Actuality, Possibility, and Necessity" (II, 178ff.;
(*W.a.A.* IV 202ff.; *Jub. Ausg.* IV 680ff.).

279:23   *existence is the dialectical moment*. See Himmelstrup's "Terminologisk Register," *SV* XV 764ff., under *"Virkelighed"* ("actuality"):

> *Actuality*. The concept of actuality can as a rule be understood partly
> as the fact of being actual and partly as the sum total of everything
> that possesses actuality.
>
> The actual was by Aristotle called something that was ἐνεργείᾳ
> in contrast to what was only κατὰ δύναμίν, the potential. The
> problem thus concerned two forms of being but on the contrary
> not a difference in essence. Kierkegaard seems to agree with this
> way of thinking when he says: "But such a being, which is never-
> theless a nonbeing, is precisely what possibility is; and a being that
> is being is indeed actual being or actuality" ([*SV*] IV 266 [*Frag-
> ments*, p. 91] . . .).
>
> In Hegel's system the *concept* of actuality appears in the second
> section of the *Logic*, where the concept *Wesen* (essence) is treated.
> The opposition between the concept of force and its articulation,
> or between inner and outer, may be conceived as annulled in a
> synthesis in which outer and inner merge. This synthesis is *actual-
> ity*, an important concept in Hegel's *Logic* and also an expression
> for the [motive] force of the "Idea." . . .
>
> Kierkegaard does not approve of the Hegelian method of mak-
> ing "actuality" emerge through a kind of logical process. With him
> there rather exists an affiliation with the Greek way of thinking.
> Whereas actuality in Hegel is, as mentioned, a qualification of es-
> sence, in Kierkegaard it becomes a qualification of being. Kierke-
> gaard's concept of actuality is emphatically qualified by the stand-
> point of "existence" [*"Eksistens"*], and he even perceives a certain
> danger in the "logical" qualification of it. The actual is that which
> has "come into existence" [*det "tilblevne"*] through a separation of

the factor of the idea or necessity and consequently has freedom as its standard and the accidental or contingent as its insignia. Kierkegaard expresses it as follows in [SV] IV 314 [*The Concept of Anxiety*, pp. 9ff.] . . . : "Thus when an author entitles the last section of the *Logic* 'A c t u a l i t y,' he thereby gains the advantage of making it appear that in logic the highest has already been achieved, or if one prefers, the lowest. In the meantime, the loss is obvious, for neither logic nor actuality is served by placing actuality in the *Logic*. Actuality is not served thereby, for contingency, which is an essential part of the actual, cannot be admitted within the realm of logic. Logic is not served thereby, for if logic has thought actuality, it has included something that it cannot assimilate, it has appropriated at the beginning what it should only *praedisponere* [presuppose]."

280:33   *Greek skepticism . . . modern idealism.* Kierkegaard read about the Greek skeptics, especially Sextus Empiricus, in Tennemann, vol. V, 267ff. The reliability of sense perception is repudiated in "modern idealism." See for example Hegel's *Phenomenology of Spirit*, pp. 149ff. (*W.a.A.* II 84ff.; *Jub. Ausg.* II 92ff.).

281:12   *cogito ergo sum.* See *Pap.* V A 30 (*JP* I 1033) where in 1844 Kierkegaard wrote in connection with his studies of Jacobi:

> From the logical point of view, the Cartesian formulation: I think, therefore I am [*er*]—is a play on words, because the "I am" logically signifies nothing other than "I am thinking" or "I think."
> Cf. Jacobi *S.W.*, II, 102n.

282:6   *In Greece, the philosopher was. . . .* The draft then has (*Pap.* VI B:54:10; *JP* I 1039):

> That an abstract thinker in our age does not think about such things [existing and abstraction] is irrelevant, but the Greeks were at any rate aware and their skeptical ataraxia was at any rate a serious attempt to abstract from existing [*at existere*], completely different from unthinkingly not becoming aware of it at all and continuing to live in this manner because lack of awareness has become habit and custom. If I did not exist [*existerede*], my thought would never add to existence [*Existents*]; on the contrary, it subtracts from it. The being [*Væren*] which specifically is the being of thought is within possibility, is possibility's representation of actual being, but it is not the being which relates itself as actuality to the whole sphere of abstraction as possibility. The annulled being

Hegel himself calls essence [*Væsen*], and the medium of thought is not being but essence.

282:7   *ataraxy of the skeptics.* Imperturbability or peace of mind was considered as the supreme good by the ancient skeptics, for example, Pyrrho (see Diogenes Laërtius, IX, 61). The draft adds here (*Pap.* VI B 54:12; *JP* II 1608):

> I here request the reader's attention for an observation I have often wished to make. Do not misunderstand me, as if I fancied myself to be a devil of a thinker who would remodel everything etc. Such thoughts are as far from my mind as possible. I feel what for me at times is an enigmatical respect for Hegel; I have learned much from him, and I know very well that I can still learn much more from him when I return to him again. The only thing I give myself credit for is sound natural capacities and a certain honesty which is armed with a sharp eye for the comical. I have lived and perhaps am uncommonly tried in the *casibus* of life; in the confidence that an open road for thought might be found there, I have resorted to philosophical books and among them Hegel's. But right here he leaves me in the lurch. His philosophical knowledge, his amazing learning, the insight of his genius, and everything else good that can be said of a philosopher I am willing to acknowledge as any disciple. —Yet, no, not *acknowledge*—that is too distinguished an expression—willing to admire, willing to learn from him. But, nevertheless, it is no less true that someone who is really tested in life, who in his need resorts to thought, will find Hegel comical despite all his greatness.

282:20   *Aristotle.* A quotation from *Poetics* 1451b.

282:35   *a teleology.* The study or doctrine of ends or final causes.

283:15   *not only capable of thinking reality but of bestowing it.* This is explained in the draft (*Pap.* VI B 54:13; *JP* III 3654:13): "actuality in the sense of existence [*Existents*]."

284:17   *God knows how many hairs.* See Matt. 10:30.

284:21   *a tyrant . . . content to decimate.* Kierkegaard was thinking of the form of punishment employed in the Roman Empire in cases of mutiny: every tenth soldier in the mutinous company was executed.

285:4   *which is impossible.* The draft then has (*Pap.* VI B 54:14; *JP* III 3654:14):

> 14. The only actuality which I do not change into a possibility by thinking it is my own, because my actuality *allem meinem Denken zuvorkomt* [precedes all my thinking], so I do not get hold of

my actuality by thinking and only by thinking, an actuality which is preserved essentially not by thinking it but by existing [*existere*].

285:20   *Stages on Life's Way (p. 341). Stages*, p. 398 (*SV* VI 452).

285:21   *ab posse ad esse.* . . . From possibility to actuality . . . from actuality to possibility.

285:31   *sensu laxiori* . . . *sensu strictissimo*. In a broader sense . . . in a stricter sense.

286:14   *The Scriptures teach*. Matt. 7:1.

286:20   *Stages*, p. 399 (*SV* VI 463).

288:28   *the external?* Here in the sense of environment.

291:11   *quam maximum* [omitted by S/L after "faith is to become"]. To the highest possible degree.

291:23   *these simple words of Diogenes*. Diogenes Laërtius in *Diogen Laërtses filosofiske Historie*, trans. Børge Riisbrigh, ed. B. Thorlacius, I–II (Copenhagen, 1811–1812; *ASKB* 1110–11), I, 66, the edition generally used by Kierkegaard. It is quoted in the *Fragments*, p. 182, from *Loeb Classical Library*, I, 149–51.

292:10   *a thing-in-itself eluding thought*. The draft adds to this (*Pap*. VI B 54:16; *JP* II 2235):

> The Kantian discussion of an *an sich* [thing-in-itself] which thought cannot get hold of is a misunderstanding occasioned by bringing actuality as actuality into relationship with thought. But to conquer this misunderstanding with the help of pure thought is a chimeric victory. In the relation between Kant and Hegel it is always apparent how inadequate immanence is.

293:9   *a stupid attack*. Note Hegel's objections in *Encyclopaedia of the Philosophical Sciences* (*W.a.A.* VI 111ff.; *Jub. Ausg.* VIII 149ff.; *Logic*, pp. 107ff.) to Kant's criticism of the ontological proofs of the existence of God. In the *Logic*, p. 108, Hegel writes as follows:

> Still it may not unfairly be styled a barbarism in language, when the name of notion is given to things like a hundred sovereigns. And, putting that mistake aside, those who perpetually urge against the philosophic Idea the difference between Being and Thought, might have admitted that philosophers were not wholly ignorant of the fact. Can there be any proposition more trite than this? But after all, it is well to remember, when we speak of God, that we have an object of another kind than any hundred sovereigns, and unlike any one particular notion, representation, or however else it may be styled. It is in fact this and this alone which marks everything finite:—its being in time and space is discrepant from its

notion. God, on the contrary, expressly has to be what can only be "thought as existing"; His notion involves being. It is this unity of the notion and being that constitutes the notion of God.

293:14   *In the same spirit.* Compare Hegel's *Science of Logic*, II, 68 (*W.a.A. IV* 70; *Jub. Ausg.* IV 548):

In movement, impulse, and the like, the simplicity of these determinations hides the contradiction from imagination; but this contradiction immediately stands revealed in the determinations of relations. The most trivial examples—above and below, right and left, father and son, and so on without end—all contain Contradictions in one term. . . . Opposite terms contain Contradiction in so far as they are negatively related to each other in the same respect, or cancel out and remain indifferent to each other.

295:4   *Plato placed the idea in the second rank.* According to Plato's view existence constitutes a well-regulated whole, a Cosmos of increasingly comprehensive forms of being, and this also holds true of the world of ideas. Ideas consequently do not have the same status or rank but are arranged by gradations, so ultimately they depend on the highest or supreme idea. He then theorizes that the supreme and principal idea is the idea of the good.

Kierkegaard's statements in the present text are presumably related to the following lines in Tennemann's *Geschichte der Philosophie*, II, 370ff., to which Kierkegaard makes reference in *Pap.* IV C 12 (*JP* III 2339):

Because Plato regarded the idea as original innate concepts, which however were inexplicable as a function of reason, he had no other alternative than to regard them as concepts derived from the divine intelligence . . . hence God is the creator of the ideas, that is, God has endowed man with reason and by this means made the ideas the principle of all cognition.

Reference may be made especially to David Ross, *Plato's Theory of Ideas* (Oxford, 1951), pp. 213ff.; Paul Friedländer, *Platon*, 2nd ed., I (Berlin, 1954), passim (see *"Eidos"* in his index); and W.K.C. Guthrie, *A History of Greek Philosophy*, vols. IV–V (London, 1975–1978), passim.

295:6   *but he is not himself an idea.* The draft adds (*Pap.* VI B 54:17): "and yet [he is] existing [*existerende*], and thus existing and thinking [he] asked about the relationship between thought and being, and philosophy replied with something quite different."

295:29   *has won through to a perfect victory.* Here the sense is, "is over and done with it." Kierkegaard borrowed this rather singular phrase (*har sin Seier forvunden*) from a barker who performed at Deer Park (*Dyrehavsbakken*), an amusement park in a northern suburb of Copenhagen, where a model of *Fæstningen Fredriksten* (Fredriksten Fort) was on exhibition. (In the barker's mouth it became *"Festungen Frederikssten,"* an odd mixture of Danish and German.) The real fort in Norway was besieged by King Charles XII of Sweden in 1716 and 1718 and again by the Swedes in 1814—all three times in vain. Before exhibiting the model, the barker, who in the 1830s was familiar to everyone in Copenhagen, gave a speech that began with: "Don't monkey with the fort, boy with the green cap! You won't give anything, will you? Let the other gentlemen through so they can put something in the dish!" He ended his story of the battles with this remark about the wounded: "yet they are happy, for they have won through to their victory!" (*"dog ere de glade, thi de have forvundet deres Sejr!"*) See A. Arlaud, *Bevingede Ord*, 2nd ed. (Copenhagen, 1906), p. 420.

296:6   *as phrased by a poet* [S/L: in a comedy]. Steen Steensen Blicher, *Fjorten Dage i Jylland* in *Samlede Noveller*, I–V (Copenhagen, 1833–1840; see *ASKB* 1521–23), V, 212. See *Pap.* II A 140 (*JP* II 1702).

296:11   *what the Jews feared so much.* That Israel "shall be a proverb and byword among all people" (1 Kings 9:7) and "become an astonishment, a proverb, and a byword, among all the nations whither the Lord shall send thee' (Deut. 28:37).

296:26   *If Hegel had published his Logic.* Kierkegaard owned Hegel's *Wissenschaft der Logik*, ed. L. v. Henning, I–III (Berlin, 1833–1834; *ASKB* 552–54), which figures as vols. III–V of *W.a.A.* A few days before his death on November 14, 1831, Hegel was occupied with a new edition, but he managed to revise only the first part (see his preface to the second edition, *Jub. Ausg.* IV 20–36; *The Science of Logic*, I, 33–51). Kierkegaard's copies were bought by the Royal Library of Copenhagen at the auction of his private library in April 1856. For a description of Hegel's logic, see above, Introduction, chap. 4.

297:3   *nature sounds . . . Ceylon.* G. H. von Schubart, a disciple of Schelling, writes in his *Die Symbolik des Traumes*, 2nd ed. (Bamberg, 1821; *ASKB* 776), p. 38, about the "voice of nature, the ethereal music of Ceylon, which in the tone of an animal-like, lamenting, and heart-rending voice sings fearfully merry minuets." Kierkegaard mentions these nature sounds in several places, first in the draft of a letter to P. W. Lund (*Breve* I, 35), and later in, for example, the *Fragments*, p. 135 (*SV* IV 300).

297:11   *a letter purporting to have come from heaven.* In older popular belief the word *Himmelbrev* (heavenly letter) was used to denote letters that were supposed to have fallen from heaven and to contain a divine command to man. In 1818 Poul Møller wrote a parody of Grundtvig that is rather well known in Danish literature; "Forsøg til et Himmelbrev i Grundtvigs nye, historiske Smag, fundet af Poul Møller." It is reprinted in *Poul Møllers efterladte Skrifter*, 2nd ed., ed. F. C. Olsen, I–III (Copenhagen, 1848–1850), I², 218ff. Kierkegaard owned the first edition of this work, also in three volumes (1839–1843; *ASKB* 1574–76). On the subject of "heavenly letters" see Kristian Sandfeld's essay in *Dania*, III (Copenhagen, 1895–1896), pp. 193–228.

298:3   *God must possess all perfections.* This is the classical formulation of the ontological proof of the existence of God, such as it appears in Anselm of Canterbury. Hegel considers it especially in *Lectures on the Philosophy of Religion*, II, 249ff.; III, 351ff. (*W.a.A.* XII 210ff., 539ff.; *Jub. Ausg.* XVII 210ff., 539ff.). See Erik Schmidt, *Hegels Lehre von Gott* (Gütersloh, 1952), especially pp. 111–40, and J. N. Findlay, *Hegel* (London, 1964), pp. 135ff.

298:30   *The explanatory paragraph is entitled Actuality* [S/L: Reality]. "Actuality" is treated in Section III, Part II, of Hegel's *Science of Logic* (II, 173ff.). See my commentary on *The Concept of Anxiety* in *Krankheit Kommen.*, p. 704.

298
(note *):1   *Hegel . . . in connection with Descartes.* Kierkegaard may have had in mind Hegel's usual characterization of Descartes in *Lectures on the History of Philosophy*, III, 221 (*W.a.A.* XV 331ff.; *Jub. Ausg.* XIX 331ff.), where he writes:

> The extent of the influence which this man exercised upon his times and the culture of Philosophy generally, cannot be sufficiently expressed; it rests mainly in his setting aside all former presuppositions and beginning in a free, simple, and likewise popular way, with popular modes of thought and quite simple propositions, in his leading the content to thought and extension or Being, and so to speak setting up this before thought as its opposite. This simple thought appeared in the form of the determinate, clear understanding, and it cannot thus be called speculative thought or speculative reason.

299:10   *Schelling put a stop to the self-reflexive process.* It is doubtful whether Kierkegaard is aiming at a specific passage in Schelling. His description of Schelling's intellectual intuition is applicable to several passages; for instance, in *System des transcendentalen Idealismus, Werke*, ed.

M. Schröter, I–VI (Munich, 1927–1928), II, 369ff. See Karl Jaspers, *Schelling: Grösse und Verhängnis* (Munich, 1955), pp. 74ff.

299:13   *Hegel . . . speaks absprechend* [S/L: contemptuously] *of . . . intellectual intuition.* See for example *The Science of Logic*, I, 79 (*W.a.A.* III 60; *Jub. Ausg.* IV 70).

299 (note *):1   *presupposed in all skepticism.* See the Index.

299 (note *):5   ϑητιϰως. This should read: ϑετιϰῶς, positively, unconditionally, as an assertion (Diogenes Laërtius, IX, 75).

300:5   *the infinitesimally small angles of the astronomers.* If we observe the same fixed stars at different points of time the lines of sight will form angles if the stars are close enough. If the stars are further from the earth the lines of sight will appear as parallel lines with ordinary measuring instruments, the angles being too small to be perceptible.

300:30   *a Greek philosopher.* Kierkegaard was thinking of the anecdote in Cicero, *De natura deorum* (I, 60), concerning the poet Simonides who was asked what God was.

301:11   *by begging or postulating. (bittweise).* See the Index.

301:33   *the bad infinite.* See the Index.

302:4   *the pixie that moves.* See the Index.

302:11   *Black Peter.* Following this the draft has (*Pap.* VI B 54:19; *JP* III 3702, modified):

> Self-reflection [*Selv-Reflexionen*] was a skepticism; it is overcome in pure thought. But pure thought is a still more extreme skepticism. Despite all the introspection [*Indadventhed*] involved in self-reflection, it nevertheless could not forget its relation to actuality in the sense of actuality, its relation to the *an sich* which pursues it. Pure thought, however, is positive through having taken the whole matter imaginatively into a sphere where there is no relation to actuality at all. Pure thought does not even dream that it is skepticism—but this itself is the most extreme skepticism. If, without pressing the comparison, one were to compare skepticism with insanity,* a person who has a notion of being insane and whose life goes on amid this conflict is less mad, however, than one who triumphantly jubilates as the cleverest of all.
>
> * *In margin*: And Danish readers will not forget that Poul Møller regarded Hegel as mad.

302:21   *exploiting . . . "to think."* More literally: "which makes itself guilty of [*forskylder*] a duplicity in its use of the term 'to think.' " The verb *at forskylde*, which is now used only in the perfect participle (*forskyldt*), is generally employed by Kierkegaard in the above sense and with the meaning of "to cause." See *ODS*, V, cols, 851ff., where examples are taken from other passages in Kierkegaard's works.

303:14   *the jealous watchfulness of the good.* This phrase appears in Ex. 20:5.

303:21   *gives away a kingdom.* Like Shakespeare's King Lear—who, however, did not do so out of charity.

303:21   *the Levite.* Luke 10:30ff. The man traveled from Jerusalem to Jericho, not the other way around. Junghans in his note to this passage raises the question of whether Kierkegaard here and in other places purposely allows his pseudonyms to make such minor errors to stimulate the reader's attention. Even though this hypothesis cannot be summarily dismissed, since Kierkegaard always worked while in an extreme state of concentration, it is nevertheless quite possible that this and similar instances may be due to ordinary slips of the memory. Kierkegaard always concentrated his attention on the inner aspects of the case, thus in this instance on the attitude of the Levite rather than on the direction in which he rode.

304:3   *Believing God.* That is, that God exists (*er til*).

304:31   *Dion.* The famous Syracusan statesman, born 409 B.C. He was banished by the younger Dionysius in 366 B.C., but in 357 B.C. he landed near Syracuse with a mercenary army and forced Dionysius to take flight. Aristotle relates in *Politics* 1312a (trans. H. Rackham, *Loeb Classical Library*) that:

> When he made war upon Dionysius, he took with him very few troops, saying "that whatever measure of success he might attain would be enough for him, even if he were to die the moment before he landed; such a death would be welcome to him."

305:10   *supremacy.* The thought expressed in this section is comparable to Kant's theory of the supremacy of practical reason over theoretical or speculative reason. See for example N. H. Søe's *Fra Renæssancen til vore Dage*, 3rd ed. (Copenhgen, 1960), pp. 108ff., and Frederick Ferré, *Basic Modern Philosophy of Religion* (New York, 1967), pp.182–236. See also Kant's *Critique of Pure Reason*, pp. A471ff. (B499ff.).

305:10   *Gnosticism.* Here the word is to be taken in the broad sense of cognition of the transcendental world. Concerning Gnosticism see the Introduction, chap. 1 and references to the literature.

305:18   *acosmism.* Actually, the theory of the nothingness of the world. Hegel called Spinoza's philosophy acosmism (*Enc.*, §50; *Jub. Ausg.* VIII 148; *Logic*, p. 106), but here Kierkegaard has in mind Fichte. In a defensive writing from 1799 Fichte replied to his opponents' accusations of atheism by describing his philosophy as acosmism. See

Kuno Fischer, *Geschichte der neuern Philosophie*, 4th ed., IV (Heidelberg, 1914), pp. 175ff.

305:23 *"heaven and earth and all that therein is."* A quotation from a textbook authorized at that time, N. E. Balle's *Lærebog i den Evangeliskchristelige Religion, indrettet til Brug i de danske Skoler* (Copenhagen, 1824; *ASKB* 183), chap. I, §I, p. 2: "Under the term World are generally included both heaven and earth and all that therein is."

306:1 *The transition from possibility to actuality.* See in this connection *Pap.* V C 1–9 (*JP* I 2345–51) and especially the "Interlude" in the *Fragments*, my edition, pp. 89–106 with commentary. Aristotle deals with this problem in, for example, *Physics* 200b ff. Reference is likewise made to the Introduction and to the literature referred to there.

306:20 *the possible constitutes a mere appearance.* The word "possible" (*Muligheden*) should probably read "transition" (*Overgangen*). The draft for this passage has *Overgangen*, whereas both the manuscript, which is in Kierkegaard's handwriting, and the original edition have *Muligheden*. The first edition of Kierkegaard's Collected Works in Danish (*SV* VII 297) has *Muligheden*, which is corrected to read *Overgangen* in the second and more critical edition (*SV* VII 332). "Transition" makes more sense in the present context. (Note by R.J.W.)

307:2 *Philosophical Fragments.* Pages 90ff. in my edition. The draft has in addition (*Pap.* VI B 54:21; *JP* I 199):

> Very likely what our age needs most to illuminate the relationship between logic and ontology is an examination of the concepts: possibility, actuality, and necessity. It is hoped, meanwhile, that the person who would do something along this line would be influenced by the Greeks. The Greek sobriety is seldom found in the philosophers of our day, and exceptional ingenuity is only a mediocre substitute. Good comments are to be found in Trendlenburg's *Logische Untersuchungen*: but Trendlenburg was also shaped by the Greeks.

307:4 *The Simultaneity.* There is a good analysis of this important concept in Per Lønning, *"Samtidighedens Situation": En studie i Søren Kierkegaards kristendoms-forståelse* (Oslo, 1954), especially pp. 29–82.

307:7 *Granted that speculative thought . . . in pooh-poohing.* Kierkegaard was thinking of Karl Rosenkranz's *Psychologie oder die Wissenschaft vom subjectiven Geist* (Königsberg, 1837; *ASKB* 744), in which the following appears in the Preface:

> The usual conceptual trichotomy of the subjective spirit [*Geistes*] as body, soul, and spirit does not exist in Hegel. . . . On the con-

trary, Hegel already in the science of subjective spirit presupposes that the concept of corporeality pertains to natural philosophy, and so he subdivides spirit into soul, consciousness, and spirit. It is this self-same subject that . . . appears in these various degrees of development.

See Arild Christensen, "Om Søren Kierkegaards Inddelingsprincip," *Kierkegaardiana*, III (Copenhagen, 1959), pp. 21–38.

308:4   *assign . . . marriage, its proper place in the system*. Part III, Subsection I, Item A, §§161–69, of Hegel's *Philosophy of Right* (pp. 111–16; *W.a.A.* VIII 223–33; *Jub. Ausg.* VII 239–49), is titled "Marriage" (*"Die Ehe"*).

308:21   *Let us . . . not confuse the historical development . . . with particular individuals*. This is a direct thrust at Hegel who in his system, and most plainly in *The Phenomenology of Spirit*, made the universal and individual developments of spirit identical. See in this respect the Introduction to the present volume, chap. 4 above.

308:24   *In the animal world the particular specimen*. See in connection with this Arild Christensen's essay, "Søren Kierkegaards Individuationsprincip," *Dansk teologisk Tidsskrift* (Copenhagen, 1953), pp. 216–36.

308:30   *Or may we assume that Christian parents give birth to Christian children?* This is a polemic against Martensen, who in his booklet against the Baptists, *Den christelige Daab* (Copenhagen, 1843), p. 23, maintained among other things that

> It is inherently clear that at the time when the essential task was to establish the Church in the world much had to take another form than in succeeding ages, after the Church had become firmly rooted in the world and the Kingdom of God so to speak had become nature . . . [and] innate in the national character.

In this connection see *Pap.* V A 10 (*JP* I 452) and my note to the *Fragments*, pp. 254ff.

309:35   *to rise in abstract-dialectical psychological determinations*. The sequence is the same as that outlined by Karl Rosenkranz in *Psychologie oder die Wissenschaft vom subjectiven Geist* (Königsberg, 1837).

310:9   *the expectation of an eternal happiness*. Efforts to ascertain what Kierkegaard had in mind here have been in vain.

310:28   *Faith is said to be an immediacy*. Kierkegaard was surely thinking of Hegel's argument in *Enc.*, §§63 and 573 (*W.a.A.* VI 228ff. and VII² 452; *Jub. Ausg.* VIII 266 and X 458ff.; *The Philosophy of Spirit*, pp. 187ff., and *Logic*, pp. 124ff., respectively), and in *The Philosophy of Religion*, III, 339ff. (*W.a.A.* XV 513ff.; *Jub. Ausg.* XVI 528ff.). In the

latter work Hegel also turns against Jacobi's identification of immediate knowledge and faith. See the Index.

310:33   *Frater Taciturnus complains.* In *Stages*, p. 435 (*SV* VI 506).

311:26   *Poetry is crowded aside and dismissed.* In all likelihood this is an allusion to the position assigned to art in Hegel's system, and thus also
to poetry, which is a subdivision of art. As the first term in the triad
Art/Religion/Philosophy, it is overcome or transcended.

312:6   *Non omnes omnia possumus.* "Not all of us can do everything." A
quotation from G. Lucilius via Virgil's *Bucolica*, VIII, 63.

In the paragraphs concluding this section of the book Climacus elaborates on his definition of a subjective thinker, at the same time elucidating the problem with which Christianity is beset as a result of the intrusion of speculative philosophy into its domain. He opens paragraph four with an outline of the subjective thinker's task, form, and style.

If a person's efforts with respect to pure thought are the only criteria for whether or not he is a thinker, we will have to reject the subjective thinker. But in rejecting him we likewise remove all the difficulties of existence.

To be a subjective thinker one must have imagination, feeling, and passionate dialectics in the inwardness of existence. The subjective thinker is not a scientist but an artist who strives to understand himself in existence. This is a task that was considered essential by the Greeks, and it is also a Christian principle. A believer is then a subjective thinker. The only difference allowable in this respect is that between the simple man and the simple wise man, which merely consists in the fact that the wise man is aware of the relationship.

It is thus a strenuous job to be a subjective thinker; and yet from all of these efforts one may expect only a very meager yield in the traditional sense of a result. The subjective thinker will of course have a specific form, and this may be said to constitute his style (p. 319), which varies in accordance with the contrasts he must hold in combination. Moreover, he is faced with the decisive difficulty arising from the fact that the *actuality* of existence does not admit of communication.

Modern speculation, Climacus maintains, seems almost to have performed the trick of progressing far beyond Christianity, or of understanding Christianity in such a way as to have just about returned to paganism. As opposed to this tendency, the intention in the *Fragments* was to make a true advance beyond paganism and arrive at Christianity. The author refrained, however, from mentioning Christianity by name, for speculation had already taken the entire Christian terminology into its service, and of course it was necessary to take this circumstance into consideration when planning the work.

What has happened in the theoretical field has also occurred in the practical: everybody thinks he is a Christian. Now if these people are really to be won over they must first be deprived of their illusions and discouraged, indeed even frightened away, from Christianity. Climacus accordingly expounds his view of baptism and arrives at the conclusion that Christendom is in fact nothing more than a sort of "baptized paganism." This is why in the *Fragments* he had recourse to paganism pure and simple and to its greatest representative, Socrates.

Now in the New Testament the claim is made that salvation is determined in time by a relationship to something historical. There is no room for doubt on this point. Whether or not Christianity is justified in making such a claim is another matter and, as far as the author's present work is concerned, beside the point. Speculative philosophers, too, appeal to the New Testament, but they have still failed to clarify in just what sense they intend to use it. Sometimes it would seem from their arguments that one cannot appeal to the New Testament at all; and yet at other times they freely avail themselves of Scriptural passages as a source reference in support of their conclusions.

It is essential, Climacus continues, not to turn the question of what Christianity is into a subject for scholarly investigation. The moment we let this happen we will enter into the realm of approximation with no possibility of escape, and such an investigation might last a lifetime, leaving the investigator no time to tackle the more important problem of whether or not to *become* a Christian. The question must therefore not be formulated philosophically and confounded with objective problems concerning the truth of Christianity.

Does this mean, Climacus asks, that it is impossible to know what Christianity is without being a Christian? In reply Climacus affirms that it is possible. But whether a man can know what it means to be a Christian without himself being one is an altogether different matter. Here the answer is no.

As to mediation, before doing any mediating we must first decide what both philosophy and Christianity are. Speculation, however, skips over this problem, casually proclaiming that it is mediation or reconciliation[1] without bothering to delve into the natures of the factors it mediates; it thereupon claims that it is Christianity. Our speculative philosophers have accomplished this trick by simply assuming that Christianity is an objective doctrine belonging to the same conceptual sphere as speculation, and that the two are merely relative

---

[1] *Forsoningen*, which may mean mediation, reconciliation, or atonement.—R.J.W.

opposites. Point by point, Climacus cuts this speculative assumption to pieces. He ends by observing that if the claim put forward by speculation were true, we would be confronted with the problem of whether mediation (*Mediationen*) in the sense of atonement (*Forsoningen*) is a clever invention made in the sphere of speculation or whether it originated in Christianity. He moreover asseverates that Christianity's very idea on the contrary involves a paradox, indeed an absolute paradox (p. 338). Climacus' real opponents here are disclosed by the phrase "so-called Christian speculation" (ibid.); principally he means the right-wing Hegelians.

Christianity, then, is not a doctrine in a purely philosophical sense. (He elaborates on this in an important footnote.) Rather, Christianity expresses the fact that existence involves a contradiction because the individual must settle the matter of his eternal happiness by a decision made in time and by relating himself to something that is historical (p. 340). Consequently he must transform his life into a communication of existence, participating in and committing himself to existence. This is the very opposite of speculation.

*   *   *

314:25   *Poul Møller has rightly remarked.* In one of his *Strøtanker* ("Random Thoughts") from the period 1819–1821, in *Efterladte Skrifter af Poul M. Møller*, ed F. C. Olsen, 2nd ed., I–III (Copenhagen, 1848–1850), III, 9ff.:

> Extemporaneous wits and other such oral poets possess more genius than the writing poets, but less awareness of it. They are rich men who amuse themselves by casting gold out among the crowd without themselves knowing its worth. Most of the time poets who write are not filled with inspired thoughts but are connoisseurs of their genuineness. Every fortunate idea that strikes them is noticed and employed in an expedient manner. But even the most prolix comic authors do not have as much wit as an excellent court jester needs in one year.

314:36   *that I count for less than nothing.* Quoted freely from Oldfux's lines in Holberg's *Den Stundesløse*, Act II, Scene 2:

> I am Jonas Andersen, the correct person's unworthy first cousin on the father's side. I am only a maggot compared with him in bookkeeping and accounting. I have him to thank, and I ought to kiss the dust beneath his feet for what I know about bookkeeping.

315:19   *All skepticism is a kind of idealism.* Idealism is here used in the epistemological sense of philosophical rationalism. See the Introduction, chap. 1, concerning the Greek philosophers of nature who, disregarding empirical observations, reasoned in the same way.

315:19   *the skeptic Zeno.* Diogenes Laërtius tells the following story about Pyrrho (trans. R. D. Hicks, *Loeb Classical Library*, XI, 66): "When a cur rushed at him and terrified him, he answered his critic that it was not easy entirely to strip oneself of human weakness."

315:31   *it is impossible not to write a satire.* See Juvenal, *Sat.*, I, 30: "difficile est satiram non scribere."

315:37   *To express existentially.* The draft has the following marginal note (*Pap.* VI B 54:25):

A play by Scribe [i.e. *Oscar*] ends with a masterly line by a servant girl who has given impetus to the intrigue by saying individually to each character in the play: I know everything—although she herself knows nothing. [The line goes:] "Is that so? It seems that everybody except me knows what I'm going to say." A modern speculator who has explained all of existence might get into the same awkward position in which everybody knows whom he is talking about—except him.

316:6   *unum noris, omnes [noris].* "If one is known they all are." The quotation is from Terentius' *Phormio* (I, 5), where the meaning is: since the one is neither better nor worse than the other, it is sufficient to know one. B. Kirmmse in *Kierkegaard's Psychology* (Pittsburgh, 1978) has investigated this phrase as a motto for Kierkegaard's theories of psychology.

316:21   *an eternal God-becoming.* See the commentary on the *Fragments*, pp. 174–80, and my essay, "Die historische Methode in der Kierkegaard-Forschung durch ein Beispiel beleuchtet," *Orbis Litterarum* (Copenhagen, 1955), pp. 280ff.

318:7   *Napoleon.* A. Thier's *Den franske Revolutions Historie*, trans. F. C. Rosen, I–X (Copenhagen, 1841–1845), VII, 291:

Bonaparte . . . began a gallop in front of the soldiers' ranks and, pointing at the pyramids, he exclaimed: "Bear in mind that from the tops of these pyramids forty centuries look down on you."

Kierkegaard owned a German edition of this work, *Geschichte der französischen Revolution*, trans. Ferdinand Philipps, I–V (Leipzig, 1836; *ASKB* 2024–28).

319:9   *the theocentric nineteenth century.* The printed manuscript then has the following (*Pap.* VI B 98:62):

> What our age needs, to talk badly about something I usually do not undertake to talk about, is not a new contribution to the system but a subjective thinker who relates himself to existing [*det at existere*] *qua* Christian just as Socrates related himself to existing *qua* human being. He himself, however, must be unaware that the age needs him, or at any rate must not want to be aware of it, for that very moment he too will have steered off course, misled by the world-historical.

320:22   *esse . . . into a posse.* Actuality . . . into a possibility.

320:32   *si placet.* If it so pleases.

321:11   *an exceptional case.* In Danish *excipere*, a loanword meaning to make an exception of or an objection in point of law; to demur. The word stems from Roman law in which *exceptio* is an exception granted a defendant to the law according to which judgment is to be passed.

321:36   *Themistocles was rendered sleepless.* Plutarch in *Themistocles* (III, 3) relates the story that when Miltiades' name was on the lips of everyone following his victory at Marathon, Themistocles spent his nights in sleeplessness. When his friends inquired as to the reason, he answered: "Miltiades' triumphs do not let me sleep."

323:16   *the discovery that there is no "beyond."* In *The Science of Logic,* in the section "The Reciprocal Determination of Finite and Infinite" (I, 151–56; *W.a.A.* III 149–55; *Jub. Ausg.* IV 159–65), Hegel defines the two concepts mentioned as reciprocally conditioning each other; but an absolute disavowal of the infinite in the sense of the "beyond" does not appear in Hegel.

324:19   *current book catalogue.* Kierkegaard is referring to lists of new publications (*Messecatalog*). They were published in Leipzig until 1860 and listed works offered for sale at the booksellers' fairs held annually at Easter and Michaelmas in Leipzig and Frankfurt.

325:19   κατὰ δύναμιν [S/L: as a possibility]. Potentially, as a possibility.

326:7   *in the Christian ideology.* The draft has (*Pap.* VI B 54:30; *JP* II 1609. "Christian categories*" and the marginal note are not included in the Hong translation):

> Christian categories.*
> All that was lacking was for Hegelian philosophy to have also a visible custom such as baptism, an act which could be performed with small children; thus one could bring it to the point where babies fourteen days old would be everything—Hegelian as well.

And if a person baptized at fourteen days as a Hegelian were to announce himself as a Hegelian, if a watchman, for example, had his child baptized as a Hegelian and then brought the child up to the best of his humble abilities and the child had no special aptitudes and grew up to become a watchman, too—but also a Hegelian—would this not be ridiculous. Let it be true ten times over that, unlike Hegelian philosophy, Christianity is not based on differences, that it is Christianity's holy humanity that it can be appropriated by all—but is this then to be understood to mean that everyone is a Christian automatically?

* *In margin*: The distinction between the visible and the invisible Church.

327:2   *an Anabaptist heresy.* The reference here may be to either the Anabaptists of the time of the Reformation or, which is more likely, the Baptists who precisely in the 1840s drew attention to themselves in Denmark. The latter, however, taught adult baptism, not rebaptism. See the Index.

327:18   *baptized in childhood.* The printed manuscript has in addition (*Pap.* VI B 98:63):

The dubiousness of being a Christian in relation to becoming a Christian will appear, moreover, as an analogy to the differences between individuals: an apathetic individual will feel tempted to regard the matter as settled; an ardent individual will feel tempted to want to renounce and abandon Christianity decisively, simply in order to belong to it in a decisive manner; to those of medium quality Christianity will be a kind of unhappy consciousness that makes existence [*Existentsen*] much too hard for them, even though they do not have the strength to throw off the yoke again. This last relationship is perhaps much more common than people believe, and the best comparison is probably with an unhappy marriage in which one neither is happy nor has the courage to break out because it is a crime, and so puts one's trust in the separation of death.

327:38   *the terrible thunderstorm.* Kierkegaard is alluding to Luther's famous experience of July 2, 1505 in the village of Stotternheim near Erfurt. During a violent thunderstorm lightning struck close to him, and in his sudden mortal fear he cried out to St. Ann for help, promising to enter the cloister. It is not a historical fact that his friend Alexius was killed at his side. See for example Otto Scheel, *Martin Luther*, 2nd ed. I (Tübingen, 1917), pp. 248ff.

328:3   *"But these hair-splitting Sophists. . . ."* Kierkegaard quotes in German. Kierkegaard owned and used Otto v. Gerlach's edition, *Luthers
Werke. Vollständige Auswhal seiner Hauptschriften*, I–X (Berlin, 1840–
1841; *ASKB* 312–16). In the Weimar edition the quotation appears in
vol. VI, p. 571, and reads as follows in the original Latin:

> Verum Sophistae nostri de hac fide nihil in sacramentis tractant,
> sed in uirtutibus ipsis sacramentorum totis studiis nugantur, sem-
> per discentes et numquam ad scientiam veritatis peruenientes.

Kierkegaard commented on this passage in an undated journal entry from 1845 (*Pap.* VI A 141; *JP* V 5855, modified):

> Somewhere in the book *Concluding Postscript* I quoted some words
> of Luther (on the Babylonian captivity). It reads: *"in diesen Sacra-
> menten,"* and without doubt Luther meant thereby the five Catholic
> [sacraments]. Now someone rushes forward and protests, etc. Well,
> go ahead. That is just what I wanted. I did not wish to begin a
> scholarly investigation in the book or use my best weapons. Now
> the prospect of a little advantage is a temptation for some honor-
> able gentleman: and so I can quote the far more significant lines in
> the same book which I have noted in my copy (Gerlach's edition).

See Regin Prenter, "Luther and Lutheranism," *Kierkegaard and Great
Traditions*, vol. VI of *Bibliotheca Kierkegaardiana* (Copenhagen, 1981),
especially pp. 127ff.

328:6   *if objectivity is truth.* The printed manuscript has after this (*Pap.* VI
B 98:64):

> Suppose the Hegelian philosophy also had such a visible custom
> as baptism, an act that could be performed with little children;
> what if someone who had thus been baptized a Hegelian when he
> was fourteen days old were to report as a Hegelian; suppose a
> watchman had his child baptized a Hegelian and now brought the
> child up to the best of his humble abilities, and the child had no
> special aptitudes and became a man and thereupon also a watch-
> man—but a Hegelian, too; would this not be ridiculous?

328(note   *Fragments. SV* IV 287; pp. 118ff. in my edition.
*):1
329:12   *two weeks after birth.* The following note is added in the printed
manuscript (*Pap.* VI B 98:65):

> *Note.* I will recall to mind a couple of words by Luther but only
> with some uncertainty and also against my will. I am always in
> fear of entering into a perpetual learned quoting that will never
> come to an end. Therefore, should this brief quotation occasion

anyone to try to begin any such thing I hereby at once retract the quotations and give up appealing to Luther.

330:1   §2. To this the following is added in the draft (*Pap.* VI B 54:31):

The piece (the *Fragments*) did not lecture, nor does what is written here. There is no lecturing here on the fact that Christianity is the truth; I am merely seeking to find a decisive expression for the Christian standpoint, which may well be significant, since it seems that in the middle of Christendom people have forgotten what Christianity is.

330:21   *in presenting the problem.* The draft continues with (*Pap.* VI B 54:32):

But now I will here seek to clarify the problem in another way so that its difficulty will become really clear, for the problem presupposes inwardness in existence [*Existents-Inderlighed*] and dialectics simply to be understood.

Inwardness in existence presupposes the problem in the sense of the phrase: an eternal happiness; dialectics presuppose it in the sense of [*in margin*: grasping the difficulty by] putting it together with a decision in time, which becomes the decision of eternal happiness. The dialectical difficulties were especially emphasized in the piece (the *Fragments*), and therefore I will not dwell on them any longer.

Modern speculation's admired discovery was that there is no Hereafter, that the Hereafter consisted of uncertain requirements that no one honored and thus finally no one issued. Such being the case, it is easy to see what answer to the problem may be expected from that quarter: that the problem itself is an undialectical narrow-mindedness. My rejoinder remains unchanged: whether a speculator will take the trouble to deal with me and, in that event, whether I might have the honor of asking whom I have the honor of speaking with, whether he is a single existing human being—in short, the rules of safety necessary to prevent being made a fool of by talking to a fantastic pure I = I. Insecurity in the world of speculation has become widespread in our day, for fantastic beings are the most dangerous of all to deal with. And next I would have to ask him whether he will deny that in the N.T. Christianity teaches an eternal happiness [*in margin*: Hereafter], and if so whether he will direct his accusation of narrow-mindedness against Christianity itself; for I am not lecturing but exploring.

330:29   *the New Testament lies in the sphere of representative thought.* Kierkegaard may have been thinking of several passages in Hegel, for example, *The Phenomenology of Spirit* (pp. 789ff.; *W.a.A.* II 573ff.; *Jub.*

Ausg. II 581ff.) and *Lectures on the Philosophy of Religion* (I, 142ff.; *W.a.A.* XI 137ff.; *Jub. Ausg.* XV 135ff.). Hegel maintains that religion—and under this category, Christianity—embodies the absolute truth in the inferior and imperfect form of "figurative thinking," whereas in speculative philosophy the truth emerges in the higher and fully adequate form of the concept.

330:38   *decisive importance.* The draft continues with (*Pap.* VI B 54:33; *JP* III 3307):

> Xenophon [in *Memorabilia*, III, 6] tells of a young man who wanted to assume the government of a city. Socrates halted him by asking if he had the requisite preparation, if he knew how many ships the city had, etc. This preparation is of great importance if a mediation between Christianity and speculation is to amount to anything; to mediate between speculation and speculation is not so difficult but is rather meaningless.

330:38   *Commission of Arbitration* [S/L: arbitrator]. This commission (*Forligelses-Commissionen*) was established in Copenhagen by the mandate of July 10, 1795, to undertake obligatory attempts at arbitration before a trial could begin in the courts.

332:8   *the contemporary generation of adults.* The draft has the following addition (*Pap.* VI B 54:34):

> [. . .] in order at once to get hold of the new generation of children, let us then take a pagan philosopher who at a man's mature age was in possession of the entire Greek culture. Christianity was preached to him. But the person who preached it to him must certainly have told him what Christianity is and thus made it possible for him to deliberate. Apostle Paul indeed also says [1 Pet. 3:15] that the believer must be prepared to give an account of faith to those who inquire about it.

332:21   *The possibility of knowing what Christianity is.* This passage is found in the draft in a version that is more detailed and somewhat different, especially in the sequence of thoughts. It concludes with the portion below in penciled brackets (*Pap.* VI B 54:35).

> There was certainty in the generation contemporary with Christianity, for Socrates correctly makes the distinction that whoever knows what he knows or knows that he does not know it is firm and certain, whereas the man who believes that he knows something he does not know is faltering. And so Christianity is faltering

in our age—presumably because we are all Christians as a matter of course.

333:10   *the twin Cerberuses.* In Greek mythology Cerberus was a three-headed dog that guarded the entrance to Hades.

333:21   *(nomen dare aliqui).* To give (one's) name. The phrase was used in Roman military parlance in the sense of "to report for war duty."

335:20   *speculative philosophy is the atonement, is mediation.* On the concept of mediation, see the Index and regarding Hegel's identification of Christianity with his own philosophy see the Introduction, chap. 4. In several passages Hegel, applying the concept of *Versöhnung* (reconciliation, atonement, mediation), stresses that his philosophy and Christianity have the same content, namely, universal reason existing in-and-for-itself. For example, he writes (*Lectures on the History of Philosophy*, I, 63; *Jub. Ausg.* XVII 94):

> Worship is only the operation of reflection; Philosophy attempts to bring about the reconciliation [*Versöhnung*] by means of thinking knowledge, because Mind [Spirit] desires to take up its Being into itself. [Square brackets inserted by R.J.W.]

336:11   *the doctrine of the Eleatics and that of Heraclitus.* Kierkegaard's knowledge of the Eleatics' and Heraclitus' philosophical theories derives chiefly from W. G. Tennemann's *Geschichte der Philosophie* (Leipzig, 1798), I, 150ff. and 209ff., as well as from Hegel's *Lectures on the History of Philosophy* (I, 239–98; *W.a.A.* XIII 280–353; *Jub. Ausg.* XVIII 296–369). See my commentary on *Die Wiederholung* (Cologne, 1956), p. 684, note to p. 272.

The totally opposite theories of the Eleatics and of Heraclitus have as their background the efforts by the earlier Ionic philosophers to provide an essentially nonmythical or rational solution to the problem concerning the universal principle or substance of things. Some replied to this question by saying that water, air, or fire, by way of example, constituted the common substance. But in the wake of such replies another question arose: How are we then to explain the transformation of an immutable substance into the visible world's incalculable multitude of different individual entities in all their ascertainable changeableness? The solution to this problem was sought by assuming that two opposite forces like rarefaction and condensation set substance into motion, thereby producing the world of mutability. This answer in turn gave rise to a new problem, this time not concerning the essence of things but the knowledge of them. It was axiomatically assumed that reason is only able to know something of its own kind and self-identical, that is, something that is immutable. In assuming this to be the case they had to inquire as to whether real being was changeable or unchangeable. It was to this question that the Eleatics and Heraclitus gave completely different answers.

The Eleatics—with Parmenides (see Plato's dialogue of the same name) as their most salient spokesman—took their point of departure in what actually is and not in what merely apparently is. They felt that the apparent in fact is not, for "apparent" denotes something that is not what it seems to be. Employing purely rational ("speculative," as it is called in the *Postscript*) reasoning, Parmenides arrived at the result that being always has been and will be, and that it is immutable and immovable. He reasoned as follows (Justus Hartnack, *Filosofiske Problemer* [Copenhagen, 1956], pp. 17ff.):

> If there was any point of time when being [*det værende*] was not, it must have originated from not-being [*det ikke værende*]. But this thought is impossible, for there is nothing that can be called "not-being"; no meaning can be joined to the concept "not-being." It is therefore meaningless to say that being originates from not-being. Either being has always been or it has never been and never will be. It thus follows that since being is, it must necessarily always have been. It likewise follows that it also always will be and that it is eternal and imperishable; for to say that being could become not-being would be to admit that not-being is. Nor does being consist of parts with interjacent empty space; for if by empty space we mean that not-being is contained in it, it certainly does not exist. And since there is no empty space, being cannot be moved either; there are indeed no places to which it can move. Space in itself must be regarded as being [*værende*], and Parmenides even attributes a definite form to it. The result of Parmenides' argument is thus that what actually is, is eternal, imperishable, and immovable.

The Eleatics thus held that sense perception is merely a source of error, whereas reason is able to penetrate and know actual being. Indeed, Parmenides asserts straightforwardly that thought and being are one and the same thing. See fragments nos. 3 and 8, *Ancilla to The Pre-Socratic Philosophers*, trans. Kathleen Freeman (Oxford, 1948), pp. 42, 44, and G. S. Kirk and J. E. Raven, *The Presocratic Philosophers* (Cambridge, 1960), p. 277. The Eleatics' answer to the question of whether actual being is immutable or mutable was that only the immutable is.

Heraclitus, by contrast, held the theory that only the mutable is, and that the world substance that philosophers were seeking consisted precisely of inconstancy; that is, motion. In his view there is nothing substantial that can retain its self-identity irrespective of external change; on the contrary, the only thing constant is change itself. Heraclitus' opinion was that there really is no such thing as being at all; there is only coming-into-being, a becoming that is not concluded and cannot be concluded. These changes take place by means of opposites that, holding each other in equilibrium, result in a harmony filled with tension. The changes occur with a regularity that reason is able to know and of which it unerringly realizes the necessity.

Common to both of these theories is the fact that they were developed exclusively by means of speculation and from a basic conviction that cognition by way of empiricism contributes only to erroneous cognition and superficial knowledge. This is also correctly noted in the *Postscript*. The additional assertion that "speculation" (namely, Hegelian) mediates between the doctrines of the Eleatics and that of Heraclitus should hardly be interpreted as an allusion to any definite statement by Hegel; rather, it points to Hegel's usual theory of the dialectical development in the history of philosophy. Hegel has briefly expressed it as follows in his *Lectures on the History of Philosophy* (I, 30; *W.a.A.* XIII 43; *Jub. Ausg.* XVII 59):

> I maintain that the sequence in the systems of Philosophy in History is similar to the sequence in the logical deduction of the Notion-determinations in the Idea. I maintain that if the fundamental conceptions of the systems appearing in the history of Philosophy be entirely divested of what regards their outward form, their relation to the particular and the like, the various stages in the determination of the Idea are found in the logical Notion. Conversely in the logical progression taken for itself, there is, so far as its principal elements are concerned, the progression of historical manifestations.

In the present context this means that the doctrines of the Eleatics and Heraclitus represent relative and not absolute opposites, and so they can be annulled in a higher synthesis.

The extant sources of the philosophies of the Eleatics and Heraclitus are found in H. Diels's *Die Fragmente der Vorsokratiker*, 7th ed., ed. W. Kranz, I–III (Berlin, 1954). W. Capelle's *Die Vorsokratiker* (Stuttgart, 1953), contains only translations and not the Greek texts; this also holds true of Kathleen Freeman's translation of Diels mentioned above. The chief older work is Eduard Zeller, *Die Philosophie der Griechen in ihrer geschichtlichen Entwicklung,* 5th ed., I¹⁻² (Berlin, 1892); this is the last edition attended to by the author himself. A more modern work is Werner Jaeger, *The Theology of the Early Greek Philosophers,* trans. Edward S. Robinson (London, Oxford, and New York, 1967); chapters VI and VII deal with Parmenides and Heraclitus. See also W.K.C. Guthrie, *A History of Greek Philosophy,* I–II (Cambridge, 1962–1969), vol. I and II.

The Greek texts with English translations and interpretations are available in the work by Kirk and Raven mentioned above, which also includes an excellent selective bibliography (pp. 446ff.). John Burnet in *Early Greek Philosophy* (Cleveland and New York, 1961), pp. 130–96 and 320–29, gives both translations and an interpretation but not the Greek texts. See also the Introduction, chap. 1.

337:5   *tasks . . . proportioned to the capacity.* The meaning here is that the task of becoming a Christian is more difficult for a highly talented person than for one who is less talented, so capacities are not an advantage for becoming a Christian.

337:20   *usus instrumentalis.* Use as an instrument, that is, in demonstrating that absolutely correct doctrines do not conflict with reason. The expression may be intended as an allusion to an earlier designation of formal logic as *philosophia instrumentalis.*

337:21   *that philosophy which . . . assumed . . . that some things were true in philosophy which were not true in theology.* The intention here may have been a philosopher such as Petrus Pomponatius. But the theory of the double truth, which originated from an attempt to combine Aristotelian philosophy and Church doctrine, is also found in the Averroists and Nominalists in the late Middle Ages. See also note to p. 271:11.

337:30   *the inhabitants of Mols* [S/L: Gotham]. Mols is a region of East Jutland about whose inhabitants many humorous anecdotes are told. The story related here by Kierkegaard appears in a frequently reprinted work, *Beretning om de vidtbekiendte Molboers vise Gierninger og tappre Bedrivter* (Copenhagen, 1807).

339:6   *an existential contradiction [Existents-Modsigelse].* Existence has two meanings here. First, it stands in contradiction to a previous existence; second, it is a communication that entails participation in a new existence.

Climacus now refers to the *Fragments* and the problem of becoming a Christian. Both in that work and here he is merely presenting the problem and providing an introductory approach to it. He has no intention of explaining it, for an explanation would imply that a direct transition from the introduction to becoming a Christian is possible, whereas the act of becoming a Christian on the contrary involves a leap. Consequently the introduction will be based on psychology and not on world history (p. 342). It is not intended for those of limited intelligence but for people whose education and knowledge make it difficult for them to become Christians. The author discerns an analogy to this form of introduction in Plato's dialogue *Hippias*.

In Section II Climacus tackles the problem itself. There are two aspects to the problem: pathos and dialectics. An individual's passion culminates in a pathetic relationship to an eternal happiness, whereas the dialectical aspect lies in the fact that a relationship to something historical also must be taken into account. The decisive difficulty of this situation now consists in putting the two aspects together (p. 345). Climacus thereupon proceeds to deal with the pathetic and dialectical aspects in turn.

He opens the part on pathos by asserting that pathos consists in allowing the conception of an eternal happiness to transform the individual's entire existence; it is not merely a matter of words or understanding. This means, then, that religious pathos consists in existing and in doing so ethically, and not in singing psalms or writing song books (p. 348).

The most intense ethical pathos results from interest and personal commitment, whereas the greatest esthetic pathos arises as a result of a lack of self-interest. The ethical is not difficult to understand; the difficulty lies in acting ethically (p. 350).

Existence is a synthesis of the infinite and the finite. Now if we agree that an eternal happiness is the greatest good possible for an existing individual it will follow that all finite considerations are *eo ipso* reduced in importance to the status of what may have to be renounced in favor of an eternal happiness. Thus an eternal happiness should not be confused with goods of fortune either by wishing for it or by desiring it while also wishing for finite goods. Unlike goods of fortune, which are distributed unequally, an eternal happiness is subject to another dialectic that assures equal distribution.

Now if an existing individual is to relate himself to an eternal happiness, his existence will have to express this relationship. Indeed, if the relationship does not transform his existence completely, he is not really relating himself to an eternal happiness (p. 353). Just as all relative acts of the will are recognizable by the fact that they will something for the sake of something else, so all *absolute* acts of the will are recognizable in that they will something for its own sake. This is what we call the Supreme Good (p. 353).

This existential pathos is "poor man's pathos, pathos for every man" (p. 353), for everyone is capable of inward action. To see how things stand regarding his eternal happiness a man needs merely to allow resignation to make an inspection of his immediacy with all its longing. If he finds one hard spot, a point that refuses to budge, he will know that he does not relate himself to an eternal happiness. In this context there is no room for mediation (that "wonderful discovery"), for whenever resignation is present mediation falls by the wayside. Indeed, Climacus calls mediation "a miserable invention of a man who was unfaithful to himself and to resignation" (p. 355).

The author then develops the point that a true ethical attitude entails indifference to results, for only a resolve and a choice have ethical relevance (pp. 355ff.).

Climacus suggests that the Medieval monastic movement in particular helped indirectly to promote mediation. Mediation was employed as a means to halt the monastic movement. Although the movement may have been in error, it nonetheless does not follow that mediation is the right path. Climacus feels that the Middle Ages and Ancient Greece at least had one thing that mediation lacks: passion. The mistake made under the influence of paganism lay in not willing to venture everything, whereas the Middle Ages misunderstood the significance of venturing everything. By contrast, our author concludes, "The hodge-podge wisdom of our age mediates" (p. 362).

The services supposedly rendered by the monastic movement are in themselves a delusion, Climacus maintains. But quite apart from this, the movement was questionable because it gave a conspicuous expression for absolute inwardness by means of a special exteriority that as such was only relatively different from any other externality (p. 363).

Now if the individual is not simply to depart from this world once he has absolutely oriented himself toward the absolute telos, he must accept the task of expressing this relation in his existence. Yet the expression must not simply consist in a direct or conspicuous externality, for in that case the whole thing will result in a monastic movement or in mediation. The individual must therefore accomplish his task by simultaneously relating himself absolutely to the absolute telos and relatively to relative ends—but of course without mediating them.

Consequently a continuous double movement will be required (p. 366). In his immediacy the individual is rooted in finitude. But once resignation has brought about the conviction that the individual has acquired the absolute direction toward the absolute telos, everything will be changed and the roots will have been severed (p. 367). Although still living in the finite world, the individual no longer has his life in it. He now lives so to speak incognito, for he still looks just like everybody else.

In the event that God were to establish a direct relationship as an ideal for human existence, it would be correct to want to express this fact directly. But this is not the case, as there is an absolute qualitative difference. The supreme expression of a man's God-relationship is therefore worship, since it indicates that God means everything to the worshiper (p. 369).

So no external sign of true inwardness is required at all. Indeed, the error of the monastic movement consists precisely in its use of external signs and recognizability. All things taken into consideration, however, Climacus sees no particular reason to warn his contemporaries against the monastic movement; on the contrary, it behooves them to show it respect.

After a digression on the religious discourse, Climacus continues his examination of the ethical. He maintains that it is possible for a man to be both good and bad simultaneously but impossible for him simultaneously to strive to *become* both good and bad.

The intention with mediation, Climacus insists, was to make existence easier for the individual by eliminating an absolute relation to an absolute telos. As a result the individual becomes entangled in a self-contradiction, for with the help of mediation he relates himself absolutely to a relative telos.

The establishment of an absolute relation to an absolute telos involves a tremendous risk, since it is impossible to obtain certainty concerning an eternal happiness. Therefore the eternal truth is the one and only truth that is exclusively definable in terms of the mode of acquisition. The way is the decisive factor—otherwise we have esthetics.

Thus the pathetic aspect must not be omitted. But we cannot simply skip over the dialectical factor either, for if we do we turn the whole thing into "mere prattle and old wives' bawling" and the Gospel into a rumor and local gossip (p. 385).

*   *   *

340:15   *Neither here nor in the Fragments.* This introduction has the following form in the draft (*Pap.* VI B 55):

> *The decision of an eternal happiness in time by relating oneself to something historical*—this is then the problem, the difficulty of which I will now do my humble best to demonstrate. For I readily perceive that the difficulty must be demonstrated, otherwise everybody will say: "Nothing else? Are these difficulties? Why, what he is talking about is something that everybody talks about, an eternal happiness in the hereafter following a life well led, or something like that. No, pure thought, astronomy, the fortifications, foreign languages—see, these are difficulties." And undeniably they really are difficulties, glittering difficulties, but the misfortune is that nobody will attend to the simple thing that concerns every human being, presumably for fear of being in bad company with everybody. "For doesn't each and every simple man talk about an eternal happiness, too? And what's the big idea of letting a brilliant mind use time and energy to think about such things and then finally get no further than the simplest man?" "But indeed nobody is asking him to advance any further, even though we do not understand this to mean that he is supposed to arrive at astronomy and the like, for if he attaches a definite clear thought to an expression that the simple man also uses—well, he at any rate will always have gained something." The misfortune of our age lies in its having refused the inwardness of existence [*Existents-Inderlighed*] in relation to thought, which is why it chases after what glitters. The art of being able to speak one's mother tongue [*thereafter essentially the same as Pap. VI A 150 to p. 63, line 27 (JP III 3467, p. 582, line 11*): He is not supposed to preach to] arty dilettantes.* Is it then not true [*Pap. VI A 150, p. 63, lines 31–34 (JP III 3467, p. 582, lines 31–35, modified*) that there is and is supposed to be solemnity in God's house? Yes, of course. And although every bungling preacher can say, "How solemn!"——the most experienced preacher must not dare to say anything else, and yet there should be an

infinite difference between what they say,] because the person being tried is supposed to know how to attach a definite thought to that solemnity. Common chatter about solemnity will perhaps please the dilettante and wound the faithful listener, because the latter despairs over not being able to succeed. The usual church cere-mony is a counterpart to the stiffness and stupidity that prevail at burials. And now why is it that the parson doing the preaching can persist in a certain abstract idea that everything is normal, that one is solemn in God's house in precisely the right way (which a regular church-goer knows is something in which he is far from succeeding every time, whereas an infrequent church-goer perhaps does not feel devotional but is merely affected sensuously; that is, he is astonished), that one is festively disposed during the impor-tant festivals, and so on; in short, that in the house of God it is completely normal for those congregated there to include practi-cally no human beings but saints—why is this, if not because the parson merely thinks momentarily** about some particular theme or other without himself existing [*existerer*] in his thinking; for in that case he would be far better informed as to how the greatest differences intersect. If he then is going to talk about spiritual trials [*Anfægtelse*], about human imperfection, he again momentarily knows how to scrape something together, but he completely for-gets this when he speaks about solemnity in the house of God where, after all, imperfect people are again present. I will take still another example from the devotional [*gudelige*] sermon, because this must after all be the closest thing to existing. With an acciden-tal contact [*balance essentially the same as Pap. VI A 152 (JP III 3469)*].

* *In margin*: But suppose a man sat apart by himself (spiritually understood), concerned that he might not be able to be devotional at the time of devotions, that a certain anxiety [*Angest*] for the appalling prospect of being unable to succeed might simply cause him to be unsuccessful, so he easily could be tempted [*fristes*] to stay away from God's house that day, but he went anyway: in short, a man being tried—there was no sermon about him.

** *In margin* [*Pap. VI B 56*]: Note. That existence [*det at existere*] is a protest against pure thought and that an existing individual's thought is incapable of acquiring eternal continuity were shown under a. But to think momentarily is something else again; it is to understand the perpetual varying of objects so as to think first about one thing and then about another, without holding any one thought fast in the passionate exertion of existing in it.

Continuation to [Pap. VI B] 55, bordered in pencil [Pap. VI B 57]:
Two things are required to grasp the difficulty of the problem: (a)
an actual conception of what an eternal happiness means; (c) *passion in
thought to be able to grasp the dialectical contradiction that this is decided
in time by a relation to something historical.*

(a) an actual conception of what an eternal happiness signifies.

* *In margin:* (b) the dialectical difficulty of *expecting* an eternal
happiness.

342:29   *Hippias. Hippias Major,* which deals with the concept of beauty. Its
Platonic authenticity has been much disputed. Paul Friedländer in
Platon, 2nd ed., I–III (Berlin, 1954–1960), II, leaves this question open.
See his bibliography on p. 259 and Guthrie, *Greek Philosophy,* IV,
175ff.

345:7   *the first part . . . the second part*: (a) in relation to an eternal happiness; (b) in the mode whereby the individual's eternal happiness is
determined with respect to the composition of this particular historical fact.

346:32   *risk anything in this direction.* Danish: *at have vovet sig ud paa den
Galei.* This phrase is formed around an expression that owes its origin to a line in the Danish translation of Molière's *Les Fourberies de
Scapin* (Act II, Scene 7). Géronte, falling for a wild story about the
servant Scapin's son, asks Scapin: "Mais que diable allait-il faire dans
cette galère?" ("But what the deuce was he doing there?") The play
was performed in Copenhagen in French in 1723 and finally translated into Danish in 1787 under the title of *Scapins Skiælmsstykker.*
The line reads in Danish: "Hvad skulde han ogsaa paa den Galei?"

347:2   *respect.* Junghans notes here that the usual meaning of respect, to
honor or esteem, is in the following passages combined with the
basic meaning of the Latin *respicere*: to look back, to look toward.
The situation for the existing individual here is that he has strayed
from God and is now looking back in order to begin again, which
can only be done by turning away from and renouncing externals.

347:2   *telos.* Goal, end (plural, τέλη).

349:23   *Hence when a man says.* Paul in 2 Cor. 11:23ff. (*The New English
Bible*):

Are they servants of Christ? I am mad to speak like this, but I can
outdo them. More overworked than they, scourged more severely,
more often imprisoned, many a time face to face with death. Five
times the Jews have given me the thirty-nine strokes; three times
I have been beaten with rods; once I was stoned; three times I have
been shipwrecked, and for twenty-four hours I was adrift on the

open sea. I have been constantly on the road; I have met dangers from rivers, dangers from robbers, dangers from my fellow-countrymen, dangers from foreigners, dangers in towns, dangers in the country, dangers at sea, dangers from false friends. I have toiled and drudged, I have often gone without sleep; hungry and thirsty, I have often gone fasting; and I have suffered from cold and exposure.

349(note *):13   *so that if I hoped for this life alone.* 1 Cor. 15:19.

350:35   *and then, too, an eternal happiness.* The printed manuscript has after this (*Pap.* VI B 98:66):

> Note. And maybe it is already a great thing that it is ranked in a class with such priceless goods. Before long it will probably be demoted to a class along with butter, cheese, sausage, and delicatessen, which housekeepers go shopping for once in a while; things will go so far that whenever someone uses this expression people will look at him in amazement and inquiry, wondering whether what he mentioned is something to eat or put on.

351:32   *qualification of essence.* Danish: *Væsenheds-Bestemmelse.* The word *Væsenhed* in the sense of substantiality, the phenomenal, and the essential was in vogue among Danish philosophers of Kierkegaard's time. Kierkegaard, however, always uses it in the sense of "essence." See *ODS*, XXVII, cols. 993ff.

351:37   *"while I shave."* A quotation from Poul Møller's essay of 1837 on immortality. See my commentary on *Das Buch Adler* in *Einübung u. Anderes* (Cologne, 1951), pp. 696–98.

352:24   *tertium non datur.* In the present context, "there is no third possibility."

352:26   *the individual himself, in his own consciousness of himself.* In other words, in communion with himself.

353:30   *a point of resistance.* Something he is unwilling to renounce. See "The Parable of The Great Supper," Luke 14:15–24.

355:20   *sleepy as a foolish virgin.* Matt. 25:1–13.

356:9   *born in a wishing individual's head.* This expression is from 1 Cor. 2:9.

356:18   *Thiers.* Adolphe Thiers (1797–1877), a French politician and historian. In one of his chief works, *Histoire du Consolat et de l'Empire* (Paris, 1845–1862), Thiers frequently makes statements such as "Fortune always plays a role in undertakings of war." See *Consulatets og Kaiserdømmets Historie*, translated into Danish by J. C. Magnus, I–VII (Copenhagen, 1845–1847; *ASKB* 2016–23, II, 243.

357:25   *when death passes over his grave.* The allusion is to the same assumption made in the *Fragments*, pp. 28ff. Mathias Claudius mentions it in the dedication to his "friend Hain" in *Sämmtliche Werke des Wandsbecker Boten*, Part One.

357:34   *All that is said.* The following parenthetical phrase from the draft was not used (*Pap.* VI B 58:6): "(by way of reference to the Sophist Gorgias' third proposition)." Kierkegaard may have read this in Tennemann's *Geschichte der Philosophie*, I, 363; see pp. 371ff.

358:8   μέτριως πάθειν. To permit oneself to be only moderately influenced. The ancient skeptics taught that wise men allow themselves to be only very slightly influenced by absolutely necessary evils. Compare for example Sextus Empiricus, with whom Kierkegaard was acquainted mainly through Tennemann's comprehensive account (ibid., V, 267–96).

359:13   *dramatic club.* The reference here is to *Det bestandige borgerlige Selskab* (The Perpetual Civic Society), which was founded in 1798 and which in 1824 was renamed *Den bestandige borgerlige Forening* (The Perpetual Civic Union). It held entertainments, including private theatricals, and it was most likely these that Kierkegaard had in mind.

360:6   *the anxious father who wrote.* Knud Gad, a shipping broker and commission agent in Helsingør, published a little work with the same title: *Hvor skal jeg sætte min Søn i Skole?* (Copenhagen, 1833). It was much discussed, among others by J. L. Heiberg in his *Valgerda*, II, 2.

360:23   *Mediation claims to. . . .* The draft has (*Pap.* VI B 58:8; *JP* III 2749):

> Meanwhile I willingly concede the dubiousness of the monastic movement, for it went too far in externalizing what ought to be inward; but then, instead of comprehending the dubiousness and rejoicing in the truth, to get mediation established in the place of honor makes a poor solution.

360:36   *chiliasm.* The doctrine of the millennium (see 1 Cor. 15:20–28 and Apoc. 20:1–6). The meaning here is a visionary expectation of the millennium.

361(note *):2   *The New Testament also speaks.* Matt. 7:14.

361(note *):4   *a committee . . . in Copenhagen.* H. N. Clausen (1793–1877), a celebrated Danish theologian and liberal politician, was in 1841 joint founder of such a committee. It was dissolved a couple of years later. See H. N. Clausen, *Mit Levneds og min Tids Historie* (Copenhagen, 1877), pp. 241–43.

362:9   *the temple at Delphi.* The inscription read: μηδὲν ἄγαν. Terentius translated this by *ne quid nimis* in *Andria*, I, 1; that is, "nothing too much," or, "do not exaggerate in any way; be moderate!"

363:6   *exhaustively into . . . predicates.* As Junghans observes, "predicate" is used in this passage in a logical sense. Junghans then goes on to assert that the word "exhaustively" recalls to mind the Gnostic and Neoplatonic doctrines of emanation (see above, Introduction, chap. 4) in the sense that, as concerns mediation, the absolute telos is finally exhausted in relative ends. Undeniably, there is indeed a very close similarity between Hegel's and Plotinus' worlds of thought. Junghans, however, overlooks the fact that the ethical consequences were different. Irrespective of any dissimilarities, both Gnosticism and Neoplatonism made escape from the world an ideal; on the other hand, Hegelian speculation—here called mediation—despite any similarities establishes civic life as an ideal.

363:8   *title-page.* (*Titelbladet.*) There can be no question here of a "dust cover" (*et Smudstitelblad*), as Lowrie proposes in his note on p. 568 of his and Swenson's edition, but of the most important part of a book that is left out either knowingly or through plain stupidity.

364:7   *respect (respicere).* See above, note to p. 347:2.

364:17   *this disciplinarian of existence.* Danish: *denne Existentsens Retnings-Major.* Literally, "existence's major in charge of direction" or "of fire control." Here the sense is simply "commanding officer."

364:21   *standing there like the genius of death.* Inasmuch as Kierkegaard was reading Lessing while preparing the *Postscript* he probably had in mind Lessing's essay from 1769, "Wie die Alten den Tod gebildet," *Lessing's sämmtliche Schriften*, I–XXXII (Berlin, 1825–1828; *ASKB* 1747–62, III, 75ff. The first engraving in this essay shows the figure mentioned by Kierkegaard.

364:22   *the dim sight of the individual.* After this the draft has (*Pap.* VI B 58:9):

> The supreme moment of decision, in which the individual acquires his absolute direction toward the absolute τέλος, is not an *übersvenglich* [presumably *überschwenglich*, effusive or gushing] moment from which life is supposed to subtract, but a maximum that life if possible must manage to be constantly expressing.

366:21   *a yawning chasm.* See Luke 16:26.

366:31   *the inviolate stillness.* This expression is common in the pastoral letters for example, in 1. Pet. 3:3–4.

368:37   *needs no external proof.* The draft has the following annotation (*Pap.* VI B 58:10):

Note. Only it must be remembered that since love is not the absolute τέλος the wife must tolerate her husband holding forth in the following manner: "Yes, my little missus, you really will have to put up with the fact that I at the same time am a Councillor, a flute player, and so on—and your husband, too." And she dare not complain of any high treason. But it is high treason to talk like this concerning the absolute τέλος, for the absolute τέλος (well, what I am going to say now even a syllogist like cousin Charles in Scribe is able to grasp, as when he says: Either you have an uncle or you don't have an uncle)—either the absolute τέλος is the absolute τέλος or it is not the absolute τέλος. And so people mediate.

369(note
*):3   *"Biblische Legenden der Muselmänner."* By Dr. G. Weil (Frankfurt am Main, 1845; *ASKB* 865), the edition owned by Kierkegaard. The Danish edition, *Mohammedanernes bibelske Legender*, trans. E.G.W. Faber (Odense, 1855), p. 134 note, has: "the story is told that the Israelites wanted to stone Moses, until angels bore his coffin in the air, in front of which God Himself walked in mourning."

373:31   *an institution for the aged.* Kierkegaard wrote "in a *Vartou*" (*Vartov* in modern Danish). This was originally a congregational house founded shortly before 1300 by Bishop Johannes Krog. In 1666 it moved to its present location in Farvergade in the center of Copenhagen and became chiefly an institution for the care of the old and infirm. It lasted until 1934 when it moved out. N.F.S. Grundtvig was priest there from 1839–1872, and Vartov became a seat of the Grundtvigian congregation.

374:21   *a New Year's congratulant.* The printed manuscript then has (*Pap.* VI B 98:67): "as one at times is also tempted to ask oneself whether it is a parson who steps forward and bows or one of those with a barrel organ who bow with a plate."

374(note
*):17   *And so likewise with hope and love.* See 1 Cor. 13:13.

374(note
*):18   *the first medieval essays in the dramatic art.* About the year 1000 performances of the day's text in the form of a dialogue were introduced into France in connection with divine services on important holy days. The priests acted scenes from the Bible for the congregation and for its edification, and the language of this so-called liturgical drama was Latin. In the twelfth century significant changes took place: Latin was replaced by the national language, the scene was shifted from the church to the church square, and the clerical actors were replaced by lay folk. During the Middle Ages this drama expanded both in scope and in importance. By degrees material was taken not

just from the Gospels but also from the Old Testament and from stories about the saints; it was these latter plays that came to be called Mysteries (*ministerium sacrum*). A distinction is made between Mysteries of the Bible and those of the saints (also called Miracle Plays) in accordance with the source of the theme.

Note Kierkegaard's collection of esthetic, dramaturgical, and theatric-historical works in *ASKB* 1364–1406a.

374(note *):19   *precisely in the church.* The following reference in the printed manuscript was deleted (*Pap.* VI B 98:68): "(See [Karl Friedrich] Flögel, *Geschichte der comischen Literatur*, [I–IV (Liegnits and Leipzig, 1784–1787)], vol. IV, 198.)" See *ASKB* 1396–99.

376:3   *existence is even produced, on paper.* Kierkegaard is obviously thinking of Hegel's definition of the concept of existence in *The Science of Logic* (II, 109ff.; *W.a.A.* IV 120ff.; *Jub. Ausg.* IV 598): "For Existence is that immediacy which emerged from the transcendence of the mediation whose relating activity operates by means of Ground and Condition, and in emerging it transcends this emergence."

376.20   *Esthetically the requirement has been imposed.* Probably an allusion to Heiberg and his school of esthetic critique who emphasized that Goethe was the ultimate neoclassical ideal of a poet. See Paul V. Rubow, *Dansk litterær Kritik* (Copenhagen, 1978).

377:9   *the exultation . . . of our own age over having overcome reflection.* Kierkegaard is referring to the Kantian method of thought that Hegel called "the philosophy of reflection" and that he had criticized as early as 1802 in his dissertation "Glauben und Wissen oder die Reflexionsphilosophie der Subjektivität" (*W.a.A.* I 3–157; *Jub. Ausg.* I 279–433).

377:14   *the principle of identity . . . is basic to the principle of contradiction.* The usual formulation of the principle of identity is A is A; or, S, which is A, is A. Hegel, however, asserted that there is no reason to uphold the classical principle of contradiction (A is not not-A; or, S, which is A, is not not-A) at the same time, since it is embodied in the principle of identity, which may also be formulated as follows: A is not not-A = A; therefore, A is A.

Kierkegaard is willing to go along with Hegel up to this point. Hegel and his faithful adherents, however, sought to transfer the principle of contradiction to the principle of exclusion (A is either B or not-B), whose validity they repudiated. Kierkegaard rejects this view, as Mynster and Sibbern had done earlier. See V. Kuhr, *Modsigelsens Grundsætning* (Copenhagen and Kristiania, 1915).

377:21   *terminus a quo . . . terminus ad quem.* Border from which . . . border to which.

377:28 *as Hegel so often says.* In *The Science of Logic,* II, 58ff. (*W.a.A.* IV 73ff.; *Jub. Ausg.* IV 551ff.).

378:2 *the most general expression for madness.* Don Juan in *Either/Or,* I, 54ff. (*SV* I 45ff.) can be included in this characterization.

379:7 *recruits.* General compulsory military service was introduced into Denmark in 1849. *Landsoldat* (soldier) was until then a designation for those soldiers who were conscripted in the native country itself, in contrast to the foreign mercenary soldiers.

379:15 *a thoughtless chatterer who.* *Vrøvlevad* (chatterer) is a now archaic word that Baggesen invented; the modern equivalent is *Vrøvlehoved.* See *ODS,* XXVII, col. 600, no. 51.

379:21 *discrimen* [S/L: decisiveness]. Decisiveness, crisis, turning-point, definitive difficulty.

379:23 *a gulf.* Luke 16:26.

380:24 *shysters* [S/L: Rogues]. *Lommeprokuratorer* (literally, "pocket-attorneys"; German, *Taschenrichter*) was formerly a deprecatory term for lawyers or persons with no real education in law who gave legal assistance to others dishonestly or merely with an eye to their own advantage. *Vinkelskriver* (literally, "angle-writer") has the same meaning.

381(note †):9 *the sphere of reflection.* In Hegel's philosophy reflection denotes a lower step than thought on the ladder of cognition. "In figurative thinking we have before us, too, an affair in its external, inessential Being Determinate. In Thought, on the contrary, we segregate from this affair the external, purely inessential." (*The Phenomenology of Spirit,* pp. 116ff.; *Jub. Ausg.* III 36 and X 328–58.)

382:29 *change in the value of the currency.* The Danish state had to declare itself bankrupt as a result of the failure of the National Bank on January 5, 1813. Paper money, which had been issued by the currency bank, was devaluated to approximately one-sixth of its nominal value, and a Bank of the Kingdom (*Rigsbank*) was set up that then issued its own rix-bankdollar bills (*Rigsbankdalersedler;* abbreviated *Rbdl.*). These did not attain par value, however, until 1838. Domestic bonds, on the other hand, were only devaluated to about two-thirds of their nominal value, and since their price had been considerably under par at the outset, owners of these bonds were lucky enough to be able to save their fortunes. Kierkegaard's own father, for example, had previously invested a substantial portion of his assets in these securities, whereby his fortune actually increased as a result of the bankruptcy.

382:32 *a conscious clarity . . . which is acquired only slowly.* The way to this consciousness (*Gjennemsigtighed*) is described especially in *The Sickness Unto Death*.

383:28   *favorites of fortune.* Danish, *Pamphilius*, which derives from the Greek πάμφιλος meaning "beloved by all."

384:27   *mediator.* Compare this with the title of Emil Brunner's work on christology, *Der Mittler* ("The Mediator"; Tübingen, 1927).

385:24   *its yoke is easy and its burden light.* These expressions are taken from Matt. 11:30ff.

In the previous sections Climacus argued that the individual's task consisted in relating himself absolutely to the absolute telos and relatively to relative ends. Now since the individual lives in the immediate he will have to make a beginning by training himself to renounce the relative ends; only then will it be possible to tackle the ideal task mentioned above. The criterion of this inward action in pathos will be suffering. In this connection Climacus now proceeds to distinguish between esthetic and ethical pathos.

Immediacy corresponds to fortune, because the immediate consciousness recognizes no contradiction or adversity that does not come from without, and in this view, which conforms to the esthetic outlook on life, suffering is merely a whim of fate. The ethical and ethical-religious attitudes, on the other hand, regard suffering as something essential.

The religious speaker must take this situation into account. He will employ suffering as a means to elevate the listener, and he must be correct in his use of the categories. If the speaker follows these guidelines he will have "the entire compass of the poetic" at his disposal (p. 393), and indeed he will even be able to assume a position superior to that of poetry and use the comic. Climacus then develops the point that the religious address, like death, deals quite simply and directly with individuals as human beings. Thus the religious address must above all avoid using an abbreviated perspective (p. 395). Rather, it ought to be a communication directed to an acting individual who is supposed to work on the task of acting in accordance with the discourse when he gets home.

Climacus now returns to the problem of suffering, again with reference to the religious discourse. Suffering must be understood as something determinative and as an essential part of the pathetic relation to an eternal happiness, whereas from an esthetic viewpoint it is of course merely incidental (p. 398). The humorist on the contrary grasps the meaning of suffering in relation to existence, and thus his position is the closest approximation to existence. Nevertheless, he fails to understand the deepest meaning of suffering (p. 400), since "he revokes everything because the explanation lies behind" (p. 402). Religiously, suffering is a sign of the relation to an eternal happiness, in the same way as the certainty of faith in connection with an eternal happiness is signaled by uncertainty (p. 407).

The author then turns his attention to spiritual trial (*Anfægtelse*), which is also a type of religious suffering, and to temptation (*Fristelse*). The difference between the two is that in temptation it is the lower that entices the individual, whereas in the case of a spiritual trial it is the higher that "as if jealous of the individual, tries to frighten him back" (p. 410). Temptation is in continuity with the individual's ethical character, whereas the spiritual trial lacks continuity and is a mark of the resistance offered by the absolute as it lays down the limit (p. 411). Here it is necessary to grasp the fact that one is nothing before God—and then to continue to be thus before God. If this consciousness of being nothing before God vanishes, the individual's religiousness will vanish at the same time (p. 413).

Suffering is indeed a dying away from immediacy, but it is not self-torture, an external act that would imply that a man after all is something before God and is able to do something on his own. Thus the religious speaker will have to proclaim that the greatest exertion is as nothing—and yet require it (p. 414). The difficulty is increased all the more because "it is in the living room that the battle must be fought, not fantastically in the church" (p. 416). Climacus, who does not pretend to be a Christian himself, explains this by means of a few examples showing among other things that from a religious standpoint the positive is always recognizable by the negative and seriousness by jest (p. 422).

A man's conception of God or of his eternal happiness should enable him to transform his entire existence accordingly. This will consist in a slow dying away from immediacy (p. 432). The religious individual of course does continue to live but is captive in finitude like a fish on dry land, for he is faced with the difficulty of holding together two incompatible factors: the idea of God and daily life, such as "a pleasure outing in Deer Park." This situation may in turn engender a crisis or an illness that it is, however, possible to overcome. Climacus explains the cure as follows (p. 437):

> in suffering the pain of his annihilation, the religious individual has learned that human indulgence profits nothing, and therefore refuses to listen to anything from that side; but he exists before God and exhausts the suffering of being human and at the same time existing before God.

As a lowly creature man is a temporal being and unable to endure leading an uninterrupted life of eternity while in time. Thus the monastic movement may seem tempting to him (p. 439). If this should happen, he will have to adhere to the truth that there is an absolute difference between God and man. He will then be confronted, however, with the problem of how to express the equality necessary in love. The solution will be found in humility, which constitutes the form of this absolute difference, provided that it be a humility that frankly admits its human lowliness.

Climacus thus leaves us two options: amusement in humility and exertion in despair; "the way to Deer Park and the way to the cloister" (p. 440). Now the cloister is too dignified for our religious individual, so he goes to Deer Park to amuse himself. Why? "Because it is the humblest expression for his God-relationship to admit his humanity, and because it is human to enjoy oneself" (p. 440). Climacus submits that the God-relationship itself urges the individual to seek withdrawal for a moment, since there is so to speak "an agreement entered into between God's solicitude and man's necessities" (p. 444).

The truly religious person thus also has his life in a contradiction, for with all his inwardness concealed within him he nevertheless looks just like anyone else. He therefore to a certain degree lives incognito, with humor serving as his mask. But it is a deceptive mask, since humor alone is inadequate to determine whether or not a person is truly religious; the observer may have before him simply a humorist and thus someone who is qualitatively lower than a religious person. Climacus himself is a case in point.

At this juncture Climacus briefly outlines the three spheres of existence and the two border regions or confines. The three spheres are the esthetic, the ethical, and the religious. Irony forms a *confinium* between the esthetic and ethical spheres, and humor performs the same function between the ethical and the religious spheres (p. 448). The author then turns to a description of irony and the ironist's inward and outward lives, in this connection correcting the view of Socrates presented in *The Concept of Irony*.

Climacus now takes another look at the religious person. Since such an individual has his life in absolute passion and has reflected himself out of the entanglements of external relativities, it will be impossible for others to understand him. In fact, to him a third person is just such a relativity. Of course the question might arise as to whether such a religious person exists at all or has ever existed, or whether everybody is religious or nobody is. This is a question, however, that no human is in a position to answer.

This brings us to a consideration of the comic, which emerges when we observe the religious individual's relationship to his environment, at the same time keeping his inwardness *in mente*. The comic will actually be present in every stage of life, only the relative positions being different, for wherever there is life there is contradiction, and wherever there is contradiction we have the comic. The tragic and the comic are identical insofar as both require contradiction; but the tragic is a suffering contradiction, whereas the comic is a painless one. Climacus thereupon permits himself a lengthy digression in a footnote of several pages (pp. 459ff.) to give examples of the comic.

Returning to his main presentation, Climacus asserts that the various stages of existence may be classified in accordance with their relation to the comic. Clearly, he emphasizes, the religiousness that consists of hidden inwardness is *eo ipso* inaccessible to a comic conception (p. 465). In the religious sphere the comic is a servant, provided the religiousness be kept pure in inwardness (p. 467).

✳   ✳   ✳

387:25   *from having been a lieutenant he becomes an emperor.* As in several other passages in the *Postscript*, Kierkegaard is referring to Napoleon Bonaparte.

387:26   *from street peddler becomes a millionaire.* In all probability this is an allusion to Heiberg's vaudeville *Kong Salomon og Jørgen Hattemager.* See above, note to p. 126.

387(note ✳):1   *A revelation is signalized by mystery.* There is here a rather close resemblance to Luther's *Theologia crucis*, in the way that it is interpreted by Walther von Loewenich in a monograph of the same title (Munich, 1929; 4th ed. 1954). There is also a similarity to Hamann's thoughts; see my article, "To af Forudsætningerne for Hamanns Opgør med sin Samtid," *Dansk teologisk Tidsskrift* (Copenhagen, 1960), pp. 77ff.

387(note †):2   *which holds that He, Himself unchanged, changes all.* This is a slightly inaccurate rendering of Aristotle's definition of the divinity. Aristotle elaborates on his theology in *Metaphysics*, 1071b ff.

According to Aristotle, everything in motion is moved by something else, a process that can occur in two ways. The second object can in turn be moved by a third, and so on; or, it is not moved by anything else, in which case there must be a "prime mover." Such a first, unmoved mover must be assumed to be, and Aristotle thereupon identifies the "prime mover" with God, who is pure actuality and pure intellect without any residue of potentiality. Potentiality is not only present in the rest of the universe but also constitutes the principle of motion. To Aristotle, then, God is He, who Himself unmoved, moves all (ἀκίνητος πάντα κινεῖ).

In his *Journal* for 1843 Kierkegaard made an entry (*Pap.* IV A 157; *JP* II 1332) that indicates that he has not taken the expression from a reading of Aristotle but from secondary sources, namely, from Schelling's lectures in Berlin and from Tennemann's history of philosophy (III, 159ff.). As to the Aristotelian concept of God, see in particular W. D. Ross, *Aristotle*, 5th ed. (London, 1949); Ingemar Düring, *Aristoteles* (Heidelberg, 1966); and Werner Jaeger, *Aristotle: Fundamentals of the History of His Development*, 2nd ed., trans. Richard Robinson (London, Oxford, and New York, 1967).

389:29   *call.* There is a play on words here. The Danish word *Kald* means first, a vocation or call; and second, a living or benefice.

389:29   *to become a religious speaker, one needs only to pass three examinations.* That is, the so-called second examination (*artium* was the first examination) with Hebrew, a certificate in theology, and tests in practical theology at the pastoral seminary. The last of these includes the examinatory sermon that Kierkegaard himself held in Trinity Church on February 24, 1844.

389(note *):2   *the Mohammedan Biblical legends published by Weil.* See above, note to p. 369. The trait mentioned here is found on p. 150 in the Danish translation.

390:3   *goes out to catch men.* Compare this with like expressions in Luke 5:10 and Matt. 4:19 and 13:47ff.

392:4   *"Come hither all ye who labor and are heavy laden."* Matt. 11:28.

393:6   *Lafontaine sat weeping.* Kierkegaard has in mind August H. J. Lafontaine (1758–1831) who played the same role with respect to the novel as Kotzebue did with the drama, and who wrote a number of touching family novels. None of this voluminous literature figures on the list of Kierkegaard's book collection, though many of these works had been translated into Danish. But Kierkegaard could easily have become acquainted with them in the *Athenæum*, a reading club of which he was a member. As an example of how widely read Lafontaine's novels were, it may be mentioned that Hans Christian Andersen's father read them aloud in the evening in Odense where Hans Christian spent his childhood. Among these novels was *Der Sonderling.* See Hans Christian Andersen, *Mit Livs Eventyr*, ed. H. Topsøe-Jensen, I–II (Copenhagen, 1951), I, 28.

393:16   *the clergyman's mélange. Mélange*, which is of course French and means "mixture," is here used in the sense of hotchpotch, jumble (see *ODS*, XIII, col. 1233). Mélange was also the name of some cheap pipe tobacco that was used in large quantities by the clergy.

393:39   *signs and symbols of distinction.* In Danish, *Kryds og Slange*, meaning the mark of distinction conferred on pupils and students.

394:10   *the bold recklessness of despair.* Junghans asserts that the thought here concerns a person who enthusiastically strives for greatness without inquiring as to whether it also is the good. The condition of this person is a form of despair.

394:13   *the fury of a man's.* The allusion here is presumably to Festus' outburst to Paul in Acts 26:24.

395(note   *undertaker. Bedemand,* which was earlier the person who issued in-
*):7   vitations not only to burial ceremonies but also to the baptism of children. The verb *at bede* means both "to pray" and "to ask."

396:19   *a matchless falcon's insight.* A dig at Grundtvig, for whom a "falcon's insight" was a favorite expression in his writings on history and mythology.

397:24   *a poetic existence . . . confinium. Confinium* means "border region" or "confine."

In Kierkegaard's theory of life's stages a *confinium* (frequently translated as "frontier") represents a transitional phase in which thought and interest intersect, and thus is a psychological state. See for example *Stages,* p. 404 (*SV* VI 469); *The Sickness Unto Death* (*KW* XIX 78; *SV* XI 213); and Robert Widenmann, "Confine," *Concepts and Alternatives in Kierkegaard,* vol. III of *Bibliotheca Kierkegaardiana* (Copenhagen, 1980), pp. 43–5.

398:1   *he cannot explain himself.* The meaning here may be either "to transfigure himself" or (more likely) "to be clear about himself."

398:13   *a poet-existence.* That is, an individual who merely relates himself to existence poetically. With respect to this concept reference is made to Himmelstrup's *Terminologisk Register* (*SV* XV 549ff.) and especially to Emanuel Hirsch, *Kierkegaard-Studien,* I–II (Gütersloh, 1930–1933), I, 133ff.; W. Rehm, *Kierkegaard und der Verführer* (Munich, 1949), pp. 346ff.; E. Pivčevič, *Ironie als Daseinsform bei Sören Kierkegaard* (Gütersloh, 1960), passim; and V. Sechi, "The Poet," *Kierkegaardiana,* X (Copenhagen, 1977), pp. 166ff.

398:15   *among his papers.* The lines in *Pap.* VI A 103 (*JP* V 5840) are used here in a slightly altered form.

398:23   *to drag it down to its death.* Junghans holds that the comparison here, either knowingly or unknowingly, has not been carried through. The significance inherent in the first two comparisons is clear: for a poet-existence spirit is equivalent to life and the body to death. If the body perishes, then, says the poet, the spirit is free; he has liberated himself from the body. This is also the intention with the third parallel: the body clings to the spirit in the same way that a drowning man clings to a swimmer. Paul's elaborations in Rom. 7:24ff. provide an excellent comparison with this entire passage.

399:3   *the Scriptures say that God dwells in a contrite heart.* Literally, in a "crushed" (*sønderknuset*) heart. Compare Isa. 57:15:

> For thus says he who is high and exalted, living eternally, whose name is the Holy One: on high I dwell, and in holiness, and with the crushed and dejected spirit, to revive the spirits of the dejected, to revive the hearts of the crushed.

399:16   *the subscription which his reverence . . . started . . . in The Advertiser.* See above, note to p. 72. As late as in Kierkegaard's time it was quite common to try to assure the publication of books by means of subscriptions made in advance, whereas in the previous century it had almost been the rule for publishers to use this means to avoid economic risk when publishing. Holberg expressed his opinion of this system quite plainly in his Epistle no. 3 (1748), and with irony in Epistle no. 126 (also 1748) titled *Fiduser til Forlæggere* ("Tips for Publishers"), from which the following may be cited (*Ludvig Holbergs Epistler*, ed. F. J. Billeskov-Jansen, I–VIII [Copenhagen, 1944–1954], II, 150ff.):

> I call those books useful that make the bookseller active, promote business, and bring their pots to boil. I do not mean those books whose sole purpose is vain erudition, books that the common man, who is the strength of the country, does not understand, and that to the great exasperation of the booksellers therefore generally are warehoused and lie about in the bookshops growing musty. Nowadays the world is unfortunately so learned that it is ready to burst from sheer erudition . . . for, seeing that the world is already filled to the bursting point with immensely learned works, so no more are needed, the aim of writing books from now on should be the promotion of trade alone. . . . The idea of advance subscriptions to publications is capital, and it is to be hoped that we will learn who the founder was, in order to perpetuate his name; for by this means the business, which previously had been uncertain, acquires considerable security. When a bookseller has supplied himself with sufficient advance subscriptions, he can snap his fingers at all the criticisms and biased opinions of journalists, since it no longer stands in their power to discredit a book and turn it into trash.

399(note *):17   *we are born yesterday and know nothing.* The expression comes from Job. 8:9.

399(note
*):18   *Seydelmann* [S/L: Sydelmann]. The German actor Karl Seydelmann (1793–1843), who was active in Berlin around 1838. Kierkegaard may have come across this incident in a work by Heinrich Theodor Rötscher (1803–1871), a celebrated Hegelian esthetician; namely, *Seydelmanns Leben und Wirken* (Berlin, 1845), p. 126.

402:7   *respice finem*. From the Latin proverb, *quidquid agis, prudenter agas et respice finem* (whatever you do, act with reason and look toward the end). This is in turn supposed to have derived from the following in Sir. 7:36: "In whatever you do, remember your last days, and you will never sin."

402:26   *Prince Ferdinand*. The heir presumptive, Frederik Ferdinand (1792–1863), a very simply-minded and somewhat improvident but extremely popular man.

403:2   *the Jew who fell down*. Efforts to find out what Kierkegaard means by this have been to no avail.

403:28   *Den Frisindede, Freischütz* [S/L: the periodicals]. *Den Frisindede, Ugeblad af blandet Indhold* was a weekly published from 1835 to 1846 by Claudius Rosenhoff (1804–1869), a very active writer who was the leading journalist of the lower middle class. *Der Freischütz* was a German weekly that came out in Hamburg from 1839 on.

405:11   *But we read in the New Testament*. Acts 5:40ff.:

and calling in the Apostles and having them scourged, they charged them not to speak in the name of Jesus, and then let them go. So they departed from the presence of the Sanhedrin, rejoicing that they had been counted worthy to suffer disgrace for the name of Jesus.

405:17   *Scaevola*. Tradition has it that Gaius Mucius Scaevola, on being taken prisoner after an unsuccessful attempt to murder the Etruscan King Porsena, showed his indifference to physical pain by putting his right hand in a fire and letting it burn to a char without wincing (Livius, II, 12–13).

405:37   *an Apostle*. Kierkegaard's thoughts on the concept of an Apostle are found in a temporary form in *The Book on Adler* (*Pap*. VII[2] B 5–230), which he did not publish himself, and in a definitive form in his essay, "On the Difference Between A Genius and an Apostle" (*SV* XI 109ff.). Of the literature on this subject special reference may be made to Eduard Geismar, *Søren Kierkegaard*, IV, 45ff. and 81ff.; Emanuel Hirsch, *Kierkegaard-Studien*, II, 852ff.; Valter Lindström, *Efterföljelsens teologihos Søren Kierkegaard* (Lund, 1956), especially pp. 242–50; and M. Mikulová Thulstrup, "The Two Guardians of Christianity: Apostle and Auditor," *The Sources and Depths of Faith in Kier-*

kegaard, vol. II of *Bibliotheca Kierkegaardiana* (Copenhagen, 1978), pp. 130–46.

406:28   *the passage in the Epistle to the Corinthians*. 2 Cor. 12:7: "And lest the greatness of the revelations should puff me up, there was given me a thorn for the flesh, a messenger of Satan, to buffet me." The next sentence in the text refers to 2 Cor. 5:2ff.

406:29   *the thorn in the flesh*. Concerning the significance of this phrase of Paul, reference is made to the Danish commentary by L. J. Koch to 2 Cor. (Copenhagen, 1927), pp. 433ff., and to the annotation in the Confraternity Bible, Part Two, p. 199. This concept has played an important part in the biographically and psychologically oriented research on Kierkegaard. A significant work in this respect is Gregor Malantschuk's essay, "Pælen i Kødet," *Frihed og Eksistens* (Copenhagen, 1980), pp. 11–19. Dr. Malantschuk focuses his attention on the relationship between suffering and eternal happiness, which he brings together in his discussion of St. Paul.

407:3   *exceptionally distinguished*. Junghans observes correctly that the word employed by Kierkegaard (*udmærket*) is used in two senses: first, in the usual sense of someone prominent by virtue of his qualities and achievements; second, in the special sense of someone marked (*mærket*) and thereby distinguished from the masses by the symptom of suffering.

407:36   *the Latin phrase*. The draft has (*Pap*. VI B 59:10): "and between them there is, if I may say so, a devil of a difference."

407(note *):1   *cum grano salis*. "With a grain of salt," that is, with a little common sense.

408:1   *interest inter et inter*. There is a difference between one thing and another.

408:20   *it is indifferent whether one is a Jew or a Greek*. The expression is from Paul in Gal. 3:28.

408:36   *the illusion that comes after the understanding*. That is, when the understanding is unable to advance further. The understanding holds that religiousness is just as much an illusion as poetry. It may be observed that Climacus, a humorist, is here expressing himself experimentally, whereas elsewhere Kierkegaard speaks of the same subject directly. See for example *Pap*. VIII[1] A 650 (*JP* VI 6135).

409:3   *advice for everything and everybody*. The draft continues with (*Pap*. VI B 60:1):

Everybody—yes, they are stupid. They have lost their imagination, which is why they have advice for everything whenever they see everything only to a certain degree. But this is precisely the stupidity.

409:14   *an entire movement in French poetry*. Kierkegaard was probably thinking of *la frénésie burlesque*, whose most prominent representative was Paul Scarron (1610–1660), a writer famous for his virgilian travesties of 1648. See for example R. Lebégue in *Littérature Française*, new ed. T. Martino, I (Paris, 1948), pp. 344ff.

409:25   *executes the movement of infinity*. According to the view advanced here Socrates does this by first making a movement through irony to infinity and the attainment of the eternal and then seeking to actualize the eternal in temporality. On this concept see especially Eduard Geismar, *Søren Kierkegaard*, II, 57–81 and 90ff.; III, 59ff.

409:27   *the relation to the eternal*. The draft has (*Pap.* VI B 60:2; *JP* I 634):

> Insofar as the religious address is confused with worldly wisdom or with the doctrine of calculation and results, it is to be regarded as an estheticizing lecture on the ethical. In a strict sense it is not even ethical, much less religious. It is by no means my opinion that a religious speaker should pooh-pooh what he in so many ways must naturally be occupied with, but he should never dare to forget the totality-category of his sphere, and that this is what he should use and have with him throughout, however mildly he admonishes the happy one that the religious lives within man and that suffering will also come if he is religious, and speaks likewise to the unhappy one. But if he becomes so complexly involved in the traffic of finitude that he forgets suffering as essentially different from the dialectic of happiness and unhappiness, then he also transforms the church, if not into a robber's den then into a stock-exchange building. This is the reason that the religious address in these times treats happiness, unhappiness, duty, the seven last words, uses the name of God and of Christ—and almost never draws attention to trials [*Anfægtelser*]. Trials belong to the inwardness of religiousness, and inwardness belongs to religiousness; trials belong to the individual's absolute relationship to the absolute τέλος. What temptation [*Fristelse*] is outwardly, trial is inwardly. I will permit myself a psychological experiment.

410:7   *spiritual trial* [S/L use the German word *Anfechtung*]. A spiritual trial (*Anfægtelse*) repels, whereas temptation (*Fristelse*) attracts. Kierkegaard has explained the difference between the two in great detail in a series of journal entries (see *JP* IV 4364–84); he writes, for example (*Pap.* VIII¹ A 93; *JP* IV 4367):

The difference between sin and spiritual trial [*Anfægtelse*] (for the conditions in both can be deceptively similar) is that the temptation [*Fristelse*] to sin is in accord with inclination, [the temptation] of spiritual trial [is] contrary to inclination. Therefore the opposite tactic must be employed. The person tempted by inclination to sin does well to shun the danger, but in relation to spiritual trial this is the very danger, for every time he thinks he is saving himself by shunning the danger, the danger becomes greater the next time. The sensate person is wise to flee from the sight or the enticement, but the one for whom inclination is not the temptation at all but rather an anxiety about coming in contact with it (he is under spiritual trial) is not wise to shun the sight or the enticement; for spiritual trial wants nothing else than to strike terror into his life and hold him in anxiety.

411:32   *one of the older works of edification.* Perhaps Kierkegaard was think-ing of Johann Arndt's *Sämtliche geistreiche Bücher vom wahren Christen-tum*, 2nd ed. (Tübingen, 1777; *ASKB* 276), which he also owned in a Danish translation, *Fire Bøger om den sande Christendom*, translator unknown (Christiania [Oslo], 1829; *ASKB* 277). The concept of a spiritual trial is discussed in several passages in these works. See Marie Mikulová Thulstrup, "Søren Kierkegaard og Johann Arndt," *Kier-kegaardiana*, IV (Copenhagen, 1961), pp. 7–17.

411:34   *Robinson.* In Campe's Danish edition, *Robinson Kruse* (Copenhagen, 1855), p. 181.

412:35   *and to exist thus before God.* The draft continues with (*Pap.* VI B 60:3): "and the jest appears to the religious individual himself when in the external world it happens to seem as if he is capable of doing something."

413(note *):3   κατὰ δύναμιν. In accordance with (its) possibility.

413(note †):2   *make a show of itself.* The Danish *tager sig ud* is a jibe at Danish Hegelian philosophers who frequently used this expression as a trans-lation of *Das Erscheinende* (appearance or show), an important aspect of Hegel's doctrine of essence. See Hegel's *Logic*, pp. 239–42, and *Science of Logic*, II, pp. 20–31. (Note by R.J.W.)

414:17   *self-torture.* The reference is to self-whippings such as the flagellants inflicted on themselves, especially in Italy in the thirteenth century. Kierkegaard was acquainted with this through church history. See for example H. Haupt in *Realencyklopädie für protestantische Theologie und Kirche*, 3rd ed., VI (Leipzig, 1899), pp. 432ff.

416:35   *to electrify the congregation, startling it galvanically.* An allusion to, among other things, H. C. Ørsted's experiments with electricity.

419:27 *Socrates . . . gave up astronomy.* Diogenes Laërtius (II, 5, 21) tells us that Socrates "worked with stone" and "investigated matters of physics," but he makes no mention of astronomy. Kierkegaard undoubtedly had in mind Heiberg who from the beginning of the 1840s was passionately taken up with astronomy and who, as mentioned above, published his annual, *Urania*, in 1844, 1845, and 1846.

419:34 *ex cathedra.* In an official capacity. The phrase is employed in particular concerning the Pope who is said to speak *ex cathedra* when expressing himself on matters of faith in his capacity as the highest authority in the Roman Catholic Church.

423:33 *turns . . . to exist in a finite ethic.* This possibility forms a parallel to the Lutheran doctrine of *iustitia civilis* (*Confessio Augustana*, art. XVIII).

424:31 *once in a while a note will be in colorata.* That is, sometimes uses coloratura. Kierkegaard has employed the word *Trille* (trills) in an unusual sense that is not found in Danish dictionaries; namely, that of repetition of the same tone. *Trille* usually means a rapid oscillation of two tonal steps in which the lowest is the principal note.

425:14 *the city gates were closed and the tollgates likewise.* The walls and four city gates of Copenhagen were not demolished until 1857. The city gates and adjoining octroi houses were closed from midnight until sunrise, and the keys to the gates were delivered to the king at Amalienborg Castle at night and brought back again in the morning.

426:29 *abominates the Baptists.* See the Index.

427:17 *the clergy are accustomed to meet in conventions.* In Denmark clerical conferences (or conventions) made their appearance in the beginning of the nineteenth century. The establishment of the Roskilde Conference in 1842 and the Copenhagen Conference (*Kiøbenhavns geistlige Convent*) in 1843 were especially important events. The latter was from its very inception opposed to Mynster, particularly with regard to the composition of a new hymnal.

The hymnal that had been in use since 1798, *Evangelisk-christelig Psalmebog til Brug ved Kirke- og Husandagt*, was soon exposed to harsh criticism, and not without good reason. Mynster sought to remedy its defects by publishing a supplement containing 58 psalms; this became authorized in 1845. The Copenhagen Conference, however, had a new trial hymnal prepared the same year with older psalms that Grundtvig had liberally readapted. (From 1837 to 1870 Grundtvig edited his own *Sang-Værk til den danske Kirke* consisting of five volumes with about 1,500 psalms and biblical poems.) The very next year the Roskilde Conference took up the matter of a new hymnal and prepared a proposed hymnal that came out in 1850. It was examined twice, and then in 1855 became authorized as the *Psalmebog til Kirke- og Hus-Andagt* ("Hymnal for Church and Home Worship"). See N. M. Plum, *Københavns Præstekonvent 1843–1943* (Copenhagen, 1943), and the articles in *Bibliotheca Kierkegaardiana*, vol. XIII (Copenhagen, 1983).

427:22   *a new hymnal.* The printed manuscript has (*Pap.* VI B 98:74):

> When a child becomes tired on a country road and there is no carriage to be had, one is in trouble; yet I did see a practical father find a way out. He suggested to the little one that he ride on Dad's walking stick—now he went hopping at a gallop; the child was not tired at all any more.

428:17   *particular private conventicles.* Kierkegaard was here thinking chiefly of the congregation that in 1839 began to gather round Grundtvig in the Vartov institution (see note above). Grundtvig published a volume, *Fest-Psalmer*, that in ever newer and expanded editions was—and still is—used in Vartov and in the many independent and voluntary congregations.

428:30   *What was it that destroyed the Assyrian Empire? Dissension, madam.* This is taken from Holberg's *Hexerie eller blind Alarm* (Act IV, Scene 4), where Herman von Breman gives a political lecture to Apelone:

> The strength of an empire and a republic consists in harmony between its subjects and is destroyed by dissension. There have been four great monarchies in the world, all of which were ruined by dissension. What ruined the Assyrian Monarchy? Dissension, Madam! What ruined the Persian? Dissension, Madam! What destroyed the Greek? Dissension, Madam! What finally ruined the Roman? By my soul, nothing but dissension. Alexander Magnus was guilty of disloyal statesmanship, and did wrong.

430:39   *moderators. Danish, Moderatores,* "a regulative force." The leaders in the organized Presbyterian churches in Scotland are called "Moderators."

431:3   *and the gods piled mountains.* The giants, not the Titans, wanted to storm Olympia, and on that occasion they piled Pelion on top of Ossa. They were defeated, however, by Zeus and as punishment confined beneath, among others, Mount Etna. See Hesiod, *Theogony*, 690, and W. Vollmer, *Vollständiges Wörterbuch der Mythologie aller Nationen* (Stuttgart, 1836; *ASKB* 1942–43), p. 774.

431:25   *transforms the temple . . . into a den of robbers.* Matt. 21:13.

432:33   *but no mutuality.* The reason is that whether or not God will establish a relationship with an individual depends on God alone.

432(note
*):2

the special interest of my present exposition has not yet begun. The *Post-script* is a work that is introductory to becoming a Christian.

433:2

to see God was to die. Compare Ex. 33:20: "But my face you cannot see, for no man sees me and still lives."

433:2

pagans thought that the God-relationship was the precursor of madness! Kierkegaard may have had in mind the very dubious—and certainly ironically intended—etymologies in Plato's *Phaedrus* 244, where among other things he advances the theory that madness may originate from the gods.

434:25

Absit. Far from it.

436:6

this sickness is not unto death. Compare Acts 11:4.

436:24

a little moment away. This implies that the individual is once again in the world. Kierkegaard writes in *Pap.* VII² B 235, p. 163 (*On Authority and Revelation*, p. 130):

> The eternal is of infinite value, and yet it must be made commensurable with the temporal, and the contact is the instant. Yet this instant is a nothing. Thinking here comes to a stop with the most dreadful contradiction, with the most taxing of all thoughts, which, if it were to be held for long at the highest pitch of mental exertion, must bring the thinker to madness.

436(note
*):12

very careful about making vows. Eccl. 5:4: "You had better not make a vow than make it and not fulfill it."

437:5

each moment be threatened with the loss of it. The draft has as a continuation (*Pap.* VI B 66):

> To some extent one can put knowledge aside and then proceed to collect new [information], and the naturalist can put his insects and flowers aside and then go on. But whenever an existing individual puts aside a decision in existence: then it is *eo ipso* lost and he is changed.

438:32

the difference between knowledge and ignorance collapses. The implication is that in ignorance knowledge and lack of knowledge merge, since the scrap of knowledge that one does possess is immediately absorbed and destroyed by lack of knowledge.

440:16

deliberation. Here the sense is contemplation (*Betragtning* or *Overvejelse*). Note the title of Mynster's popular work on dogmatics: *Betragtninger over de christelige Troeslærdomme* ("Reflections on the doctrines of the Christian Faith").

444:6

whoever is silent before God. See Eccl. 5:1–2: "Be not hasty in your utterance and let not your heart be quick to make a promise in God's presence. God is in heaven and you are on the earth; therefore let your words be few."

444:32   *sensu eminenti*. In a decisive sense.

445:4   *So much for the religious suffering*. A rough sketch to a continuation to this passage reads (*Pap*. VI B 64):

> To p. 1 of the rough draft.
> . . . I will not dwell further here on how the ethical (which, after all, is already somewhat removed from the absolute God-relationship) must intervene as a regulative and take command. This is not in the interest of my purpose, and I have nothing to do with that phase—therefore I am using the foreshortened perspective.

445:30   *at least there is no one who notices anything in their manner or behavior*. The draft then continues with (*Pap*. VI B 67):

> But if anyone were to shrink from such an exertion—still, it seems odd to me that people want to have such a poor opinion of the great things they achieve (for, since the secret of course lies in the fact that nobody must notice them, it is indeed possible that they do them; for nobody will notice anything) that they regard them as nothing and even want to go further.

446(note   *(in Either/Or)*. Kierkegaard's memory has obviously failed him. It
*):1   is the pseudonym Johannes de Silentio who advances this theory of the ethical and self-revelation. See *Fear and Trembling*, pp. 91ff. (*SV* III 145ff.).

447:4   *as Frater Taciturnus says in Stages on Life's Way*. *Stages*, pp. 363ff., in "Epistle to the Reader" (*SV* VI 442ff.).

447:6   *the confusion pervading recent speculation*. See above, note to p. 18.

448:13   *stricte sic dictus*. Taken strictly.

449:20   *like Magister Kierkegaard*. In his dissertation, *The Concept of Irony*, Kierkegaard's thesis was that irony as purely negative was a part of Socrates' nature and not just a form of expression.

449(note   *peat-cutters*. *Tørvegnidere*, a now obsolete pejorative term for the
*):7   peat-cutters (*Tørvebønder*) of Copenhagen who drove very slowly because of their load. It is formed around the verb *at gnide*, to rub, which in figurative speech also means to drive slowly. See *ODS*, XXV, col. 127, which refers to this very passage in Kierkegaard.

450(note   *The derelict Hegelian ethics*. Kierkegaard has in mind especially *The*
*):1   *Philosophy of Right*.

450(note   *Socrates adopted a negative attitude toward the State*. See for example
†):1   the point of indictment mentioned in Plato's *Apology* 24A.

451:34   *but he does not himself stand related to God.* To this the printed manuscript adds a note (*Pap.* VI B 98:77; *JP* II 2116, slightly modified.
Inderlighed and *Inderliggjørelse* inserted in brackets by R.J.W.):

> *Note.* Thus the humorist still has an inwardness [*Inderlighed*] which
> is undialectical and only approximates the dialectical actualization
> of inwardness [*Inderliggjørelse*] of religiousness. The spheres are or-
> dered in relation to the dialectical development of inward deepen-
> ing [*Inderliggjørelse*], and to the degree an individual [*Individ*] keeps
> himself on the outside, fortifies himself against it [inwardness] or
> even partially fortifies himself, to the same degree his religiousness
> is less. The inwardness of the immediate person is externality; he
> has his dialectic outside himself. The man of irony is already turned
> inward in the exercise of the consciousness of contradiction. The
> ethical man is turned inward, but the development of inwardness
> [*Inderliggjørelsen*] is self-affirmation against himself; he strives with
> himself but does not remain dialectical to the end because he has
> fortified himself in a possibility by which he conquers himself.
> Humor is turned inward in the exercise of the absolute contradic-
> tion, is not without the inwardness of suffering, but still has so
> much of an undialectical self left that in the shifting it sticks its
> head up like a nisse and raises laughter; the religious person's in-
> wardness is a self-annihilation before God.

457:20   *paralogism.* A false inference. *Conditio non ponit in esse*: a condition
does not posit being, for in postulating a theorem as a condition one
says nothing about its actuality.

458:14   *Lord Shaftesbury.* That is, Lord Shaftesbury in *Essay on the Freedom
of Wit and Humor* (London, 1709), pp. 57ff. Kierkegaard, who did
not read English or own any translations of Shaftesbury, undoubtedly owes his knowledge of him to J. G. Herder's "Adrastea," no.
14, *Herder's sämmtliche Werke zur Philosophie und Geschichte*, ed. Johann von Müller, I–XXII (Stuttgart and Tübingen, 1827–1830; *ASKB*
1695–1705), XI, 175ff.

458:17   *the Hegelian philosophy has desired to give preponderance to the comical.*
Hegel concludes his *Vorlesungen über die Aesthetik* (*W.a.A.* X³ 579;
Jub. Ausg. XIV 579ff.):

> With the development of comedy we have now arrived at the
> actual terminus of our scientific discussion. We began with sym-
> bolic art, in which subjectivity is to be found as content and form
> and strives to become objective. We proceeded to classical sculp-
> ture, which the introverted [*für sich klar*] developing substantiality

represents to itself in living individuality. And we ended in the romantic art of feeling [*Gemüths*] and inwardness with an independent, inherently spiritual, and self-moving absolute subjectivity that, having emancipated itself, no longer conforms to the objective and particular, and so brings the negative factor of their dissolution to consciousness in the humor of the comic. Nevertheless, from these heights comedy at the same time leads to the dissolution of art in general.

458:33   *the Aristotelian view.* In *De partibus animalium* 673a Aristotle emphasizes that man is the only animal who laughs.

459(note   Following are some rough sketches to this note (*Pap.* VI B 70:10,
*):1   13, 14, 15):

> 10) When out at a cemetery one reads on a grave an inscription by a man who mourns his lost little daughter in verse, but finally exclaims in his verse: Console yourself, Reason, she still lives, (signed) Hilarius Butcher—well, this is very comical. First, the name itself (Hilarius) produces a comic effect in this connection, then the dignity: Butcher, and finally the cry: Reason! For after all it might be suitable for a professor in philosophy to take it into his head to confound himself with reason [*Fornuften*], but a butcher just cannot get away with it.
> [*JP* II 1746:13, 14, 15]
> 13) The immorality does not lie in the laughing but rather in the ambiguity and the titillation in the laughing, when one does not really know whether to laugh or not and one is thereby prevented from repenting for having laughed in the wrong place.
> 14) Thus there may be someone who is able to be comically productive only in flippancy and hilarity. If one were to say to him: Remember, you are ethically responsible for your use of the comic, and he took time to understand this, his *vis comica* perhaps would cease—that is, it would be unauthorized, without the direct implication that he actually did harm with it while he used it.
> 15) In contrast to the flippancy and wantonness (as productive) and ambiguity and sense-titillation (as receptive) of ringing laughter [stands] the quiet transparency of the comic. A person ought to practice laughing not in connection with the objects of his antipathetic passions but in connection with the objects of his gentleness and consideration, that which he knows he cannot totally lose, the area where he is protected by the opposition of all his emotions against the ambiguous, the selfish, the titillating.

459(note
*):1

The Aristotelian definition. This reads in translation (*Poetics*, 1449a; *Introduction to Aristotle*, ed. Richard McKeon, *The Modern Library* [New York, 1947], p. 630): "The Ridiculous may be defined as a mistake or deformity not productive of pain or harm to others."

459(note
*):12

"Trop." Trop, a perpetual law student, is the principal character in J. L. Heiberg's vaudeville *Recensenten og Dyret.*

459(note
*):13

The "Busy Man" . . . the ridiculous unmixed. Holberg's comedy *Den Stundesløse* ("The Busy Man") is based on the plot in Molière's *Le malade imaginaire* and concerns useless industry or diligence.

459(note
*):21

Hamlet swears by the fire-tongs. This is a linguistic mistake. In *Hamlet, Prince of Denmark* (Act III, Scene 2, v. 337) Hamlet swears to Rosenkrantz "by these pickers and stealers." According to Dover Wilson's note in the Cambridge edition (1948, p. 207), the expression originates from the catechism authorized in Shakespeare's time. In a modern Danish edition Østerberg renders this line with *"ved disse Dirkere og Stjælere"* ("by these picklocks and stealers"), whereas the edition generally used by Kierkegaard, *Shakspeare's [sic] dramatische Werke*, trans. August Wilhelm Schlegel, I–XII (Berlin, 1839; *ASKB* 1883–88), has *"bei diesen beyden Diebeszangen,"* that is, "with both these thieves's tongs"; in other words, with his two hands. According to the glossary in *The Complete Works of William Shakespeare* (New York, 1952), p. 1297, the Shakespearean word "pickers" is translatable by "the hands."

459(note
*):23

". . . fully four shillings worth of gold in the binding of this book." The manuscript identifies the book as *"Heiberg's Urania."* See the Index.

459(note
*):26

Holophernes. Holophernes, a commander-in-chief under King Nebuchadnezzar, led an Assyrian army into Israel and was beheaded by Judith while in a drunken sleep (see Judith, especially 12:10ff.). He also appears in Holberg's *Ulysses von Ithacia* (Act II, Scene 5) in which Chilian says: "Now I'm an ambassador extraordinary over the whole army and subordinate to nobody except General Holophernes, who is seven and one-quarter ells tall." A Danish ell (*Alen*) equals slightly more than two feet (24.7 inches).

460(note
*):8

Pryssing. In Heiberg's *Recensenten og Dyret* (Scene 6 and passim) the bookbinder Pryssing speaks in the third person to Trop, who to some extent is financially dependent on Pryssing. This was a disparaging form of address in the Danish of Kierkegaard's time.

461(note
*):55

Hilarius is derived from the Greek ἱλαρός, which means cheerful.

462(note
*):23

laughter can destroy everything. The printed manuscript has further (*Pap.* VI B 98:78):

And I know from personal experience that now my sense of the comic seldom disturbs me wherever I refuse to see the comic, and I know in addition that precisely because I have been attentive to myself I have more than once regretted having laughed in the wrong place.

462(note *):29   *pathetically apprehended.* That is, emotionally.

462(note *):35   *vis comica.* Comic power.

463:2   *Despairs of a way out.* In *The Sickness Unto Death* (*SV* XI 195, especially note; *KW* XIX 60 note) a distinction is made between despairing *over* something earthly and despairing *of* the eternal.

464(note †):1   *Aristotle remarks. Rhetoric* (trans. J. H. Freese, *Loeb Classical Library*, 1419b): "Irony is more gentlemanly than buffoonery; for the first is employed on one's own account, the second on that of another."

464(note †):6   *scurra.* Buffoon.

466:4   *"since now everywhere. . . ."* This phrase sounds unmistakably Grundtvigian, but it has not been possible to locate the quotation.

466:32   *Gorgias.* The famous Sophist who lived in the fifth century before Christ. In *Rhetoric* (trans. J. H. Freese, *Loeb Classical Library*, 1419b) Aristotle adduces Gorgias' rule for speakers according to which they should "confound the opponents' earnest with jest and their jest with earnest."

467:6   *pettifogger.* See note to p. 380:24.

467:28   *ne quid nimis.* Everything with moderation.

Climacus begins paragraph three with a brief recapitulation of the two previous paragraphs. Here he proposes to tackle the question of how a consciousness of guilt can become the decisive expression for the existing individual's pathetic relationship to an eternal happiness.

He regards guilt as a snare, since whoever justifies himself totally simply denounces himself, whereas the person who justifies himself partially denounces himself totally. The priority of total guilt is not an empirical qualification based on a calculation of all the transgressions. Rather, the totality of guilt comes into being for the individual as soon as he puts his guilt together with an eternal happiness (p. 471), and this essential consciousness of guilt constitutes the greatest possible absorption in existence. Nevertheless, it is still within immanence and so differs from the consciousness of sin.

As the author had emphasized previously, in the religious sphere the positive is recognizable by the negative. In the present case this implies that the relation to an eternal happiness is recognizable by means of the totality of the consciousness of guilt. The decisive expression for this consciousness is thus its essential persistence, or the eternal recollection of guilt (p. 475).

Now it holds true that to suffer when guilty is a lower expression than to suffer when innocent; and yet it is a higher expression because the negative is the distinctive mark of a higher positivity. Only with respect to the Christian paradox does it hold true that suffering in innocence is a higher expression than suffering when guilty (p. 476).

In the eternal recollection of guilt mentioned above the existing individual relates himself to an eternal happiness in such a way that he is as far as possible from his eternal happiness; but he continues to relate himself to it anyway (p. 476–77). For the very concept of guilt is a religious concept and a total qualification. It is just such a total qualification that must concern the religious address essentially, even though the speaker may begin by making use of particular offenses. Eternal recollection, however, or persistence in the consciousness of total guilt, cannot be given external expression without making it finite; it thus belongs to hidden inwardness (p. 479).

Climacus thereupon indicates some views of guilt that are lower than the eternal recollection of guilt that takes place in hidden inwardness. He mentions the following cases: when memory comes into play instead of recollection; if recollection is not eternal but momentary; if the guilt is mediated; whenever the civic conception of punishment is supposed to constitute satisfaction; wherever an esthetic-metaphysical conception of nemesis is applied; and if the satisfaction consists of self-imposed penance. On the other hand, the penitential movement and attitude of the Middle Ages were worthy of respect because the individual applied an absolute standard to his own situation (p. 486). Analogies to self-inflicted penance will appear if the individual, instead of turning outward, turns inward and toward himself (p. 487).

Humor, which borders on religiousness, apprehends the totality of guilt-consciousness and is produced by combining spiritual culture in an absolute sense with childlikeness. Now, although humor does indeed reflect on guilt-consciousness as a totality, it revokes the profound aspect as a jest; in other words, the humorous person fails to relate himself to an eternal happiness. Still, the development has at least brought him to hidden inwardness.

The religiousness of which Climacus has spoken up to now, Religiousness A, is not specifically Christian. To be sure, it is dialectical; but it is not paradoxically dialectical, since it is only conditioned by the dialectical actualization of inwardness, not by something else. The point in Religiousness B is that it must be conditioned by "a definite something" (p. 494). Climacus also insists that Religiousness A must be present in the individual before there can be any question of becoming aware of the dialectical Religiousness B.

The difficulty inherent in becoming a Christian—and Climacus' purpose is to underscore this difficulty—is a qualitative one. It is therefore essentially just as hard for everybody. All who wish to enter Religiousness B, both the clever and the simple, must be prepared to renounce their understanding, that is, immanence, and stake their lives on the absurd. Thus speculation to be consistent should insist that Religiousness A is superior to Religiousness B, since it lies within the sphere of immanence. But, Climacus asks, why then call it Christian?

Religiousness B has a higher dialectic, a dialectic "to the second power," that brings the subject to ever more intense levels of pathos and inwardness in existence. Thus "one does not prepare oneself to become attentive to Christianity by reading books, or by world-historical surveys, but by immersing oneself deeper in existence" (p. 497). The difficulty lies in using the absolute paradox to hold the qualitative dialectic fast despite any illusions of the senses. It is therefore important not to lose sight of the fact that the paradox defies comprehension.

Misunderstandings frequently arise whenever one manages to thrust Christianity back into the field of esthetics, "in which unwittingly the hyper-orthodox especially are successful" (p. 499). Climacus accuses Grundtvig and his followers of just such an error, and even avers that he would prefer speculation's misunderstanding to theirs. As a rule, the basic misunderstanding is due to the conception that the unintelligibility of the paradox is supposed to be related to the difference between the sharp- and short-witted. To counter this misunderstanding one needs merely to bear in mind that the paradox is essentially related to man as such and qualitatively to each person individually, irrespective of the individual's talents.

Of course, a Christian does use his understanding in various connections, Climacus writes, but in relation to Christianity he employs it to find the limit so that he can believe despite his understanding; and his faith serves in turn to assure him that he really is believing against the dictates of his understanding. He will be able to avoid believing nonsense against his understanding, however, simply because his understanding will discern that it is nonsense and thus prevent him from believing it.

*   *   *

469:29   *to be off like Icarus.* According to a Greek myth (see for example, Pausanias, IX, 3, 2) Icarus received from his father, the ingenious Daedalus, a pair of wings that were supposed to be an aid to him in his flight from King Minos, by whom they both were held captive. Icarus came too close to the sun, causing the wax in the wings to melt, and he plunged into the sea.

469:37   *"going back to fundamentals" (Tilbagegaaen til det Tilgrundliggende).* The phrase is Hegelian but not the meaning, which in Hegel is ambiguous. To Hegel *zu Grunde gehen* signifies in part that logically an inference is made from the conclusion back to the premises, and in part that something is annulled. In his Hegelian logic Heiberg takes as an example a house that collapses (*gaar til Grunde*) because of age; or, it sinks into its own ground! Both the German and Danish expressions are idioms that usually mean to perish or be destroyed, ruined, or lost. Thus Hegel and Heiberg have broken up their respective idioms into their component parts and used *Grunde* in the sense of a logical ground or fundamental condition. In Danish, at least, there is no precedence for this usage. See *ODS*, VII, cols. 159ff.

470:2   *I once read an account.* Kierkegaard presumably had read Hegel's very detailed review of Wilhelm v. Humboldt's "Ueber die unter dem Namen Bhagavad-Gita bekannte Episode des Mahabharata" (1826), which came out first in *Jahrbücher für wissenschaftliche Kritik* (1827; printed in *W.a.A.* XVI 362–435; *Jub. Ausg.* XX 57–131). *Bhagavad-Gita* is of course not a drama but a religious-philosophical didactic poem with a framework as that indicated by Kierkegaard. Kierkegaard owned Friedrich Schlegel's *Ueber die Sprache und Weisheit der Indier* (Heidelberg, 1808; *ASKB* 1388), in which fragments are translated into German.

471:12 *there is a catch to it.* This is perhaps an allusion to the Danish expression *Bordet fanger*, which in card-playing signifies that any card laid on the table is deemed to be in play.

471:15 *qui s'excuse s'accuse.* Whoever excuses himself accuses himself.

471:29 *(totum est partibus suis prius).* The whole is prior to its component parts.

472:12 *One reads in the older works of the orthodox theologians.* Kierkegaard cites this doctrine in several places but never divulges his source. See for example *Pap.* VI A 62 and VIII[1] A 662 (*JP* III 3633, and I 4, respectively) and *The Sickness Unto Death* (*KW* XIX 80; *SV* XI 216). The exact passage used by Kierkegaard has thus not been found, but it would appear that his source was primarily his own notes taken during H. N. Clausen's lectures. See *Pap.* I C 19 (*JP* V 5038) and *Pap.* XII, §30, especially p. 79.

The rudiments of the doctrine appear in *Augsburg Confession*, Article II, "De peccato originali." Kierkegaard became acquainted with the doctrine as promulgated by the orthodox Lutheran theologians chiefly through Karl Hase, *Hutterus redivivus oder Dogmatik der evangelisch-lutherischen Kirche*, 4th ed. (Leipzig, 1839; *ASKB* 581), §132, "Damnatio et beatitudo aeterna," and C. G. Bretschneider, *Handbuch der Dogmatik der evangelisch-lutherischen Kirche*, 3rd. ed., I–II (Leipzig, 1828), II, §175; Kierkegaard owned the fourth edition of this work (Leipzig, 1838; *ASKB* 437–38), which unfortunately has not been available.

472(note *):7 *humble before God.* An inaccurate quotation from *Stages*, p. 111 (*SV* VI 117), Judge William's essay, "Observations About Marriage."

474:29 *but has this only as an annulled possibility.* That is, in actuality. See Gregor Malantschuk's "Das Verhältnis zwischen Wahrheit und Wirklichkeit in Sören Kierkegaards existentiellem Denken," *Frihed og Eksistens* (Copenhagen, 1980), pp. 47–60.

475:7 *human justice pronounces.* According to a mandate of February 20, 1789, it was determined among other things that anyone found guilty of common theft a third time was to be punished by hard labor in a house of correction or fortification for life. A new mandate of April 11, 1840, specified that punishment for life was to be applied only to qualified theft, for example, burglary committed a third time, whereas it was to be applied to any theft after the fifth infraction.

479:6   *encomio publico ornatus.* Honored by public eulogy. The phrase was still in use in Kierkegaard's time with respect to a "summons" (*Til-kaldelse*) to receive a distinction after an examination (see *ODS*, IX, col. 353). Kierkegaard's older brother Peter received this distinction in his student examination in 1822.

480:5   *a priest in silk* [S/L: prelate]. The expression is of course deroga-tory, but perhaps Kierkegaard was thinking of Mynster, who as bishop had to wear clerical robes of silk.

481:30   *for the solution of mediation and its indulgence.* Kierkegaard was think-ing of Hegel's explanations of "The Correlation," *Logic,* pp. 252ff. (*Enc.,* §§138ff.; *W.a.A.* VI 275ff.; *Jub. Ausg.* VIII 313ff.).

482:5   *nemesis.* Junghans refers to the dominant role played by the idea of nemesis in the works of the elder M. A. Goldschmidt; but there does not seem to be any connection here. Concerning Kierkegaard and Goldschmidt reference is also made to H. Toldberg's article in *Fest-skrift til Paul V. Rubow* (Copenhagen, 1956), pp. 211–35.

482:15   *the Furies did not dare to enter the temple.* Kierkegaard is alluding to Sophocles' *Electra, Orestes,* and *Iphigenia in Tauris,* in which the story about Orestes is used very freely: Orestes flees from the gods of revenge (the Furies, the Erinyes) into the temple of Apollo in Delphi.

483:22   *Holophernes.* See above p. 365.

485:2   *the mermaids.* This is a reference to the copperplate in W. Vollmer, *Vollständiges Wörterbuch der Mythologie aller Nationen,* I–II (Stuttgart, 1836; *ASKB* 1942–43), II. Kierkegaard had already mentioned this plate in January 1837 in the Journal (*Pap.* I A 319; *JP* II 4394; square brackets inserted by R.J.W.):

> There must be a stage in the development of mythology which corresponds to that whole period in childhood when the individual is so minimally separated from the whole that he says: Me hit the horse—the stage in which the individual is so minimally separated from the whole that he comes to view only in fleeting moments, something like *"die Wellenmädchen"* [the mermaids] in the sketch found in the Vollmer prints (*Vollständiges Wörterbuch der Mythologie,* plate CXV), where the individual is correctly portrayed and ren-dered graphic as a procreative power in the process of becoming.

485:10   *float over it all like a scum.* As pointed out by Gregor Malantschuk in his article mentioned above (note to p. 474:29), this and other passages in the *Postscript* in which Kierkegaard criticizes Hegel's anti-individualism tend to echo Poul M. Møller's essay on immortality. Note for example the following from *Poul Møllers efterladte Skrifter*, ed. F. C. Olsen, 2nd ed., I–III (Copenhagen, 1848–1850), III¹, 72.

> Every finite being becomes, according to the underlying hypothesis [in Hegel], merely a vanishing ripple in an ocean of thought whose undulations are determined by an ineluctable necessity.

487:13   *invitation.* Kierkegaard writes "*Invite,*" which in Danish stems from card-playing and means to lead with a low card in order to inform one's partner of the color that should be followed.

489:26   *tertium comparationis.* Literally, "the third (factor) of the comparison," that is, the element common to two compared objects or in the interrelationship of two matters.

489:32   *deputy to parliament.* A member (*Stænderdeputeret*) of the advisory assembly of the Estates of the Realm (*Stænderforsamlinger*), which existed from 1831 to 1848.

490(note *)   The draft has in addition (*Pap.* VI B 71:3):

> *Note.* Since in relation to the little I know I have made it a principle to show definitely what is what or to show definitely why it definitely cannot be shown, I will do it once more here in a note, although I know well and rather definitely that it is a thankless labor to have dealings with such things. This is where one perhaps acquires dexterity and a measured step very slowly, while all and sundry unhesitatingly pass judgment on the same thing, that is, where humoristically enough the difference between the best developed person and a chatterer is infinitesimal, for indeed both of them speak about the same thing, about the humoristic, the ironic; whereas whoever occupies himself with Hebrew, astronomy, and the like is exempted from any fraternization with the uninitiated.

490(note *):3   *a note of pain in the rejoinder, which ironically is entirely incorrect.* Concerning this passage see Eduard Geismar, *Søren Kierkegaard. Livsudvikling og Forfattervirksomhed.* I–VI (Copenhagen, 1926–1928), II, 99ff., and Jens Himmelstrup, "Terminologisk Register," *SV* XV 592ff. and 608ff. ("Humor" and "Irony").

490(note *):12   *His sad interpretation of childhood.* The meaning is that the higher a person comes in the existential relationships the more his view of childhood changes.

491:3   *a man like Kant.* Kierkegaard was thinking of Kant's repudiation of the traditional proofs of the existence of God in *Critique of Pure Reason,* trans. Norman Kemp Smith (London and New York, 1964), pp.

495ff. (A584ff., B612ff.). In the passage immediately following allusion is made to the controversy of the 1830s among Hegelians on the subject of individual immortality (see the Index), but hardly to any definite writing.

491(note *):1   *the travail of soul.* Compare Eccl. 1:13–14.

491(note *):7   *It is related of Socrates.* This incident is mentioned in a draft for an article in Kierkegaard's conflict with *Corsaren* (*Pap.* VII¹ B 11, p. 176), but the source has been sought in vain.

492:5   *Buffon.* Georges Buffon (1707–1788), whose *Histoire naturelle, générale et particulière,* I–XLIV (Paris, 1749-1804) was very widely read and was translated into other European languages.

492(note †):1   *the race becomes higher.* That is, higher than the individual. The thought here is explained in the third part of an undated journal entry from about 1840 (*Pap.* III A 216; *JP* II 1101, modified). "The whole Christian life," Kierkegaard writes, "is a complete life and as such has its" immediacy, mediacy, and:

> 3) Identity, by which every external phenomenon of the Church is surmounted, yet not in such a way that now the individual is not merely a phase [*Moment*] in the order of things as the Church is, does not struggle through the visible to the invisible, but by virtue of the invisible (which is in the individual not merely as a phase [*Moment*] of the whole but continues in the individual) [he] penetrates the visible and consummates himself in the visible.

493:8   *when relativity rests.* To this the following is added in the draft (*Pap.* VI B 72):

> To that passage: that it is comic when total guilt underlies comparative goodness.
>
> When something firm underlies movement it is not comic, but when destruction is its basis all that scurrying around is in fact comic. The contradiction is that despite any movement and all the movement from a particular place there is no getting away from the total.
>
> for example, on a sinking ship.

494:20   *is not conditioned by anything.* That is, by anything historical, whereas Religiousness B is indeed conditioned precisely by "a something historical"—Jesus Christ.

494:37   *in the second instance.* Junghans correctly explains this as a break with immanence. Religiousness A is also dialectical, but in the first instance, in the actualization of inwardness. The new dialectic, which belongs to Religiousness B, appears after the break with immediacy and the eternity of recollection.

495:33   *distinguish . . . between what he understands and what he does not understand.* Kierkegaard also used this idea as a motto for *The Concept of Anxiety* (*SV* IV 306; *KW* VIII 3). See my commentary on this motto in *Krankheit u. A.*, p. 702.

495:36   *Socrates and Hamann.* See Plato's *Apology* 21D and Hamann in *Hamann's Schriften*, ed. Friedrich Roth, I–VIII (Berlin, 1821–1843; *ASKB* 536–44), II, *Sokratische Denkwürdigkeiten*, p. 12, "Zweite Widmung":

> He [Socrates] distinguishes between what he does and does not understand in the writings of Heraclitus, and makes a very fair and unpretentious inference from what is comprehensible to what is incomprehensible.

The above is quoted from *Johann Georg Hamanns Hauptschriften erklärt*, ed. F. Blanke, I–VII (Gütersloh, 1956–1959), pp. 77ff. In his notes the editor of this edition quotes this passage from Thomasius' German translation of Charpentier's biography of Socrates, which is the one used by Hamann. See also T. Schack, *Johann Georg Hamann* (Copenhagen, 1948), pp. 90ff.; W. Leibrecht, *Gott und Mensch bei Johann Georg Hamann* (Gütersloh, 1948), pp. 165ff.; my essay, "To af Forudsætningerne for Hamanns Opgør med sin Samtid," *Dansk teologisk Tidsskrift* (Copenhagen, 1960), pp. 77ff.; and R. G. Smith, *Johann Georg Hamann* (London, 1960).

496:21   *Too trifling a one to propose to the god.* To this a marginal note is added in the printed manuscript (*Pap.* VI B 98:81; *JP* II 1344): "In this case the Incarnation would have direct analogies in the incarnations of paganism; whereas the distinction is: incarnation as man's invention and incarnation as coming from God."

497:30   *although it belongs to subjectivity it is not arbitrariness.* See in this respect Valter Lindström, "Problemet objektivt-subjektivt hos Kierkegaard," *Nordisk teologi, idéer och män. Till Ragnar Bring* (Lund, 1955), pp. 85–102.

498:3   *God is the basis.* That is, the creator. See in this connection Valter Lindström, *Stadiernas teologi* (Lund, 1943), chaps. I and III.

499:9   *interprets the Runic inscriptions.* That is, interprets obscure sayings. This entire passage is composed with typical Grundtvigian locutions.

499:25   *the hyper-orthodoxy.* Kierkegaard means the Grundtvigians, who at the time were generally regarded as such. It was not so much Grundtvig himself who provided the occasion for this characterization as his adherent A. G. Rudelbach (1792–1862), who nevertheless was rather independent of Grundtvig.

499:29   *a higher position in time.* Junghans justifiably considers this a polemic against Grundtvig who—just like speculation—had history behind him. Christianity, however, can only lie before one as a task that reason is unable to solve.

500:12   *the females take off their hats.* An allusion to 1 Cor. 11.

501:36   *to want to be like God.* Gen. 3:5.

502:2   *tertium comparationis.* The third term in a comparison.

503:31   *one who is really a Christian.* Kierkegaard is usually the best interpreter of his works; so too here. In a long journal entry from 1850 he quotes and fully endorses a statement by Hugo de St. Victor (d. 1141) that he had read in Adolph Helfferich, *Die christliche Mystik in ihrer Entwickelung und in ihren Denkmalen,* I–II (Gotha, 1842; *ASKB* 571–72), I, 368. The quotation and Kierkegaard's comments read as follows (*Pap.* X² A 354; *JP* I 7):

> Hugo de St. Victor states a correct thesis (Helfferich, *Mystik,* Vol. I, p. 368): "Faith is really not supported by the things which go beyond reason, by any reason, because reason does not comprehend what faith believes; but nevertheless there is something here by which reason becomes determined or is conditioned to honor the faith which it still does not perfectly succeed in grasping."
>
> This is what I have developed (for example, in *Concluding Postscript*)—that not every absurdity is the absurd or the paradox. The activity of reason is to distinguish the paradox negatively—but not more.
>
> *In an earlier journal or in loose papers* [*Pap.* VI A 17, 19; *JP* I 627, 628] from an earlier time (when I read Aristotle's *Rhetoric*) I was of the opinion that a Christian art of speaking should be introduced in place of dogmatics. It ought to relate itself to $\pi i \sigma \tau \iota \varsigma$. $\pi i \sigma \tau \iota \varsigma$ in the classical Greek means the conviction (more than $\delta \delta \xi a$, opinion) which relates itself to probability. But Christianity, which always turns the concepts of the natural man upside down and gets the opposite meaning out of them, relates $\pi i \sigma \tau \iota \varsigma$ to the improbable.
>
> This concept of improbability, the absurd, ought, then, to be developed, for it is nothing but superficiality to think that the absurd is not a concept, that all sorts of absurdities are equally at home in the absurd. No, the concept of the absurd is precisely to grasp the fact that it cannot and must not be grasped. This is a negatively determined concept but is just as dialectical as any positive one. The *absurd,* the *paradox,* is composed in such a way that

reason has no power at all to dissolve it in nonsense and prove that it is nonsense; no, it is a symbol, a riddle, a compounded riddle about which reason must say: I cannot solve it, it cannot be understood, but it does not follow thereby that it is nonsense. But, of course, if faith is completely abolished, the whole sphere is dropped, and then reason becomes conceited and perhaps concludes that, *ergo*, the paradox is nonsense. What concern there would be if in another realm the skilled class were extinct and then the unskilled found this thing and that to be nonsense—but in respect to the paradox faith is the skilled. It believes the paradox, and now, to recall the words of Hugo de St. Victor, reason is properly determined to honor faith, specifically by becoming absorbed in the negative qualifications of the paradox.

Generally it is a basic error to think that there are no negative concepts; the highest principles of all thought or the proofs of them are certainly negative. Human reason has boundaries; that is where the negative concepts are to be found. Boundary disputes are negative, constraining. But people have a rattle-brained, conceited notion about human reason, especially in our age, when one never thinks of a thinker, a reasonable man, but thinks of pure reason and the like, which simply does not exist, since no one, be he professor or what he will, is pure reason. Pure reason is something fantastical, and the limitless fantastical belongs at home where there are no negative concepts, and one understands everything like the sorcerer who ended by eating his own stomach.

Πίστις means belief, faith, confidence; δόξα means opinion, conjecture. See also the entire Introduction to the present volume and the references given there, especially N. H. Søe, "Søren Kierkegaards Lære om Paradokset," *Nordisk teologi, idéer och män. Till Ragnar Bring* (Lund, 1955), pp. 103–22 (reprinted in English as "Kierkegaard's Doctrine of the Paradox," *A Kierkegaard Critique*, ed. Howard A. Johnson and Niels Thulstrup [New York, 1962], pp. 207–27); Cornelio Fabro's important article, "Fede e ragione nella dialettica di Kierkegaard," *Dall'essere all'esistente* (Brescia, 1957), pp. 127–87 (reprinted as "Faith and Reason in Kierkegaard's Dialectic," *A Kierkegaard Critique*, pp. 156–206); and J. Heywood Thomas, "Paradox," *Concepts and Alternatives in Kierkegaard*, vol. III of *Bibliotheca Kierkegaardiana* (Copenhagen, 1980), pp. 192–220.

Résumé (pp. 505–554)

Climacus begins this part by emphasizing that existence is accentuated paradoxically because the eternal itself has come into existence at a point in time. This in turn absolutely qualifies the distinction between Here and Hereafter, a conception that is decisive for every communication of existence.

Speculation, the author continues, annuls the distinction between Here and Hereafter, whereas in Religiousness A reflection on existence leads to reflection on the distinction; but at this stage we are still within immanence. It is, however, Religiousness B—the paradoxical religiousness—that finally qualifies the distinction absolutely by accentuating existence paradoxically. Thus a man's conception of the distinction between Here and Hereafter is basically the same as his conception of what it means to exist. Now speculation views existence as an annulled abstraction, whereas in Religiousness A existence is emphasized as actuality at the expense of eternity. Religiousness B, however, not only attaches itself to both existence and the eternal but also posits an absolute contradiction between them.

Climacus then asserts that "all conceptions of existence rank in accordance with the qualification of the individual's actualization of inwardness." He thereupon applies this view schematically, demonstrating it by means of reference to the various spheres of existence (pp. 506ff.).

In the realm of thought the eternal is superior to anything historical, since it is the basis of everything. Thus in Religiousness A the individual bases his existence on his relation to the eternal, expressing this by transforming himself in actuality. Whereas speculation loses itself in pure thought, thereby dissipating all contradictions, the person in Religiousness A bases his existence on his relationship to an eternal happiness. But in Religiousness B a new dialectical contradiction emerges because the individual bases his eternal happiness on something historical, hence on approximate knowledge, which otherwise would be possible only if the individual did not himself possess an eternal qualification (p. 509). As the author has already pointed out on several occasions, all historical knowledge amounts to no more than an approximation, and this also applies to the individual's own external history. His only actuality is his own ethical actuality (p. 509).

A difficulty thus arises whenever subjective passion (not to be confused with the historian's objective passion) is put together with something historical. The difficulty is compounded because the historical fact in this case is not a simple historical fact but is made up of something that can only become historical contrary to its nature, hence by virtue of the absurd. This historical fact is that the god, an eternal being, came into existence at a definite point of time as a particular human being, thereby constituting a datum that became historical contrary to its very essence (p. 512).

Speculation has in this respect spoken of "something eternally historical" that is supposed to be readily understandable. The phrase itself, however, is a play on words; it amounts to transforming the historical into a myth, "even though in the same paragraph one contends against the mythical tendency" (p. 513).

Religiousness B is discriminative, selective, and polemical, for it lays down certain conditions that the individual must fulfill to attain to eternal happiness. This intensifies the pathos that was already present in Religiousness A. More precisely, this intensified pathos is the consciousness of sin, the possibility of offense, and the pain of sympathy.

Climacus has in his work made it difficult to become a Christian. The number of Christians among the educated is perhaps not very large, but about this Climacus can know nothing. He does know, however, that "to go further than Christianity and to fumble with the determinants with which the pagans were familiar, to go further and then, so far as concerns existence-efficiency, not to be able by far to compete with the pagans—this, to say the least, is not Christian" (p. 520). Those addressed here are the right-wing Hegelians, and first and foremost Martensen. Although Climacus has indeed made things difficult, we must not allow this to occasion a new confusion and think that the author's intention was to become important to another, let alone to the entire human race. Climacus rather regards himself as a teacher in a *Socratic* sense.

Christianity did not come into the world during the childhood of mankind but in the fullness of time. So too no person begins life as a Christian; each individual becomes one in the fullness of time—if he does (p. 523). The Christianity taught to and assimilated by a child is not Christianity strictly speaking but "idyllic mythology" (p. 523). Of course, some do appeal to a certain Scriptural passage, but unjustifiably in Climacus' view, for if we put a literal interpretation on being a child it would be nonsense to preach Christianity to adults. Childlike Christianity is certainly lovable in a child, but in an adult it results in a childish and fantastic orthodoxy that merely brings confusion in its wake. By way of example, Climacus points out that this childish orthodoxy draws attention to the fact that Christ came in the person of a lowly servant, and then assumes that the paradox consists in the contrast between lowliness and splendor. This is confusion, however, for essentially the paradox consists in the fact that God, an eternal being, came into existence in time as a particular man, so whether this man was a servant or an emperor is completely irrelevant (p. 528). Similarly, this same orthodoxy emphasizes Christ's sufferings incorrectly, ignoring the fact that in this case the paradox attaches to the circumstance that Christ came into the world *in order* to suffer. Such a childishly imaginative view is rooted in commensurability, and since commensurability is essentially paganism, the orthodox preacher who allows himself to slide into these qualifications ends up by presenting a comic form of paganism.

Following this, Climacus returns to "that Biblical passage," on this occasion sharply criticizing those scholars who exploit the Bible merely to find texts that they can use to substantiate the results of their research (p. 533).

In conclusion, Climacus sums up his deliberations by observing that objectively there are three ways in which one may define how to become or be a Christian: (A) A Christian is a person who accepts Christianity's teaching—but then along comes approximation, and this could continue without end. (B) Everything depends on assimilation, but an assimilation understood purely in categories of immediacy instead of as a specific category. (C) Whether or not a man is a Christian is determined by whether he has been baptized—but then an approximation also commences with respect to this datum. Climacus thereupon turns to the subjective definition of what it means to be a Christian. In this case the decision rests with the subject, and assimilation is not an immediate but a paradoxical inwardness that differs from any other inwardness because it is suitable to the absolute paradox. This in turn rules out approximation, at the same time making it clear that to be a Christian does not depend on directly communicable information, since no individual is able to communicate faith directly (p. 542).

Climacus does not pretend to be a Christian. He is a humorist, and as emphasized earlier a humorist will revoke everything he has said. The book concerns Climacus only; let no one appeal to it, for whoever does so will simply disclose that he has misunderstood it (p. 546).

Everything considered, Climacus the humorist is merely a private person. He detests democracy, regarding it as the most tyrannical form of government, for it obliges everyone to take a positive part in governing. Climacus prefers to remain as he is, "a learner in the art of existence" (p. 550). This brings us to the end of Climacus' work.

In a final declaration, Kierkegaard, writing directly and above his own signature, acknowledges that he is the author of the pseudonymous works. At the same time he explains that the pseudonymity was not accidentally caused by anything concerning him personally, but that it is an essential part of his authorship. There is not one single word by Kierkegaard himself in the pseudonymous books, he insists, and thus he can only entertain an opinion about them as a third party, as a reader. He requests that when quoting, the name of the respective pseudonymous author be cited.

Kierkegaard concludes his final declaration by offering thanks to Governance (God), by commemorating his deceased father, and by sincerely expressing gratitude to everyone who has kept silent and to Mynster for having spoken out (p. 553). He feels that he and the pseudonymous authors would have to agree that their only desire was to "read solo the original text of the individual, human existence-relationship, the old text, well known, handed down from the fathers—to read it through yet once more, if possible in a more inward way." He also feels that this has been accomplished, and so his final words in the book consist of an entreaty that no "half-learned man [might] lay a dialectical hand on this work, but . . . let it stand as it now stands!"

*   *   *

505
(note *):2
  all other faith is only an analogy. In *Fragments* Kierkegaard operates both with a broader concept of belief as a sense for the historical and with a stricter Christian concept of faith (*Fragments*, pp. 118ff., 129ff.; *SV* IV 286ff., 295ff.). In this passage in the *Postscript* he uses the concept of faith in the Christian sense only.

506:25
  the concealed immanence of the eternal. The meaning here is that the eternal was present in immanence but concealed, and now in Religiousness B it emerges from this concealment, revealing itself as God in time.

506:26
  ubique et nusquam. Everywhere and nowhere.

506:36
  All interpretations of existence rank in. . . . If we put the author's thoughts here into the conceptual scheme possibility/actuality, we can interpret this to mean that in the stages qualified as lower than

Christianity a person is able to approach the true being of human nature only as a potentiality. Christianity alone is able to yield actual being.

507:4   *unum noris omnes.* In knowing one, one knows them all. It is from Terent, *Phormio*, 265: "Unum cognoris, omnes noris."

510:24   *hating father and mother.* Luke 14:26.

510:32   *a new creature.* Compare 2 Cor. 5:17.

512:6   *(for at the time . . . this was not necessary).* The printed manuscript has the following note (*Pap.* VI B 98:82; *JP* III 3086):

> [*Note.*] And the difficulty involved in the miracle of creation as something happening to an existing person is thrust aside as much as possible by being baptized as a child. The thinking probably goes something like this: An infant of eight days is scarcely an existing being [*Tilværende*] and if by being baptized it becomes a Christian (at an age when usually it is hardly looked upon as a human being), all difficulties are over. But this reasoning is not the paradox; it is much, much easier to show that it is nonsense. It attempts to thrust becoming a Christian so far back esthetically that to be born and to become a Christian amount almost to the same thing. And the dark discourse about grown men becoming children again is cozily exchanged for a little very charming flattery and baby talk about an eight-day infant's superabundant meritoriousness in being an infant of eight days, not a bit older.

This is also found in the following variant in another draft (*Pap.* VI B 73:2; translation based on *JP* III 3086 above):

> And people have thrust aside the difficulty involved in the miracle of creation by being baptized as a child, probably with this thought: An infant of eight days is of course not an existing being [*en Tilværende*]; and if by being baptized it becomes a Christian, all difficulties are over. But this reasoning is unfortunately not the paradox, for it is easy to show that it is rubbish. It attempts to thrust becoming a Christian so far back esthetically that to become a Christian and to be born amount almost to the same thing.*

> * and the dark discourse about becoming a child [is] cozily exchanged for a little very charming esthetic flattery about an eight-day infant's superabundant meritoriousness in being an infant of eight days.

512:26   *To transform . . . speculatively . . . the Deity in time.* See my commentary on the *Fragments*, pp. 149ff.

513:13   *it must be formed conversely.* The printed manuscript has the following continuation (*Pap.* VI B 98:83):

> Thus I also heard a parson [*essentially the same as* Pap. *VI A 156, line 3 to p. 67, line 6;* JP III 3471, *lines 3–9:* preaching about a miracle, who, in order to make the report of it credible, first developed [the idea] that the disciples had seen it with the eyes of faith, but then, doubting the credibility of the argument himself, concentrated all his mimetic gifts, his eloquence, and perspiring efforts on the last point—that they had even seen it with their physical eyes. His Right Reverend Sir seemed to think that the certainty of the physical senses is higher than the certainty] of faith (this is already confusing enough) even with respect to a miracle which is precisely dialectical in diametrical opposition to the senses. It was a good thing he said Amen; it was the best thing he said, for he really seemed to be just as well informed about Christianity as Peer Degn was about the Greek language. Peer Degn was once able to recite the entire Lord's Prayer in Greek but now could only remember that the last word was Amen. In the final analysis things will probably end up with this becoming the definition of a sermon: It is a speech by a parson that ends with the word: Amen.

513:27   *"all theology is anthropology."* This is the main thesis in Ludwig Feuerbach, *Das Wesen des Christendums,* 2nd ed. (Leipzig, 1843; *ASKB* 488). The following appears in the Preface:

> What in these writings has so to speak been proved *a priori* (that anthropology is the secret of theology) the history of theology had long since proved and corroborated *a posteriori.*

514:3   *factual actuality.* In other words, Christianity as a historical fact.

514:6   *intermediate dialectical determinant.* Here in a positive sense.

514:8   *entered into the heart.* Compare 1 Cor. 2:9.

514:23   *actuality is the highest.* This must be understood in accordance with what was presented earlier: everything treated conceptually is thereby changed into possibility, here Christianity because it is a historical fact. (Junghans, note 792a.).

514:36   *the free-thinker asserts that Christianity is a myth.* This is David Strauss's theory in *Das Leben Jesu.*

515:26   *the requirement of the times.* After this the printed manuscript continues with (*Pap.* VI B 98:84):

> It is also possible to regard the matter differently, and although I will always be willing to admit that up to now my works have

not had any influence or been of any importance, I am also equally prepared to console myself with the consideration that, after all, they might possibly acquire such, and that judgment has not already been passed on them—for having satisfied the requirements of the times.

515:34   *the pure man.* Ideal man as viewed immanentially. A human being is unable to advance beyond immanence by means of his own strength.

515:37   *a humorous distinction.* This means the difference between those who exert themselves in order to transform their existence into Religiousness A and those who do not do anything. Essentially, they are alike, since they both remain within immanence.

516:16   *presumption of predestination.* In other words, the individual considers himself as predestined—for salvation.

516:29   *in the place of an Apostle.* See the Index.

518:20   *the autopathic collision.* An encounter in which the individual himself suffers.

520:2   *among people of culture . . . the number of Christians.* This may be an allusion to Schleiermacher, *Ueber die Religion: Reden an die Gebildeten unter ihren Verächtern,* 5th ed. (Berlin, 1843; *ASKB* 271). See above, Introduction, chap. 4.

521:1   *"a friend of tiny tots" à la Uncle Franz.* These were the principal characters in two German children's books, which had been translated into Danish: J. C. Grote, *Onkel Frants's Reise giennem alle fem Verdensdele* (Copenhagen, 1827), and K. T. Thieme, *Godman eller den danske Børneven* (Copenhagen, 1798).

521:21   *Christ . . . attracted to the young man.* Matt. 19:20ff.

521:38   *If it has happened that a father. . . .* This and the following concerning Christianity and children derive from Kierkegaard's personal experience. His father not only believed in an unusually strict upbringing but also insisted on so rigid an adherence to orthodox Christian principles that it marked Søren Kierkegaard for life. See for example *The Point of View for My Work as An Author,* p. 76 (*SV* XIII 604), *Pap.* IX A 411 (*JP* VI 6274), and the following entry (*Pap.* X¹ A 8; *JP* VI 6298):

> The joy of being a child I have never had. The frightful torments I experienced disturbed the peacefulness which must belong to being a child, to have in one's hands the capacity to be occupied etc., to give his father joy, for my inner unrest had the effect that I was always, always, outside myself.
>
> But on not rare occasions it seems as if my childhood had come back again, for unhappy as my father made me, it seems as if I

now experience being a child in my relationship to God, as if all my early life was misspent so dreadfully in order that I should experience it more truly the second time in my relationship to God.

522:12   *the people who besought.* The Gerasenes in Mark 5:17.

523:5   *that he keep silent.* Compare Faust the doubter in *Fear and Trembling*, pp. 116ff. (*SV* III 171ff.).

523:9   *the fullness of time.* Gal. 4:4.

523:28   *It is the idea of childishness.* The printed manuscript has (*Pap.* VI B 98:85):

> It is the idea of femininity and childlikeness, it is the lovable meeting of the generations the moment one generation becomes aware that it is deposing the other. When the vague aspirations of youth are over, when there is a pause within maturity and the eternal shines back in existence [*Existentsen*], then the love of mother and father transfigures [*forklarer*] itself in religiousness.

524:24   *easy for a child to enter into.* An allusion to Matt. 18:3.

524:28   *"Suffer the little children."* Matt. 19:14.

525:2   *teleological suspensions of the ethical.* In other words, an intentional and temporary invalidation of the ethical. See the description of Abraham in *Fear and Trembling*.

525:15   *the disciples who rebuked the children.* Matt. 19:13.

525:31   *turn Christianity into moonlight.* That is, into something fantastic.

525(note *):1   τοιοῦτοι. Kierkegaard's explanation of the correlative itself is taken from C. G. Bretschneider, *Lexicon manuale graeco-latinum in libros novi Testamenti*, 2nd ed., I-II (Leipzig, 1829; *ASKB* 73-4). This extremely doubtful interpretation, however, is his own.

526:27   *An orthodoxy.* Perhaps the target here is Grundtvig.

527:15   *the objection raised by Nicodemus.* John 3:4 and 5:18ff.

527:22   *the determinant faith.* That is, the concept or definition.

527:37   *Such a childish orthodoxy.* Whether or not a definite allusion is intended here has not been determined.

527:39   *in the lowly form of a servant.* The phrase is taken from Phil. 2:7. See H. Roos, "Søren Kierkegaard und die Kenosis-Lehre," *Kierkegaardiana*, II (Copenhagen, 1957), pp. 54-61, and A. Grillmeier and H. Bacht, *Das Konzil von Chalkedon*, I-III (Würzburg, 1979), III, 531-611.

529:7   *an army of analogies.* Here the meaning is "the last reserves."

529:19   *a fantastic view of life (the transmigration of souls).* Kierkegaard's description seems almost to fit the doctrine of reincarnation as found in the *Upanishads*. Kierkegaard, however, was not very well acquainted with Indian thinking, though he did own Friedrich Schlegel, *Ueber die Sprache und Weisheit der Indier* (Heidelberg, 1808; *ASKB* 1388). As to Buddha, who taught liberation from the evolutionary cycle and from the suffering that he believed constituted life, Kierkegaard may have read about him in Hegel's *Lectures on the Philosophy of Religion*, II, 63ff. (*Jub. Ausg.* XV 415ff.).

530:23   *not John the Baptist even.* John 1:31, 33.

530:25   *Isaiah had prophesied.* Isa. 53:4: "Yet it was our infirmities that he bore, our sufferings that he endured, while we thought of him as stricken, as one smitten by God and afflicted."

530:34   *bona fide.* In good faith.

533:24   *the abundant time of eternity behind him.* One may compare this with the first paragraph of a journal entry from 1848 (*Pap.* IX A 42; *JP* VI 6152):

> God be praised, there will be time in eternity to think every thought through to the smallest particular. There, thinking will not mean anything but to think; it will not mean earning a living, acquiring honors and status—and being understood by others—by means of a few half-digested thoughts.

533:27   *Lot's wife was turned to stone.* Gen. 19:26.

533:28   *the abomination of desolation.* In Dan. 8:13 and passim. This is actually a designation for the altar of Zeus Olympios, which Antiochus Epiphanes had erected on the holocaust altar in the Temple of Jerusalem. The phrase, however, is often employed—as here—in a misunderstood figurative sense.

534:33   *Cromwell, who indeed was a practised Bible-reader.* Presumably this is merely something that Kierkegaard remembered from his school days.

534:36   *Protector.* This was Oliver Cromwell's and his son Richard's title from 1653 to 1659.

535(note   *an intermediary determinant.* Here the meaning is "common denom-
*):3   inator." In the religiousness of immanence the relationship to God is direct; immanence, in which there is no leap, is the common denominator for any direct relationship to God.

538:4   *the Turk and the Russian and the Roman yoke.* Kierkegaard is referring to Grundtvig, who in *Nordens Mythologie eller Sindbilled-Sprog*, 2nd ed., rev. (Copenhagen, 1832; *ASKB* 1949), pp. 45ff., had explained that "the Danes sought refuge so far north because they had sworn rather to bury themselves in the waves than to bend beneath the Roman yoke." In a speech titled *Om Nordens historiske Forhold* ("On the Historical Circumstances of the North" [Copenhagen, 1843],

p. 19) he maintained that without the migrations from the north "the Middle Ages would have had to be content with the exploits and world histories of the Byzantines and Arabs, and modern times with those of the Russians and the Turks."

538:17   *the category "quite differently."* Junghans in his note to this passage recalls to mind the part played by the concept *das ganz andere* in the so-called dialectic theology of the 1920s and 1930s, remarking that by means of his pseudonyms Kierkegaard here repudiates an erroneous use of this category. We must note, however, that even though the phrase in the *Postscript* is the same as that frequently employed during the interwar years in German philosophy of religion and systematic theology, the same thing is not understood by it. In the *Postscript* it is used within the sphere of immediacy, whereas in Rudolf Otto, *Das Heilige* (Munich, 1917), for example, it is used to denote the divine *mysterium tremendum et fascinosum*, which corresponds to the absolute paradox in Kierkegaard.

539:23   *by the witness it bears with his spirit.* Compare Rom. 8:16.

539:32   *the orthodoxy which especially has made baptism the decisive mark.* Grundtvigianism.

540:5   *This how can only correspond to one thing.* See in this respect the Index: subjectivity.

540:16   *He who within a higher knowledge . . . faith as an annulled factor.* That is, annulled in speculative philosophy.

541:10   *the Danish Government transferred the English three percent loan.* In 1825 the Danish government negotiated a loan that was underwritten by the English banking firm of Wilson. When that firm went bankrupt in 1837, L. N. Rothschild took over the loan contract.

542(note   The draft has (*Pap.* VI B 82): "for the person who says it directly
*)   betrays himself, because it must be said indirectly, and this will prevent any cheating and all the parroting afterwards, at seventh hand."

543:3   *a scoffer attacks Christianity.* In all likelihood the target is Ludwig Feuerbach; see the Index.

543:13   *the talent which Socrates so much admired in Polos.* See Plato's *Gorgias.*

543:15   *The ironist then is on the watch.* Kierkegaard touches on this subject in *The Book On Adler* (*Pap.* VII² B 235, p. 158):

Ironic artfulness culminates in the stratagem with which one makes a person speak about himself, denounce himself, reveal himself, just when in his own mind he is not speaking about himself at all and, what is more, has even forgotten himself. It is one thing to become acquainted with a man's inner [self] when he opens himself up to one in confidence, and it is another thing to direct his attention to another point at the very moment one is speaking with his inner [self] with each word of his. Whenever a man says something extraordinary about himself it is ironically correct to believe him (the negative lies in not resisting him directly, in not denying it by yelling positively) in order by this means and with the help of one's own ingenuousness to make it evident that it is false and to coax the lie out of him. The ingenuousness appears to be an affirmation, precisely in order to bring the denial out in the open. It is easy to see how the concept veers around. By means of his ingenuousness the ironist makes the boaster careless: and so he is caught.

543:28   *lose his life for this opinion.* Compare John 10:12, 15.

544:23   *once in this work.* On pp. 57–58.

545: title   *APPENDIX.* The preliminary draft has this heading and observation (*Pap.* VI B 83:1):

Revocation
Johannes Climacus and His Reader

In margin: This little appendix should contain the humoristic revocation—for all humor is revocation.

545:20   *the whole work.* The preliminary draft then has (*Pap.* VI B 83:2):

From the foregoing the reader (if I have any, let alone any on this last page) will recollect that there were two events in my life that made me decide to be an author: first, when it dawned on me at the café out at Frederiksberg Gardens that I had to try to make something diffcult, in order at least to be doing something, too; and then the scene in the graveyard,* which decisively brought my attention to bear on Christianity. The whole. . . .

   * *In margin:* a couple of months later.

546:20   *So then the book is superfluous.* The preliminary draft has the following (*Pap.* VI B 83:3):

In margin:
Let no one trouble himself to appeal to me; for whoever appeals to me has *eo ipso* misunderstood me. But still less let anyone take the trouble to attack me§—for I say it before[hand,] I revoke everything. What a man does for the sake of enjoyment should not cause him worries.† If, for example, the censor should take it into his head to suppress anything, even the slightest thing, I will revoke the whole book; and just as when a man wants to take a drive one day and it threatens to rain, and he thinks: It's not worth the trou-

ble, and he then stays home and saves his money—this is the way I think, and I revoke the book. I can well imagine that whoever writes a book might prefer to change a single passage to have the whole book come out; but why should I, since I do it solely for the sake of my own enjoyment? For the enjoyment is the main thing; if a man is going to spend his money he also ought to get enjoyment out of it, and if he does not, he at least ought to have the enjoyment of saving his money.

§ in a way that will oblige me to reply (still less by prosecuting me according to the law and justice of the land).

† and I do not feel within me the remotest disposition or inclination to become a martyr, or even to resemble one. Should I happen to be put to death as a martyr, then one may be sure that it darned well [sgu] is not my fault; for I revoke everything.

The final draft (Pap. VI B 86:2) has this variant:

And above all let him not appeal to me in such a way that through him* I might become the object of attacks, perhaps even of legal proceedings. If that should happen, I will revoke everything; I do not feel the remotest disposition, inclination, or need to become a martyr, or to resemble one in any way.† Should it nevertheless so happen that I am put to death as a martyr: then one may be sure that it darned well is not my fault.

In margin: And above all I protest against any violence, against anyone appealing to the book in such a way.

* In margin: in these religiously turbulent times.

† The person who regards it as a nuisance even to acquire significance must find it far too offensive to acquire significance in this way.

The final draft then has the following in connection with "For An Understanding with the Reader" (Pap. VI B 87):

All I need is for a party-liner to appeal to me in such a way that I would be dragged away and executed. But this would after all be completely impossible—that I should become a martyr or be executed for an opinion, I, who have no opinion at all and always revoke on the third page what is said on the two preceding, insofar as anyone might think that it was my opinion.

I desire no proof from actuality of the fact that I really have an opinion (a follower, a hurrah, being executed, and so forth), for I have no desire to have any opinion at all.

547:11   *a Revocation.* The printed manuscript then has (*Pap.* VI B 98:87):

> Above all I protest in advance against any violence, against any-one appealing to the book in such a way that with his quoting in these religiously turbulent times I might become an object of at-tacks, perhaps even of legal proceedings. If that should happen, I will revoke everything; through an earnest self-examination I have assured myself that I do not have the slightest disposition, com-petence, or need to become a martyr or to resemble one in the remotest way. If it is a nuisance even to acquire significance, it is really too offensive to acquire it in this manner. Should I never-theless happen to be put to death as a martyr, then one thing is certain: it darned well is not my fault!

547:13   *not even a publisher.* The *Postscript* was published on commission by publisher C. A. Reitzel. In August 1847 he also took over the re-maining stocks of the other books on consignment that Kierkegaard had published through this publishing house and on which he earned 2,000 *Rdl.* all told. See Frithiof Brandt and Else Rammel, *Søren Kier-kegaard og Pengene* (Copenhagen, 1935), pp. 17–20.

547:25   *"Only the positive."* The preliminary draft has in addition (*Pap.* VI B 83:4):

> and of course only the positive is an encroachment on the personal freedom of another; the negative is a politeness that deters a man from calling one single real person his reader.
>
> *In margin*: to say nothing of inconveniencing an entire reading public that, even if it never regrets the inconvenience because the importance of the writing is so great, nevertheless ought to be regarded as fully employed. One should not inconvenience people without producing results.

> *Continuation to 83 [Pap. VI B 84]*:
> What if I put the conclusion of the Preface here [*in pencil*: pp. 5 and 6].
>
> > For if I must tell you myself, My Dear Reader—and then the whole thing.
> >
> > Such a fictitious reader under-stands one; one can speak with him in complete confidence.
>
> My Dear Reader, I am anything but a devil of a fellow in spec-ulation.

The final draft then has the following (*Pap.* VI B 88):

Nor can I see why anyone should be so desirous of participating in the government of the country. I think as follows: As long as somebody is willing, then I am darned [*sgu*] happy, and one of my private concerns is rather how it would all end if no one were willing.

It is also curious that our age is so prone to pull great men down; it seems to me that one of life's conveniences consists in the very fact that there are such distinguished men. We do not ourselves have to entertain an opinion about things that do not concern us directly; we can accept the distinguished man's as correct without further ceremony.

548:32   *If I have to say it myself.* This statement is explained as follows in *Pap.* VI A 140 (*JP* I 1038, except marginal note, which was omitted):

The meaning of the last section in the Introduction (or if it comes to be in the Appendix): "For if I say so myself, I am anything but a devilish good fellow," etc., is that on the whole there can be no schoolmaster, strictly understood, in the art of existing [*at existere*]. This is said often enough in the book, but it is said here in such a way that many will understand it straightforwardly, and yet probably no one will raise an objection. Barbs bristle in the words: "the ambiguous art"* and farther on, "be this a joyful or sorrowful sign," joyful, namely, that there is no one, because he who will straightforwardly be this is a fool, and finally, "far be it from me, the vain and empty thought of wanting to be such a teacher" (vain here in the biblical sense).—With respect to existing, there is only the learner, for anyone who fancies that he is in this respect finished, that he can teach others and on top of that himself forgets to exist and to learn, is a fool. In relation to existing there is for all existing persons one schoolmaster—existence itself.

* *In margin*: thereupon: then something will darned well come of it. The meaning is either that someone might learn something by being a witness, for being a witness is not direct communication; or it would become clear that there is no instructor.

548:36   *casibus.* Here the meaning is the tribulations of life.
548:39   *Stygotius.* In Holberg's *Jacob von Tyboe* (Act II, Scene 5) Magister Stygotius boasts that "all the *literati* talk about me out in Rostock, Helmstad, and Wittenberg."
549:1   *disputations.* The meaning here is either that he participated in ex-

ercises in the art of disputation or that he held a disputation for the Magister degree, as Stygotius.

549:17   *If only among us.* The final draft reads (*Pap.* VI B 94):

> In case there is an instructor among our philosophers who will take me in charge, not an instructor in the classical disciplines, for we have one and I am by no means worthy to be his student; not in historical philosophy, for which I perhaps do not have the necessary preliminary knowledge; but an instructor in thinking about existence [*Existents*] and existing [*existere*]: then I can safely guarantee that something will come of it, all right [*essentially the same as SV VII 614, lines 6–14*]. But since no such instructor so far has tendered his services, I myself will hazard the attempt to present something as a learner [*essentially the same as SV VII 614, lines 22–26*]. Perhaps in this respect I will not even be believed. For whenever someone in our age says: I know everything, he is believed, but he who says: There is much that I do not know—he cannot be trusted. In Scribe a man experienced in love affairs relates that he [*essentially the same as SV VII 614, lines 35–38*].

549:18   *teacher of classical learning.* Kierkegaard was thinking about Johan Nicolai Madvig (1804–1886), a classical philologist who even in his own time had earned European celebrity, especially as a textual critic. His editions of Cicero are still very well known.

549:21   *teacher of the history of philosophy* [not philosophy of history as S/L have]. Presumably this is aimed at Martensen, but there is also the possibility that Kierkegaard was thinking about Christian Molbech (1783–1857), a historian who from the beginning of the 1840s allowed himself to be somewhat influenced by Hegel's philosophy.

549:23   *teacher in . . . the religious address.* Mynster.

549:29   *teacher in the fine art of poetry.* Probably J. L. Heiberg.

549:35   *by Jove.* The Danish *sgu* is a contraction of *saa Gud,* "by God," and even today is hardly used in good company. See *ODS,* SVIII, cols. 333, 1157ff. (Note by R.J.W.)

550:4   *offers.* The Danish *profiterer* means both "to offer instruction" and "to make a profit." See *ODS,* SVI, cols. 1356ff. (Note by R.J.W.)

550:17   *"There is much I do not know."* See in conjunction with this *Pap.* V A 46 (*JP* III 3299):

> Danish philosophy—if there ever comes to be such a thing—will be different from German philosophy in that it definitely will not begin with nothing or without any presuppositions whatsoever or explain everything by mediating, because, on the contrary, it be-

gins with the proposition that there are many things between heaven
and earth which no philosophy has explained.

By being incorporated in philosophy, this proposition will provide the necessary corrective and will also cast a humorous-edify-
ing warmth over the whole.

550:18   *a play by Scribe*. *Une chaîne*, translated into Danish under the title
En Lænke ("A Fetter"; Act IV, Scene 1). With respect to Kierkegaard's use of Eugène Scribe see Ronald Grimsley, *Søren Kierkegaard
and French Literature. Eight Comparative Studies* (Cardiff, 1966), pp.
112–29.

551: title   *A FIRST AND LAST DECLARATION*. The printed manuscript has (*Pap.* VI B 99):

[In pencil: No!]

Note. *[In pencil: No!]*

As a matter of form, and for several other reasons that are not
worth the trouble to enumerate, I formally acknowledge what in
reality cannot interest either anyone to know or me that they know
it: that I am the author of an article in *Flyveposten*, and so forth,—

---

and also that I have never written anything else; and with this I in
addition take leave of the reader, if I ever had any at all.†

For, to use an expression from ninepins: Now that I've hit all
nine, that's the end of that game.

S.K.

† To the reading public I fortunately do not owe much regarding
either pecuniary income or a mark of honor. On the other hand, I
do feel bound to thank the God who granted that I might express
what I wished to express exactly as I desired it, the God who
favored [me] in external circumstances, the God who blessed the
efforts of laboring thought, who often transformed [*omskabte*] mute
pain into a refreshing expression—to thank Him, something I ordinarily prefer to do in secret but which I now do openly as if in
the presence of others, whether or not they smile or wonder at it,
remain ignorant of it, or are moved by it.

If God turns the whole thing into
a jest for me, if the work is not
going to be of any importance at
all to anyone, and if I am not going
to have any readers at all, it will
not on that account be a jest or less

> sacred and serious to me, since for
> me it was my work, and it would
> not have been more sacred to me
> if I had known that I was going to
> have a great number of readers.

551:1   There are several more drafts to "A First And Last Declaration" in *Pap*. VII¹ B 74–80 (see *JP* V 5864), to which the reader is referred. See also *Pap*. VII¹ A 2 (*JP* V 5871) with references, which is quoted above in the note to the title page.

551:9   *an article in Fædrelandet*. The first of these articles, "An Expression of Gratitude to Herr Professor Heiberg" (*SV* XIII 448–52; *Fædrelandet*, no. 1168, March 3, 1843), was a biting reply by Victor Eremita to Heiberg's maladroit review of *Either/Or*. The two articles by Frater Taciturnus are "The Activities of a Travelling Esthetician, And How He Nevertheless Happened to Pay for the Banquet" (*SV* XIII 459–67; *Fædrelandet*, no. 2078, December 27, 1845) and "The Dialectical Result of A Literary Police Transaction" (*SV* XIII 468–71; *Fædrelandet*, no. 9, January 10, 1846). In the first article Taciturnus attacks P. L. Møller's *Gæa* and challenges *Corsaren* to abuse him; the second article continues his attack on *Corsaren* (see above, Introduction, chap. 9). These are, however, not the only articles that Kierkegaard published pseudonymously or anonymously.

553:6   *the evasively dialectical doubleness* [S/L: with paralogistic insolence]. The word *eviterende* is the present participle of *evitere*, a foreign word derived from the Latin *evadere*, to evade. The meaning here is to avoid a direct relationship. See Ludvig Meyer, *Kortfattet Lexicon over fremmede . . . forekommende Ord, Konstudtryk og Talemaader . . .* (Copenhagen, 1837), p. 192. Kierkegaard owned the second and third editions of this work (Copenhagen, 1844 and 1853; *ASKB* 1034 and 1035).

553:27   *the honorarium has, to say the least, been rather Socratic*. Socrates did not exact payment for his instruction. Kierkegaard made a profit of about 2,000 *Rdl*. from his books on consignment and a little less than 3,000 *Rdl*. from royalties after 1847. See Frithiof Brandt and Else Rammel, *Søren Kierkegaard og Pengene* (Copenhagen, 1935), p. 36. The following may be quoted in connection with Kierkegaard's own remarks here and elsewhere (ibid., pp. 48–9):

> But of course an author also has to live. On this subject, too, Kierkegaard had an opinion that completely agrees with academic thinking. It proceeds from the simple fact that a man is worth his work, a fact that applies as much to an author as it does to anybody

else. It is quite in order that an author who serves an idea likewise earns money, and Kierkegaard has nothing against an author earning a fortune as an author. The only thing an author may not do in his authorship is pare down the requirements of the idea *in order* to earn money. If the author is "an essential author" and lives in a small country, he will be unable to make a living from his activity as an author. In that case it is reasonable for the state to assist him, if the state would otherwise call itself a cultured state. This is Kierkegaard's basic point of view concerning what it means to be an author and to earn money as an author.

553:42　　*the signature Kts.* That is, Mynster, who in periodicals signed his articles "Kts" (Jakob Peter Mynster).

554:13　　*half-learned man.* The Danish *Halvbefaren* is a nautical term that was applied to a seaman who had sailed for eighteen months and made at least two major voyages. The more commonly used *Helbefaren* (experienced) once denoted a seaman who had sailed for thirty-six months and made four major voyages. See *ODS*, VII, cols. 771, 1069. (Note by R.J.W.)

INDEX

Abelard, Peter, 24, 27
abrogation, 266, 268
absolute (the), 44, 95
absolute idea, 56, 94
absolute relationship, 337-38
absolute telos, 337-38, 348ff., 357
abstract thought, 300, 302, 311
abstraction (see also thought), 57, 260, 377
absurd, 253, 264, 368-69, 375-76, 378
Academy, 171
acosmism, 318
actuality, 11, 35, 93-94, 100-101, 300ff., 310-11, 312-13, 316, 317, 319, 326, 351, 382
Adelard of Bath, 27
Adler, Adolph Peter, 78-79, 187, 227
Adresseavisen, 205, 354
Aenesidemus, 169
Agrippa of Nettesheim, 33
ἀκίνετος πάντα κινεῖ, 352
Aladdin, 234, 249
Albert the Great, 27
Alberti, Leone Battista, 31
Alcibiades, 209
Altenstein, Karl zum, 51
Ambrosius, 21
amusement, 350
Anabaptists, 192, 327
Anaxagoras, 299
Anaximander, 5
Anaximenes, 5
Andersen, Hans Christian, 353
Andersen, Vilhelm, 153
Anfægtelse; see spiritual trial
Anselm of Canterbury, 25-26, 75, 316
an sich (see also *Ding-an-sich*), 313, 317
anthropology, 102ff., 201, 246, 382
antinomies, 41
Antiochus Epiphanes, 385
Antisthenes, 10
antitheses (see also contrasts), 53
Antoninus, Marcus Aurelius, 237

anxiety, 105, 285
apathy, 171
apeiron, 5
apologetics, 19, 159
Apostles, 176-77, 355
approximation, 163, 164, 173, 264, 323, 377, 379
Aquinas, Thomas, 26, 28ff., 164, 198, 289
Arcesilaus, 169
Aristippus, 10
Aristophanes, 9n, 218, 245
Aristotle, 11ff., 23-24, 27ff., 50, 54, 99, 103, 155, 160, 181-82, 201, 215, 224, 234, 241, 262, 291, 298-99, 301, 303, 307, 308, 310, 312, 318, 319, 351-52, 364, 366
Arndt, Johann, 358
art, 44, 53, 60, 83, 204, 309, 321, 363-64
assimilation, 251ff., 379
astronomy, 238-39, 241, 242, 249
ataraxy (ataraxia), 171, 311
Atomists, 8
atonement, 169, 277, 324, 331
Augustine, 18ff., 21-22, 24, 26-27, 29, 32, 200
authority, 166
autonomy, 75
autopathic, 281, 383
Averroes, 27, 334
Avicenna, 27

Baader, Franz von, 33, 45, 72, 75-76, 230, 240, 306
Bacon, Robert, 27
"bad infinity," 87, 92, 97, 225-26, 317
Baggesen, Jens I., 155, 305, 346
Bailey, Herbert S., Jr., xi
Balle, Nicolai E., 217-18
baptism, 127, 173, 191-92, 193, 323, 326-27, 328, 381, 386
Baptists, 191ff., 320, 327, 359

Barfod, Povl Frederik, 240
Barth, Karl, x
Baur, Ferdinand Christian, 74
Beck, A. F., 79, 266
becoming, 54, 82-83, 92, 96-97, 168, 205, 206-207, 213, 222, 266, 333
beginning, 158-59, 221, 225ff., 228, 237-38, 309-310
being, 6, 9, 27, 33, 54, 93, 96-97, 168, 206-207, 222, 225, 227, 251, 255, 268, 304, 310, 311, 313, 331-32
belief (see also faith), 164-65
Bengel, J. A., 229
Berengar of Tours, 25
Bessarion, Cardinal, 31
Bhagavad-Gita, 370
Bible, 25, 38, 55, 74, 81, 102ff., 163ff., 167, 173, 174ff., 184, 188, 189, 323, 329
Biel, Gabriel, 30
Billroth, J.F.F., 64
bittweise, 197-98, 317
Black Peter, 317
Blicher, Steen Steensen, 315
Boccaccio, Giovanni, 31
Boehme, Jacob, 33, 44-45, 52, 54
Boesen, A. F., 236
Boethius, 24, 27
Bonaventura, St., 27
border region; see confine
Bornemann, Johan Alfred, 88, 306
Borup, Morten, 126
Brandt, C. J., 125
Breman, Herman von, 360
Brorson, Hans Adolph, 167
Brunel, Sir Marc I., 166
Bruno, Giordano, 32
Brutus, 181
Bruun, Thomas C., 217-18
Buddha, 385
Buffon, Georges, 373
Bultmann, Rudolf, x

Caesar, Julius, 281
Callicles, 217, 292
Calvin, John, 200
Campanella, Tommaso, 32
canon (χανών), 165
Carl Emanuel, Duke, 236
Carneades, 93n, 169

Carové, Friedrich Wilhelm, 63
Carpocratians, 14
catechumen, 216
Catherine II, 290
Cato the Elder, 205
cause, 12, 40, 42, 164
Celsus, 20
"center" Hegelians, 63, 65, 79
Cerberus, 331
Cervantes, Miguel de, 174
change, 6ff., 8, 11ff., 54, 331ff.
chaos, 3
Charles XII, King, 315
Charron, Pierre, 33, 169
childhood, 371, 372; Kierkegaard's, 383-84
childlikeness, 368, 384
children, 330, 378-79, 381
chiliasm, 342
China, 233, 238, 282
choice, 105, 108, 157, 336
Christ, 18, 20, 29, 48, 86, 106, 109-10, 154, 200, 271, 273, 277, 379
Christendom, 323, 329
Christensen, Peter Wilhelm, 124ff., 129-30
Christian VIII, King, 193
Christianity, 60-61, 66, 68, 72ff., 81, 109ff., 132ff., 156, 158, 163, 232, 253-54, 260ff., 265, 270-71, 278ff., 285, 296, 303, 322ff., 327, 329, 330, 369, 375, 378, 380, 382
Chrysippus, 93n
Church, 157, 165, 173, 174ff., 189, 190, 199-200, 373; visible, 200
Cicero, 156, 270, 317
Clapperton, Hugh, 272
Claudius, Mathias, 342
Clausen, Henrik Nicolai, 71, 74-75, 157, 189, 191, 229, 342, 370
Clement of Alexandria, 20, 204
clergy, 287
Climacus, Johannes, 109-10, 113, 117-18, 133-34, 154, 156, 263, 280, 356, 379-80
cogito ergo sum, 311
cognition (see also knowledge), 28ff., 33-34, 53-54, 75, 81, 104, 161, 168
coknowledge, 75, 241
comic, 291, 348, 350-51, 363, 366, 373

coming-into-existence, 6, 99ff., 164, 202, 221, 300, 333
Commission of Arbitration, 330
communication, 102, 111, 113ff., 118, 202, 219, 253, 278-79, 283, 284, 290, 294, 324, 334
concepts, 27, 30, 40-41, 53-54, 57, 69, 92ff., 94, 98, 159, 314, 330
confine (confinium), 350
Confucius, 238
Constantius, Constantin, 284, 285, 294
contemporaneity, 112, 154, 247, 303
contingency, 311
continuity, 73, 301, 339, 348
contradiction, 38, 55, 82, 88ff., 93-94, 98, 168, 212, 229, 259, 271, 306, 307, 314, 340, 350-51, 363, 377
contrasts (opposites), 55ff., 94, 168-69, 314, 333
conventions, 359-60
Copernicus, Nicholas, 33, 120
copula, 254
Corsaren, 118ff., 130-31, 373, 393
cosmology, 3, 9, 13, 22-23, 32-33, 80, 94, 109n
cosmos, 3-4, 11, 32, 44, 94, 314
creation, 25, 103-104, 106, 381
credo ut intelligam, 25, 75
Creed (Apostles'), 173, 175ff.
Crito, 274
Critobulus, 275
Croesus, King, 170
Cromwell, Oliver, 383
Cromwell, Richard, 385
Cullmann, Oscar, 200

Daub, Carl, 63, 67-68, 75, 304
death, 242-43, 343
decision, 159, 329, 338, 343, 361
Deer Park, 240, 348
Delbrück, Ferdinand, 175ff.
democracy, 380
Democritus, 8
demon, 205-206
Den Frisindede, 355
Descartes, René, 22, 26, 33ff., 70, 75, 169, 256, 311, 316
despair, 105, 108, 112, 353, 366
determinate being, 92, 95-96, 268, 346
determinism, 58

dialectical doubleness, 393
dialectics, 25-26, 199, 329, 335
difference, 337, 350
difficulties, 338-39
Ding-an-sich (see also an sich), 42, 51
Dion, 318
Dionysius, 318
disputations, 24, 229, 390
divine idea, 92ff.
Döbler, Ludwig, 256-57
Døbler; see Döbler, Ludwig
docents, 210-11, 299
doctrine, 324
dogmatics, ix, 42, 46, 68, 375
Don Juan, 346
Don Quixote, 174
double movement, 109
double reflection, 205, 219, 283, 294
doubt, 22, 34-35, 82, 108, 169
δόξα, 375-76
Drachmann, Anders Bjørn, 144
drama, 227
dualism, 14, 44-45, 66
Duns Scotus, John, 26, 29-30
dying from, 349

earnestness (see also seriousness), 262, 366
Eckhart, Meister, 76
edification, 278ff., 288, 289
edifying discourses, 282
ego, 42-43, 228, 230
Eiríksson, Magnús, 130ff., 210
ekklesia, 199-200
Eleatics, 307, 331ff.
Elrod, John W., 109n
Elysium, 296
emanation, 15-16, 18, 25, 44, 56, 343
Empedocles, 8-9, 235
empiricism, 41
ends; see telos
engagement, 285
epistemology, ix, 40-41, 70, 91-92
Erdmann, Johann Eduard, 64, 295
Erigena, John Scotus, 24-25, 54
erotic, 285
essence, 92-93, 188, 310, 312, 341, 358
esthetic (esthetics), 60, 348ff.
eternal, 47, 106-107, 202-203, 259-62
eternal happiness, 193, 213-14, 329,

eternal happiness (*cont.*)
335ff., 338, 340, 341, 349-50, 367ff., 377
eternal unhappiness, 213-14
eternity, 285, 357, 385
ethics (the ethical), 9, 59, 108-109, 113, 232, 235, 239, 278ff., 281, 302, 305, 335, 350, 362, 384
Eunomius, 21
Eusebius, 20
evil, 14, 18, 33, 37, 45, 59, 230
ex cathedra, 359
exclusion, principle of, 89, 306, 307, 345
existence, 26, 91-92, 96, 98ff., 104, 108, 188, 197, 221-22, 271, 276, 278, 283, 284, 300ff., 304, 310, 311, 322, 327, 334, 339, 345, 361, 377ff., 380, 384
existing individual, 212, 260ff.
externality, 336-37, 363

Fædrelandet, 393
faith, 17, 20ff., 24-25, 28-29, 38, 69, 73, 75, 105, 107ff., 157-58, 163, 165, 252-53, 260-63, 302-303, 307, 320, 330, 375-76, 380, 386
Faust, 248, 384
feeling, 157, 303, 364
femininity, 294, 384
Fenger, Rasmus Theodor, 125
Feuerbach, Ludwig, 65ff., 79, 133, 244, 382, 386
Fibiger, Johannes, 78
Fichte, Immanuel Hermann, 64ff., 72, 244
Fichte, Johann Gottlieb, 42-43, 49, 159, 161, 201, 226, 228, 254, 255, 318
Ficino, Marcilio, 31
Fischer, G. Philipp, 65
Fischer, Kuno, 63
flagellants, 358
forgiveness of sin, 263
Frederik VI, King, 249
Frederik Ferdinand, 355
freedom, 41, 45, 47, 59, 100-101, 106, 243, 311
Fridrichsen, Anton, 200
Friendly Society, 276
Fry, Elisabeth, 192, 257
fullness of time, 378

Gabler, Georg Andreas, 62-63
Gad, Knud, 342
Gans, Eduard, 63
Ganzheitsdenken, 56
Garrick, David, 241
Gleim, Johan Wilhelm Ludwig, 218
Gnosticism (Gnostics), 13-14, 19, 318, 343
god, the, 263, 264, 276, 302, 378
God-becoming, 325
God-relationship, 104ff., 252, 337-38, 350, 362
Goethe, Johann Wolfgang von, 8, 44, 75, 77, 248, 293, 345
Goeze, Johann Melchior, 212, 222
Goldkalb, Salomon, 235, 297, 298
Goldschmidt, Meïr Aaron, 371
good, the, 9-10, 33, 230
Gorgias, 170, 342, 366
Göschel, Karl Friedrich, 244, 258
Gregory of Nyssa, 20-21
Grundtvig, Nikolaj Frederik Severin, 24, 71, 125ff., 161-62, 173, 174-75, 178-88, 194-95, 236, 316, 344, 353, 359, 360, 369, 374, 375, 384, 385
guilt, 107, 111, 198, 367ff., 373
Guldberg, Ove Hiegh, 217
Günther, Anton, 65
Gyllembourg, Thomasine, 126, 132, 245, 287

Hamann, Johann Georg, 38, 102, 153, 277, 284, 295, 351, 374
Hamlet, 365
Hartspring, Dr., 233, 247
Haufniensis, Vigilius, 246, 284
Hegel, Georg Wilhelm Friedrich, 3, 14-15, 24, 32ff., 36, 45, 48ff., 130, 149, 152, 157, 160-61, 170, 172, 199, 201, 215, 218, 220, 228, 237, 243, 248, 259, 297, 299, 303, 304-305, 306, 307, 312, 316, 317, 319-20, 321, 326, 329-30, 331, 343, 363-64, 369-70, 371, 372; and Denmark, 70ff.; and ethics, 362; and Germany, 62ff.; and history, 233-34, 235, 236, 238, 282; and Kierkegaard, 91ff.; and logic, 92-98, 158-59, 168, 198-99, 215, 223-24, 226, 268,

309ff., 313-14, 345, 346, 358, 369; biography, 49ff.; his system, 51-61
Hegelianism; *see* Hegel, left-wing, right-wing
Heiberg, Johan Ludvig, 14, 77, 81-82, 85ff., 99, 120, 126, 155, 208, 220, 226-27, 233, 235, 237, 239, 241, 245-46, 247ff., 275, 297, 298, 306, 342, 345, 351, 365, 391
Heiberg, Johanne Luise, 244
Helveg, Pastor, 240
Helweg, Friedrich, 209
Helweg, Ludvig, 208-209
Hemsterhuis, H., 258
Hengstenberg, Ernst Wilhelm, 71
Henning, Leopold von, 63
Henry IV, King, 236
Heraclitus, 6, 55, 307, 308-309, 331ff.
Herder, Johann Gottfried, 38, 46, 277
Hereafter, 326, 329, 377
Hesiod, 212
hierarchy, 11, 13, 22-23, 37, 44, 54
Himmelstrup, Jens, 310-11
Hinrichs, Hermann F. W., 63
Hippias Major, 340
Hirsch, Emanuel, 249
history (historical), 57, 161-62, 198-99, 203, 215, 232, 233, 235, 236, 239, 240, 258, 320, 323, 326, 338, 373, 377ff., 382
Hoffmann, Ernst T. A., 242
Holberg, Ludvig, 156, 168, 170, 210, 243, 257, 293, 324, 354, 365, 390
Holck, Hans, 205
Hölderlin, Friedrich, 49
Holkot, Robert, 307
Holophernes, 365, 371
Homer, 205
Hong, Howard V., 164
hope, 296
Hostrup, Jens Peter, 235
Hotho, Heinrich G., 51, 63
How, 252, 263, 302, 386
Hubert-Becker, Dr., 246
Hume, David, 30, 32
humility, 350
humor (humorist), 113ff., 348, 350, 363, 368, 387
hymnal, 359-60

I = I (*see also* ego, identity), 221, 228, 300, 329
Icarus, 369
idea, 10-11, 27, 41, 44, 57, 66, 95-96, 199, 236, 314
idealism, 10-11, 31, 35, 42, 45, 48, 50ff., 99, 311, 325
identity, 35-36, 44, 52, 55, 66, 88-89, 197, 199, 221, 228, 229-30, 254, 255, 304, 345, 373
ignorance, 9, 361
imagination, 303
immanence, 114, 214, 255, 278, 285, 367-68, 373, 377ff., 380, 383, 385
immediacy, 157, 158-59, 226, 320, 336-37, 348ff., 373
immortality, 64ff., 84, 243-44, 246, 300, 373
imprimatur, 170
Incarnation, 29, 61, 87, 374
incognito, 337, 350
infinity, 87, 97, 357
inner (*see also* outer), 93-94, 199, 234, 297, 310
inspiration, 166
instant (*see also* moment), 361
intellectual intuition, 36, 44, 54, 160, 220, 228, 237-38, 316-17
intellectuality, 302-303
inter-esse, 310
interest, 301, 335
invitation, 112
inwardness, 72, 111, 197, 251ff., 260-61, 262ff., 272, 276, 278ff., 284, 299, 302, 329, 363; hidden, 351, 367-68
Ireneus, 19
irony, 113ff., 350, 362, 363, 366, 386
Isaiah, 385
Isis and Osiris, 219, 224-25
iustitia civilis, 359
Ixion, 257

Jacobi, Friedrich Heinrich, 38, 157, 202, 204, 216ff., 277, 283, 284, 311, 321
jest, 349, 358, 366
Job, 288-89
John the Apostle, 270
Jørgensen, Jørgen, 156
Josty's, 249

Judith, 365
Junghans, H. M., 161, 168, 198, 230, 234, 243, 265, 269, 318, 340, 343, 353-54, 356, 371, 375, 382, 386
Juno, 257
Justinian, Emperor, 171

Kant, Immanuel, 26, 32, 40ff., 46, 49, 51, 70, 95, 109n, 153, 201, 235, 303, 309, 313, 318, 345, 372
κατὰ δύναμιν, 326, 358
Kierkegaard, Ane Sørensdatter Lund, 273
Kierkegaard, Elise Marie, 273
Kierkegaard, Kirstin Nielsdatter, 273
Kierkegaard, Magister (Søren), 211, 212, 285, 288, 362
Kierkegaard, Maren Kirstine, 272-73
Kierkegaard, Michael Pedersen, 273, 346, 383
Kierkegaard, Niels Andreas, 273
Kierkegaard, Peter Christian, 126, 144, 189-90, 273, 371
Kierkegaard, Peter Severin, 273
Kierkegaard, Søren Michael, 273
King Lear, 318
knowledge (see also cognition), 10-11, 20-21, 40ff., 60, 157, 159, 163, 244, 251-52, 264, 361
Købner, Julius, 191-92
Kofod, Hans Ancher, 240
Kotzebue, August, 352
Krog, Bishop Johannes, 344
"Kts" (= Mynster, J. P.), 282, 283, 394

Lactantius, 20
Laërtius, Diogenes, 169, 208, 313, 325
Lafontaine, August H. J., 352
Lander, John, 272
Landsoldat, 346
Lao-Tse, 238
laughter, 364, 365-66
Lavater, Johann Caspar, 202, 204
leap, 107-108, 115, 149, 157, 188, 203, 213, 215-16, 335
lecture (see also privatdocent), 276, 329
"left-wing" Hegelians, 63, 65ff., 79
Leibniz, Gottfried Wilhelm, 26, 30, 32, 37, 56, 75, 99
Lenau, Nikolaus, 75

Lessing, Gotthold Ephraim, 38, 46, 107, 175ff., 202ff., 209, 215, 219, 221, 222, 230-31, 270, 343
Levin, Israel, 144
Ley, Christian S., 179, 195
Lichtenberg, Georg Christoph, 293
Lindberg, Jacob Christian, 125ff., 178, 184, 189ff.
Linton, O., 200
Locke, John, 32
logic, 27, 55ff., 91-101, 158-59, 221, 223-24, 226, 271, 305, 310-11
logos (λόγος), 14, 19, 55, 92, 184
love, 350
Lowrie, Walter, 145, 207-208, 343
Lucian, 211
Lucilius, G., 32
Luno, Bianco, 150
Luther, Martin, 30, 241, 327, 328, 351

macrocosmos, 38, 61
madness, 361
Madvig, Johan Nicolai, 166, 193, 391
maieutic, 206
Malantschuk, Gregor, 109n, 223, 254-55, 267, 356, 371
Mann, Otto, 39
Marheineke, Philipp Konrad, 51, 63, 68ff., 75
Marlborough, Duke of, 237
Martensen, Hans Lassen, 35n, 45, 67-68, 72, 74ff., 88ff., 99, 117ff., 130-31, 157, 161, 193, 198, 240, 245, 249, 255-56, 266, 269, 291, 305-306, 320, 378, 391
Marx, Karl, 32
masculinity, 294
masterthief, 156
"matchless discovery, " 173, 178ff., 236
mediation, 55ff., 168-69, 201, 207, 226, 310, 323, 330, 331, 336, 342, 343, 345, 371, 391
Medici, Cosimo, 31
Melanchthon, Philipp, 30, 279
mélange, 352
memory, 368
Mendelssohn, Moses, 216, 218
Menschenschreck, Diedrich, 243
mermaids, 371

μετάβασις εἰς ἄλλο γένος, 215, 226, 234

metaphysics, ix, 46, 236

metempsychosis, 14

method (the), 54, 98, 224, 228

μέτρον, 308

μετρίως πάθειν, 342

Michelet, Karl Ludwig, 51, 63, 228, 277, 284

microcosmos, 38, 61

Miltiades, 326

mimic, 153

Minos, King, 369

miracle, 248, 249

Miracle Plays, 344–45

μισέω, 161

Mohammedan legends, 344, 352

Molbech, Christian, 238, 292, 391

Molière, Jean-Baptiste, 340, 365

Møller, Peder Ludvig, 121ff., 128-29, 393

Møller, Poul Martin, 75, 83ff., 172, 174, 179, 195, 223, 243, 246, 316, 317, 324, 341, 373

Mols, 334

moment (*see also* instant), 106

monad, 37

Monaphysites, 21

monastic movement, 336-37, 342, 349-50

monism, 14, 19, 44, 66

Monomotapa, 238

Monrad, Ditlev Gothard, 193

Mønster, Peder Christian, 191-92

Montaigne, Michel de, 33, 169

morality, 46, 59

Moravian Brethren, 190

Mosbech, Holger, 165

motion; *see* movement

movement, 6-7, 91-92, 94, 98, 206, 223, 301, 308, 314, 351, 373

movement of infinity, 357

Mure, G.R.G., 268

Mynster, Jacob Peter, 71ff., 88-89, 99, 118, 124, 134ff., 157, 192-93, 282, 283, 288, 305-306, 345, 359, 361, 371, 380, 391, 394

Mysteries of the Bible, 344-45

mystery, 351

myth (mythology), 371, 382

Nanking, 223

Napoleon, 242, 325, 351

nature, 41, 57-58, 101, 105, 199, 259, 357

Nebuchadnezzar, 365

necessity, 60, 100, 215, 236, 319

negation, 97, 207, 229

negative, 91, 93, 206-207, 209, 211, 212, 349, 367, 389; concepts, 376

nemesis, 368

Neoplatonism, 21, 26, 160, 343

Nero, 181

Nestorians, 21

New Testament; *see* Bible

Nicholas of Cusa, 31, 44, 54

Nicodemus, 384

Nielsen, Rasmus, 79, 117-18, 133, 154-55, 240

Niethammer, Friedrich, 51

Nominalists, 27, 334

Norvin, William, 206

Notabene, Nicolaus, 285, 288

nothing, 54ff., 83-84, 168, 206-207, 227, 268; before God, 348

notion; *see* concepts

objective (objectivity), 164, 202, 263, 264

objective spirit, 58ff., 235

Oehlenschläger, Adam, 234, 249, 292-93

offense, 111, 378

Old Testament; *see* Bible

Olshausen, Hermann, 166

Omar, Caliph, 282

Oncken, J. G., 192

One (the), 6, 15-16, 53

ontology, 70, 223, 319

opposites (*see also* contrasts), 54ff., 314

Orestes, 371

Origen, 20, 215

Original sin, 38, 109, 252

Ørsted, Anders Sandøe, 126, 193

Ørsted, Hans Christian, 358

orthodoxy, 200, 370, 374, 379, 384, 386

Osten, F.v.d., 205

Otto, Rudolf, 386

outer (*see also* inner), 93-94, 199, 234, 297, 310

Overskou, Thomas, 265

Pabst, J. H., 65
paganism, 170, 257ff., 261-62, 323, 374, 379
πάμφίλος, 347
pantheism, 32, 45, 53, 66, 222, 230
Paracelsus, Theophrastus, 33
paradox, 111, 169, 252-53, 258, 259-62, 263, 265, 266, 285, 296, 324, 367, 369, 375-76, 381; absolute, 324, 368
paralogism, 363
Parmenides, 6-7, 55, 332
parson (see also clergy), 339-40
particular, 27, 29, 84, 300
Pascal, Blaise, 35ff., 102, 259
passion (see also pathos), 107, 110, 153, 193, 259-62, 281, 308, 335, 340, 378
pathos (see also passion), 104, 110-11, 281, 304, 335-36, 348, 378
Paul, St., 330, 340-41
Paulli, Just H., 193
penance, 368
peras, 5
periissem nisi periissem, 295
Petrarch, 31
pettifogger (see also shyster), 366
"Philadelphia System," 156
Philip, King, 181
Philo, 21
Philolaus, 6
philosophicum, 257
philosophy, lx-lxi, 53, 61, 66, 81, 85-86, 96, 152, 223, 226, 331, 391-92
Piazzi, Guiseppe, 50
Pico della Mirandola, 31-32
pietism, 46, 201
πίστις, 262, 375-76
pixie, 189, 317
Platen, August von, 245
Plato, 10ff., 44, 49-50, 54, 99, 171, 198, 209, 234, 237, 262, 275, 281, 314, 335, 361
Pletho, 31
Plotinus, 3, 14ff., 19-20, 21, 23, 44, 53-54, 230, 343
plurality, 7-8
Plutarch, 171, 181, 205, 224-25, 235, 286, 291-92, 326
poet-existence, 353-54
poetry, 43, 227, 309, 321, 348
Polus, 237, 386

Pompanatius, Petrus, 334
Pontius Pilate, 270
Posidonius, 4, 13-14, 54
positive, 45, 93, 207, 212, 348, 367, 389
possibility, 301-302, 310ff., 319, 326, 380
Potemkin, 290
potentiality, 11, 100, 269, 300, 326, 351, 381
practical reason, 40-41, 309, 318
prayer, 241
predestination, 383
predicate, 343
prepositions, 218
presuppositions, 149, 158-59, 197, 198, 221, 391
prime matter, 3, 5
prime mover, 13, 44, 301, 351
privatdocent, 209ff., 255
Proclus, 4
proofs, 26, 28, 215, 313-14, 316, 372
Protagoras, 6, 170-71, 280, 298-99
Pseudo-Dionysius, 24
pseudonymity, 112-13, 154, 288, 294, 380
psychology, 47, 335
Ptolemaeus, 23
pure being, 82, 206, 225, 310
pure reason, 40ff., 55ff., 92
pure thought, 55, 152, 301, 309, 317, 339, 377
Pyrrho, 169, 325
Pythagoras, 5, 307-308

Quidam, 294, 295
quodlibet, 24, 229, 287

"R—", 293
race, 373
rationalism, 37, 41, 71-72, 74, 87-88, 306, 325
Realists, 27
reality (see also actuality), 11, 26, 36, 38, 101
reason, 24-25, 28-29, 37, 58, 73, 157, 257ff., 331ff., 375-76
recollection, 11, 107, 262, 367-68, 374
reconciliation, 54-55, 323n, 331
redemption (see also atonement), 29, 47-48, 109

reduplication, 108, 243, 254-55, 275
reflection, 89, 94, 221, 305, 345, 346
reflection-into-another, 304
reflection-into-itself, 304, 309
Reimarus, Elise, 216
Reimarus, Hermann Samuel, 212, 222
reincarnation, 384
Reinhold, Karl Johan, 49
Reitzel, Carl Andreas, 150, 284, 292, 389
relative ends, 335-36, 348ff.
relative relationship, 337-38
relativism, 170
religion, 46, 53, 60, 69, 73, 82, 86-87, 330
religious address (discourse), 348ff., 357, 367
religiousness, 286, 368-69
Religiousness A, 111, 368, 373, 377-78, 380, 383
Religiousness B, 106-107, 113, 368-69, 373-74, 377-78, 380
repetition, 107, 108, 278
representative thought, 329-30
resignation, 108, 336
resolve, 108, 226, 336
respect, 340, 343
results, 235, 280-81
revelation, 38-39, 48, 68-69, 74-75, 81, 108, 110, 158, 203, 253, 257-58, 351
revocation, 387
Richter, Friedrich, 65, 244
Richter, Jean Paul, 196
"right-wing" Hegelians, 63, 65, 87, 159, 324, 378
Rigsdaler (Rigsbankdaler), 150n, 346
Robinson Crusoe, 358
Rohde, Peter P., 144
Romanticism (Romantics), 43, 106
Roos, Carl, 235
Rosenhoff, Claudius, 120, 239, 355
Rosenkranz, Karl, 58, 159, 205, 304, 319
Rossini, Gioacchino, 246
Roth, Friedrich, 277
Rothschild, L. N., 386
Rötscher, Heinrich Theodor, 63, 227, 355
Rudelbach, Andreas G., 71, 374

Sack, Karl Heinrich, 159

sacraments, 29, 289, 328
Sakkas, Ammonius, 20
Salutati, 31
salvation, 323
Sanchez, Thomas, 169
Scaevola, Gaius Mucius, 355
Scarron, Paul, 357
Schaller, Julius, 65
Scharling, Carl Henrik, 166
Schelling, Friedrich Wilhelm von, 14, 33, 36, 43ff., 49, 51, 72, 152, 207, 220, 228, 230, 237, 277, 316, 352
Schilling, Friedrich, 235, 246
Schink, Johann Friedrich, 203
Schlegel, Friedrich, 43
Schleiermacher, Friedrich Ernst, 45-46, 61, 63, 67-68, 72, 75, 166, 198, 383
Scholasticism, 24ff., 31
Schönheyder, Dr. J. C., 218
Schubart, G. H. von, 315
Schubart, H. E., 244
science, ix, 94-95, 152-53, 226, 232, 237, 293
Scipio, Cornelius P., 269
Scribe, Eugène, 237, 325, 344, 392
Scriptures; see Bible
seduction, 294
self, 106, 201
self-affirmation, 363
self-annihilation, 349, 363
self-consciousness, 34-35, 67
self-knowledge, 10, 37, 53, 57, 61, 66-67, 103, 105, 111
self-reflection, 317
self-revelation, 362
sense perception, 10, 53, 202, 301, 311, 332
Separatists, 192
seriousness (see also earnestness), 108, 349
sermon, 279, 282, 288, 382
Sextus Empiricus, 169, 311, 342
Seydelmann, Karl, 355
Shaftesbury, Anthony Ashley Cooper, 363
Shakespeare, 154, 216, 239, 243, 274, 275, 318, 365
"show," 358
shysters (see also pettifoggers), 346
Sibbern, Frederik Christian, 75, 77,

Sibbern, Frederik Christian (*cont.*) 80ff., 99, 126, 220, 228, 245, 306, 345
Silentio, Johannes de, 282-83, 362
Simonides, 317
simple (wise) man, 108, 322
simultaneity (*see also* contemporaneity), 319
sin, 18, 75, 104, 108-109, 158, 198, 252, 263, 279, 285, 358, 367, 378
single individual, 302
skepticism, 22, 99, 169, 301, 311, 317, 325
Skovfoged, Jens, 305
Sløk, Johannes, 106
Socrates, 9ff., 102, 114-15, 124, 154, 172, 181, 198, 205-206, 208, 209, 212, 217, 230, 236, 239, 247, 258, 261, 262, 264, 274ff., 280-81, 288, 290, 292, 308, 326, 330, 357, 359, 362, 373, 374, 386
Soldin, Salomon, 243
Solger, Karl W. F., 277
Solon, 170, 230
Sophie Frederikke, 249
Sophists, 9, 25, 170, 280, 298, 328, 342
Sophocles, 270, 371
sorites, 93n
space, 32, 101, 198, 215, 332
specimen, 320
speculation (speculative), 11, 32, 86ff., 94ff., 98, 109, 149-50, 158, 160-61, 174, 197, 222, 232, 253, 260-61, 264, 276, 278ff., 284, 285-86, 303, 308, 322ff., 329, 330, 332, 362, 368-69, 377ff., 386
speculative Good Friday, 55
Spengler, Oswald, 59
Spinoza, Benedict (-Baruch), 16, 24, 31-32, 35ff., 45-46, 56, 58, 66, 207-208, 230, 266, 303, 318
spirit (*see also* Hegel; and logic; his system), 44, 53ff., 319-20
spiritual trial, 271, 339, 349, 357-58
stages, 25, 53, 57, 60, 108, 110, 113ff., 267, 380ff.
state (the), 59-60, 297, 362
Stefens, Henrich, 75
Stilling, Peter Michael, 79-80
Stoicism, 171, 243
Strauss, David Friedrich, 66, 67, 75,

167, 219, 266, 382
Stufenkosmos, 44, 60
subjective (subjectivity), 108, 164, 168, 197, 202, 251ff., 259, 262ff., 363-64
subjective spirit, 58
subjective thinker, 322ff., 326
sublation, 54, 168, 268
sub specie aeterni (aeternitatis), 36, 153, 207-208, 245, 260, 300, 303, 308
substance, 11-12, 36, 40, 266, 331ff.
suffering, 114, 280, 286, 294, 348ff., 357, 363, 367
suicide, 308
Supranaturalism, 60, 72, 74, 87-88, 306
suspension, 384
Swenson, David F., 145
Sygotius, 390, 391
syllogism, 234
synthesis, 40, 54, 106ff., 168, 197, 201, 255, 267, 303-304, 310
system, 91-92, 95ff., 149-50, 157, 221-22, 223, 229, 240, 260
systematists, 230, 240

Taciturnus, Frater, 122, 229, 235, 321, 362, 393
teleology, 47, 94, 312, 384
telos (τέλος), 241, 308, 309, 337-38, 343, 344
temporal, 303-304
temptation, 349, 357-58
Tennemann, Wilhelm G., 314, 352
Terentius, 325
Tertullian, 19-20
Thales of Miletus, 5
Themistocles, 326
theology, 47, 66, 258, 306-307, 382
Theophrastus of Eresus, 286, 291
theoretical reason, 40-41, 309, 318
Thielicke, Helmut, 39
Thiers, Adolphe, 341
thing-in-itself (see also *Ding-an-sich*), 42, 51
"thorn in the flesh," 356
thought, 35-36, 38, 54ff., 81, 202, 222, 251, 255, 300ff., 304, 310, 313, 340, 346
time, 40, 57, 101, 197, 199, 213-14, 236, 258, 263, 285, 329, 349, 378, 380
Tivoli, 239, 276, 292

τοιοῦτοι, 384
tragic (the), 351
transcendence, 214
transcendent (in Kant), 40–41
transcendental (in Kant), 40–41
transition, 12, 100, 188, 203, 215, 319
transmigration, 384
Trebizond, 293
Trendelenburg, Adolf, 65, 93, 184, 219, 224, 226–67, 304, 319
Trinity (triune), 26, 29, 69–70, 83, 87, 92, 101, 307
Trop, 365
truth, 28, 73, 92, 109, 164, 168, 197, 215, 251ff., 257ff., 262–63, 283, 302–303, 330; Christian, 278ff.
Tryde, Eggert Christopher, 192, 240, 245

Udlevelse, 296
Ulysses, 205
understanding (the), 55, 58–59, 94, 356, 369
universal, 84
universals, 27, 29, 300, 305
unscientific, 152
Upanishads, 385
upbuilding; *see* edification

Valla, Lorenzo, 31
Vartov, 344, 360
Versöhnung, 54n
Victor, St. Hugo de, 375

Victorines, 27
Victorinus, Marius, 21
Virgil, 321
Vogelius, Peder, 218
vows, 361

Weber, Carl Maria von, 292
Weil, Dr. Gustav, 344, 352
Weis, Carl, 249
Weisse, Carl Heinrich, 64–65
Werder, Karl, 65
Wessel, Johan Hermann, 167, 236
Westphaler, Geert, 265
What, 252, 263
Widenmann, Robert J., xi
Wielandt, Jr., 205
Wilhelm, Judge, 105, 108, 247
William of Ockham, 29–30
Wilson, Dover, 365
Wolff, Christian, 30, 37
Word (*see also* logos), 18, 101
worship, 331, 337

Xenocrates, 171
Xenophanes, 6
Xenophon, 237, 275, 330

Zahn, Theodor, 166
Zealots, 168
Zeller, Eduard, 63
Zeno of Citium, 291
Zeno of Elea, 78, 286, 325

LIBRARY OF CONGRESS CATALOGING IN PUBLICATION DATA

Thulstrup, Niels.
Commentary on
Kierkegaard's Concluding unscientific postscript.

Translation of: Søren Kierkegaard, Afsluttende
unvidenskabelig efterskrift.
"English translations of Kierkegaard": p.
"English translations of Hegel": p.
Includes indexes.
1. Christianity—Philosophy. 2. Apologetics—19th
century. I. Kierkegaard, Søren, 1813-1855. Afsluttende
unvidenskabelig efterskrift. II. Title.
BR100.T4813 1984   201   83-43095
ISBN 0-691-07180-2